MORE

THAN YOU EVER WANTED TO KNOW

ABOUT

GLASS BEADMAKING

by James Kervin
GlassWear Studios
1197 Sherry Way
Livermore, CA 94550-5745
Phone (925) 443-9139
Fax (925) 292-8648
glasswearstudios@comcast.net

More Than You Ever Wanted To Know About

Glass Beadmaking

by James E. Kervin

Published by:

GlassWear Studios
1197 Sherry Way
Livermore, CA 94550
(925) 443 9139

First Printing 1994
Second Printing 1995, completely revised.
Third Printing 1996, completely revised.
Fourth Printing, 1999, completely revised
Fifth Printing, 2003, completely revised

Library Cataloging Data

Kervin, James E., 1950-
Glass beadmaking: more than you ever wanted to know about
by James E. Kervin 310p
Includes bibliographical references and index
ISBN 0-9651458-8-3
1. Glass blowing and working. 1. Title
TP859.K 2003
748--dc20

Library of Congress Catalog Card Number 99-094346

Images on front cover

Top left	Azalea Bonzai Vessel, Artist: Leah Fairbanks, 2002 Size: 1¾" long, Photo: George Post
Top Center	Dog head bead, Artist: Al Janelle, 1998 Size: 1¾" long, Photo: Al Janelle
Top right	Fused earrings, Artist: Bernadette Mahfood, 1999 Size 2" long, Photo: Larry Sanders
Lower left	Dichroic Angle, Artist: Pat Hoyt, 2002 Size 2½" long, Photo Rich Images
Lower Center	In the Shallows, Artist: Sharon Peters, 2002 Size: 1½" diameter, Photo: Janice Peacock
Lower right	Three dichroic beads, Artist: Stevi Belle, 1996 Size: 1½" to 3¼" wide, Photo: Jerry Anthony

Image on back cover
Lower left Curved dichroic beads, Artist: Cay Dickey, Size: 1¼" to 2" long, Photo: Carl Tamura

Image on this page
Center Rugrose Coral, Artist: Patti Dougherty, Size: 1½" long, Photo: Jim Kervin

Preface

Beadmaking is rapidly becoming one of the hottest new trends on the glass art scene, and with good reason. Beads themselves are a wearable art form whose beauty excites many. In addition, getting started making beads is relatively inexpensive. For about $50, you can get started using a small handheld torch and a few home-made tools and with it you will be able to wind, shape, and decorate beads of your own design. You will soon find yourself dazzling your friends with your new creations and if you choose, you can develop your artwork into a small business of your own. Either way, you will soon find yourself one of the many "glassoholics" hooked on the fascinating pastime of manipulating glass in the flame of a torch.

I was first introduced to the potential of wound glass beadmaking by Brian Kerkvliet of Gossamer Glass Studios in a beadmaking class that he presented at Fenton Glass Studio in 1992. Brian made it all look so easy and his work was like nothing I had ever seen before. He was also an excellent instructor and I learned a lot. I came away from that class inspired to make beads.

Brian still teaches a lot of classes out of his studio, Inspiration Farm in Bellingham, Washington. Look up Inspiration Farm on the web to find out more. There are also many other classes in beadmaking springing up all over the place and I would definitely recommend searching one out to augment what you will learn by reading this book. Before you sign up for one of these classes, check out the artist's work and compare it to some of the gorgeous work advertised in Bead & Button, Lapidary Journal or Ornament magazine to get a feeling for their skill level. You want to learn from someone who knows his or her stuff. Also realize that not everyone who can do something well can teach it well, so ask previous students whether they felt that they got what they wanted out of that artist's class.

Also, as the number of glass beadmakers started to grow, they became aware of each other and saw how diverse the field was. To help out themselves and each other, it was decided to form a society through which to interact. This group, the International Society of Glass Beadmakers (ISGB), is an excellent way to meet other beadmakers. Joining one of its many regional groups and going to its annual convention is an excellent way to learn new skills and marketing ideas. Visit their web site (www.isgb.org) for more information.

Anyway, after that class with Brian, I was hooked and came back again the next year when he taught again to learn more. Meanwhile I examined the work of others for ideas on technique as well as content and in the process really fell in love with beadmaking. One of the really nice features about wound glass beadmaking is that you have results relatively quickly. You can make a number of beads an hour, rather than the one piece in a number of days that I had been used to achieving with other glassworking processes. As I searched for more information on glass beadmaking and started seeing some of the books that were coming out on the subject, I was really disappointed. As I read through them, I felt like that old lady in the hamburger commercial, "Where's the beef?" I decided that what was really needed was a complete guide to glass beadmaking techniques, equipment and tools.

That vision served to start me on the long and difficult journey of compiling the information for this book. As I researched the glass bead scene, I realized that there was a lot more out there than just wound beads and decided to expand this work to include these other glass beadmaking techniques. The work that you see before you continues to grow and will never really be complete, because the art form itself continues to develop. The first edition of this book was then been updated with information shared by many of the leaders of the American glass beadmaking movement. Subsequent editions have continued to benefit a great deal from the generous information from artists such as Loren Stump, Pati Frantz, Mary Mullaney, Ralph Mossman,

Don Schnieder, Tom Holland, Patricia Sage, and Jim Smircich. I also want to thank all the artists who provided pictures of their work or allowed me to use pictures of their work. This book has benefited from layout suggestions from Jaret Elbert, the patience of my loving wife, Peg BonDurant, and the editing of one of my favorite glass bead artists, Sharon Peters.

I have tried to include many exhaustive details on the techniques and equipment involved in glass beadmaking not found in any other source — thus the name of this manual. Equipment and safety are very important areas that especially did not seem to be covered sufficiently in other sources, books or videos. Hopefully you will find all the information you need on these topics in this book. The National Institute for Occupational Safety and Health (NIOSH) personnel have recognized this book as a good source for safety information and have referenced it in their past reports on safety in beadmaking,

If there are things that you do not understand because I have not explained them well enough, let me know and I will try to improve it in future editions. If you think that there are other areas that should be covered or more figures are needed to explain certain concepts, again let me know. If you think something is wrong, I would very much appreciate hearing your opinion. This fifth revision of this book continues to incorporate suggestions that I have already received from other readers like you. At the same time, I hope that you will find this effort and the many months that were spent initially preparing and revising this edition will be of some benefit in helping you learn the exciting art of glass beadmaking.

Many people have requested including more step-by-step beadmaking instructions. I felt that this change would have greatly increased the size or diluted the content of this book. To address this need, I have instead chosen to start a companion series of smaller booklets on individual bead artists, their work and the techniques used to create it. In these you will find detailed step-by-step directions if you want them.

This book was designed to provide information in regard to the subject of glass beadmaking. Although I have tried to present this subject in as great depth as possible, it is impossible to cover everything. You are urged to read all available material on the subject. Check out the many references listed herein to supplement this text. Be aware that, even though I have attempted to provide as complete and accurate a source book as possible, **there may be some mistakes** present both typographical and in content. Therefore use it as a guide and if something seems wrong, realize that it just might be. This manual was written to educate and entertain. The author shall have neither liability nor responsibility to any person or entity with respect to any loss or damage caused, or alleged to be caused, directly or indirectly by the information contained in this book. **If you do not wish to be bound by these and the following restrictions, you may return this book with a copy of your receipt to the publisher for a full refund.**

It should also be mentioned that discussion of particular equipment or supplies in this book does not constitute a recommendation. They are just some of those used by or known by me. Results will vary among individuals depending upon their skill level, so no warranty is implied for these products. Instead, this information is supplied so that you, as an educated consumer, can make your own choices.

Because of the nature of this art form, injuries can occur and you as user of this information have sole responsibility for your safety as well as that of other individuals who could be injured by your actions. Neither the equipment nor I are responsible for injury resulting from equipment misuse. You need to learn as much as you can about how to operate your equipment, to follow any recommendations from the manufacturer, and to take classes from qualified instructors. Watch videos to learn the rhythm and movements required to work with this magical material. With this attitude and preparation, you will be able to safely enjoy the fascinating world of glass beadmaking.

Table of Contents

Introduction to Glass Beadmaking

Figure 1. Eye bead, Length 3.1 cm. Carthage 5th-3rd century B.C. Courtesy of Corning Museum of Glass.

The history of the use of beads for decoration is almost as old as that of man himself. Prehistoric beads were made from teeth, bones, seeds, wood, and other pierceable objects. Originally, they were probably used as amulets with sympathetic magical powers rather than as ornaments. As such, they may have been thought to possess the attributes of other creatures, such as the strength of a bear or the courage of a vanquished foe.

The oldest recorded objects, which appear to have been pierced and used for adornment are small marine mollusks that have been determined to be 100,000 years old. As a rule, these types of objects are generally not considered to be beads, unless they have been worked into a regular form. Glass beads obviously came much later.

The exact origin of glass is unknown but it is believed to have been discovered in Egypt around 1400 BC. It probably came from some ceramic artisan's understanding of and experimentation with glazes. These artisans were already making faience beads from powdered sand, clay, and limestone that were packed into small balls or tubes around a stick and coated with a glazing solution of soda. During firing, the sticks would be consumed leaving a hole in the bead. The limestone combined with the sand to form the body of the bead. If there was a little copper or iron oxide in the mix, the bead would also end up being colored. Through experimentation, the artist must have observed that if he added more soda, he ended up with a shiny clear surface. This substance was a crude glass.

These new glass artisans must have been struck by the resemblance of this material to naturally occurring gemstones and found themselves trying to duplicate the colors they saw in nature. As they became more accomplished, they learned to make batches of glass in thick earthenware crucibles. They found that they could form vessels by dipping clay forms into the glass and soon learned to make

Figure 2. Mosaic hawk's head, Height 4.3 cm. Egypt 3rd-1st century B.C. Courtesy of Corning Museum of Glass.

beads by dipping a metal rod into the crucible and winding the glass clinging to it around a stick or similar core material. This stick or core was then removed by burning or digging it out. With that the glass bead adventure began. That is likely the process that was used to make the bead in Figure 1.

The adventure continued and expanded through many different societies, each bringing its own unique addition to glass beadmaking. With the Greeks and Romans, we see the development of glass mosaic cane techniques similar to those being used by modern-day Fimo clay bead artists. The application of different layers of colored glass into patterns allowed them to build up of images in the cross section of a piece of glass. Chips from this piece could then be used to decorate many beads with this image. By successive bundling and stretching the bundle, the image could be made as complex and as small as desired.

Figure 3. Twentieth century chevron beads made by ancient techniques used by the Venetians.

The art of glass beadmaking really began to flower in Venice, Italy in the 11th century. There, they used the flame of oil lamps and later simple natural gas torches to melt glass and wind it into beads. It is from this practice that the term for working glass in a torch got the name, lampworking or flameworking. Beadmaking was so important to the Venetian economy that its secrets were protected under a threat of death. Even today, beads of this style are often referred to as Venetian beads.

From there, glass beadmaking has continued to develop. It has spread to the far corners of the globe. In addition, glass is no longer a precious material reserved only for the wealthy. Shaping glass into beads is no longer a state secret. The information on how to make glass beads is now freely shared with other beadmakers and you will learn much of that information in this book.

Simple beads are mass-produced and sold all over the world. But in that process, they have lost some of their charm and beauty. People long for the hand-made objects of art that beads once were. They want these types of beads to wear and display. The techniques for making these unique art objects are presented in this book.

Bead terms

There are a number of terms used to describe the parts of a bead and bead shapes. Bead terms are defined and explained in this section to enhance your understanding of glass beads and beadmaking techniques. All of these general terms are illustrated in Figure 4.

An imaginary line drawn down the center of the hole in a bead is referred to as the **axis** of the bead. Going up or down this line is referred to as moving down the axis or **moving axially**. The largest distance across the bead when looking down that axis is the **diameter** of the bead. The edge of the cross section perpendicular to the axis is known as the **perimeter** or, if round, the **circumference** of the bead. Moving around this edge is thus referred to as **moving circumferentially** around the bead.

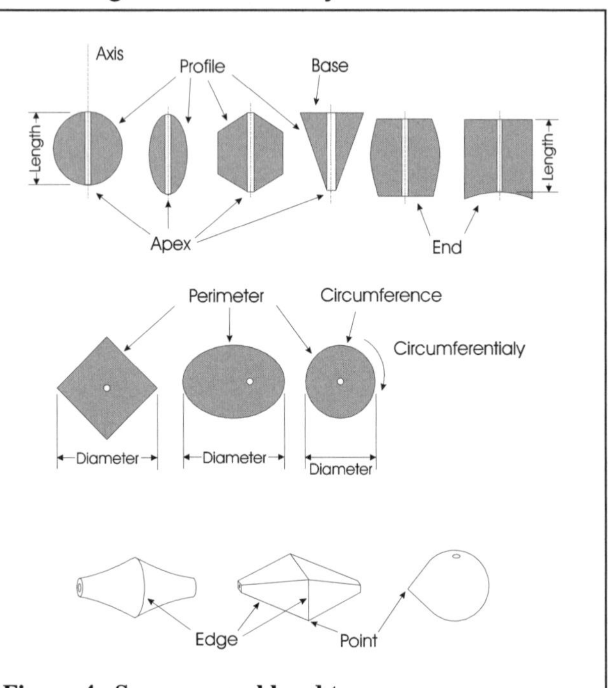

Figure 4. Some general bead terms.

If one end of the axis of the bead ends in a point, that point is referred to as an **apex** of the bead. If the end of an axis ends in a flat or semi-flat surface, its called an **end** of the bead unless the other end of the bead ends in an apex in which case it is called the **base** of the bead. The shortest distance from one end or apex of the bead to the other is called its **length**.

The contour of the bead along its length is referred to as its **profile**. A sharp meeting of surfaces on a bead is known as an **edge**. Edges may have any orientation to the axis. A sharp meeting of three or more surfaces or the tip of a cone that is not an apex is referred to as a **point**.

Bead shapes

A whole naming system was developed for bead shapes by Beck. He defines the **standard bead** as one whose diameter is equal to its width. Figure 5 shows the shapes that he has defined for standard beads.

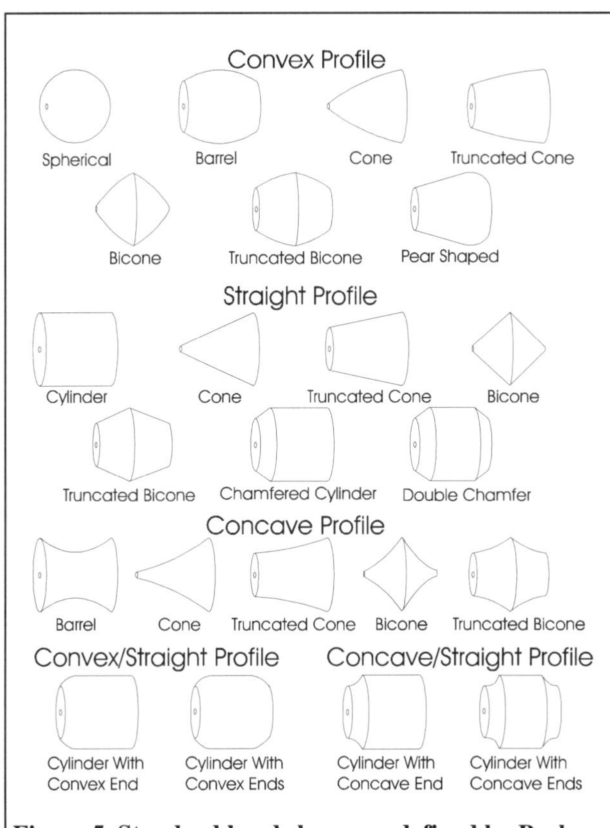

Figure 5. Standard bead shapes as defined by Beck.

A bead that has a length greater than its diameter is referred to as a **long bead**, and one with its length shorter than its diameter as a **short bead**. If the length of the bead is a third or less of its diameter, it is called a **disk bead**. Beck also has names for how beads are faceted and ornamented.

Glass beadmaking techniques

Glass beads are also categorized by the technique used in their manufacture. At this point, I will give just a brief description of each technique, which we will then go into greater detail in this book.

The first of these beadmaking processes is that of **winding** beads. Here heat softened glass is wound about a mandrel. By working the glass with tools and decorating it with glass of other colors, the variations with this technique are endless. Winding is probably the most wide spread beadmaking technique being practiced today.

The next process, that of **blowing** beads, is where small bubbles of glass are blown, decorated, and shaped without the help of a mandrel to stabilize the glass. As a result, this process is a little more difficult than winding but it results in larger beads that are lightweight.

If a much larger bubble is blown and decorated, it can be stretched out to form a long tube that can be cut up into small individual beads. This is the basis for the process of **drawn** beadmaking.

A different kind of process, called **pressing**, was traditionally performed by taking two blobs of glass and sandwiching them in a mold around a hole former to make a bead. The pressing mold was often decorated with raised designs that would be duplicated in the face of the bead.

A variation of this technique, called **folding**, used a single blob of glass that was folded over the mandrel in the mold. We will not discuss this technique. The only beadmaker that I really know who currently uses this process is Tom Holland.

We will briefly discuss a variation of pressing known as **press molding**. In this technique, a single blob of glass is put into one half of a mold and formed into shape by pressing the second half of the mold down on top of the blob. This half incorporates a needle that pierces the blob to form a hole in the bead.

Kiln casting of glass is the last traditional technique that will be discussed in this book. Also known as **pâte de verre** beadmaking, it involves filling a small mold with small piles of finely broken glass, known as frit, and melting it at high temperature in a kiln. Then when it cools down and you break the mold away, you have your bead. The hole is made by placing an easily removed, temperature-resistant material down the center of the pile of broken glass.

A non-traditional variation of kiln casting is used to make what I refer to as **fused** beads. It involves heating up larger pieces of cold glass in a kiln to form your bead (or bead stock to cut up into beads). This technique may or may not also include the use of a mold in a second firing to shape the beads.

Another variation of casting that we do not discuss in this book is **hot glass casting**. Here you have a mold with pore former that is filled with molten glasses rather than cold glass frit. The only advantage of this technique over that of pâte de verre beadmaking is in the clarity of the glass in the final bead.

In this book, you will find information about wound, blown, drawn, press molded, pâte de verre, and fused glass beadmaking. This is actually pretty much the range of techniques being practiced today. Hopefully, with the information presented in this book, you will be able to get up and running with any of these techniques. Because of its great popularity, the main focus of this book is on wound glass beadmaking. Before we go on to discuss these techniques, you need to learn a lot about the equipment that is used in beadmaking. That is what is presented next.

Suggested further reading

Dubin, Lois Sherr. **The History of Beads**, Harry N. Abrams Inc., 1987

Erikson, Joan Mowat. **The Universal Bead**, W. W. Norton & Company, 1993

Francis, Peter Jr. **Beads of the World**, Schiffer Publishing Ltd., 1994

Gordon, Albert F. & Kahan, Leonard, **The Tribal Bead**, Tribal Arts Gallery, 1976

Jargstorf, Sibylle, Baubles, **Buttons and Beads**, Schiffer Publishing Ltd., 1993

Karklins, Karlis. **Glass Beads, The 19th Century Levin Catalogue and Venetian Bead Book and Guide to Description of Glass Beads**, National Historic Parks and Sites Branch Parks Canada, 1985

Kucukerman, Prof. Onder. **Glass Beads - Anatoliann Glass Beadmaking**, Turkish Touring and Automobile Association, 1988

Liese, Gabrielle. **The Work of Contemporary Glass Beadmakers**, The Bead Museum, 1993

Liu, Robert K. Ph.D. **Collectible Beads**, Ornament Magazine, 1994

Poris, Ruth F., **Advanced Beadwork**, Golden Hands Press 1990

van der Sleen, W. G. N. **A Handbook on Beads**, George Shumway Publisher, 1964

Torches and Gas Systems

The first area of discussion in this book is on the different pieces of equipment that you will use in making glass beads. This is an area that does not always get covered as well as it should in classes, videos, or books. It is hoped that if this book serves no other purpose, it will be to provide you with the knowledge that you should have about your equipment, the principles behind its operation, the dangers involved in its use, and how to operate it safely.

This presentation is divided into three chapters. In this first chapter I discuss torches, what they are and how to set them up. In the next, I present many of the different tools used in lampworking. In the third, I examine larger pieces of equipment like kilns and glory holes.

In your first reading of this book, you may want to skim through these sections and go on to find out more about how beads are made. Then come back and reread them when you are ready to start setting up equipment in your studio.

Work area

Before starting our discussion of torches, let's look at how to set up a studio work area. In developing a workspace for beadmaking, you should keep at least two factors in mind: safety and convenience. Safety is utmost because there is nothing more precious than your own well being and that of your loved ones, and convenience is a factor because a well-organized work area helps make everything easier.

The space doesn't have to be very large, a small portion of one's garage or basement is more than good enough. I know some nationally known beadmakers who worked in an area the size of a closet for years, so the size of your work area should not be limiting.

The safety issues that you should consider in setting up your work area are those that are required to prevent fires and avoid material toxicity, etc. Safety considerations are so important that they have also been brought together and elaborated on in their own chapter at the end of this book. The minimum required safety items necessary for your work area are covered in this section.

First, try to rid your workspace of any unnecessary combustibles. The floor in your work area should be non-combustible. If not cement, then some other form of protective covering should be used. Molten glass can start fires when dropped on a combustible floor if not handled immediately.

Keep a ceramic or metal waste container on your workbench reserved exclusively for any hot glass you might pinch off or have to get rid of in a hurry. It could be filled with water if you like to quench your tools as you work. Never put any combustibles like paper in it. It does not have to be very large — even

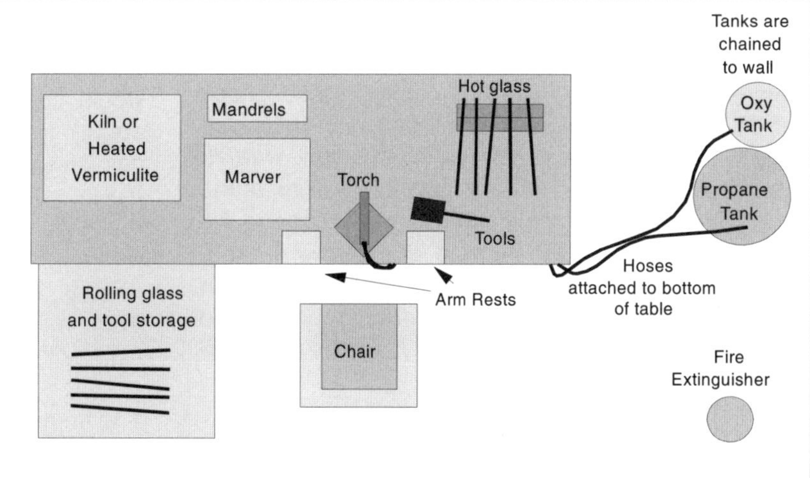

Figure 6. Example workbench layout for propane-oxygen system.

Figure 7. Example studio layout.

a medium sized vegetable can will do.

Since you will be working with open flames, you should move all combustible materials away from your work area. All flammable liquids should be kept in tightly capped containers and stored in a flammable liquid storage cabinet that prevents any vapors from leaking out into your work area. Check all natural gas lines, if any, to make sure that none are leaking. If working in your garage, pull your car out of the garage while you are working.

If these efforts were to fail and a fire were to break out, the next piece of required safety equipment for all beadmakers, a fire extinguisher, would come in handy. Your fire extinguisher should be prominently displayed in some easy to reach place and not buried away. Check it occasionally to insure that it is properly charged.

Another thing to consider is that your beadmaking torch can give off carbon monoxide and unburned hydrocarbons during use. Breathing these gases and fumes is unhealthy. For this reason, make sure that you have proper ventilation in your work area. If you don't have an industrial ventilation system, at the very least have a window and a fan to exchange the air. Don't have the fan blowing into your work area, instead have it in the window blowing air out of your work area. This is because sudden drafts can thermal shock your work and may result in cracked beads.

If you are going to use a fuel-oxygen torch with oxygen bottles, you will need to set up a storage rack to hold your oxygen bottles. This rack should allow for easy addition and removal of bottles, but at the same time should ensure that no bottle can be accidentally knocked over. The bottles should be securely held in place by stringing chains around them that attach to hooks on the rack. It should be located in a shady dry location to prevent overheating or corrosion of the tanks. If you keep more than one tank of oxygen at any time, the rack should also prevent them from banging against each other. Your oxygen and propane tanks should not be located near furnaces, hot water heaters, or other sources of ignition.

To make your work area an easier place in which to work, you should construct an easy-to-reach rack where you can keep glass rods already cut to working length. Have individual bins for different colors and types of glass with which you will be working. Do the same for your tools. Al Janelle recommends using magnetic strips to hold your tools within reach.

Workbench

Your workbench should be large enough to fit all your equipment comfortably. I use a 2' x 6' table that I got at a school auction. Some flameworkers use inexpensive 6' banquet tables. Another alternative is to build your own bench from plywood and 2" x 4" studs. Modify it to fit you and your work style. Hooks can be added underneath the table to keep the torch hoses from getting under foot.

The surface of the workbench should be at a comfortable working height either while seated or while standing. When standing, the ideal workbench would be about waist high. You will want it to be about mid abdomen level when seated so that you can rest your elbows on it. You may even want to mount cushions on the workbench for your elbows. (Consider treating any cushions with flame retardant.) A stool or swivel chair is preferred to a normal chair because it is much easier to back off from a stool than from a chair if you should accidentally drop some molten glass into your lap.

The flameworking area of your workbench should be covered with some fire resistant material. A number of such materials are available: sheet metal, asbestos board, non-asbestos board, etc. Sheet metal is not the best material for this application because it conducts the heat away from any dropped glass to a larger area, possibly leading to burning yourself. Asbestos board is not desirable because of the associated cancer risk.

Both Wale Apparatus Company and Ed Hoy's carry rigid non-asbestos work surfaces that are a good choice. Another commonly available alternative is to use Wonder Board or Dura Rock. These are some of the brand names for the moisture resistant and noncombustible concrete board that is used in construction of showers. It usually has a rough side to which tile is glued and a smooth side to go against the studs in the wall. A sheet of Wonder Board can be cut to fit your workbench using a carbide scribe and installed smooth side up.

If your bench is to be up against a wall, you should cover the wall behind your workbench with the same board. Space the board off the wall about ½" with noncombustible fittings to allow air circulation behind the board to carry away any heat that might build up. In addition, your flame should not be directed onto the board but should be at least a foot away.

Lighting

Lighting is important for a number of reasons. The first is probably fairly obvious, to see your work. Lighting from above and slightly behind you is best as it avoids getting either light shining in your eyes or distracting reflections off your glass. Diffuse lighting such as fluorescent lighting is recommended because it is easier on the eyes. Try to use as full a spectra bulb as possible so that you can see the true colors of the glass that you are working with. Use Chromolux incandescent bulbs or daylight balanced florescent bulbs.

Lighting is also an important factor in being able to see the torch flame and reading the temperature of the glass. When making beads or any other flameworked item, control of how much you heat the piece and its components is very critical to the final results. Thus you need to know where you are in the flame. Sometimes you want the bead directly in the flame, sometimes beneath the flame, sometimes off to the side of the flame, etc. To control this requires good lighting.

Almost as important as the lighting in being able to see the flame is the background behind it. The flame is most visible if your background is flat black. Against a light background the flame is nearly invisible. If you want to paint your background darker, use of heat resistant wood stove paint is recommended. Another option is to use flat black tiles against the wall.

Torch gases

Now that we have a workplace in which to use our torch, let's move on to a discussion of the different gases used in beadmaking. The gases vary in properties, cost and availability. You may have reasons for preferring one over another. First we'll discuss oxygen, which supports fuel gas combustion, and follow with a discussion of the various fuel gases.

Oxygen

Oxygen is the gas that all living things use in the metabolism of foods for energy to stay alive. It makes up 21% of the air we breathe. If that value is reduced to 15% or below, the air can no longer support a candle flame. Increase that value to 25% and cotton fabric will burn eight times faster than normal. This in fact is one of the hazards of working with oxygen. Cloth fabrics in a near pure oxygen atmosphere will burn rapidly with an almost explosive force.

Oxygen enrichment allows all materials to burn faster and hotter. This is why we like to use mixed gas torches to make beads. Depending upon the adjustment of your torch, not all of the oxygen may be consumed by your flame and it may build up in a confined work area. Thus the purpose of workspace ventilation is not only to remove combustion fumes but also to vent excess oxygen.

Another danger in using oxygen is its reactivity to the presence of oil or grease. Violent spontaneous combustion can result from such an exposure. This response is particularly dangerous if it occurs in the confined space of a piece of equipment such as a regulator. Therefore only equipment “cleaned for oxygen service” should be used with it.

> **Safety Note***: Never use oil or organic lubricants on oxygen valves or regulators. In fact, always use clean gloves or freshly washed hands, free of any oils or grease when handling oxygen equipment.*

Pure oxygen is generally considered to be nontoxic, but long exposures to high concentrations may

Table 1. Physical properties of oxygen.

Physical Property	Value
Chemical formula	O_2
Molecular weight	31.9988
Specific gravity (relative to air) at 70°F	1.105
Specific volume (cu ft/lb) at 70°F, 1 atm	12.08
(cu m/kg)	0.6996
Density, saturated vapor (lb/cu ft) 1 atm	0.27876

actually damage your respiratory track. This is a factor to which some people are more susceptible than others. It is not so much a danger to beadmakers as it is to those of you who may be "technical" scuba divers or respiratory patients on oxygen. As a matter of fact, I had to pass an oxygen tolerance test before being admitted to hard hat diving school back in my old Navy days.

Oxygen is the most abundant element on earth, but most of it is not in the gaseous form but is instead bound up as oxides. Natural gaseous oxygen exists as a colorless, odorless and tasteless gas. Unless of course you are somewhere where the temperature is below approximately -300°F, where oxygen is a transparent, pale blue liquid slightly denser than water. If you know of any such a place, let me know so that I can stay away from there.

Without oxygen, combustion or life as we know it would not be possible. It reacts with all elements, except the inert gases, to form oxides. Table 1 presents some of its physical properties.

Fuel gases

A number of different fuel gases can be burned in a torch. They may be mixed either with air, or with oxygen for better performance. The most common of these gases are propane, acetylene, propylene, natural gas, and stabilized methylacetylene-propadiene (MAPP Gas®).

Because of their flammability, all fuel gases should be considered potentially hazardous. They should be used, handled, and stored in accordance with the recognized safety practices that I will try to summarize in this manual. If you want more information, I suggest consulting some of the following recognized standards for welding:

ANSI 249.1 Safety in Welding and Cutting

NFPA 51 Oxygen-Fuel Gas System for Welding and Cutting

Some of the physical properties of these fuel gases are listed in Table 2. As you examine the data in this table, some of the reasons one fuel gas may be preferred over another may become apparent. One property very important to beadmaking is the flame temperatures of the fuel gas. Acetylene, propylene, and MAPP Gas® burn much hotter than either natural gas or propane. Yet, pound per pound, they all provide about the same amount of heat.

Due to their low vapor pressure at 70°F and their higher boiling temperature, propane, propylene and MAPP Gas® can be provided in liquid form. This allows their cylinders to be constructed with much thinner walls, and makes these cylinders lighter.

For those of you not familiar with the term **psig** used in the table, it is a unit of pressure and means pounds per square inch as read on a gauge or gauge pressure. In other words, it is the pressure of

Table 2. Some physical properties of typical fuel gases.

Physical Property	Fuel Gas				
	Propane	Acetylene	Propylene	Natural Gas	MAPP Gas®
Chemical formula	C_3H_8	C_2H_2	C_3H_6	CH_4	C_3H_4
Specific gravity of gas relative to air at 60°F	1.55	0.906	1.476	0.554	1.48
Vapor pressure at 70°F (psig)	120	635	133	NA	100
Specific gravity of liquid relative to 60°F water	0.507	NA	0.522	NA	0.573
Specific gas volume at 70°F(cu-ft/lb)	8.6	14.7	9.05	23.6	9.0
Liquid density at 60°F (lb/gal)	4.22	NA	5.0	NA	4.77
Boiling range for liquid at 1 atm (°F)	-44	-84	-54	-259	-36 to -4
Flame temperature in oxygen (°F)	4579	5589	5193	4600	5301
Heat of vaporization at 25°C (BTU/lb)	184	NA	188	NA	227
Total heating value (post vaporization) (BTU/lb)	21,800	21,500	21,100	23,900	21,000
Total heat value of vapor (BTU/cu-ft)	2498	1470	2371	900-1000	2404

Table 3. Some safety properties of typical fuel gases.

Safety Property	Fuel Gas				
	Propane	Acetylene	Propylene	Natural Gas	MAPP Gas®
Shock sensitivity	Stable	Unstable	Stable	Unstable	Stable
Explosive limits in oxygen (%)	2.4-57	3.0-93	2.3-55	5.0-59	2.5-60
Explosive limits in air (%)	2.2-9.5	2.5-80	1.9-11	5-15	3.0-11.0
Max allowable working pressure (psig)	Cylinder	15	Cylinder	Line	Cylinder
Burn velocity in oxygen (ft / sec)	12.2	22.7	15.4	15.2	15.4
Tendency to backfire	Slight	Slight	Slight	Large	Slight
Toxicity	Low	Low	Low	Low	Low
Reactivity with common materials	None	Alloys with 67% Copper	None	None	Alloys with 67% Copper

the gas over that of the surrounding air pressure. This surrounding pressure varies with altitude, but at sea level it is 14.7 psi.

Looking at the specific gravity of their vapor relative to that of air, we see that propane, propylene, and MAPP Gas® are heavier than air. Gases that are heavier than air will sink and collect on the floor of your work area. On the other hand, acetylene and natural gas are lighter than air. Their vapors will rise, get stirred up, and disperse more quickly than the other gases and won't need floor ventilation.

> **Safety Note:** ***If you are using fuel gases that are heavier than air, you need to consider ventilation near the floor to prevent explosive levels of vapors from building up.***

Besides its physical properties, you should also consider a gas's safety properties when choosing which one to work with. Some of the safety properties for fuel gases of interest are listed in Table 3.

As you can see, none of these gases are really very toxic and most do not backfire much. One major consideration is the allowable working pressure restriction for acetylene. In concert with its shock sensitivity, this should convince you to avoid its use. The shock sensitivity of natural gas is not as much of a concern because we tend to pipe that into our studio at very low pressure (¼ to 2 psig). Also, note that acetylene gas has a much wider explosive range than the other fuel gases. This equates to a much higher likelihood of developing explosive mixtures, most likely in the fuel gas line.

Another property of interest to a flameworker is that of reactivity of the gases with other materials. Looking at the table, we see that both acetylene and MAPP Gas® react with alloys (usually brasses) that have a copper composition greater than 67%. What this means is that you cannot use just any torch with them. You have to check to see that the torch is rated for use with these gases. On the other hand, you can use any torch rated for these fuel gases with all of the other gases. As we will see later the Hot Head® and the QuietTorch™ meet this requirement and are rated for MAPP Gas®.

A safety concern not listed in the table is the danger of frostbite from the fuel gases that are provided in liquid form because they cool small containers to near freezing under heavy use. To see this you have to look back into the physical property table to see that propane, propylene and MAPP Gas® are so provided. Let's now look at each of the fuel gases in turn.

Propane

Propane is the fuel gas most commonly used by glass beadmakers because of its ease of availability, handling, safety, and low cost. It is a saturated hydrocarbon gas with three carbon atoms and eight hydrogen atoms on each molecule. Propane is also much cleaner burning than some other fuels, such as acetylene.

Table 4. Typical propane cylinder sizes.

Feature	Dimension		
Size (lb)	20	33	100
Empty weight (lb)	26	36	77
Length (in)	19	27.3	48.9
Diameter (in)	12.2	12.2	14.5

Propane is a single-component, liquefied fuel gas obtained from crude oil and gas mixtures emanating from either oil or natural gas wells. In addition, it is also produced in certain oil refining processes and in recycling natural gas. Propane itself is odorless, but for safety's sake, a smelly oil is added to it that can be easily detected by anyone. This oil is a derivative of garlic.

Propane is available in small one-pound disposable cylinders as well as in bulk quantities. The fact that it liquefies under pressure allows the bulk cylinders to be light and easy to handle. Dimensions and weights of typical refillable propane cylinders are listed in the table on the previous page.

Propane is generally considered to be nontoxic. Short exposure to its vapor is not harmful, although high concentrations may produce a slight anesthetic effect. Avoid contact with liquid propane because it can cause frostbite-like burns. Propane gas has relatively narrow explosive limits from 2.2 to 9.5% in air. Mixtures outside of this range are safe.

Acetylene

Acetylene is a fuel gas commonly used in industry for oxygen-fuel gas welding and cutting. It is not used much for beadmaking because it is more dangerous. It is colorless and tasteless, but has a garlic-like odor. Like any of the fuel gases, it is flammable and can asphyxiate you if released in enough volume to displace your breathing air. The garlic-like odor is easily apparent at levels well below those that are hazardous.

Standard commercial grade acetylene (grade D) is only 98% pure. Its use can leave your glass looking dirty. Some manufacturers do carry higher purity gas, at increased cost of course, which burns cleaner.

The heat and flame temperature produced when burning any fuel gas depends upon the amount of oxygen with which it is mixed. Mixing acetylene with air at 21% oxygen produces a flame temperature of around 4000°F (2200°C.) This is hot enough for most glasswork. But if it is burned in combination with pure oxygen, flame temperatures as high 5730° F (3166°C) are achievable. Varying the oxygen to acetylene ratio will vary both the flame temperature as well as the amount of heat you can transfer to your work. Acetylene can generate the full gamut of flame types, from reducing to oxidizing.

Table 5. Typical acetylene cylinder sizes.

Feature	Dimension					
Size (lb)	MC	B	3	4	4.5	5
Empty weight (lb)	8	25	43	70	120	168
Length (in) w/o cap	13	19.5	25.5	34.3	38	41
Diameter (in)	4	6	7	8	10	12

Since acetylene is shock sensitive at pressures greater than 15 psig, it is not supplied as a liquefied gas as is propane. Instead, it is supplied dissolved in acetone. This mixture is packaged in heavy-walled cylinders filled with porous packing material to prevent sloshing. Acetylene cylinders should be handled carefully and not dropped in order to avoid damage to this packing material. This construction results in much heavier cylinders as can be seen from the weights in Table 5.

Acetylene should never be used at regulator pressures higher than 15 psig because of its shock sensitivity. It can react explosively to mechanical shock or ignition sources under such conditions. Acetylene can also react with copper, silver or mercury to form explosive compounds. Therefore, gauges, tubing and fittings should be steel, stainless steel, or brass with a copper content below 67%.

Propylene

Propylene is a single-component, liquefied fuel gas like propane. It is produced as a by-product at oil and petrochemical refineries. Its main commercial use is in the production of plastics (polypropylene) and chemicals. Propylene can serve as a fuel gas with outstanding performance, safety, and economy. As you can see from Table 2, propylene has a flame temperature considerably higher than that of propane, which may make it desirable for some applications such as borosilicate work.

Propylene, like propane, is very stable. It is not shock sensitive nor will it react with copper. It can be stored for long periods of time since it will not decompose without oxygen. Short exposures to its vapor are not harmful, but high concentrations may produce an anesthetic effect. Direct skin contact with liquid propylene can cause frostbite-like burns.

Natural gas

Natural gas is a fuel gas readily available in most urban areas. The primary combustible component of natural gas is methane. Because it is a natural product, its chemical composition varies depending on the location from which it is mined. It is obtained from wells that tap pockets of the gas trapped in the rock above petroleum deposits. After bringing it to the surface, it is purified and piped to our homes at low pressure of about ¼ to 2 psig.

The flame temperature achievable with natural gas is approximately the same as you can get with propane, but it is much cheaper. Because of its wide availability, it is a good choice as a fuel gas for use in beadmaking and the convenience of not having to refill one's tank is much appreciated.

Natural gas and its prime constituent, methane, are generally considered to be nontoxic. Breathing high concentrations can induce a feeling of pressure in the forehead or sinuses. Natural gas is relatively odor-free so a smelly hydrocarbon is added to make it more apparent when leaks have occurred.

MAPP Gas®

MAPP Gas® is a mixture of methylacetylene and propadiene. It is a stable high-energy fuel gas offering excellent performance, especially for use with handheld torches. A neutral MAPP Gas®-oxygen flame has a flame temperature of 5301° F (2927°C). It is insensitive to shock. A cylinder of MAPP Gas® will not detonate if dropped, dented, or incinerated; I would not suggest trying this at home.

It has relatively narrow explosive limits, 3 to 11% in air. MAPP Gas® can be used safely even up to full cylinder pressures of 100 psig at 70°F. Regulations in some locations may limit its use to the traditional 15 psig required for acetylene.

MAPP Gas® is available in one-pound disposable cylinders as well as in bulk quantities. The refillable cylinders are easy to handle because they are light like propane cylinders. If you use a lot of it, you may want to search around to find a source for larger tanks.

Like acetylene, MAPP Gas® reacts with copper, silver, or mercury to form explosive compounds. Therefore, gauges, tubing, and fittings have to be made from steel, stainless steel or brass with a copper content below 67%. Because of this, any torch usable for MAPP Gas® will be so marked. **If not so marked, do not use it for MAPP Gas®.**

MAPP Gas® is nontoxic, but exposure to high concentrations may produce a slight anesthetic effect. Skin contact with liquid MAPP Gas® can cause frostbite-like burns. Unlike some of the fuel gases, MAPP Gas® has a natural distinctive odor that smells just terrible if any leaks are present. This odor is detectable in concentrations as low as 100 ppm (parts per million) which is a concentration 1/300th that of its lower explosive limit. This means that you will usually smell it well before it becomes any sort of explosive hazard.

Table 6. Typical MAPP Gas® cylinder sizes

Feature	Dimension			
Size (lb)	7.5	30	70	115
Empty weight (lb)	7.5	25.5	56	72
Length (in)	22	35	44	48.5
Diameter (in)	6	9	12	14.75

Chemtane 2

Chemtane 2 is a blended fuel gas developed and marketed by Jalapa Gas and Chemical Corporation. I was introduced to this fuel gas by Peggy Prielozny, who uses it almost exclusively. It is made from a propane base. Jalapa hopes to market this fuel nation-wide in the near future with refueling stations as for propane. Chemtane 2 uses the same equipment as propane but burns with a much hotter flame.

Chemtane 2 has a flame temperature of 6000°F with oxygen and is much hotter than any of the naturally occurring fuel gases listed in Table 2. This factor combined with its total heat value of 24,812 BTU/lb means that you can work faster with less effort than with propane. It is a multipurpose fuel that works well both with handheld torches and mixed gas torches. With this fuel you will find the power to muscle your way through large borosilicate beads.

Because this fuel is propane based, you will find many of its physical and safety properties to be nearly the same as propane's. For example, it has the following physical properties: a vapor specific gravity of 1.5, a standard vapor pressure of 125 psi, a liquid specific gravity of 0.505, a standard specific gas volume of 8.83 cu-ft/lb, a liquid density of 4.24 lb/gal, a boiling point of -43.6°F, a standard heat of vaporization of 180 BTU/lb, and a standard total heat value of 2,810 BTU/cu-ft.

Like propane, Chemtane 2 is very safe to use. It is not shock sensitive. It has a narrow set of explosive limits in air of 2.3 to 9.4%. It has no working pressure limitations. It is resistant to backfire, is non-reactive, and has low toxicity. Like propane, it will produce a slight anesthetic effect if released into your work area. You can even use your old propane tank for this fuel.

Chem-o-lene

If you cannot get Chemtane 2 in your area, then you might want to get an additive to use with your propane system that gives many of the same benefits. It increases the flame temperature of a propane-oxygen system from about 4300°F to about 5800°F. It was originally designed for industrial use around oil fields as an alternative to acetylene. It is packaged in a proprietary bottle for use in lampworking by a company from Georgia called Chemweld and is distributed by Ricky Charles Dodson and Wale Apparatus.

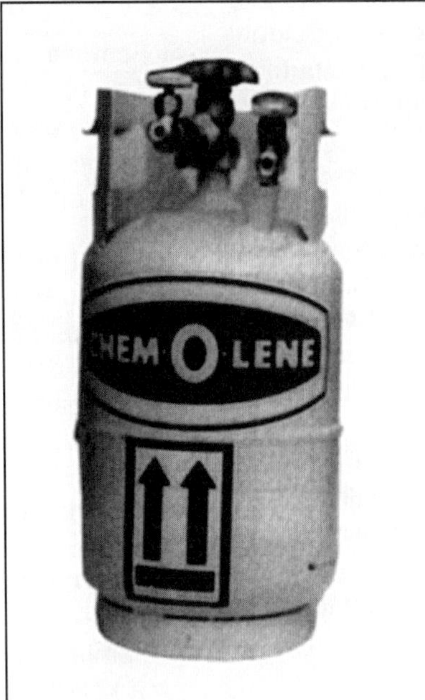

Figure 8. Chem-o-lene Cylinder.

Chem-o-lene is a sticky, oily, transparent yellowish liquid, about the consistency of motor oil. It comes in the five pound bottle seen in Figure 8 and gets hooked up in the propane line between the propane regulator and the torch. As the propane flows through the bottle, it picks up some Chem-o-lene into the gas flow.

When burned in the torch, things do not appear any different, but the heat output is much greater than normal. It has been reported that you can work twice as fast or with half the usual flame when using Chem-o-lene. Of course, this may not be right for everyone, especially those of you who like to work with a small sharp flame. But for those who specialize in large borosilicate beads, it may be a major boon.

A five pound bottle filled with Chem-o-lene currently sells for about $330 and will treat about 800 pounds of propane. When the chemical runs out, the bottle can be refilled for about $225. This price can easily be recovered in fuel savings. When you finish working for the night, make sure that the additive bottle gets closed or it can get into your gas system. This will require draining it back out into the proprietary bottle before you can start work the next day.

Handheld torches

Several videos and booklets have popularized the use of handheld torches in glass beadmaking. These torches have been derived from those normally used for soldering copper pipes, and although some do work for beadmaking, they are not as desirable as a fuel-oxygen system for a number of reasons.

- The lower flame temperature, which they provide, makes working glass a much slower process than with a propane-oxygen system.
- They generally provide a slightly reducing flame that may reduce many of the metal oxides used to color glasses and resulting in undesired color changes.
- They tend to be much noisier than surface-mixed, propane-oxygen torches.
- These torches do not have a very adjustable flame and this can prove very frustrating when you want a small pinpoint flame for detail work.

I will provide some introduction in their use as a way to get you started into glass beadmaking cheaply. But, I suggest that you to consider moving on to a more sophisticated, although unfortunately also a more expensive, fuel-oxygen torch system when you really commit to glass beadmaking for the long-term. As usual, there are some exceptions—there are a few beadmakers who really like these torches and have worked almost exclusively with them for a number of reasons:

- their inexpensiveness
- their lower heat output keeps the glass cooler and thus easier for beginners to handle
- the portability of the torch allows it to go with you almost anywhere, for example on vacations
- their simplicity. Some people are scared off by the complexity of mixed gas systems.

Disposable fuel gas tanks

The handheld torches tend to be used mainly with the liquefied fuel gases stored in small, disposable, cylindrical tanks weighing about a pound. These tanks are constructed with thin steel walls that are rolled and welded. The thickness of the tank walls is sufficient to contain the pressure of the liquefied fuel under normal conditions, but these walls are not thick enough though to contain the fuel if the tank is heated up. This is because the pressure inside a tank of a liquefied fuel gas increases drastically when heated. This is the result of more and more of the liquefied fuel gas boiling off into its vapor phase as the temperature rises. If the tank is heated hot enough, the pressure in the tank could get so high that a cylinder could burst.

To prevent this from happening, the disposable fuel tank manufacturers build a small pressure relief valve recessed into the top of each tank as seen in Figure 9. This pressure relief valve is set to bleed off fuel gas vapor at pressures substantially below the burst pressure of the tank.

Of course bled-off fuel vapors are very flammable, creating a risk of fires. For this reason, you should always store these fuel tanks in a cool place. You should also ensure that this storage area is dry so that rusting does not weaken the tanks.

A handheld torch is connected to a disposable fuel gas tank by way of a threaded joint on the top of the tank. If you look down inside the threaded joint, you will see an opening into the tank. At the top of the opening, you can see a short taper in the throat leading to a hollow white teflon washer. Beneath that, you see a small valve like those on bicycle tires.

The way that the seal between the torch and the tank works is that the torch head has a shaft that sticks down into the teflon washer. As you screw the head onto the tank, the shaft pushes in the bicycle valve to let fuel gas out of the tank. The teflon washer seals around the shaft to help reduce leakage of fuel gas around it. The torch head also has a washer that seats against a flat on the top of the tank as you screw the two together finger-tight. The washer on the torch is the final and most important seal to prevent fuel gas from leaking out of the joint between them. If you ding the flat on the top of a disposable tank, it can cut into the washer as you screw the torch onto the tank. This can ruin the torch washer and allow the joint to leak fuel gas from then on.

For this reason, you need to protect the flat on the top of each tank when in storage. When you get the tank from the hardware store, it should have a protective plastic cover on it. Store the tank with that cover in place to protect the flat. Once you screw the torch head down onto the tank top, take a second to listen for leaks. If you detect none, then the torch is ready to use.

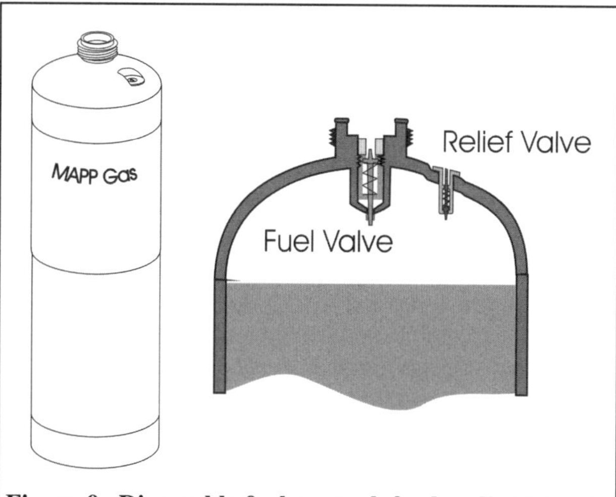

Figure 9. Disposable fuel gas tank for handheld torch

From the description of the tank, it sounds pretty simple and seems like nothing could go wrong with it. Well, that is almost true. I have read of situations where after use, a person was removing a camping stove from such a disposable propane tank for storage and the bicycle valve got stuck open. So, here is this person holding a hot stove in one hand and the disposable propane tank spewing propane in the other.

To make matters worse, as propane (or any of the liquefied fuel gases) evaporates, it sucks heat out of its surroundings to get that little bit of extra energy needed to change from a liquid to a vapor. This causes the tank to cool and if the fuel gas is evaporating fast enough, cool can become freezing. Have you ever heard about children licking frozen signposts? Yes, you guessed it, the tank can freeze to your hand. This is a sobering image, isn't it? So, treat these disposable tanks with respect.

Let's examine that situation for a second. How could it have happened? What could have caused that bicycle valve to get stuck open? The most likely scenario is that dirt somehow got stuck in the valve. So always make sure that the seat of the torch and the throat of the tank are clean before you screw them together. That's another reason for keeping the protective plastic cap on your disposable fuel tank during storage.

Another possibility for what could have happened, is that the end of the shaft on the torch that pushes in the bicycle valve may have gotten a burr on it, perhaps by dropping it. Then when it was screwed into the propane tank, the burr could have caught the top of the valve and bent it. This may have caused the valve plunger to get bound up when it was pushed in, preventing it from closing after removal of the stove. So, make sure that you carefully check out your torch head before each use to look for damage.

This leads to the issue of how you should store your disposable fuel tank and torch. Should you store them separately or connected? I believe that the joint between the torch and the tank is probably less reliable than the valve built into the propane tank. So I always store them separately as is recommended. You may also have small children around that might play with the torch if they find it assembled. So, it makes sense for you to always disassemble the two after use and store them separately.

Before you disassemble them, move to a well-ventilated space. Then, unscrew the torch from the tank. After disassembly, listen for leaks, smell for gas, and hold your thumb over the top of the tank to feel if any fuel gas is leaking out. Remember to put the plastic protective cover back on the top of the tank.

Some general rules for the use of disposable fuel tanks are as follows:

- Only use them in well ventilated areas
- Do not store them in living areas
- Do not store them near appliances with open flames such as water heaters, furnaces, or gas dryers.
- Do not store them in direct sunlight or areas that get above 120°F (49°C)
- Never puncture or burn them even if you think they are empty
- Discard empty ones in a safe place, do not try to refill them
- Detach them when not in use
- Make sure to close the torch burner valve before detaching.

The other thing that can be frustrating with those small one-pound tanks is that when you have used up about two-thirds of the tank, it will cool very quickly with further use. This results in pressure loss and an increasingly softer flame even though you still have plenty of fuel. Because of this, you can rarely use up a tank efficiently. Not only that but you have all those tanks to dispose of.

Handheld torch head

If you decide to try using a handheld torch for making beads, by far the best choice is a Hot Head® shown in Figure 10. Don't go out and get a

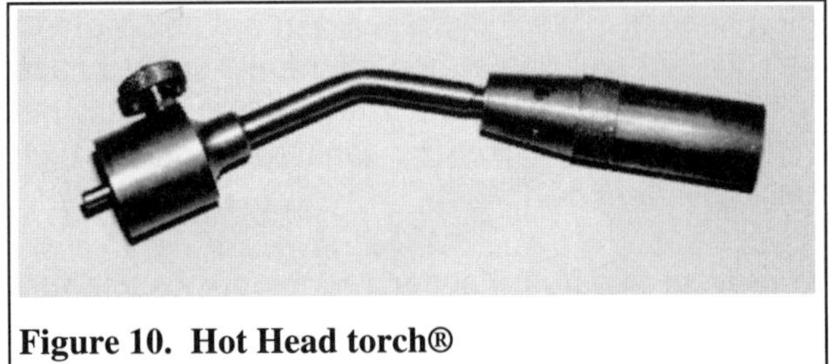

Figure 10. Hot Head torch®

plumbing torch from a hardware store because it just does not get hot enough. Another relatively new handheld torch on the market is the "QuietTorch™" or "Fireworks" that is seen in Figure 11.

Basically, the function of a handheld torch head is to control the flow of the fuel gas, to mix it with air for burning, and to direct the flame away from the tank and onto our bead. It mixes the air and fuel together using a venturi mixer to accomplish this. An example of a venturi system with which most people are probably familiar is that of a perfume atomizer.

The way that venturi mixers operate is that a jet of working liquid (air for the atomizer and fuel gas for the torch) goes by a suction hole at high speed. As it goes by the holes it creates a low-pressure region that pulls material in through the holes. This is very similar to how air moving over the wing of a plane creates lift. Thus when you squeeze the bulb on the perfume atomizer, you shoot a fast moving jet of air over the top of the tube that goes down into the perfume. This causes the perfume to be sucked up the tube and pulled into the air stream. With a Hot Head®, a high velocity jet of fuel pulls air into the jet as It goes by the holes on the side of the head.

A Hot Head® torch provides a nice hot flame with which one can work, but with a lot of extra flame washing over your work. If one stays in the proper position, past the blue cone, one can be reasonably

Figure 11. QuietTorch™or Fireworks Torch

successful in making glass beads with soft glass. The QuietTorch™ flame is more directed and by rotating the air-mixing valve on the side of the barrel you have some control over the flame chemistry. This control can be a little tricky to master so give it a little time and you have to have gloves or pliers available to adjust this on the fly because the barrel gets real hot.

Torch stands for handheld torches

Some beadmakers actually used these torches by holding the tank tightly between their legs while allowing the torch head to just stick up over the top of their fireproof work surface. I cannot caution you strongly enough against this work practice. There will be times when you are making beads that you will drop some molten glass into your lap. If you are holding the tank in your lap, what are you going to do when you have to get up quickly to avoid getting burned? Also the tank gets pretty cold as the propane evaporates, making holding it this way uncomfortable. Some persistent artists have gotten around these problems by using a towel in their lap to protect and insulate their legs.

For these reasons, I suggest that you purchase or build some sort of a torch holder if you are going to use a handheld torch. Some suppliers offer a bracket that can be screwed to your workbench and will clamp onto the propane tank. The one problem that I see with this arrangement is that it ends up holding the tank out over your lap. This can prevent quick escape from the bench and puts the torch in a very vulnerable position. But, this is probably the best that can be done with a disposable tank because of its awkward size. If you try to position one on your workbench, the torch is too high to work with unless you are going to work standing up. Make sure that whatever stand or bracket you end up using gets rigidly attached to your workbench so that it can not fall to the floor if you make a sudden dash from your chair.

You can also make a stand similar to the one currently on the market, using a right angle bracket purchased from the hardware store. I suggest using about a 3" or 4" bracket. One end gets screwed down to your workbench as illustrated in Figure 12. The other end of the bracket is fastened to the disposable fuel tank using two large hose clamps. These clamps are tightened to the fuel tank by screwing the screw head of the clamp clockwise. To adjust the angle of the torch for your work, you can change the angle of the bend in the bracket.

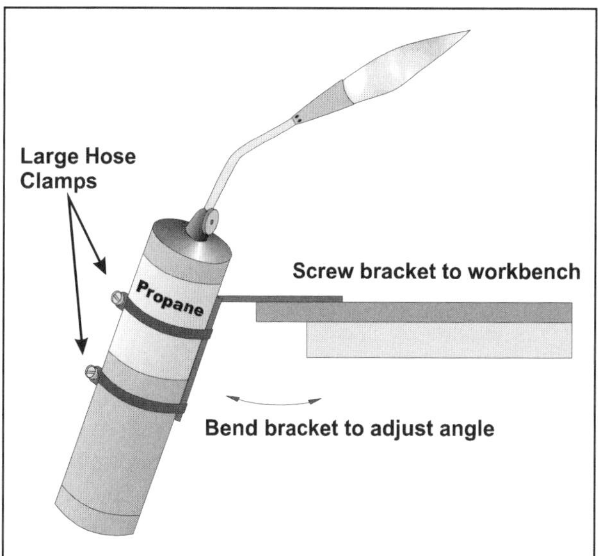

Figure 12. Homemade stand for a handheld torch.

Tank adapters

If you do not want to be restricted by the limited amount of gas in a one pound disposable tank, you might consider purchasing an adapter hose to feed fuel to your handheld torch from a larger tank. Coleman makes adapter hoses that have a fitting that hooks up to a normal propane tank on one end and a fitting that looks like the top of a disposable tank on the other end. They come in a number of different lengths: 4', 6', etc. One of these fittings is shown in Figure 13.

This is what the real long-term users of this torch do. It removes all the limitations incurred with the one-pound tanks. It also allows you to switch to a fuel other than those that are available in the disposable tanks. Peggy Prielozny, one such long-term Hot Head® user, says that she would have switched long ago if she had not been able to use a tank

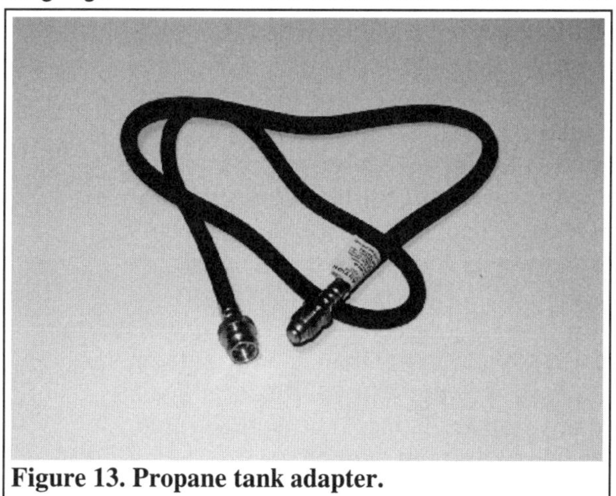

Figure 13. Propane tank adapter.

adapter with Chemtane 2. She says that it is the perfect fuel for these torches and it is only available in bulk. So she would not be able to use it without a tank adapter.

If you decide to use an adapter connected to a larger tank instead of a disposable tank, you will have to modify your torch stand to grip the adapter or torch head instead of the tank as shown in Figure 14.

When you use a tank adapter, it is not mandatory, that you use a regulator on the bulk fuel tank. The reason that I would consider one is that bulk fuel tanks do not cool as much as disposable tanks and thus the pressure in them can be a lot higher, especially on a hot day. This can result in uncomfortably large torch flames without regulation of the feed pressure. You regulator would have to be controllable in the range of 60 to 90 psig.

The Hot Head® and the QuitTorch™ are designed to operate at normal tank pressures of about 100 psi. They do not contain a regulator but instead use a small orifice drill through a brass button or "spud" to control the amount of gas released. This orifice can wear over time resulting larger flames and may eventually need replacement. Because it is so small, this orifice can become blocked by foreign materials so be sure to keep your connections clean and to clean the tank connections before mating them.

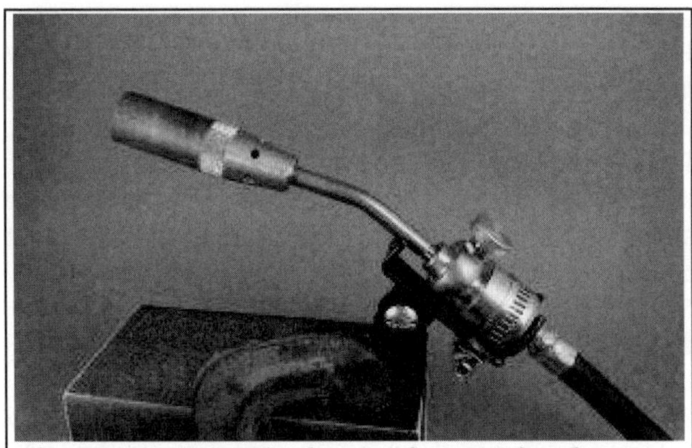

Figure 14. Stand when using tank adapter.

Fuel-oxygen systems

To be able to make beads quickly and easily, you need a mixed gas torch system. These have both a fuel and an oxygen source. Without both, it is just not possible to provide enough heat to the glass to quickly soften it for easy manipulation. For a fuel gas, most glass beadmakers use propane although natural gas is also a good choice if you have it available. In this section, I will mainly focus on setting up a propane-oxygen system but will also provide some discussion of the issues is setting up to a system to use natural gas.

Using oxygen rather than air in your torch provides a hotter flame. This is a result of two factors. First, since air is only 21% oxygen by volume, it does not provide as much oxygen per volume to burn the fuel. Second, oxygen is the only gas consumed from the air. Thus, when you use air as the source of oxygen for your torch, you waste energy heating up the other gases in the air that are not part of the combustion process. This results in a much cooler flame. In addition, I suggest that you get into the habit of calling oxygen, "oxygen." The bad habit of calling it air causes a lot of confusion when trying to communicate with others.

The gas system that you will work with in making beads is probably the most dangerous part of the whole operation. It stores an awful lot of energy that could, if abused, do a great deal of harm. On the other hand, when handled properly, the risks of its use are not excessive. Because of this reason, it is very important to understand how your equipment works and how to operate it safely. The components of a completely assembled propane-oxygen torch system are illustrated in Figure 15. Let's go over each of these components in detail.

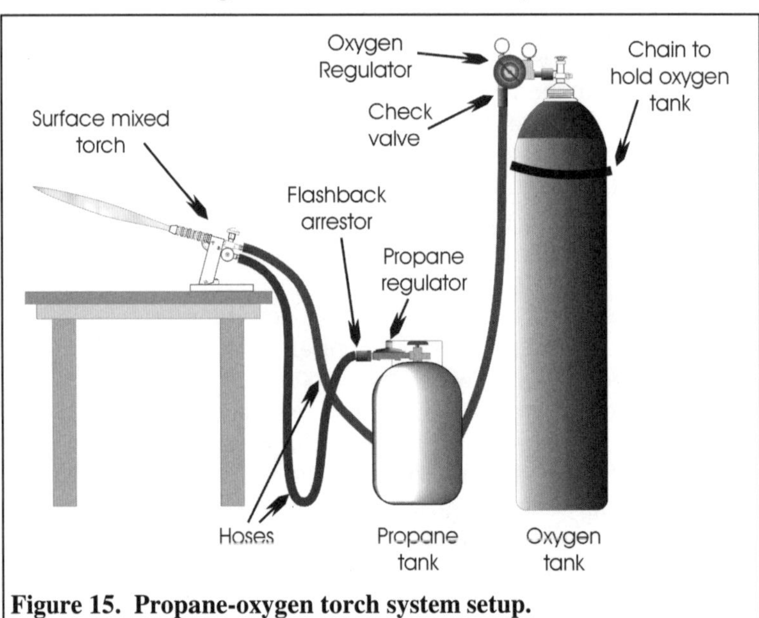

Figure 15. Propane-oxygen torch system setup.

Propane tanks

Being a liquefied fuel gas means propane is a dense energy source with a lot of energy in a small lightweight volume. The mixed gas systems use propane from the same refillable containers as those used for barbeques. These tanks, as described in Table 4, are available in 5, 20, 30, and 100-pound sizes from camping, hardware, or recreational vehicle centers. The weight designator represents the approximate weight of propane when full. The size of the tank you need depends on how often you are going to make beads. A 5-lb. tank will last a long time and is very portable. But, if you are going to be doing a lot of flameworking, you may want to go to a 20-lb. size.

You can get tanks refilled or exchanged at many of the same places that sell them as well as some gasoline stations. When getting your tank refilled, check to see how pure the propane is. The higher the percentage of propane, the cleaner burning it will be. Not everyone carries the same grade of propane. Ask, if they know how pure the propane they are selling you is.

Components of a propane tank

On the top of your propane tank, as seen in Figure 16, is a valve with a round or triangular handle. This is the tank on/off valve. It is usually protected from damage by a lifting collar welded to the tank. The handle will probably be marked with arrows showing the correct direction to open and close the valve. They are turned counterclockwise to open the tank and clockwise to close it.

The handles on the on/off valve all used to be round, but triangular ones were added to indicate if the tank has the new overfilling protection device (OPD). It is a safety device designed to provide an automatic means of preventing overfilling of a propane cylinder in excess of the proscribed 85% full. It is recommended by the National Fire Protection Association (NFPA 58) and became mandatory in most states after March 2002.

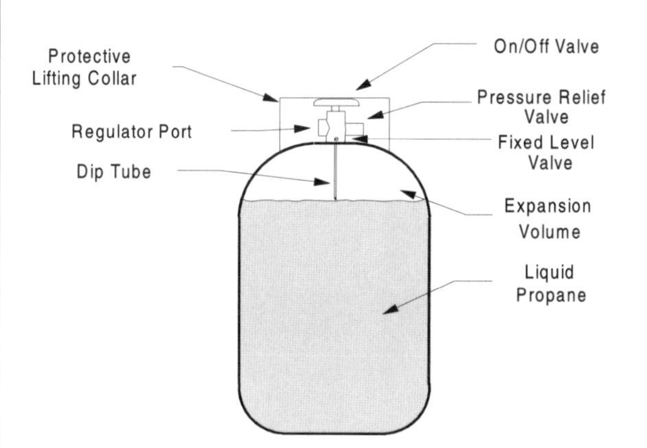

Figure 16. Cross sectional view of a typical older propane cylinder

They are only available for vertically standing propane tanks and are required on tanks from 4 lb through 40 lb. Some earlier models of OPD valves had flow problems. If you should have flow problems, try a different tank to see if the OPD valve could be the issue. If it is then you will need a new valve or tank.

To one side of the vertical shaft of the on/off valve is an open port into which your propane regulator screws. If you look closely at the regulator port, you will see that the threads on the inside of the port go in the opposite direction of normal pipe threads. Normal pipe threads are right-handed and screw together by turning the fittings clockwise. Propane regulator port threads are left-handed threads and screw together by turning the fittings in the opposite direction, counterclockwise.

Left-handed fittings are distinguished from right-handed fittings by a groove notched into the fitting as seen in the one on the left in Figure 28. The fittings are made left-handed to try and prevent you from accidentally making a wrong connection such as connecting a fuel-contaminated hose to your oxygen source. Left-handed fittings are sometimes hard to get used to. If you have trouble tightening or loosening the fittings, double check to see that you are turning them in the correct direction.

The other appendage on the on/off valve, opposite to the regulator port, is the pressure relief valve. It serves the function as the relief valve on the disposable propane tanks. It vents gas from the tank if the pressure rises too high for some reason. This prevents the tank from rupturing. This safety valve should only be adjusted by qualified personnel. It is usually set to release at 250 psig.

In between the pressure relief valve and the pressure regulator port may be what looks like a brass screw with a hole in it. This fitting is called a 10% or fixed level valve. In normal operation, this valve should always be closed (screwed in). Its function is to make sure that a tank does not get overfilled.

Ideally, a properly filled propane tank is only filled 85% full with liquefied fuel gas. The remaining 15% of the tank is occupied by fuel gas vapor. This remaining space is known as the expansion volume. It provides some room for the liquefied fuel gas to expand into if the tank should be overheated. If your tank got overfilled, there would be no room for the liquid to expand. If overheated, expanding liquefied gas would then push out against the walls of the tank. This could allow it to generate large enough pressures to burst your tank. The expansion volume also serves as space for a sufficient amount of vapor to accumulate to readily feed your torch. If it were not large enough, the flow to the torch would be limited.

Filling a propane tank

Not overfilling your propane tank is so important, that you should only have them filled by qualified personnel. In addition, you should understand the filling procedures so that you can ensure that it is being done properly. The regulator has to be removed to fill the tank. It is best to do this at home before going to get the tank filled. When going back and forth to the fill station, always screw the plastic protector plug into your regulator fitting to prevent any damage to the threads that might cause them to leak.

Filling by fixed level valve is one of the two methods used to fill propane tanks. The fixed level valve is that fitting which looks like a screw with a hole in it that was discussed earlier. It is attached to a tube, called the dip tube. This tube extends down into the tank to the designed 85% fill level. The fixed level fill method is done in well-ventilated areas, preferably outside, because propane will be released during the procedure.

To use this filling method, the tank is first connected to the fill station and the on/off valve is opened. The person filling the tank will then start the transfer pump and open the fixed level valve. When the propane reaches the designed fill level, liquid propane is forced up the dip tube and released as a white mist out of the fixed level valve. At this point, the tank on/off valve and the fixed level fill valve are closed. The transfer pump is turned off and all fittings are disconnected. The fixed level valve should then be checked to see that it is closed using a soapy water solution. You should do this when you arrive home if they did not do it at the fill station.

In theory, it should not be possible to overfill the tank with this method because once it is filled all the extra propane would be forced up the dip tube and out the fixed level valve. But in practice, it is possible to pump the propane in faster than it can come out the fixed level valve, especially if the valve is not opened enough or the pumping pressure is high. Therefore, the filling person should remain in attendance while filling the tank and avoid becoming distracted.

Filling by weight is the other fill technique. In this method the full weight of the tank is calculated ahead of time and the tank is filled until it reaches the correct weight. To determine the full weight, one first needs to get the water capacity (WC) and tare weight (TW), or empty tank weight. These two numbers are usually stamped on the outside of the lifting collar around the tank on/off valve along with the dip tube length (DT). For my 20 lb. tank, the WC=47.1, the TW=18, and the DT=3.9. The water capacity and tare weight values are in pounds. The dip tube length is in inches.

To calculate the full weight, multiply water capacity by 0.42 and add the product to the tare weight. This value (0.42) is 85% of the specific gravity of liquid propane at room temperature (which in other words is the ratio of the density of propane to the density of water). Therefore 0.42 times the water capacity is

Figure 17. Overfill Protection Device operation

the weight of the propane to be added for an 85% fill. Thus, in my case, the weight of the tank full is 47.1 x 0.42 + 18 = 37.78 lb. With this method, math errors or inaccurate scales can cause problems.

OPD valve operation is designed to be a backup mechanism in preventing overfilling of a propane tank when using one of the two previously described procedures. Its operation is sketched in Figure 17. Before the tank is full the float, at the bottom of illustration 1, hangs down causing the pin that is riding on its attached cam to be pushed up. This pin is essentially a check valve like we will discuss later in Figure 26. When it is held up by the cam, it cannot close. Then as the tank starts to fill, the float starts coming up by rotating about a pivot point in the cam as seen in illustration 2. Eventually it rotates up to the point where the pin can drop into the dip in the cam surface as in illustration 3. When the pin drops it allows the check valve to become functional and seal off the flow of propane into the lower valve from the regulator port. Sealing is assisted by the pressure of the propane trying to get in. When pressure is removed and you hook up the tank to your regulator, pressure on the backside of the check valve is relieved and propane can now flow in the allowed direction of the check valve up and out of the tank. As propane is used from the tank, the OPD valve will again drop toward the starting position.

Tank certification

As you looked around for the WC, TW, and DT values, you may have noted a date stamped on your tank such as 9 88. This is the date of manufacture of your tank. Twelve years after this date, you will have to get your tank recertified before you can get it refilled any more.

Many suppliers of industrial propane bottles can do recertification. They will check the tank inside and out for any signs of corrosion or other indications of impending failure. If it passes, a new certification date will be stamped on the tank. It will have to be recertified every five years from then on.

Using a propane tank

Whenever you use your propane tank, it should always be standing straight up, although there are some propane tanks for RVs that are made to be mounted sideways and could be used for glass beadmaking. With standard propane tanks, the vapor is admitted to the on/off valve at the top of the tank. If the tank is on its side, the liquid level may be high enough to allow liquid propane through the valve and into the system. This could result in a build up of pressure inside the hoses as the liquid vaporizes, possibly causing them to burst. It could also result in damage to the OPD mechanism or cause it to close depending on the tank orientation.

Most of the propane in your tank is in liquid form. But, since it has such a low boiling point, -43.8°F, you will always have plenty of propane vapor over the surface of the liquid, just as you have plenty of steam over the surface of water when you boil it. As the vapor evaporates off the surface of the propane, it cools the local area of the tank. Because of this, you can often tell the liquid level of the propane in your tank by looking for a sweat line (condensation ring) around your tank. There are even liquid crystal strips available that change color with temperature that you can attach to the side of your tank to make the cooler region near the propane liquid level more readily visible.

The pressure of the propane vapor in the tank and thus the pressure available to supply propane to your torch is a function of the bottle temperature. Table 7 lists the vapor pressure over liquid propane at several selected temperatures. From the table, we see that the pressure available at normal room temperature is about 110 psig. Alternately, you keep your tank outside and in winter, you may only have 11 psig available.

Table 7. Temperature variation of propane vapor pressure.

Temperature (°F)	Pressure (psig)	Temperature (°F)	Pressure (psig)
-44	0	70	110
-40	2	90	150
-20	11	100	172
0	24	110	197
20	41	120	225
32	54	130	257

If you store your cylinder next to your hot water heater (definitely not recommended), your pressure may soar to over 250 psig in the heat of summer. Under such conditions, your pressure relief valve may release some of the pressure rather than allow the tank to rupture. This presents a safety problem of another sort because now you have propane venting out into the room and it could cause an explosion. So, try to keep your propane tank in a location where it will neither get too hot nor too cold and is well ventilated.

Safety Note: ***Store your propane in cool, dry locations and never near natural gas appliances.***

Many areas have fire regulations that require storage of propane tanks out-of-doors, which is really a good idea. NFPA 58 states that propane tanks should be stored outdoors at least five feet from a source of ignition and no closer than three feet from an opening to a structure. It further recommends that it not be enclosed more than 50% (two sides). If you do this, be sure to protect the tank from the elements—thermal, rain and snow, but make sure that the shelter includes plenty of ventilation. Also try to hide it from prying eyes so that children will not play with it. Other beadmakers have used things like garbage cans with holes in them or garden hose houses to disguise and protect their propane tanks. They also bury the hoses in a way as to protect them from water damage and feed them through a hole in the wall or a window to their workstation.

Another thing you may notice is that the smelly garlic-derivative oil called methyl mercaptan, which is added to propane so you can smell it, is not as volatile as propane. Therefore, as you get near the bottom of the tank, the propane tends to get stinkier and you may be able to smell it in the torch combustion gases. After a number of propane tank fills, more and more of the stinky oil builds up in your tank and the smell gets even worse. When it starts to get really obnoxious, you may want to drain the oil out of your tank at the next opportune time. Do this only when your tank is empty. Vent the tank outside for a while first to get rid of any propane vapors that might still remain. Then, lean the tank over a tray to catch the oil and drain it. After it is all drained, clean up the tank and dispose of the oil properly.

Natural gas hookup

There are a few things that you need to understand before you consider switching over to natural gas. The first is be prepared to get the runaround because this is not widely done and your gas company and plumber are not going to understand your needs and may fight you some on it, especially if you try to lobby for higher gas pressure to your studio.

One of the first things that you probably want to know is the gas pressure available to you. The regulated natural gas pressure to most homes is between about 1/4 and 2 psig with most being on the lower end of that range. These pressures are also commonly quoted in terms of inches of water in which case 1/4 psig translates to about 7 inches of water. This pressure is lower than what most of the torches that we use in beadmaking were designed for. As an example, a minor bench burner was designed to operate at about 2 psig. Because of this you will have to open your torch fuel value more than you are used to in order to get the same sized flame. Also the maximum flame size and heat output of your torch will be lower at this pressure because you can just not get enough gas to the face of your torch. This will also limit the size of torch you can use. At 1/4 psig I would not try to use something much larger than a minor bench burner. You may find you flame looks and burns different than you are used to.

Before you hook up to natural gas you should talk to a plumber and find out if there are any local restrictions. Then if required get a building permit. Basically what will be done in most situations is that you will have to first tap into your natural gas line. How that is done depends upon the configuration of the pipes in your home but usually amounts to:

- Turning of the gas at the meter
- Sawing a section of pipe in half to remove it
- Adding a Tee to that section of line by adding back three shorter sections of pipe, a Tee and a union
- One section of pipe goes into one of the old connectors and another into the other
- The Tee then mounts to one of the pieces and the remaining section into the other side of the Tee
- At this point there will be a short gap between the two sections of pipe that is just large enough to fit the union
- One half of the union screws onto one side and the other half onto the other side
- Then the union is screwed back together.

You will then add an extension coming out of the Tee to go to your workstation. At the end of the extension, before the connector where you connect your hoses you want to have a shutoff valve. This will allow you to shut off the gas in case of an emergency like your hoses spring a leak. It is also a lot more convenient to be able to turn off the gas here when you change your hoses than having to go out to the meter.

Although some people do not think it is necessary, I advocate installing some protective devices on the system to prevent the possibility of flashback. This is especially needed if you are to ever use a premixed torch but damage to a surface-mixed torch could also occur that would allow flashback conducive conditions to develop. You cannot use the same kind of flashback arrestor that you use on regulated propane systems because the pressure is not high enough to compress the spring in the integral check valve so you will not get any flow them. There are arrestors and check valves made for the natural gas industry using different technology that will work for this application. What I would suggest is to install a check valve and a coil flash arrestor in the system. You can get check valves that open with a fraction of a psi. One source for this equipment is N. M. Knight Company in New Jersey.

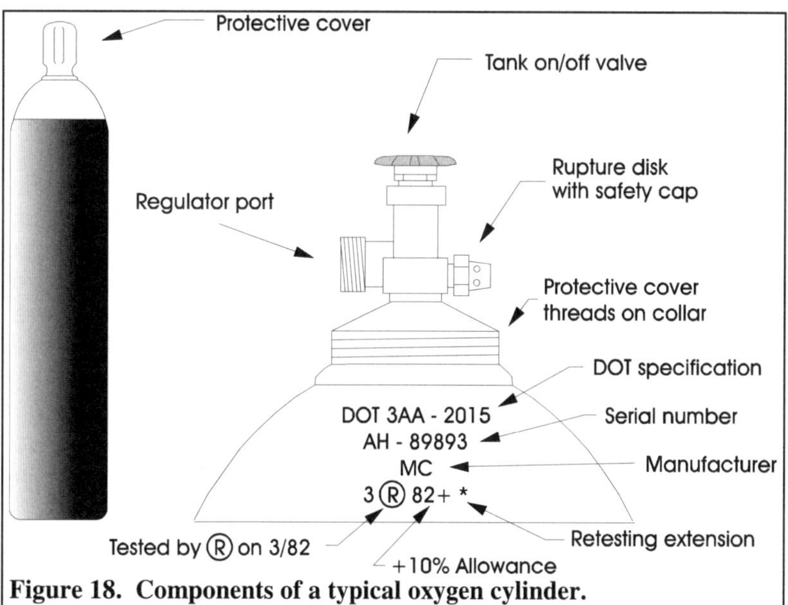

Figure 18. Components of a typical oxygen cylinder.

If you decide to pursue having higher natural gas pressure to your workstation than is currently being fed to the rest of the house this is where the battles come. To do this, you will need to get the gas company to install a slightly higher-pressure regulator to the whole house or add an extra branch in your gas system downstream from your current regulator. To this branch they will have to add a higher-pressure (about 15 psig would be reasonable for larger torches) regulator and likely a second meter. You would then have to add piping from that meter to go to your workstation. Be prepared for resistance because this is out of the ordinary and they will be sure that they know more than you do and will not want to do it. Your gas company may or may not let you have a dual pressure system unless it is going to a separate building. There may also be zoning and local building code regulations to deal with and last but not least, there will probably a good-sized bill for all these non-standard special circumstances requests.

Oxygen cylinders

Oxygen is available in cylinders from your local welding supply company. They will normally sell you the oxygen and rent you the tank it is in for a nominal monthly fee. This may or may not be the preferred situation. Some companies might require that you buy the cylinder. This is not always desirable, depending on whether or not you are then responsible for its upkeep, which includes things like cylinder valve maintenance and hydrostatic testing. Buying your tank is usually cheaper but you may not be allowed to just drop off your old cylinder and get a new one, you may have to wait for them to fill your cylinder. Check the policies of your local welding supply company to see how they handle owner tanks.

Oxygen cylinders come in a number of sizes that are rated by their oxygen capacity in cubic feet at standard atmospheric pressure and temperature (STP). The most common size cylinders are listed in Table 8 along with related characteristic data. The service pressure of your cylinder will be marked near the top in accordance with Department of Transportation (D.O.T.) regulations. Do not accept a cylinder where the label is not legible.

As an example, you may see the marking D.O.T.3A-2015. This indicates that the cylinder has been manufactured in accordance with D.O.T. regulation

Table 8. Data on common oxygen cylinder sizes.

Oxygen Content *(cu ft)	Cap Height (in)	Outside Diameter (in)	Weight Full (lb)	Weight Empty (lb)	Inside Volume (cu ft)
20	19	5 3/16	13 ½	12	0.115
80	35	7 1/8	70	65	0.463
150	51	7 3/8	92	80	0.858
251	56	9	153	133	1.453
337	60	9 ¼	172	146	1.950

* Final oxygen volume at 70°F & 14.7 psi assuming initial tank at 70°F & 2200 psi.

3A and that the cylinder fill pressure is 2015 psi at 70°F. Current D.O.T. regulations on non-liquefied, non-flammable gases permits a 10% overfilling of cylinders. Your oxygen cylinder falls into this case and will usually be filled to about 2200 psig.

Components of an oxygen cylinder

On the top of your oxygen cylinder, as seen in Figure 18, is an on/off valve similar to the one on your propane tank. It is constructed of forged brass and screws into the cylinder with a ½" or ¾" thread. In addition to the on/off valve, there is a regulator port off to one side and a pressure relief feature to the other. The cylinder has no fixed level valve because the oxygen in your cylinder is a gas and is filled to a fixed pressure.

The on/off valve is protected during shipping by a protective cover that screws onto threads cut into the collar at the top of your cylinder. Always keep this cover and put it on whenever transporting your cylinder. Don't take it off until you have secured the tank to an immovable object.

In looking at the regulator port, you will first notice that its threads are on the outside of the port where they are more susceptible to damage. When you get the cylinder from your supplier these threads will be covered with a plastic cap to protect them. Save this cap and use it to prevent damage to the cylinder valve during transportation. You may get that cylinder back someday, so it is to your benefit to do so. If you look closely at the fittings on your regulator port, you will see that they are right-handed. This prevents you from accidentally mixing up oxygen fittings with propane fittings. All of your right-handed fittings will be smooth and do not have the notch in them that the left-handed fittings do.

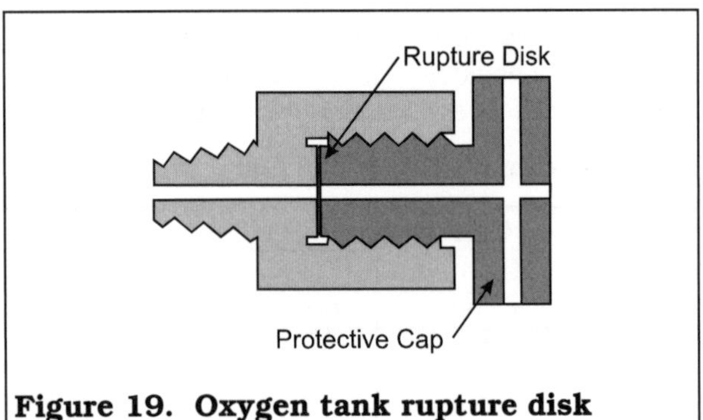

Figure 19. Oxygen tank rupture disk

The pressure relief feature is also different on an oxygen cylinder from that on a propane tank. Oxygen cylinders use a rupture disk. The safety cap, which you see over the rupture disk in Figure 20, prevents access to the disk and also prevents you from getting hit by flying pieces of the disk if it were to rupture. The disk is a thin piece of metal that bursts if subjected to too high a pressure.

The rupture disk thickness is sized to fail at about 3000 psig. This is considerably above the cylinder service pressure but well below the hydrostatic test pressure of the cylinder. The object here is again to provide a controlled way for a cylinder to fail if it should somehow become over pressurized. Notice how the rupture disk is connected directly to the inside of the cylinder and not through the valve. This means that it is always on the job protecting against over-pressurization of the cylinder. Again you should not play with this fitting.

> **Safety Note:** ***Never tamper with the rupture disk or its protective cap.***

Filling a cylinder

Oxygen cylinders must only be filled by trained personnel. They are filled by connecting them to a gas system and allowing the gas to flow into the cylinder until it reaches the right pressure. You should not have to worry about this procedure, as much as with propane, because the facilities at which they are filled are more specialized and the personnel that fill them tend to be better trained.

You may notice that the pressure in a freshly filled cylinder may vary a little from the 10% over 2015 psig, or 2200 psig, nominal value that is allowed by the DOT regulations. These cylinder fill variations are due to factors such as the temperature at which it was filled or the speed with which it was filled.

Cylinder certification

Hydrostatic testing is the recertification method required for oxygen cylinders. It is required ten years after manufacture of the cylinder and every five years thereafter. During hydrostatic testing, a cylinder is intentionally pressurized with water to about 3300 psig to test its continued integrity. The cylinder, which is constructed from a single forging of at least one-quarter inch thick high-carbon armor plate steel, expands under this pressure. The amount of expansion of the oxygen cylinder while pressurized and its permanent expansion after the pressure is released is recorded. They are used to determine whether the cylinder is safe to put back into use.

Occasionally, it may also be necessary to heat up the cylinder to anneal out any stress that may have been put into it during this operation. Additionally at times it may be necessary to clean the cylinder out using a caustic solution. The professionals that service your cylinder will perform these operations.

Using oxygen cylinders

Cylinders for other compressed gases should never be used to hold oxygen. This is because some other gases are pumped using oil. This can allow a film of oil to build up on the inside of the cylinder. If this equipment is used with oxygen, a fire or explosion may result. Generally the cylinder that you get will be painted green. Unfortunately this is not always the case and cylinder color-coding is no longer considered reliable. Instead, look for a paper shoulder label on the top portion of the cylinder where it starts to narrow down. This label will give information on chemical content, any health hazards and gas reactivity, such as oxidizer, flammable, or non-flammable, etc.

You may have heard horror stories about cylinders taking off and flying through brick walls like a rocket when a valve got broken. These stories have some basis of fact, so you should always treat your cylinders with some degree of respect. This type of reaction can occur because the oxygen in the cylinder is a pressurized gas, and all of it is immediately available to do work if the valve should be damaged. Realize that in a full cylinder each cubic foot of oxygen has been compressed down to about 10 cubic inches. This is $^{1}/_{173}{}^{nd}$ of its original volume and thus if there is a leak it will come rocketing out.

Because of this danger, treat your oxygen cylinder with respect. Put the protective cap on whenever you move your oxygen cylinder. Make sure that it cannot fall over or bang against other objects by chaining it in a rack. Do not drag your cylinder. If you don't have a handcart with which to move it, move it by standing it almost upright and rolling it on the bottom rim.

Safety Note: ***Always put the protective cap on your oxygen cylinder whenever you move it.***

Whenever you are using oxygen, you should open the on/off valve completely. This is because the on/off valve is what's called a back reacting valve. This type of valve only prevents leakage around the valve stem when the valve is completely open or completely closed. Although sometimes the valve may leak even if it is completely open, because it has been mistreated previously. For this same reason, it is best to completely close the on/off valve whenever the cylinder is not in use.

Figure 20 shows a cross sectional view of this valve. By examining it, we can see how the back reacting valve works. When closed, as shown in the figure, the lower valve forces the front seal down against the sealing surface of the oxygen inlet port. At this time, the only thing that is sealing the back seal is the force of the spring loading in the handle, but since there is no oxygen inside the valve body this is not a problem.

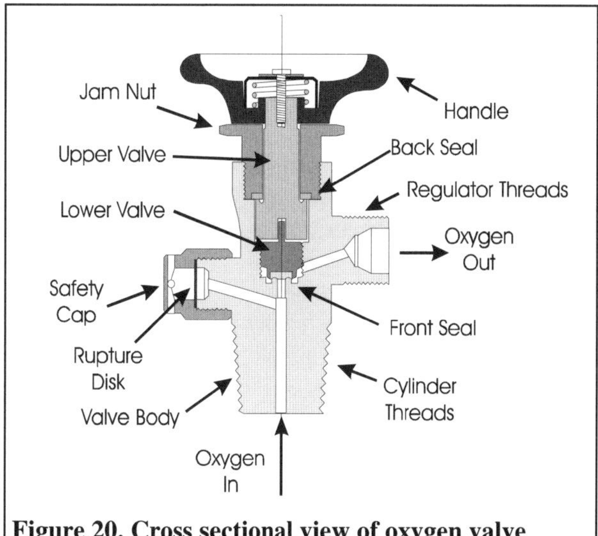

Figure 20. Cross sectional view of oxygen valve

Turning the handle causes the upper valve to turn, which in turn causes the lower valve to turn in the same direction. This is because the connection between them is not round. But since the lower valve is threaded, turning it counter-clockwise also causes it to move upward, opening the inlet port and allowing oxygen to fill the valve body. Although this is not apparent in the drawing, oxygen can get to the back seal. With only the force of the spring in the handle on the seal, high-pressure oxygen can leak out past the seal and around the upper valve. But, if you completely open the valve, the lower valve will go higher and push up against the upper valve. This extra push will put more pressure on the back seal and prevent any leakage.

Tip: To save on oxygen costs, always fully open you oxygen tank valve when in use and close it when not in use.

If a cylinder has a leak around the valve or the rupture disk, tag it to indicate the problem and move it out to a safe well-ventilated area immediately.

As a courtesy to your oxygen cylinder rental company, you should return your oxygen cylinders to them with 50 to 100 psig of oxygen remaining in them. This helps to prevent getting any foreign material into the cylinder. Also if you have more than one cylinder, mark an empty one with a chalk "MT" written on its side after it is taken out of service. This can avoid possible confusion later.

Oxygen concentrators

As you work with beadmaking for a while, you may decide that you are tired of lugging oxygen tanks to your welding supplier and may want to get an oxygen concentrator or oxygen generator instead. Small medical systems are called oxygen concentrators and larger industrial systems go by the name of oxygen generators. They both really operate by the same principle and the main difference is in the quality of the systems. I will use the general term of concentrator to refer to both types of systems. Oxygen concentrators are able concentrate the 21% of oxygen present in the air that we breathe to a high enough concentration for use with a lampworking torch. The purity of the oxygen produced by these systems will vary somewhat from about 90% to 95% depending upon how fast you are using it and your operating pressure. Oxygen concentrators, such as shown in Figure 21, have become popular with the medical community and more and more systems are becoming available. They are able to separate the oxygen from air's other main constituent, nitrogen, through the magic of gas adsorption.

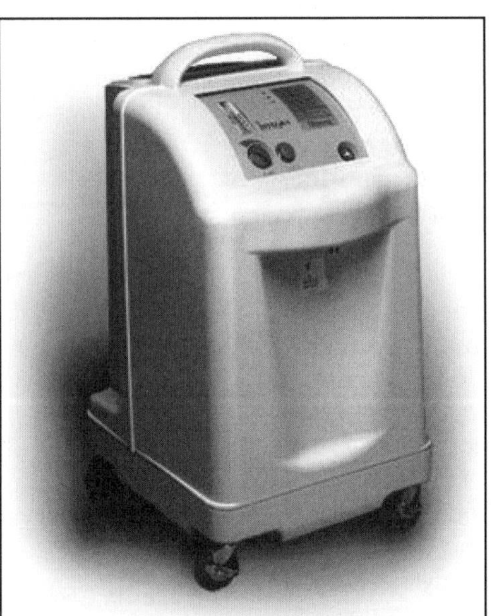

Figure 21. Small medical oxygen concentrator

How oxygen concentrators work

Adsorption is the term given to the fact that many gas and vapor molecules want to stick to solid surfaces. The molecules stick to the surface by way of a weak set of forces called Van der Wall forces that are much weaker those in chemical bonds, but strong enough to hold the molecules in place for seconds, minutes, and even longer. Almost all solid surfaces exposed to air are coated with one or more layers of adsorbed molecules. The affinity of some molecules to a surface is greater than others, a fact that makes it possible to use adsorption to separate molecules from one another.

With oxygen concentrators, the surface that the gases stick to is a light, porous material known as a zeolite. This material has a vast network of tiny interconnecting holes and tunnels resembling a microscopic sponge. If you add up all the surface area of these holes and tunnels, it represents an enormous amount of surface area onto which gas molecules can stick. At ordinary temperatures and pressures, air molecules stick to these surfaces for a short time before they are knocked off. Nitrogen molecules stick for slightly longer times than oxygen molecules because they bind more strongly to the zeolite surface than do the oxygen molecules. For this reason, as you pass air through fresh zeolite, the gas that comes out is concentrated in oxygen and most of the nitrogen molecules are left behind on the zeolite surface.

To increase the efficiency of the process, oxygen concentrators pass the air through containers of zeolite (known as beds) at higher pressures that push the molecules closer together. The air coming out is almost pure oxygen until the zeolite surface become saturated with nitrogen and can hold no more. Then to continue the process, the concentrator switches the air feed into a second zeolite bed. Meanwhile, the concentrator control system vents the first bed to atmosphere. There are then more nitrogen molecules sticking to the zeolite than the equilibrium conditions of the adsorption process can support and most of the nitrogen molecules gradually get knocked off of the surface and vented to atmosphere. This is called regenerating the bed and about the time that it is complete, the second bed is starting to become saturated and it is time to switch the flow back to the first bed. By switching back and forth like this every few seconds, one zeolite bed is always concentrating oxygen while the other is regenerating.

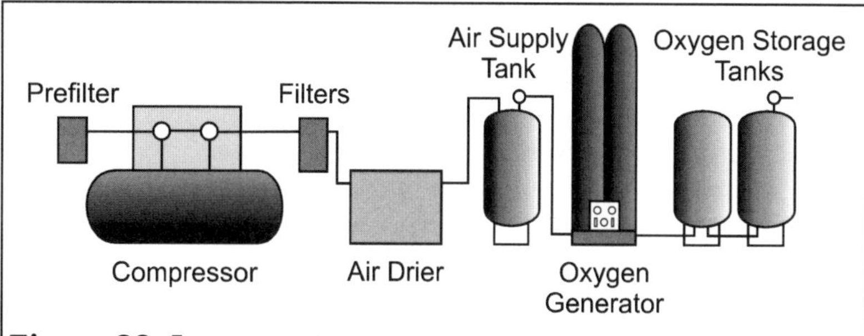

Figure 22. Large oxygen generator system components

This concept may smack of magic or perpetual motion to some but it works and you are paying for it with the electrical energy required to compress the air. The cost of this electricity is usually a lot less than what we are paying the welding supply shops for tanks of oxygen and you can often pay for the equipment investment within a year or two. The beauty of these systems is that they will work indefinitely if you provide them clean dry air to work with. The truth of the situation is that our air will often contain impurities such as oils or solvents that can, if not well filtered, deposit onto the zeolite and poison it over time, requiring replacement of the zeolite every couple years.

There are basically two main classes of concentrator systems: small portable medical systems that are made to supply about 5 liters per minute (lpm) at low pressure to a patient and larger commercial systems that provide two to hundreds of times more oxygen at high pressure. Which system you want depends upon a number of factors that we will discuss shortly.

System Components

An oxygen concentrator system may be composed of a number of components laid out as in Figure 22. They include:

Prefilter to filter large particles out of the input air.

Compressor to pressurize the air to the right levels required for operation of the system.

Air filter/drier to filter any oil or particulates that the compressor may have introduced into the air and to remove moisture. All of these things can coat out on the zeolite surface greatly decreasing its useful life.

Air supply tank or flow restrictor to smooth spikes out of the air supply that could cause packing of the zeolite bed and resulting in increasing its resistance to air flow.

Zeolite beds in pressure vessels to filter nitrogen out of the air.

Control system to control the flow between the beds, which is usually based upon a fixed time interval.

Storage tank to smooth out the pressure spikes in the oxygen supply to your torch and supply surge requirements for temporary large flames.

Depending upon the kind of system that you purchase, it will have some or all of these components. Smaller, more portable systems may not have a number of these components.

Table 9. Conversion table for liter per minute (LPM) to standard cubic foot per hour (SCFH)

LPM	SCFH	LPM	SCFH
1	2.1	11	23.3
2	4.2	12	25.4
3	6.4	13	27.5
4	8.5	14	29.7
5	10.6	15	31.8
6	12.7	16	33.9
7	14.8	17	36.0
8	17.0	18	38.1
9	19.1	19	40.3
10	21.2	20	42.4

Factors to consider in choosing a concentrator

If you look at the table at the end of this article you can see that there are a number of oxygen concentrator systems to choose from, which can make choosing among them difficult. Let's discuss some factors that you can consider in making your choice.

Flow: The size of torch that you use will dictate this factor. Entry-level mixed-gas beadmaking torches like the Nortel Minor Bench burner are perfectly happy with one a good small medical concentrator systems that supplies about 5-lpm systems. For bigger torches, you have to use larger more expensive concentrators to get the flow that the torch needs. Again, these are usually called oxygen generators even though they work on the same principle. Entry-level borosilicate torches usually require at least a 15-20 lpm oxygen generator. Capacity specifications for medical devices tend to be given in lpm and for industrial systems in standard cubic feet per hour (SCFH). To assist in comparison between these types use the conversion table. One way to increase the flow capability of your system is to add additional units that you plumb in parallel into your system by connecting the output of two concentrators into a Y fitting the other end of which goes to your torch.

Pressure: Another torch related factor is what oxygen pressure the concentrator puts out. With an oxygen tank the general rule of thumb was to set your regulator at 25 psig for premixed torches and 5-10 psig for surface-mixed torches. Now–a-days some manufacturers are recommending a little higher oxygen pressure both to help keep the face of the torch cool and to prevent build up of carbon on the face of the torch. This might be a problem with some of the medical systems, which only deliver oxygen at a few psig. Realize that some systems can deliver higher flow rates and pressure in trade for slightly lower oxygen purity.

Oxygen Storage Tank: If you are running a torch off of a concentrator that is just marginally within its flow capability, adding a storage tank or even two allows continuous use at a low flow levels with occasional surges for good part of an hour to higher levels. Whether this trick will work for you depends a lot on your work style. The other thing that a storage tank does for you is to smooth out pressure and flow variations in the delivered oxygen, preventing any pulsation in the operation of the torch.

Compressors: With some systems, you will have to also purchase a companion air compressor and associated filters to keep oil and moisture out of the bed, others come with these as part of a self contained unit. If you have to provide a compressor, you should use a high-quality, industrial compressor. Some manufacturers recommend oil-free compressors, others say that is not necessary and a good industrial cast iron compressor is sufficient for their equipment. You should also be sure that your compressor is sized to handle the needs of your system. In doing so, you may need to take into account the altitude of your studio; at high altitudes you will need at least a 10% more capable compressor. A good rule of thumb for helping choose the motor horsepower (HP) requirement for your compressor is that it should be equal to, or greater than, the output flow divided by 4. Also consider the compressor's efficiency and noise level. Whether you choose to get a self-contained unit with a built-in compressor or purchase components separately is a personal choice and should be based on a number of other factors such as:

- are you mechanically minded enough to assemble a system,
- do you already have an air compressor that meets the specification requirements, or do you need one for a future activity such as sandblasting.

Weight: Let's face it, more capable systems are heavier and will be harder to maneuver around into position. But if you need the flow, then you will have to pay the price. The only thing that you can do about this is to get equipment that comes in multiple pieces, one of which could be a separate compressor.

Size: More capable systems will be larger and finding room for them in your studio may be challenging. The difference is usually in the height of the system. When calculating the footprint area that you will need for commercial systems based upon vendor data, be aware that the actual system footprint may more than double when you add in the auxiliary equipment. In addition, concentrators are somewhat delicate systems and need to be housed in an enclosed space out of the elements. Depending upon your geographic location this space may also need climate control since concentrators do not operate as well if the beds are colder than ~40°F or warmer than ~130°F.

Electrical Requirements: Many of the units are available in either 110-V or 220-V versions and the amperage requirements are not too high. In the table I have only listed data for the 110-V versions. If you go with a 220-V version, make sure that your workspace is wired for it. If you need a compressor, also consider its power requirements in sizing the system current loads because most of the power consumption in oxygen concentration is really in compressing the air input to the zeolite tanks.

Sound Level: Although you probably will not think of it, sound level can be very important. You don't really want a noisy workspace. Besides being unhealthy, it is also distracting and can cause you to make mistakes. Medical concentrators are usually quieter (about 50 dba) and with ones where you have to provide the compressor, it is not really relevant because most of the noise comes from the compressor. But remember, when you use the compressor it can be positioned remotely to keep your workplace quiet. Use a muffler if they make one for your system.

Operating environment: The longevity of your concentrator greatly depends upon the quality of the air that you feed into it. You need to ensure that the air is clean, oil-free, and dry. The first requirement can be satisfied by filtering the air through a particulate filter that will remove particles down to about 15 microns in diameter. The second will require getting a coalescing filter capable of keeping oil vapor levels below 5 ppm (parts per million). The last requirement is usually specified by a dew point for the input air of about 37°F. If you live in a humid environment or are getting a very large system over about 200 SCFM, meeting this requirement may entail purchasing an air drier for your system. It is important to include these three pieces of equipment as needed because if your bed becomes contaminated, it will cost several hundred to a thousand dollars to replace the zeolite in the beds. Also if you move from one part of the country to another, be sure to reevaluate your needs make any required changes to you system.

Medical Concentrators: One of the things that you have to understand with medical concentrators is that you are paying for a lot of bells and whistles that you really do not need. (One example is a stopped flow alarm that goes off when the system is feed into a turned off torch. This alarm will actually shut down some systems.) These additions are driving up the cost of your equipment and unless you are getting a good deal by buying a used or reconditioned concentrator it may not be worth it. Check eBay to see what kind of a deal you can get. For many of you this might be the right choice, but realize that you are never sure what you are getting. You have no idea how many hours the machine was run, under what conditions, and how well it was maintained. For this reason you may want to get a reconditioned one with a guarantee because it can be hard to get replacement parts for some medical concentrators.

Price: Again, don't let the sticker shock scare you off. You get what you pay for. Think of the cost of the oxygen concentrator as an investment. Do the numbers to compare it to what you are paying for tank oxygen. For example, with my provider and all the taxes and hazardous material fees imposed by the state, I am now paying about $38 per tank fill and $13 per tank rental a month. At a tank per every other week, this amounts to $1144 per year. At this rate, it does not take long for one of the larger concentrators to pay for itself. If you are strapped for cash, ask the company representative if they have a lease to own program.

Warranty: The industry standard warranty appears to be about one year but check to see what your company representative offers.

Others: Since this is a big-ticket item, be sure to ask all the hard questions. Find out what the equipment's mean time to failure is. Get references of other lampworkers that use their equipment. Find out what kind of technology it is based on, mechanical- or computer-based controls. Always ask if there is something else you should know.

If you decide to go ahead and purchase an oxygen concentrator, consider also whether you are planning a torch upgrade any time in the near future. That might affect your concentrator choice. Then weight all the factors that we have discussed and decide which system is best for you. Remember, you will always get better performance by a slightly bigger more capable system than an underpowered one.

Using an oxygen concentrator

When you receive your oxygen concentrator, unpack it, read all the instructions and test it out. See how noisy it is and decide where you should keep it in your studio. The operating procedures will vary with the type of concentrator.

For a small medical or industrial concentrators, hook up your oxygen concentrator directly to the oxygen input of your torch. Do not add a regulator or flashback arrestor to it or you will likely not get any flow. If you have more than one concentrator, hook them in parallel as I discussed earlier to feed your torch.

Before lighting your torch, you have to warm up the bed. This basically means starting it up and letting it run for about a few minutes with the torch oxygen valve open to get flow through the system. Then when it is time to light your torch, briefly turn off the oxygen valve on your torch while you light the propane, and then immediately turn it back on. This is because if you have a medical system turned off too long it might decide that the patient has stopped breathing and set off an alarm.

For larger, commercial generator systems, with air supply and oxygen storage tanks the system will cycle automatically as oxygen is drawn out of the storage tank. For these types of systems, you can just turn them off at night when you are done working and turn them on again when you are ready to start up in the morning and they will cycle as necessary to fill up the oxygen storage tank.

Table 10. Comparison of Oxygen concentrators and oxygen generators.

System	Company	Max Oxygen Output (SCFH)	Max Output Pressure (psig)	Storage Tank Size	Weight (lb)	Electrical Requirement (Volts/Amp)	Power Consumption (kWatt)	Size W x D x H (in)	Sound Level (dba)	Compressor Requirement (SCFM/PSIG)
Elite[a]	Air Sep	10.6	8.5	None	54	110 / 4	0.35	16x15x29	48	Built in
New Life Elite[a]	Air Sep	12.7		None	54	110 / 4	0.35	16x15x29	52	Built in
AS-12	Air Sep	12	9	None	55	110 / 3	0.35	17x10x27	55	Built in
AS-12A	Air Sep	24	18	30 gal	290	110 / 6.3	0.7	45x20x48	55	Built in
AS-20	Air Sep	20	45	60 gal	134	110 / 1.5	0.18	13x11x57	60	5.3 / 90
AS-45	Air Sep	45	45	60 gal	235	110 / 1.5	0.18	17x15x58	60	13.3 / 90
AS-80	Air Sep	80	45	60 gal	338	110 / 1.5	0.18	20x16x60	60	15.0 / 90
OG-15	OGSI	15	12	None	78	110 / 4.0	< 0.5	17x10x30	62	Built in
OG-15NC	OGSI	15	30	None	53	110 /0.4	0.05	17x10x30	63	4 / 30-50
OG-25	OGSI	25	60	60 gal	190	110 / 0.4	0.05	16x13x51	70	6.5 / 90
OG-50	OGSI	50	60	60 gal	275	110 / 0.4	0.05	19x14x63	70	12 / 90
OG 75	OGSI	75	60	60 gal	310	110 / 0.4	0.05	19x14x69	70	17 / 90
OG-100	OGSI	100	60	60 gal	500	110 / 0.4	0.05	24x24x69	70	22 / 90
OC-1.2 1/3 HP	OnSite	12	40	None	130	110 / 3	0.3	10x18x27	55	Built in
OC-1.2 1 HP	OnSite	15	40	None	130	110 / 3	0.3	10x18x27	55	Built in
Pro-2	OnSite	20	40	60 gal	220	110 / 0.3	0.03	26x26x62	64	6 / 65
Pro-4	OnSite	40	40	60 gal	250	110 / 0.3	0.03	26x26x62	64	15 / 65
Pro-8	OnSite	80	40	60 gal	300	110 / 0.3	0.03	26x26x62	64	21 / 65
Integra 6323[a]	SeQual	10.6	5	None	54	110 / 4	0.45	26x15x19	52	Built in
Integra Ten[a]	SeQual	21.2	7	None	57	110 / 4	0.45	26x15x19	52	Built in
Workhorse-8	SeQual	8	9	None	43	110 / 4	0.45	16x17x16	52	Built in
Workhorse-12	SeQual	12	9	None	47	110 / 4	0.45	17x17x16	52	Built in
Workhorse-15	SeQual	15	7	None	49	110 / 4	0.45	22x17x16	52	Built in
Workhorse-15 Profile	SeQual	15	7	None	67	110 / 4	0.45	22x17x10	52	Built in
Workhorse-23 Profile	SeQual	23	7	None	78	110 / 4	0.45	22x17x10	52	Built in
Quad 40	SeQual	40	9	None	85	110 / 0.4	0.05	19x21x24	52	12 / 25
Quad 60	SeQual	60	7	None	95	110 / 0.4	0.05	22x21x24	52	13 / 18
Quad 100	SeQual	100	15	None	95	110 / 0.4	0.05	22x21x24	52	24 / 35
Solaris 3[a]	DeVilbiss	6.4	8.5	None	37	110 / 2	0.225	14x12x	49	Built in
Solaris 5[a]	DeVilbiss	10.6	8.5	None	52	110 / 4	0.4	16x14x	50	Built in
Mark 5[a]	Nidek	10.6		None	62	110 / 4	0.4	15x15x26	48	Built in
HOS-1[a]	BetterThanAir	10.6		None	54	110 / 4	0.35	16x15x29	62	Built in
BTA-1[a]	BetterThanAir	10.6	9	None	73	110 / 4	<0.5	17x10x30	62	Built in

[a] = Medical Concentrator

Maintenance

Most systems need some maintenance. This usually consists of daily draining any condensers on the compressor, periodically cleaning the particulate filters, and blowing out the coalescing filter as necessary to maintain the quality of the input air to the system. These steps are very important in maintaining your system's performance and you need to do them religiously. Some filters will change color making it easier to tell when it is time to change them. Some manufacturers also offer maintenance programs to help remind you when it is time to change filters.

There are lots of concentrator systems out there and I have listed a number of them in the attached table. Check out eBay because you can sometimes get a real bargain on a used medical concentrator, but realize that there is no guarantee on the number of hours it will have on it or the current oxygen purity it is putting out.

Regulators

The pressure in your oxygen cylinder and your propane tank is too high to be used by your torch without modification. If hooked directly to your torch, the gas would be coming out so fast that it would blow the flame out. Therefore, both the fuel and the oxygen tanks use regulators to lower the pressure supplied to your torch down to a few psig. At this pressure, the gas comes out slowly enough that the flame will not blow out.

Propane regulators

The propane regulator screws into the propane tank with a male fitting. Before attaching the propane regulator to the tank, blow out the regulator port on the tank. This can prevent any foreign material from getting into the regulator that might interfere with its operation. When blowing out the opening, be sure to do it in a well-ventilated area where no flames are present. Blow out the valve by pointing it away from anyone and then quickly opening and closing the cylinder on/off valve a crack and letting some gas come out. Now you are ready to attach the regulator to the tank. Once it is in place, propane from your tank can enter the regulator as shown at the left side of the figure. It leaves the regulator from the right side to go to your torch.

How propane regulators work

Regulators work by using a balance of pressure forces to control the opening and closing of a valve. To explain this process, let's look inside a typical pancake propane regulator, which can regulate your gas pressure up to a maximum of about 10 psig. Figure 23 illustrates a cross sectional view of a pancake propane regulator. The movement of the lever arm up and down acts as an on/off valve to control the gas flow. It opens and closes the high-pressure port. The lever arm rotates about the pivot, which in this view is shown as a circle under the left side of the lever arm.

The regulator operates as follows:

- When the right end of the lever arm is pushed down by the adjusting spring, the left end of the arm rotates up. This opens the high-pressure port.
- Propane vapor then flows into the low-pressure chamber faster than it is flowing through the exit to the torch.
- As excess propane fills up the low-pressure chamber, it pushes up against the diaphragm.
- The diaphragm in turn pushes upward against the adjusting spring, pulling the right end of the lever arm up with it.
- This continues with the lever rotating around the pivot point until it closes the high-pressure port.
- At this point, the force exerted against the diaphragm by the pressure of the propane in the low-pressure chamber equals the applied force of the adjusting spring. Thus this spring force directly controls the pressure in the low-pressure chamber.
- As propane flows out of the low-pressure chamber to the torch, the adjusting spring once again pushes the lever arm down opening the

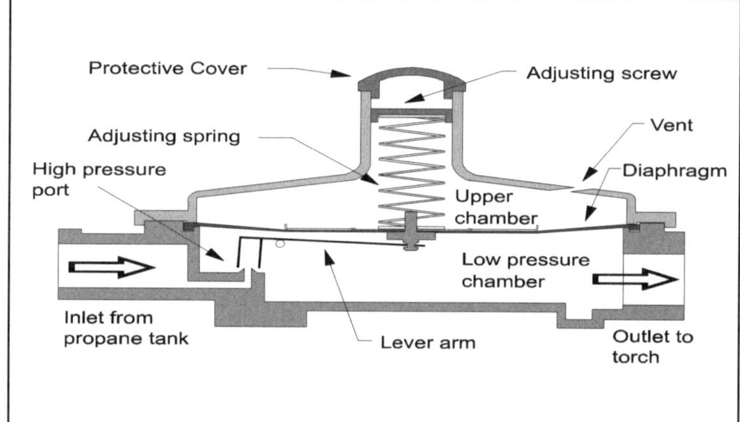

Figure 23. Cross sectional view of a pancake propane regulator.

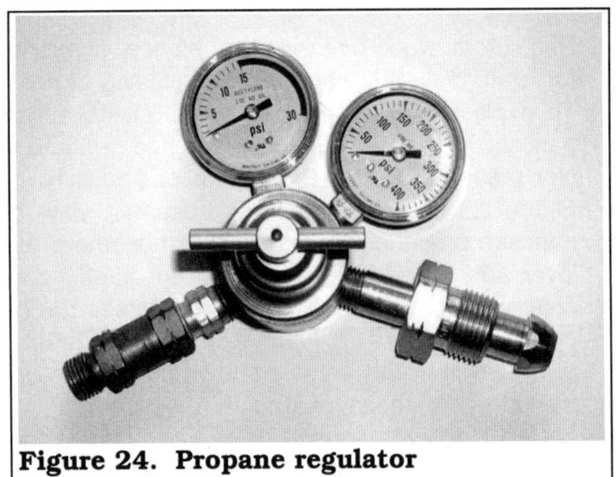

Figure 24. Propane regulator

high-pressure port and the whole cycle start over again.

From this explanation, you see that the propane pressure that is fed to the torch is controlled by the adjusting spring tension. Screw down clockwise on the adjusting screw and the tension of the spring increases. Because of this, the pressure in the low-pressure chamber now has to be higher to push back against the spring and close the high-pressure port. Likewise, if you reduce the tension on the spring by unscrewing the adjusting screw counter-clockwise, the pressure fed to the torch will be reduced.

You may notice that the upper chamber, in which the adjusting spring is located, is vented to the outside atmosphere. This prevents any backpressure from being exerted on the diaphragm by the air in this chamber as the volume is decreased.

If you think about it, the propane also has to push against this atmospheric pressure when it pushes against the diaphragm. Thus the pressure setting of the spring is that over and above atmospheric pressure. This is what is meant by gauge pressure, that which is over and above atmospheric pressure.

Propane regulator settings

The normal pancake propane regulator that many of you will use in beadmaking has a spring that allows adjusting of the output pressure between about 1 and 10 psig.

- If you are using a <u>surface mixed torch</u> you will typically set to about 4 psig.
- If you are working borosilicate on a <u>premixed torch</u>, you typically set the propane pressure up a little higher, in the range of 5 to 8 psig.

These different torch types will be discussed shortly.

Note that some torches have recommended operating pressures greater than 10 psig. For these torches you cannot use a pancake regulator because it cannot go up that high. For these torches you will have to use a regulator with attached gauges like that seen in Figure 24, which allows higher and more precise regulation of pressure.

For a regulator with an attached gauge, adjust the spring tension by turning the tee handle clockwise until the outlet gauge reads the pressure given above.

Adjusting a pancake regulator

A pancake propane regulator as seen in Figure 23 can be adjusted as follows:

1. With the propane tank on/off valve closed, remove the protective cover from the propane regulator. Unscrew the adjusting screw on the propane regulator. (On some propane regulators, there may be a handle like the tank on/off valve instead.) Clear away any combustibles from the end of your torch because the flame could get almost a foot long during this process.

2. Open the gas valve on your torch all the way. No gas should be coming out yet. Open the propane tank. Some gas might start coming out of your torch now. If so, go ahead and light the torch. If not, gradually screw down on the adjusting screw until you can just light the torch.

3. After the torch is lit, continue to slowly screw down on the adjusting screw. As you do so the flame will get larger as the gas flows out faster. Continue screwing down until the flame just leaves the end of the torch or blows out.

4. Immediately close the torch gas valve and then the propane tank on/off valve. Back off on the adjusting screw just a little bit because a flame that leaves the end of a torch is unstable. Your propane regulator is now adjusted.

5. Put the protective cover back over the adjusting screw. If your regulator has a handle but no gauge, tighten the locking nut on the handle to prevent it from being turned unintentionally.

This setting is permanent and does not have to be repeated unless someone changes it on you or you change torches.

If you have a propane regulator with a gauge, it is better to adjust your propane pressure each time you use it. You would also back off the adjustment handle when the system is not in use, as is explained in the following section for oxygen regulators, because this will prevent damaging the regulator and allow it to last longer.

Oxygen regulators

The operation of an oxygen regulator is very similar to that of the propane regulator. Its construction is a little bit different though, because of the much higher pressures involved. Your propane regulator drops the pressure from about 100 psig to 4 psig. Your oxygen regulator has to be able to lower the pressure from 2200 psig to about 10 psig. These higher pressures require more positive closure of the high-pressure port. You can see the differences in construction by studying the cross sectional view of the oxygen regulator in Figure 25.

Installing an oxygen regulator

Before attaching your oxygen regulator to the cylinder, you should flush out the regulator port just like you did for the propane tank. Sometimes debris gets into the regulator port during filling of the cylinder that you do not want to get into your regulator. To flush this port, secure the cylinder in its rack, and take off the protective cover. Turn the cylinder so that the regulator port is not pointed at anyone. Quickly open the on/off valve just a crack (about an eight of a turn). You will get a loud burst of oxygen. Close the valve immediately.

Now, you can connect your oxygen regulator to the cylinder. Do this by sliding the regulator nut back, inserting the round fitting of the regulator into the regulator port on the cylinder valve, and screwing in the nut clockwise. Screw it down finger tight first. Then, while holding the regulator in the position you want it with one hand, tighten the nut with a well fitting wrench in the other hand.

Because of the ball and socket design of the fitting on an oxygen regulator, you do not need to tighten them too hard. Never use any lubricants on these or any oxygen fittings. Also try to keep your hands free from oil when attaching your regulator. Remember oils can spontaneously undergo combustion with pure oxygen to produce serious fires.

Safety note: ***Do not lubricate oxygen fittings.***

How oxygen regulators work

As I stated, the operation of a oxygen regulator is very similar to what we have already discussed for a propane regulator. Let's discuss its normal operation:

- When you start, the adjusting handle is screwed out and the high-pressure valve is shut from the force of the high-pressure chamber spring.
- After the cylinder is opened, high-pressure gas fills the high-pressure chamber.
- The needle on the cylinder pressure gauge, the gauge on the right, will slowly swing to indicate the cylinder pressure. The needle swings slowly because the opening from the line to the gauge is made very small to admit the gas slowly. This protects the gauge from damage that could occur from sudden applications of pressure. A full cylinder will register about 2200 psig. You use this gauge to tell when your cylinder is out of oxygen.
- At this point, the high-pressure valve is closed. It will stay closed until the adjusting handle is screwed down enough onto the adjusting spring to apply a force equal to that of the valve spring

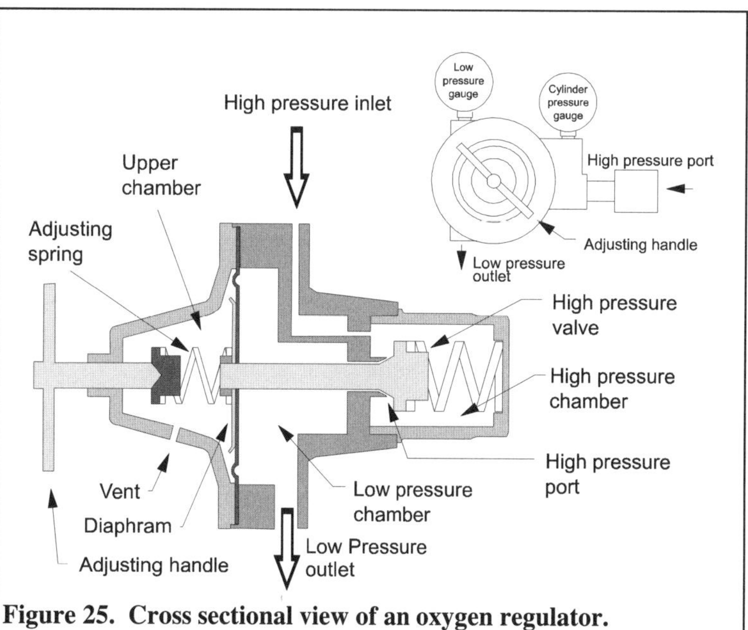

Figure 25. Cross sectional view of an oxygen regulator.

and that of the high-pressure gas pushing on the back of the valve.

- A small amount of oxygen will then be admitted into the low-pressure chamber and it will register on the low-pressure gauge.
- The needle on the low-pressure gauge, the gauge on the left, will then slowly swing to indicate the pressure in the low-pressure chamber of the regulator. You use this gauge to set the oxygen working pressure.
- As the gas in the low-pressure chamber builds up, it will push up against the diaphragm.
- When the force of the low-pressure gas against this diaphragm is greater then the difference of the spring forces and the high-pressure force mentioned above, then the valve will get pushed closed.
- As some of this gas is bled off from low-pressure chamber out into the gas lines and is consumed by your torch, the pressure in the low-pressure chamber will drop. As it drops below the difference value, the high-pressure valve will again open.
- And so on and so on and so on.

The oxygen pressure that is required in the low-pressure chamber to close the valve is a function of the degree of compression of the adjusting spring. The more this spring is compressed the higher the gas pressure in the low-pressure chamber has to be to push the valve closed. Thus, the more you screw the adjusting handle in clockwise, the higher will be the regulated low pressure.

Oxygen regulator settings

The setting for your oxygen regulator depends upon what type of torch you are using:

- For beadmaking using a surface-mixed torch, you will typically set the pressure regulated somewhere between 5 and 10 psig.
- When working borosilicate using a premixed torch, you will typically increase the regulated pressure to about 25 psig.

Some torches may have higher recommended operating pressures. Check your manufacturers recommendations.

To keep the oxygen pressure regulated correctly, you may find that you have to readjust the adjusting handle slightly once your torch is operating and constantly consuming oxygen. The exact pressure required by your torch might also vary slightly depending on the size tip you might be using.

Using an oxygen regulator

The steps for opening and adjusting your oxygen regulator are as follows:

1. Before you open your oxygen tank on/off valve and admit oxygen into the regulator, you should always completely unscrew the adjusting handle counterclockwise until all spring compression is removed from the adjusting spring.

2. Stand off to one side of the regulator before you open up the oxygen cylinder. This is because regulators have been known to blow out upon pressurization.

3. Slowly open the oxygen cylinder on/off valve to allow oxygen into the high-pressure chamber in the back of the regulator body. You open the valve slowly to avoid sudden pressure surges, which can weaken the valve body over time. Be sure and remember to completely open the on/off valve so you do not lose oxygen around the valve stem.

4. Now slowly screw the adjusting handle in to start letting oxygen into the low-pressure chamber. It will turn freely at first until it starts to tighten up against the spring. At that point, you should start reading pressure on the low pressure gauge. Continue to do turn the handle until the low pressure gauge reads whatever level you want it.

5. If you go too high, back off on the adjusting handle a little and vent off some of the oxygen in the lines at the torch. Then readjust to get the desired pressure.

At this point, you are probably wondering why we just don't leave the adjusting handle screwed in and the adjusting spring under compression in the first place. The reason is that when there is no gas pressure in the high-pressure chamber and the adjusting spring is under compression, the valve ends up being a lot more open than it is in normal operation. Then when the tank is opened and 2200 psig oxygen is suddenly introduced into the regulator, much of this gas quickly flows into the low-pressure chamber and causes the high-pressure valve to slam shut with a much greater force than normal. Slamming the valve shut like this can damage the seat of the valve on the high-pressure port.

A damaged valve seat can leak and allow higher than normal pressure to build up in the low-pressure chamber. If this happens, you will have to take your regulator into the shop to get it fixed. Therefore, to prevent damage to your oxygen regulator, always unscrew the adjusting handle out to the point where it is no longer exerting force on the diaphragm after you close your cylinder and double check that it is screwed out before opening your cylinder.

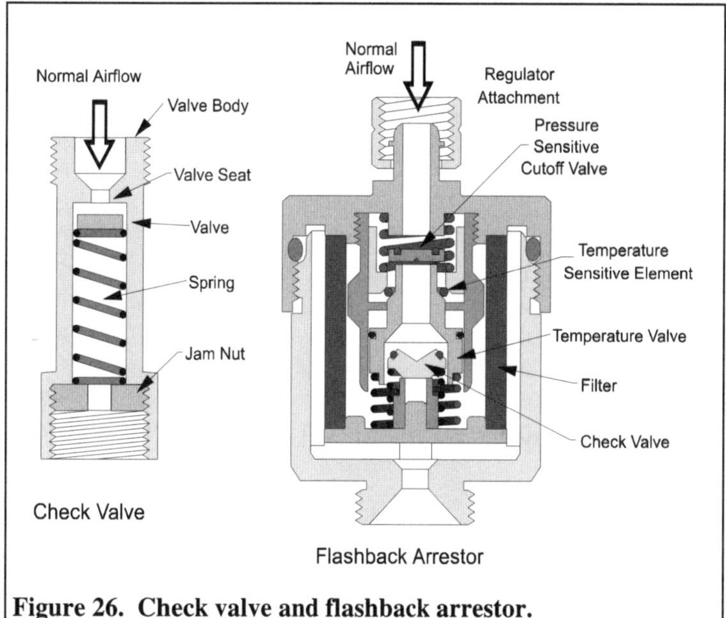

Figure 26. Check valve and flashback arrestor.

Check valves and flashback arrestors

Another set of fittings that need to be included in your gas system is either check valves or flashback arrestors. The purpose of these fittings is to prevent backflow of gas, possibly resulting in a fire in your hoses, regulators, or tanks. One or the other should be included in both the oxygen and the fuel gas line. Many glass beadmakers use check valves because they are cheaper and because they use surfaced mixed torches that are much less likely to flashback than premixed torches.

Flashback is a phenomena in which the flame burns back from the tip of your torch into the rest of the gas system. It can burn back inside the tip to the torch and even on into the hoses. If not protected against, it may proceed all the way into the fuel tank or oxygen cylinder with explosive results. Again, flashback is mainly a problem for concern with premixed torches for reasons that will be explained later.

Warning signs of a flashback in progress include squealing or abnormal hissing sounds and a sudden smoky or sharp pointed flame. These are indicators of tip blockage. If you experience a flashback, there may be major problems with your system, the most likely of which is a partially plugged tip.

If you get a flashback:

- Immediately extinguish the torch by first closing the torch oxygen valve and then the fuel valve.
- Allow the torch to cool for a few minutes.
- Check your torch for leaks and tip blockage.
- Purge each of the hoses separately.
- Recheck the regulator settings.

When you have found and corrected the problem, then and only then can you safely relight your torch to resume working.

A check valve is a valve that only allows gas flow in one direction, from the regulator to the torch. It may be mounted on either the torch or the regulator. The preferred location is on the inlet of the torch because that prevents any back flow into the hoses. But this is not easy to do on most torches, so they are usually mounted onto the outlet of your regulator.

As illustrated in Figure 26, a check valve operates through the action of a spring-loaded valve. Gas flowing in the normal direction compresses the spring and flows around the valve. Gas trying to flow in the opposite direction assists the spring in pushing the valve against the valve seat, thus closing off flow. This reverse flow can happen if the tip of the torch gets plugged and the higher-pressure oxygen pushes its way up towards the fuel tank.

Check valves are sensitive to dirt and damage to the seating element. To assure their proper operation, they should be checked regularly, at least every six months. You can check the proper functioning of your check valves by blowing into both ends and seeing that air will only flow in one direction. A check valve should not be reused if it is exposed to a flashback.

> **Safety Note:** ***Your equipment should be checked very carefully after a flashback. Hoses or check valves exposed to a flashback flames should not be reused***

A flashback arrestor is the more complex device illustrated in the right side of Figure 26. It combines a number of safety functions into one unit. These

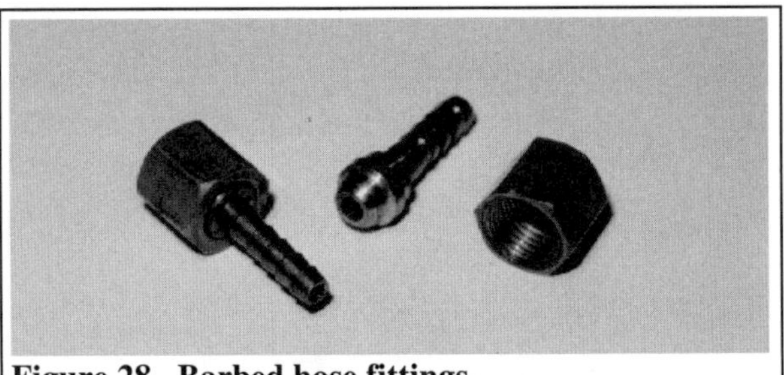

Figure 28. Barbed hose fittings.

include the following: a pressure cutoff valve, a check valve, a stainless steel filter, and a heat sensitive element. It also has a small internal volume to absorb the energy of a flashback as it travels up the hose.

The proper place to install a flashback arrestor onto your gas system is onto the regulator. It will eliminate any chance of explosion in your regulator or tanks. In the event of a flashback, the small orifices in the stainless steel filter prevent propagation of a flame and the incoming pressure wave pushes the cutoff valve closed, preventing any further flow of oxygen to the flame.

The check valve portion of a flashback arrestor performs the same function as explained previously; i.e. that of preventing any back flow of gas into the regulator. If a flashback arrestor is exposed to excessive heat, the temperature sensitive element will melt allowing the temperature valve to close the pressure cutoff valve. Because of the multiple safety functions incorporated, it is suggested that you use them on your gas system.

A flashback arrestor is reusable after a flashback but not after a fire where the thermal sensitive element has melted. You'll know if this has happened because it will no longer allow gas to pass through the hoses.

Tubing and fittings

Connecting your torch to your regulated gas supply requires tubing and fittings. The type of fitting used most by glass artists in connecting their hoses are barbed hose nipple fittings with hose nuts as shown in Figure 28. The most common barb size is a ¼". You will need some of these if you purchase any of the low-pressure fittingless tubing that I will discuss.

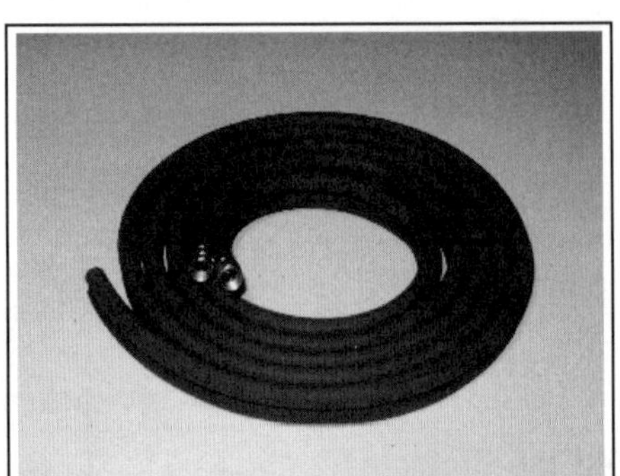

Figure 27. Illustration of industrial high-pressure hose and fittings.

These fittings are available with both right and left hand threads on the hose nuts for connecting to your oxygen or your propane supply respectively. The way to tell them apart is to look for the notch on the nut portion of the fitting as to the left of Figure 28. This is a left-handed fitting. Hose barbs are also available with male pipe fittings on the other end if you need them. You may also have a set of hose barbs on the gas inlets to your torch. Tubing is attached to barbed fittings by slipping it onto the fitting and clamping it into place using hose clamps as shown in Figure 29. It is easiest if you loosely slide the hose clamp over the hose before attaching the hose onto the barb.

Figure 29. Using hose clamps with hose fittings.

The best type of tubing available is that used for commercial welding and cutting operations. It incorporates high-pressure tube fittings of the ball and cup type, as seen in Figure 27, and is available in various sizes. The hoses are of a heavy double wall construction reinforced with fiber. It is available as either single tubes or double tubes of various lengths and is color-coded; red for fuel and green for oxygen. The fittings are left and right-handed to match. Because of its higher-pressure rating and integral end connectors, it is the only type of connector and tubing endorsed by the National LP Gas Association. Make sure that you purchase type T hoses that are approved for all fuel gases and not type R, which are only approved for acetylene. One disadvantage of this tubing is that it is less flexible than others, making it is a little more awkward to use. This is not usually a problem in beadmaking since you do not move your torch around as you work.

A number of types of fittingless tubing are also available for use with lampworking torches. The most common tubing size has a ¼" inner diameter (ID) and a wall thickness between $^{1}/_{16}$th and $^{1}/_{8}$th of an inch. The most widely used tubing is made from black neoprene rubber and is preferred because of its flexibility, lightweight, ruggedness, and durability. Another popular choice is pure gum rubber tubing like that on your Bunsen burner from high school chemistry. This amber colored tubing is flexible and light, but is not as durable. It eventually darkens and becomes hard and brittle.

Another good choice in tubing is Tygon® tubing. It is available as paired color-coded Tygon® tubing bonded together called Twintube®. The tubes are orange and green color-coded. The green is conventionally used on the oxygen connection and the orange on the propane connections. Although slightly heavier than rubber tubing, Twintube® is still quite flexible. It can soften a bit when heated, so be sure your hose clamps are tight. Using a bonded tubing set results in fewer tangles of tubing around your studio. It also provides a neater and safer atmosphere.

When connecting up your system, blow out the hoses to clean out any foreign material that may be in them. Use two wrenches when tightening fittings; one on each side of the joint that you are connecting. This will prevent loosing another fitting down the line and reduces chances of damaging a fitting. After connecting your hoses, check them all for leaks using a solution of liquid dish detergent and water. Paint it on all your fittings while they are pressurized. Any leaks will cause the solution to bubble. You may want to repeat this procedure periodically to check for cracks or punctures in your tubing.

Safety Note: ***It is very important to ensure that your gas system connections are leak free. Be sure to bubble test each joint.***

Keep your tubing out from underfoot by hanging it from the underside of your workbench. Never walk on it if you can help it because this can cause eventual splitting of your hoses.

If a hose is ever damaged or burned in a flashback, replace it. Flashbacks often burn the inner wall of a hose, weakening it. Also, don't even think about trying to repair a hose by wrapping it with tape. This can allow pinhole leaks over time, creating dangerous situations.

Fuel-oxygen torches

The fuel-oxygen torch is the most important piece of equipment a glass bead artist has. The whole purpose of having a gas system is to supply the torch with gas. The type and size of torch that you select will limit the type and scale of work you can do. Therefore, it is important to think about what other areas you may expand into in the near future (like flameworked sculptures, neon, etc.) before purchasing a torch.

Premixed torches

The type of torch most commonly used by borosilicate flameworkers is a premixed torch. Premixed means that the oxygen and the fuel are mixed inside the torch prior to being burned at the tip. Many premixed torches are also multipurpose, meaning they can use either oxygen or air to burn the fuel gas. This is accomplished by changing the tip. Though as mentioned earlier, oxygen is preferred because of the higher flame temperature and more complete combustion it provides.

One of the advantages of a premixed torch is that its "hard" high-velocity flame transfers heat to the surface of your work so rapidly that the inside of your piece initially remains relatively cool in comparison. This allows attaching glass constructions to the work without getting the whole thing so hot that it droops.

Another advantage of premixed torches is that they will usually have many different tips available. The wide choice of tips allows better shaping of the flameworkers most important tool, the flame. Different operations require different flames shapes and size, thus the different tips. (Note: some manufacturers use the term burners instead of tips.) With a large tip you can work glass rod up to an inch in diameter. Anything larger than this may require a larger torch than you may have. Smaller scale work can be accomplished by changing to a smaller tip.

One of the disadvantages of a premixed torch is that the flame tends to be slightly reducing and can deaden the color of soft beadmaking glasses. This problem can be overcome with practice by adding extra oxygen to the torch flame but it is tricky to master.

When using a premixed torch, remember to adjust your propane pressure and oxygen supply pressure up to about 5-8 psig and 25 psig respectively. Otherwise your flame may get too close to the tip, allowing it to heat up and possibly ignite the fuel prematurely inside the torch. This condition is very dangerous because it can lead to flashback.

Because the fuel and oxygen are mixed inside a premixed torch, a plugged tip can cause pressure to build up inside it. This can lead to possible backflow of gas up whichever hose is at the lower pressure. Without a check valve at the torch inlet, this would normally allow oxygen to push its way up into your fuel regulator and possibly fuel tank. On the other hand, if you had an almost empty oxygen tank, fuel gas could conceivably push its way up your oxygen hose.

For this reason, many premixed torches will have check valves integral to their construction. But integral check valves can become damaged over time and for this reason, you may want the backup of flashback arrestors on your regulators. A partial blockage of a premixed torch can result in a flashback for similar reasons.

Premix torches are also very susceptible to backfire. A backfire is an instantaneous extinguishing and reignition of a torch flame. It is usually the result of holding your work too close to the tip of your torch and is confined to the torch head. Blocking the flow at the tip causes the gas velocity to slow enough that it no longer feeds enough gas to keep the flame lit. Then as the gas again builds up, the hot tip may relight the gas. Otherwise, the torch flame will stop burning immediately.

If the torch does not relight, turn off your torch and check out your system as discussed for a flashback. Look for loose connections, leaky hoses, incorrect gas settings of the regulator, or anything else that could cause gas starvation at the tip. Under certain conditions a backfire can progress to become a flashback, so if you should have a backfire, watch out for symptoms of a flashback.

Surface mixed torches

The type of torch preferred by most wound glass bead artists is a surface-mixed torch. In this type of torch, the oxygen is typically directed up to the burner tip through sections of stainless steel tubing formed into a tapered nozzle. The propane flows around and between the tube cluster to the end of the nozzle. The gases then mix for the first time at the surface of the torch. Surface-mixed torches are used with lower gas pressure settings than those for premixed torches — about 4 psig for propane and 5-10 psig for oxygen.

Ideally, the barrel around the stainless steel tubing should act as a heat sink and radiator to prevent the tubing from getting too hot and melting. With proper design most of the heat of the flame is projected away from the torch and the barrel does not heat up very much.

I have heard of people trashing their surface-mixed torches by trying to use them with acetylene. The flame was just too hot and melted the burner face. This could also be a problem with Chem-o-lene. If run with slower gas flow, surface-mixed torches can suffer from carbon buildup on the face of the torch. This buildup is consists of deposition of impurities in the fuel gas being burned. Accumulated carbon can be removed by quickly scraping the front of the torch with a tool like a pair of tweezers. If your torch has this problem a lot, it can often be compensated for by increasing the gas pressures to your torch slightly.

Surface mixed torches are preferred for beadmaking over premixed torches for a number of reasons:

- The flame is spread out.
- The slower gas flow out of the torch tip results in a more uniform and quieter flame.
- It does not transfer heat to your work as quickly as a premixed torch so the heat has more of a chance to penetrate into your work. This allows it to achieve a more uniform temperature.
- They do not suffer from the irritating popping backfire that the premixed torches do if shut off incorrectly (i.e. if you turn the propane off first).
- It is easier to control the flame chemistry so that you do not get reduction of you glass colors.

Hybrid torches

There are torches on the market that combine features of both premixed and surface mixed torches. One example of this type is a Carlisle CC torch, which has a central premixed torch core surrounded by a surface-mixed ring. Controls on the torch allow individual adjustment of either portion of the flame.

National now also has a torch that can be either a surface-mixed or a premixed by changing out the heads. Torches are continuing to evolve and lots of changes will be forthcoming as manufacturers try to make them cheaper and better.

Factors to consider in choosing a torch

Today's beadmakers looking for a torch are fortunate to have a wide variety of good ones from which to choose, but making that choice can be a daunting task. How can one choose between them? Let's discuss a number of factors you should consider when choosing a torch and then review most of the lampworking torches currently on the market.

The first factor to consider is how sure are you that you really want to be a beadmaker? This can be a relatively expensive hobby and you may want to control costs until you are ready to commit. In that case, you would probably want to choose a handheld torch, like a Hothead® or QuietTorch™. They are simple to use, portable, easy to learn on, inexpensive ($30-$35) and good for beginners, but they are still relatively noisy and harder control flame chemistry on than fuel-oxygen torches. Simplicity is a good feature to look for no matter which torch you end up getting, especially for beginning beadmakers.

Once you make a long-term commitment to glass beadmaking, you will likely want to graduate to a mixed-gas torch. It will allow better control of flame size and chemistry, but will require getting a source of oxygen. Most people start with oxygen tanks but many are moving on to oxygen concentrators or generators that separate oxygen from air. If you go this route, which equipment you buy will limit the size of torch that you can use.

Next you have to choose between the two main types of torches: premixed and surface-mixed. You will also hear the term triple mixed but that is just another other form of surface-mixed torch. Premixed torches produce a hot pointed flame that tends to be reducing. This type of torch is generally used with borosilicate (hard) glass and not soda-lime (soft) glass because controlling the reducing tendency can be tricky. With surface-mixed torches control of the flame chemistry is much easier so this is the kind of torch that most soft glass beadmakers use.

Besides flame chemistry, glass beadmakers, because of the scale of their work, need good control of the size of their flame. They want to be able to change their flame from a large soft bushy flame for overall heating to a sharp needle flame for detail work. This is one area where the triple-mixed (oxygen-fuel-oxygen) torches excel. The extra high-velocity oxygen jets can really focus the flame, but this does add a measure of complexity to learning and maintaining these torches over the simpler surface-mixed torches.

The other end of the flame-size characteristic is how large of a flame you can get. When making larger solid glass objects, a glass artist wants a torch that can produce a larger flame. This translates to a torch with a larger face and usually a much higher price tag. These larger torches will usually have two components to them, a smaller detail flame and a larger bulk heating flame. These two components may be separate as in the Nortel torches or concentric as with most of the other torch brands.

The last flame characteristic that you want to consider is that of flame temperature. Since all the torches use the same fuels, typically propane or natural gas, higher flame temperatures are generally achieved by having a larger or a more focused flame. This is important if you are considering working with hard glass because borosilicate glass melts at a much higher temperature than soft glass and needs the hotter flame.

Lastly, look for other features that make use of the torch easier or make it more versatile.

- Look at how easy the stand is to mount to your worktable.
- Look for ease of positioning the torch on the stand.
- Look for how hot the torch body gets.
- Look at how many controls it has.
- Look at its construction.

Review of beadmaking torches

Let's now examine a sampling of today's mixed-gas beadmaking torches. A summary chart of the most common beadmaking torches used in the U.S. is given at the end of this chapter for side-by-side comparison. They are all good torches and differ mainly in options. They can be divided into six general groups that I have defined by their capability and cost as follows:

- Entry level soft glass torches
- Entry level borosilicate torches
- Entry level dual capable torches
- Medium level borosilicate torches
- Advanced borosilicate torches
- Production borosilicate torches

I will next discuss each of these groups and the torches in them. Note that the prices given are as of the summer of 2002 and are only for comparison

Entry level soft glass torches

These torches are the kind owned and used by most glass beadmakers. On them, beadmakers can make good-size soft glass beads and some limited-size borosilicate beads, although they can only work borosilicate slowly. These torches can be supplied oxygen by tanks or by oxygen concentrators of the 5-liter/min medical variety.

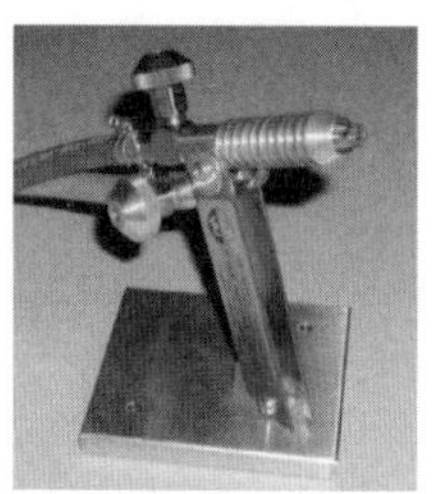

The first of these torches is the industry standard, the Nortel **Minor Bench Burner** that sells for $169. This is the torch that most of today's beadmakers learned on and which continues to be very popular. It is a good versatile surface-mixed torch with 7 jets that has good flame size (1/8" to ¾" diameter) and chemistry control. It is easy to use and relatively rugged. It has an adjustable base that is fixed into position by tightening a machine screw. Nortel has made a few small changes to increase its longevity. They have modified the side plates to capture the cooling fins so that they cannot slide forward into the flame and increased the wall thickness of the center tube to reduce heat erosion.

A similarly priced torch is the **Carlisle Mini CC**. It also has 7 surface-mixed jets and sells for $170. It has a ball-joint mount that allows easy aiming of the torch during set up. It allows good control of its similar size flame. Its brass outer casing can get relatively hot so Carlisle has developed a stainless steel head to reduce heat conduction back to the body of the torch. This also reduces face erosion.

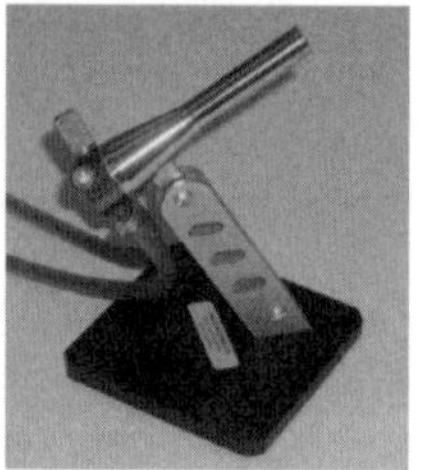

The **Glass Torch Technology (GTT) Bobcat** is slightly more expensive ($195) because of its stainless steel construction and it has the sleek look of the entire GTT line of torches. It is also a 7-jet surface-mixed torch that gives flame sizes and chemistry control comparable to the rest. It has an adequate friction base adjusted using machine screws.

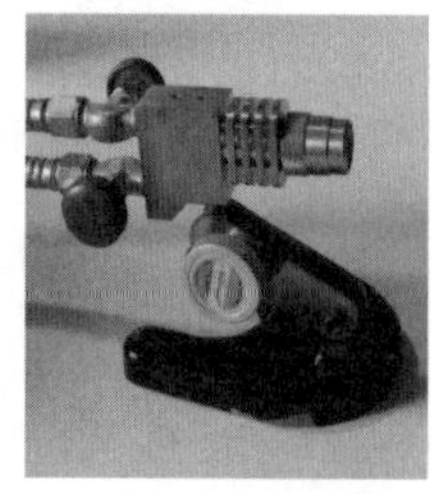

The next torch in this series is the **National 8M**. It differs a lot from the rest because of its replaceable head technology. The basic torch body and base sell for $129 and then you can purchase any of a number of different sized heads to give you the maximum flame size that you want. There are currently four surface-mixed heads and a premixed adapter. The four surface-mixed heads range from a smaller 7-jet head for $65 to a larger 29-jet head for $85. The $39 premixed adapter can be used with any of the National tips for their other premixed torches. Many people buy this torch for its adaptability but most only use the smallest head because the heads cannot be changed until they cool down. The smaller heads do not quite provide as large a flame as you would expect because the flow becomes turbulent when the oxygen is opened past a certain point. National is developing a small companion premixed torch to ride on the top of the body to allow a pinpoint and large flame in the same set up. I found the ball joint base on this torch hard to lock into position.

Entry level borosilicate torches

These torches are simple premixed glass torches used by many clear borosilicate workers. They are primarily used for small work but have a wide variety of tips that can modify that statement. Tips come in a number of different sizes from a micro single orifice of 0.035" in diameter to a #5 with a 0.100" orifice. Using single-orifice tips larger than about a #3 gives diminishing returns, you would probably be better off switching to a multi-hole tip. With small tips, these torches can be used with oxygen concentrators. Larger ones would require oxygen generators. Because of the reduction tendencies of a premixed flame, they are not generally a good choice for working colored soft glass.

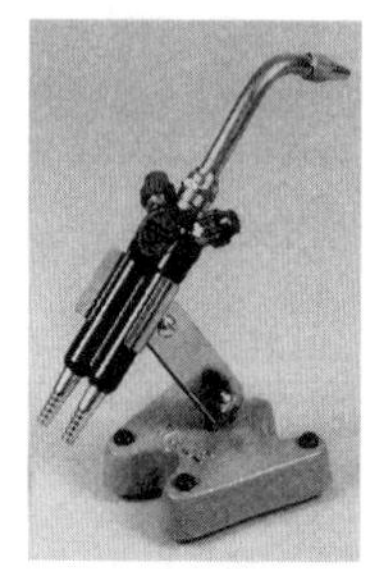

A good multipurpose premixed torch is a **National 3A–B Blowpipe**, which sells for $60. It is widely used as a hand torch but by purchasing the optional stand it quickly converts into a bench torch. With all the available tips it can be quite versatile. It comes with either hose barbs or size B hose fittings.

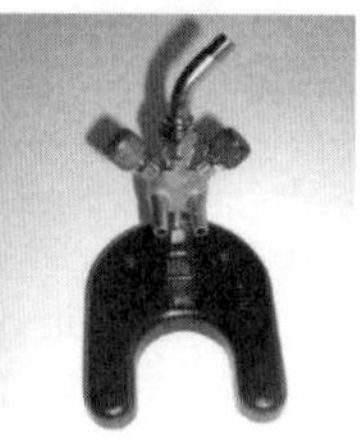

If all you really want is a small premixed bench burner, then the **National 6B** is the torch that you want. This torch sells for only $89 and can use the same set of premixed torch tips. It has a rotatable elbow that allows you to help position the torch although it does not allow you to adjust the height.

Entry level dual capable torches

These torches are the next step up in the hierarchy of beadmaking torches. They are still affordable soft glass bead torches but they also allow production of borosilicate beads. Their oxygen flow characteristics are such that the medical type of oxygen concentrators are no longer adequate; instead one of the entry-level oxygen generators or a tank is required.

The first of these torches is the $270 **Nortel Mid-Range Bench Burner**. It is a surface-mixed 25-jet torch that is arranged in a square grid. It does not have a good pinpoint flame requiring a beadmaker to have a second torch ready for those needs. If you try to work too small with it, you will get excessive carbon buildup that will require frequent cleaning. Because of its lack of pinpoint flame many artists will go with its sister torch described next.

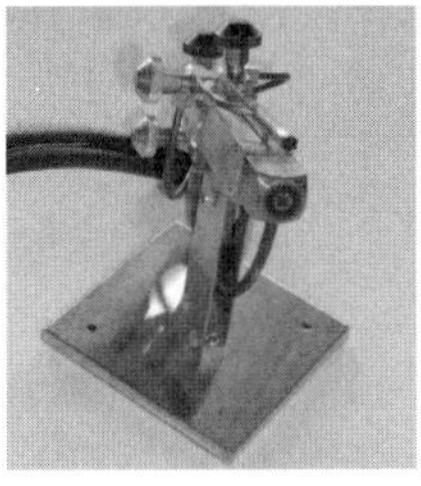

This torch is the **Nortel Mid-Range Plus** for $379. It has the same bottom surface-mixed 25-jet head as the Mid-Range but with a smaller companion upper torch. For this you can choose a Minor Bench Burner head if you are going to mainly work in soft glass or a small premixed head if you are going to specialize in hard glass. This torch is much more versatile and compact than running a Mid-Range alone or with a second torch. Both torches have a good secure friction adjustable base.

For a little larger flame than the Mid-Range, there is the **Nortel Major Bench Burner** for $399. This has the same companion rider head options as the Mid-Range Plus with a larger bushy bottom head of either 48 or 64 surface-mixed jets arranged in a square grid that provides a flame up to 1½" in diameter. Which head you choose depends upon how hot of a flame you want. The 48-jet head reduces carbon build up by increasing the required jet velocity for the same heat output.

The next entry in this class, the $360 **Bethlehem Glass Bead Burner** (GBB) uses a smaller focused 5-jet surface-mixed head to provide a hotter flame to work hard glass. Because it only has 5-jets, the size of the flame is restricted to about ⁵/₈" in diameter. This means it is mainly for smaller borosilicate work but it provides a full range of flame control for soft glass. The wing nut tightened friction base on this torch is easily adjusted but is currently too small and light to provide enough stability to allow use without clamping it to your workbench. I was told that the manufacturer is correcting this problem.

The last torch in this category is the **GTT Lynx** for $435. This is the first in Glass Torch Technology's line of triple-mixed torches. These torches have each of their jets arranged in concentric rings of oxygen-fuel-oxygen. The center high velocity oxygen jets allow improved combustion, focusing of the flame, and reduced carbon build up. The Lynx has 7 of these triple-mixed jets that provide the most adjustable flame available up to a maximum diameter of ⁷/₈". The added complexity of triple mixing makes these torches a little harder to learn and clean.

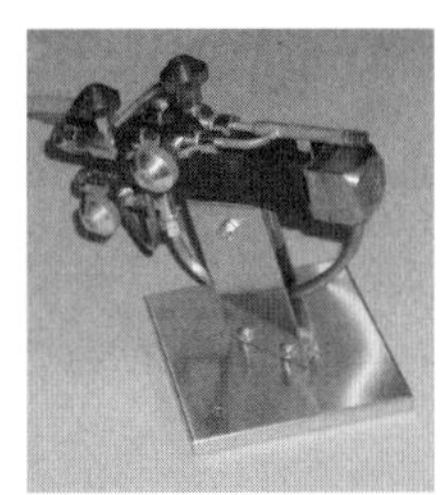

Nortel has recently previewed the new **Red Max Major Bench Burner** that will be in this category. They have not even named or priced it yet, although it probably will sell for about $499. It looks similar to the Major Bench Burner except the bottom 47-jet surface-mixed head is arranged in concentric focused rings with improved mixing to provide a hotter flame that should be better for borosilicate. It has the same companion heads to choose from as the Major Bench Burner and should also be less susceptible to carbon build up.

Medium level borosilicate torches

This class of torches is still usable for making soft glass beads but it allows larger borosilicate work. Their oxygen flow is such that the entry-level oxygen generators may no longer be adequate and instead one of the larger oxygen generators or a tank is required.

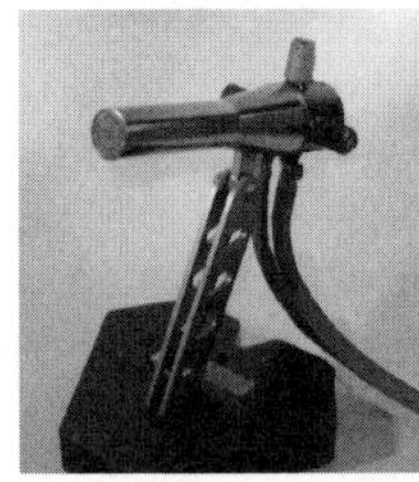

The first of these torches is the $625 **GTT Phoenix**. It has a 21-jet triple-mixed head, which gives hot flames up to 1¼" in diameter but has no detail flame. Because of this, it is not really a good choice for beadmaking. It was designed mainly for scientific lampworking.

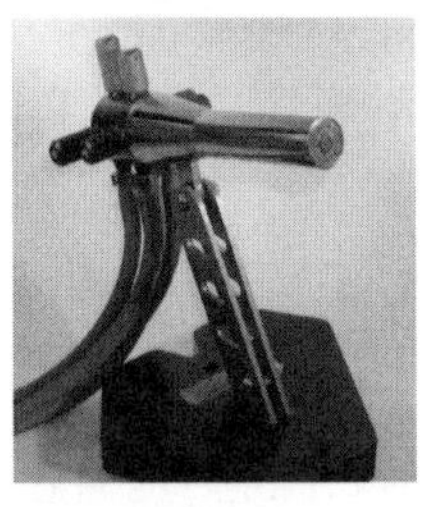

The other Glass Torch Technology entry in this category is the $1125 **GTT Phantom**. It has a concentric triple-mixed head where the inner flame is the same 7-jet triple-mixed flame as the Lynx and 14 triple-mixed outer jets that are controlled separately. This produces a very versatile flame that can go from a pinpoint to 1¼" in diameter. It has the typical sleek GTT design, but again the added complexity of triple mixing makes it a little harder to learn and clean.

The last torch in this category is the **Carlisle CC Burner** whose price varies from $932 to $1054 depending upon which base you choose; ball & post or the nicer rack & pinion. Water-cooling is also an option. Its concentric head consists of a premixed center flame of one of two sizes and an outer 34-jet surface-mixed flame. The center premixed flame means that this torch is harder to use on soft glass.

Advanced borosilicate torches

These torches are still usable for making soft glass beads but they are capable of very large borosilicate work. Their oxygen flow is such that a much larger oxygen generator or a tank is required. They are of a size such that they are less applicable to beadmaking and more suitable for solid borosilicate sculpture.

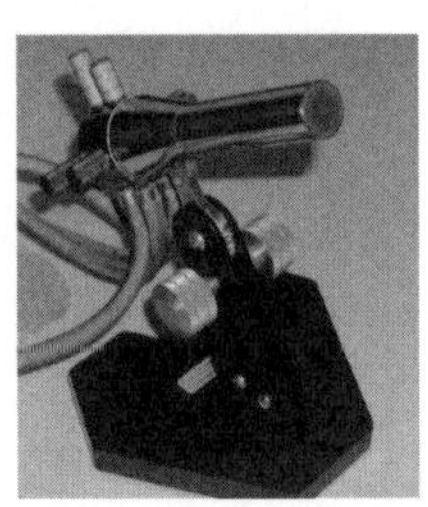

The first entry in this category is the $1625 **GTT Mirage** of the typical sleek GTT design. It has a concentric triple-mixed head with an inner Lynx 7-jet triple-mixed flame and an outer separately controlled 28-jet triple-mixed one. This produces a very controllable flame that can go from a pinpoint to $1^5/_8$" in diameter. Again the added complexity of triple mixing makes it a little harder to learn and clean but its versatility makes the effort well worth it.

The **Carlisle CC Plus Burner** varies from $1453 to $1607 depending again upon which base you choose; the ball & post or the nicer rack & pinion one. Its concentric head consists of a center premix flame of one of two sizes and an outer 63-jet surface-mixed flame. The center premix flame means that this torch is harder to use on soft glass. Water-cooling is also an option.

The last torch **in this category** is the **Bethlehem PM2D Burner** whose price varies from $1555 to $1755 depending upon whether you choose to get the optional water-cooling package. The concentric head consists of the same 5-jet surface-mixed flame as the GBB and an outer 69-jet surface-mixed flame. The oxygen and fuel jets are balanced to give this torch even flame temperature with good control.

Production borosilicate torches

These torches are for those that continually strive for the ultimate flame size for very large borosilicate work. Scientific lampworkers also use them for their quartz capability. Again, they would require a much much larger oxygen generator or tank.

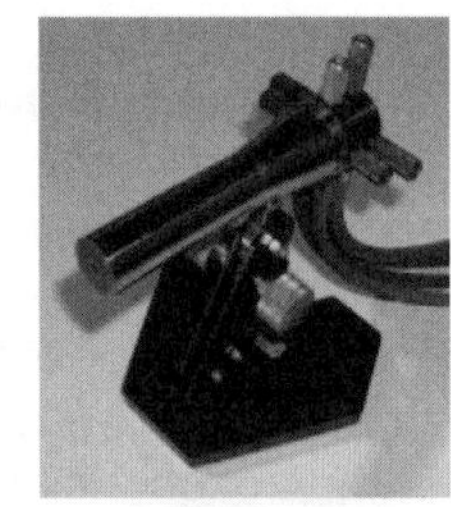

The first of these torches is the $2250 **GTT Delta Elite**. Like all the of the larger GTT torches it has the same sleek design and the inner triple-mixed 7-jet Lynx head. Its outer head consists of 39 triple-mixed jets organized in three concentric rings. This produces a very controllable flame that goes from a pinpoint to 2¼ " in diameter. It comes with a nice rack and pinon base that allows great position control.

The other torch in this category is the **Herbert Arnold Zenit 40** for $2500. It is a master of German engineering. It has a center inner head of 10 surface-mixed jets surrounded by an outer head of 63 surface-mixed jets. It is interesting in that after making a number of setup adjustments, it allows control of the flame size by swinging a single lever while maintaining constant flame chemistry with variability in flame size similar to the Delta Elite. It also has a good adjustable base.

Summary

Try to pick a torch that satisfies your immediate or near-term needs. Don't project out five years into the future when you hope to be a large borosilicate sculptural artist because you will pay for it in larger fuel and oxygen costs on a torch that may be more than you can really handle for a while. Be realistic in your expectations and desires. Biggest is not always best. I know beadmakers who have worked on Minor Bench Burners for over a decade and are still happy with their capabilities. So I wish you luck in making the correct torch choice for your needs.

Suggested further reading

Airco Gas and Gear. **Product Catalog**, 1989

Althouse, Andrew D., Turnquist, Carl H., Bowditch, William A. and Bowditch, Kevin E. **Modern Welding**, Goodheart-Willcox Company, Inc., 1997

Dodson, Rick. ***It's Hot - It's Cool - Its New*****, Glass Line** Vol. 9 No. 1 (Jun/Jul) 1995

Dodson, Rick. ***Chem-0-Lene Revisited*****, Glass Line** Vol. 10 No. 2 (Aug/Sept) 1996

Hammesfahr, James E. and Stong, Clair L. **Creative Glassblowing**, W. H. Freeman and Company, 1968

Hoyt, Homer. **Glassblowing, An Introduction to Solid and Blown Glass Sculpturing**, Crafts & Arts Publishing Co. Inc., 1989

Jalapa Gas and Chemical Corp. **Chemtane 2 Product Specifications**, 1999

Table 11. Fuel-oxygen torch comparison table

Torch	Manufacturer	Cost	Fuel Gases	Oxygen Source	Primary Flame	Secondary Flame	Config	Soft Glass	Hard Glass	Max Flame	Base
HotHead		\$30	Mapp/P	None	Pm 1	None	N/A	Yes	No	¾"	Sep
Minor	Nortel	\$169	P/NG	T/OC	SM 7 jets	None	N/A	Yes	Some	¾"	FF
Bobcat	GTT	\$195	P/NG	T/OC	SM 7 jets	None	N/A	Yes	Some	¾"	FF
Mini CC	Carlisle	\$170	P/NG	T/OC	SM 7 jets	None	N/A	Yes	Some	¾"	Ball
3A-B	National	\$60	P/NG/B	T/OC	PM 1	None	N/A	Some	Yes	Var	Sep
6B	National	\$89	P/NG/B	T/OC	PM 1	None	N/A	Some	Yes	Var	RE
8M	National	\$129+ ~\$65	P/NG	T/OC?	SM 7,21 PM 1	PM 1 jet	Sep	Yes Some	Some Yes	Var	Ball
Mid Range	Nortel	\$270	P/NG/H	T/OG?	SM 25 jets	None	N/A	Yes	Yes	1"	FF
Glass Bead Burner	Bethlehem	\$360	P/NG/H	T/OG	SM 7 jets	None	N/A	Yes	Yes	⅝"	FF
Lynx	GTT	\$435	P/NG	T/OG	TM 7 jets	None	N/A	Yes	Yes	⅞"	FF
Mid Range Plus	Nortel	\$379	P/NG/H	T/OG?	SM 7 jets	SM 25 jets	Sep	Yes	Yes	1"	FF
Major	Nortel	\$399	P/NG/H	T/OG?	SM 7 jets	SM 48/64 jets	Sep	Yes	Yes	1½"	FF
New Nortel	Nortel	\$499	P/NG/H	T/OG?	SM 7 jets	SM 47 jets	Sep	Yes	Yes	1⅜"	FF
Phoenix	GTT	\$625	P/NG	T/OG?	TM 21 jets	None	N/A	Yes	Yes	1¼"	FF
Phantom	GTT	\$1125	P/NG	T/OG?	TM 7 jets	TM 14 jets	Conc	Yes	Yes	1¼"	FF
CC	Carlisle	\$1100	P/NG/H	T/OG?	PM 1 jet	SM 34 jets	Conc	Some	Yes	1½"	B&P, R&P
Mirage	GTT	\$1625	P/NG	T/OG?	SM 7 jets	SM 28 jets	Conc	Yes	Yes	1⅝"	F, R&P
CC Plus	Carlisle	\$1700	P/NG/H	T/OG?	PM 1 jet	SM 63 jets	Conc	Some	Yes	1⅝"	B&P, R&P
PM2D	Bethlehem	\$1550	PNG/H	T/OG?	SM 5 jets	SM 69 jets	Conc	Yes	Yes	1¾"	R&P
Delta Elite	GTT	\$2250	P/NG	T	SM 7 jets	SM 39 jets	Conc	Yes	Yes	2¼"	R&P
Zenit 40	Herbert Arnold	\$2500	P/NG/H	T	SM 10 jets	SM 63 jets	Conc	Yes	Yes	2"	R&P

Manufacturers: GTT = Glass Torch Technology
Cost: Prices are those of the summer of 2002 and are for comparison only
Fuel Gases: Mapp = Mapp Gas, P = Propane, NG = Natural Gas, H = Hydrogen, B = Butane
Oxygen Source: T = Tank, OC = Oxygen Concentrator, OG = Oxygen Generator, OG? = Larger Oxygen Generators
Primary & Secondary Flame: SM = Surface Mixed, PM = Premixed, TM = Triple Mixed
Configuration: N/A = Not Applicable/Single Head, Sep = Separate Heads, Conc = Concentric Heads
Max Flame: Var = Depends upon the head
Bases: FF = Friction Flat, B&P = Ball & Post, R&P = Rack & Pinion, Sep = Separately Purchased, RE = Rotating Elbow

Lampworking tools

There are a number of tools that you should consider having on your workbench when making lampworked beads. You may already have some of them around your shop or alternatives, which may work almost as well. Let's discuss some of these tools and what they are used for, starting with glass cutters.

Glass cutters

To work glass in a torch, it helps if the glass is first cut into manageable pieces. The appropriate tool to use for this purpose depends a lot upon what kind of glass you are using. Sheet glass requires a much different cutter than rods or tubing.

Sheet glass cutters

If you use sheet glass in your work, the appropriate tool is a standard glass cutter like that used in stained glass. Some artists use scrap sheet glass from fusing to make their beads and this cutter is just fine for that application. Also since most of the dichroic glass being used in beadmaking is manufactured in sheet form, the stained glass cutter will be used by artists working with dichroic glass.

Stained glass cutters come in many shapes and sizes. Some are especially designed to make them easier to use. Since oil is used to lubricate stained glass cutters, some may also have self-oiling features. I recommend against this because you will have to clean the oil back off. I use my cutter dry to avoid oil residues.

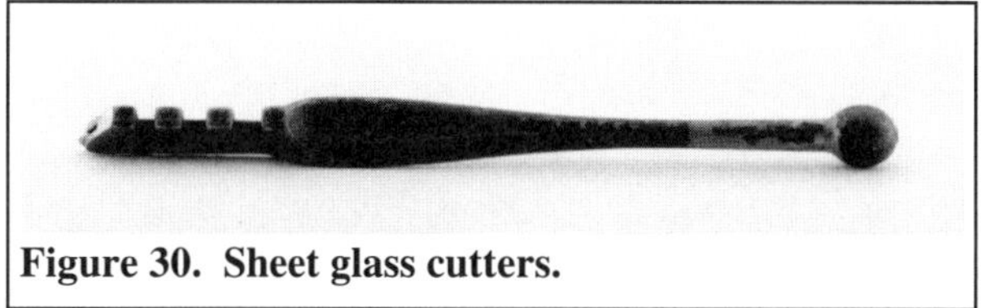

Figure 30. Sheet glass cutters.

You use a standard stained glass cutter as follows:

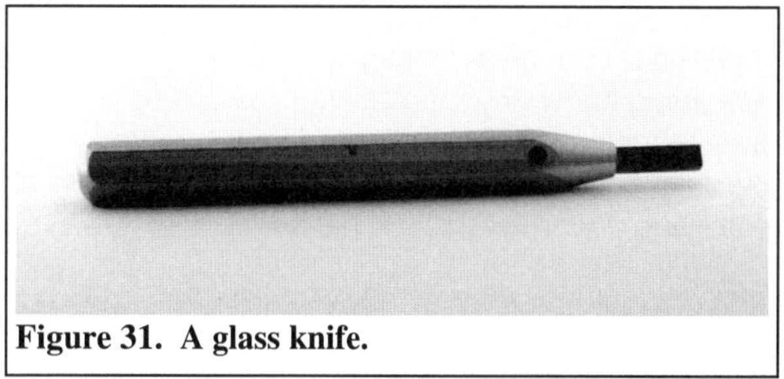

Figure 31. A glass knife.

- Hold it such that the shaft extends up through your index and middle finger.
- Squeeze the flat area near the tip of the cutter between the tips of these fingers and your thumb.
- Use a straight edge to guide your cut to get a consistent result
- Press the wheel of the cutter down against the glass and
- Pull it smoothly toward you.

You should hear a noticeable scratching sound and get a visible score in the glass. Try to get this right the first time, as going over the score a second time is bad for the carbide wheel on the cutter.

The score is then run (forming a crack through the thickness of the glass) from one end to the other. This is done by bending the scored glass with the score positioned upward over the edge of a table. If the piece is small, use a set of running pliers, which does essentially the same thing. Running difficult scores is aided by pulling slightly outward on either side of the score as you bend the glass. You can find more information on this subject in any good book on stained glass techniques.

Glass knifes

Other artists prefer to use glass that has been specifically manufactured for lampworking. There is an increasing number of sources for such glass which include Effetre, Haselbach, Lauscha, Bullseye or Satake glass. This glass comes in the form of rods up to three feet in length. A standard glass cutter does not work well for cutting rods into manageable lengths. There is a tool manufactured specifically for this task, called a glass cutoff knife, which is pictured in Figure 32.

A glass knife consists of a rectangular tungsten carbide blade mounted in an anodized aluminum handle. The blade is removable and can be reversed to expose four new cutting surfaces. Tungsten carbide is an extremely hard material used primarily for things like machine tools. In fact, used lathe tools can be a cheap alternative to a cutoff knife if you know any machinists. Besides being very hard, tungsten carbide is also a brittle material. If you drop your knife, you can break off a section of your blade. I learned this the hard way.

To use your cutoff knife, hold the handle with the four fingers of one hand and push a rod against the blade with your thumb. Then make a score around the rod by twisting the rod all the way around with your other hand.

To "run" the score or break the rod, take it in both hands and position your thumbs about one half inch to either side of the score. Bend and break the rod by pushing with your thumbs and pulling the rod on either side toward you with your fingers.

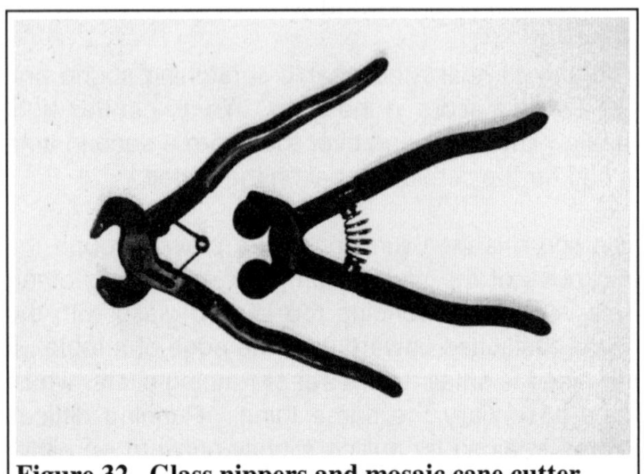

Figure 32. Glass nippers and mosaic cane cutter.

Nippers

Nippers are hand tools made for working on ceramic tile. They are used to nip out small sections of tile, similar to the way that grozing pliers are used in stained glass to nibble out small sections from a piece of glass. As seen to the left in Figure 32, tile nippers have a set of short tungsten carbide blades mounted perpendicularly at the end of their jaws. Make sure that you get nippers with tungsten carbide blades even if they are slightly more expensive because the ones with steel blades dull quickly.

Tile nippers are used a lot like scissors. When you squeeze the handle the blades, which again are mounted perpendicular to the way blades are mounted on scissors, come almost together. They are used to nip off a section of rod by holding the handles parallel to the rod with the blades straddling the rod. Squeezing the handle brings the jaws together. Watch out as you do this because small pieces can really go flying and some dust is generated. You can keep the cut pieces from flying if you hold one finger on the end of the cane while cutting. Try not to pinch yourself though.

A new type of nippers made specially for cutting glass cane, called a Leponitt Mosaic Glass Cutter. As seen to the right in Figure 32, it has two replaceable tungsten carbide disk blades. The carbide disk blades have a sharpened, 85° included angle all the way around each cutting edge. With a diameter of ¾" this means that each disk has a total cutting surface of about 2½" compared to the usual ½" on most tile nippers.

When a portion of the disk that you are currently using becomes dull, you just grab the included Allen wrench, loosen the screw holding the disk, and rotate the disk to bring a fresh cutting surface into play. The cost of a replacement set of disks is about ¾ that of a new tool.

I find that this tool cuts cane more uniformly and with more control than a tile nipper. This is probably because the blades are much thinner and sharper than on my nippers, and they don't tend to shoot cane slices across the room like the tile nippers do. But being a specialized tool, it tends to be a lot more expensive than tile nippers.

Triangular files

If you are on a budget, a triangular file is an

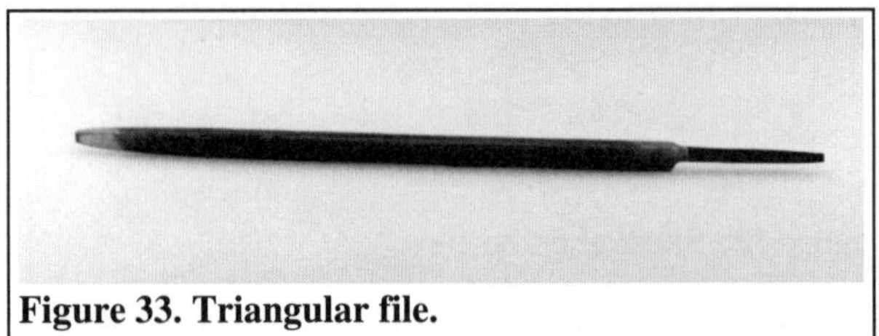

Figure 33. Triangular file.

inexpensive tool that can be used to score your glass rods for breaking. To use it for this purpose, hold the rod down on the table with one hand and take the triangular file in the other. Push the triangular file perpendicularly across the top of the glass rod away from you. This should put a short score in the rod. Then rotate the rod slightly and continue scoring it with the file until it runs about ¼ to ½ way around the rod. Next wet the score. Then break the glass rod with your hands as described for the glass knife, holding the short score away from you.

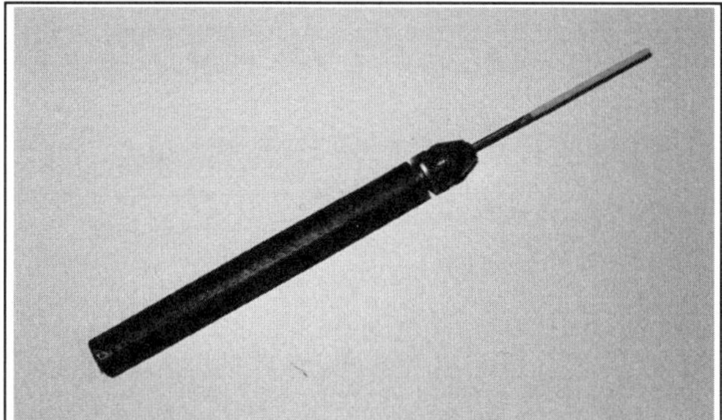

Figure 34. Winding mandrel holder.

Holding tools

The next set of tools that we want to discuss is those for holding hot glass. Without them we would all have a lot of burned fingers.

Winding mandrels and mandrel holders

The easiest of the beadmaking techniques available to a typical glass artist, as will be described later, is that of making wound glass beads. In this technique, glass rods are melted in the flame of a torch and wound around a mandrel to form a bead. The most common kind of mandrel used by wound glass beadmakers is made from stainless steel filler rod used in TIG welding. This filler rod can be purchased from any welding supply house and is commonly available in 3-foot lengths and diameters of $^{1}/_{16}{}^{th}$, $^{3}/_{32}{}^{nds}$, and $^{1}/_{8}{}^{th}$ of an inch. Copper coated steel filler rods are also another good alternative, but be sure you do not get the flux-coated rods.

Stainless steel is always the recommended mandrel material for a number of reasons.

- It holds up well to the heat without distorting.
- It does not oxidize appreciably.
- Its surface remains smooth under repeated use.
- Lastly it is a poor conductor of heat. This allows you to hold the rods relatively close to the bead without burning yourself. Try this with copper and see what happens.

Some artists like to attach handles to their mandrels by sticking them into center drilled wood dowels or by using a pin vise as shown in Figure 34. This can be especially important when making those big heavy “monster” beads, where after a while it can actually get to be a little painful trying to hold the mandrel. Another convenient option is to use one of the mechanical pencils made for drafting which has a normally-closed pin-vise like mechanism that opens when you press the button on the end of the pencil. You can wrap the barrel of the pencil in tape to make it larger in diameter and easier to handle.

The extra thickness gained from any of these options helps give you more control during winding by making the rods easier to handle. They may also help prevent putting stress on your ligaments and joints, reducing chances of repetitive motion injuries. What all beadmakers probably really need is a powered mandrel holder that turns the rod for us. This would help prevent the repetitive motion injuries that some beadmakers are starting to incur.

The other thing that you may want to think about doing is adding weights to the end of your mandrels or mandrel handles to counterbalance the weight of the bead on the other end of the mandrel. This would also help to make the mandrel easier to handle. Tom Holland has suggested using a mandrel rest at your workstation. This is a block of wood with a bent coat hanger mounted in it that has a loop on the end of it. You rest the mandrel in the little loop as you turn it. The loop is used like the fulcrum on a seesaw. This way you do not need to support the weight of your bead but only use the weight of your hand to hold the bead up.

If you are interested in making buttons, you can bend a $^{1}/_{16}{}^{th}$-inch mandrel in two to form a mandrel

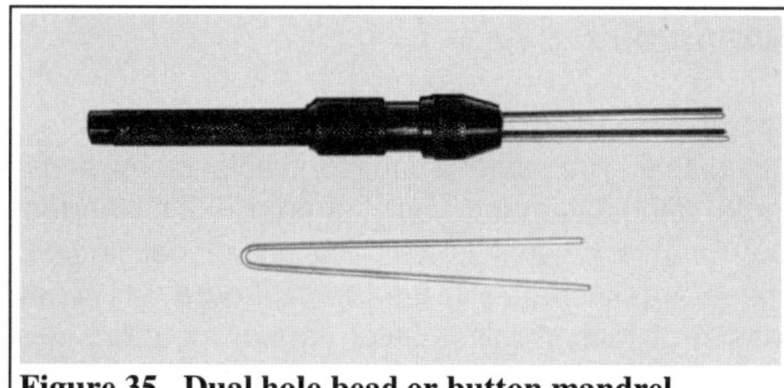

Figure 35. Dual hole bead or button mandrel.

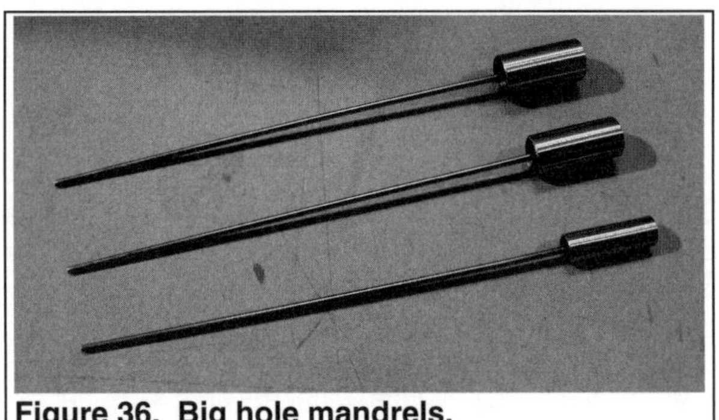

Figure 36. Big hole mandrels.

on which to wind two holed buttons. This type of arrangement can also be used to make beads with two through-holes for use in multiple stranded necklaces or bolo ties. This tool, which is shown in Figure 35, is used similarly to a regular mandrel.

Make sure that you keep the mandrel prongs parallel to each other and that you apply a good coating of separator compound so that you can get the bead or button off afterwards. To make them easier to handle and more rigid they are held in a pin vise as shown. This also helps to keep the rod bent properly. If you do not want to make your own someone will be glad to sell you one.

For beads with holes larger than $^{1}/8^{th}$ of an inch, you have two options: you can use thin-wall stainless steel tubing or some of the new big hole mandrels inspired by Emiko Sawamoto. Tubing is available in $^{3}/16^{ths}$ ad $^{7}/16^{ths}$ inches in diameter. The big hole mandrels, like those see in Figure 36, are two inch long sections of thick wall stainless steel tubing with an end cap welded onto $^{5}/32^{nds}$“ diameter mandrels. This arrangement allows faster rotation than with tubing and avoids the problem of steam released from partially drier release from traveling up the tubing and burning your fingers. These mandrels are good for making large holed beads, rings, napkin holders, scarf slides, and core formed vessels. Personally, I find that with large work that they are heavy, hard to hold and should be used with mandrel holders.

Hot fingers

Sometimes when you are making beads, marbles, or vessels, you need a tool to cradle them in the flame without burning your fingertips. The perfect tool for this is what is called a set of hot fingers. These are illustrated in the top of Figure 37. They consist of four stainless steel fingers mounted in a handle. They grip the glass object by adjusting a slide. Moving the slide forward brings the fingers together, and sliding it back allows the fingers to open. As always, you can purchase one of these tools or make your own.

The one pictured here was made using round cross section brass tubing to form the handle and a slightly smaller square cross section tubing that can fit down into the handle to form the slide. A ring is soldered onto the end of the adjusting slide to prevent it from completely sliding down into the handle. The fingers themselves are made from steel wires that could be old bead winding mandrels. These components can be seen in the bottom of the figure.

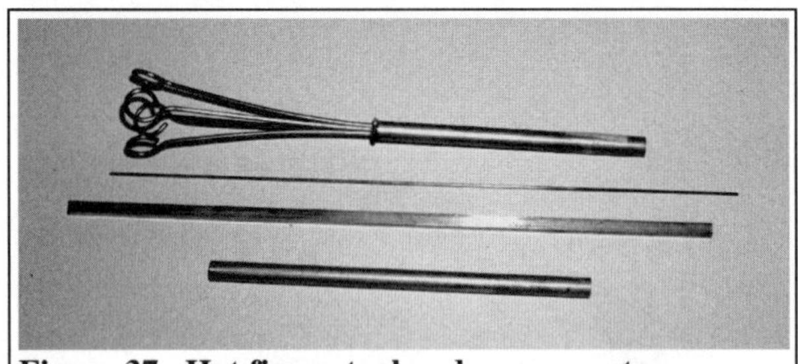

Figure 37. Hot finger tool and components.

To make your own set, you first bend the tips of the fingers to suit the job at hand. The circular tips shown are good for handling spherical beads or marbles. Ends with outward pointing V's are used for objects like goblets. Next, you slip the slider over the other end of the fingers, ring end on first and then followed by the handle. The ends of the fingers are soldered into the aft end of the handle being careful not to solder the slide in place. The fingers are lastly given a slight outward bend to them so that they open when the slide is slid back.

In their book listed at the end of this chapter, Hammesfahr and Stong give alternate fabrication techniques for making hot fingers that anyone should be able to use. In addition, they show some alternative fingertip configurations that can be used for other glass working purposes.

Manipulation tools

There are a number of tools that can be used to manipulate hot glass. They can be to squeeze it, stretch it, rake it, or cut it. We use them to give complex shapes to our beads. Let's discuss some of these tools.

Tweezers

Tweezers, like those seen in Figure 38, are used to pick up and hold hot constructions that you want to add to your beads and to preheat them in the outer

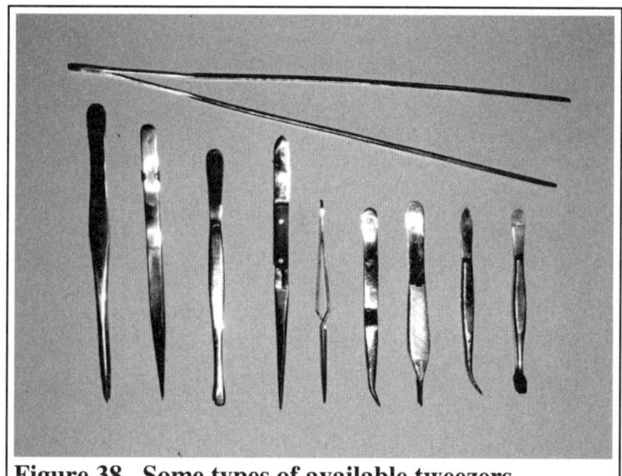

Figure 38. Some types of available tweezers.

reaches of your flame. As such, they could also be defined as holding tools but they are more often used to shape and form one's beads or to pick unwanted features off of a bead. The special long tweezers shown in the figure are very useful in flameworking and come in 6, 8 and 10-inch lengths.

Tweezers are usually made of thin steel and thus will not stand up to a direct flame. Most, if heated in the flame, will get soft and bend. For this reason, remove a bead from the flame before you use your tweezers to form and distort it. This is true with most metal tools.

Removing the glass from the flame as you manipulate it will also help prevent the glass from sticking to the tweezers. This can happen with any metal tool if both the tool and the glass are hot. If you do get them hot, dipping your tweezers into water will quickly cool them.

There are many kinds of specialized tweezers that are used for other purposes that may be useful in shaping beads. Some tweezers, like those in the center of the figure, are self-locking and have to be squeezed to open the jaws. This can be helpful in holding onto tiny pieces that you are trying to add to a bead. Tweezers for stamp collecting, like those seen to the right of the figure, have small flat ends that can be useful for shaping. Others have small pointed ends that come in handy for pulling out feature details. You may want to collect a wide variety of tweezers for your work. I find them to be invaluable tools.

Pliers and mashers

Pliers can be used like tweezers to shape your glass and they are a little more resistant to the heat because of their greater mass. This also means that they will chill the glass faster and are more likely to thermal shock it than tweezers. Therefore, you may want to preheat them slightly before touching them to your bead to prevent thermal shocking it. But not too much or they may stick to the glass. This is more of a problem when the glass is really hot. Pliers can be used to add twists and ridges, or to pull out and stretch sections of a bead. The ideal pliers for this type of work are good needle-nosed pliers.

If you do not want striation marks from the pliers gripping surface on your beads, you can buy pliers with a flat surface or you can file them off.

Special jawed pliers can be made by brazing different kinds of shaped plates onto cheap swap-meet pliers or can be purchased premade. Examples of such pliers are illustrated in Figure 39. They are called mashing or squashing pliers. They are used to mash molten beads to flatten them out. A smaller version, called a "mini-masher", is also available. It has small square jaws that are used for squishing small details into sculptural beads.

Flat jawed mashers are also available, whose jaws do not come together parallel. They close at the inside of the jaws where they are brazed on but they are open at the outside end of the flat. This type of masher can be used to make star millefiori and Chevron beads.

Variations on the flat jawed mashers are ones with curved jaw faces. These are used to give a little curvature to tableau beads (discussed later). Pati Walton also sells a version of mashers with jaws made from spoons that can be used to help shape lozenge-shaped beads. She calls them Pati-wackers.

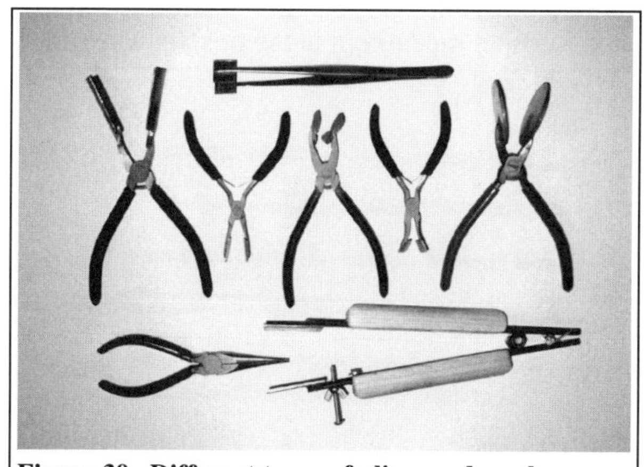

Figure 39. Different types of pliers and mashers.

You can also make special pliers with jaws that have textures or shapes. I call these types of pliers, "pinchers" for lack of a better name. They texture the glass as well as shape it. Commercial pinchers are available to make leaf-like ridges, squiggly lines and square lines, but with a little imagination I am sure that many other ideas may come to mind. They come with the pinching surface of the pliers either perpendicular to the end of the jaws like a normal mashing pliers, or aligned along the jaws, whichever is easier for you to use.

If you decide to make your own specialized pliers, try making your jaws out of brass as it does not seem to leave as much scum on glass as some other materials. If you want to make your own pliers that texture the glass as you squash it, try brazing on sections of a wood rasp (file). This puts in a number of parallel lines like veins on a leaf.

Reamers and shapers

Reamers are primarily used to flare out or ream the ends of blown beads. They come in a number of different types. The most common type is simply straight graphite rods with a point on one end, as seen in the bottom of Figure 40. I often add a handle of some sort on the other end to keep your hands from getting dirty. For my handle, I just wrap one end of the rod with tape as seen on the top rod. Graphite rods are available in a number of different diameters from any flameworking supplier. Graphite reamers are also available with a hexagonal cross section as seen in the second from the top. This reduces contact area with the glass and thus reduces heat loss as you twist it in the hole.

Another type of reamer for large holes is shaped like a triangle at the end of a rod. One of this type is seen in the upper left of the figure. The best ones of this type have the triangle made from brass. When using reamers made from brass or steel, lubricating the tip with beeswax prior to use helps prevent it from sticking to the glass and vice versa. This type of reamer will not cool a bead much as you are reaming out the end of a blown bead, as some of the others will. This type is also very useful for shaping and distorting the surface of a bead by pushing the reamer into the bead.

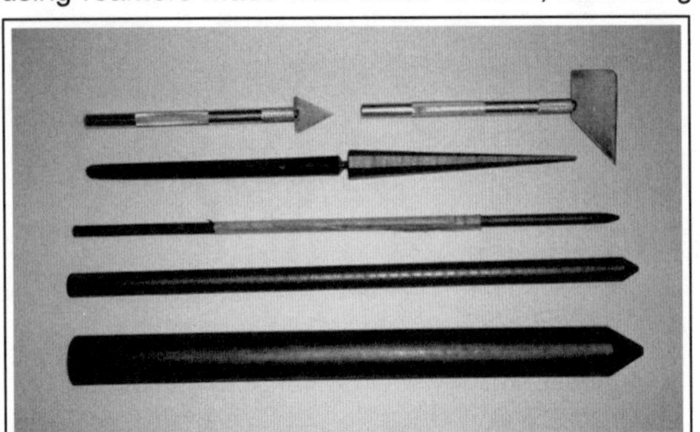

Figure 40. Various reamers and shapers.

There are many variants of this tool that can be used for shaping and sculpting beads. One of them can be seen in the upper right of the figure. It has a nice flat surface for pushing into the bead and a point to drag across it. Other tools that can be used to sculpt glass include razor blades, exacto knifes, screw drivers, and ordinary butter knives.

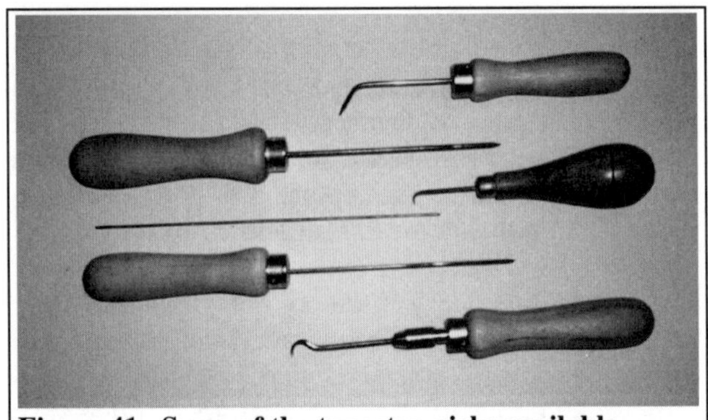

Figure 41. Some of the tungsten picks available.

Tungsten picks

Tungsten picks are used in a number of ways. They can be used to rake glass, pick off unwanted elements, shape features, and drill holes through the glass. A good straight pick can be constructed using tungsten wire like that used for tig welding. It is easily obtained from a welding supply house. They come in pieces of various diameters and seven inches long. I get ones about $^{1}/_{16}$" in diameter. This wire can then be mounted into a wood dowel handle or a pin vise.

A pin vise is a small handle used to hold things like small reaming tools, scribes, drill bits, etc. The handle has a hollow at one end into which fits a collet—a slotted tapered tube. Over the collet a screw-on cap is applied that causes the collet to tighten on whatever is inserted into it as the cap is tightened.

Tungsten is used with glass for two reasons. First, it is very resistant to heat. Second, it does not stick to glass as much as other metals (unless both the pick and the glass are hot). If one is cooler than the other, then it will not stick. This feature can be put to good use to allow a pick to act as a temporary mandrel in building up beads out of tubing. Here you can temporarily bond the tubing to the pick by heating one end of the tubing and the pick. The bead can be released later by heating the pick really hot and twisting the bead off.

Tungsten picks are also available with small hooks on the end, as seen in the right side of Figure 41. These picks are used to shape features and put indentations into the surface of the glass, and I will discuss their use when I talk about making a face bead. Picks are also available with right angles on the end, to be used for raking. They are not really necessary because you can always rake your bead with a stringer, but you may want to purchase one anyway. Bent and curved picks are hard to make on your own since tungsten is very brittle. You have to get it really hot to bend it and it is hard to do, so you may want to purchase these.

To drill a hole in a piece of glass with a straight tungsten pick, you get the pick white hot and poke it through the hot glass twisting it back and forth as you push. You may have to repeat this operation more than once to get the pick all the way through the glass. You will also need to warm the glass in the outer reaches of your flame to soften it and prevent thermal shock.

To prevent distorting the exit side of your bead, it helps to go half way through from one side and then the other half from the other side, trying to meet in the middle. This gets easier with practice. If you get trapped in the middle, just heat up the exposed portion of the pick until it is white hot and twist it out. For making larger holes, it helps to make a pilot hole first with a smaller diameter pick and them ream it out with a larger one.

If your straight tungsten pick gets dull or the tip breaks off, you can sharpen it by dipping the hot end into a product called Chem Sharp. This material can be purchased at your local welding supply house and comes in either powder or stick form. It is a mixture of sodium nitrate and potassium nitrate. Both of these materials are hygroscopic (suck water out of the air) so be sure to keep them tightly capped when not in use.

To sharpen your tungsten pick, first rough shape it on a grinding wheel. Then heat it to a dull red in a flame and immediately plunge it into the Chem Sharp powder or rub it across the stick. When you do this, it will spit and sputter so be sure to wear glasses and possibly gloves. If your pick was hot enough, the mixture will react with it and eat away at the tungsten. After a few seconds remove the pick and rinse it off in water. Repeat as necessary until it meets your approval. This works like a miracle.

Scissors

Another tool that you will occasionally need for beadmaking is a pair of scissors. In addition to the obvious uses such as cutting metal foils or leaf, scissors can also be used for cutting molten glass. You can use them to square off ends of components or to make cuts into the molten glass where you want to pull out sections into things like feathers on wings.

When looking for a set of scissors to use in making glass beads, look for those with thin blades. This helps minimize the heat conducted away from the glass when cutting it. This will allow you to cut further with the scissors before the glass cools enough to get hard. Bonsai scissors are perfect for this job and are easy to obtain.

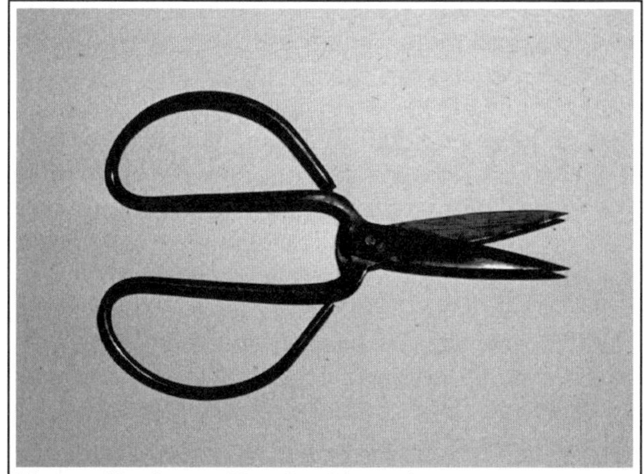

Figure 42. A set of beadmaking scissors

Shaping tools

The next set of tools provides working surfaces on which to shape beads, and will differ in size, shape, and composition. Let's look at some of these.

Marvers

Often when making beads, you need a bench surface on which to work the glass. In hot glass shops, this working surface is called a marver because traditionally it was made of marble. You will use a marver primarily to help shape and work air out of your beads. The marver also serves a secondary function as a surface from which you can pick up surface decorations, such as fine glass frit.

The preferred material for a marver is a sheet of graphite because it can withstand high temperature and hot glass will not stick to it. With graphite, you can also preheat your decorations by setting it on a hot plate or directing a handheld torch on them without problems.

If you cannot get a big graphite pad, you could resort to a thick piece of iron or brass. Make sure that you clean as much rust or other surface corrosion off the metal as much you can so that your beads do not pick it up. Another alternative is to use marble tile.

There are also small graphite blocks (mini-marvers) available that mount on the top of your torch. There they are always conveniently available for use without having to hold them in your hand.

Paddles

Paddles are portable smooth surfaces on which to marver or shape glass while it is hot and pliable. Hot glass workers often use wet cherry wood paddles for shaping glass. They are soaked in water to prevent the wood from burning. This is too messy for our work. Instead, the paddles that lampworkers and beadmakers use are made from graphite. Graphite is used because it is a good heat conductor and it will not stick to hot glass, as metal will when it gets hot.

Paddles can also be used as marvering plates on which to form the glass if you don't have a marver for your workbench. For handwork, small paddles on the order of about 1½" x 1¾" are preferred by most beadmakers but paddles are also available in many other sizes, such as 1" x 4", 2" x 3", 3" x 4", etc. You may want to have a variety of sizes.

Most paddles have rectangular solid faces but there are some on the market shaped like small rubber spatulas with an increasingly sharp edge on one side, a rounded edge on the other side, and a sharp end as seen in the left of Figure 43. These paddles, sometimes called Stump Shapers after Loren Stump, allow you to poke groves and creases into hot glass, shaping it to your will. Because they have sharp fragile edges some of these paddles are made from brass for greater durability.

If desired, paddles can be shaped for other purposes. As an example, those seen at the bottom

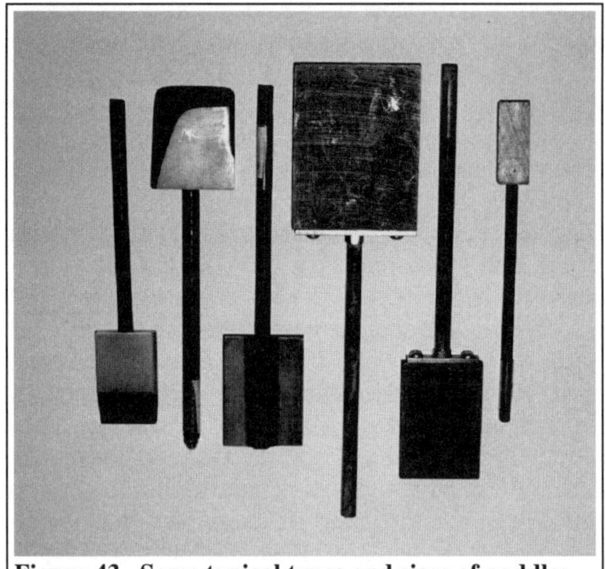

Figure 43. Some typical types and sizes of paddles.

middle of the figure have been given sort of an upside down T shape. This type of paddle is used to shape cylindrical beads with rounded ends. Rolling in one of the two rounded creases shapes the sides of the cylinders. Which edge you use depends upon the size of the bead. To form a nice rounded end, you turn the mandrel perpendicular to the crease and roll the end of the bead along the crease. Most beadmakers just shape cylindrical beads on a flat paddle and get the rounded ends by jockeying the paddle around to form it, but you might find you like using these shaping paddles better.

Textured rollers

As you can imagine, texture can be put onto a bead's surface by rolling the hot bead on an object with the desired texture. There are a number of textured surface rollers that are commercially available, and if you look around, you may find other things that you can use. Three commercial ones are shown in Figure 44. The one in the upper left is

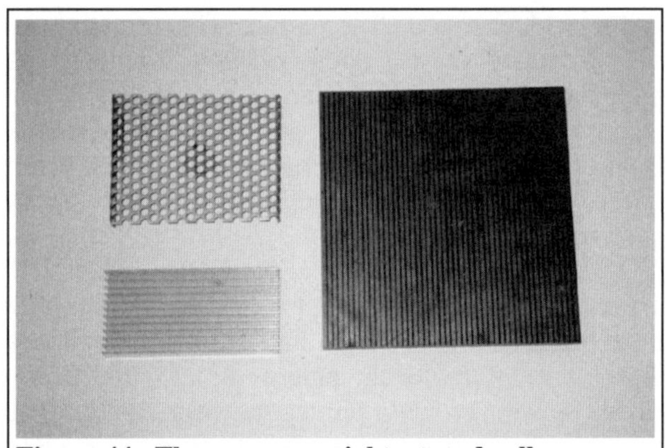

Figure 44. Three commercial textured rollers.

known as a Holy Roller for obvious reasons and leaves a texture of lens-like shapes on the surface of the bead. The one beneath it will put deep linear indentations into a bead. The third is a small graphite surface plate that creates shallow linear indentations. It can also be used as a marver from which to pick up evenly spaced glass stringers.

Changing the direction that the bead is rolled on the textured surface can vary the orientation of each of the applied textures. The depth or degree of the texture is controlled by how hard you press the bead onto the textured surface and how hot the bead is as you roll it.

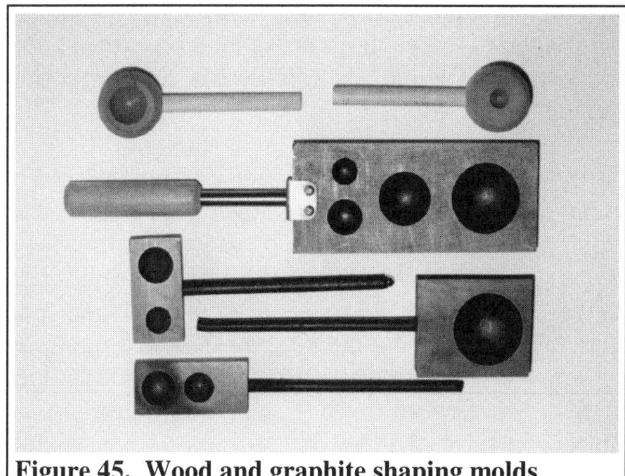

Figure 45. Wood and graphite shaping molds

Shaping molds

Another class of shaping tools used for making beads and other objects is that of shaping molds. Figure 45 shows a number of shaping molds. The upper two are wooden marble molds. The one beneath them and the two at the bottom are graphite marble molds. Marble molds can also be used for making hemispherical cabochons. They have hemispherical cavities cut into the graphite surface and a handle for holding them. The one in the center left is a mold for making buttons. It has short cylinders with partial spherical bottoms cut into it.

In addition to hemispherical bottomed molds, there are also graphite molds available with other shapes cut into them, such as ovals, tear drops, etc. Some of them even have cut outs across the surface in which a bead mandrel can ride. This allows you to be able to get the bead close to the mold so you can form a complete bead.

Graphite shaping molds need to be kept clean and you have to avoid chipping the edges of the cavities because as we will see this is the surface on which

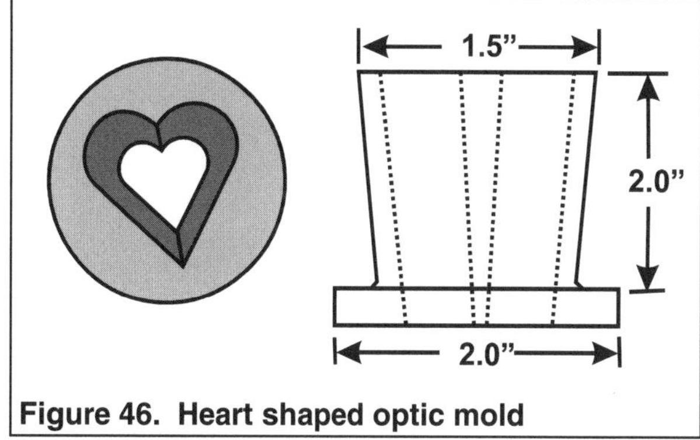

Figure 46. Heart shaped optic mold

we will do most of the forming. The use of these molds to make marbles, buttons, and cabochons is described in a later chapter.

Besides these relatively simple shapes, there are also other types of molds that have been made with more complex shapes cut into them. Three types of these that I will discuss are deep optic molds, shallow figurative molds, and graphite shapers.

Optic molds are designed to make relatively long complex cross sectional constructions. They are used primarily in making simple mosaic canes as will be described in a few chapters. They are basically a metal cylinder with a shaped cavity cut into them like a heart cut into them as seen in Figure 46. By dipping hot glass into them the glass takes on the shape of the cavity over a small length. To prevent capturing the glass in the mold, the cavity is tapered so that it is larger at the top and smaller at the bottom.

Figurative molds, like those seen in Figure 47, are

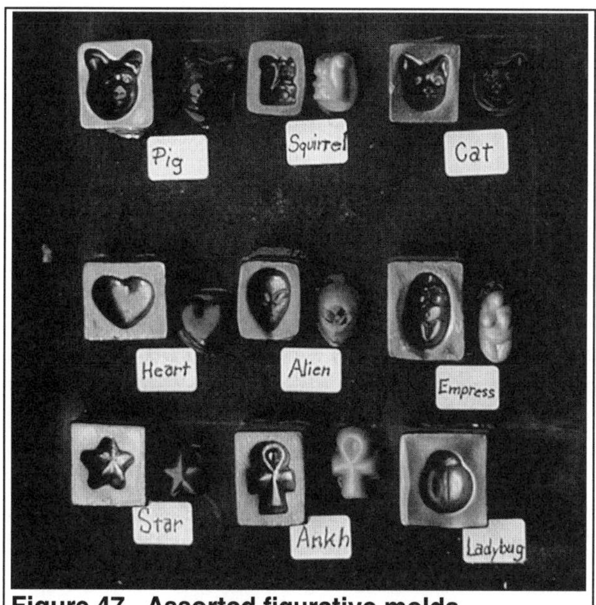

Figure 47. Assorted figurative molds

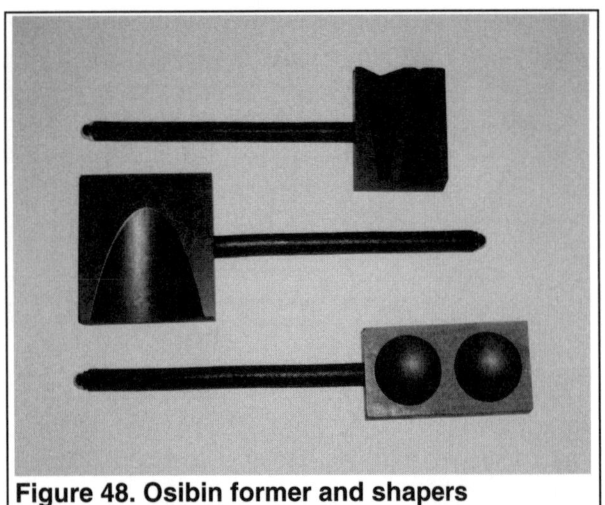

Figure 48. Osibin former and shapers

used to make shallow complex glass images about ½" cube by again plunging hot glass into them. These molds are machined out of brass and again have a slight taper to the image so that it will not trap the glass inside the mold. Some of the images that are available include faces, insects, etc. They are use to make cabochons, button, etc.

The last tools are a new set of graphite formers and shapers designed by and named after Kim Osibin with help from Craig Milliron. The first of the new tools is Kim's Cone and Vessel Shaper in the top of Figure 48. It is a versatile tool for shaping axisymetric conical beads and vessels. The tool has two deep tapering V-shaped grooves on one side of the tool; one going in opposing directions across the face of the tool allowing one to easily switch from one groove to the other when making torpedo or biconic beads. By tilting the mandrel in relationship to the face of the tool you can change the angle of the cone. Because you are really riding on a line in the V, you will not get folding of the glass like when you overfill a marble mold.

The nest tool, in the middle of the figure, is the Osibin Former to assist in forming round, oval and olive shaped beads. Each side of the tool has a deep ovoid depression in it that starts out as a narrow, shallow curve that widens and deepens as it progresses across the face of the tool. The depressions are different on each side so it is like getting two tools in one. By changing the orientation of the bead to the tool you change the oval working surface that shapes the bead. The second tool is the Lentil Shaper used for making lentil shaped beads or buttons. The tool is two sided and has two shaping cavities on each side all with a different spherical radius to them. By moving the bead around in the cavity you can make beads larger than each cavity.

Curved shaping cups

You can also make your own shaping tools to help form your beads to specific shapes that give similar to the last set of shaping tools discussed. René Roberts has developed such tools for use in her work. To make these tools, she takes 24-gauge brass sheet and shapes it into a shallow cup shape using a dabbing mold. She then mounts the cup onto a piece of brass tubing to serve as a handle, as seen in the upper left of Figure 49. The tool is shaped like a cup to give it more rigidity. This is also the reason that 24-gauge brass is used. Any lighter gauge and the cup is just too flexible; any larger and it is too hard to form.

To make one of these tools, get a dabbing mold of about the shape that you are looking for in the bead cross section. If you have a good wood turner for a friend, you might be able to get them to make one for you. Then cut a circle out of brass sheet just slightly larger that the dabbing cavity and smooth up its edges with sandpaper. Now, use a wood dabber (a short section of ½ to 1" diameter doweling on which you have slightly rounded one end) and start shaping around the edge of the disk. Slowly work around the edge of the disk and then inward toward the center. Take it slow and form a good shape into the cup. You start at the edge to prevent folding, which can happen if you try to start at the center.

Now clean the oxide off the underside of the cup with some sandpaper and paint an area slightly larger than the handle you are going to attach there with some flux. Set the cup upside down on some mandrels on your marver and add a couple of small pieces of silver solder onto the fluxed area. Slowly heat up the whole cup with a small flame until the solder flows.

Figure 49. Curved shaping cups.

Then hang a couple of mandrels off the side of your workbench by sliding one end under your marver or some other heavy object. Set the cup up on them again, but this time upside down. Clean off the end of your brass tubing handle and apply flux to it. Lightly heat the end of the handle and cup (from the bottom this time) until the solder flows again. Then quickly touch the handle to the cup and hold it there to finish the tool. Try to make sure that the handle straight up and down as you touch them together as it is hard to use if it is crooked. Reheat the joint as necessary to adjust the handle.

Clean up the flux and your tool is ready to go. You will use the upper surface of the cup as a curved surface on which to shape your beads. This is a good tool for shaping long gentle oval torpedo beads. If you do not quite have the shape that you were looking for, you can tweak it some by bending it with your fingers. I will discuss use of this tool more later when I discuss shaping beads. René also makes dabbed cups like the other two tools in the right side of the figure. She attaches these to wooden blocks and uses them as press molds. She says that these molds can be tricky to use because it is hard to bring them together parallel.

Bracelet and ring formers

If you want to get into making additional forms of solid glass jewelry besides beads, buttons, and pendants, then you might want to consider making bracelets and rings. The king of bracelet making is Kevin O'Grady and you can see a demonstration of him at work in Lewis Wilson's video, "*Lampworking, Advanced Beads, Bracelets, Marbles.*"

A new tool that you will need to make bracelets is an oval former like that seen in Figure 50. It is a heavy steel shaper about a foot and a half long that has a varying oval cross section down its length in the approximate ratio that you would see on a wrist. Unlike mandrel you do not wrap the glass around the shaper and decorate it on the shaper. Instead you use it to shape a decorated borosilicate rod into a bracelet shape of a specified size. With this tool you can make almost any size you might need except for a doll bracelet.

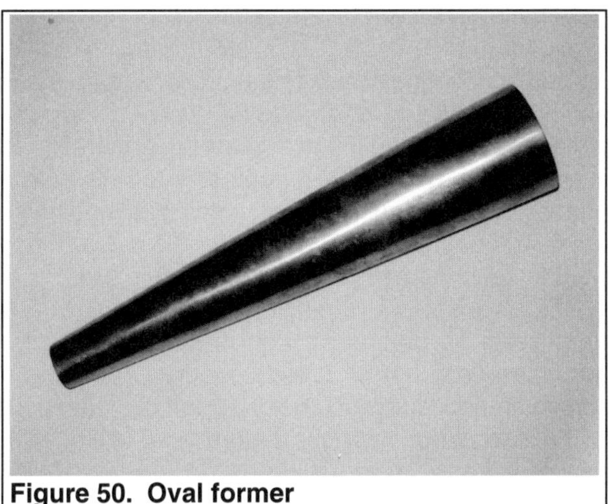

Figure 50. Oval former

There are similar tool for rings. They consist of a tapered cylinder with a circular cross section that covers virtually all ring sizes. With this tool you can either use it like the oval former to only shape the final ring or you can apply bead release to it to wind a ring of whatever size that you want on the tool. This second technique allows you to make a little more decorative ring. Because these are larger objects you have to be much more aware of thermal shock or consider using borosilicate glass to reduce the likelihood of it.

Casing molds

A casing mold is a tool somewhat similar to a shaping mold, in that it is formed by a cavity cut into a block of graphite. A simple casing mold is illustrated in Figure 51. It is known as a "Stump Sucker" because Loren Stump helped develop it. It has a cylindrical cavity with a conical tapered bottom that is hollowed into a block of graphite. A small graphite screen sits at the bottom of the cylindrical portion of the cavity resting on the conical taper to stop flow of the glass and the bottom is connected by a small hole to tubing with an attached mouthpiece. There is a filter in the tubing line so that you do not suck in any hot graphite particles.

Objects to be cased are placed in the bottom of the cavity on top of the screen. The mold is then preheated on a hot plate or something similar.

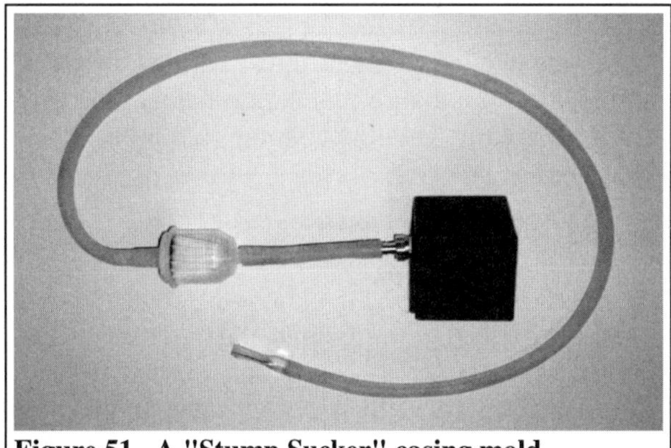

Figure 51. A "Stump Sucker" casing mold.

Figure 52. Kiln with built-in casing mold.

Another preheating technique for this tool can be seen in Figure 52. Here the casing mold is built into the side of a crucible furnace, which preheats the mold as part of its normal operation. After proper preheat of the objects to be cased, hot molten glass is fed into the cavity and air is sucked out by way of the tubing. The cased object is then pulled out of the casing mold and either worked in a flame or put into an annealer.

Larger versions of casing molds can be used to make paperweights. But as the size gets larger, you may want to consider using a small vacuum pump to draw out the air.

Controlled cooling aids

Beads need to be cooled slowly after lampworking or they may crack from induced stress. The best method to cool them is to keep a small annealer on your workbench into which you insert your beads as soon as you finish them. But beginning beadmakers cannot always afford this and are willing to accept an occasional cracked bead for their own use, so let's discuss some alternate methods that they can use.

> **Tip:** Anyone who sells their beads should anneal them to ensure that they will not crack at some later time. See the chapter on annealing.

Vermiculite pan

The most common cooling aid used by beginners is vermiculite. A pan of vermiculite several inches deep is kept on an easy-to-reach portion of your workbench. Vermiculite is a clay mineral that has been expanded from ten to fifteen times its original volume into light airy pellets resembling mica by a high temperature process. It is an inert material often used for insulation or for providing loft to planting soil in gardening. Beginning beadmakers use it for its insulative properties to slow down the cooling of their beads. This helps reduce bead loss from immediate thermal shocking or later cracking. Heating the pan of vermiculite on a hot plate will help to slow down cooling even more. Some novice beadmakers use an old crock-pot or electric skillet instead of a hot plate but that may not be hot enough. A hot plate gets the vermiculite much warmer and if large enough allows an area on which to preheat glass rods or construction components.

Using the vermiculite to slow down cooling is relatively simple. As soon as the bead is flame annealed and allowed to cool just enough to harden its outer surface, as seen by losing its glow when held in a shadow, it is buried in the vermiculite. This slows down heat loss from the surface of the bead, allowing the temperature distribution throughout your bead to remain more uniform as it cools. Slower, more uniform cooling minimizes introduction of residual stress into the bead. The trick is that you have to let the outer surface harden enough first or you will dent it up.

Cooling in vermiculite will not completely alleviate all residual stress in your beads, therefore it is highly recommended that you kiln anneal your beads later. If you do not, they may crack at some later time, even months to years later. If you sell your beads, this can result in you getting a bad reputation as well as the whole glass beads art movement. I have known one beadmaker, though, that made a tube filled with vermiculite that he wrapped with heater wire that got so hot that he was actually able to anneal his beads in it. This worked well but did not have the versatility of an annealer.

A good container in which to keep your vermiculite is an old roasting pan or one of those disposable turkey-roasting pans found in most supermarkets. It is big enough that you can work quite a while before running out of room. A pan of vermiculite resembles a cat litter box, so if you have a studio cat you may want to keep the pan covered when not in use.

Vermiculite as purchased from the hardware store or nursery may not be completely dry. Therefore it is recommended that you bake it in an oven at about 350°F for about an hour before you use it with beads. Otherwise, the moisture in the vermiculite may cause the beads to cool too quickly and crack.

Ceramic fiber

Another slow cooling method used by many novice beadmakers is to have a fold of ceramic fiber blanket, such as Fiberfrax®, on their workbench instead of vermiculite. This ceramic blanket material is what is used as the insulative liner on many glass kilns. After finishing work on a bead, they tuck it into a fold in the blanket to slow down its cooling. Like the pan of vermiculite, this fiber blanket can be kept warm on a hot plate to further slow cooling of the beads. Some beadmakers have reported to me that they were getting a lot of cracked beads using this technique, but others say it works just fine for them. Again this does not anneal the bead.

Virtually all glass bead artists advocate switching as soon as possible from vermiculite or fiber blanket to a small annealing kiln that you keep on your bench. This is prompted because of concern about possible health hazards of using either vermiculite or ceramic blanket. These materials have physical structures similar to that of asbestos and might lead to similar health problems. Therefore, you may want to consider purchasing a kiln or annealer as you expand your beadmaking equipment to minimize any possible health hazards. In addition, by sticking your beads directly into a kiln hovering at the annealing temperature of your glass, you will minimize the chances of getting any thermal shock. If the annealer is then cooled down slowly at the end of your beadmaking session, no subsequent annealing will be necessary.

Lighters

A torch may be lit in any of a number of ways. You might think that most people would just light the torch with a match, but the National Fire Protection Agency and the National Safety Council consider this method to be neither safe nor reliable. The reason for this is not immediately obvious. You would think that everyone would be familiar enough with the use of matches, that this would be the preferred method.

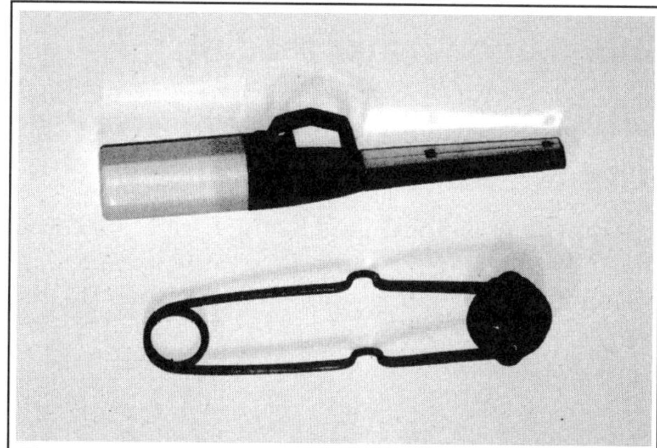

Figure 53. Different types of lighters that can be used to light torches.

The problem with matches, besides the fact that they get your hand too close to the flame, is that they can be blown out if the gas velocity on your torch is turned up too high. Then if the torch is not turned off, it may release enough gas into your workspace to cause a small flame up or explosion by the time the second match is lit. Therefore, the use of matches to light your torch is discouraged.

The most common tool used to light a torch is a striker. Seen in the bottom Figure 53, a striker works by scraping a small piece of flint across an irregular metal surface similar to a file. This is the same technique used to spark a cigarette lighter. Scraping the flint causes a spark to jump that can ignite the gas from the torch. In most strikers, the spark is generated in a small cup, which serves to trap a pocket of gas to make lighting it easier. Some People find strikers really hard to use. Part of the secret is pulling the flint inward against the file slightly as you squeeze it.

Another device used by some artists to light a torch is a butane lighter like those used for barbecues. This uses pressure on a piezoelectric crystal to generate a high voltage spark that then lights a small butane flame from a refillable reservoir, all at the pull of a trigger. It is a very reliable mechanism but can be a hazard. If you are the kind of person who uses something and does not immediately put it back in its proper place, this tool can be dangerous.

Suggested further reading

Dunham, Bandhu, **Contemporary Lampworking, A Practical Guide to Shaping Glass in the Flame**, Salusa Glassworks, 2002

Hammesfahr, James E. and Stong, Clair L. **Creative Glassblowing**, W. H. Freeman and Company, 1968

Wilson, Lewis C., **Lampworking, Advanced Beads, Bracelets, Marbles**, Crystal Myths, Inc. 1994 (two video set)

Kilns and glory holes

Up to this point, the pieces of equipment that we have discussed have been fairly small and relatively inexpensive. That will change with the equipment that we will discuss next—kilns and glory holes. Since they are larger and more specialized pieces of equipment, they may not be needed initially or by all beadmakers. But, as you get into larger beads or different types of beads, you may want to consider investing in them. If nothing else, get a kiln to anneal your beads. Ideally, every wound glass beadmaker should have a small annealing kiln sitting on their workbench.

Kilns and annealers

A kiln or annealer is an insulated container in which glass can be heated in a non-reducing environment. Unlike torches, a kiln allows precise temperature control over the whole bead from room temperature to over 2000°F. As a beadmaker, you will primarily use kilns for annealing stress out of your beads, as will be discussed later. Of course, you might also decide to pursue fabrication of beads by one of the more common kilnworking practices such as fusing or Pâte de Verre.

Table 12. Temperature ranges for various kilnworking processes.

Temperature Range (°F)	Process
200-300	Removal of physically bound water from molds and kiln furniture (212°F)
300-400	Removal of chemically bound water from molds and kiln (375-450°F)
400-500	Paper burns (451°F)
600-700	Lusters stop smoking (600-625°F)
900-1000	Organic materials finish burning off
	Firing bright metal lusters on lead glass (960°F)
	Annealing beads (950-1000°F)
1000-1100	Firing Reusche high-lead, low-fire enamels (1080°F)
	Firing Thompson low-fire enamels (1050-1150°F)
	Firing bright metal lusters on soda lime glass (1040-1100°F)
1100-1200	Firing Fuse Master enamels (1125°F)
	Firing low temperature lusters (1100°F)
1200-1300	Firing bright metal lusters on Pyrex or quartz (1200-1250°F)
	Firing most lusters (1250-1325°F)
	Slumping Bullseye glass (1300°F)
1300-1400	Firing high-fire Thompson enamels (1350-1450°F)
	Firing most clear overglazes
	Devitrification range for susceptible glasses
	Tack fuse Bullseye glass (1350°F)
1400-1500	Paradise paint matures (1450°F)
	Full fuse Bullseye glass (1450°F)
1500-1600	Flat fuse Bullseye glass (1550°F)
1600-1700	Pâte de Verre casting (1600°F)
1700-1800	Raking hot glass in a kiln
	Squeezing fine air bubbles out of glass melt
1900-2000	Melting and fining glass in a crucible (2000°F)

You will also find a kiln useful in fabricating millefiori, in making drawn beads, and in applying lusters or glass paints to your beads. There are quite a number of operations that can be done in a kiln that cannot be done in a flame. Each of these processes has its own characteristic temperature. Table 12 provides a list of some temperature ranges and kiln processes done in each of them.

Kiln construction

Kilns are composed of three main components: a structural framework, an insulating liner, and a heat source. There is nothing really complex about a kiln, so don't be afraid of them. They are really nothing more than a high temperature oven.

Kiln framework

The main framework component of a kiln consists of its exterior metal skin. The exterior skin serves a number of important purposes. The most important of them is to act as a framework onto which you mount your insulation and protect it from mechanical damage during normal operation. The exterior skin also serves as a convenient place to mount control boxes, lids, and doors.

The other significant structural component is a stand. Kilns are mounted off the floor on stands for two reasons. The first is so you will not have to bend down as far to put things into and take them out of the kiln. The second is to allow air to circulate underneath your kiln. This helps keep the exterior skin of the kiln cool.

Kiln insulation

The insulation of a kiln will generally be composed of a number of layers of different materials that may vary with the location in the kiln. The bottom of the kiln is typically made from firebrick. This provides a strong, heat-resistant surface upon which to stand all your kiln hardware. The inner walls of most ceramics kilns will also be made from firebrick because of the much higher process temperatures needed for ceramics.

The insulation in the walls and ceilings of most glass kilns these days are usually made from alumina fiber blanket that has been rigidized to provide strength. Fiber blanket is acceptable for this purpose because processing temperatures of glass is typically 500°F or so lower than that used in ceramics. The alumina

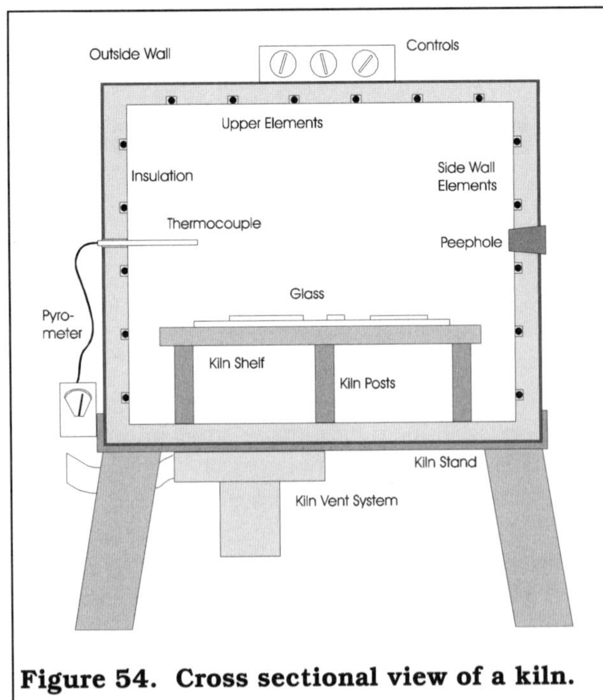

Figure 54. Cross sectional view of a kiln.

fiber can withstand these temperatures without breaking down too much.

The use of alumina fiber blanket for kiln insulation provides advantages over firebrick in that it has a much lower heat capacity, meaning that it soaks up less heat. This allows faster temperature changes in a kiln cycle. Fiber blanket is also less vulnerable to handling damage than firebrick, but there is still some concern that alumina, whose fibers are similar structure to asbestos, may also be carcinogenic and may become more so with repeated exposure to high temperatures. Because of this, many safety-conscious glass artists choose to use firebrick-lined kilns instead.

Firebrick-lined kilns take much longer to heat up because firebrick's higher heat capacity requires much more energy be added to heat it up. For the same reason, a firebrick-lined kiln also takes much longer to cool down. This phenomenon is called rebound and it can be used to good purpose in helping to provide slow cooling of your beads after a firing, without the use of power.

Behind the inner exposed layer of either firebrick or fiber blanket may be additional layers of other insulation materials such as ceramic wool. Even the outside walls of a kiln may be made from insulating fiber pressed into rigid board to provide that extra bit of insulation. With all this insulation, the inner surface of a kiln can be as hot as 2000°F while the outside remains cool enough to touch.

Kiln elements

The heat source for almost all glass kilns is electrical. This is because of its many advantages over gas. These include:

- More uniform heating
- Easier control of temperature and atmosphere
- Quieter
- Safer
- Lower maintenance.

The main difference between different glass kilns, besides insulation type, seems to be where the elements are placed. Some only have elements on the ceiling of the kiln. This arrangement provides a more uniform heat distribution over the surface of the glass. It allows faster heating rates on large glass projects without risk of cracking from thermal stress. A disadvantage of this configuration is that it does not allow heating a second shelf of glass beneath the top one. For this reason, top firing kilns are usually fairly shallow but larger in length and width.

The other fairly common element configuration is to have the elements mounted on the side of the kiln. Here, the rate of temperature rise has to be slowed slightly for large glass projects to allow the heat from the elements to penetrate to the center of the shelf. If this is not done, stresses can build up from faster expansion of the edges than at the center of the work and cause thermal shock. This configuration also allows for heating of stacked shelves, although you have to make sure that the spacing between them is sufficient to allow proper air circulation and heat convection. For this reason, kilns of this configuration will tend to be taller inside than top fired kilns but not as long or as wide.

These two configurations can also be combined as was shown in Figure 54, to make a versatile kiln applicable for either situation. For the purpose of glass beadmaking, either configuration will work just fine. This is because the pieces that you will be making are usually relatively small and will not develop large temperature variations.

If you are using your kiln as an annealer, you will find yourself reaching in and out of it quite frequently. Since you do not want to get shocked, you will want to make sure that you can never touch a live element. One way to do this is to have a "dead man's" switch (contact switch) mounted to the door in such a way that whenever the door is opened, power to the kiln is turned off. This will not work for artists who like to work with the door open for long periods of time because this would allow the annealer to cool too much.

Alternatively, you could try to hide the elements down in grooves in the sides of the annealer. But this is not fool proof and no one likes playing the fool in this situation. A safer configuration is to encase the elements in quartz tubing as shown in Figure 55. The heat from the elements will easily pass through the walls of the tubing since most of the energy is in the form of electromagnetic radiation.

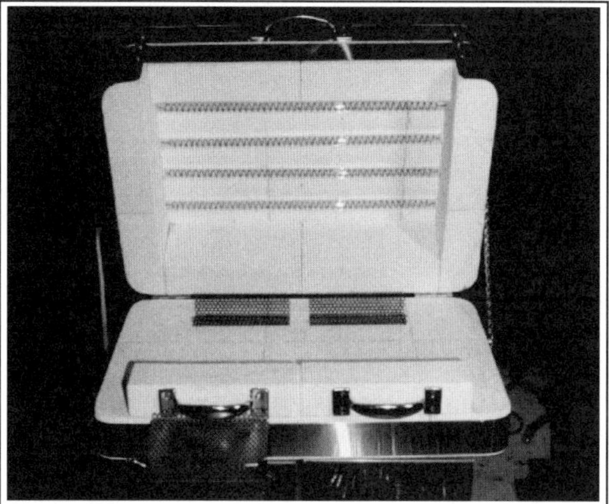

Figure 55. Annealer elements enclosed in quartz.

This arrangement is not as good for a fusing kiln. In fusing, we are working at higher temperatures where the heat can build up enough in the tubing to cause the elements to overheat. This can cause them to burn out a little sooner. Here, a dead man's switch would be the preferred safety option. Although, since we do not go into a kiln as much for fusing, it might be as acceptable to manually switch off the power whenever you have to go into the kiln.

Element control

The heating elements in your kiln work just like those in your stove or oven. As electricity moves through the wire, its flow is slowed or resisted by the atoms in the wire. The energy expended in pushing against this resistance to flow is released as heat. Infinity switches mounted on the front of your kiln help control the electricity flow through the elements and thus the heating of your kiln.

Infinity switches are typically numbered from 1 to about 10 where the higher the number, the higher the fraction of time power to the kiln is on. Their control capability ranges from about 5% to 100% of the time. These switches operate by using interior bimetallic strips similar to those in a thermostat. As power flows through the strips, they heat up and bend. This opens the electric circuit shutting off power to the kiln. They then cool down, unbend, and reestablish the electric circuit. Rotating the infinity switch controls the amount of time that the kiln is on by controlling how far the strip has to bend to pull away from the contact and shut off the power.

The electrical power required for your kiln may be either 110 or 220 volts, depending upon the size of your kiln. Small annealers used by most bead artists only require 110 volts or ordinary household current. Larger kilns for fusing may require 220 volts. This is the same voltage as used by an oven or clothes drier and such a kiln might even be plugged into a drier receptacle.

Kiln doors

Your kiln may have its door on either the top or the front. Opinion is divided as to which configuration is better. Top-loading kilns are touted as being easier to load and use because they provide complete access to the inside surface of the kiln. Others say burns to the face and arms are more likely when using a top-loader. These occur as you peek into the kiln to see how the firing is progressing. During peeking, top-loaders are also more susceptible to having particles fall off the lid onto your project. This can be really annoying and may lead to pitting or cracking of the glass during cool down.

In a front-loading kiln, where the door is positioned on the front of the kiln, you may not be able to completely view the kiln's interior when you peek into it, but this configuration provides a better view of the side to make sure that your beads are not slumping or sagging. This is the configuration used by most beadmakers because it allows them easy access to reach into the kiln. Front loaders often suffer from heat leakage from poor seating of the door. Having a side-firing front-loader is definitely not the best kiln configuration because the missing elements on the door can cause large temperature variations within the kiln.

Crucible kilns

Some of you may want to consider purchasing another type of kiln especially made to heat up and melt crucibles of glass. An example of this type of kiln can be seen in Figure 56. A number of crucible kilns are now on the market. They can come in very handy in making such things as millefiori, filigrana and latticino. They are also invaluable when making drawn beads.

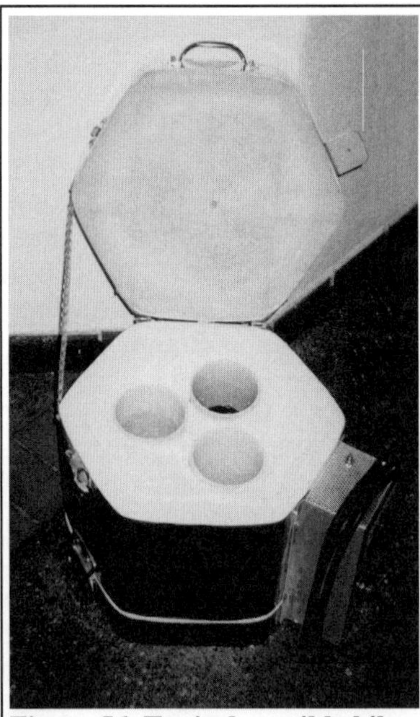
Figure 56. Typical crucible kiln.

These kilns are usually small because they only have to heat up one or a very few crucibles. They will generally only have a few inches of air space between the crucibles and the inside wall of the kiln. They can often be adapted to accommodate different or more glass crucibles. Since they are primarily used for glass dipping operations, most are low to the ground.

Because you're reaching into a live kiln when you dip into a crucible kiln, it is best if your kiln has a dead man's switch that turns off the power when you open the lid. If not, you will have to keep turning it off and on all the time, which can be a real drag. This is absolutely necessary because glass and firebrick conduct electricity at high temperature. They can form a conductive path causing you to get a shock as you dip if the power is on. I learned that from experience when working with an experimental crucible kiln. This is not a very desirable thing to have happen when you are handling molten glass.

Most crucible kilns will usually have a fiber blanket or firebrick insert that fits around the top of the crucible and the kiln wall. This piece serves some important functions.

- It helps protect against thermal shock of the crucible when you open the kiln.
- It also helps prevent the glass in the crucible from cooling too fast when the kiln is open.
- The insert helps stabilize the crucible from falling over in the kiln and spilling molten glass all over the place. Since many small crucibles tend to be tall skinny cylinders, this can be a real concern if you are trying to use your fusing kiln for this purpose.
- Lastly, it helps prevent drips of molten glass that is dipped from the crucible from falling back into the kiln. Hot glass is highly corrosive and will

quickly attack the walls and elements of your kiln.

Because of the potential for dropping glass and the high temperatures at which crucible kilns are run, some manufacturers include an extra set of elements with each kiln.

To melt a crucible of molten glass for use in your work, you can start either from cullet or batch. Cullet is small scraps of glass while batch is a mixture of the raw ingredients that are melted together to make glass. I would suggest that most of you should work from cullet, but do not want to discourage you from using batch if you really want to give it a try.

Melting cullet is easier on your kiln because you do not have to go to as high a temperature as you would with batch and there will not be as many bubbles. Also, some of the ingredients in batch are toxic and I always avoid handling such materials when I can. Bullseye has a nice, clear, non-lead, crystal cullet (#1401) available in chunk form. You can use it in conjunction with their fusing sheet glass and lampworking rods. It is compatible with both of them.

If you want to work with Effetre, you may have trouble finding cullet because not much is available, otherwise you will have to chop up rods or sheet glass to make your own cullet. If you have trouble locating Effetre cullet, I have been told that East Bay batch does have a formulation for Effetre compatible batch that they will put together for you.

No matter which way you decide to go, cullet or batch, try to control the temperature of the crucible kiln very closely and not overfire it. You will be working right near the upper capability of the kiln elements and even an extra 50 degrees higher can make a big difference on the element life of your kiln. Expect to have to occasionally replace the elements, especially if you do not have the kiln on a good controller. This is another reason why some crucible kiln manufacturers will provide you with an extra set of elements when you purchase their kiln.

Melting cullet

Start by filling up the crucible in your kiln pretty much to the brim. If you use glass strips, stack them in vertically to allow the air to flow out as it melts. The material must all be the same kind of glass or the melt will not be uniform. It may result in final pieces with visual defects because of refractive index changes or cracks from compatibility problems. For that reason, I also suggest that you always use the same type of glass in a particular crucible from firing to firing.

Your cullet must be clean. You need to wash it to remove any dirt or metal. These can cause the formation of tiny seed bubbles, which are hard to remove. If you see a lot of these bubbles in your cullet melt, you may have to resort to an old glassblowing trick and stick a small potato on the end of a punty into the melt. This will release a large volume of steam that will bubble up through the melt, gathering up the seed bubbles with them. Don't try this on a full crucible though, or you may have quite a mess to clean up.

After filling the crucible with cullet, heat it up as you would a fusing project. You start out venting the kiln to let any moisture come out, heating it at a rate of up to 300 to 400°F/hr. After you pass 300°F, you can close the lid. When you get to about 1700°F, check the crucible to see if you need to add a little more cullet. The volume will probably have reduced considerably because the air space between all the cullet pieces will be gone.

At this point, add more glass cullet if desired. The pieces should be small because large ones may shatter from thermal shock and send fragments flying. Then, continue heating up the kiln to about 2100 to 2200°F. Hold the kiln at this temperature for a couple of hours to allow as many of the fine bubbles as possible to rise to the surface of the melt. This process is call refining or fining of the melt.

At the end of this period, the temperature is dropped to about 1800 to 1900°F. Gas is a little more soluble in the melt at this temperature and most of the fine bubbles that remain will be reabsorbed into the melt. This process is called squeezing because it squeezes the gas bubbles out of the melt. We then raise the glass back to a working temperature between 2000 and 2100°F. The glass is now ready to use.

Melting batch

If you choose to work with batch instead of cullet, start as before except do not completely fill the crucible with batch. This is because batch releases a tremendous amount of gas, up to 1400 times its own volume at 1800°F. This could result in overflow of the melt if the crucible is filled to the brim. Instead only fill it about $^7/8^{ths}$ full. Adding just a bit of cullet to the batch will help speed up the melting process. Commercial batches generally use around 30% cullet.

Heat up the kiln as before, but keep it vented to release all gases that will be released. At 212°F, any moisture in the batch will evaporate out. Soda ash will melt and release its carbon dioxide over the temperature range of 932°F to 1560°F. It will start to react with the grains of sand and gradually dissolve them. Then, at about 1650°F, the lime (calcium carbonate) will start to decompose and release its carbon dioxide which helps mix the melt. At about 2190°F the lime will start to react with the rest of the melt. By 2370°F, the melt should be fully reacted and ready to work, with the exception that it will probably have many seed bubbles in it.

As the batch stops bubbling (about 4 hr), the level of the melt will reduce down to approximately ¾th's of its original volume. The timing of this change is a function of the kind of glass and the percent of cullet in the mix. Add more batch, if needed, until it is just below the top of the crucible. When the batch is completely melted and fined, squeeze it as we did for cullet and get to work.

Shutting down a crucible kiln

When you are finished working for the day, you should empty out the crucible as much as possible before cooling the kiln. You do this by repeatedly gathering glass from the crucible with a punty and getting rid of it by dipping the punty into a bucket of water. This is done because glass's coefficient of expansion is much larger than that of the crucible.

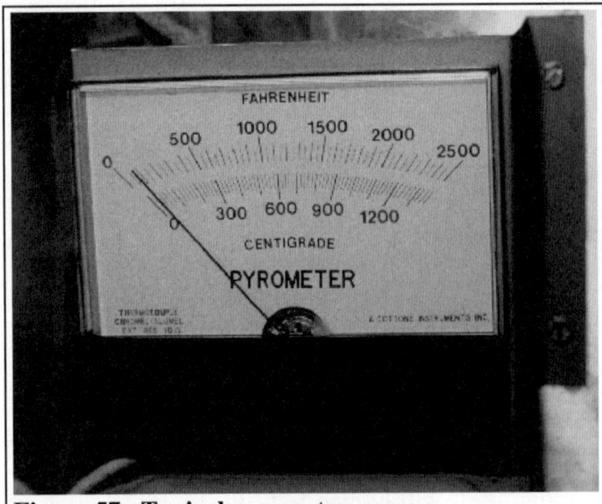

Figure 57. Typical pyrometer gauge.

Thus it will exert force on the crucible as it tries to shrink away from the crucible that could be strong enough to crack the crucible. Therefore don't melt more glass than you can really use or it may end up wasted.

Measuring kiln temperatures

Since the whole purpose of a kiln is to heat things up in a controlled manner, let's discuss the different choices that we have to precisely measure the temperature in a kiln. They include pyrometers and cones.

Pyrometers

A pyrometer (literally translated to mean fire meter) is a convenient device to monitor the temperature inside your kiln. It allows you to monitor your kiln temperature so that you do not end up heating it too high or at too fast a rate. It uses a thermocouple made from wires of two dissimilar metals welded at the tip, which is inserted into the kiln.

Heating the welded junction between the two wires causes the metal in one of the wires to pull electrons from the other wire. This physical effect, called the Seebeck effect, causes electricity to flow around the loop from the thermocouple through the pyrometer and back to the thermocouple. It is actually a quite common effect between metals, but certain metals produce a much higher voltage potential than others. Some specially developed alloys, like chromel, alumel, and constantan, make thermocouples so sensitive that they can measure the temperature increase caused by holding them in your hands.

The pyrometer gauge actually measures the amount of current flowing through it, not temperature. But since that is directly proportional to the temperature of the thermocouple, the readout can be calibrated in temperature. The wires used to connect the thermocouple to the gauge have a calibrated resistance and they should not be shortened or exchanged except with acceptable replacement parts.

The scale on the pyrometer looks something like the one in Figure 57 and is generally calibrated both in degrees Fahrenheit and Centigrade. They usually have a range of about 0° to 2500°F. The pyrometer and thermocouple are sensitive instruments and therefore should be treated respectfully. It should not be subjected to dust, moisture, or being bumped around. Never connect anything else across the

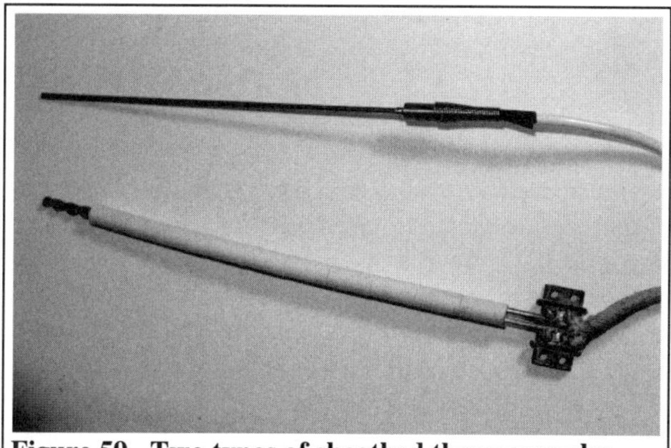
Figure 59. Two types of sheathed thermocouples.

pyrometer terminals except the connecting wires to the thermocouple. You can break the pyrometer if you do

To test to see if your system is hooked up correctly, hold a match under the thermocouple junction and see if the temperature reading on the pyrometer rises. If the gauge needle is reading below zero, then you have the wires to the pyrometer reversed. Switch them and it will then record correctly. There is often a little resistance to needle movement that can be overcome by tapping slightly on the face of the pyrometer. This will help give a truer reading.

If you look at your thermocouple, you will see that it is encased in a metal sheath as at the top of Figure 59 or a ceramic body as at the bottom. This sheath provides insulation from accidental contact with the elements. The thermocouple is generally inserted into the kiln though a hole drilled into one of the conical firebrick plugs made to be put in a peephole. It should be inserted well into the kiln away from the sides and the elements, preferably out over your work. Try to always position it in the same place so that the conditions that you will get inside the kiln are consistent for the same pyrometer reading.

Figure 58. Properly fired cone

After a thermocouple has been used a lot, it will start to oxidize and can eventually even be completely consumed by the oxidation process. The oxide layer can insulate the thermocouple junction and should be cleaned off by light abrasion using 0000 steel wool. Try not to flex the junction or you may crack it. If you don't get a reading with a match test of the thermocouple and you are sure everything is hooked up correctly, it is possible that the junction is broken or that the metal has been completely oxidized. If this happens, you will need to purchase a new thermocouple.

The meter of the pyrometer needs to be kept cool to read correctly. If mounted to the kiln, it should be positioned in a place where it does not get heated when you open the door to peek in. If the outside of your kiln gets hot, then you should not mount the gauge there. Wherever you keep the meter, mount it firmly so that it can not be accidentally knocked to the floor.

Cones

Another method used to measure kiln temperature, the use of cones, does not really measure temperature. Instead it measures what is commonly referred to as heat work. Cones are slender pyramid-shaped objects of clays that have been carefully formulated to react to heat work in a predictable manner. They are placed inside your kiln where they can be viewed through the peephole. As they heat up, they soften and bend under their own weight after a certain amount of heat work.

The temperature at which a cone deforms is also a function of the heating rate. These values are published by the manufacturer of the cone and should be controlled for about the last 200°F of the firing. As an example, Orton's large and self-supporting cones are calibrated for a heating rate of 270°F/hr. A properly fired cone will have its tip bend over in a smooth curve until its tip becomes even with its base as in Figure 58.

Cone values range from 022 to 42. The larger the number, the more heat work that is required to deform the cone. You might wonder at the leading 0 on 022. Originally the cone numbering started at 1, which was used for a processing temperature of about 2100°F. Demand soon developed for lower temperature cones to serve as indicators during firing of decorations, lusters, and enamels as well as for use in glass fusing. Rather than renumbering all the cones from 1 again, it was decided to number backwards from 1 by adding an 0 in front of the number to indicate it is a heat treatment less than 1. So a 022 is a lower number cone than a 015 and thus requires less heat work.

Cones come in three different types:

- large regular cones which are 2½" high and require mounting in cone plaques or clay pots.

They are inserted such that exactly 2" of the cone sticks out of the plaque and it is at an angle of eight degrees.

- small regular cones are 1 1/8" high and are mounted so that 15/16" is exposed.
- self supporting cones already have their own preset base such that they are mounted at the right height and angle.

A guide should be used to ensure that either of the regular cones are mounted at the correct angle. They should also be positioned such that they will not fall against each other during the firing.
The recommended way to use cones is in sets of three as illustrated in Figure 60.

- The center cone is chosen to indicate when the proper heat work for your process is complete. This is referred to as the firing cone.
- The first cone is one number lower than the firing cone. This "guide" cone's bending will indicate that you are approaching the proper heat work condition and need to pay more attention to the kiln.
- The third cone is to guard against overfiring your project. If you see it start to bend, then you are getting too hot and need to reduce the temperature in the kiln as soon as possible.

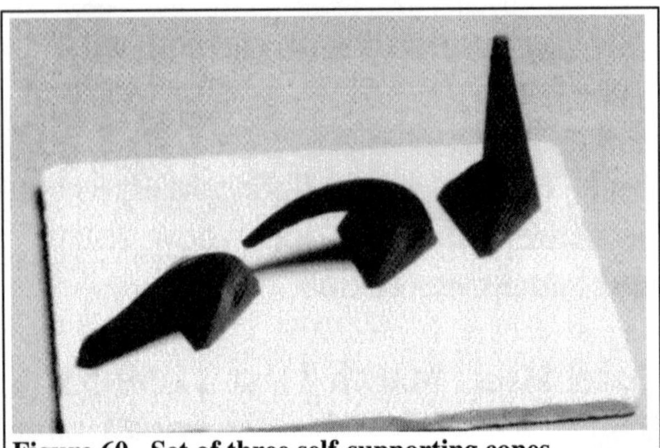

Figure 60. Set of three self-supporting cones.

The performance of a cone may vary somewhat from its established value if kiln conditions vary from those for which they were calibrated. Besides the effect of heating rate, which we have already discussed, cone performance is also affected by temperature soaks and kiln atmosphere.

Soaking at temperature increases the required cone value for a given temperature. Soaking for one hour at temperature requires using a cone that is one cone number higher to indicate proper heat work. A three-hour soak requires a cone two cone numbers higher and a nine-hour soak three cone numbers higher. This is because you are putting in a lot of extra heat work during any temperature soak.

Kiln atmosphere can also affect cone performance. If for some reason you have a very reducing environment in the kiln, say because you are burning out organics, you may need to use an iron-free cone. They do not require oxygen to mature properly as do standard cones. If you don't, you will underestimate the amount of heat work that you are putting into your beads.

You will actually probably not use cones much in your work with glass. The main thing that glass artists use them for is to check the calibration of their pyrometers. Here we just compare the pyrometer reading to how the cone is responding. Cones are also useful in determining how evenly the inside of your kiln is heating. To do this, scatter a number of the same value of cones around the inside on the kiln and watch how much differently they respond at these different locations.

Controlling your kiln

For most beadmaking situations, except in making fused and pâte de verre beads, all you usually need to do is hold your kiln at a constant temperature while you work. As an example, we hold glass pieces at a constant temperature in preparation for adding them to a bead. Similarly, we hold a kiln at the annealing temperature during a beadmaking session so that we can put our beads directly into the kiln as we finish them.

Either situation does not require a very sophisticated controller. But to be complete and since I am a very controlling person, let's discuss the different kinds of controllers and what they do.

Infinity switches

The standard control mechanisms used on most kilns are infinite range switches. They are the dials that have low, high, and a bunch of other settings in between on them. They are seen on the left of the kiln in Figure 54. They control the amount of time that electricity is flowing through the wires of your kiln elements.

Infinity controls, as we discussed earlier, work in a similar manner to the thermostat for your house. Inside they have a bimetallic strip (two metal strips welded together) that bends as it heats up from the current flowing through it. Current will flow through it for a while until the strip heats up enough to bend and break electrical contact. Then as the strip cools, it straightens out enough to again make contact. By rotating the dial on the switch, you control how far the bimetallic strip has to bend before it breaks contact and thus the fraction of time that the kiln is on.

Figure 61. Infinity control.

You might think that this would be a good way to control the temperature of your kiln, but unfortunately it isn't. It doesn't read what is happening in the kiln and has to be manually adjusted. You have to work a lot with your kiln to get a feel for how the different infinity-switch settings will control the rate of temperature rise.

The rate of temperature rise for different infinite range control switch settings varies with the task temperature. It gets slower and slower as you get to higher temperatures until it reaches a plateau and will not go much higher. Thus, you might think it possible to just choose an infinity switch setting that plateaus out at the temperature that you want. There are two problems with this approach. First, the rates and final plateau temperature vary some with the mass of the material in the kiln. Second, you usually want to get done as fast as possible because kiln time consumes electricity, which isn't free. This means that you want to raise temperature as quickly as possible regardless of final plateau temperature. For that reason, you may want to consider some sort of electronic controller.

Set point controllers

The simplest form of "intelligent" controller is a set point controller. It holds a kiln at a dialed in temperature indefinitely. It will keep your kiln within a few degrees of your set temperature by turning the power off when it is too high and turning it back on when the temperature drops too low.

The controller will not regulate rates of temperature rise or fall. You have to do that by adjusting the infinite range control switches. They act as a governor for your kiln, setting the maximum operating power fraction and keeping the kiln from getting out of control. In this way, they can be used to act as a manual override over any electronic controller.

With a set point controller, you can set your infinite range control switches for the approximate rate of temperature rise that you want and the set point controller for the final temperature. Then when the kiln reaches the set temperature, it will hold at that temperature indefinitely. If the kiln is already at that temperature, it will stay there by allowing the elements to come on and off as necessary to remain there.

Set point controllers are not nearly as expensive as they used to be and many kiln manufacturers now include them as a standard option. They are really the only kind of controller needed for most wound glass beadmakers.

Programmable controllers

Programmable controllers can control just about every aspect of your firing — ramps, dwells, etc. They vary in the following features:

- How much power they are rated for.
- Number of program segments a firing program can have.
- How many programs they can store.
- How many kilns they can control.
- How they control ramp segments.

Let's discuss each of these points in greater detail.

Most kilns will run either on normal household power of 110 volts or on larger appliance power of 220 volts. A controller cannot just be switched from one to the other. At the very least, the power relay of the controller, the device that turns the power to the kiln on and off at the command of the controller, will have to be changed to a new one of the proper voltage and power rating to match the kiln.

By power, we mean that besides voltage, the relay will also have to be rated to carry the current required by the kiln to heat the elements. The product of current (amps) and voltage is power and is measured in watts. So when you go looking for a kiln controller, be sure that it is rated for the current and voltage required for your kiln.

The next features under consideration have to do with how versatile you will find your controller. The first of these, the number of segments allowed in a program, is the number of ramps and dwells that you will be able to have in a firing. This can be important for pâte de verre where a typical firing may have as many as thirteen segments or more. For other operations, like being on your worktable while winding beads, you don't need many segments. Some controllers only offer a limited number of control segments, and therefore are not quite as versatile.

If you do more than one kind of firing with your kiln, it would be nice not to have to completely reprogram the controller every time you want to do a different operation. This is where the feature of being able to store more than one program in the controller comes in handy. You could have programs already entered for a number of different operations and just punch a button for whichever one you want at the time.

As your studio grows, the number of kilns that you have may also grow. You might start doing techniques that require more than one kiln to be operating at a time — like dipping molten glass from a crucible kiln that you blow into a bubble, draw out into tubular bead stock, and anneal in another kiln. Alternately, the long firing times of large pâte de verre pieces may convince you that you need more than one kiln.

Kiln operation and care

Lastly there are a number of items that need to be discussed on how to prepare your kiln for use and how to care for it. Also, I would like to point out what you need to know in order to operate it safely. Then in later chapters, I will explain how to use kilns in specific applications. So let's start with setup.

Setting up your kiln

Start by reading your kiln instruction manual to develop an understanding on how to use and set up your particular kiln. How you set it up can greatly affect the safety of its operation. It should be kept at least one foot away from any flammable materials and ideally should have one foot of air space all around it to carry away excess heat. It should be located on a fireproof surface, preferably concrete. If not, install some sort of insulating fireproof material underneath the kiln. It should not be located near gasoline, oils or other flammable materials. It should not be set up in a damp area.

The space in which you set up your kiln should have plenty of ventilation because there are times when items that you are firing in it may release toxic vapors. You may want to consider installing a ventilation system if you decide to do a lot of work with glass paints or lusters. The kiln should also be out of the way so that you or others are not continually tripping over it. It should have plenty of room around it so that you can access it safely.

Get the kiln all set up before connecting it to power. Make sure that you hook the kiln into a circuit with the right voltage and current capacity. Also, you should try to hook it directly into a circuit receptacle without using an extension cord if at all possible. Make sure that the power cord is not in contact with your kiln so that it will not melt during use. If you have to use an extension cord, make sure that it is properly constructed for the voltage and current used by your kiln. As an example, a 110 volt 15 amp kiln requires an extension cord of at least #12 copper wire.

If you have to install an extra circuit to provide power for your kiln, make sure that a certified electrician does it. Your plug receptacle should not be more than about 50 ft from the junction box. The power line should have a minimum of other outlets on it to prevent overloading your circuit. Also, other items on the same circuit may cause variations in a firing that could ruin it. Likewise, power delivery to your house may vary somewhat during the day and change the amount of power available to your kiln at any one time.

Kiln care

If your kiln has never been used or has not been used in a long while, you should do a tempering run before using it. A tempering run is a slow heat up and dwell at a low temperature to drive off all moisture in the insulation. To do this, first empty and clean out your kiln. As when you do any work on a kiln, make sure that it is off and consider unplugging it. Next, vacuum the kiln out. A soft brush nozzle works best for this.

Check to see that there is a good layer of kiln wash on the floor of the kiln. Kiln wash is a refractory separator material like that used on winding mandrels. If the kiln wash layer is not in good shape, scrape off the old kiln wash layer and apply a new one. Its application is described shortly

Now close the kiln lid, but vent it by propping it open about an inch with a piece of ceramic kiln furniture. Turn the kiln on low. Allow it to heat up slowly to about 300°F and hold it there for an hour to get rid of the physically attached water. Then proceed on up to 400°F and hold it there for another hour to get rid of the chemically attached water. At this point turn off the kiln, close it, and allow it to cool slowly back to room temperature. Besides helping to make your kiln last longer, this process also reduces the amount of moisture released during a kiln firing. Moisture can cause bubbling if it is trapped beneath the glass and can react with the surface of hot glass to corrode it.

You should occasionally check over your kiln to see that everything is in good shape. Check out the exterior structure to see that nothing is coming loose. Check out the inside of the kiln. Again, always turn off the kiln power by unplugging it whenever you are doing any maintenance on it.

Cracks in firebricks are part of normal wear and tear. They allow expansion and contraction during the firing cycle and do not need to be repaired. Chips and crumbled areas are another thing altogether. They reduce the thickness of the thermal insulation and should be repaired. They can be patched using repair cement available from your ceramics supply store. Spatula it into place. Let it dry overnight and then sand it lightly to smooth it.

If the damage is extensive, you may have to remove part of, or a complete brick. For a partial brick replacement, cut a piece from a new brick to fit and fill in around it with repair cement. For an entire brick, replace it with a new brick that you have trimmed to size to match the old brick. There should be a slight gap between the bricks to allow for thermal expansion, so don't make it too tight of a fit.

Figure 62. Element bulging out of groove.

Next check out the elements. Are they bulging out of the grooves as above? Sometimes all that has happened is that the element staples have come out. If so, just push them back into position using a screwdriver. Other times the coils may have actually grown in length from thermal cycling. If this is the case, they will need to be resized slightly and anchored back into their grooves.

To resize bulged out sections, use a needle nosed pliers to slightly shorten the distance between each coil loop by squeezing them together. Try to make the gaps between loops the same so that you do not have hot spots that could burn out quicker. Do this carefully because elements tend to become brittle with age. As the bulged out area is shrunk, insert them back into the grooves. When done working the elements back to size, anchor them in place with an element staple. Put the staple over the bottom portion of the loop in a groove. Push it part way in with some needle nosed pliers at a slight angle so that the staple will hold better. Then use the tip of a small screwdriver to push it to the bottom of the groove.

If your elements are coming out at the corners, you need to lengthen them to fit. This uses essentially the same procedure. Use a snap ring pliers (one that opens when you squeeze the handle) or a screwdriver to open up the distance between a number of loops. Then staple them in place.

If you have had your kiln for a long time and it seems that the firings are starting to take longer and longer, the elements may be starting to wear out. With time, they will not be able to carry as much energy as they used to and will need to be replaced. This process is accelerated if you have been doing reduction firings.

I suggest that you consult your kiln manual as to how to replace any elements, or else get a qualified repairperson to do it for you. Elements can also become damaged if they make contact with glass during a firing and the glass can short across the elements. So if you have thermal shock kiln explosions, I suggest that you clean out the kiln afterward to remove any glass that may have gotten near the elements.

Occasionally, you will have to replace an infinity switch. This is because the contacts in the switch that turn the power on and off deteriorate over time. As they open, the electrical flow does not stop immediately and a spark jumps across the gap at the contacts. This is the muffled pop that you hear as your kiln cycles. This arcing concentrates the electrical flow over such a very small area that a little metal on the switch actually gets melted. Arcing is made worse by a damp or dusty environment. Over time, the contact area gets so pitted and corroded that they build up a heavy resistive layer and no longer work correctly.

To remove the switch, first remove the knob by gently prying it off the shaft at the face of the switch using a screwdriver under the base of the knob. Unplug the kiln and open the protective switch box in which the switch is mounted. Remove wires from the old switch, one at a time, and either mark where they came from or install them directly onto the new switch to keep their order correct. Remove the locking nut on the outside of the shaft housing and slip the old switch out. Slip in the new switch, lock it in place with the locking nut, close up the protective housing, replace the knob, and you are back in business.

These are the simplest and most common repairs that may be needed on a kiln. For anything more extensive than this, see your kiln manual or get a repairman.

Kiln safety

There are a number of safely aspects to using a kiln that we have not yet discussed. First and foremost, a kiln uses a large amount of electricity that can be dangerous if not used correctly. Therefore always operate your kiln according to the manufacturer's directions. Never reach into a kiln unless the power to it is shut off.

Make sure that the wires that come out of the kiln are in good shape. On a 110-volt kiln that plugs into a normal wall socket, the plug should have a ground pin (i.e. that third round pin beneath the other two flat ones). Never use one of those three pin to two pin adapters that are available in the hardware stores to plug your kiln into a socket with only two prongs. That third wire is hooked up to the exterior of your kiln to carry away any current that may somehow leak to the exterior if you develop a short in the kiln wiring somewhere. Without that ground properly hooked up, a short can potentially become a very shocking experience. In fact it would probably be a good idea to check that this ground is hooked up correctly by using an ohmmeter to measure the resistance between the round pin on the plug and the exterior of the kiln. It should be a low number.

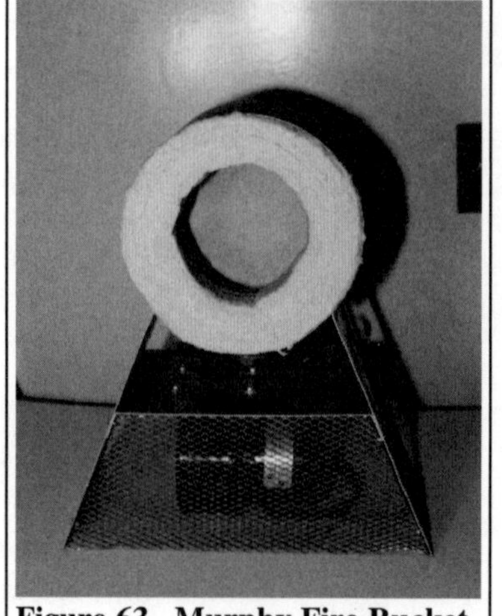

Figure 63. Murphy Fire Bucket.

The next safety concern about working around a kiln is how to dress properly. A kiln puts out a lot of heat and when opened during a firing, it can very easily burn you. So you definitely need to wear protective clothing on your hands and arms when you reach into it. On your hands, you should wear some of the new non-asbestos, high-temperature gloves. Check them over to make sure that they have not developed any holes. To protect your arms and upper body, you should wear some heavy clothing made from natural fibers. Natural fibers are a must because man-made fibers can melt and can become fused to your skin, resulting in some nasty burns.

The last thing that you need to protect from the heat of the kiln is your eyes. Welder's shades of at least a #3 are required to prevent damage to your eyes from exposure to infrared radiation coming out of an open kiln. Just using didymium glasses is not good enough for this type of situation.

Glory holes

Glory holes are large heating chambers that are fired by propane rather than electricity. They are used by glassblowers to heat and reheat glass as they work with it. Beadmakers primarily use them to make components, most notable of which are millefiori, for inclusion in their beads. If drawn beads are your thing, then you will also find one useful for that purpose. Glory holes provide a much larger heated volume than a torch that is over 2000°F. This allows rapid heating of glass to temperatures at which it can be manipulate. Glory hole operation can be approximated by directing torches into a small, insulated chamber.

Glory hole construction

A glory hole can be considered to be composed of the same three main components as a kiln: a metal framework, a refractory lining, and a heat source. The design of each of these components involves tradeoffs to meet the designer's requirements. Factors to consider include heating capability, ease of use, durability, safety, and of course cost.

There are a few glory holes currently on the market that are fine for the kind of work that we will be talking about in this book. They include the Murphy Fire Bucket made by Fusion Glass, Inc. as seen in Figure 63 and another by Denver Machinery. Sundance Art Glass offers insulated chambers that can be used with a Hot Head® torch or a minor burner as seen in Figure 64. Its nice to finally have a use for all those old Hot Head® Torches out there. The chambers come in 4 to 10" diameters.

Figure 64. Glory Hole fired by a torch. Courtesy of Sundance Art Glass.

More rugged and efficient glory hole designs use multiple layers of different fibers and possibly even firebrick or castable refractory liners. The inner liner should have the highest temperature rating possible since it is directly exposed to the flame. Successive outer layers can be of lower and lower density materials to provide higher insulative capability.

You could also, if so inclined, build your own glory hole. For plans, see one of the references listed at the end of this chapter: "Advanced Glass Fusing" by Boyce Lundstrom, "Glory Hole is Heart of Glassblowing" by Karl Platt, "Glassblower's Companion" by Dudley Giberson, or Glass Notes by Henry Halem. Figure 65 shows a cross sectional view of a typical glory hole. You will want to keep things small for most beadmaking applications.

Glory hole framework

The first of the glory hole design components, the framework, provides strength and durability for the system. It consists of a metal cylinder and stand, usually constructed from steel to withstand the high temperatures and the erosion incurred in daily use. The most common sources for such cylinders are large pipes or small steel drums.

The cylinder wall protects the fragile refractory lining from mechanical damage during use. Mounted to the cylinder is the rest of the stand framework, which positions the glory hole at the proper height for work and to which the burner system is mounted.

Glory hole insulation

The choice of the second component of the glory hole, the refractory insulation, involves tradeoffs in durability, cost, and energy efficiency of the system. Most glory holes are insulated strictly using alumina fiber blanket material rigidized with some refractory cement. This is because fiber blanket is cheaper and easier to work with than many other types of refractory materials. But, remember that this material may be carcinogenic and needs to be handled carefully. It especially needs to be kept from overheating.

If your glory hole has a castable liner, you should make sure that it has been properly prefired prior to first use. Otherwise you will want to take it easy and fire the glory hole at a low temperature the first time you use it to make sure all the chemical reactions that occur during a typical curing cycle have been done completely and gradually. This is like breaking in a new car, where you don't push it too fast right away or you will regret it for the rest of your life. Even after curing, a castable refractory lined glory hole should be heated up slowly during each use to prevent cracking its liner from thermal shock. Practicing this precaution will pay you back with increased equipment life.

Glory hole heating system

The heating and combustion system feeds both air and fuel, usually propane or natural gas, to the burner in the side of the cylinder. Most likely, you will have a propane-fueled glory hole that will use a propane tank and regulator identical to that, which has already been described in the discussions of propane-oxygen torch systems. The burner is

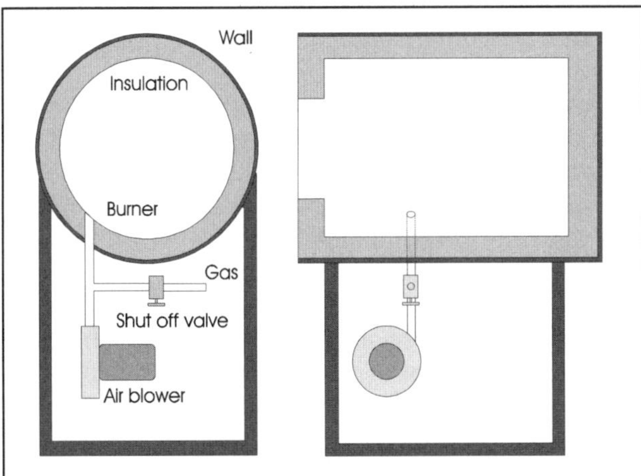

Figure 65. Cross sectional view of a typical glory hole.

located off center from the center of the cylinder and feeds the flame into the chamber tangentially to the surface of the wall. This causes the flame to make a swirling vortex inside.

The burner may simply consist of a piece of pipe or it may have a nozzle to increase the speed of the incoming combustion gases. It will be buried inside the insulation to protect it from erosion by the flame. A mechanical blower supplies airflow. A gas regulator and a throttle valve will regulate gas feed.

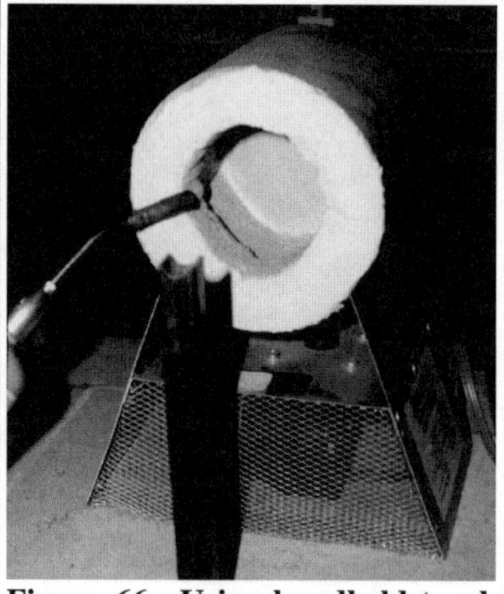
Figure 66. Using handheld torch to light a glory hole.

If you are using one of those torch-based systems, there are two things your have to be careful of. First, make sure that you do not stick the torch head too far into the chamber. If you do, you can ruin the torch head by overheating it. Second, if you are using a mixed gas torch, you need to keep the torch flame temperature from getting too hot or you can overfire the ceramic fiber insulation liner and transform it into its carcinogenic form.

Glory hole operation

The materials that we will be using in the glory hole will, because of their size, usually require the use of either preheated components or annealing them after they are formed in the glory hole. For this reason, a glory hole should be located in close proximity and without obstructions to your kiln. There should also be plenty of room available to turn around, back up, and do the operations that will be required. This is especially important as you are lighting it with a handheld propane torch and it lights off with a loud roar.

The use of a glory hole involves an open flame that produces a lot of heat. For this reason, it should be located away from combustible materials and fuels (oils, paints, etc.). Have your propane supply tank located as far away from the glory hole as practically possible, but position it so that you have easy access to the tank for on/off control. Always keep a fire extinguisher close at hand. The flame contains some unburned fuel byproducts so use it only in a well-ventilated area. Make sure that all your propane connections are leak tight.

If this is your first time using an a glory hole, you are in for a thrill. It sounds really powerful and can scare you. But, if you are careful, understand your equipment, and follow all the correct operating procedures, you should not have any real problems. The basic operating instructions are as follows:

1. Check to see that the fuel throttle valve to the burner is closed.
2. Turn on the propane at the propane tank. Check for any hint of propane smell in the air or the sound of any leaks. (You did leak check all your fittings when you set up the system.)
3. Turn on the air blower. Hear how noisy it is. Could you have heard any propane leaks if you turned it on first?
4. Some glory hole blowers may have a valve to throttle the blower air. If yours does, throttle it down to prevent it from blowing out the flame while you are lighting the glory hole.
5. Light a handheld propane torch like those discussed earlier to light the burner. You use this instead of something like a match since it is less likely to blow out.
6. Hold the torch with its tip as far inside the mouth of the glory hole as necessary to ensure that the flame reaches the burner as you point the flame at it. Make sure that you are not so close that the flame is blown out by the airflow from the blower inside the glory hole.
7. Slowly open the gas throttle valve. The burner should light almost immediately. If not, close the gas throttle valve and try to determine what the problem is. Do you have propane? Is your regulator adjusted correctly? Can you smell gas? Is the torch still lit?
8. Adjust the propane so that you just have a small blue-yellow flame at the outside of the burner.
9. Allow the glory hole to warm up. (In just a couple minutes it will be glowing red.) Then turn up the throttle on the blower.

10. Adjust glory hole temperature and atmosphere by throttling your propane feed.

Turning off the glory hole is much easier. Turn off the propane first at the throttle valve and then at the tank. Never turn off the air first because gas flow could then be slow enough that the flame front could travel into your gas system. Allow your blower to continue running for a few minutes to cool everything down.

Suggested further reading

Fournier, Robert. **Electric Kiln Construction For Potters**, 1st ed., Van Nostrand Reinhold Company, 1997

Fraser, Harry. **Electric Kilns**, 2nd. ed., Watson-Guptill Publications, 1974

Gibberson, Dudley F. **A Glassblower's Companion**, The Joppa Press, 1999

Halem, Henry **Glass Notes** ***A reference for the glass artist***, 3rd edition, 1996

Nickerson, John. "***A Glory Hole Design***", in **Hot Glass Information Exchange** 1979 John M. Bingham editor

Olsen, Frederick L. **The Kiln Book** 3nd ed., Materials, Specifications and Construction, Krause Publications, 2001

Platt, Karl. "***Glory Hole is Heart of Glassblowing***" Glass Art Vol. 3 No. 3 (March/April), 1988

Rhodes, Daniel, **Kilns; Design, Construction & Operation**, Chilton Book Company, 1981

Riegger, Hal. **Electric Kiln Ceramics**, 1st ed., Van Nostrand Reinhold Company, 1978

Ritchie, Ralph W. and Ritchie, Fern J. **Electric Kiln Handbook**, 2nd ed., Ritchie Unlimited Publications, 1996

Glass

Now that you know a little about beadmaking equipment, let's talk about the material with which you will be working, glass. Glass is a unique material formed by melting and mixing a number of oxides together. When heated, this brittle material will get softer, gradually deform or slump, and eventually melt to form a viscous liquid.

Unlike other materials, this transition does not occur as a sharp transition at a specific temperature. Instead, it occurs gradually over a temperature range. When the molten glass is cooled, this process occurs in reverse and whatever shape that was introduced into the glass while soft is retained when it hardens. To understand glass better, we need to spend some time discussing its chemistry and how this affects its properties.

Glass chemistry

As just stated, glass is made from a mixture of oxides. The main oxide used in these mixtures is silica or silicon dioxide (SiO_2). If it were the only oxide present, you would have what is known as fused silica or quartz.

Silica based glasses are not composed of distinct molecules but instead consist of an interconnected, random, three-dimensional matrix. The basic structural component of this matrix is the silica tetrahedron. This is a four-sided pyramid with oxygen atoms at each vertex of the pyramid shielding a silicon atom at the center. Each oxygen atom is part of two tetrahedrons that are orientated randomly with respect to each other and is thus referred to as a bridging oxygen atom.

The silicon and oxygen atoms in fused silica are held together by strong covalent bonds (electron sharing between atoms), which results in a relatively sharply defined, high melting point (3115°F). Melting occurs at a much higher temperature than that which you will use in your studio. Most of the refractory materials used in the manufacture of glass kilns would not stand up to repeated exposures to such extreme temperatures.

To lower the melting temperature of silica glass, a number of other oxides are added to randomly break up some of the covalent bonds between the bridging oxygen atoms by attaching them to a metal atom instead. This will end one section of the chain making the whole chain less rigid and more mobile. These metal oxides will also strain the glass matrix as it cools because of size differences between the metal atoms and the silicon atoms.

Not all of the additives form strong covalent bonds with oxygen, some instead form weaker non-directional ionic bonds. When heated, these weaker bonds and the less rigid structure they bring allow the silica tetrahedrons to move about at much lower temperatures (about 1800°F). Variations in chain length within the glass matrix widen the temperature range over which this happens.

The types of other oxides added and their proportions in a glass determine when it starts to soften and when it will effectively melt. The weaker the bonds, the lower the temperature at which softening will occur. Also, the more of the modifying oxides that are added, the shorter the resulting silica chains in the glass and the more fluid the glass becomes once it starts to soften. Glasses that soften at lower temperatures are said to be softer while those that soften at higher temperatures are said to be harder.

Types of glass

Let's examine some of the most common art glasses and discuss how their composition affects some of the properties relevant to glass beadmaking. These properties are summarized in

Table 13. Let's start this discussion with the simplest glass, quartz glass, which is composed only of the basic building block, SiO_2.

Quartz

Quartz, or fused silica as it is sometimes called, is made by heating pure silicon dioxide to about 3137° F. The resulting liquid is so viscous that any gas bubbles trapped between the grains of sand as it melts come out very slowly if at all.

When cooled, the rigid three-dimensional matrix of this material causes it to have a very low coefficient of thermal expansion (COE). This also accounts for its relatively high softening, annealing, and strain points. It is much too viscous and has too high a melting point to be useful in beadmaking.

Soda-lime glass

In order to decrease the viscosity of fused silica and thus make it more workable, fluxes or network modifiers in the form of metal oxides are added to the formulation. In soda-lime glasses, the metal oxides that are added are sodium oxide in the form of soda ash and calcium oxide in the form of lime carbonates; thus the name soda-lime glass.

Both of these materials release large volumes of gas as they react with the molten silica. Soda (Na_2CO_3) releases carbon dioxide to form Na_2O. Lime does likewise transforming from $CaCO_3$ to CaO. Typical soda-lime glass compositions are between 70 to 80% by weight silica, 8 to 12% by weight lime, and 12 to 17% by weight soda.

As discussed earlier, these materials modify the silica network in a way that lowers the melting point and spreads it over a temperature range. The exact amount of modifier added needs to be closely controlled. Too much lime can make the glass susceptible to devitrification and too little results in a glass that is susceptible to chemical attack. In addition to soda and lime, other additives are included to make the mixture more workable. One of these is alumina (aluminum oxide) which helps improve the glass's chemical durability.

Breaking up the silica chains into shorter sections will lower the viscosity, making the glass easier to shape into beads. It also results in a glass with a higher COE. The consequence of this is that more annealing is required for our beads to remove residual stress. Most commonly available fusing glasses and Effetre glass (that glass which is used by most wound glass beadmakers) are of this type.

Table 13. Average properties of some basic glass types.

Glass Property	Quartz glass	Soda-lime glass	Borosilicate glass	Lead glass
Softening point (°F)	2876	1337	1400	1145
Annealing point (°F)	1983	1022	1000	840
Strain point (°F)	1753	940	775	775
Thermal expansion coefficient (10^{-7} in/in/°F)	3.1	50	27	50
Density (lb/ft^3)	137	156	144	218
Refractive index	1.459	1.51	1.49	1.6

Borosilicate glass (Pyrex)

Boron oxide forms a plane triangular matrix unit that can also be used to help break up the rigid silica matrix. It also tends to migrate to the surface of the glass where its structure reduces the surface energy of the glass. This property makes the glasses to which it is added as a modifier, chemically more stable.

The smaller size of a boron atom compared to that of calcium and sodium atoms in soda lime glass allows more freedom of motion and thus less stress is introduced into the glass matrix as it cools. This also results in a glass whose coefficient of thermal expansion, although higher than quartz, is much less than other glasses.

Unfortunately, its more stable structure also makes borosilicate glass a harder glass that requires a hotter flame to work. It remains much more viscous and has to be really pushed around to shape it in comparison to soda-lime glass. Because of its higher working temperature, many of the metal oxides used to color soda-lime glass will burn out of borosilicate glass. Therefore, its color palette is different and more limited than soda-lime glass.

The reason that it is used by many beadmakers is that its lower COE makes it much less susceptible to thermal shock. This makes it much more forgiving to work with. You can actually stop working when the telephone rings, put the bead down on your workbench to talk, pick it back up afterwards, and resume working without disastrous results. Try this with Effetre and watch out.

Lead Glass

Lead oxide is usually used as a network modifier of the silica matrix, but when added in high enough concentrations, it can also act as a network former. It is a good flux that gives the glass a much larger temperature range over which it can be worked and over which it changes very little in viscosity.

This glass can be worked in cooler flames and is just plain easier to manipulate than soda-lime or borosilicate glass. It is also easier to create a good clear formulation with lead glass. For these reasons and the extra sparkle that it gets from the higher index of refraction, it was the glass of choice used for centuries to produce fine tableware and art work.

In flameworking, lead glass finds its main use in neon tubing. Satake beadmaking glass imported from Japan is lead-based and is being used by a number of American glass beadmakers. It has many colors available and as expected, is easy to work.

When working lead glass in a flame you have to be very careful that the flame is not reducing. If it is some of the lead will reduce and darken the glass. This will give it a dull metallic look.

Colorants

The colors in glass are formed by three basic processes: dissolution of metallic oxide molecules, colloidal suspensions of fine particles, and inclusions of crystalline materials.

Metallic oxides can be dissolved uniformly into molten glass just like sugar dissolves in water. They actually become part of the solution and will not settle out again. When the molten glass is cooled and allowed to solidify, the oxides remain dissolved in the solid glass phase. Each metallic oxide atom will absorb some light of characteristic wavelength and let the rest pass by. The result is color.

Larger colorant particles, which may not dissolve, can still be dispersed uniformly throughout a melt as a colloidal suspension. They will also interact with light of a characteristic wavelength range to produce color. The sizes of the suspended particles dictate the wavelengths of light that they can reflect. The remainder of the light is absorbed.

Although a colloidal suspension may seem the same as dissolution, it is not. This is more like the mix of fine silt in river water. There, the particles are suspended because of the motion of the water molecules, but they never really become part of the solution. If you were to take that water and run it through a centrifuge, you would be able to separate the particles out. Likewise if you held glass with these colorants at high temperature for a long time, these colorant particles could settle out.

The third way that glass is colored is through the addition of the kinds of materials that form tiny crystalline inclusions in the glass. These crystals refract light much differently than the bulk of the glass. This leads to an opalescent appearance.

As you work with many different colored glasses, you will find that some of them will change color after being worked in a flame. I am not talking about the temporary change of color that you get when a rod is hot. I am speaking of those glass rods that might be a pale transparent color when purchased but change to a deep rich color after being heated correctly. Such colors are referred to as striking colors. They can be correctly "struck" either in the flame or during kiln annealing.

If you try to use some of your scrap stained glass for making beads, you may find that these may also change colors. Unless formulated for fusing, these glasses may not have stable colors and many times may end up looking really ugly after being worked in a flame. Also you may sometimes find that when one color of glass is applied over another that they react to form a third color at the interface between them.

All of these effects are due to changes in the oxidative state of the metallic oxide colorants. A similar thing happens if you heat some glasses in an oxygen poor flame (reducing flame) where oxygen is stolen from the colorant to produce a dull metallic colored glass.

If you'd like to try adding your own color to glass using metal oxides, here's how you would go about it. (See Table 14 fir color and oxide information) First lay out some colorant oxides on your marver. Heating the oxides on the marver before mixing them with the glass will make them easier to pick up.

Next form gathers on the ends of two glass rods and roll them in the colorant powder. You can use clear soda lime or borosilicate glass, but borosilicate glass will not necessarily work well with all colorants because as we discussed earlier they may burn out. Bring them together in the flame and twist the rods in opposite directions to uniformly mix the colorant into the gather. As you see the striations of colored powder go away and blend in, reroll the gather in the colorant and mix in the flame. Repeat this process until you get the depth of color that you are looking for. Then stretch the gather out into cane or rod of the desired thickness.

If you have clear tubing available, fuse one end closed and attach a clear rod. Then fill the tube with the colorant and fuse a second clear rod onto the other end of the tube, taking care not to fuse the second end shut. It would shatter from the expanding air upon reheat if you did this.

Now heat the tube in the largest possible flame starting at the fused end. As the tube starts to soften, force the ends together and rotate them in opposite directions as before to mix up the colorant. When satisfied with the uniformity of the final mix and its depth of color, pull out the molten blob into cane of the desired thickness.

Be careful whenever mixing your own colors because the metal oxide fumes released are not necessarily good to breathe. In fact, some oxides like lead, cadmium, and uranium are highly toxic. Mixing should always be done in an area with good local ventilation set up such that you are pulling the fumes produced in the process away from you. In addition, the workspace itself should have good general ventilation to prevent buildup of any stray fumes. As an even further precaution, consider wearing a respirator that provides protection from metallic fumes.

Table 14 lists a number colorant materials you can add to get the listed colors and approximate amounts of the colorants that are needed. Try some and see what you end up with.

Table 14. Glass colorants and colors they produce.

Color	Shade	Colorant	%
white		fluoride opals (fluorspar)	
		phosphate opals	
		tin oxide	
	cream	silver oxide	2-4%
yellow		vanadium oxide	
	greenish	silver nitrate	0.2%
	transparent	silver oxide	
		selenium	
orange		cadmium & selenium	
red	ruby	gold	
		copper oxide (red)	
	flat	copper oxide (black)	
		cadmium & selenium	
	pink	tin oxide & chromium oxide (2/1)	
purple		manganese dioxide	0.5-1%
		nickel	
blue		cobalt oxide	0.05%
		cobalt carbonate	0.2-1%
	greenish	copper carbonate	0.4-1%
	pastel	cobalt carbonate & tin oxide (1/3)	
green	yellowish	iron oxide	0.4-1.5%
		iron chromate	0.5-1.7%
		potassium dichromate	0.2-0.8%
	dark	chromium oxide & cobalt carbonate (1/1)	1-2%
	pastel	chrome oxide & tin oxide (1/1)	
		chromium oxide	0.2%
		copper oxide (black)	0.2-0.4%
	transparent	copper oxide (red)	0.2-0.4%
black		manganese dioxide	6+%
amber		sulfur	1.5%
		iron oxide	2-5%
brown		silver nitrate	
		nickel carbonate	0.2%
		copper oxide (red)	
gray		nickel carbonate	0.2%
	smoky	nickel oxide	0.2-0.6%

Enamels

Custom colors can also be added to your beads and glass rods through the use of enamels. Enamels are really nothing more than finely ground colored glass. They are usually formulated to have intense colors and to flow very easily. The first attribute is achieved by having an abundance of colorant. The second by having fluxing agents that lower the melting temperature and the viscosity of the enamel.

They can be used to coat the outside of your bead or can be blended with the glass rods to make custom colors.

When choosing to work with enamels, you have to consider a few things. First you need to make sure that the enamels that you choose to work with are compatible with your glass palette. The term compatibility will be explained in great detail shortly. For Effetre glass, which is the choice of most of wound beadmakers, the 9000 series of Thompson Enamels is the right line of enamels to work with. They were specially formulated to be compatible with this glass. If you want an even wider enamel color palette, you might want to consider working with Kugler and Zimmerman powders. These can essentially be considered to be enamels and can be applied over a base of clear Schott glass.

The next thing to consider in choosing an enamel is its grind. The grind is usually expressed as a mesh number. This is the number of wire fibers per inch of the screen through which the enamel will pass. The larger the number the finer the enamel. The 9000 series of Thompson enamels is only available in an 80-mesh grind but there are 32 different opaque colors.

Kugler and Zimmerman colored glass is available in a couple of grinds as well as chunks. Most of the time you will use them as powders. They are available in a multitude of colors since this is the material that many glassblowers use to color their glass.

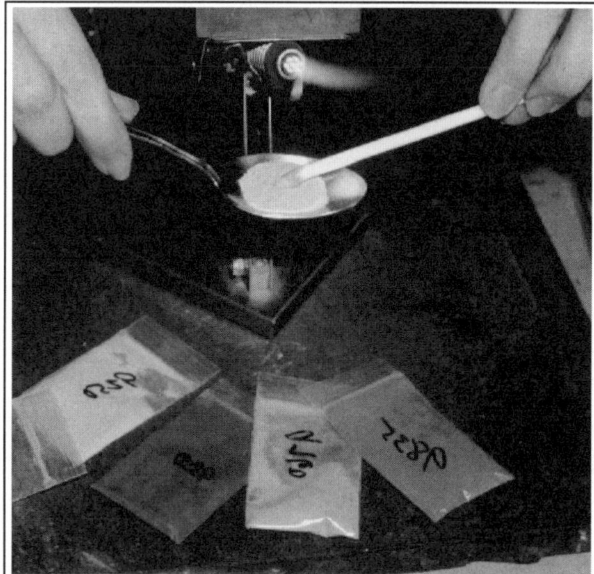

Figure 67. Coating a glass rod with an enamel.

The third thing to consider is safety. When using finely ground enamels, you invariably will have some powder floating in your breathing air. These can get trapped inside your respiratory tract and absorbed by the body. The danger here is from the toxic effect of some of the metallic oxide colorants or fluxes in them. Thompson enamels are lead free, but Kugler and Zimmerman powders are not. There are also other metallic oxides like cadmium and cobalt, which are used as colorants in some of the enamels that should concern you. This also goes for glass paints.

The enamel manufacturer or distributor will usually label the containers if any toxic materials are present, but don't be too bashful to ask. These materials can be harmful to the body and you should always consider wearing a respirator when using them.

Blending colored rods with enamels

If you want to coat the surface of a rod with an enamel, just heat it up until it just starts to glow and roll it in the enamel. Then reheat the rod as necessary to add more. If you want to use them to make custom colored glass rods, then you need to mix them like paint. Here the pigment is the enamel that you add to the base tint glass rod.

You add a little of the pigment to the rod by heating the rod till it is at least just glowing. Then bring up a small container of enamel just beneath the flame and roll the hot end of the rod in the enamel. Some artists use a teaspoon to hold the enamel but I like those small kitchen scoops made out of cast iron because they do not have a lip on one end. This makes it easier to roll a bead or rod in them as well as to pour the enamel back into its storage container afterward. Another convenient tool that I have seen used in enamel application is a frit and powder trough. These are basically alike a large M in cross section where the center is a nice smooth U shape. The open ends allow easy access to the powder and easy clean up afterward.

So, heat up the coated rod and mix it with the enamel powder as was done with the metallic oxide colorants, using a second rod of the same base color to help. Be careful not to boil the glass because this may result in the lower melting temperature enamel losing some of its color. Add more enamel by repeatedly rolling the rod in it until you get the depth of color that you are looking for.

The tint rods that we usually mix with enamels are light opaque colors but don't dismiss trying to mix them with transparent colored rods. This combination can produce translucent colors similar to the alabaster Effetre colors. You can also try mixing them incompletely to get striations of color in the glass.

If you are going to use this enamel-colored glass as stringers, you do not really need to mix the enamel into the rod, but could get by with just coating the rod with the enamel. Here you roll the rod in the enamel just after it is glowing and then return the rod to the flame to melt the enamel into the surface. As you heat the enamel, it will get less angular, start to spread out over the surface, taking on an orange peel appearance, and finally smooth out. Any residual bumpiness can be smoothed out by rolling the bead on a paddle and several layers of enamel can be added for greater depth of color. This rod is then pulled out into thin cane for decoration of your beads. The rod can be cased first to ensure that color loss from overheating the enamel is minimized.

Be sure to remember to wear your respirator when blending color using enamels. For more information on the use of enamels in beadmaking, refer to my booklet **The Enamel and Electroform Decorated Beads of Kate Fowle Meleney**, which is part of my ***Beadmaker Series***.

Blending colored rods

Most of you will work almost exclusively with precolored glass rods such as Effetre and do not want to bother with enamels to expand your palette. But the Effetre color palette is limited enough that you may find that you will not have all the shades that you may want for constructing highlights in a bead. To alleviate this limitation without using colorants or enamels, what you will need to do is learn to mix different colored rods together to get new colors. This will allow you to develop a number of color variations for shading and shadowing as well as more realistic vegetation and flesh tones — a place where the Effetre palette is definitely lacking.

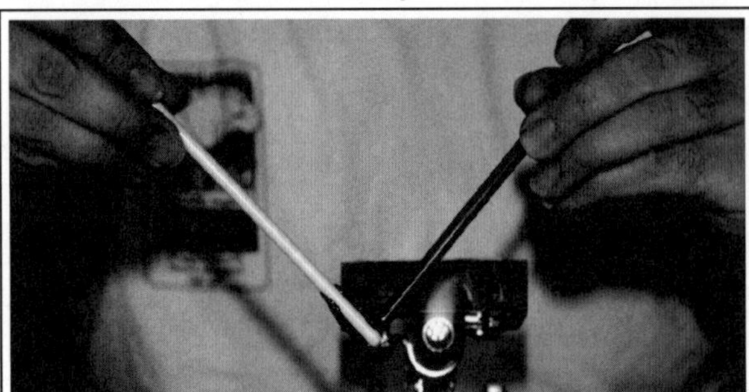

Figure 68. Applying a thick coating of the pigment color rod onto the base tint rod.

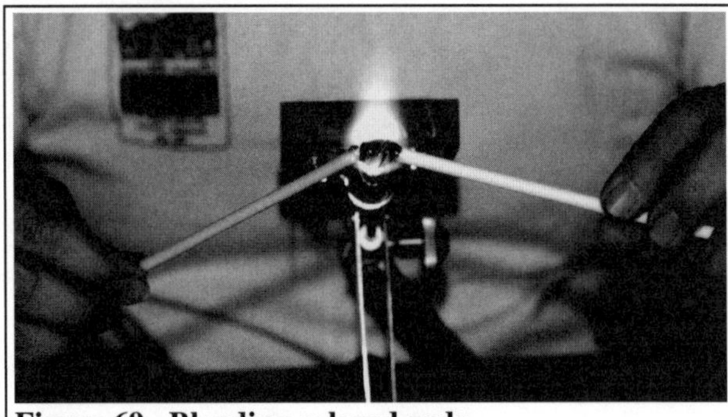

Figure 69. Blending colored rods.

To blend colors, start with two rods of your base tint (usually the lighter color) and one of a darker "pigment" color. Paint some pigment color onto the outside of a base tint rod for a length of about an inch. For a thin coat, this is done by getting the tip of the pigment rod red hot and then painting it on by pushing down and towards you on the base tint rod directing the flame into the junction between the two as you apply it. To apply a thicker coat, paint the pigment rod away from you while heating the outside of the applied pigment rod. At the end of each paint stroke, lift the pigment rod off the base tint rod and burn off any stringers in the flame.

Once you have applied enough pigment to the base tint rod, you are now ready to mix it up to get a nice uniform color. Grab another base tint rod and attach it onto the pigment colored end of the first rod. Heat up the whole pigment colored region until it is hot and globby. Twist one rod in one direction and the other in the opposite direction. To assist in mixing you can swirl one rod around the other. Stretching the glob out and pushing it back together also helps.

You will not be able to see what you have at this point but you should be able to tell if it is well mixed or not by looking for striations in the red hot glob. Striations are good indication of incomplete mixing, just as they were when we were mixing colorants and enamels. When done mixing, pull out the glob into a fairly thick cane. If you want a continuous range of shades, you could save just part of the cane and mix the rest with more base tint. Repeat this a number of times and you should achieve any distribution of shades you desire. For more information on color mixing see my booklet, **The Classic Bead Shapes of Jim Smircich and His Amazing Control of Heat**, which is another title in the ***Beadmaker Series***.

As you start blending colors, you will find that you won't always get the color that you would expect from consulting a color wheel. For example, blue and red won't necessarily make purple. The different metal oxide colorants may interact in unpredictable ways. Some colors, like reds, may break down after prolonged mixing into an ugly brown. Likewise, once turquoise starts to sparkle, it will burnout.

Some colors are not necessarily what they seem either. For example, Effetre black is actually a very dark purple. Transparent colors mixed with opaque colors will usually result in streaky transparent colors. To start getting a feel for what you can achieve with blending, try blending white or ivory with a little red to get better flesh tones or green with a little "black" to get more natural greens for vegetation.

When blending colors, as in mixing your own colored glass, you have to be concerned with toxic heavy metal fumes coming out of the very hot glass. Make sure that you always use proper ventilation.

Coatings

The appearance and color of a glass can also be modified by the addition of coatings onto it. Like a mirror coating, they change the reflective and refractive properties of the glass. Some of these coatings will stand up to the heat of the torch allowing them to be incorporated into beads — others will not. So, let's look at some of these coatings.

Irridized coatings

Irridized coatings are surface coatings, usually of stannous chloride, that are sprayed onto the surface of the glass when it is still fairly hot. They give the glass a little extra sparkle. The Favrile glass of Tiffany Studios is an example of this kind of coating.

Stannous chloride is some pretty nasty stuff so most beadmakers do not use it. They instead will use a product called thermoluster or mother of pearl. It is a mixture of a number of chemicals that includes 1,1,1-trichloroethane and tetraisopropyl titanate. This coating matures at temperatures around 800°F. The color achieved with this material will vary some with temperature. As you increase temperature, the applied coating will change from a rainbow bronze to a steel gray.

These coatings may be lost with continued working in a torch, but will stand up to the heat of annealing in a kiln. Such coatings should always be applied as the last step after shaping of the bead is complete.

Dichroic coatings

A relatively new coating technique that has become more common in all kinds of art glass to give jazzy color effects is that of vapor deposition. It is generally applied to sheet glass that you then incorporate into a bead, but a few artists, such as Sharon Peters, have had it applied to part of the exterior of finished beads. The process deposits alternating thin coatings of high and low refractive index materials on the surface of the glass. Refractive index is a measure of how fast light moves in a material. This also affects how well the material can bend or refract light. By bending light, the different colors can be separated just as with a prism.

Each of these layers is very thin, on the order of the wavelength of light, which is really small. Even with multiple layers, the coating may only be a few millionths of an inch in thickness. Because of this extreme thinness, the coating itself has very little strength and can be scratched when cold or broken apart as it is stretched hot. It is the glass it is deposited on that gives it any strength at all.

These optical coatings were developed for use as "interference filters" and have some interesting refractive properties. When viewed by looking through the glass at a light source, the glass will appear to be one color as you look straight through it. If you move your head so that you are looking through the glass from a slightly different angle the color will change. These colors are referred to as the transmitted colors of the coating since the light is being transmitted through the glass. If instead of looking through the glass, you view the glass by light reflected off of it, you will see the complimentary color. This is called the reflected color.

Dichroic coatings form partially reflecting surfaces like two-way mirrors, only the effect is limited to one color. Which color depends upon the thickness of the coating layers. The thicker the individual deposited layers, the longer the wavelength of the reflected light. The reflected colors in order of decreasing coating thickness are red, yellow, green, blue, and violet. With dichroic glass, none of the light is absorbed by colorants. So, if you were able to add the reflected and the transmitted colored light back together, you would get the original white or colorless light.

Each layer reflects only a fraction of the total possible reflected colored light. So the more layers that are added, the greater the amount or depth of color achieved. Also since it is almost impossible to make all the layers exactly the same thickness, the reflected light really ends up not being of a single wavelength but of a small range of wavelengths centered around the average layer reflected wavelength.

Dichroic glass is available in a number of transmitted colors, the most common of these colors tend to be blue, cyan, magenta or yellow. Red, orange and green are also available but are more expensive because they require thicker coatings and thus more deposition time. Because of the high-tech nature of the coating process, the cost of dichroic glass tends to be relatively high. But those artists who use this material in their work feel that it is worth the price, about $2 to $5 a square inch. They feel that it adds a new dimension to their beads and puts them in higher demand.

The method of applying dichroic coatings, called vacuum vapor evaporative coating, was developed to make optical filters and partially reflective surfaces for scientific applications such as lasers. It starts with abrasive and chemically cleaning the glass very well. The glass is then put into an ultra-high vacuum chamber on a planetary rotation system that will uniformly expose the whole surface of all the glass to the vapor. Here the glass is heated up and cleaned again by bombarding it with high-speed electrons that have been accelerated by a high voltage potential.

Coating companies go through all this cleaning because the glass has to be ultra clean for the coatings to stick to it. Otherwise, they might peel off as the coatings are heated or abraded. After preheating the glass to about 500°F, the electron beam is next directed onto targets containing the material that is to be deposited onto the surface of the glass. This material will either be a high or a low refractive index material. The high refractive index materials used are usually metal oxides like titanium oxide, zirconium oxide, tantalum oxide, or aluminum oxide. The low refractive index material is usually quartz or silicon dioxide. The electron beam heats up the surface of the targets to incredibly high temperatures, as high as 3000°C. At these temperatures the surface of the target vaporizes. These vapors travel across the vacuum chamber to the clean glass surface. Here they deposit on the cooler glass surface just as steam from the shower condenses on your mirror. If the chamber were not at high vacuum, the vapors would not be able to cross this gap, or if they did they would be cooled to the point where they would not hit the glass with enough energy to stick to it. The materials will also stick better if the glass is heated properly. These and other processing parameters affect the nature of the coating and how dense it is.

All during the deposition process, the glass is being rotated in order to achieve a more uniform coating. This will affect the uniformity of the colors of the coating. The deposition rate of the coating material is controlled by the temperature to which the target is heated and the vapor pressure in the chamber. The thickness of each layer is controlled by the deposition time. The number and thickness of the different layers deposited on the glass determine the resulting optical properties. By masking the glass coatings with stainless steel shields placed over the glass, patterned coatings can be made.

Almost any type or form of glass can be evaporative coated on one side. You can find dichroic coatings on both rods and sheet glass, although sheet dichroic is much more common. Because of limitations in size of available vacuum chambers, most glass sheets are between 16" and 24" on a side. Also since it is hard to maintain coating uniformity, the color may vary somewhat over the sheet or a lot if the sheet was not rotated. This is how rainbow dichroic is made.

Coating glass with heavy texture can further enhance variation of color in a dichroic coating. Since the amount of coating material applied is constant with respect to the planer surface area of the glass, it will vary on textured surfaces. As the textured surface tilts with respect to the flat side, the coating gets thinner.

Compatibility of dichroic glass is a function of the base glass to which the coating was applied. Much of what is available has been made for fusing work and can be used in beadmaking but has a COE of 90. Dichroic Effetre sheet glass is now becoming available from some suppliers but it can be a pain to work with. This is because the glass is usually pretty thick.

Be sure to ask your dichroic supplier if the coating is appropriate for beadmaking because some are not.

This is determined by which oxides are applied to the surface as well as whether high temperature overcoats of quartz are applied. These will greatly increase its flame resistance. Quartz overcoats on each oxide layer perform even better. How the layers are laid down on the glass also affects its performance under heat. The denser and more crystalline the layers the more stable they will be.

Because there is no industry standard for describing dichroic glass colors, you cannot always be sure exactly what color you are going to get. Each manufacturer may describe their colors a little differently. One may specify their color by the transmitted color, while another may define it by the reflected color. This can make it confusing when trying to mail order dichroic glass. The best thing is to look at some samples of the glass before ordering. At the very least send them a chip of what you are looking for so they can match it. Some dichroic manufacturers keep records on each coating run and mark this on the glass. If you give them this number they can provide you with consistent materials.

When you heat dichroic glass to use in a bead, you may notice a number of changes taking place. First, you will usually get a color shift down the rainbow toward yellow. This happens because as you heat the coating, it becomes denser and thus thinner. It loses a little of its refracting power. Thus, the color that you get in the bead is a little different than the color that you purchased. Second, as the coating densifies, it also shrinks in the plane of the glass. This will cause the coating to develop many small ribs or crazing.

A lot of people have a hard time determining which side of the glass the dichroic coating is on. For opaque base glass, which is usually black, it is obvious which side is coated and there is no confusion. On textured glass, the dichroic side is always on the textured side. It is really only a problem with flat transparent glass. There are two ways of determining which side has the coating on it.

The first way is to touch the piece of glass with an object like a tungsten pick and look for the reflected "shadow." If the shadow meets the object at the touch point, the top surface is the coated side. If there is a gap between the shadow and the tip of the object, the bottom surface is the coated side.

The other technique, besides being a little more difficult to describe, is often a little more difficult to judge. Here you hold the glass such that you can see a strong reflection off of the coating. Then you look through the glass toward an edge on the opposite side to see if you can see the lower edge of the cut. If you can see it, the lower surface is the coated surface. If not, the top side is the coated side.

Since either of these tests can be hard to do on the spur of the moment at the torch, it is a good idea to figure it out ahead of time. I either mark the glass side or organize all the pieces with coating up or down on my workbench before starting. Then problems only occur if I drop the piece when I am getting ready to apply it.

Temperature regimes of glass

As you work with any glass, you will develop a feeling for how many of its physical properties vary with temperature. The variation in properties can be described in terms of different glass temperature regimes.

The brittle solid regime

The temperature regime in which you are probably most used to working with glass is that around room temperature. In this temperature regime, glass is a solid material that breaks in a brittle manner when stressed. A small scratch or crack will propagate quickly through the material with great ease.

Glass in this regime expands and contracts with changes in temperature at a near constant rate. The amount of expansion is known as the glass's Coefficient of Expansion (COE). This number, which is expressed in units of 10^{-7} inches per inch per degree centigrade, is the average expansion over a defined temperature range. The usual range that is tested in the laboratory is from 0° to 300°C (32°-600°F). The upper end of the temperature range for the brittle solid regime is somewhat higher than this. For soda-lime glasses, it is on the order of 700°F.

As the temperature of the glass is changed in the brittle zone, the parts of the glass that get warmer faster will try to grow in size relative to the cooler glass around it. This causes the silica tetrahedrons to try and slip and stretch past each other until they lock up on a larger colorant atom. These slippages build up at locations like this, straining the natural order of the atoms in the glass and resulting in

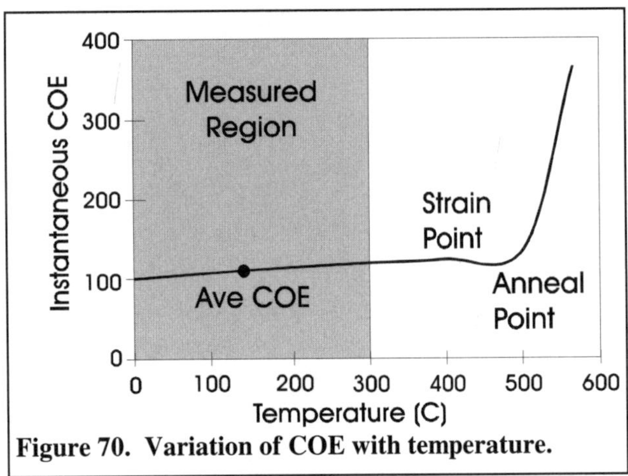

Figure 70. Variation of COE with temperature.

stress. In the brittle regime, the only way that any stress in glass can be relieved is by fracture.

The non-brittle solid regime

As the glass is taken higher in temperature, the atoms become more mobile as their vibrations and tetrahedron rotation increase. They start to be able to jump around any obstructions that may have pinned them previously in the brittle solid regime. This does not happen all at once, but gradually as the vibrations of the glass atoms increase with increasing temperature. This motion allows any built up stress to start to relieve itself.

For soda-lime glasses, this temperature regime extends roughly from 700 to 1000°F. Within it, the glass will continue to expand and contract with temperature change, but the COE is different than it was in the brittle solid regime. In fact, the COE is never really a constant and varies throughout both temperature regimes as shown in Figure 70. The increase in the atomic mobility at these higher temperatures allows any stress build up to relieve itself. But it is still possible to change the glass temperature faster than the movement of the atoms can reduce the stress. In other words, you can still get thermal shock in this regime.

This is the temperature regime in which glass is annealed. Many artists have been taught to think that annealing (stress relief) takes place at a particular temperature, but that is not correct. What that annealing temperature actually represents is a compromise. The compromise is a temperature at which the atoms are mobile enough to allow relief of the stress in a reasonable amount of time, minutes, without being so high that the actual glass itself starts to flow in the same sort of time period.

The flexible regime

As you heat a soda-lime glass to temperatures above 1000°F, it begins to become more and more pliable. Left at this temperature, it will droop or slump under the influence of gravity or muscle power. The atoms in the glass are now so mobile that it is no longer susceptible to thermal shock. Its properties start to resemble something more like soft, sticky taffy than a hard solid. It will begin to stick to other pieces of glass or to other materials with which it may come in contact, such as separator coatings or kiln wash. These effects become more pronounced as the temperature is raised until about 1400°F when soda-lime glass starts to enter the last temperature regime.

The fluid regime

In this last temperature regime, the glass exhibits fluid like properties and hand manipulation of it becomes possible. This is the regime that you are operating within as you wind, shape, and decorate beads in the flame of your torch. This regime is also the one in which full and flat fusing takes place in a kiln. By careful control of the temperature of your piece, you can determine how the glass can be worked. You can make it so soft that it flows like a thick fluid or have it sufficiently viscous that it can be sculpted like clay.

Glass compatibility

As mentioned earlier, the kinds and amounts of oxide modifiers used in making a particular glass modify the silica matrix differently and affect the rate at which the glass shrinks when cooled. This rate, as mentioned earlier, is commonly known as the

Table 15. Coefficient of Expansion (COE) of some common art glasses.

Manufacturer	COE (in/in/°C)
Northstar	32
Pyrex	33
GNA	81
Shott Clear	83 & 87
Bullseye	90
Wasser	90
Uroburos	90
Kugler	82-94
Zimmerman	74-94
Spectrum	96
Morreti	104
Satake	120

coefficient of expansion (COE) and is usually expressed as a whole number.

As an example, the Bullseye compatible glasses all have a COE of 90. This means that in the solid regime, a 1-inch long piece of one of these glasses will shrink 0.0000090 inches (90×10^{-7}) for each 1°C reduction in temperature. Thus, a 10 inch piece of glass will shrink about 0.051 inches in cooling from its annealing temperature (about 1100°F) to room temperature. Similarly, a 10-inch piece of Effetre glass with a COE of 104 would shrink 0.060 inches.

Therefore, if you were trying to fuse together 10-inch strips of these two types of glass, the difference between the shrinkage of one strip and the other would be 0.009 inches. This is about the thickness of 5 sheets of paper. That may not seen like much on our ordinary macroscopic level, but when you compare it to the size scale of reference, atoms, it is enormous. As a result, the piece will literally pull itself apart.

As anyone who has done hot glasswork knows, you have to make sure that whatever glasses you use are compatible. Some manufacturers cater to hot/warm glass artists and have initiated good quality controls to ensure a consistent self-compatible glass line.

For beads, which are pretty small pieces of glass, small variations (1-3 points) in COE will probably not cause any major problems. But as most good fusing manuals will recommend, you probably should check the compatibility of your glass yourself for large beads. Table 15 lists published values of COE for many of the common art glasses.

In actuality, the concept of a constant COE value for a given glass is a highly simplified version of what really happens. As mentioned, the COE is not a constant and it varies considerably with temperature, as was illustrated in Figure 70. What is reported in Table 15 is the average value for the shaded test region from room temperature to 300°C. But if the glasses are of similar composition, they will also behave similarly over the rest of the temperature region of interest. If not, they may vary widely in that region. Even if they had the same average value in the shaded region, they may not be compatible because of the differences at higher temperatures outside of the shaded region.

Differences in annealing temperatures between two glasses can also lead to compatibility problems. If one glass hardens before the other, it can push that other soft glass around — stretching it at will without introducing much stress in itself. The second will trap that residual stress because it cannot budge the hardened first glass. This leads to a strained boundary between the two glasses that can initiate cracks later. Both of these are reasons why it is always a good idea to check out compatibility of your glass, especially if it comes from a number of different manufacturers.

Also, be aware that not all the glass from a manufacturer will have the same COE and be compatible. As an example, unless labeled as compatible, there is no guarantee that a particular sheet of Bullseye glass is compatible. Also some people have tried to tell me that all GNA is compatible and I have learned the hard way that this is not true. So, unless a glass is labeled as compatible, don't assume it is.

Compatibility Testing

If you want to test whether your glass is compatible yourself, you can pull long cylindrical threads as will be discussed in the next chapter. The two glasses must be joined down the length of the thread and equally divided in the cross section. If the glasses are compatible (shrink at the same rate), the thread will remain straight. If the thread bends by more than about one quarter of an inch over a twenty-inch length, they are on the borderline of being incompatible and probably should not be used together. The glass on the inside of a bow has the higher COE. If you use glass with one-eight or more of an inch of deflection as a surface decoration, it likely will break off.

If you want a quantitative value for the COE difference of the two glasses, you need to carefully measure the length of the thread, its diameter (this will require a micrometer to do accurately) and the bow. Substitute these values into the following equation to get a good approximation of COE difference:

$$\text{COE diff} = \frac{16 \cdot 10^7 \cdot \text{thread diameter} \cdot \text{bow}}{\text{length squared} \cdot \text{temperature difference}}$$

The term 10^7 is equivalent to 10,000,000. All dimensions should be in the same units, such as inches. Thread length squared means the thread length multiplied by itself. For a temperature difference, you might assume that you would use a value expressing the difference from when the glass

Table 16. COE difference values from 2' thread test.

Thread Diameter (in)	Bow (in)				
	0.125	0.250	0.375	0.500	0.625
0.010	0.2	0.4	0.6	0.8	1.0
0.020	0.4	0.8	1.2	1.6	2.0
0.030	0.6	1.2	1.8	2.5	3.1
0.040	0.8	1.6	2.5	3.3	4.1
0.050	1.0	2.0	3.1	4.1	5.1
0.060	1.2	2.5	3.7	4.9	6.1
0.070	1.4	2.9	4.3	5.7	7.1
0.080	1.6	3.3	4.9	6.5	8.2
0.090	1.8	3.7	5.5	7.4	9.2
0.100	2.0	4.1	6.2	8.2	10.2

solidifies back down to room temperature. This would be about right if the COE values did not have the large non-linear changes above the strain point that we saw back in the last chapter. By trial and error, I found a value of 1700°C to be a good approximate temperature difference to use in this equation.

If you are not the type of person that feels comfortable with using equations, you can use Table 16 on the next page to help determine the COE differences from a test of a two-foot long thread. For bows larger than those in the table, multiply the table COE value in the last column for that thread diameter by the ratio of your measured bow to the largest bow listed (your bow/0.625). For shorter threads, divide the table value by the ratio of your thread length to two feet.

There are some things that may cause problems with determining COE differences by thread testing. They include cracking or non-ideal thread geometry. When you have very large COE differences, even small diameter threads may develop very small cracks or crazing that will release some of the stress in the thread that causes bowing. This will result in an underestimate of the COE mismatch.

In deriving this equation, I had to make a number of assumptions about the thread geometry. Violations of these assumptions affect the accuracy of the calculated value. The first assumption that I made was that the thread diameter was constant along its length. If this is not true, try to break the thread into a shorter one of more constant diameter. A second assumption was that the cross section of the thread was round. If not, approximate an average diameter for the cross section. Lastly I assumed that the cross section was split equally between the two glasses. Large differences in viscosity of the two glasses may make one side pull thinner than the other, which will result in an underestimate of the COE mismatch.

Suggested further reading

Bramford, C. R., **Colour Generation and Control in Glass**, Ceramic Book and Literature Service, 2002

Bray, Charles. **Dictionary of Glass Materials and Techniques**, 1st ed., A & C Black Ltd., 1995

McLellan, George W. and Shand, Errol B. **Glass Engineering Handbook** 3rd ed., McGraw-Hill Book Company 1984

Newton, Roy, and Davidson, Sandra. **Conservation of Glass**, 1st ed., Butterworth-Heinemann Ltd., 1989

Pfaender, Heinz G., **Schott Guide to Glass**, 2nd ed., Chapman and Hall, 1996

Scholes, Samuel R., and Greene, Charles H. **Modern Glass Practice**, 7th ed., Ceramic Book and Literature Service, 1993

Shelby, James E., **Introduction to Glass Science and Technology**, RSC Paperbacks, 1997

Weyl, W. A. **Coloured Glasses**, Brady & Serban, 1954

Flameworking techniques

Now let's turn our attention on how to operate your equipment and then on learning some of the basic flameworking skills that will be needed in beadmaking. To begin with, let's discuss how to operate some different torches.

Handheld torch operation

Operation of a handheld torch is relatively straightforward. They are generally used with disposable canisters of propane, but they can also be used with propylene or MAPP Gas®.

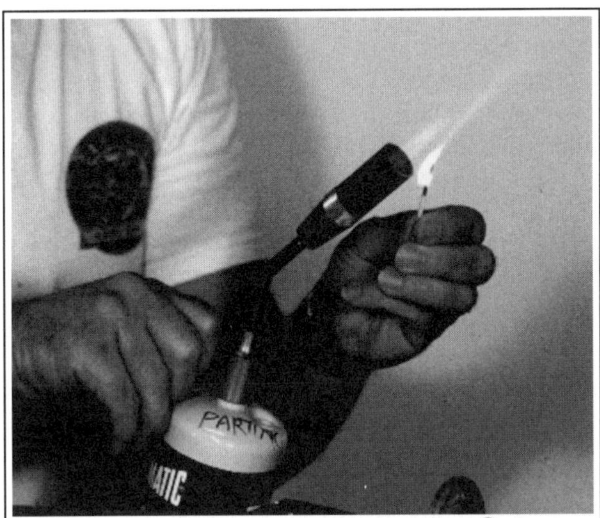

Figure 71. Turning gas on with Hot Head® torch.

Start by assembling the torch head onto the disposable canister or fuel tank. Ensure that the torch on/off valve is turned off. You can tell which way to turn it by looking closely at the handle on the on/off valve. It may be labeled with the direction to twist the knob to turn it off. That direction is usually clockwise. Next, insert the shaft of the torch head into the throat of the fuel tank and screw the torch head on. The torch head will screw on in a clockwise direction. In installing the torch onto the tank, try not to tilt it, and hand tighten it only. Overtightening the torch head on the disposable tank can distort its threads.

Whenever attaching or removing the torch, do it in a place where no open flames are present. This is just in case any fuel is released at the connection between the torch and the tank. Also, always allow the torch to cool before removing it from the tank. But please do remove it when you are done working — do not store them attached together.

To light a Hot Head®, set it down upright or in its stand on the worktable. I will describe using a match to light your torch because many handheld torch users may not yet have purchased a striker. But using a striker is the safer lighting technique and the one that I recommend. It can be used to light a handheld torch just as is described for lighting the fuel-oxygen torch later. So to light a handheld torch with a match, start by lighting a match and holding it slightly below the front edge of the opening on the torch head. Have the match head slanted slightly down to make it less likely to blow out. Turn the fuel gas on medium low by barely turning the on/off valve counterclockwise. Slowly lift the burning match into the flowing gas and the flame should catch. If the rush of fuel gas blows out the match, turn off the gas and start over.

Lighting a Fireworks torch is much easier. You set it up in the torch stand, turn on the gas, and push the light button. The piezoelectric lighter will throw a spark that is sufficient to light the gas.

Once lit, adjust the gas flow using the on/off valve until you can no longer see any yellow in the flame. When you are done, turn the torch off by twisting the on/off handle fully clockwise. Be aware that the torch will continue to burn for a couple of seconds after the knob is in the off position, so don't crank down on the knob too hard. These torches have what's called a needle valve. As you open the valve, you are withdrawing a needle out of a tapered hole

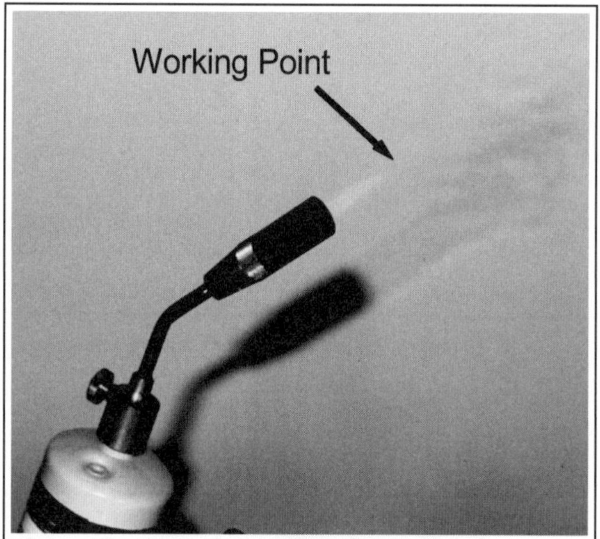

Figure 72. Flame from a Hot Head® Torch.

in the valve seat. This effectively changes the size of the hole and thus the amount of gas that flows through it. Cranking down too hard can damage the valve seat.

In these small handheld torches, you will want to work out in the flame just past the inner blue portion where you lose all signs of color, as can sort of be seen in Figure 72. This is the hottest portion of the flame and is generally about 1½" to 2½" from the tip of the torch. Most people tend to find themselves drifting back closer to the tip of the torch because they can see this portion of the flame better or they just want the bead closer to them where they can see better.

Force yourself to keep pushing the bead back out into this hotter portion of the flame. Besides being easier to work the glass in this location, this is also a less reducing portion of the flame. As such, it will be less likely to cause the colorants in the glass to be reduced. Reduction is where the flame steals oxygen from the metallic oxide colorants, reducing them to metal atoms that look dull and gray. This seems to be more of a problem with propane or propylene than with MAPP Gas® or Chemtane 2, possibly because of the oxidizer they contain. It is also worse in a poorly ventilated space but we're not supposed to be working in spaces like this.

With the Fireworks torch, you can adjust the flame chemistry somewhat by rotating the air mixing valve as seen in Figure 73. Use pliers because the barrel gets quite hot. This valve controls how much air gets pulled into the flame. Closing the valve makes the flame more reducing. Around 50% closed is reported to result in a neutral flame out at the tip of the yellow cone. The smaller flame on this torch restricts the size of the beads that you can make, but the lower heat output slows down the whole process making it easier for beginning beadmakers to control what they are doing.

It's important to position your torch correctly. Always keep the fuel canister upright or slightly tilted from upright, so you do not push liquid fuel out the torch tip. Remember that most of the fuel gases exist as liquids inside the canister until they evaporate or boil. You can actually tell the liquid level inside the tank because the tank will be cooler and will develop a sweat ring at this level on a humid day. You do not want liquid propane coming out of the torch because it will cause the torch to flare up. This is why the stands that I have discussed for use with these torches always position the canister slanted upward at an angle.

As you use up the fuel in your canister, you will find that your flame will get smaller and softer. This is because evaporation of the liquid fuel from the canister cools it. This reduces the vapor pressure in the canister, which in turn reduces the flow of fuel to your flame. The cooling becomes more pronounced as the amount of fuel in the canister is reduced. You may find that you have to stop frequently when near the bottom of the tank to allow it to warm up some to get enough pressure feed the flame.

Fuel-oxygen torch operation

With a fuel-oxygen torch, you have much more adjustability than you have with a handheld torch. You are able to control both the fuel and the oxygen

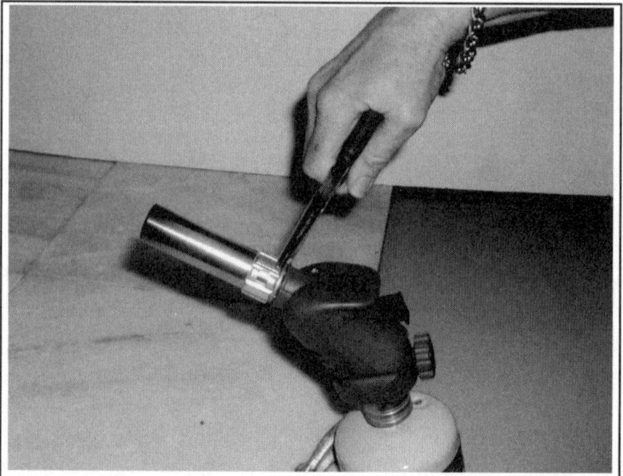

Figure 73. Adjusting the air mixing valve on a Fireworks torch.

that you burn in the torch. The different adjustments allow you to more completely control the size and the shape of your flame. You can make the flame larger or smaller, sharper or bushier as desired for whatever operation you are currently pursuing. These changes are accomplished by changing the gas flows or by working in a different section of the flame. Learning to make these adjustments will help in gaining mastery over your work. It is also a good idea to occasionally clean your torch to get rid of any carbon buildup.

Turning on the gas

If you have never used a fuel-oxygen torch before, don't worry, it's not that difficult and you will soon get the hang of it. Begin by getting a feel for how the valves operate. Start with the valves on your torch while your fuel gas, usually propane, is turned off.

Look at the valves on your torch. There are usually just two of them, one for the propane and one for the oxygen. The propane is usually connected up to a red valve (which is conventionally on the right) and the oxygen is connected to a green valve (on the left). These valves are needle valves that screw a tapered needle in and out of a soft tapered seat when they are operated and like those on the Hot Head®, they should never be turned off really hard because that can cause the needle to deform or scratch the soft valve seat. Either of these conditions can lead to developing a leaky valve that will need to be replaced.

With the gases turned off at the cylinders, try opening and closing your torch valves. They are opened by turning the handle counterclockwise and closed by turning them clockwise. Try to develop a feel for this. If your valves are difficult to turn and you are sure that you are turning them in the right direction, then they may need some adjustment. **Remember that we do not want to use any lubricants with oxygen fittings because this can cause a fire.**

Valve adjustment is done by slightly loosening the locking nut under the valve handle, which can be seen in Figure 74. Tightening this nut will also make the valve a little harder to turn. This adjustment should always be made with the valve open so that you are not jamming the needle deeper into the valve seat as you tighten the nut. Tightening this nut is also the adjustment to make if you notice any gas coming out through the valve handle.

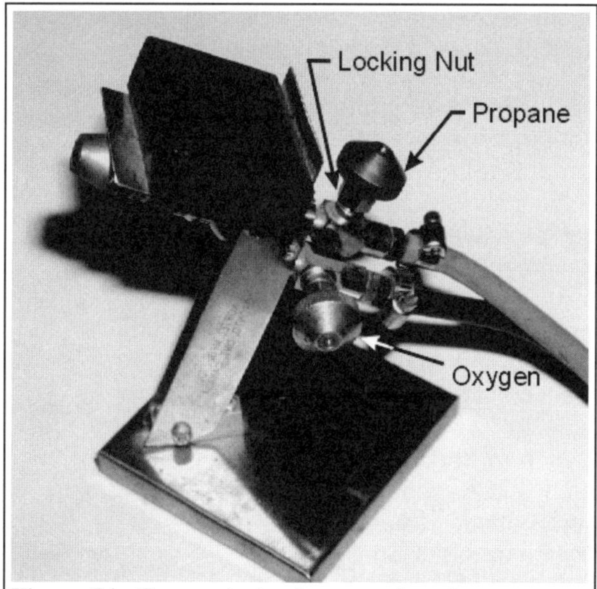

Figure 74. Gas control valves on minor burner.

Now, close the torch valves. Look at the adjusting handle on your oxygen regulator. Check to see that it is screwed out and is not exerting any force on the adjusting spring. Fully open the on/off valve on the oxygen cylinder by turning it counterclockwise until it will not open any further. You should not hear any rushing or hissing of gas. If you do, close the on/off valve and check for leaks. At this point, the only place that could be leaking is the connection between your oxygen cylinder and the regulator. If you have any leaking, unscrew the regulator from the cylinder. Clean the fittings with a clean dry cloth. Examine the fittings for scratches. If the tank seat is damaged, take it back to the supplier. If everything looks okay, fit the regulator back into the tank valve connection and screw down a little tighter this time on the regulator nut.

If you can open the oxygen cylinder valve and do not hear any sustained leaks, you should see the cylinder pressure gauge slowly register the pressure inside the cylinder. **Remember that you have to completely open the oxygen on/off valve to prevent leakage around the valve stem.** No pressure should show on your low pressure gauge at this time. Now slowly screw down on your regulator-adjusting handle. After you start to feel resistance on the adjusting handle, you should start to see pressure register on the low pressure gauge. Set it in the 5-10 psig range for a surface mixed torch.

If you hear a leak at this point, first check to see that your torch oxygen valve is turned off. If it is, check to see that the oxygen hose is connected properly to all fittings and that there are no holes in it. Check also to see that all your hose clamps are tight. Try closing the oxygen cylinder valve and seeing if you can detect any perceptible drop in the pressure reading on the high pressure gauge. If you see movement but cannot hear anything, leak check your fittings with liquid detergent and water to find the leak as will be described shortly.

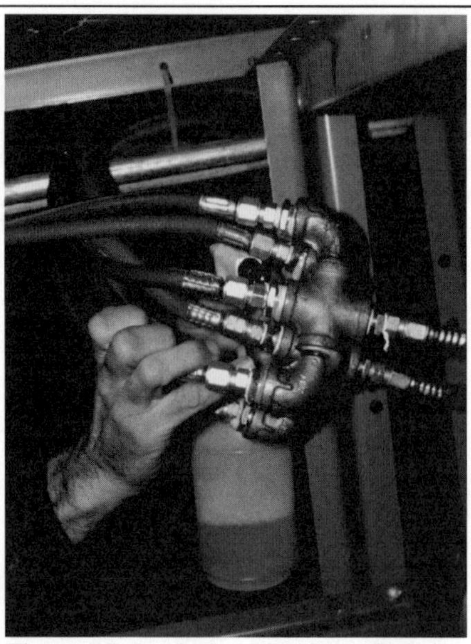
Figure 75. Leak checking hose fittings.

Let's now check out how your torch valves operate. Don't worry about releasing a little oxygen in this operation as it is perfectly safe to do so and you will only lose a few cents worth. Think of your torch valves as water faucets. The further you open a faucet, the more water flows out and the faster it rushes out. Now, try slowly opening and closing your torch oxygen valve. Listen to the sound of the oxygen flow as you open and close it. Observe how you don't have to close the valve very hard to stop the gas flow. Get a feel for this. Your propane valve operates exactly the same way, but you do not want to play with it like this because you would be releasing propane out into your workplace, creating a possible explosive hazard.

Once you feel comfortable with the operation of your torch valves, you are ready to proceed on to the next step, turning on the propane. Check to see that the torch propane valve is closed. Reach down and open the propane tank on/off valve between one to two full turn, no more. This allows plenty of flow but makes closing the tank quicker in an emergency. Take a second to listen and smell for any leaks. If you detect any gas, quickly check to see if the torch valve is open. If not, immediately close the tank on/off valve and check over all the propane connections. Those of you with T handle adjustable regulators will now adjust it to the proper pressure. For a surface mixed torch, you generally keep the oxygen to gas ratio at about 2 to 1.

Once you have corrected any gross leaks, again open the tank valves. Check all your fittings and tubing for small leaks by painting or spraying a solution of liquid dish detergent in water on them as shown in Figure 75. Of course, you will probably not have as many fittings clustered together as can be seen in the figure. But if you see any bubbles, then you have a leak at that joint that must be fixed before lighting the torch. If you don't detect any leaks, then you are ready to go. This procedure should be repeated any time you disconnect and reconnect your fittings. You do this on your propane fittings for two reasons. First, to prevent explosive propane hazards. Second to prevent biological hazards of propane. Propane vapors can give you a terrible headache or worse in large exposures. You check your oxygen fittings for leaks to prevent wasting oxygen.

With these procedures completed, we are now ready to proceed on with discussing how to light your fuel-oxygen torch.

Lighting the torch

Flint strikers are the tools used by most artists to light their torches. Strikers are inexpensive and very reliable once you become accustomed to them. To light the torch with a striker, hold it a couple inches in front of the tip of the torch with the hollow of the cup facing the tip of the torch as shown in Figure 76. Open the gas valve on the torch slightly by turning it about one quarter turn counterclockwise or less. Any further may cause the flame to deflect off the cup once lit and may lead to burns.

Now light the gas in the cup by immediately squeezing the arms of the striker together. This scrapes the flint across the file in the cup and strikes a spark. You may want to practice this ahead of time because it is not quite as easy as it sounds.

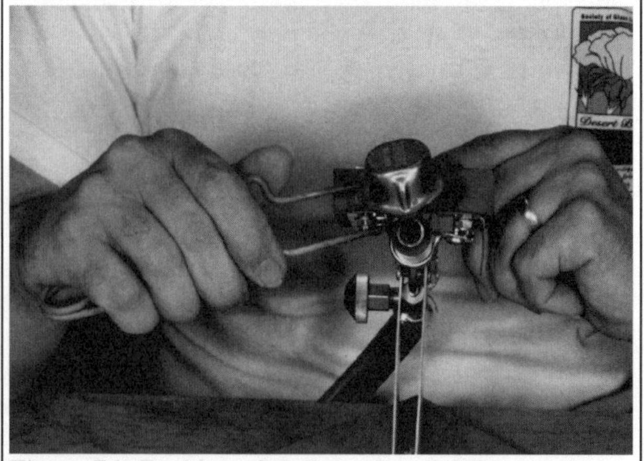
Figure 76. Position of striker when lighting torch.

You should be able to get a spark every time you try because as you are trying to light the torch, the propane is continuing to be released. If you take too long to get a good spark, enough propane will build up around the end of the torch to cause a flameup that can be frightening as well as dangerous.

There are a number of problems that can occur when using a striker. If you are not familiar with their use, you may not exert enough force on the arm to hold the flint against the file. Without that contact, you cannot strike a spark. Also, if your flint has worn down, you may not get a spark. In this case, you will need to replace the flint by unscrewing it and screwing on a new one. I have also had a problem with some strikers where the flint gets caught at the leading edge of the file and cannot be pulled across it. This problem can be fixed by bending the little bar at the left side of the file slightly inward so that the flint does not get trapped in the gap at the leading edge of the file.

Operation of an electronic lighter is similar. Open the torch fuel valve such that the flow of gas is low. Then depress the button on the lighter and the high voltage arc should light the flame. If it doesn't work, immediately turn off the propane and check to see if the lighter is arcing. A weak battery may be the culprit. They have to be changed after about 50 hours of use. You may also have had the gas on too high. These lighters are more expensive initially and over their lifetime than the flint strikers. But their ease of operation may make them worth it to you, especially if you are having trouble getting the hang of using the flint striker and are being constantly exposed to those frightening flameups.

If you decide to use one of the butane lighters, ignite the pilot flame on the lighter by first turning on the gas and pulling the trigger. Next, open the gas supply to the torch and immediately light it with the pilot flame. Then, let go of the trigger and turn off the gas to the lighter. Remember to put this lighter off to the side, outside of your work area, and well away from hot glass before starting to work.

If this is the first time that you have had the torch lit, and you have a pancake propane regulator, you should now go through the procedure for adjusting the propane regulator that was explained in the previous chapter on regulator operation. Otherwise, let's proceed onward and learn more about how to use your torch.

Flame chemistry

Before we start working with your torch flame, let's briefly discuss what is going on in there to help you better understand what is happening as you stick glass in the flame. This understanding will also allow you to better control the results you get using your torch.

We have already discussed some of the fundamentals on fuels and their properties. Basically, the chemical energy that is contained in the fuel gas that we use releases heat when it is burned with oxygen to produce carbon dioxide and water vapor. In chemistry short hand this would be written as:

$$1\ C_3H_8 + 5\ O_2 \rightarrow 3\ CO_2 + 4\ H_2O + 2200\ \text{kcal/mole}$$

propane+ oxygen → carbon dioxide + water + energy

As you may remember from your high school chemistry, the numbers out in front of each molecular formula indicate how many of the molecules take place in the complete reaction and the lower numbers tell us how many of each kind of atom (C=carbon, O=oxygen and H=hydrogen) are in the molecule.

So what does all this tell us? First, you can see that we need five times as much oxygen as propane to get complete combustion. Do you think that your torch is providing that much oxygen? Well its not and we will get into that later. The other thing that we see is that heat energy is released in the process. How much energy is released depends upon the comparison of how much energy is in the bonds between the atoms of the reactants compared to that in the bonds of the products.

In actuality, the combustion process is really a two-step one. The first step consists of breaking apart the propane molecule and partially burning it to carbon monoxide with the released hydrogen recombining to form hydrogen gas. In our chemistry shorthand this is written as

$$1\ C_3H_8 + 1.5\ O_2 \rightarrow 3\ CO + 4\ H_2 + 225\ \text{kcal/mole}$$

This is the portion of combustion that occurs in your inner blue or primary flame at the face of the torch. It is the region where the oxygen that you supply to the torch is used. As you supply more or less oxygen this part of the flame will shorten or lengthen. The tip of the primary flame is the hottest part of the flame.

The second step of the combustion process completes the burn of the carbon monoxide to carbon dioxide and of the hydrogen gas to water vapor. This step is expressed as

$$3\,CO + 4\,H_2 + 3.5\,O_2 \rightarrow 3\,CO_2 + 4\,H_2O + 1895 \text{ kcal/mole}$$

This reaction step occurs in the portion of the flame, called the outer or secondary flame. The oxygen for this step comes from the air around you and you can see that we use twice as much oxygen here than in the inner flame. Looking at these equations the first question that you probably have is that if more energy is released in the outer flame, why isn't it this the hottest part of the flame? The reason for this is that the energy production is spread out over a much larger volume and this volume is larger because the oxygen has to be drawn into it by mixing with the air around it.

The flame temperature is a physical property of the fuel gas based upon the molecular structure of the material and is usually quoted at the two points listed in the Table 17, neutral flame temperature and maximum flame temperature. Neutral flame temperature is that inside a properly adjusted neutral flame while maximum flame temperature is the maximum that can be reached in a highly oxidizing flame. These temperatures are usually calculated because there is no easy method to measure them.

In your flame there is a race going on between how fast the gases are coming out of the torch and the speed of the flame front burning the gas. This is reflected in the length of the inner flame. The longer the inner flame the faster the gas is moving. If the gas were coming out at the same speed as the flame speed then the burn front would be approximately right at the face of the torch. Here the gases would be moving about 12 ft/s or 8 mph. Since our inner flames are not burning here you can see that the gases are moving much faster.

You can affect the length and shape of the inner flame coming from each orifice by speeding up the gas velocity. You do this by upping the pressure on the regulator. When you up the pressure to the torch, the flame will become more pointed. This pointiness indicates the speed distribution of the gas coming out of the orifice. The gas coming out of our torches is essentially in something called laminar flow. This means that all the gas molecules are essentially moving in the same direction because they have just come out of a long tube. But they are moving at somewhat different speeds. The gas near the wall of the tube is moving slower because of the friction of the gas along the wall of the tube. That in the center is moving the fastest. There is also friction within the gas that then establishes how much faster adjacent molecules can be moving. This results in establishing a gradient of gas velocities in the flow. As seen in Figure 77, at low speed the flame will look blunted. At higher speeds it becomes more and more pointed.

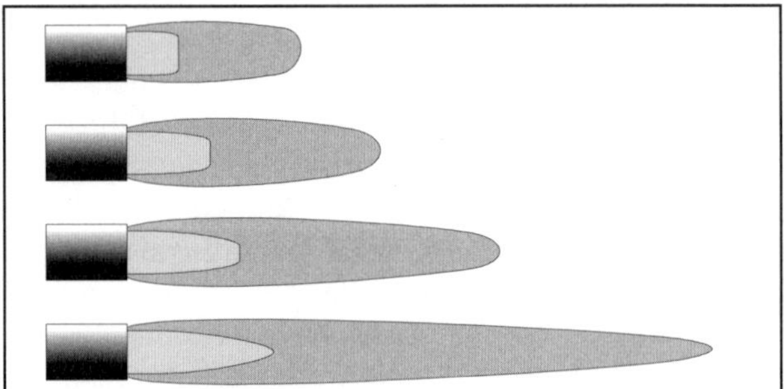

Figure 77. How inner and outer flame would look as you increase gas speed for a single orifice.

This might be important if you want a small detail flame. Increasing the gas pressure slightly allows using a smaller flame with enough velocity to keep combustion away from the face of the torch. This reduces carbon build up on the face of the torch. Higher velocity pointed flames also are a harder flame pushing more heat into the glass and thus are good for working harder glass. Be careful though, because if you increase the gas velocities so high that the flame leaves the face of the torch, it can

Table 17. Table of Fuel Gas Parameters

Fuel Gas	Molecular Formulae	Heat of Combustion		Max Flame Temp		Neutral Flame Temp	
		MJ/m^3	BTU/ft^3	°C	°F	°C	°F
Acetylene	C_2H_2	55	1470	3102	5612	3100	5612
MAPP Gas#	C_3H_4	91	2460	2902	5255	2600	4712
Propane	C_3H_8	104	2498	2777	5030	2450	4442
Propylene	C_3H_6	89	2400	2857	5174	2500	4532
Natural Gas (Methane)	CH_4	37	1000	2742	4967	2350	4260
Hydrogen	H_2	12	325	2871	5200	2390	4334

Methylacetylne-propadiene (stabilized)

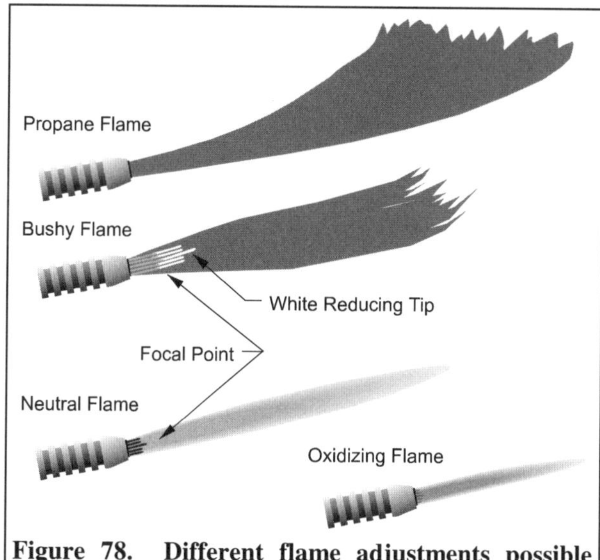

Figure 78. Different flame adjustments possible with a fuel-oxygen torch.

become unstable and can go out unexpectedly while continuing to spew propane and oxygen into your workspace.

Another thing that you will notice in some torches is that you will be going along fine with a nice flame and you add just a little bit more gas to it and the flame all of a sudden goes weird on you with flames going everywhere. What has happened is that the flow just became turbulent. The gas molecules are no longer all moving in the same direction. This can happen if the design of the torch has not been optimized correctly or if the face of the torch has gotten dinged. The National 8M suffers from this problem.

The other thing that I am sure that you know we can control in the flame is its chemistry. We can make it more reducing or oxidizing by changing the oxygen-to-propane ratio as we adjust the flame.

Adjusting the flame

Slowly open the propane valve until you have a yellow flame about 4 to 6 inches long as shown in the top of Figure 78. This produces a flame that varies in color from yellow at the face of the torch to orange-red in its outer reaches. The flame may be a little smoky or sooty because without any oxygen the propane is not being completely burned. This is called a **propane flame** and about the only thing that this flame is ever used for is to purposely apply a layer of soot onto a borosilicate sculpture that you then burn off during flame annealing. Burning off the soot aids in gauging that you have added the proper amount of annealing heat into the piece. This flame is also very reducing and will cause the metal oxides that color your glass to be reduced (lose oxygen) and change color.

Open the oxygen valve on the torch slowly. Soon, you will get a flame that looks like the second picture in Figure 78. Be careful not to add the oxygen too quickly or you might blow out the flame, in which case you have to turn off the gas valve on your torch and start over. This flame is a **bushy flame.** A soft outer blue flame will surround the inner flame. This soft reducing flame is called "bushy" because it has very little force and it has a relatively low temperature. It is a good flame for reducing the metal oxides in reduction frits to make them shiney

As more oxygen is added the inner flame will continue to shrink and will divide into two portions. A bright section next to the torch face that changes to a pale-green streamer that trails out in a pointed manner into the outer blue flame. This streamer is an indication that the flame still has an excess of propane in it and will disappear as the flame approaches a neutral flame. This flame has more force to it and will still reduce sensitive colors of glass. It is called a **reducing flame**.

Add some more oxygen to the flame and the blue cone will become more pronounced and draw in toward the tip of the torch. At the same time, the white tip will also become smaller. When the flame looks about like the third picture in the figure, it is what is referred to as a **neutral flame**. This is the flame that has a oxygen-to-propane ration of 1.5/1. The blue tips have been reduced to about one quarter of an inch in length and are relatively equal in length. It can be safely used on your colored glass without worry of reducing it. It is also the type of flame most commonly used in beadmaking and the portion of the flame that you will be working in is about two thirds of the way out in the flame. It is a harder flame and its inner flame will appear more blunted and will no longer trail into a soft point. Discerning between this flame and an oxidizing flame is difficult because they have a similar appearance.

Adding still more oxygen will result in a more pointed flame called an **oxidizing flame** as is seen in the bottom illustration in Figure 78. As you add more oxygen to get this pointed flame, you will also begin to notice that your minor burner will get a little hissy from the oxygen flow. This flame can be used for detail work where you want to limit the area over which the flame is applied. You can also quickly get a small pointed oxidizing flame from a neutral flame by cutting the propane flow of a neutral flame.

If you add too much oxygen and propane by setting the pressure regulator too high, you can start to get your flame to separate from the torch face. As mentioned earlier, avoid this kind of situation because it is unstable and may result in you flame blowing out. If this happens sometime at your normal operating pressure, check your orifices because they may be partially plugged.

Experiment with adjusting both the propane and the oxygen. Watch how the flame changes size and shape. Play with this enough to become familiar with the variety of flame shapes available to you. Usually, one shape is best for a particular operation you may be doing. Through experience, you will learn to be able to quickly adjust your torch to get the flame that you desire. Another thing to be aware of is that different portions of the flame are hotter than others. The focal point is the hottest part and you should be working out past it. The normal working position is two thirds of the way out in the flame. The area closer to the torch is more reducing and working here may change the color of your glass as well as possibly boiling it. As you move toward the edges of the flame, it is cooler and good for slow heating. Figure 79 illustrates where you should work in a neutral flame for various operations.

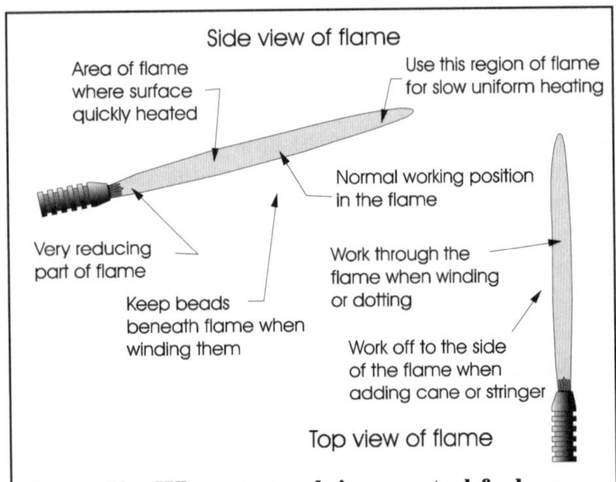

Figure 79. Where to work in a neutral fuel-oxygen torch flame for different processes.

One common mistake that beginners make is that they concentrate so intensely on manipulation of the beads and glass rods, that they completely forget about the possibilities open to them through flame adjustment or operating in different positions in the flame. Try to be aware of your flame and adjust it as needed to make your work easier. In most of your beadmaking work, a medium flame with blue cones about one quarter of an inch long are indicative of the proper size flame. Also, listen to the noise generated by your torch. A noisy flame probably has too much oxygen.

Shutting off your equipment

Shutting off your torch is a lot simpler than turning it on. The only thing that you need to remember is to turn off the oxygen first and then the propane. If you reverse this order, you can get a loud popping on premixed torches. Again, do not overtighten the valve knobs on your torch or you can damage the valve seats. Then turn off the fuel gas and oxygen at the tanks and unscrew the adjustment handle on the oxygen regulator and the propane regulator (if it has one).

Lastly, bleed any pressure from the hoses by opening the torch valves one at a time. To avoid releasing propane vapors into your workplace, you may want to burn these up as you bleed off the propane pressure. Remember to close them before starting up next time.

General torch care tips

After you have been using your torch for a while (about one half hour or so), you may notice a build up of some glowing material on the end of the torch. This build up is carbon and should be cleaned off to prevent the possibility of transferring it to your beads. It is cleaned off by scraping your tweezers or any other tool, but not glass, across the face of your torch. You do not have to turn off your torch when you do this, but be aware that this may produce a snapping sound so don't let it bother you.

You will also be developing a build up of carbon in your torch. A small cleaning tool is usually included with your torch to ream this out. You should do this regularly but do not attempt to do this while the torch is running. This may seem obvious, but I have been told of one instance where this was done and the tip cleaner melted off inside and ruined the torch. Although, how that person was able to do this without getting themselves burned is beyond my comprehension. The tip cleaner that comes with the torch is kind of wimpy, so, you might want to invest in a better set of tip cleaners, like those seen in Figure 80. These can be purchased at a welding supply house. Just run them in and out of the holes in the tip of the torch to clean them.

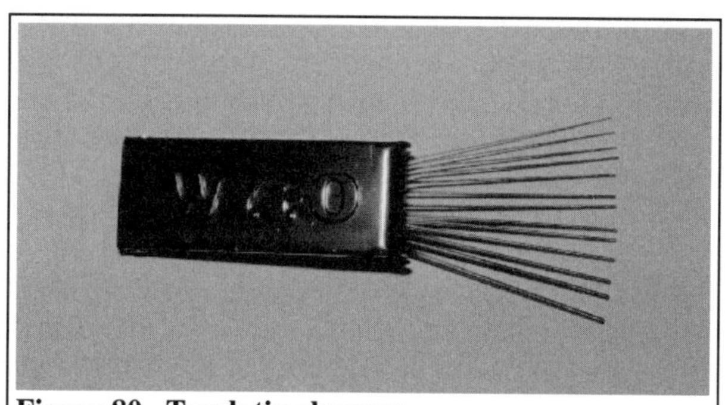
Figure 80. Torch tip cleaners.

If you should happen to get some glass on the tip of your torch while you are making beads, immediately turn off your torch. Cool it off and clean any glass off the tip. This may require a sharp tool like a knife so be careful. If you don't do this, the hot glass can wick into the tip of your torch and block the holes in the tip, possibly causing irreparable damage to it.

Glass manipulation basics

Now that you know how to safely operate your torch and a little about different types of glass, you are ready to start working glass in a flame. In this first section, you will start to develop an understanding of how glass behaves in a flame and some basic flameworking techniques that you will need in order to become proficient. After that, you will practice these skills by making some components that can be used later on in decorating your beads. At that point, we will move into different beadmaking techniques.

Holding the glass

In most lampworking situations and in beadmaking, you will hold the glass rod feed stock in your dominant hand. Your right hand, if you are right-handed, or your left, if you are left-handed. How you hold it in that hand depends on what operation you are doing at the moment. In some operations you will hold the glass rod like a pencil, in others you will hold it like a tennis racket. In all cases, though, you will hold it lightly not firmly.

You will have to get used to rotating the rod in the flame when you start to work with molten glass. The rod should be rotated constantly during heating for two reasons. The first is to evenly heat the rod around its circumference, which allows glass to flow uniformly. If you only heat one side of the rod, the other side will not flow or stretch. This can cause the glass to pull and exert force on objects to which you are trying to add glass. The other reason that you need to rotate the glass rod as you heat it is to prevent the heated glass from sagging under the influence of gravity. As the glass forms a molten drop on the end of your rod, it will want to bend down and drip off. By rotating the rod, down continually changes direction and the drop stays centered on the end of the rod.

Some artists like Jim Smircich can get by without rotating the rod as they apply glass to a bead. They do this by super heating the end of the feed rod so that the glass just runs off of it. This can take a lot of practice and therefore is not for everyone, but it can be done. Rotating the rod is the more common practice because it is easier to control, especially for beginners.

Now that you know why you want to rotate the rod, you need to learn how to rotate it. In the **pencil grip**, you rotate the rod by sliding it between your thumb and ring finger while using the index finger to steady the rod as shown in Figure 81. Here the rod is rolled by sliding the thumb back toward the palm of the hand and the ring finger is slid away from the palm. During this motion, each finger will move between a quarter and a half of an inch. At this point, the thumb is lifted and moved back out to the starting position while the rod is temporarily held in position between the index finger and the ring finger. The thumb is then placed back against the rod and holds it against the index finger. Lastly, the ring finger slides back to its original position and we are ready to start the whole motion over again. In actual

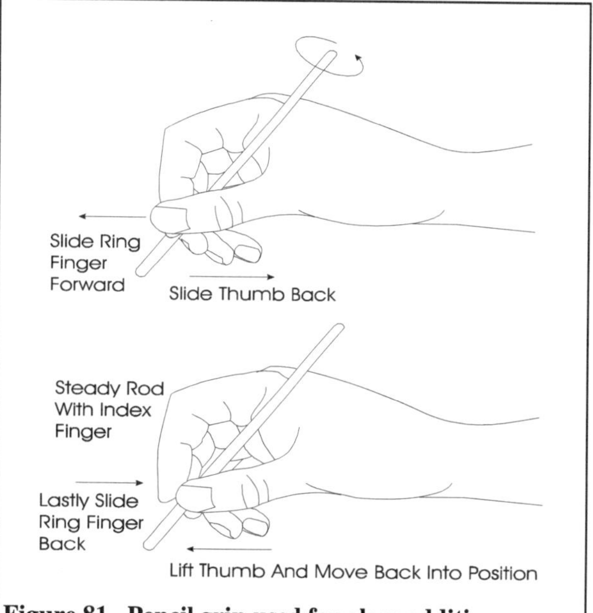

Figure 81. Pencil grip used for glass addition.

practice, this becomes one continuous motion. The process is hard to describe but with a little practice you will understand it and the motion will become automatic. It is easier to do once it becomes automatic and you stop thinking about it. This is the grip that we use when adding glass to a bead or decorating it.

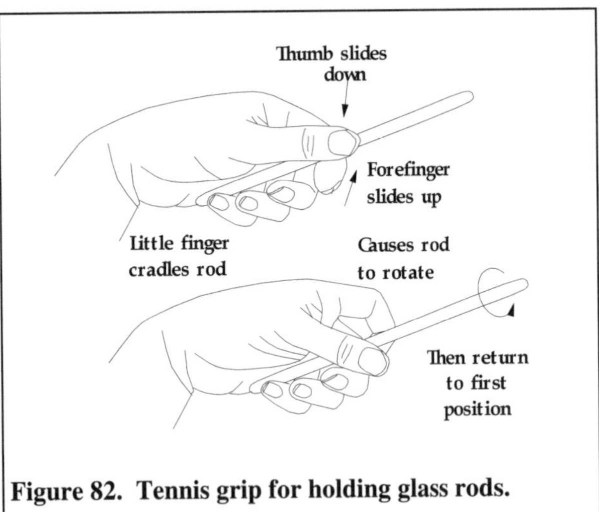

Figure 82. Tennis grip for holding glass rods.

In the **tennis racket grip**, the motion is a little bit different and a lot easier. Here, the rotation is accomplished by rolling the rod between your thumb and your index finger as illustrated in Figure 82. The thumb, which is pointing toward the end of the rod, slides downward while the index finger and maybe also the ring finger, which are pointing downward perpendicular to the rod, slide upward. The rod rotates between them while at the same time being cradled between the remaining fingers and the palm of your hand. This cradling allows both the thumb and the index finger to be lifted and moved back to the starting position simultaneously without losing control of the rod. We primarily use this grip when we are gathering glass on the end of a rod.

Heating the glass

Now that you know how to hold and rotate a rod, let's discuss how to safely get it into the flame without thermal shocking the glass. This has to be done before you can work with it. Thermal shock happens when heating builds up stress in the glass larger than it can withstand and it shatters. As explained earlier, this is a problem mainly in the low temperature regime where glass still reacts as a brittle solid. So the objective is to heat the glass rod slowly through this regime and on into the non-brittle solid regime where all stress flows easily through the material. This is especially important with filigrana and aventurine because they seem to have a lot of residual stress in them. Thermal shock is also more common with large diameter glass rods or rods with freshly cut ends. Strips cut from sheet glass, as our dichroic beadmakers are well aware, can also be a problem.

There are three general ways that I know of to preheat your glass to flame temperature. The first is to take the glass rod in your dominant hand in a tennis grip and wave it in and out of the flame. You will want to start out near the end of your flame where it is cooler. Do this until you can start to see the sodium flare over the top of your didymium glasses. Some types of glass will also change color as they heat up which serves as additional indications of correct preheat. As the glass heats up, slow down your waving and bring it into the working point, about two thirds of the way out in your flame. The tip of the glass rod should start to glow. At this point, you can stop waving the glass and hold it in the flame. As the end of the rod becomes molten, you would start rotating it.

Another way to introduce the glass into the flame is to start by holding the glass rod way out at the end of the flame. As it starts to change color or glow a little bit, you can slowly slide it through the flame toward you until you get it into the proper working position. The last and easiest way to preheat your glass is to have a section of your hot plate or annealer available to do this. Some annealers come with little racks to help balance the portion of the rod that protrudes out of it. Just set the rod down here and let it get hot. Be careful of short rods, which may become too hot to handle.

With some glasses or operations, you may have to heat up more than just the tip of the rod. You may have to heat up as much as an inch of the end of the rod to prevent getting thermal shock. You can do this by plunging the rod repeatedly into the flame and pulling it back out instead of waving it.

Gathering

The first step in building many decorative glass components is to gather a molten glob of glass at the end of a rod. The gather is made up of glass from the rod itself that is collected and held at the end of a rod as it melts. This is achieved, as illustrated in Figure 83, by introducing the rod into the flame as was just explained and keeping the end in the flame. By rotating the rod, you can keep the molten drop that starts to form at the end from dropping off. As you keep the end of the rod in the

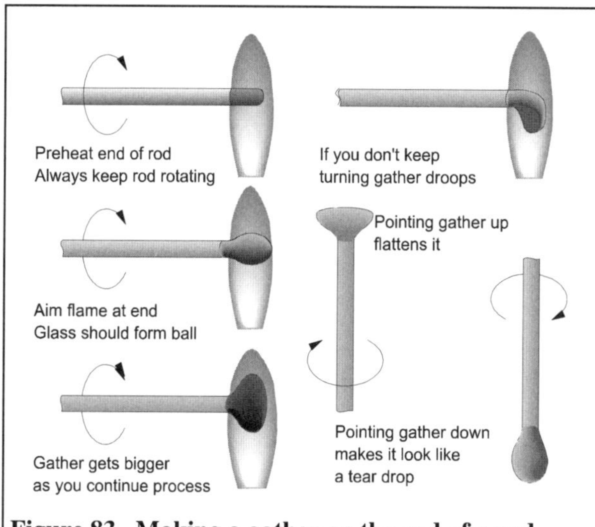

Figure 83. Making a gather on the end of a rod.

flame longer and longer, more of the rod will melt and become part of the drop at the end of the rod. In most beadmaking situations, you will not gather more than about a $^3/_8$" diameter drop before using it. With practice of your rotating skills, gathering this much and more will be simple.

There are also times that you might want to develop a gather somewhere else along the rod, rather than at the end. To do this, hold the rod in one hand and introduce it into the flame at the point where you want to form the gather. You do this by slowly waving this point through the flame just as if it were the end of your rod. As you get it to the point where you can continuously to hold it in the flame, you want to grab the other end of the rod with your other hand. Start rotating the rod with both hands to keep it from drooping as it gets soft.

As the center softens, you will have to be careful to rotate both ends at the same speed or the gather will be twisted and distorted. As it melts, you can speed up the gathering process by gently pushing the two ends of the rod together as you rotate them. When the gather is of the desired size, lift it out of the flame and continue rotating it while you allow it to cool. Rotation is necessary because it can still droop at this point. Also, you may want to be careful to keep the two ends of the rod aligned as the gather cools.

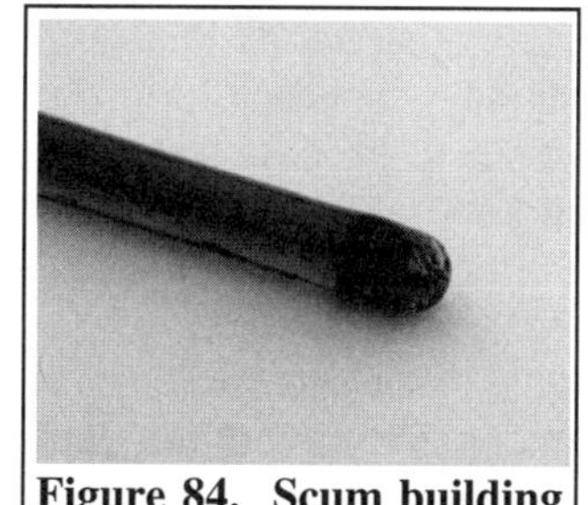

Figure 84. Scum building upon the end of a rod.

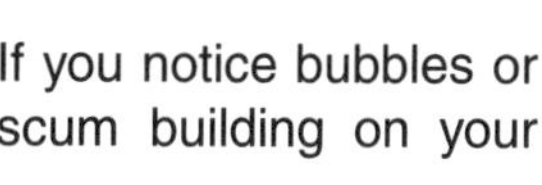

If you notice bubbles or scum building on your gather as seen in Figure 84, this is an indication that you are overheating the glass. To prevent this, you need to work out further in the flame from the tip of the torch. Remember the ideal location to work is about two thirds of the way out in the flame.

Joining rods

One way to practice gathering is by joining two shorter rods together to make a longer one. This will allow you to use up all those short rod ends that you will soon be generating. Practicing this skill will help improve both your rotating and your gathering skills, as well as your whole feeling for how the glass responds in a flame. To do this, cut two short pieces, each about six inches long, from one of your rods. Take one piece in each hand and introduce an end of each into the flame as was explained earlier. Then, gather a small drop on each just barely bigger then the end of the rod.

If while doing this, one piece gets ahead of the other, just remove it from the flame for a few seconds or hold it out further in the flame. It can even be allowed to stop glowing and be put immediately back into the flame without thermal shock damage, but if the rod if left out of the flame too long, it might cool so much that slow reentry would be necessary. You will develop a feeling for this as you get more experienced. If not, the glass will let you know by shattering when you introduce it back into the flame.

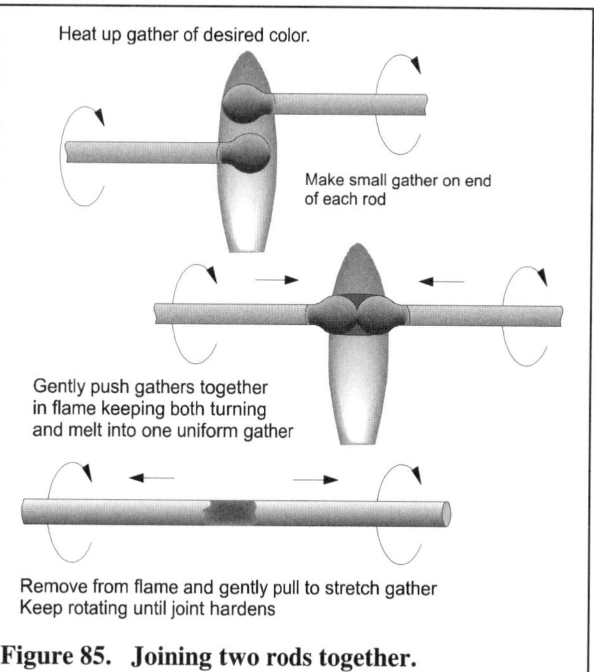

Figure 85. Joining two rods together.

After you have a small gather on the end of each of the rods, you are now ready to join them. Do this by bringing the two gathers together in the flame and holding them there just long enough for them to join together into one gather in the center of what is now one rod. While doing this, you will have to continue to rotate both rods to keep your gather from drooping. Once touched together, the rods have to be rotated at the same speed or the gather will twist and distort. Increase the size of the gather until it gets to be just slightly larger than the rod diameter.

Once the gather at the junction is the right size, remove it from the flame. Lifting it up is the easiest way to do this. Continue rotating both rods while also keeping the aligned until the glow starts to go away at the joint. Then gently pull on the ends of both rods just enough to shrink the gather down to the original diameter of the rod. Keep it aligned and rotating until it chills enough to become solid.

If your rod is not of uniform thickness, just stick the gather area back into the flame, reform the gather and try again. If it is not straight, lightly reheat it and hang it straight. This skill will allow you to use any short rod ends without burning yourself.

Drawing points

There are times in beadmaking when you might want a small glass point, a narrowed down section of rod, to apply glass in a controlled manner or to use as a tool in manipulating a bead. There are two ways to draw such a point: either from a gather at the end of a rod or from one in the middle of the rod.

To draw a point from a gather at the end of a rod, start by forming such a gather. Then grab another rod with your other hand. Pull the gather out of the flame and touch it to the cold rod. Give it a second or two to chill and then slowly pull it away from the cold rod. The slower that you pull it away, the thicker the point will be that you draw out of the gather. Larger gathers and longer points might require you to rotate the rod slightly while pulling.

When the point is of the desired length, hold it stretched out for a couple seconds to allow it to get hard before you put it down. Once cool, you should be able to break the point free from the cold rod because it will not have formed a good joint. If the other rod had been hot, this would not be the case. Alternately if you grab this end with some cold tweezers, it should chill fast enough to thermal shock and will break off at this point.

You can pull longer points from a rod, which are called either stringer or cane depending upon the diameter, by continuing to heat the first rod as you pull the point from the end of gather with the second rod. This process is illustrated in Figure 86. To start, heat the rod on the other side of the gather from the point. The gather itself is just outside of the flame. Continue to feed more rod into the flame as you continue to pull cane from the gather. This can be tricky until you perfect it.

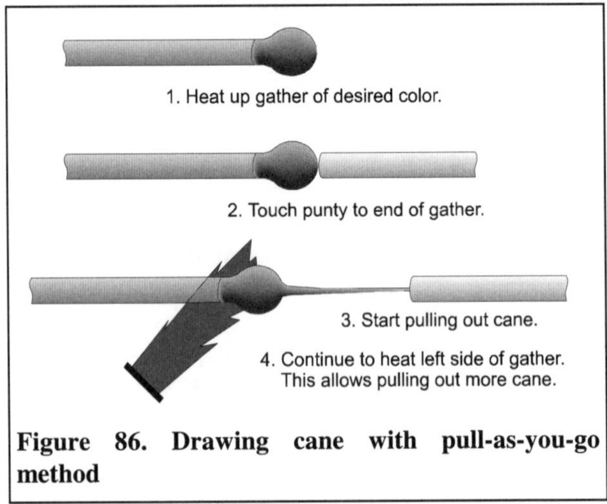

Figure 86. Drawing cane with pull-as-you-go method

To pull a point from the middle of a rod, start by forming a gather there. Remove the gather from the flame while continuing to rotate both ends of the rod. Allow the gather to cool slightly and then slowly draw it out as in the previous case. When to the desired length, stop pulling and hold it outstretched a couple seconds to allow it to cool. Then break it in the middle and you have two points to use. Remember that the longer you wait before pulling and the slower that you pull, the thicker your point will be. Thin lengths of glass that you pull are called stringers and thicker ones are called canes.

Flame cutting

Flame cutting is very similar to drawing a point from a central gather. Start with a rod, get it into the flame and just to the point where the central area is starting to gather. Lift it out of the flame and pull just slightly. This will form a stretched region in the rod. Allow it to cool slightly and put this thinned out region back into the flame slightly more on one side than the other. This area, since it is thinner, will heat faster than the thicker region around it. If this region was made thin enough in the first draw by having minimized the gather, you should now be able to pull the pieces apart in the flame without much stringing.

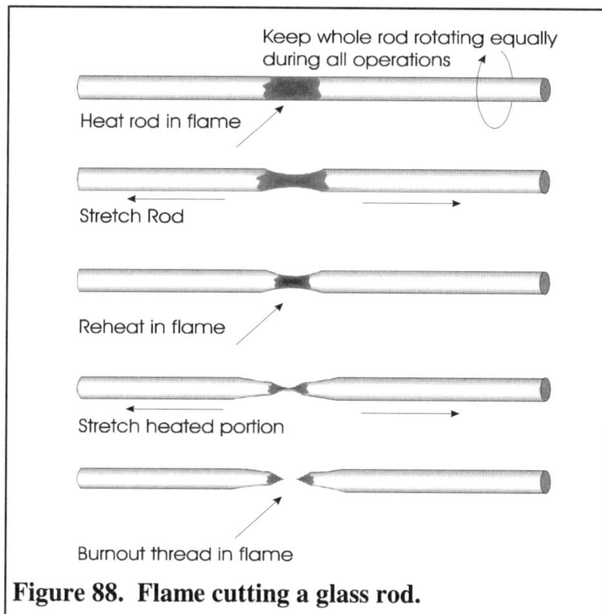

Figure 88. Flame cutting a glass rod.

If it is stringing out, wind the string around the other with a small circling motion. Do this until the flame burns through the string and then separate the two pieces. You may want to take a second to melt the string into a gather on the piece you wound it about before putting it down.

Punty use

There may be times when you have been working on a glass bead or a decoration on a glass rod and you want to work on the area where it is attached to the rod. To do this, you need to temporarily attach another rod to the bead at a different location to act as a handle. This handle is called a punty.

To attach a punty, you make a small gather at the end of a new rod and touch it to the bead at the desired location. This action is often referred to as puntying, but I am not sure if that is a real word. How permanent this attachment becomes depends upon how hot the bead was at the attachment point. If the bead was pretty warm, then the glass will flow from the rod to the bead and make a good permanent attachment.

But many times you do not want a permanent attachment. In those cases, you will keep the bead a little cooler so that material will not flow from the rod to the bead as readily. If you look closely at such a temporary punty joint, you will be able to see the temporary joint between the two. The glass on the punty will have drawn in at the attachment point, leaving a sharp meniscus all the way around that will be easy to crack off later, as shown at the bottom left of Figure 87.

If you want to make a more permanent attachment, get both the rod and the attachment point hot (slightly glowing) and press them together so that they form a slight bulge. Then gently pull on the joint until it contracts down to form a smooth joint as shown in the bottom right of the figure. If it still has some sharp undercut to it as in the bottom left picture, you will need to sharpen up your flame point and reheat this area. Sharp joints are crack initiators and will almost never last.

Sometimes the object that you are handling is so large that you want a pretty substantial and strong glass punty. But Effetre rods, if that is what you are working with, mainly come in about one quarter inch diameter, which are not quite big enough. What you can do here is use a large diameter pyrex rod as your punty. Compatibility is not a problem because you are going to remove it before it cools. Just be sure to remove all traces of the punty when you are done and throw away the last little bit of what you are making that was attached to the pyrex.

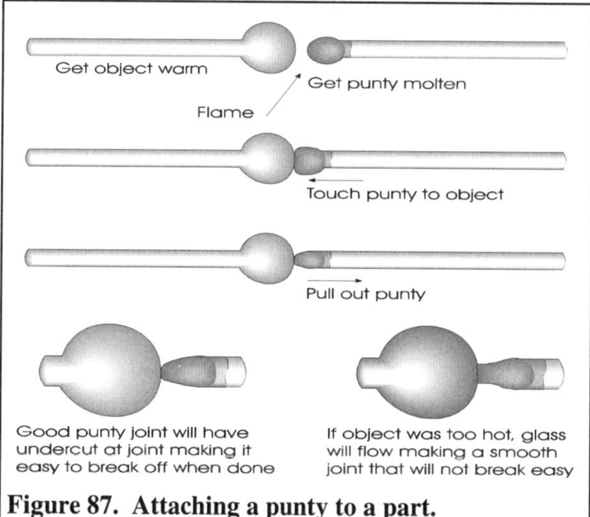

Figure 87. Attaching a punty to a part.

Pulling compatibility test threads

With the basic skills that you have just learned, you have the skills necessary to be able to test the compatibility of your glass. To do this, heat about the three-quarters of an inch of any two glass rods which you want to test for compatibility. Start to get a gather on the end of one of the rods and attach it to the other rod about one half of an inch from the end. Then fuse the two rods together by aiming the flame onto the joint between the two rods.

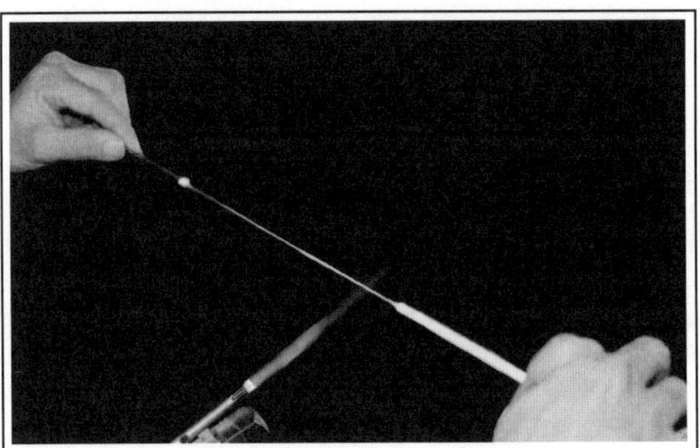
Figure 89. Pulling thread for a compatibility test.

Rotate the rods to evenly heat both sides of the joint. Heat one of the rods at the joint surface where it connects with the overlap area to soften it and move it down on center of the joint region between the two rods. These steps are the same as the initial steps used for making latticino that are illustrated in Figure 90. Refer to it if you are unclear on this explanation. Repeat this operation with the rod on the other end. Keep heating the overlap area of the two rods until the joint area contracts into a molten glob shaped like a football. While heating the joint, you will have to keep the two rods rotating to prevent them from drooping.

You have to also be careful to rotate them uniformly so that you do not develop any twist in the molten glass. You may find it helpful to tilt the rods back and forth to keep the glob in the right position. Also, if the center is hot but the ends are not fully joined, you may want to remove it from the flame to let the center cool down a little before working on the ends. Once you have properly heated and formed the glob, pull it out from the flame and let it cool slightly. You will have to continue to rotate the rods to prevent the glob from drooping.

Next, slowly pull the glob out into a long thin thread as in Figure 89 without twisting the glob as you do so. After it is stretched to full length, hold it tight for a few seconds until it solidifies. If you have done this right, you will have a long thin thread with a stripe of one color on one side of the thread and a stripe of the other color on the other side of the thread.

You want to make sure that the threads are circular in cross section and are equally divided between the two glasses. Break off the thread from both of the original rods and measure deflection of the thread. Then use this information as explained in the last chapter to determine the COE difference between the two glasses.

Flame annealing

When making large beads, a lot of stress can build up in the glass when one part of the bead is almost molten and the other end is solid. Also, there may be times that you spend a lot of time on one portion of a bead, while the rest of the bead is cooling. In these cases, the stress may get so large that the bead can crack during its initial cooling before it can be kiln annealed.

To help prevent this, you should flame anneal your beads out in the outer reaches of your flame before burying it in the vermiculite or sticking it into the annealer. Get the bead uniformly hot just at or below the temperature where it starts to glow (the dull red state). If you start building up soot or getting a color change in your bead, the flame is too reducing and you need to add just a little more oxygen to it.

After you have heated the bead uniformly, pull it out of the flame and allow it to cool slightly, so that it is not glowing. To be able to see when the glow has gone away, it helps to hold the bead down in the shadow under your workbench. Once the glow disappears, bury the bead in your heated vermiculite or your annealer to let it finish cooling. If you put the bead into the vermiculite or annealer when it is too hot, the vermiculite or kiln floor will dent or stick to it. The pot of vermiculite should be heated to about 300 to 400°F to slow down cooling. Then when done for the day, turn off the hot plate under the vermiculite and allow it to cool for about one half hour, depending on the size of the bead, before you remove it. Be sure that you feel the top of the vermiculite to see how warm it is before you pull the bead out. Try to refrain from peeking at your masterpieces before they are cool, to prevent thermal shock. Kiln anneal them afterwards.

General glass manipulation comments

One thing to always be aware of when working on a bead or other glass construction is to keep the whole thing warm. Every once in a while go back and rewarm the whole project to about the dull red state if possible. It is very easy to get so absorbed in one area of decoration that you forget the rest of the bead and let it cool off. Nothing is worse than seeing your bead crack before your eyes as you rewarm a section that got just a little too cool. If you

Figure 91. Some examples of twisted canes
Artist: Al Janelle Size: $^{3}/_{16}$ to ¼" in diameter.

suspect that a portion of the bead has cooled off, try to reenter the flame gradually as if the bead were a cold rod of glass.

You can sometimes fix cracks by reheating the region to lightly glowing red, but this will mean loss of any surface details in the process. If you do not become aware of the crack until after the bead has cooled, you will have to reheat it in your annealer to the annealing point before grabbing your mandrel and bringing the bead into the flame for rework. Be careful because the mandrel will be hot. You may want to wear gloves for this and dip the mandrel in water to cool it right away.

Along those same lines, you can vary the viscosity of the glass through careful control of its temperature, such that it can be sculpted like clay. To do this, you really have to get a feel for reading the heat in the glass and where to heat it in the flame. Overheat it and the glass will run away from you. Control its heat well and you will be able to do anything with it. Heating the bead very fast will get the outside hot while leaving the inside relatively cool. To uniformly heat a bead, you have to heat it slowly out in the end of your torch flame, removing it from the flame occasionally to let the heat sink into the bead.

Component construction

As a way to practice some of the skills that you have just learned, you can make some constructions that can be used to decorate the beads that you will make later. We have already discussed pulling cane and stringer but there are many other decorations that can be premade. So let's discuss how to make a number of other kinds of decorative constructions.

Latticino or twisted canes

One of the easiest constructions that you can make to decorate your beads is a basic latticino. Latticino translates literally from Italian as "little milk-white glass strands." This describes the traditional latticino, which is made by twisting white and clear rods together to create small white candy cane stripes suspended in clear glass. Now-a-days beadmakers use almost any color combination imaginable to make similar twisted cane constructions, as seen in Figure 91. In this book, I have generalized the term latticino to apply to these structures too. All glass artists do not universally accept this generalization. Some prefer to call them twisted canes.

The overall latticino manufacturing process is illustrated in Figure 90. It is very similar to the process that was used in thread testing for compatibility. The process is as follows:

- Start by preheating about an inch of two rods and getting a gather on the end of each
- Attach them together with an overlap by touching a gather on one rod to the other rod about an inch in from the end of that rod.
- Bend the rod over to touch the gather on the other rod (a & b).
- Join the two rods in their overlap region by heating along the joint.
- Heat the rod handles and move them onto center (c).
- Melt the joined area down into a uniform glob that looks like a football.
- Lift the glob out of the flame continuing to rotate it to prevent droop.
- Let the glob cool slightly.

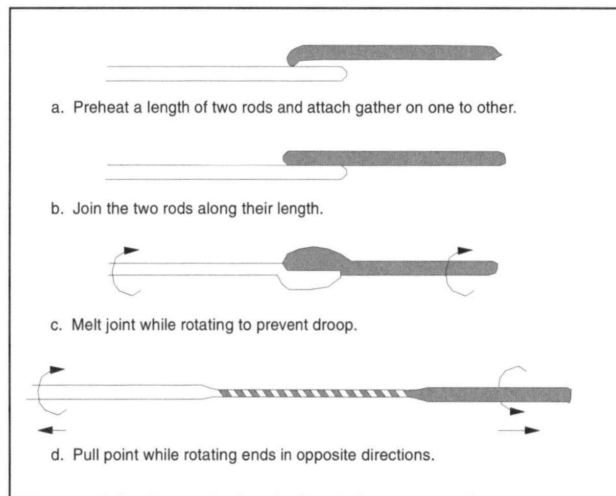

Figure 90. Steps in basic latticino manufacture.

- Start to introduce a counterclockwise twist by rotating one rod in one direction and the other in the opposite direction (d).
- Slowly pull the glob apart.
- Twist faster and faster as you stretch it farther and farther.
- When done, hold the latticino stretched out for a few seconds to allow it to finish hardening up.
- Cut the latticino up into manageable lengths of about a foot.

You can control the thickness of the latticino as you pull it out, just as you did in pulling points for cane. You do this by controlling the speed with which you pull it out of the glob. The slower that you pull it, the thicker it will be. Slightly thicker sections and ends can be pulled out some more by lightly reheating those sections in the edge of the flame and repulling. This can be tricky though, because the small diameter sections heat very quickly. It may help to hold the end on an angle in the flame as you reheat it.

There is another way to make a basic latticino besides the pull-all-at-once technique that we just described. This method is what I call the pull-as-you-go technique. For this technique, you get the two rods hot as you did before and join them together with an overlap of about an inch, but this time do not melt them into a ball. Instead get one end hot, then pull and twist out latticino again in a counterclockwise direction. Keep the flame off the region that you are pulling out, instead be preheating the area just ahead of that region. This is very similar to the pull-as-you-go cane techniques illustrated back in Figure 86.

This method can be made a little easier by holding the rod at angle to the flame because it allows preheating of a larger area. An advantage of this method of making latticino over the last is that the latticino can made with surface texture. By keeping the glass a little cooler, a texture resembling that of a rope can be developed that gives the latticino just a little more uniqueness when lightly fused onto the surface of a bead. A disadvantage of this technique is that it is a little harder to keep the latticino uniform as you pull it out.

The next technique can be done using a single short piece of rod, as illustrated in Figure 92. In this illustration, the rod we are using on is a piece of filigrana that looks really good when twisted and results in something like a traditional latticino. Here you heat the short piece of rod in the middle and

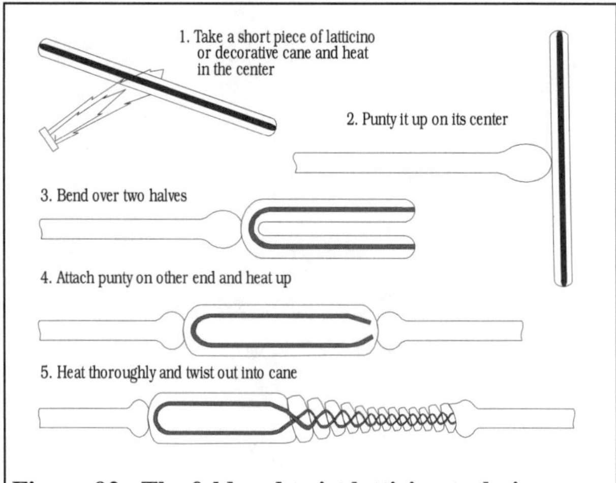

Figure 92. The fold and twist latticino technique.

punty up at this point onto another rod. Next, continue to heat the middle of the short rod, and bend it in half to bring the ends together and lightly join them along their length. Now attach a punty to the two ends. Heat up the whole length and pull it out while twisting at the same time, using either the pull-all-at-once or the pull-as-you-go technique.

As you make latticino, one problem you might have is that it will change from looking like a stripe of one color on the second to that of a stripe of the second color on the first. This problem usually comes from not moving the rods at the end of the overlap back on center or not shrinking the joint down uniformly into the football shape before pulling it out. One way to eliminate this problem, if you just can not make good latticino the normal way no matter how hard you try, is to join a short section of the second color to the center of a longer rod of the first. Then, when you pull it out, you will always have more of the background color than the stripe color and your latticino should look more consistent. Use this only as a short-term solution though and continue to try to make them the more "correct" way.

Latticino can also be made from more than just two colors. As an example, let's discuss making a latticino using three colors. To do this, start out by joining two rods together as before, but do not heat them up to form a glob. Instead, flame cut off the remaining portion of one rod. Now, add another color by heating a thick rod and attaching it along the joint of the first two rods. Move the attachment rods back onto center and work the three rods together into one glob by heating and melting the rods. Try to prevent trapping air down the center of the joint of the three rods by working the heat from one end to form the glob until you finally reach the other. The reason that you do not want to trap any

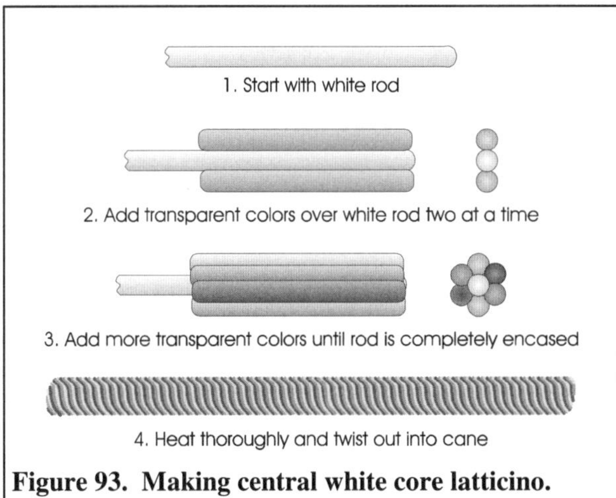

Figure 93. Making central white core latticino.

air bubbles is that they will pop and shatter the latticino when you reheat it to apply as decoration to your bead. Once you have the glob fully formed, you pull it out, pulling in a counterclockwise twist as before. Latticino can similarly be constructed from four colors, but after four colors the effect starts to be lost.

There are many different variations to the latticino theme. Basic latticino made from filigrana are very impressive looking. This makes a latticino with very fine well-defined lines that spiral around each other in a clear casing. Another variation is to make a rainbow colored latticino with a white or light core. The white core emphasizes the transparent colors. For example, a red, yellow, and blue white-core latticino could be made by applying sections of color onto a central white rod as shown in Figure 94. This process works best if all the glass rods are of the same diameter.

To make this latticino, you start by preheating the white rod and applying two stripes of transparent red on opposite sides of the central white core. Use the pencil grip on the red rod as you apply it, twisting slightly to evenly heat the rod. The thickness of the transparent layers can be controlled by how much you stretch and push the transparent rods as you apply them to the white rod beneath the flame. Next, paint two stripes of yellow alongside the two red stripes. Push the yellow rod down into the joint area between the white and red to try to completely fill the joint and not trap any air. Lastly, apply two stripes of blue, again pushing down slightly to completely fill the void between the red and yellow stripes. Attach a rod handle to the other end of the white core and heat up the striped area into a homogeneous blob. Then, twist it and pull it out like any other latticino.

Another variation you can make are latticinos with internal twisting ribbons. Al Janelle has a video that goes into this technique in great detail, in case you have questions after reading this explanation. To make this type of latticino, start by flattening out a large gather. Then pull it out into a short ribbon a little over an inch long. Get the end of the ribbon hot and square it off with your scissors. This will become the ribbon that will spiral down the center of the latticino. At this point, you can decorate the ribbon however you want. You could add stripes down the center or the sides, or any of a number of different options. The example, shown in Figure 94, has stripes added down the centers and the sides.

Once the ribbon is decorated, case the whole ribbon in clear glass by adding successive stripes of clear, pushing down to fill the voids. It helps to rock the clear rod back and forth in the flame to heat it evenly as you apply it. Remember to keep the whole ribbon warm as you do this. If it gets too warm and flops around on you, reshape and chill it slightly with your paddle. Eventually, you will get the ribbon encased in a big cylinder of clear glass as shown in the figure. Attach a handle on the other end and heat up the cylinder and pull it out into twisted cane using the pull-all-at-once or the pull-as-you-go technique. You will be able to see the ribbon twisting through this latticino. This type of latticino is good for creating any seaweed for underwater scenes or as leaf cane for floral scenes. Here, it looks good if the front and back of the ribbon are of slightly different shades of green.

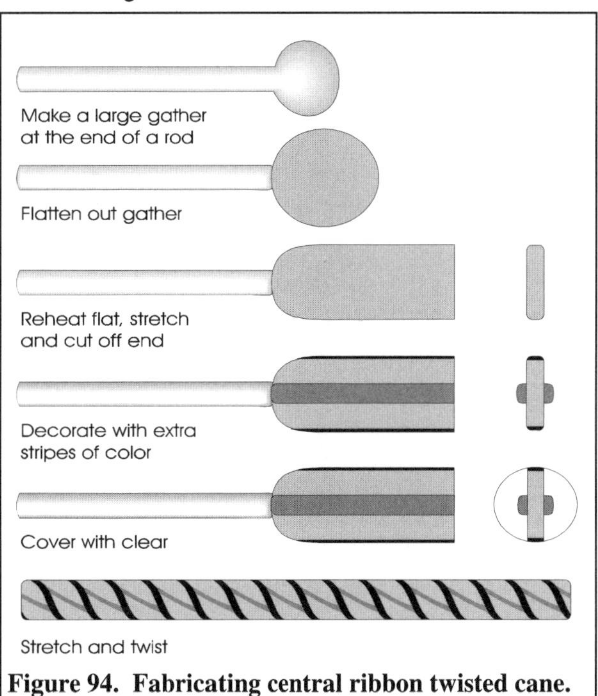

Figure 94. Fabricating central ribbon twisted cane.

If you have a crucible kiln, there is another way to make latticinos that we have not talked about. Take a couple glass rods at least two feet long. Wrap one end in some tape to hold them together. Then grab the wrapped end with a gloved hand and dip them into a crucible of clear glass as shown in Figure 95. Pull them out of the crucible and have a partner grasp the other end of the dipped rods with some pliers or a heated punty as is being readied here. Then, quickly twist the rods and gently draw the latticino out from them. You should be able to get several feet of latticino from each dip.

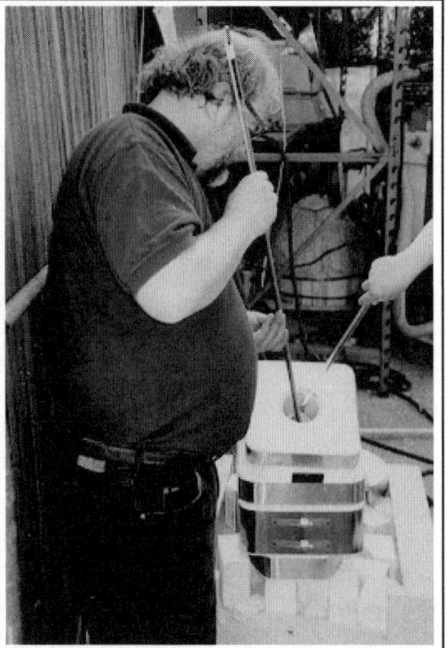

Figure 95. Dipping glass rods into crucible kiln to make latticino. Courtesy of Sundance Art Glass.

I have presented only a few of a myriad of latticino variations possible and how to make them, to get you started. Use these as a springboard to come up with your own designs. Some latticino are so beautiful in themselves that it is a shame to use them on a bead. When making jewelry, you could use that perfect latticino to make multi-colored dangles by fire polishing one end and making a loop in the other or by adding a metal cap. To make a loop, just heat up a small section of the latticino and bend it down on itself. Flame cut off the extra latticino. With a fine pointed flame, join the looped end to the main body of the latticino. Then shape the loop by lightly heating it in the flame and manipulating it with a reamer or pointed tweezers. This will be better described in the section on making looped pendants in a later chapter.

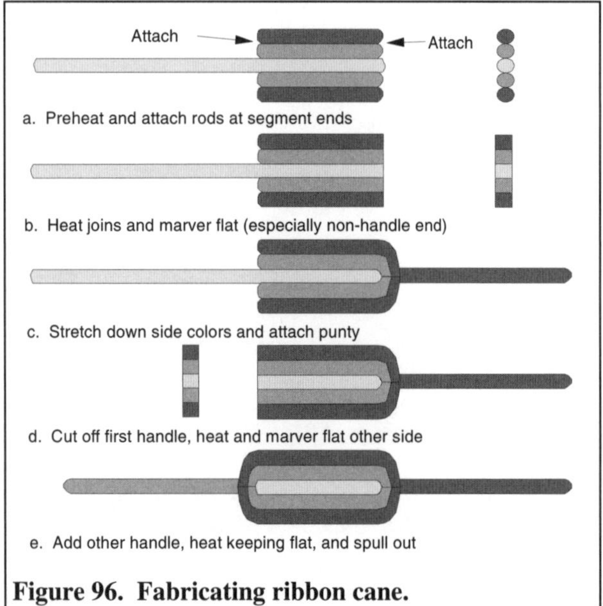

Figure 96. Fabricating ribbon cane.

Ribbons

A construction that is formed in a manner similar to latticino is ribbon. Here, you lay up a number of rods one on another as you did for latticino, but you keep the lay-up flat in a paddle-like arrangement as shown in part (a) of Figure 96. As you add each section of rod, you join them on the "paddle." Try to keep it hot and straight. You do not attach an additional handle at this time because it is easier to shape and flatten the ribbon on the marver without a handle. After you have added all the rod segments, you then heat the rods along the jointed areas and marver the ribbon flat (b). You want to remove all the creases between the rods to prevent the ribbon from stretching unevenly as you pull it out.

Now, attach a handle to the well marvered end. When you do this, pull down some of the outside colors as illustrated in the figure before attaching the new handle on center (c). Pulling the ends down helps the ribbon stretch more evenly when you pull it out later. Otherwise you can end up pulling the center out of the ribbon. Now, burn off the original handle and flatten that end of the paddle (d). When the whole paddle is flat, reattach the handle to that side, again pulling down some of the outer color, as shown in part (e) of the figure.

Next, heat up the paddle evenly by waving it in small circles in the flame, flipping it back and forth as it starts to droop. When it is uniformly heated, bring it out of the flame and cool slightly, all the while continuing to flip it back and forth to prevent any droop. When cooled to the right temperature, start to pull it out. Like with cane, the size of the finished ribbon is controlled by the speed with which you pull it out. If the ends start to cool and don't get pulled out quite enough, you can wave them through the flame to reheat them up enough to continue the pull.

Cased rods

Often when you make decorations like flowers, you want a subtle blending of colors on the petals of the

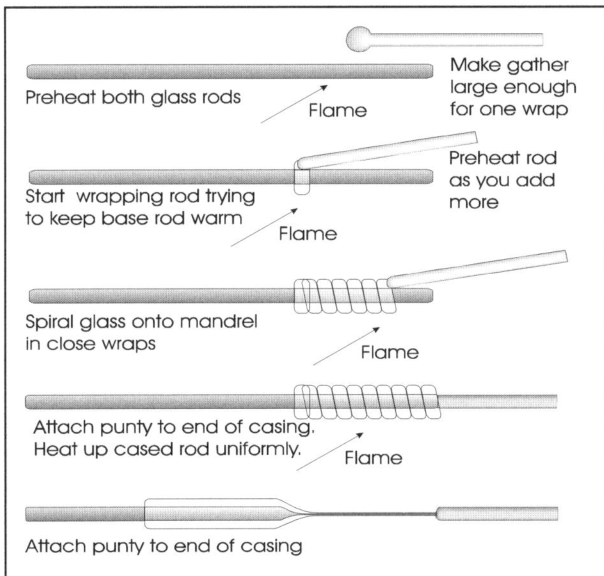

Figure 97. Making thickly cased cane by circumferential wrapping casing glass.

flower. One way to achieve this is by using multi-colored rods, where one color is cased or covered with another. Start out by preheating two rods as if you were going to make a latticino. Hold the rod of the color that you want on the inside in a tennis racket grip in your non-dominant hand. You want to lightly heat it just enough so that it will not thermal shock when it is cased. You do not want to get it soft.

Heat the color that you want coated onto the outside and start to make a gather. Now start to wrap the cooler rod with material from the gather on the hotter rod. Do this by touching the gather on the hot rod, which you are holding in the pencil grip, to the cooler rod and rotating the cooler rod away from you as shown in Figure 97. This is very similar to the basic wound bead technique to be described later. You may want to read that section before attempting this construction. When casing, it is very important to keep the hot rod in the flame and the cooler rod below the flame. Make sure that you do not trap air between wraps as this can cause popping of the cane as it is applied. To make thinner outer coatings, try pushing down with the hot rod for wider application or pulling a point from the gather as you wind it on the cooler rod. Rotate the hotter rod in the flame as you apply it to ensure that it is evenly heated.

The other method of casing is to apply the casing color with lengthwise applications of color. Here, as before, you start by warming up the rod to be cased and heating up just the tip of the casing rod. If you want a thin casing coat, you heat up about ½ inch on the end of the casing rod red hot while holding it in the pencil grip. Then, apply the casing by pushing down onto the outside of the rod to be cased with the casing rod pointed slightly toward you. Quickly draw the casing rod down the length of the rod to be cased and then pull it away from the cased rod through the flame to burn off any stringers that develop as you pull away. For long cased areas, the flame can be situated such that it is pointing along the outside of the cased rod and onto the casing rod to continue heating the casing rod as it is being applied. Apply as many thin stripes as is needed to fully case the outside of the center rod. This technique is illustrated in Figure 98.

To apply thick layers lengthwise, warm the rod to be cased as before and about ½" of the casing rod but not quite as hot as before. Now apply the casing rod to the cased rod pushing down lightly (while holding it in a pencil grip) and having the casing rod pointed slightly away from you. Slowly apply the thick casing by drawing the casing rod toward you. The torch flame should be directed onto the junction where the two rods are meeting but mostly onto the casing rod.

To keep the backside of the casing rod from getting too cool and pulling as you apply it, it helps to slowly rotate it. At the end of the stroke, pull the casing rod away from the cased rod again burning off any stringers in the flame. On subsequent coats, gently push into the interface between the cased rod and the previous casing stripe to ensure not trapping any air between them. This was not as much a problem

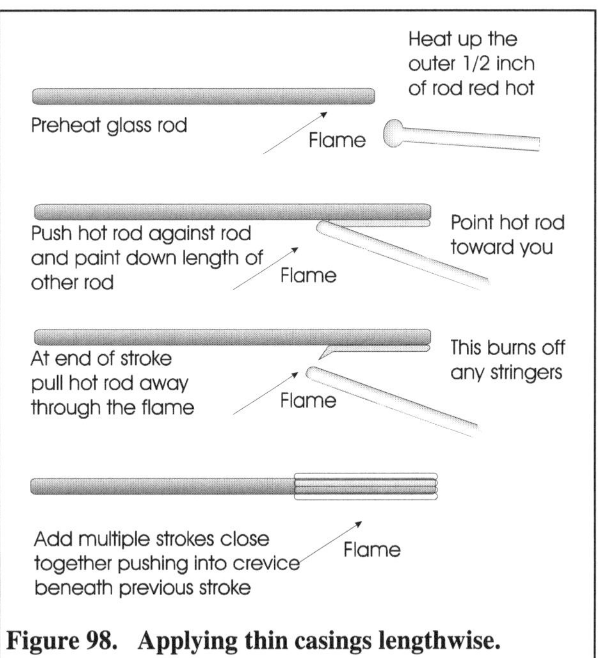

Figure 98. Applying thin casings lengthwise.

with the thin coats because the casing rod was hotter and you were pushing harder.

Once you've completed the casing coat, fuse a rod onto the end of the cased section and thoroughly heat it. Get the glass to flow and fill in between the wraps. You will have to rotate the rods as you heat them to prevent droop. When a uniform hot glob is formed from the cased section, remove it from the flame and pull it out to whatever diameter cane you desire. While pulling it out, you may find it easier to prevent drooping by rotating it back and forth instead of all the way around.

One form of cased rod that really looks good are encasements of opalescent white with a deep transparent color like rubino oro or bleu cobalto. These white core canes allow some beautiful transitional effects between the transparent colors by themselves, contrasted to the regions of transparent glass over the white.

Another form of cased rod that is really versatile is filagrana. You can purchase ready-made filagrana, but the number of colors that are commercially available are limited. Therefore, you may want to make some new colors of your own by casing opalescent rods with clear. If you have a crucible kiln you can make whatever color of filagrana you want by just dipping the opalescent rod into a crucible of clear glass.

Another thing that you might want to make using your newly learned casing skill is really good aventurine. The stuff that you can buy is really pretty wimpy in comparison to what you can make yourself. To do this, you need to first purchase some nice chunks of goldstone, greenstone or bluestone. I use chunks about one half to three-quarters of an inch in diameter. Grab a piece of this with your large tweezers and slowly heat it up out in the far reaches of your flame or prewarm them in the front of your annealer. Because of its size, you will have to really take it easy. When it is hot enough, attach it to the end of a glass rod by pushing the hot areas together. Then get the goldstone nice and hot. Use your mashers to shape the goldstone chunk roughly into a cylinder. Now, case this cylinder with clear glass and pull it out into a nice cane. You have to coat the goldstone with clear glass or it will burn out. You will find this cane to be much stronger in color than any of the aventurine that you can purchase. It can also be stretched much thinner without getting lost.

Suggested further reading

Burton, John. **Glass - Hand Blown Sculptured Colored Philosophy and Method**, 1st ed., Bonanza Books, 1967

Carberry, Edward. **Glassblowing An Introduction to Artistic and Scientific Flameworking**, 2nd ed., M G L S Inc, 1994

Dunham, Bandhu Scott, **Contemporary Lampworking - A Practical Guide to Shaping Glass in the Flame**, 3rd ed., Salusa Glassworks, 2002

Hasluck, Paul N. **Traditional Glassworking Techniques**, 1st ed., Dover Publications, Inc., 1988

Hoyt, Homer L. **Glassblowing - An Introduction to Solid and Blown Glass Sculpting**, 1st ed., Crafts & Arts Publishing Co. Inc., 1989

Roberts, N. H. **The Complete Handbook of Lamp Glass Art**, 1st ed., Tab Books Inc., 1981

Schuler, Frederic. **Flameworking - Glassmaking for the Craftsman**, 1st ed., Chilton Book Co., 1968

Townsend, Milon, **Advanced Flameworking Volume 1**, 1st ed., Blue Moon Press, 2001

Millefiori and Mosaic Cane

The term millefiori is translated literally from Italian as “a thousand flowers”. It is a term that was established by the German scholar, Heinrich Freiherr von Minutoli, in 1827. He used it to refer to canes being produced at that time which in cross section contained stylistic floral images. Many artists now refer to any decorative glass cane, which has simple patterns in the cane cross-section as being made by millefiori techniques or as being millefiori. That is how I use the term in this book.

When the image gets much more complicated and is constructed of discrete elements, the cane is then usually referred to as mosaic cane. Millefiori and mosaic canes are usually used as thin slices that are applied as external decorations on beads. These thin slices are referred to as murrine (the singular is murrina). It is the pattern or image in the cross section that is the desired design element.

Figure 99. Computer generated image of final Roman mosaic face cane of first century. 3.3 H x 1.5 cm W Courtesy of The Corning Museum of Glass

Figure 100. Some examples of Effetre murrine slices

Mosaic cane manufacture is nothing new. The ancient Romans were masters of the technique and used it in much of their fused work. The face that you see in the figure to the left was created in ways similar to those that you will learn in this chapter. It was made from components that were assembled into a complete image. The hair, the headpiece, the eyes, the nose, the mouth were each made separately and then assembled into half a face. Those two halves would then be put together to make a whole face as has been done in the computer generated image seen in Figure 99.

If you don’t want to make your own millefiori, simple ready-made compatible murrine are commercially available for use in your work, made by the Effetre glass factory in a wide variety of patterns. Figure 100 shows some of the patterns that they have available. Effetre murrine can be purchased by the ounce or the pound. You can get all of one design or mixtures of patterns graded according to size or coloration (clear or opaque). You can also purchase the millefiori cane instead of murrine, to cut to whatever thickness you want. Or instead, you may choose to make your own millefiori and thus your

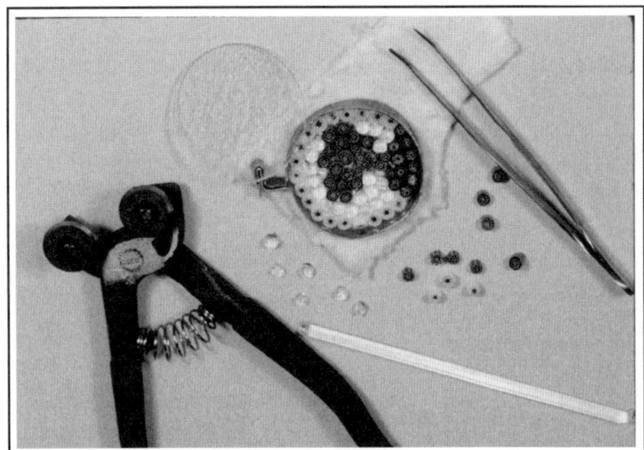

Figure 101. Laying up murrine to fuse into a pendant.

own murrine. Construction of millefiori and mosaic cane is the subject of this chapter.

Besides being used in beadmaking, murrine can also used to build up mosaic images, such as those made in Murano, Italy for pendants. To do that, the murrine are arranged on a kiln shelf and fused together in a kiln. For this application, you want the murrine to be sliced a bit thicker, on the order of ¼" thick or more. If not, the glass will not flow to fill in the gaps between them to form a uniform fused pendant. Alternately, you can fuse murrine cut for beadmaking onto a piece of clear Effetre sheet glass, as is being done in Figure 101. To keep the

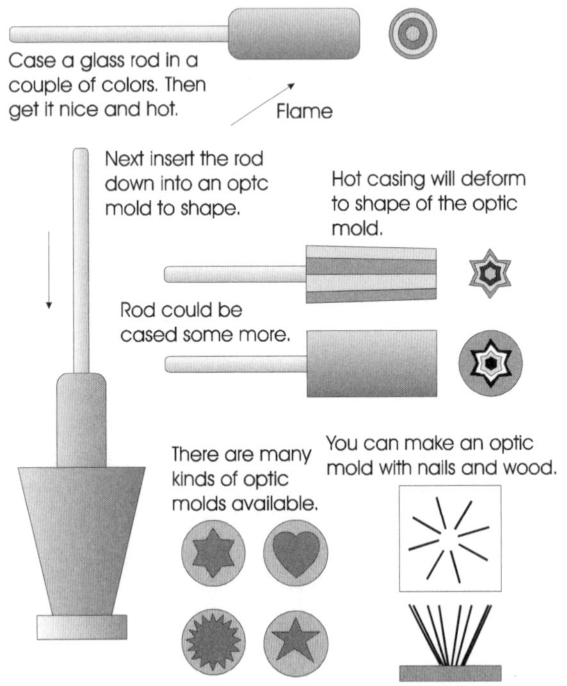

Case a glass rod in a couple of colors. Then get it nice and hot.

Flame

Next insert the rod down into an optc mold to shape.

Hot casing will deform to shape of the optic mold.

Rod could be cased some more.

There are many kinds of optic molds available.

You can make an optic mold with nails and wood.

Figure 102. Using optic molds to make millefiori.

overall shape desired for your pendant, the murrine should be enclosed in a ring of sheet copper during fusing. In making some of these mosaic pieces, I have noticed what I believe to be some incompatibility between certain types of the murrine, especially between clear and opaque, that needs further validation.

Optic mold cane construction

There are many methods that you can use to make your own millefiori caneThe first method that I will discuss is that of repetitively casing different colored layers that are occasionally manipulated for shape using optic molds. This is the technique that is used by furnace workers to form simple cross sectional patterns and it is the technique by which most of the Effetre millefiori is made. This technique is much easier to do if you have a crucible kiln with multiple pots of strong contrasting colors. A glory hole is also helpful.

Let's first discuss how you might make millefiori by this technique using a torch. Later we will go on to discuss how larger pieces of equipment might be used to do the same thing. The basic process is summarized in Figure 102. To try this technique yourself, you might want to start out with a crude, hand-made optic mold and glass heated in your torch. You can make the crude optic mold by nailing about six 4d finishing nails in a star pattern as shown in the bottom right of the figure. Note how the tops of the nails are slanted outward to prevent capturing the glass. They also must radiate outward from the center of the circle without tipping in that plane or they will trap the glass. Note that the angle of the nails has been greatly exaggerated in this drawing. They would actually look more like Figure 103.

Figure 103. Plunging cased rod into crude optic mold.

Now, you case a rod of one color with another color using one of the processes that was discussed in the last chapter, to get a bundle which you will distort in the optic mold. Heat the cased section of the rod until it is very soft. Next, plunge it into the homemade optic mold, as shown in Figure

103, to distort the casing and develop the cross sectional pattern. Allow the bundle to cool somewhat and then case it in another color.

If you are using a crucible kiln, dip the distorted bundle to add a new color. If you are hand-casing at the torch, first add the new color down in the depressions made by the optic mold. Apply the casing really hot and push down hard to avoid trapping air. Then go on to case the rest of the distorted bundle and fill it in to form a cylinder. Again thoroughly heat and distort the bundle using the optic mold. Repeat this process as many times as desired to get as large a piece as you want, filling in the valleys each time with a contrasting color. The color scheme can either be repetitive or different on each layer. Then, heat the final bundle and draw it out into the desired thickness rod or cane for your work. Allow it to cool and chop it into about one eighth inch thick murrine slices, or longer if you want to try fusing them.

So much for rough and crude, let's now discuss how you would proceed if you really want to get into making a lot of cane by this technique. First, you would get some professionally-made optic molds. These can be purchased from glassblowing suppliers. A good source of small optic molds made especially for beadmakers, is Steinert Industries, Inc. Professional optic molds are constructed similarly to the crude molds already introduced. They are of simple shapes that are tapered inward such that they are larger at the top than at the bottom. Again, the taper is so you will not trap glass in the molds as it hardens.

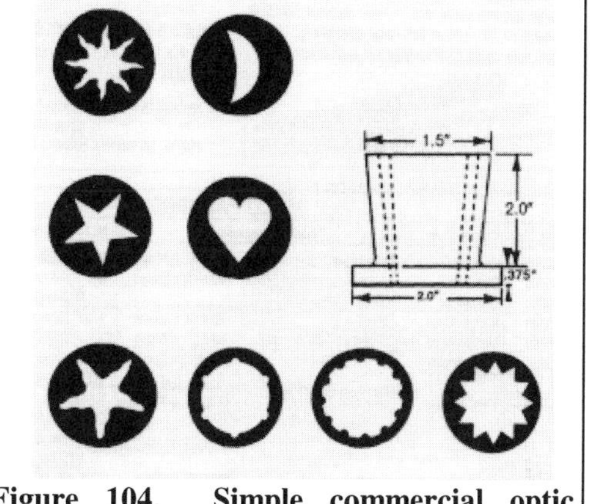

Figure 104. Simple commercial optic molds.

Optic molds are made from metals with very good heat conduction, like aluminum or bronze, so that they will quickly cool and chill the design into the glass. As stated earlier, they are usually simple shapes such as those shown in Figure 104. When used with molten glass from a crucible, the optic molds do not need to be preheated. But when working from a torch, I find that I have to preheat them to prevent the glass from chilling before reaching the bottom of the mold.

Let's now use our optic molds to form a millefiori cane using a gather from a crucible kiln. Take a small gather from one of the crucibles by dipping a small stainless steel punty into it. Remove the gather from the crucible by lifting the end of the punty and winding up whatever glass is dripping off the rod. Then, go over to your mold and hold the punty vertically over it. Allow the gather to stretch some so that it will fit down into the taper of the optic mold better. Next, stuff the hot glass down into the mold to the point where the punty is just above or just into the top portion of the mold.

If you go a little too far with the punty, use some pliers to push the gather back out onto the end of the punty. Remove the glass from the mold by pulling straight up with the punty. If you don't get a good impression of the mold cavity, then the glass on the punty was not hot enough. It may sometimes be necessary to smooth out the optic pattern with tools like paddles or to use other tools like pliers to adjust the dip so that it is centered on the punty.

> **Safety note:** ***Be careful, the optic molds get hot.***

Once a good impression has been made from the optic mold, allow the glass to harden up before you take a second dip. It has to be hard and cool enough to ensure that it will not deform when you make a second dip into a different color. Don't put the glass into the crucible too fast or you may trap bubbles. For the second dip, we go straight down into the crucible up to the top of the first dip and then bring it straight back out. Then, transfer the punty to horizontal. Rotate the punty to keep the glass from drooping. At this point, you have two choices; you can either marver it smooth or you can take a second dip into an optic mold. It does not have to be the same mold but it could be. If you are going to be making multiple dips into the same optic mold, you may want to keep track of the orientation in which you dip it. You can do this by making a mark on your punty. It may look a lot better if you consistently keep the same orientation.

In examining all the Effetre murrine in Figure 100, you can see that they use a number of different optic molds to create their millefiori canes. When making millefiori this way, you will often find that the

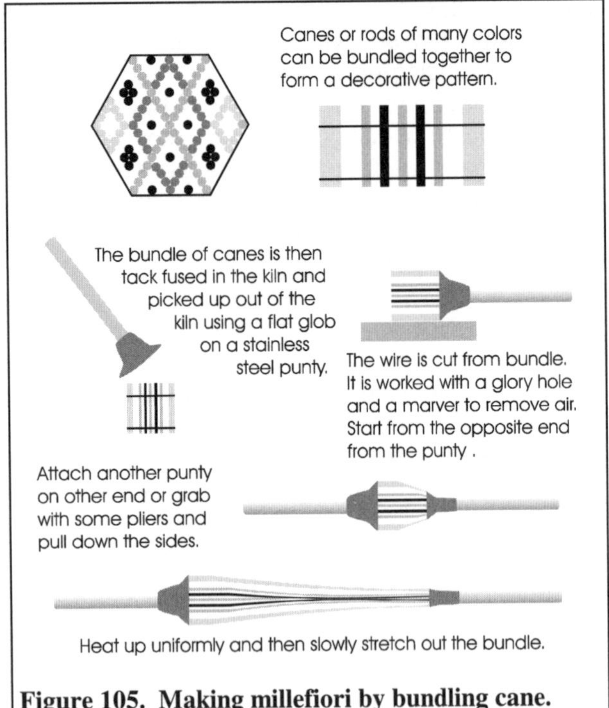

Figure 105. Making millefiori by bundling cane.

beginning section of the pull will not have a complete image in it and will have to be discarded.

After you have made as many crucible dips and optic mold impressions as you want, marver out the final dip bundle into a cylinder. Now, it is time to draw out the bundle into cane. Get it uniformly heated by heating it in the torch or glory hole and then lightly marvering it out. A glory hole is the better tool when the bundle is very large. Repeat heating and marvering until it seems about right for drawing out. We do the marvering to chill the outer surface so that the bundle does not get out of control as we wait for the heat to penetrate into its core. When ready, have an assistant grab the end of the bundle with a set of pliers or by puntying up onto it. Have him or her draw it out slowly so that it does not get too thin. About the diameter of a pencil is what is usually desired.

Kilnforming cane techniques

Bundling cane is one kilnforming technique that can be used to make more complex millefiori that may contain images like people or animals. This technique, more commonly used by fusers or furnace workers, is a bit complicated and involves bundling strips, rods and/or cane together cold and then fusing the glass in a kiln to form the desired image before being stretched out in a flame. Some glass historians and technicians have suggested that complex cane images created by this technique should more correctly be referred to as mosaic glass.

The basic process is illustrated in Figure 105. In the first section, a number of canes and rods of various sizes have been bundled together using copper wire to create the desired pattern or picture. They are put into a kiln and tack fused together so that they will stick together. If you set up multiple bundles of cane in the kiln at one time, you need to separate each bundle with ceramic fiber paper. Use a gather on the end of a punty to stab the end of the tack-fused bundle and remove it from the kiln. Make a molten glass collar around the punty end of the bundle. Then quickly cut the wire from the bundle and get it hot.

Slowly heat up the bundle in your torch or glory hole, starting on the opposite end from the punty and work all the air out of it as you work from one end to the other using your marver. If working in a torch, attach another punty to the other end with a gather large enough to cover the face of your bundle. Then, you can either get the bundle all nice and hot and pull it out all at once, or heat it up and pull as you go. If working in a glory hole, add a little sacrificial glass to the end of the bundle. (This could also have been part of the initial fused blank.) Then stick the whole bundle into the glory hole to about the punty end of the bundle. Rotate it as necessary to keep it from drooping. Uniformly heat the bundle throughout using your marver to occasionally chill the outer surface.

Once you have made a bundle and stretched it into cane, you can rebundle this cane with other canes and stretch it again to make more complex canes. You can also make components and bundle them together with filler cane to make detailed images. If you make half of a symmetrical image, you can combine it with the reversed image to get a

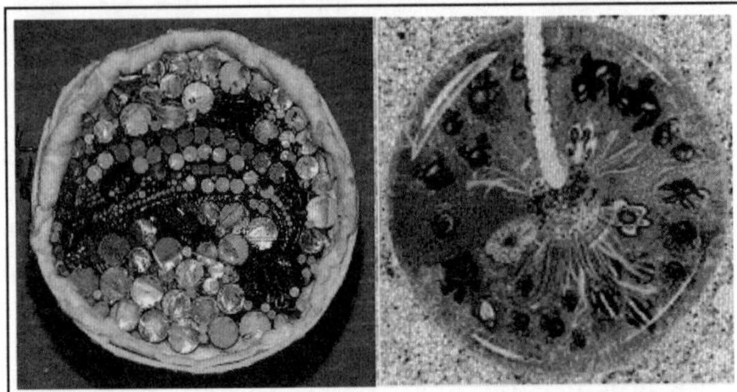

Figure 106. Mosaic cane laid up by Mary Kennedy. Photos by Mary Kennedy.

complete symmetrical image. Do this by flipping a second piece of the same pulled cane end for end and adding it to the first. These are some of the techniques that were used in antiquity to construct those famous Roman glass mosaics, like the one shown in Figure 99. Mary Kennedy is a modern practitioner of these kilnforming techniques and uses them to make kilnformed beads. An example of a killer whale cane bundle that she has laid up and an aquarium bead incorporating some of the finished cane slices can be seen in Figure 106.

If you don't have a kiln, you can try making mosaic cane starting with cold with small, wired bundles. Slowly heat one end of a bundle in the far end of your torch flame until you get it to fuse together. Next attach that end to a punty. Then slowly try to fuse together the other end of the bundle, again out in the far reaches of your flame. Continue slow heating until you feel comfortable with how the bundle is tacked together and then cut off the wire. You have to remember to go back and hit the first end of the bundle with the flame occasionally or you can lose the whole thing. Now, proceed as previously described for the bundle from the kiln. The problem with this technique is that you are almost sure to have a couple rods or canes break as you heat them and fall out of the pattern.

In either of these two bundling techniques, the final resolution of the image is dependent upon the size of the rods that made up your bundle. If you look at a mosaic image made by a bundling technique under a magnifying glass, you will always be able to see the dot or pixel structure of the canes and any lines present will not really be straight.

Another kilnforming technique for making mosaic cane is one presented by Brian Kerkvliet in one of his Glass Art Magazine articles. In it, he suggested developing an image and casting each of its components separately using the technique of pâte de verre, which is described later in this book. These components are then put together, tack fused in your kiln, and worked as any other bundle. An example of this technique in progress can be seen in Figure 107.

Figure 107. Preparing bundle components for casting of pâte de verre molds.

There are a number of pros and cons with this technique over regular bundling. In its favor, the image will not have the dot or pixel structure that normally plagues bundling techniques. On the other hand, the complexity of the pâte de verre process may force you to keep the image relatively simple. This is because pâte de verre is too much work to make a complicated image and any inaccuracies in the process will make a detailed image hard to assemble. Since it is assembled from larger, irregularly shaped pieces, you have to be much more careful when heating the bundle up in the kiln to tack fuse it together. It is very susceptible to cracking apart.

To use this process, first develop a simple image. Next, transfer the image onto the end of a short piece of high-density foam using tracing paper followed by a felt tip pen. Brian uses some of the high-density pink insulation polyurethane foam used on foundations. The piece of foam should be the height and width of the final desired bundle but it should be about 30% longer. Now cut out each of the individual components using a saw or hot wire.

A hot wire is preferred over sawing for a number of reasons:

- it is easier to cut out a complex shape
- it seals the edges of the component as it melts the pieces out of the foam
- it removes less material from the cut surface.

If your foam is not of high enough density, it may just shrivel up when you touch it to the hot wire.

When you cut these pieces out of the foam, you have to be as careful as possible to make sure that you cut as perpendicular to the top surface of the foam as possible. If not, the pieces will be hard enough to get apart with foam that has some flexibility but impossible to assemble the finished glass components which are not flexible.

A hot wire cutter cuts foam by melting a thin swatch of foam as you push it into the hot wire. The hot wire has to be adjusted just right. Too cold and it will not cut the foam. Too hot and the melt will be

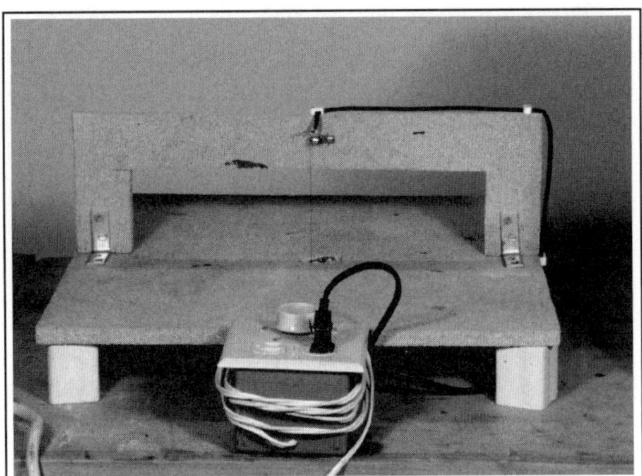
Figure 109. An improvised hot wire cutter.

coarse and seal back up as the wire passes through the foam. You can buy hot wire cutters but I suggest you make your own. To make a hot wire cutter, all you need is some nichrome wire, like that in your kiln, a little wood, some fittings from the hardware store, and an old toy transformer that puts out about 12 volts DC. It helps if the transformer has a power control on it. If not, you can use a light rheostat for this.

To make your hot wire cutter, start by constructing the base and throat of the cutter from wood as seen in Figure 109. Attach single-hole mechanical lugs at the top of the throat and at the base to act as connectors from which to string the nichrome wire. I suggest lugs for 10-14 strand wire or smaller. String thin nichrome wire-like that from an old toaster or hair drier between the lugs. Attach insulated wire to the lugs at the top and bottom to go between the nichrome wire and to the transformer. Turn on the transformer and try it out. If it does not get hot, check your connections. If it just gets warm, the current rating of your transformer is not high enough. If it gets too hot, add a light dimmer switch between one end of the nichrome wire and the transformer. Now, try a piece of foam and see how it cuts. Play with the dimmer switch as necessary to get a nice smooth cut.

After you have your image block cut up into its separate pieces, you have to cast each of these pieces in glass. Start by coating the sides of the image pieces with a good release agent, like petroleum jelly. This will help fill in any surface imperfections from the cuts as well as make removal of the piece from the refractory mold a lot easier. You want to be able to remove and save the foam pieces in case the first casting does not go well. Cast refractory molds around each of these pieces as discussed in the pâte de verre bead chapter. Clean out the molds, fill them with glass and place them into the kiln. You can use one of many types of glass to fill the mold, either crushed, rods, or strips, as long as they are all compatible. The sections don't have to be a uniform color if you don't want them to be.

Now place the molds into your kiln and melt the glass. The reason that the image block was 30% longer than the desired bundle should now become apparent. The pile of glass in each of the molds will shrink down into the cavity about 30% to fill in all the air space. Slowly cool the cast glass pieces back to room temperature, carefully break them out of the mold, clean them, and you are ready to assemble your bundle and put it in your kiln as before. Of course I skipped a lot of details here, but if you read the pâte de verre bead chapter you should be able to figure them out.

Lampworked mosaic cane

As you become more experienced in lampworking, you will find it possible to construct millefiori or mosaic cane images at the torch by adding material to a base rod and shaping it with hand tools. Some relatively simple examples of cane images made with this technique can be seen in Figure 108. As you can see, the two center canes are signature canes for the artist's beads.

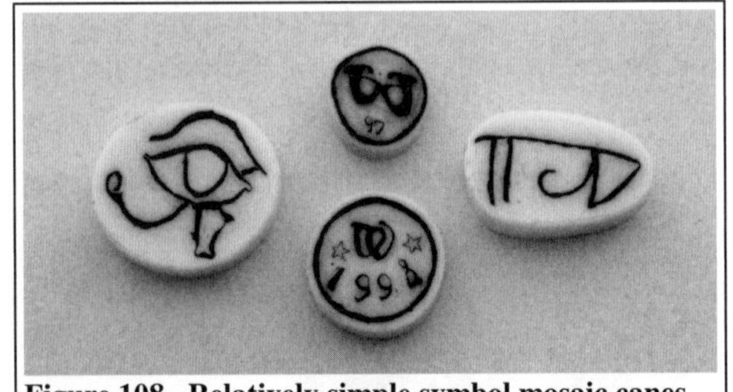
Figure 108. Relatively simple symbol mosaic canes. Artist James Weurfel Size: ¼" to ½" in diameter.

Making mosaic cane in the flame of a torch is a relatively advanced technique, and you may find the occasional help from an assistant to be beneficial. To make things easier to understand as I describe the process, I will continue to refer to the large image cane before stretching as a bundle, even though with this technique you are really no longer bundling anything.

Ribbed cane

The first kind of lampworked cane that you can try is a pretty simple one called ribbed cane. Ribbed cane usually has a very simple pattern in its cross section, such as seen in Figure 110, and it is different from most mosaic canes in that it may not necessarily be used as slices. Instead, the value of ribbed cane is often for making floral applications. It is used for the variation in the thickness of the casing color on the exterior of the cane. This variation will show up as natural looking striations of color when the cane is applied to beads to make floral decorations as will be described later.

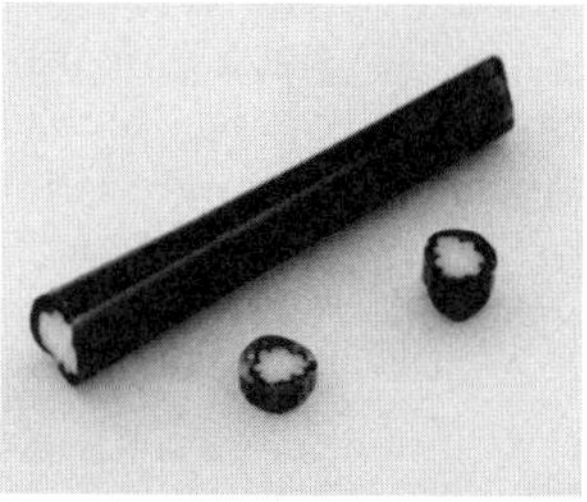

Figure 110. Ribbed cane cross section.

To make ribbed cane, start by making a good sized cylinder of a light colored glass on the end of a glass rod. Smooth it up. Then, heat up one side of the cylinder and press inward with a sharp tool like a shaper (one of those spatula shaped graphite paddles) or a knife. Next, heat up the opposite side of the cylinder and make another groove. Go on to make about eight equally spaced grooves in all around the cylinder.

Figure 111. Floral bead using ribbed cane. Artist: Kirsten Orr Size: ¾" in D x ¼"L

Now, go back and fill in those groves with a dark colored glass, like black. After the grooves are all filled, lightly coat the outside surface of the cylinder with the dark color. Then, uniformly heat the cylinder and pull it out into a fairly thick cane. When applied to a bead, the thicker sections or ribs of the darker color will be apparent as dark streaks running through the applied cane. An example of a bead with ribbed cane floral decorations can be seen in Figure 111.

Mosaic cane construction principles

When you design a complex image, it helps to break the image up into a number of component parts, which are later assembled into a more complex image. As you will soon see, doing each section individually allows you to shrink each image component in cross section separately to an appropriate size prior to final assembly. Before actually describing the construction of any complex mosaic canes, let's start out by discussing some of the basic principles to consider during construction of mosaic cane pieces.

First, it helps to **construct a mosaic cane bundle on the end of a borosilicate glass punty** because borosilicate's higher viscosity makes it stronger and more stable as you heat up the bundle. Borosilicate is also more resistant to thermal shock in case you forget to warm it occasionally. If the bundle does break off of the punty during construction, don't panic. Just pick it up off the bench or the floor with some long tweezers that you keep handy for that purpose and reattach it to the punty before you go on. Use a large diameter pyrex rod of about ½" for your punty because it is easier to handle, as a bundle can get fairly big and heavy. Thin it down to about half this diameter on the end that will attach to the bundle by pulling a short point.

Alternately, you could use a pyrex backbone down the length of the bundle as is suggested by Lewis Wilson in his video on millefiori cane construction. This appears to work best if you make this backbone as the top of a pyrex T. The bottom of the T then works as a good handle so that you can keep flipping the piece back and forth to keep it evenly heated. After you are done, you just heat up the area around the T such that the Effetre glass is fairly soft while the pyrex is just flexible. Then peel the pyrex off the bundle. If you have a problem getting the last little bit off, reheat it and try cutting it off with your scissors. Then plop the whole thing into the annealer. If you want to see a demonstration of this, buy the video or take a class. The only problem with the T-bar technique is that it violates the second principle of mosaic cane construction that we will discuss next.

The second general principle of mosaic cane construction is to **start work on any image from a simple shape at the center of the image**. This allows you to start from a single colored rod — at least for the beginning of a subcomponent. A more complex image will probably be started using a central subcomponent. By starting from a point near the center of the image, it is easier to judge and control the size of the image as you build it. You will better understand where you are going with it.

The third general principle is **don't let your bundle get too long** or you will have a hard time balancing it on the end of your punty, as well as keeping it warm enough to prevent thermal shock. One and a quarter to two inches seems to be optimum size for torch assembly. This can be adjusted depending upon the size of your torch flame.

The fourth principle is to understand that **colored layers appear to lose some of their intensity as they are stretched** out and made thinner in cross section. So use bolder colors than those you might at first choose, especially if the component is to go through multiple stretch cycles. These layers are also easier to apply lengthwise to the bundle as you build it up rather then circumferentially.

In order to properly know what the image looks like as you build it up, you need to observe the fifth principle — **keep the non-punty end of your bundle clean**. This allows you to view your image and see where you need to add more glass. For the same reason, smooth out each colored layer after you finish adding it. This allows you to really know what the image looks like. It also prevents color bleeding from below through crevices in the surface of an applied layer. Do this by marvering or shaping the bundle with a paddle. When shaping the bundle, only get the side of the bundle that you are working on hot, not the whole bundle. This gives you a rigid side against which to push and prevents the whole assemblage from bending as you push against it.

The last general principle that you need to consider is that as you stretch out a bundle into a cane, it tends to want to form a cylindrical cross section. Therefore, to avoid distortion of your image as you pull it out, it helps to **make the bundle roughly cylindrical** or at least oval to begin with before you stretch it. If nothing else, avoid wide variations in cross sectional thickness.

Beginning mosaic images — block letters

So with these principles in mind let's discuss how to go about making a fairly simple form of mosaic cane — block letters. Many glass bead artists want to add identification to their work as they get better and more widely known. They feel that it makes their work more valuable and recognizable. One way to do this is by adding a signature cane made with block letters.

There are three basic types of shapes that you will have to work with in making block letters: straight sides, partial curves and closed curves. The following letters have straight sides: A, B, D, E, F, H, I, J, K, L, M, N, P, R, T, U, V, W, X, Y and Z. The following letters have partial curves: B, C, D, G, J, P, R, S, and U. Lastly, the following letters have closed curves: O, and Q. As you can see, some of the letters have both straight sides and partial loops. Let's look at the construction of each of these types in turn.

Figure 112 show the construction technique for making one of the **straight-sided letters**. For this illustration, I chose one with straight sides only, an M. As in making all mosaic cane, it helps to start out at approximately the center of the image, in this case the wedge is at the center of the M. Do this by making a gather of your background color and making a wedge about an inch and a half long using a paddle and a marver. Then, paint one long side of the wedge with black and smooth it out with your paddle. Make sure to keep the end clear. After that, paint the second long side of the wedge with black.

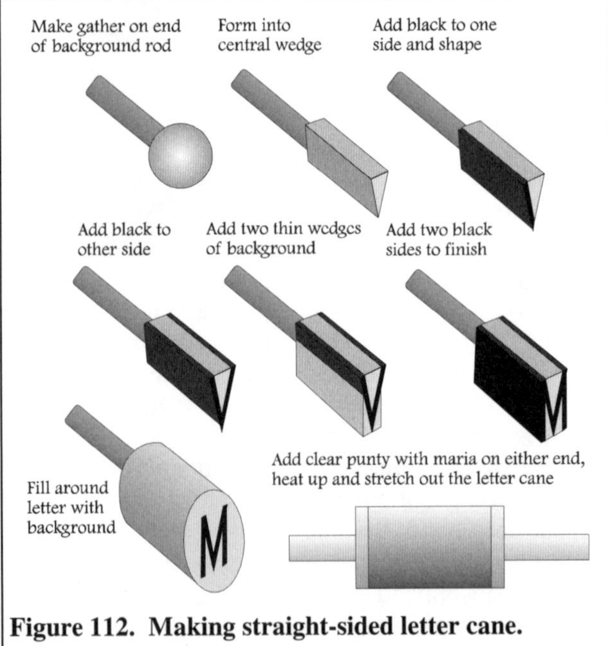

Figure 112. Making straight-sided letter cane.

If you were to stop at this point, you would have a V. Now add a narrow wedge of background color to either side of the V. (If you were making a W instead of an M you would add wider wedges.) Add the final two black sides and the letter is completed. If you were to try and pull the bundle at this point, it would try to round up the edges. Therefore, add enough extra background color around the letter to ensure that it will pull uniformly. Now, add a punty to the other side of the letter. Since letters are fairly small, you can probably get by using just a maria, a flattened gather on the end of a rod, to attach the punty onto the cane. You want to use clear glass here so that you can see what you are doing as you stretch the cane. If you want to maximize the amount of usable letter cane, then you should burn off the original rod and add a clear maria on that end also. Then get the bundle hot, remove it from the flame and pull it out.

Partial **curved letters and closed curved letters** are done pretty much the same way except that you may have multiple curved surfaces to contend with. For this example, let's look at one of the harder ones, an S, as illustrate in Figure 113. Here you pick one of the central loops as a place to start. You make a shape to correspond to this out of background color. You next coat it about three quarters of the way around with black. If you were to stop at this point, you would have a C or with a little shaping a U or a J. You should start to see how a lot of the letters are very similar. Next, add a thick stripe of background down below this. Then, carry the outside of the S around this background loop and the S is complete. Of course, you want to fill in with more background color around the letter prior to stretching it so that you keep the proper shape, and add clear rods with marias on them to the ends of the bundle so that you get a maximum amount of usable letter cane out of this pull.

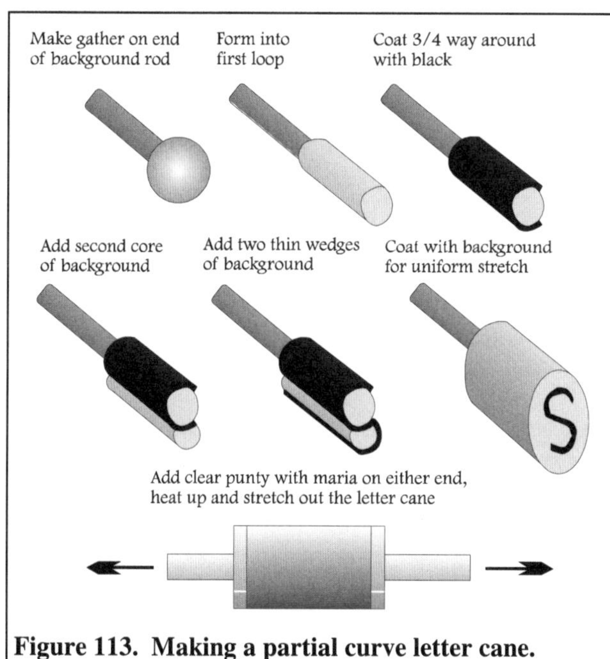

Figure 113. Making a partial curve letter cane.

Figuring out how to do the rest of the letters will be left as an exercise for you. Most of them will be pretty obvious. The B is a little bit difficult. I find it best to start with the flat side first, lay on one background stripe, cover it with black then lay on the other background stripe, cover it with more black and use a little shaping work to finish it. If you need more hints on the order of construction for block letters see the figure on this topic in Cindy Jenkin's book.

Advanced mosaic images — faces

In any mosaic image, you always start out by planning the individual subcomponents that you will need to construct ahead of time to make up your image. For faces, these components will consist of the eyes, the nose and the mouth. Figure 114 shows a collection of these components with an example face. I will discuss construction of each of these components in turn, and then describe how you combine them to make the final facial mosaic image.

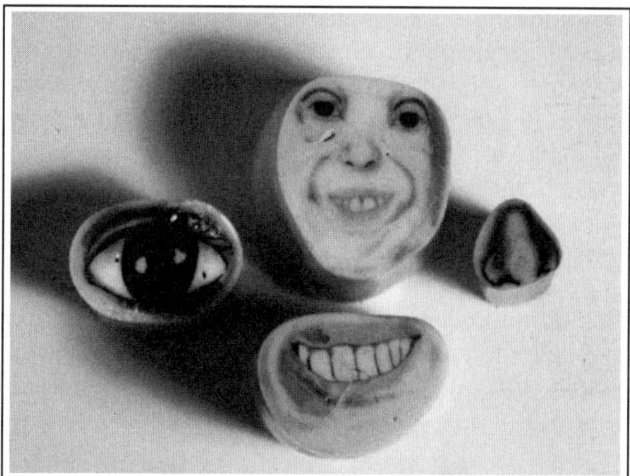

Figure 114. Mosaic components for a face.
Artist: Loren Stump Size: 3/8" to 1" in diameter

Let's start with a discussion of construction of an eye cane. Look at an eye. From inside outward, it consists of several parts: the pupil, the iris, the white, the eyelids, the lashes, and some surrounding flesh. Each of these subcomponents can be made as simple or as complex as you want. The pupil can be a simple black dot, it could have a dash of white to simulate a reflection of light, or in the limit, it could even have a small image of something that the person is looking at.

The iris can be a single color like blue, or you could try to show all the ribbing of its ligament substructure. The white can be just that or it could be the eye of the typical glass artist, who has been up all night working, with a complex bloodshot look.

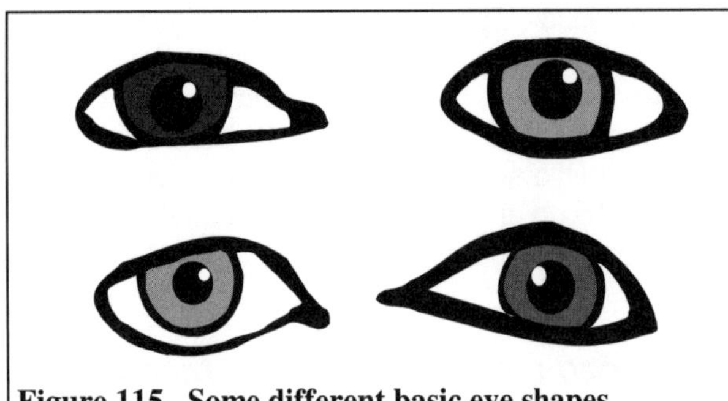
Figure 115. Some different basic eye shapes.

The lids can be thin or really baggy. Eyelashes can be represented by a single line or by any of a number of variations where you try to show the structure of the individual lashes. From this, you can see what I mean when I say that an image can be kept simple or made very complex.

With this in mind, the eye that I will describe constructing here will be relatively simple as illustrated in Figure 116. As I describe its construction, I will hearken back to some of the general principles of mosaic cane construction presented earlier. So start out with a simple black pupil. (If you want something more complex, you will have to make a sub-subcomponent with the image you desire.) Warm up the desired one and a half inches on the end of the black rod in your non-dominant hand.

Pick up an iris colored rod with your dominant hand and use it to case the pupil with the iris color. For a simple iris, this involves just applying several lengthwise casing coats of the appropriate color. Use a bold color like a dark blue, not a pale one. Remember to keep the end clean and to smooth out each layer before moving on to the next. As you build up the iris, be aware that most of the time, unless the eyes are wide open in surprise, you will not see them as being circular. They are usually clipped at the top and the bottom by eyelids. You may want to add a very thin layer of black around the iris to delineate it better.

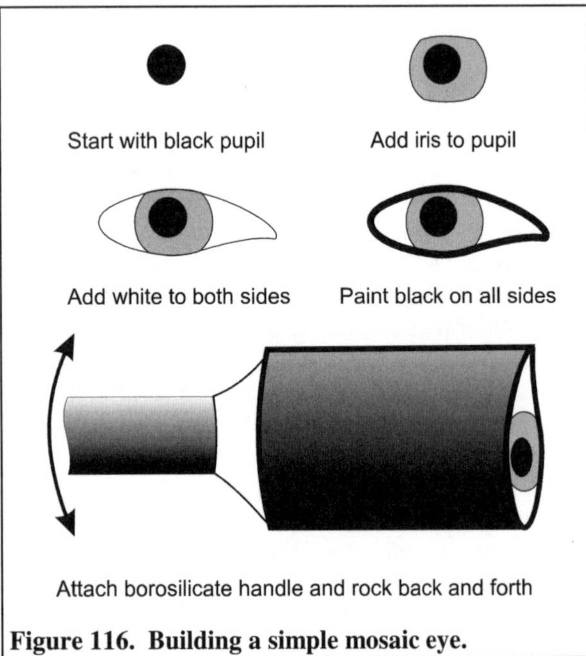

Figure 116. Building a simple mosaic eye.

Next, the white of the eye is added to either side of the iris to establish the basic eye shape. Remember that this basic eye shape, as is illustrated simply in Figure 115, may vary with either the nationality of the person that you are trying to portray or with the emotion that you are trying to show in them. Once you have this basic eye shape established by the addition of the white of the eye, it makes the eye all that more distinct if you again apply a very thin coating of black all the way around the exterior of the eye shape.

Before doing this, you may want to transfer the bundle onto a pyrex punty if you have not already done so. If you do transfer it to a pyrex punty at this time, make sure that whatever end faces out away from the punty carries a clear image of the construction to guide your work. This usually means holding the bundle with tweezers, burning off the rod handle and reattaching that same end to the punty.

If you want to get as much good mosaic cane as possible pulled from the bundle, you may want to add a little glob of any color glass (although clear glass is preferred) to that end in which you embed the punty. Then firmly implant the punty into this glob by getting the glass hot, sticking the warm punty into the glob and rocking it back and forth as well as side to side about 45°. This attaches some of the glass from the glob up the side of punty forming a good strong joint. Lastly, pull out slightly on the punty to get a tapered transition.

With the mosaic eye construction now firmly attached to the punty, we are ready to continue on by adding an eyelid and eyelash treatment to the upper portion of the eye. The eyelid will usually be at most just a thin layer of flesh, but you might try varying its thickness for effect or to show age.

The three different eyelash treatments that I will discuss are laid out vertically from top to bottom in Figure 117. The first column shows how to make large exaggerated lashes. Here you add narrow

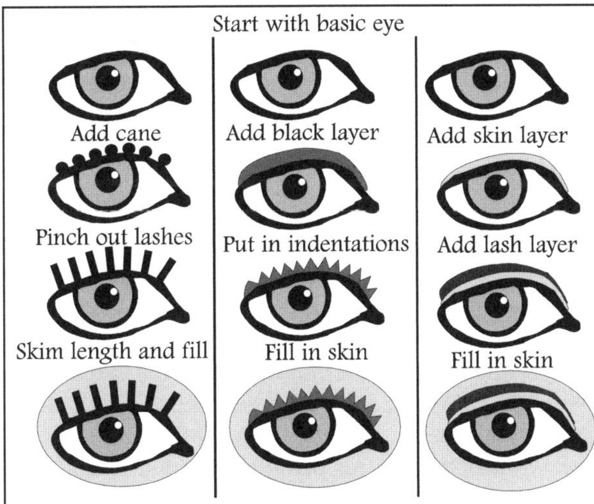

Figure 117. Some basic eyelash treatments.

stripes of black onto the top of the thin layer of black around the eye shape and squish them into tall thin ridges. A mini-masher is the ideal tool to use for this task. If the are uneven, you can even them out by heating the tops slightly and then skimming off the top evenly with the black rod. Now fill in between the lashes with some super hot flesh colored glass and you are finished.

The second lash treatment is to apply a thick layer of black to the top of the eye and then use a graphite shaper or reamer to push little grooves into this layer which you then backfill with flesh color.

The third lash treatment is to add a thin European eyelash. To achieve this effect, first apply a thin crescent shaped upper eyelid that is thinned to almost nothing on either end. Then apply a thin layer of black over this lid.

At this point, the eye is really pretty much complete, but if you were to stretch it out, it would distort badly because of the large changes in cross section. So you need to add some extra flesh color around the image to at least make it an oval shape. Once this is done, build up a cap of clear glass on either end of the bundle that goes all the way out to the edge. This will allow an even pull of the whole cross section of the bundle and will maximize the amount of usable cane that you get out of the bundle when you stretch it.

Figure 118. Murrine of women with different lashes. Artist: Loren Stump Size: 5/8" in diameter

If you don't add end caps, you may find yourself pulling out the center of the bundle and having the outside pull inward unevenly at different sections of the cane. Clear glass is the best choice for these end caps for two reasons. First, it is the least expensive color of glass, and second, it allows you to see the image underneath the end cap. This allows you see what you are doing as you stretch out the bundle. You can imagine what the final face cane might look like if the eye cane inadvertently got twisted as you stretched it out. It would result in the eye being at a different angle down the length of the pull. Then later when you add it to the face you would get the same rotation down the length of the face. This is okay if you are trying to create a Picasso face cane but not if you are trying to create a natural looking face.

As soon as you attach a second punty to the other end cap, you are ready to stretch out the bundle. Remember to firmly attach that punty to the end cap as before by rocking it back and forth and side to side after inserting it. Next, evenly heat the bundle. As you may remember, do this in the outer portion of your flame because this area has a cooler and softer flame. Make sure that you evenly heat the bundle, applying the flame not just to the barrel of the bundle, but also to the ends and the end caps. If you have problems with the bundle heating unevenly, you might want to try working out even further in the flame to slow down the heating process.

As the bundle heats up, you can monitor progress by wiggling slightly on the punty to feel if it is ready to pull. As you are heating the bundle, it also helps to remove the bundle from the flame occasionally to allow the heat to sink in and prevent the outside from getting too far ahead of the inside. You might also want to marver it lightly to chill the outside. You want to ensure as uniform heating as possible because large thermal gradients in the bundle can result in uneven stretching of the image.

Once the bundle feels right, bring it out of the flame, hold it for a couple seconds and gently stretch it out

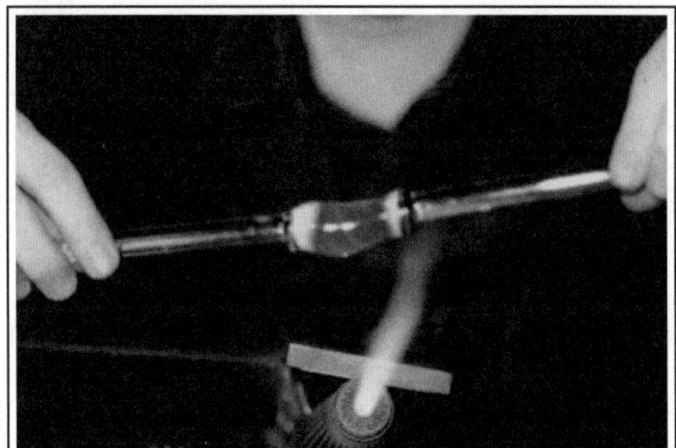

Figure 119. Sharon Peters pulling out a bundle.

as seen in Figure 119. If you hold the thick end up as you gently pull and wiggle the bundle, you can use gravity to your advantage and since heat rises, this helps retain heat in the bundle allowing slower pulls. After the stretched cane has hardened, it can be cut up into manageable lengths (1½ to 2") for further assembly. If the diameter of the pulled cane is larger than about ¼", you may have to immediately stick it into an annealer to prevent it from thermal shocking. This is mandatory with any cane over one half inch in diameter.

There are times when you may want a variable thickness, or at the very least, sections of varying thickness to your pull as when you are making letters and want to put together similar sizes to make words. Since it is very hard to consistently pull to the same size, it is easier to pull variable sized letters and to match sections of similar size when you build them up into words. For faces, there is also a nominal size relationship between the features that will appear more natural looking.

We are now finally ready to move on to construction of the nose. Noses tend to be the most difficult part of the face to get right, just because of their shape. For a simple nose like that shown in Figure 120, start out by building about an inch long mass of glass. A quick way to do this is to heat up about an

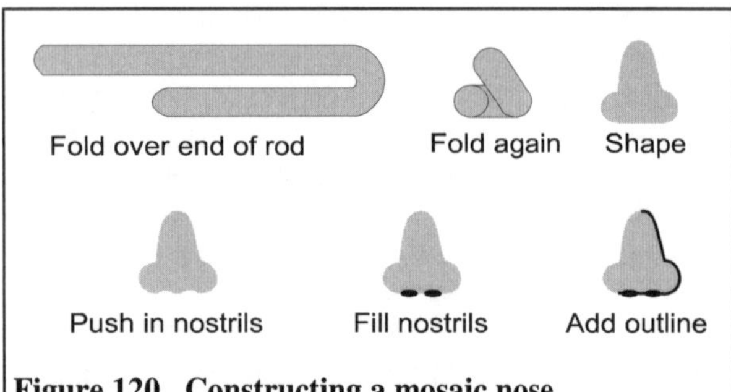

Figure 120. Constructing a mosaic nose.

inch and a half of flesh colored rod and fold it over on itself. Heat that up and fold it over again to get a mass of glass in a T-like cross sectional shape. You could have built up a cylinder and pinched it into shape but I find this easier. Smooth and shape this construction using heat, shapers, and mashers to get the basic nose-like shape. Get the bottom hot and use your shaper to push in two indentations to form the nostrils. Lay a thick black line into each of these indentations.

Apply a thin black coating about half way around the nose as shown to get the shadowing effect seen when light is shining from the opposite side of the face. In preparation for pulling this bundle, it should be made into an oval shape by adding extra base flesh color. You may want to have part of the flesh that you add on the shaded side of the nose to be darker to accent the shadow more. Then pull as before by adding end caps to punties and heating the bundle up uniformly. Anneal the resulting cane as necessary.

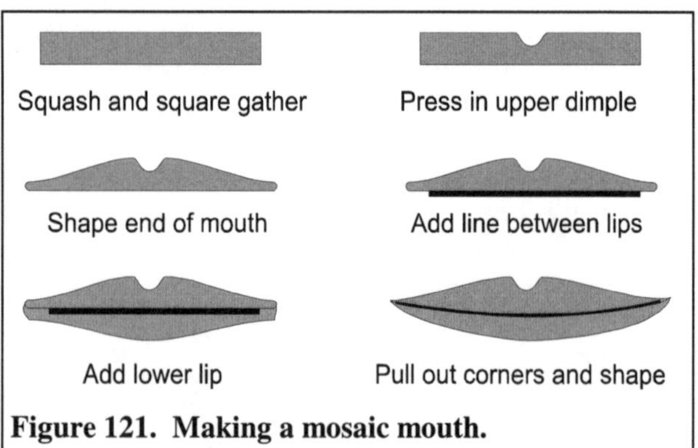

Figure 121. Making a mosaic mouth.

The last major component of the face to be made is the mouth. Begin with a gather of red that you squash and then square up to form the start of the upper lip as shown in Figure 121. After that, push in the top of the center with your shaper and marver it on both sides. Next apply a coat of black or white or both to the bottom of the lip depending upon what type of expression you are trying to convey.

When making teeth, the white is usually applied a little thicker then is the black, which is used to represent slight lip separation. You could even show shadows between the teeth as was seen in Figure 114. Apply another thick coat of red to the bottom of this to represent the lower lip. Marver it together and shape it somewhat to a point at either end. What you really want is a sharper end than you can get by marvering. To get this sharp edge, heat up one edge of the mouth and pull it out to a point with some tweezers or pliers and cut it off at the appropriate spot. Repeat on the other side.

Now you may want to shape your mouth into a smile or a frown by lightly heating the edges and pushing them around with a paddle. In preparing your bundle for stretching, you next have to fill around it with some surrounding skin color. Start by covering the delicate exposed ends of the mouth so that they don't melt down as you apply the rest of the glass. Then fill the valley at the top of the mouth and finally the rest of the surrounding flesh.

Before adding too much flesh, you might want to consider whether you will be adding a mustache or beard. If so add some or all of it at this time. Once you have your oval built up around the mouth, again add end caps, and punties. Then pull away. When stretching out this bundle into cane, try to keep in mind the size of the eyes and nose components that you have already constructed and stretch it to the appropriate size to match.

At this point, you are ready to start assembling all of your components into a completed face. When assembling mosaic components into a larger image, there are a number of things that must be considered. First, it helps if the component parts are not too small in diameter — $^3/_{16}$" or larger in diameter is desired. Otherwise, they heat up too fast when introduced into the flame and are hard to control. Pieces larger than about $^3/_8$" in diameter should be preheated in an annealer prior to assembly to avoid thermal shock. Pieces smaller than this can generally be successfully preheated on the fly in the outer end of the flame without mishap. Remember to always start assembly near the center of your image and work outward. When bringing hot components together, do not let them touch until they are exactly where you want them. Otherwise, they may get stuck in an unintended orientation.

Punty up what will be the center of the face, the nose. Hold the mouth up to the bottom of the nose and decide if extra flesh or a mustache is needed to space them correctly relative to each other. If so, add a little flesh color to the bottom of the nose. Then heat up this area to soften it and preheat the mouth. Attach the mouth to the nose by touching them together at the far ends, closest to the punty, and slowly closing the two together like the blades of a scissors until they are attached along their whole length. You do this in this manner to ensure that they are correctly aligned down the whole length of the bundle.

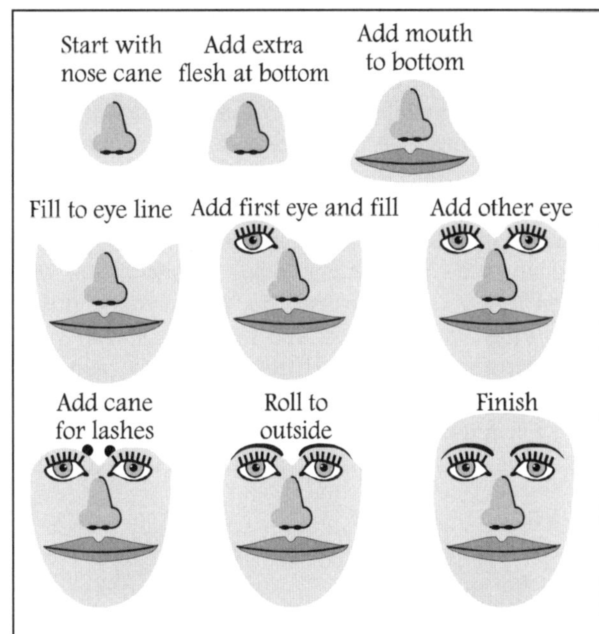

Figure 122. Assembling the final mosaic face cane.

Any valleys between these two components should now be filled with flesh and/or facial hair colored glass. Continue adding this color to build up the shape of the face from the chin to the cheek line—approximately half way up the nose, as shown in Figure 122. The facial color layers are added in thin coats applied very hot to keep control of the face shape as you build it up. Marver the face bundle as necessary, remembering to do one section at a time and to keep the end of the bundle clean to monitor assembly progress.

Make two grooves with your graphite shaper into the cheek line, one on either side of the nose, in which to set your premade eye canes. Check out the grooves to see that they are level and at the correct position. Trial fit an eye cane, without actually touching it to the bundle. Check to see that it looks orientated correctly—rounded side to the outside and that the grooves are the right depth. If okay, proceed on; otherwise, modify the cheek line and the grooves as necessary to properly position and receive the eye cane. When ready, get the groove hot and prewarm the eye cane. Scissors it into the groove as was done with the nose and the mouth cane. Fill any voids between the eye and the cheek with flesh color. Also, apply a thin layer of flesh color over the eye but so much that it interferes with placement of the eyebrow.

Now, attach the other eye cane into its groove in a similar manner. Remember that this piece will have to be flipped end-for-end from what was used on the other side to keep the rounded edge to the outside. Shape the face as necessary. Make a slight valley down the center of the forehead to allow for the eyebrows by pushing down in the center with your shaper and rolling it to the outside. In preparation for making the eyebrows, take a second to contemplate their shape. They are thicker near the nose and thinner at the side of the face. To get this effect apply a stripe on the inside of one of the two humps that you just created but not over the nose. Then, heat up the stripe and roll over it with your shaper from the inside to the outside to give it a tapered look. Repeat this on the other side of the face. Fill in the forehead with facial color.

Figure 123. Two images made from same face cane. Artist: Loren Stump Size: ½" to ¾" in diameter.

At this point, we can either go on to add hair and other features to the face, or stop and stretch out this basic face bundle. Stopping and stretching it out to a thick cane at this point would allow using this basic face cane to make a number of similar faces with different colors of hair, hats, ears, etc. that we add later. The face could be reshaped slightly each time to give it a little more or less angular appearance. When pulled small, you may not even be able to tell that the different images were made with the same basic face cane. Figure 123 shows an example of this where we have two images by Loren Stump, one a cowboy and the other a French nobleman, that both appear to have been constructed from the same face cane.

Figure 124. Example of using complex image to further build up a more complex image. Artist: Loren Stump Size: ½" to ¾" in diameter.

As you can go much further than this, you can take some of these faces and build them up into full figures, landscapes, or whatever. As an example of this, see Figure 124 where a bust of a woman has been used later to form a image of her on a path. For an extreme example of this, be sure to check out the image of the Last Supper by Loren Stump in the colored section. This image took 102 separate pulls at the torch to construct.

Advanced cane techniques

The face cane, which was just described in the last section, is a relatively basic image, and lacks color gradation and depth of image. I have already discussed how you can make an image a little more complicated by building it up from more detailed subcomponents, but there is another technique that will allow you to add even more realism to your images. It will allow addition of things like a rosy color to the cheeks. Before starting, you need to blend a number of related facial colors using the techniques for blending colors that were discussed in the chapter on glass. The Effetre palette itself is just too limited to allow developing a gradation of color in your images. What you really need is approximately twenty different variations of flesh

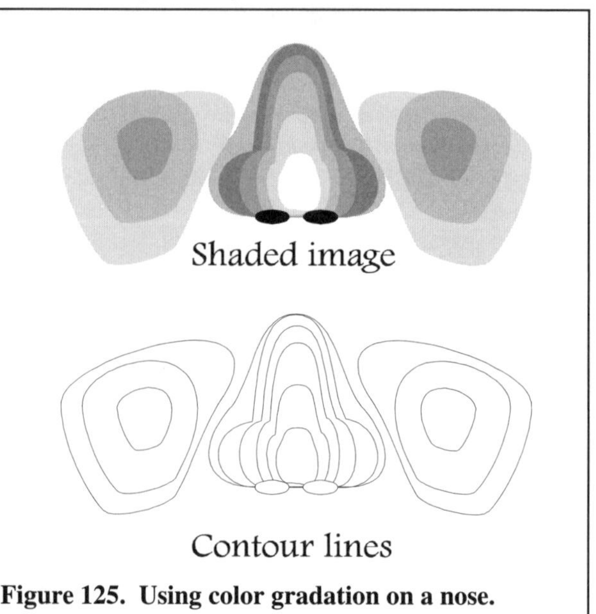

Figure 125. Using color gradation on a nose.

color to be able to develop a more natural looking portrait cane. So go back to that section, review it, and blend some colors.

Once you have a variety of facial colors, you are now ready to plan how you will use them to construct a more natural looking image. As an example, look at Figure 125 to see how you might use gradation of color to construct a more natural image of a nose and cheeks. In this image, the top surfaces of the nose are lighter colored flesh; there are gradations of color as you go from this top surface to lower ones. These both represent changes in skin tone as well as shadows.

One way that might help you to understand this is to think of the image like a topographic map with altitude contour lines. The area between lines of adjacent altitudes is colored with the same color. Thus for the image of the nose, you would start with the brightest color being the central bridge and tip of the nose. You would then work your way outward adding thin layers of slightly darker flesh colored glass. Using this approach, you have to keep track of the edge facial color of each construction so that the components will flow well from one to the next. To better understand gradation of color, you might want to go to a museum and examine some of the work of the great masters. But if your travel budget is like mine, you may instead have to settle on getting the book by Giovanni Sarpellon listed in the suggested reading list at the end of the chapter.

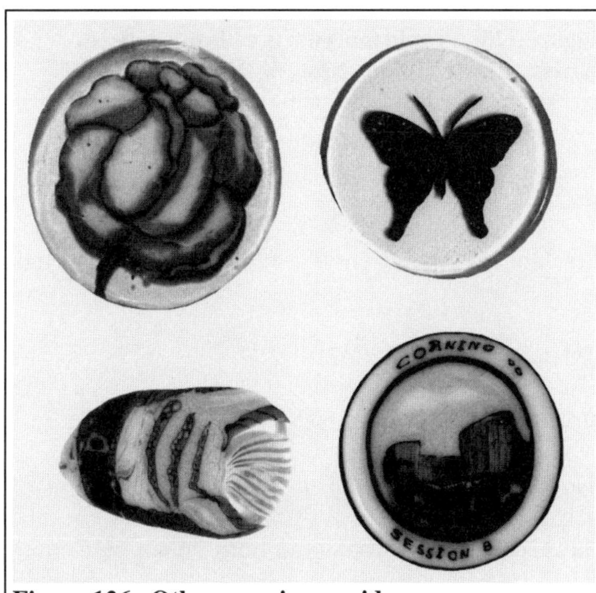

Figure 126. Other mosaic cane ideas.
Artist: Loren Stump Size: $^{5}/_{8}$" to 1" in diameter

The previous technique is still not the best that can be achieved. By studying the work of the classical mosaic cane master, Giacomo Franchini, Loren Stump came to realize that Giacomo was even going beyond the addition of multiple color layers. He noticed that he could not see the dividing lines between the different colors as he could with the work of others such as Luigi Moretti. By experimentation, Loren realized that in addition to developing a large color palette with formulations of many color variations, Giacomo appeared to be blending the colors further as he applied them so that he got gradual color variations such as those seen in paintings.

Figure 127. Aquarium bead made with fish murrine.
Artist: Pati Walton Size: 1"H x $1\frac{1}{4}$" W x $^{5}/_{8}$"T

In trying to duplicate this effect, Loren found that if he heated the surface of the bundle as he painted on the next color with stringers and worked it into the surface, that he was able to blend the applied color with that beneath it. Then by doing this with successive color additions, he could get the depth of color variation that he was looking for. During blending it's necessary, because you are applying cane to a hot surface, to frequent reshape the surface to ensure that you are not distorting your image. This is the type of technique that distinguishes the true master of mosaic cane construction from the rest of us. Go back and check out the detail of this in the cheeks of the men in Figure 123.

Other mosaic cane ideas

There are many other ways that mosaic cane can be used beyond letter and portrait cane. Figure 126 shows some image ideas that you could try making. Many bead artists are into making aquarium or underwater scene beads because glass lends itself to that look. The fish and other denizens of the deep can be fabricated as mosaic cane images and embedded into these beads. They can be applied over ocean, coral, seaweed, or other backgrounds. Building up multiple layers could allow an increased feeling of depth by applying more fish and seaweed cane. If you look at the aquarium bead in Figure 127, you can see that the fish are pieces of handmade murrine by Pati Walton. You can also add bubbles coming up from the fish by poking little indentations into the bead surface and trapping air as will be discussed later.

But, why stop with aquarium beads. You could make animal canes of all kinds and build them up to make forest or jungle beads like some of Pati's newer work. For background scenery, you would make rocks, trees, and bushes to increase the depth of the images in your beads. You could also use your animal cane to make zoo beads with animals in cages or circus beads with animals performing tricks. You could use them in religious themes, having them gathered around a manger or walking up the gangplank of the ark.

Another good image choice would be insect cane. This could be applied to beads with internal flowers. Butterfly cane such as the one shown in Figure 126 would be the perfect image to go with this type of application.

Of course, once you have portrait cane, why not continue on to make whole figures. Then you can go into comic or storybook beads. Watch out for copyright violations. Bible stories might really be popular and you don't have to worry about copyrights there. You could put these figures into other objects, as Loren Stump puts people into his cars. In Figure 128, you can see one of his police cars where he has built up the car around murrine of a policeman in the front seat and of a lady of the evening in the back seat. Why not have people peeking out of windows in houses and cottages, or peeking through portholes on boats, planes, trains, etc?

But why stop with earthly things. Why not go on to build whole new worlds in your beads as Josh Simpson builds them into his marbles. You could make mountains and volcanic canes to add to such images. Or continue on out into space where you can use planet, star, spaceship, or constellation canes. After all, once you have mastered basic mosaic cane manufacturing techniques, the sky is the limit.

Figure 128. People murrine used inside a bead. Artist: Loren Stump Size: ¾"H x 1½"L x ¾"W

Suggested further reading

Bruhn, Jutta-Annette. **Designs in Miniature**: The Story of Mosaic Glass, The Corning Museum of Glass, 1995

Kerkvliet, Brian, ***"Murrini Madness"*** from **Glass Art** Vol. 12 No. 4 May/June 1997

Kerkvleit, Brian, ***"Murrini: The Dip Stuff"*** from **Glass Art** Vol. 12 No. 5 July/August 1997

Kerkvleit, Brian, ***"The Cast Cane"*** from **Glass Art** Vol. 13 No. 5 July/August 1998

Sarpellon, Giovanni. **Miniature Masterpieces Mosaic Glass 1838-1924** (translated from Italian by Corning Museum of Glass) Prestal-Verlag, 1995

Wilson, Lewis C. **The Making of Murrini Faces, Letters, Mosaics** (Video) Crystal Myths, 1994

Wound beads

We are now ready to delve into the first of the many beadmaking techniques that will be discussed in this book that of mandrel wound beads. This technique is probably the easiest one for a novice to master. All you need is a basic torch setup and the flameworking skills that have been presented. This is also one of the largest beadmaking technique chapters in the book because it is currently the most popular technique.

Basic techniques for wound beadmaking

The basic technique of wound beadmaking consists of winding molten glass around specially prepared mandrels whose removal forms the hole in the bead. The beads are shaped using tools and the heat of the torch. They can be decorated with the items that we discussed in previous chapters as well as many other techniques to be discussed in this chapter.

Preparing for winding

There are very few special preparations required to get ready for making wound beads beyond getting a workspace ready for flameworking, as has been described earlier, and possibly making some constructions with which to decorate your beads.

The one thing that does have to be prepared before starting to wind beads is some stainless steel winding mandrels. If you prefer, you can purchase premade mandrels, but most glass beadmakers love to save money and make their own. They are made from TIG filler rod that can be purchased from any welding supplier in three-foot lengths.

The first thing that you will need to do is to cut them into about 12" lengths. Then, you have to grind or file any burrs off the ends so that the beads will be able to easily slip off of them. I grind mine all the way around on each end by holding them at a 45° angle to the grinder wheel. Be sure to also grind off any stock numbers that can sometimes be found on TIG filler rods.

Be careful when using the grinder, you don't want to end up shooting the rods back at you or jamming them into your hand. Have them tilted downward and away from you as you bring them into contact with the lower part of the grinding wheel as presented in Figure 129. The wheel is spinning downward on the side that you are working from. Therefore, if the wheel grabs the mandrel away from you, it will shoot it down and away from you. Don't work on the top of the wheel or the opposite can happen.

Figure 129. Taking burrs off mandrel on a grinder.

Next you have to coat the winding mandrels with a separator compound so that the beads can be removed from the mandrel when they are finished. Several different release formulations are available commercially, or you can develop your own. Many beadmakers use kaolin clay-based recipes similar to that used for kiln shelf separators. One such easy-to-make formula consists of a 40/40/20 solids mix by volume of kaolin clay, alumina hydrate, and whiting.

You first premix the dry ingredients and then mix them with water to about the consistency of a thick pancake batter. This mixture should sit for about a day to allow complete hydration of the alumina hydrate. You may want to always have some mixed up to the consistency of a thick paste that you can then thin down as needed, so you don't have to wait for hydration to occur. Some artists add a couple drops of sodium silicate solution to this mix to act as a fluxing agent.

If you find that your beads are not releasing well from the mandrel when using this recipe, decrease the kaolin clay/alumina hydrate ratio and add a little powdered graphite or more whiting. On the other hand, if the release layer is too fragile, increase this ratio. Instead of alumina hydrate, some artists use 200 mesh or finer flint. The Japanese typically use a 30/70 mix of porcelain clay to volcanic ash. If you already have it, you could try a commercial kiln shelf mix.

There are also a number of other mandrel separator materials to choose from. Zircon graphite, available from refractory suppliers, works well and is the main refractory ingredient of "Sludge" or "Super Sludge." It dries quicker than clay-based separators and you can almost go directly into the flame with it. I also find it to be very durable and to form fewer bubbles than clay based separator compounds. The one down side to its use is that it settles fairly quickly and needs to be mixed well before use.

I have been offered two suggestions on how to get around this problem. One is to drop some less than perfect beads into your separator container to assist in mixing the separator as you shake the container. Another good idea is to keep your separator in an old blender and whip it up a little before you dip your mandrels. It also makes it real easy in adding water to thin it down a little.

Mix up whichever separator formulation you choose to work with to about the consistency of a thick pancake batter and store it in a tightly sealed container to prevent it from drying out. Dip your mandrel into the separator and pull it out. For short dips just straight in and out works best. For long dips, tilting your release container and dipping nearly horizontal is the way to go. The coating should be smooth and uniform. If not, the separator is not mixed well enough. Allow the mandrel to air dry before use.

When drying, the mandrels should be arranged so that the drying separator coatings do not touch anything. I find that splaying the mandrels out,

Figure 130. Coating mandrels with separator.

coated end up, in a tin can works well for me. Other artists I know stick them in sand or polystyrene foam to hold them upright. Do whatever is easiest for you. Preferably, you should let the mandrels air-dry overnight. If you do not have that much time, let them air dry for a few minutes and then try passing them through a bushy flame to complete drying. If you can get them to dry without popping or cracking the separator coating on them should be safe to use.

The coating should have some visible thickness to it. I like to have it at least $^{1}/_{32}{}^{th}$ of an inch thick. If your coating is not thick enough on the first dip, you can dip the mandrel a second time after the first dip dries. Some artists advocate this, but for most purposes I prefer a smaller diameter hole in my beads and find one dip to be sufficient. If I want a larger hole, I prefer to use larger diameter mandrels instead.

Long thin olive jars, available from the grocery store, make good containers for dipping mandrels. They allow more of your mandrel to get coated when you dip an end into the separator solution without needing to prepare a large volume of separator compound. With a longer coating of separator on your mandrel, besides having the option of making bigger beads you also have the option of winding multiple beads on one mandrel.

Having longer dips also allows you the option of winding your bead on the center of your mandrel. Some artists like to do this because it allows them to hold the mandrel on either end so they can come in from all angles as they work on complex beads. Being right handed, I find the left side of a bead much harder to decorate than the right. Being able to flip the bead would make getting at the left side easier.

The other thing that you want to do before starting to make beads is to clean your glass rods. They sometimes get an oil film on them that can discolor your work. Isopropyl alcohol works well for this purpose but be aware that alcohol vapors are flammable and can flash into flame if they come into contact with an ignition source like your torch flame. So if you use it to clean your rods, do it ahead of time. If you want something to clean with at your bench, you may want to try ammonia instead. It is non-flammable although it does have slightly more toxic vapors.

Every artist has their own little twist on cleaning their glass, for example Sharon Peters is into leather. She has a nice soft piece similar to a shammie that she says does a great job of cleaning. A convenient thing to have around is one of those hospital alcohol dispensers where you just push down on the top of the dispenser with a towelette to moisten it with the contents. Note that as you consume the glass rod with which you have been working, you will reach an area of the rod where you have been holding it and will have to clean it on the fly. For this reason, you will want some cleaning material available at your bench even if it is only a dry cloth.

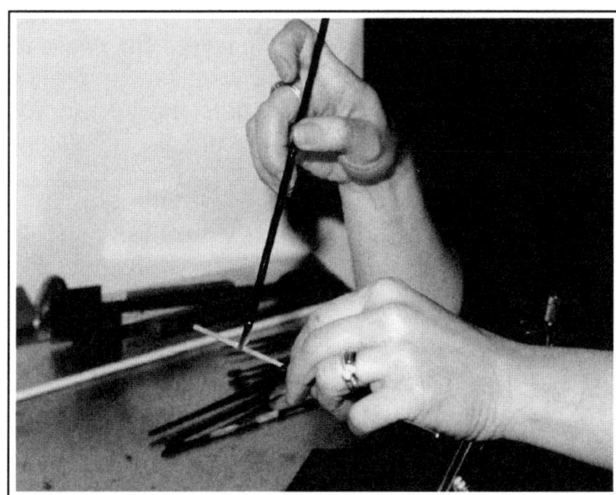

Figure 131. Hand positioning when winding a bead.

Winding a bead

Start by preheating the winding mandrel slightly to mature the separator compound. You don't have to get it really hot; just warm it enough to get rid of the last bit of chemical water and park it in the back of your flame. Most separator compounds will change color slightly as they mature. This aids in telling when they are ready. Next, take a glass rod and develop a small gather on the end of it. Then wind the molten glass from the gather onto the mandrel.

Do this by adding the glass from the feed rod, which you are holding in your right hand in the pencil mode, assuming that you are right-handed. Apply the glass from the gather through the flame onto the winding mandrel, which is just beneath the flame as seen in Figure 131. Try to make sure that this gather is large enough to wrap all the way around the winding mandrel. Wind it onto the mandrel by rotating the mandrel away from you at a rate at which the glass is able to flow evenly from the feed rod onto the mandrel. Have this first wrap going perpendicular to the mandrel and get it nice and uniform.

Once you make it completely around the mandrel, your basic pea bead is virtually done. If you want, you can go on to make it larger by continuing to wrap more glass on top of the first wrap and melting it in. Alternatively, you can make your bead longer by spiraling on more glass as illustrated in Figure 132. To do this, you angle the rod off into a helical spiral of glass along the mandrel, trying not to trap bubbles. It helps to give a little push with the rod into the edge of each previous wrap to squeeze any air out and to push the glass together before spiraling on more glass. I also find moving from left to right easier so I place my starter beads on the left

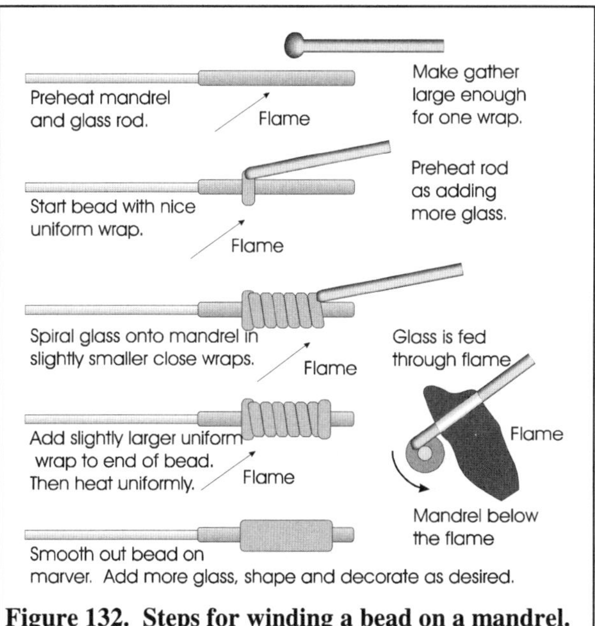

Figure 132. Steps for winding a bead on a mandrel.

side of the separator coated portion of the mandrel. As you add glass to the spiral, remember to keep the bead below the flame and the feed rod in the flame. Also be sure to rotate the feed rod in your pencil grip to uniformly heat the rod around its circumference. It is best for right-handers to rotate the rod counterclockwise because this brings the hot glass down onto the mandrel. If you don't rotate the feed rod, it will tend to be more viscous (stiffer) on one side of the rod and this can exert enough pull on the bead to break the separator coating. This problem can also be prevented by twisting the rod back and forth as you apply the glass or by superheating the glass as you apply it such that it is very fluid.

Make sure that you do not let the glass touch any bare, uncoated sections of the mandrel or it will stick to them. If this happens, you will not be able to remove the bead without cracking it and you will be the proud owner of a beaded swizzle stick.

How much glass you add is up to you. A small bead may require only two or three wraps of glass. Larger ones will require adding many more layers. Just remember that the larger the bead gets, the more it needs annealing. **Also, the wall thickness of your beads should typically never be less than the thickness of your mandrel.** Of course this rule of thumb must be used with a grain of salt when you are winding large pieces like bracelets, rings, etc.

You may find that you actually end up making a lot of small round beads. This is because they make good spacer beads to place between your more complicated beads on a necklace. Sometimes you may want to make a number of these small round spacer beads with slightly varying diameters as a design element in a necklace. This can be hard to do. If you just haphazardly make a bunch of these beads hoping that they will have enough variation, you may get lucky occasionally. The size of these beads can be controlled a little better by taking a tip from Paula Radke. She chops up her rods into short pieces of varying length. Then when she makes a bead from each of the pieces, they will have a natural variance in diameter and mass.

When adding glass to the mandrel, pay special attention to the first and last wrap at the ends of the bead. Make sure that you apply a uniform wrap all the way around the mandrel at these locations. This will help prevent developing jagged ends on your beads. During the rest of the application, apply the glass smoothly in a close spiral. Push against the previous wrap as seen in Figure 132 to prevent trapping bubbles between wraps. This ensures that the glass flows into any undercuts on the previous coil. Also slightly overlap each of them. Incomplete fill between wraps can lead to cracking of the bead later because these voids act as initiation sites for cracks.

As you add glass to the mandrel, establish the length of the bead on the first layer. Jim Smircich actually makes a little mark on his separator compound with the points of a compass to help judge how long a bead he is trying to make. Make the base layer just slightly shorter than the length you want for your finished bead. Then add a little extra glass onto the ends of the wraps to allow for marvering over into a smooth end as shown in Figure 132. Then marver the bead out to final size to get a nice round edged thread hole.

A variation on winding is to wind your bead using multiple colors side by side axially down the length of the bead. Caitlin Hyde uses this technique because she believes that it gives greater depth of color to her beads especially with transparent colors. Some of her beads can be seen in the color plates. I find that this multiple color technique can also give interesting effects when the bead is decoratively distorted by raking. Raking, which is explained later, produces some interesting swirls of colors when used on layered color beads.

Continue to work at establishing the general shape of the bead on each succeeding layer. Be aware as you are shaping that you may want to remove the bead from the heat before it gets as soft as you want. This is because heat will still be conducting

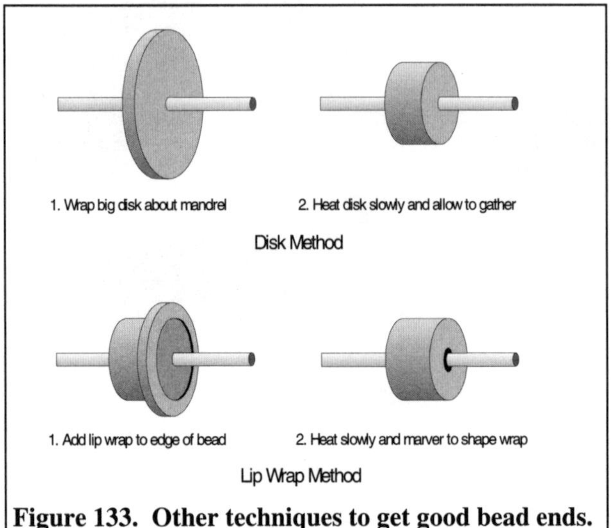

Figure 133. Other techniques to get good bead ends.

into the center of the bead from the surface after being removed from the flame. Thus if you wait until it appears as soft as you want in the center, it may become too soft on the outside.

Remember to typically hold the feed rod no closer to the torch than about two thirds of the way out in the flame so that you do not overheat the glass. If you do overheat it, the result will be many bubbles both large and small in the molten gather on the end of your glass rod, which will subsequently end up in your bead.

Remember to always keep your mandrel rotating just as you did your glass rods when gathering. This keeps the bead centered on the mandrel instead of drooping off of it, although you can also use drooping to good advantage when trying to center a bead that may have gone awry or to purposely make drooped pendant beads.

Try not to overheat the first layer of your bead. If you do, the glass may flow along the mandrel and form jagged edged holes on the end of the bead that can cut the bead-stringing thread. This happens because as you get the glass hotter, it reduces in viscosity and wants to wick out onto the mandrel, leaving thin sharp edges. Artists used to working with borosilicate glass may have a problem with this when they switch to soda-lime glass, because it is so much softer and flows so readily.

If you have this problem, don't panic. You can correct for it by reheating the bead while holding the mandrel tilted down at about a 30° angle. This will cause some of the glass in the body of the bead to flow back out to the end. Of course, if all else fails, you can grind those jagged ends off later.

I am aware of two alternate methods of winding beads to help get nice rounded bead ends, not sharp ones. These two techniques are illustrated in Figure 133. The first consists of winding a disk about your mandrel and then slowly heating the disk so that it gathers in on itself to form a nice rounded bead. Avoid overheating the disk so much that the glass wicks out onto the mandrel. The second technique involves adding glass to the end of your bead up away from the mandrel so that it looks like a disk at the end of your bead. Then with use of heat from your torch and some light rolling of the bead on your marver, this glass will roll over to extend the body of your bead. This will leave a nice rounded end and is a great way to add contrasting colored endcaps onto your base bead.

Figure 134. Using a notched paddle to steady mandrel while heat shaping bead.

To aid in holding your winding mandrel steady while heating a bead in the flame, you may want to fashion a tool to hold the bead end of your mandrel up. This can be something as simple as notching and putting a small indentation in the corner of your graphite paddle in which to stick the end of the mandrel, as shown in Figure 134, or you can purchase one of Jim Smircich's "tail stock holders." Here he is making a comparison to a lathe where you have your hand as the motor at one end and a non-powered holder at the other.

The tail stock holders have a ball at one end to slide on your bench and a flat with an indentation on the other end in which to stick the end of the mandrel. The length of the tool is about the height of the flame at the proper working distance from your flame. You can easily make a tool like this yourself if you want. Jim pinches off the separator on the end of the mandrel when it is wet so it doesn't start flaking off as you use the tool to steady the mandrel.

If you go the notched paddle route, you may want to purchase one of the brass insert kits being manufactured by Vince Henley. They prevent of the mandrel from drilling the hole deeper into the paddle with use. The kit contains everything that you need to modify a graphite paddle and install the insert. The insert has the added benefit of reducing friction during rotation.

Sometimes while winding a bead you may trap air between the wraps that forms a bubble or you may have bubbles form from damp separator compound. Interior bubbles can weaken your beads as well as being unsightly in transparent glass beads. In order to bring a bubble to the surface to remove it, get the bead soft by heating the area of the bead with the

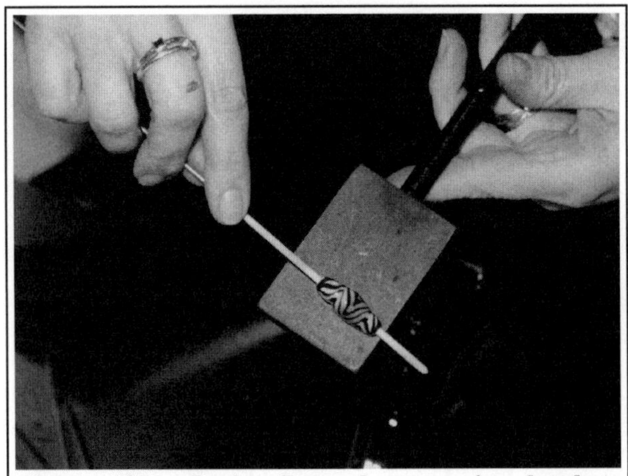

Figure 135. Janice Peacock marvering bead to shape.

bubble. Then push on the glass next to the bubble with your tweezers and try to force it to the surface. Once on the surface, chill the top of the bubble by touching your tweezers to it. Then, reheat the bubble to pop it. To fill in the void left by the bubble, it is best to evenly heat the bead and allow the surrounding glass to flow into the void rather then trying to add glass to the void. Adding glass on top of a popped bubble invariably results in trapping more air to form another bubble.

Shaping a bead

Beads, unless they are small round ones which contract into the shape that you want during a thorough reheating after wrapping, will usually require some handworking to form them into shape.

Handworking a bead into a regular shape is accomplished primarily through marvering or mashing, although master beadmakers can also do a lot of shaping just through the use of heat and gravity. As discussed earlier, marvering can be done on a number of different surfaces. Small graphite paddles are what is generally used for this purpose, because they can shape and absorb heat from a bead without discoloring it. There are also specialized paddles that have grooves and cut outs in them to form different bead shapes. These include spheres, cylinders, tear drops, etc.

To marver a bead, heat it until it's soft but not runny. (Overheating is the number one mistake made by most beginning beadmakers.) Remove it from the flame and allow it to cool for a couple of seconds while continuing to rotate the mandrel so the bead does not droop. Then shape it by rolling it on a paddle or marver. Apply very light pressure as you first roll the bead on the marver while the glass is soft, but gradually increase pressure on the bead as it hardens.

As an example of shaping beads on a marver, let's discuss making a torpedo bead, a long biconic shape. As seen in Figure 136, you first roughly shape the bead by strategically adding a few extra layers of glass in the right locations. Then heat either the right or the left cone and start shaping by rolling the bead on the marver at the correct angle. Try not to groove the separator compound as you do so because this may cause the bead to break free of the mandrel.

After roughly shaping the bead, concentrate on refining the shape at the apex of the cone by only heating the top two thirds of the cone. Once you have this end to the desired shape, concentrate on the base portion of the cone by only heating the bottom two thirds of the cone and rolling the bead on the marver on the apex of the cone. Then repeat this process on the other side. Don't forget to marver the ends if needed, as shown in Figure 137.

From this example, you see that part of the trick in marvering a bead into shape is not trying to do it all at once. It is important not to get the bead too soft

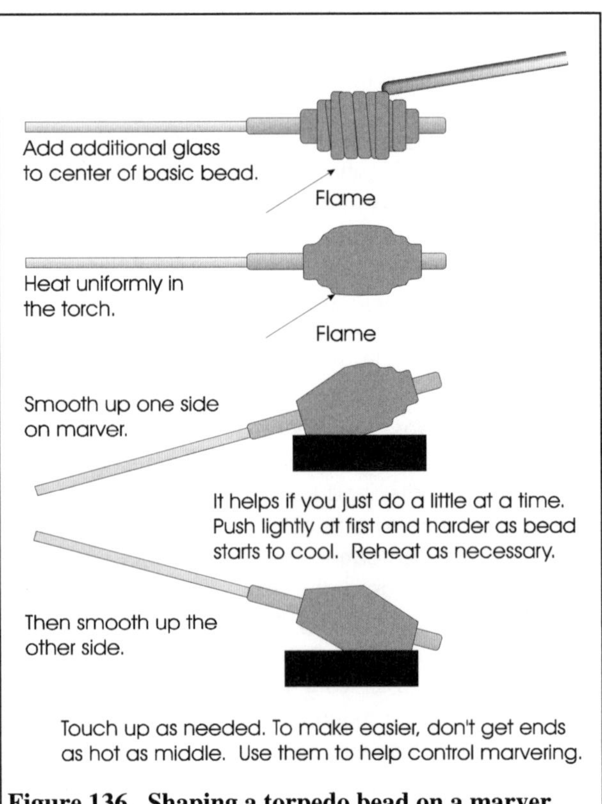

Figure 136. Shaping a torpedo bead on a marver.

Figure 137. Shaping the end of a bead on a paddle.

or it will flow too fast and may tend to form folds as you roll it on the marver. This is also the reason that you wait for a couple seconds before marvering the bead. Overheating may also result in sharp edges around your thread holes as the glass on the ends wicks out onto the mandrel. Instead, try to shape the bead little by little for better control of the process. As you shape your bead and later as you decorate it, remember to reheat the whole bead every once in a while. Otherwise, one section may get so cool that it thermal shocks as you move it back into the flame to continue work on it. This is important since both marvers and paddles really suck heat out of a bead.

In addition to rolling a bead on the marver to create round cross sectional shapes, you can also use a marver to put flat surfaces onto a bead. Juanita Dunn likes to put a flat surface on the back of some of her larger beads because she says that it makes them lay in a more controlled manner when worn.

By using this technique to add multiple flat surfaces, you can also create shapes like rectangular solids and cubes. To do this, just get the bead soft and press it down on the marver with your paddle. This forms two flat surfaces at the same time. Then flip the bead a quarter turn and press again. You can flatten or shape the end of the bead by pressing it on the end of the marver.

Whenever you flatten part of a bead with a tool you will put a set of concentric ripples on the surface of the glass. They are called chill rings and can be very distracting. They are the result of using a cold tool on hot glass. You can reduce the tendency of their formation by warming the tool ahead of time, but you may risk it sticking to the bead if the tool is made from metal. It is suggested instead that you

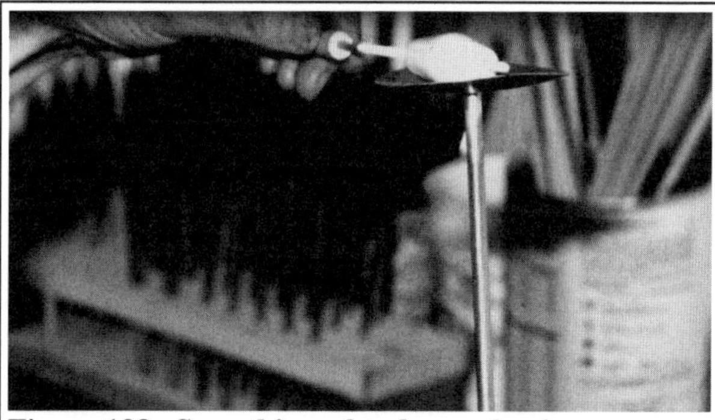
Figure 138. Smoothing a bead on a shaping cup.

go back and reheat the bead surface slightly to remove the marks.

Besides using paddles to shape a bead, you can also shape them on the home-made shaping cups like those that I discussed earlier, René Roberts likes using them because she can make them to fit the graceful curves that she likes to put on her beads. They are used like paddles, except that you do not roll the bead down the length of the cup. Instead, you spin the bead in place on the shaping cup as seen in Figure 138, as you would with paddles that have shapes cut into their surface such as marble molds, button molds, etc..

a good thing about them is that you can make shaping cups for whatever smooth arc shape that you want. You can even make shaping cups with multiple bends where you have a sharper curve in one plane than in another. You do this by hand tweaking a cup to give it a little sharper bend in one direction. With such a cup, you can subtly change the curvature of a bead to whatever you want by working at slightly different orientations on the multiple bend cup.

When using shaping cups, like any other brass tool, it helps to lubricate them with a little beeswax. This will help prevent the tool from sticking to the glass. Avoiding getting the cup too hot also helps prevent the glass from sticking to it.

Another way to shape beads is to pinch them using pliers. Mashing pliers are generally used to flatten beads, as was done by pushing the bead between a marver and a paddle. If you have a set of mashing pliers with a large throat, they can also be used to shape a bead in other ways. By gently squeezing the bead in a nibbling fashion, mashing pliers can be used to quickly rough out the shape of beads that are symmetrical on a plane that goes through the axis and is perpendicular to the axis. This means

Figure 139. Shaping a bead using mashers.

that you can use them to form cylindrical and torpedo shaped beads as well as flat ones.

You achieve different shapes by changing how you hold the mandrel relative to the jaws. By holding the mandrel parallel to the masher jaws as in Figure 139, you can make cylindrical beads. As you tilt the mandrel more and more relative to the jaws of the masher, you will get sharper and sharper torpedo beads. If you change the tilt of the mashers as you move from point to point on the bead, you can use them to form smooth arcs.

Of course mashing pliers can also be used to mash a bead flat. When you do this, you are making disk or tableau beads. When mashing, be aware that you may leave chill marks that you have to deal with.

Mashing pliers may also have textured surfaces to add another design element to your beads. The most commonly available pliers have rippled surfaces that can be used to give a leaf-like texture to little leaf beads that you make for use in floral arrangements.

Texture can also be introduced onto the surface of a bead by marvering it on a textured surface. We discussed graphite or metal marvering surfaces with parallel grooves or patterned surfaces that are commercially available to use for this process. They are used as illustrated in Figure 140. Here, Sharon Peters is using a holy roller to put a pebbly surface onto a bead.

Figure 140. Introducing ridges in a wound bead

Figure 141. Using a parallel ridge marver to put spiraling grooves into the surface of a bead.

The parallel-ridged rollers provide an even more impressive effect. They are used to put a spiral of parallel grooves into the surface of a bead, as seen in Figure 141. The surface texture that you will get from each of the surface textured rollers will vary somewhat with the angle at which you roll the bead across the surface and how hard you push. You can also make you own textured rollers or use things like files and wire brushes to introduce interesting surface textures.

To put other interesting surface images into your beads, you can try pressing them into brass figurative molds, dies that you have carved using pieces of graphite, or cast images into plaster. Alternatively, you could press things like leather dies into a bead while it is still hot and soft. This idea will be discussed in a little greater detail later.

As mentioned earlier, some master beadmakers can do a lot to shape their beads using mainly the heat of the torch, surface tension, and gravity. Jim Smircich is one of those beadmakers. He specializes in large biconic beads with dynamic colors shaped almost entirely by this technique. To lengthen and round the end of a bead, he heats up one side to the point where it just starts to glow. He pulls the bead out of the flame, allows its outside surface to cool slightly and then tilts the mandrel to get the glass to flow.

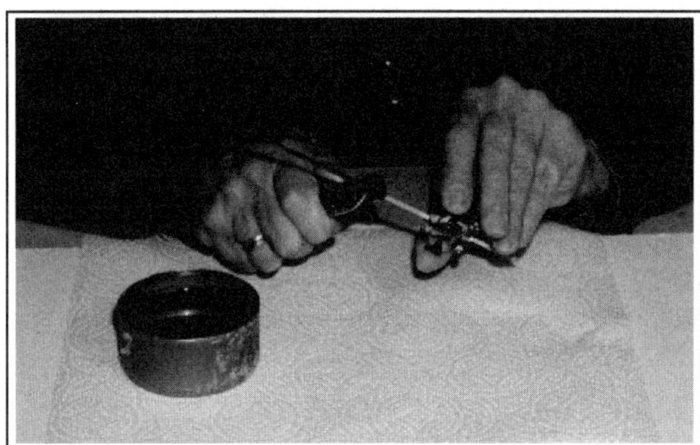
Figure 142. Removing a bead from a mandrel.

This technique can be used to move more material out to the end of a bead or back into the body depending on which way you tilt the mandrel. Of course he is keeping the bead rotating the whole time to prevent drooping. Glass can be brought into any area of a bead by heating a ring up around the bead and allowing surface tension to pull glass into this hot ring from either side of it. To find out more about these techniques, see my booklet on Jim Smircich from the beadmaker series

Finishing the bead

Once you have finished shaping and decorating your bead, flame anneal it and put it into heated vermiculite to cool more gradually. After you are through for the day, turn off the hot plate under the pan of vermiculite to allow them to cool more gradually. When it has cooled to the touch (about a half-hour or so), you can remove the beads from the vermiculite and take them off the mandrels before annealing them.

Instead of using vermiculite, some artists prefer to directly insert their beads into an annealing kiln that they have sitting on their bench. This also allows them to be able to preheat rods and decorations prior to use. It alleviates the use of vermiculite which as we discussed, some glass bead artists are starting to worry about because of its close physical structure to asbestos. Also by cooling your beads in a more controlled manner that is possible using an annealer, you will not have to go back and anneal them later.

To take a bead off the mandrel, grasp the center of the mandrel with some pliers in one hand and the bead with your other. I find that needle nosed pliers do not work very well for this purpose as they do not grip the mandrel firm enough. I use a small set of Sears Arc Joint® pliers or some Vise Grip® pliers for this purpose. Some artists put the mandrels in a vise. Once you have a tight grip on the mandrel, twist the bead to break it free from the separator compound. Continue to gently twist the bead back and forth as you pull it all the way off the mandrel. Move your grip on the mandrel as you move the bead to avoid bending the mandrel. If your mandrel has a bend or a snag on the end, you may have to pull the bead off the handle end instead.

If you cannot break the beads free by twisting them, you can try soaking them I water for about ten minutes. This can be less messy if you break off the surrounding exposed bead release first by munching on it with your pliers over a wastebasket.

You can clean out some of the separator compound by inserting an appropriately sized drill bit or one of those twisted wire cleaning tools into the bead hole and twisting it to remove more separator. Be careful as you do this though, because it is easy to crack your beads especially around the edge of the hole if the drill bit is too large. I find that just sliding the bead back and forth on the mandrel before you take it off also helps to clean the hole as well as getting the mandrel ready to redip in the separator.

Figure 143. Cleaning out the bead hole.

Since some of the separator compounds may be slightly toxic, you may want to wear a respirator with a dust cartridge when you are cleaning out bead holes—if not for the separator compound, then for the glass dust. Clean the beads directly over your trash container and dispose of the powder properly after you are done. Clean up any loose powder with a wet towelette. Some artists even recommend that you clean out the separator compound under water to avoid raising dust because of these concerns but I find that this sometimes makes it harder to get the inside of the bead clean.

Figure 144. Grinding the sharp edges on the end of a bead off with diamond tools and a Dremel®.

If you have any sharp edges on your bead holes, they need to be removed so that they will not cut the cord on which you string the beads. Of course the real solution is not to have any sharp edges in the first place. Eventually as your skill level improves, the frequency and degree of these sharp edges should decrease. The sharp edges can be removed by using a diamond grinder or by rubbing them back and forth on a file. Dressing tools in the form of small diamond coated spheres or cones mounted on a shaft and inset into a handle are commercially available to help with this task. Make sure that you lubricate them with water to keep the glass dust down and to extend the life of the diamond tools. I like to use the tapered diamond-coated needle-like tool that is seen in Figure 143.

To speed up the cleaning process, you can use a Dremel® or light handheld bead cleaners with diamond coated bits, but be careful or the bit may skip across the surface of the bead and scar it. I like the bits that have a nice cone shape to them for this purpose because they get just the inner edge of the hole. Since this should be done wet, I often add a flex shaft to the Dremel® to avoid any chance of shocking myself. That combined with a speed-control foot pedal gives me complete control over the process.

Figure 145. Ancient vessel pendant made with multiple enamels layers
Artist: Stevi Belle
Size: 3½"H x 2¾"W
Photo by: Jerry Anthony

These same tools can be used to clean up and polish the inside of your bead holes. This is very important for getting good-looking transparent beads. Some artists avoid this problem by putting an opaque core in their transparent beads. After reaming the bead holes out well, if the inside of the bead is not shiny enough for you, try applying a little Future floor wax to the inside of the hole with pipe cleaners for a real good looking bead hole.

Lastly remember to kiln anneal your beads as is discussed later in the chapter on annealing. If not, they may crack sometime in the future leading to poor client relations.

Decorating wound beads

There are many different ways to decorate wound beads. We will start by discussing simple decorating techniques like frit and dots. From there, we will move on to more complicated decorations such as trailing on colored lines, and then we will discuss how to distort these decorations. But when decorating always remember to go back and heat the entire bead every once in a while to prevent thermal shock.

Frit and enamels

One of the first decorating techniques for a beginner to learn is picking up glass frit or other materials off a marver. Frit is the name given to small pieces of glass in the size range between chunks and powders. Picking up frit can create interesting random patterns of color and will provide instant success for the novice beadmaker.

To use this technique, spread out a single color or a pleasing array of colored frit onto your marver. Get your basic bead tacky hot in the flame (just starting to glow) and roll it in the frit on the marver or in a spoon. The bead will pick up some of the frit, more if the marver is being warmed on a hot plate or by your torch. Return the bead to the flame and heat the frit to get the surface texture that you want. This can vary anywhere from smooth, where you melt and marver all the frit into the surface of the bead, to sandy, where the frit is heated just enough to barely bond it to the bead.

When you roll your bead in frit, you may want to consider whether to cover the ends of the beads or not. If you don't roll up to the ends, you can keep your ends clean but not decorated. If you roll up to the mandrel, you will invariably end up with jagged ends on your bead that will have to be ground off later, but they will be decorated.

Figure 146. Petroglyph bead with dusted enamel coating
Artist: Kate Fowle Meleney
Size: 1¼"L x ½"W x ¼"T

Reduction frit is a commercially available frit that gives a shiny finish when applied to the surface of your beads. It is so called because the metal oxide colorants in this frit easily break down in a reducing environment to form a shiny metallized layer on the surface of the glass. This frit is usually made from relatively compatible Kugler glass (COE ≅ 90) and should be applied thinly on Effetre.

Kugler glass powders and frits, as well as Zimmerman can be used to decorate the outside surface of glass beads in thicker layers. Stevi Belle uses these a lot in her work to give it a weathered appearance as seen in Figure 145. To use them this way, you will have to change your base glass to one with which they are more compatible such as Bullseye or Schott glass.

If you do not want to change your base glass from Effetre, you can still use similar techniques. Kate Fowle did a study on the compatibility of Thompson enamels with Effetre glass a couple of years ago. She found that some of the opaque window glass series enamels appeared to be compatible and produced nice colors. She got the Thompson Enamel Company interested in supplying enamels for beadmakers, so now they are supplying a whole line of Effetre-compatible enamels in assorted colors and frit sizes. These are the 9000 series enamels.

Enamels can be used to expand your Effetre color palette by either coating the outside of the bead or by blending them to create custom colors as was described earlier. Mixing the black enamel with an Effetre black rod, for example, will produce a deep black, instead of a purple, which will hold its color even when pulled out into fine stringers. You can also mix larger sized frits to achieve a granite-like look. Kate Fowle paints and stamps enamel paints onto beads and lightly fires them into the surface to produce petroglyph-like images. One of these beads can be seen in Figure 146. You can apply glass enamels or powders to the surface of a bead the same way that you apply frit, by heating the bead and rolling it in the powders. For more information on the use of enamels in beadmaking see my booklet on Kate Fowle Meleney from the beadmaker series.

Whenever using glass powders and enamels, you need to be aware of safety concerns for their use. Remember to wear your respirator and wash your hands after handling them and use a wet rag to clean up any material that you may have spilled.

Dots

Dots are added to a bead from a gather on a rod by touching the gather to the bead and pulling it away. This leaves a small blob from the gather on the surface of the bead. During this process, the bead is kept warm just beneath the torch flame to ensure a good joint to the dot. The gather is touched through the flame onto the bead below and pulled back away through the flame, as in Figure 147. You are doing this through the flame to avoid forming stringers of glass between the dot and the gather as you pull it away. If you are making big dots, which could result in big stringers as you pull the rod away, you may have to wind the stringer up as you pull away with a slight circular motion of the hot glass rod.

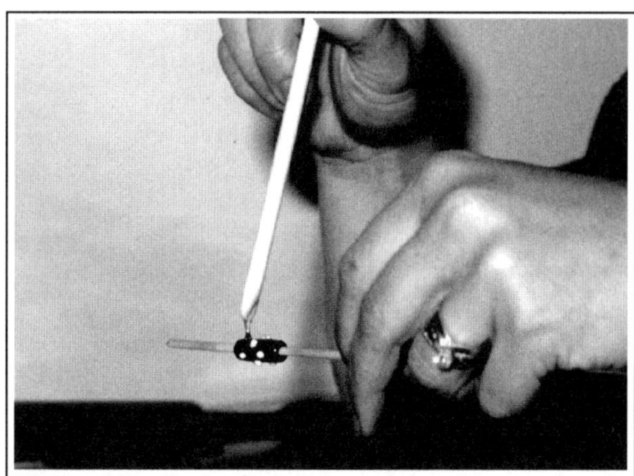
Figure 147. Janice Peacock applying dots to a bead.

Check to see that the joint between your dot and the surface of the bead is applied correctly. There should be no undercuts because this will allow the dots to break off at a later time. If there are undercuts, this indicates that you are not keeping the surface of the bead warm enough as you add the dots.

The size of your dots is controlled by a number of factors. They include:

- the size of your gather,
- how lightly you touch the bead,

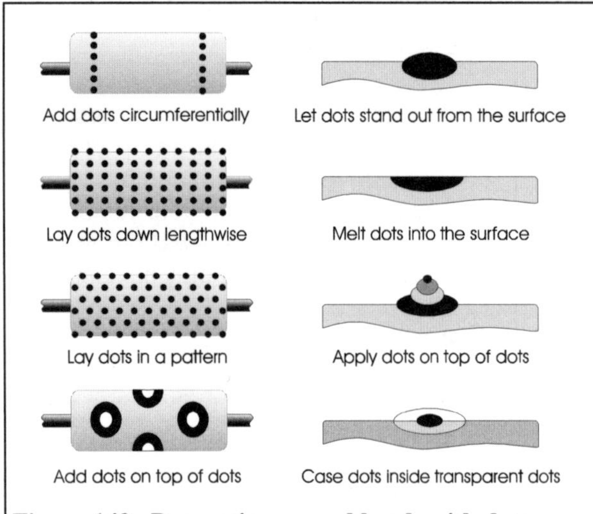

Figure 149. Decorating wound beads with dots.

- the diameter of your rod, and
- where you burn the stringer away.

When using smaller diameter glass rods or canes to apply dots, you will want to dot the bead through the sides of the flame where the heat is much less intense. Otherwise the cane will get fried by the flame and just curl up into a ball.

Figure 148. Warring state bead
Artist: Tom Holland
Size: 5/8"L x 5/8"Dia

You can make all sorts of patterns with your dots. Many glass bead artists work almost exclusively with dots and have made a real art form of it. This is also true of artists from past ages, as can be seen in the Chinese warring states beads. Many contemporary bead artists continue to work making dotted beads, and they are very beautiful. Figure 148 is an example of one of these. Dots can be added in many patterns: randomly, in lines, squares, etc. You can control the surface texture of the dot by how much you reheat the bead after application. You can even pile dots on top of other dots or encase dots within clear dots as shown in Figure 149.

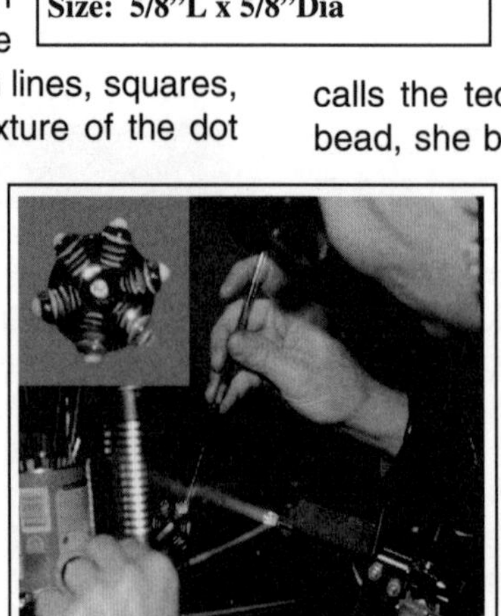

Figure 151. Sage making a stratified dot bead.

Dots can also be added in a rapid random pattern to form decorative layers on a bead. This is most often done to form things like foliage layers, as seen in Figure 150. In this case, you barely lift the rod off the bead, before going back in and applying another dot.

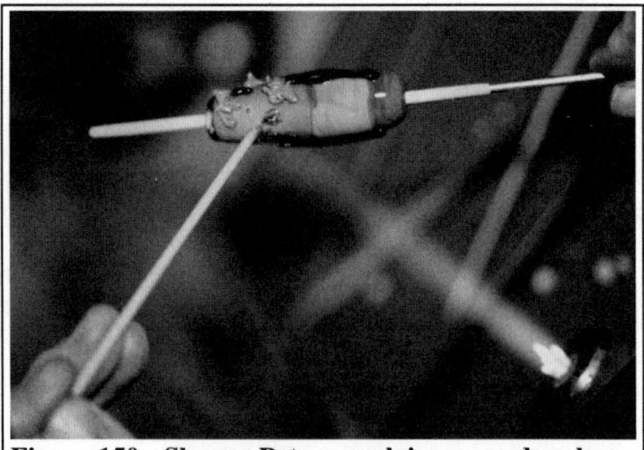

Figure 150. Sharon Peters applying a random layer of dots to a bead to form tree foliage.

I first saw Jana Burnham use one form of dotting that I really like. This was the application of transparent color dots over opaque white dots. She liked doing it on a black background but the technique is so versatile that it looks good on almost any base color. These dots can be melted into the surface to form sunken colored pools in the bead surface, or left raised. As dots are melted into the surface of the bead, they can form a net-like pattern if they are applied in a regular pattern to the bead surface. As an example of this, see the bead by Maud Mekalanos in the color plates. This is just one of the amazing things you can do using only dots. Dots can also be decoratively distorted in a subsequent step, as will be discussed later in this chapter.

Sage makes an interesting form of dot bead that I really like, and can be seen in the upper left of Figure 151. She calls the technique stratified dot weaving. For this bead, she builds up a disk bead by adding dots one on top of another to form strata-like cuts in the side of a hill. She usually uses repetitive patterns of transparent over opaque colors, often adding multiple transparent dots to each opaque dot, making the repetitive dot stratification more apparent. The thicker transparent layers make the bead appear more transparent and lighter.

The weaving portion comes from using multiple dot patterns (at least two) that she builds outward in the bead like spokes on a wheel. As she builds the disk outward, the dots from one spoke will slightly overlap those from the next spoke. After each dot is applied, it gets flattened just slightly with her paddle before she adds the next one. As she builds the disk larger in diameter, the size of the dots has to increase to keep the spoke-like pattern going.

Trailing

Trailing is the addition of decorative stripes from a gather onto a bead. To trail a simple stripe around the circumference of a bead, start by warming your bead while developing a gather on a rod of the stripe color. Pull both up out of the flame and lightly touch the gather to the bead. Then, slowly pull the gather away from the bead and spin the bead away from you at the same time.

Since you are not pulling the gather away through the flame as you did in making dots, a stringer will be pulled from the gather and laid down onto the bead. You need to pull away just slightly from the bead and twirl the bead quickly to apply the stringer. If you allow the stringer to cool too much, it will not attach to the bead. When you have gone all the way around the bead, pull the gather a little further from the bead. Then, blow on the stringer and wiggle it back and forth to break it off at the surface of the bead, or burn it off in the flame.

You need to make sure that the trailing is well attached all the way around the surface of the bead. Otherwise, when you put the bead back into the flame, the stringer will expand and break off. To ensure attachment, lightly heat the trailing in the edge of the flame and marver as necessary to get it to attach. Take your time, heat delicate trailings slowly, because they can burn off quickly if not well attached.

In doing this, you may develop a little glob at the overlap of the wrap where the gather left the bead. This glob can be fixed by using one of two techniques. The first is to remove some material by gently heating the glob till it starts to glow and touching a warm rod to it. The rod should be allowed to cool some or you will deposit more glass from it onto the bead, rather than removing glass from the glob on the bead. When you pull the rod away, material that was in the glob will transfer to the cooler rod and pull away as a stringer. You may have to do this a couple times to make it look right.

The other technique for fixing the glob is to use the remaining cooled stringer on the rod as a tool to stretch out the glob. Do this by heating the glob and using the stringer as a tool, touch the glob and stretch it to even out the circumferential wrap. At the end of the pull, let the stringer rest a second, blow on it, and break it off by rocking it side to side.

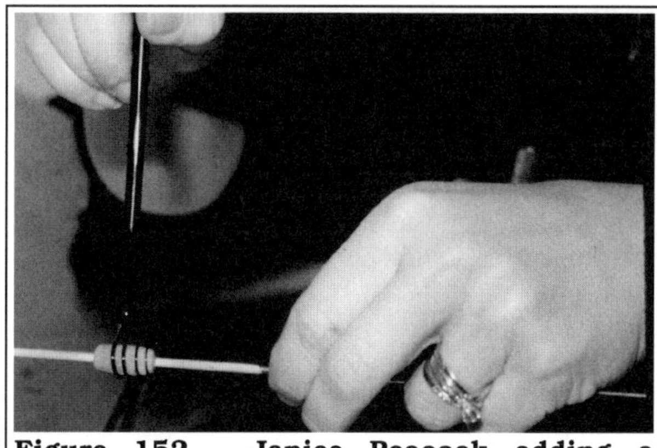

Figure 152. Janice Peacock adding a spiraled trailing.

Another way that trailing is commonly used is to apply a spiraling line onto a bead, as illustrated in Figure 153. You do this in almost exactly the same way as was done for the circumferential wrap. You start by touching the gather to one end of the bead. As you pull the gather away from the bead and twirl it into a trail, you slowly move the gather down the length of the bead. At the end of the bead, you pull

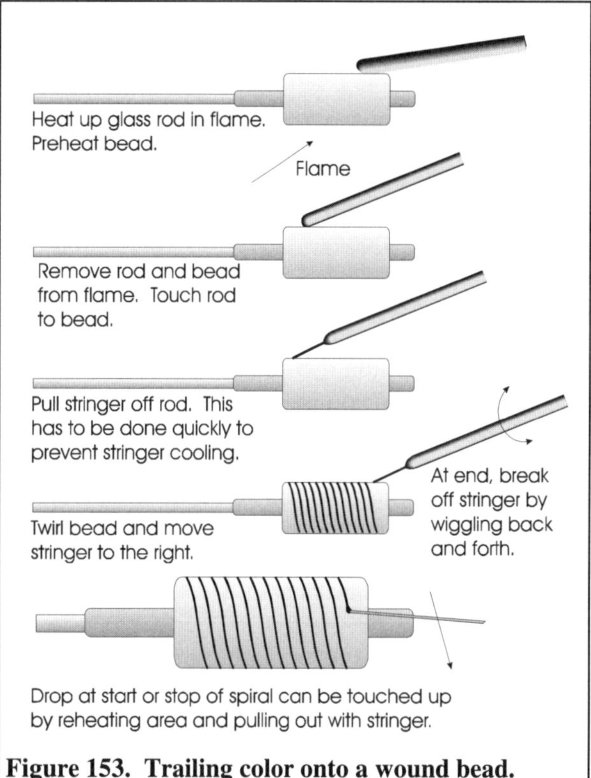

Figure 153. Trailing color onto a wound bead.

the gather away from the bead, pulling a stringer with it. You then break the stringer off at the surface of the bead. Any glob at the start or end of the trailing can be handled as before, except that if you decide to stretch it, you will have to stretch it in the direction to continue the spiral. After application, you heat the bead to work the spiral into the bead just like you did for the circumferential wrap.

There are a number of ways that you can vary the look of trailings. They can be applied in different directions. They can be added axially, circumferentially or spiraled on. You can vary the width of the trailing by the size of the gather, or by how fast you pull the trail from it. You can vary the spacing between the lines of spiral trailings. You can apply multiple spirals or spirals of different colors. You can add a second spiral in the opposite direction to make a cross hatched pattern. You can also distort them, as we will talk about next.

Distorting a bead

Sometimes you want to distort a pattern on the surface of a bead to achieve a different effect. There are many ways that the surface of a bead can be distorted. These include raking, furrowing, twisting, pressing or pinching. The first couple of these are achieved through the same general technique. The surface of the bead is heated and a tool is drawn across it to distort the surface. Note when doing this that only the surface has to be heated, not the whole bead down to the core.

Tools may be made of metal or glass. A glass tool is usually made by drawing a fairly sharp point from a glass rod of the same color as the surface feature you are trying to modify. One easy way to make a glass tool for distorting a trailing is to draw a little extra stringer from the gather at the end of the trailing. Then after breaking it free from the trailing, use what is left on the rod as a tool for distorting the trailing. Otherwise, you will have to pull a point from the rod prior to distorting.
You can also use a tungsten pick or a dental tool to drag across the surface, but I find the glass version is much easier. If you do decide to use a pick or dental tool, chill it in water between applications to prevent glass from sticking to it. An advantage in using a tungsten pick is that if it gets stuck in the bead, you can heat it up and pull it out without distorting the surface too much.

When using these techniques to distort a bead's surface, one thing that you need to be aware is that the size of the affected area varies with the temperature of the bead surface. If it is fairly hot, the viscosity of the glass will be low and the tool will easily slide through the glass, only affecting a narrow region of the glass surface. As the surface cools somewhat, the area that is affected gets larger because the viscosity of the liquid glass increases and pulls more on the surrounding surface. As it cools more, the glass gets very viscous and wants to pull large areas of the bead surface around the tool. Soon it cools even more and starts to get hard again, at which point the surface becomes undistortable.

Raking

The first technique for surface distortion that we'll discuss is called raking. In this method, you distort the surface of the bead by pulling a tool through the surface of the glass, as shown in Figure 154. You can rake through a number of different surface features. When done lengthwise across a trailed spiral a number of times in the same direction, the process is referred to as festooning. When you change direction on every other rake as shown in Figure 156, it is called feathering. You can also rake from the center to the edge of the bead or vice versa to get effects like the spider web bead seen in Figure 155.

Figure 154. Tom Holland raking surface of a bead. Photo by: Sage

There is a bit of controversy over the best tool for raking. Many beadmakers swear by a tungsten pick, while others rake beads by using a glass stringer of the same color as the surface decoration. This is the school I usually follow. To do this, start by pulling a point, and then rake the short point down the length of the bead and stop. Blow on the bead surface to solidify it and break the point free from the bead surface by wiggling it back and forth. It will usually break right at the surface. If not, use a tweezers to break the point off as near to the surface of the bead as you can.

Any undesirable stringer remaining can be removed by heating the area, removing the bead from the flame, and pulling off the excess material by touching it with a warm, but not hot, rod and pulling away. If you don't make it all the way down the length of the bead in a single rake, don't worry. Just break the point from the surface, rest the bead to allow it to set up, reheat the surface, and finish the rake. The cooling step helps prevent the bead from getting too hot and globby.

Figure 156 illustrates the effect of raking on a number of surface decorations like lines and dots. Raking through dots can create heart like images. Raking between dots creates a paisley-like effect that Carol Bugarin refers to as the old double dot drag. The figure also shows the difference between feathering and festooning.

Besides raking lengthwise down a bead you can also rake circumferentially or at an angle around a bead, as shown at the bottom of the figure. When raking circumferentially around a bead, you have to be careful not to pull so hard on the bead that you break it free from the mandrel. This is easier to do when raking circumferentially than lengthwise because there is a shorter length of separator material to react to the force in that direction.

You can prevent the bead separator breaking by not letting the bead surface get too cool. You also do not have to rake all the way across a surface. You can go just part way across, as will be discussed when we make an eye decoration for a tableau bead.

Figure 155. Spider web bead. Artist : Tom Holland Size 1½" L x ¾" W x 3/8" T

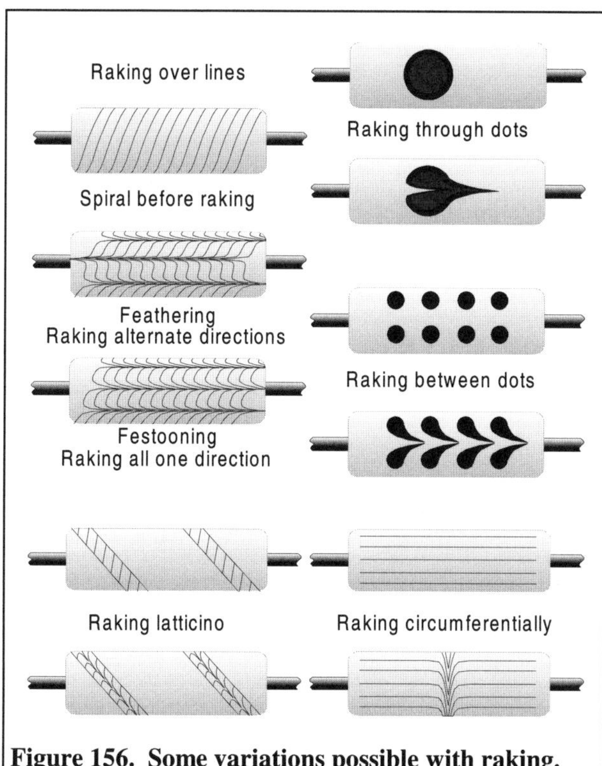

Figure 156. Some variations possible with raking.

The effect that you get when raking a bead varies a lot with the temperature of the bead and the tool. Tom Holland, who belongs to the metal tool school of raking, teaches three basic types of raking. The first is the cold rake. Here you use a cold tool on a cool bead and just barely move the surface of the bead as you glide over it. The second method is the hot rake with a cold tool. This version tends to drag more glass with it and ends with a decorative glob at the end of the rake. Last is the hot rake with a hot tool. Here, if the temperature is just right, you can glide right through the surface of the bead and exit without gathering any glass. In fact, Tom has perfected this technique to the point where, by preheating the bead ahead of himself as he goes, he can make multiple feathering rakes back and forth across the surface of the bead without ever having the tool leave the surface of the bead.

Furrowing

With raking, successive features are brought together and touch along the rake line, forming a line behind the tool. But what if you don't want them to touch and only want to distort them a small equal amount in the same direction? To achieve this effect, you can use a tool like the edge of your paddle or a knife to plow furrows through the surface of the bead. This will move the surface in a little V, something like the bow wave of a boat. It moves the entire surface in contact with the tool a little bit. The furrowing effect can change depending on the width of the tool. Furrowing with the rounded end of your tweezers gives a much different effect than using a sharp object like a knife.

In furrowing, we are not trying to drag the surface with us but only to push some of it a little ahead of the tool, so don't plow too deeply or you might drag the surface. This is really another form of cold raking, so obviously the tool and the bead must be kept relatively cool. Since you are working so cold,

Figure 157. Tom Holland furrowing a bead.
Photo by: Sage

you will also find that you may not be able to furrow the entire length of the bead in one pass. One quarter of an inch at a time may be a more reasonable goal. Then just splash on a little heat and furrow a little further.

If you want to move the surface a little more after your first pass, you can run another furrow through the surface of the bead at the same location. Running successive furrows through the same location will end up looking more and more like raking. By making a number of parallel furrows of alternate directions you will get a zig zag effect, as seen in Figure 157.

Twisting

Another way to distort a bead surface is, as was mentioned earlier, to twist it. To do this, get the portion of the surface that you want to distort hot. Remove the bead from the flame, touch the end of a stringer to the surface at the desired point, and twist it as seen in Figure 158. This will cause the local surface to be distorted in a spiral. Release the glass tool afterward by blowing on it to freeze the bead surface and then rocking the point back and forth to break it off at the surface. If it does not break free right at the surface, handle the situation as was

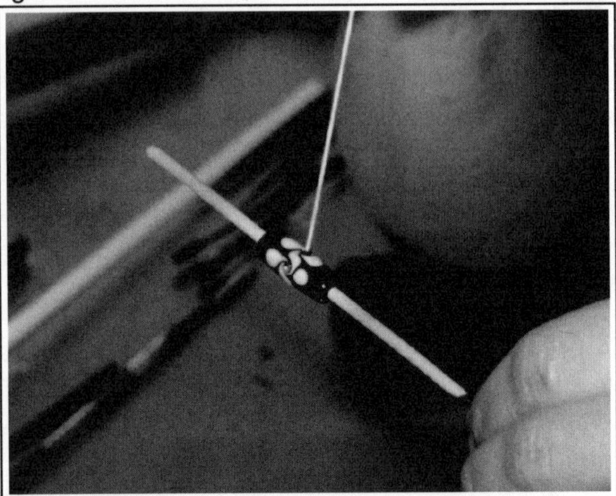
Figure 158. Janice Peacock twisting array of dots.

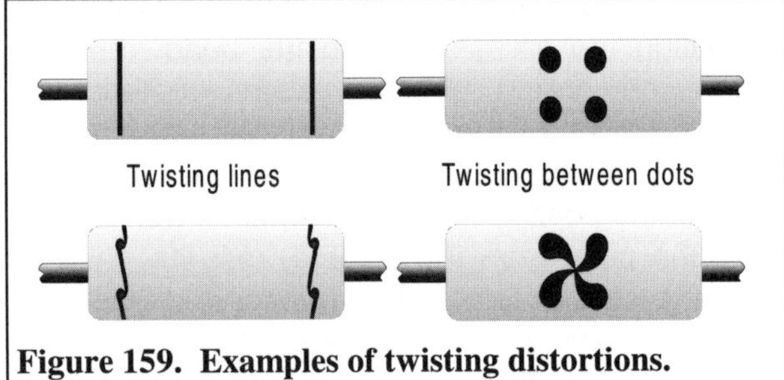

Figure 159. Examples of twisting distortions.

done for raking.

When done in the center of an array of dots this process makes a nice spiral pattern, as illustrated in Figure 159. When done on lines it makes the fancy loop pattern shown. One variation of twisting that Jim Wuerfel first showed me was to use a mosaic cane stringer as your tool. Then when you break off the tool, you get the pattern inside the cane in the center of the twist, as seen in Figure 160.

Figure 160. Result of twists made mosaic cane.
Artist: Jim Wuerfel Size: 2½"L x ¾"Dia

Poking

In addition to distortions created by moving the surface of the bead, you can also create interesting distortions by poking into it. This technique is most often used to form flower shapes in a bead. For example, you can make poppies in a clear bead as follows. After embedding a green stem in the bead and covering it with clear, you put a yellow dot on the bead surface. By getting the dot hot, poking into its center and backfilling the poked in area with clear, you end up with a flower.

A flower with multiple petals can similarly achieved by poking your tungsten pick down into the center area between a cluster of dots, as seen in Figure

Figure 161. Sage poking hole into a collection of dots to make a flower.

161. There are probably many other variations on this technique that you could develop, such as combining poking with twisting or poking into larger dots over smaller dots, or varying how deep you poke into a dot, etc.

Flow

It is also possible to make distort a bead's surface without using any tools at all. Here the effect is achieved by using gravity to your advantage to cause flow of the glass, as seen in Figure 162. All that you have to do is get your bead hot and rotate it in the torch flame just fast enough to keep its shape but slow enough that gravity exerts a slight pull on the hotter section of the bead. This will result in an effect in which lengthwise lines or dots take on a U like shape in the heated areas. You have to be very careful when doing this because it is very easy to let the bead flow out of control.

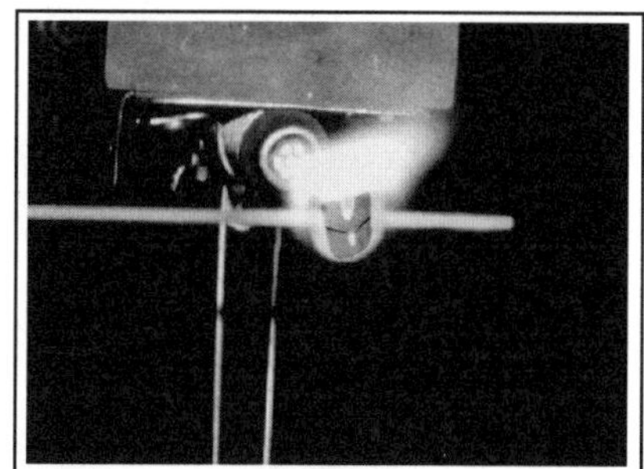

Figure 162. Distortion of a series of dots using gravity flow.

Pressing

Another interesting technique for decorating simple beads is to stamp them with leatherworking dies. These dies are available in a variety of shapes and sizes. By combining different dies or by multiple stamping with a die, a number of designs can be achieved. When selecting dies, try to ensure that there are no undercuts in them so that they will not become trapped in the glass. If you are making multiple impressions of a die into one bead, it may be necessary to chill the die in a small container of water between stampings to avoid sticking it to the glass. You might try backfilling stamped surfaces with clear glass to avoid losing the pattern as you reheat the bead.

Figure 163. Small fleur-de-lis imprint from a leather die used to stamp a bead.
Artist: Bonnie Blincoe. Size: 1¼"L x 1"W x ½"T.

I have even seen some artists use this technique to mark their signature stamp or a copyright symbol onto a bead. As an example of this, see the bead in Figure 163. Bonnie Blincoe uses the fleur-de-lis as a symbol for her beadmaking studio.

When you first purchase a die, it will probably have a rust-resistant plating over the surface of the image. With use of the die on hot glass, you will find that this plating will be eroded away, leaving them open to the possibility of rusting. To prevent this from happening, you should coat the surface of the die with oil whenever they are going to be put away for some period of time. Then before using them the next time, clean off the oil with some degreasing agents like soap and water followed by alcohol.

Pinching and stretching

Sometimes you want to really move glass around on a bead. You may want to add something like raised ridges or swirls into your bead. Alternatively you may want to stretch out sections of your bead to form things like wings, as is being done in Figure 164. These major distortions can be introduced through manipulation of the glass with tools such as tweezers or pliers. Use of any tool like this will cause some chill marking of the glass surface. Preheating the tools slightly can lessen this. After you have all the distortions put into the surface of the bead, they can, if desired, be softened slightly by reheating the bead in the flame. This will also remove any chill marks that the cold tools may have left. With a little imagination, you will find a lot of

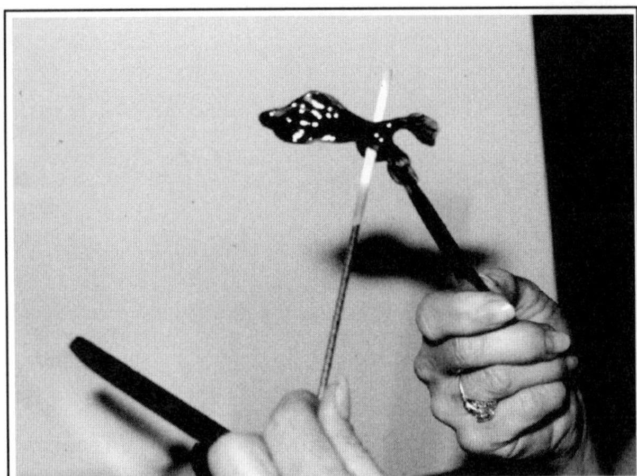
Figure 164. Carol Fonda pinching and pulling on a bead to form the wings of an angel.

things that you can do with such distortions. You can use them to make fins on a fish, wings on an airplane, collars on a clown, etc.

Sculpting

By working with the glass at just the right temperature, it can actually be moved around and sculpted like clay. This allows a whole new way of shaping or distorting the glass, and you can move features around with tools to your own satisfaction. There are many tools that can be used for this. They include: paddles, shapers, spatulas, nails, screw drivers, etc. Use your imagination but you should probably restrict you tool choices to those made of metal. Reamers and razor blades are tools favored by many bead artists for sculpting. They are great for pushing linear indentations into beads and straightening up features, as shown in Figure 165. To learn more about sculpting beads see my booklet on Sharon Peters from the beadmaker series.

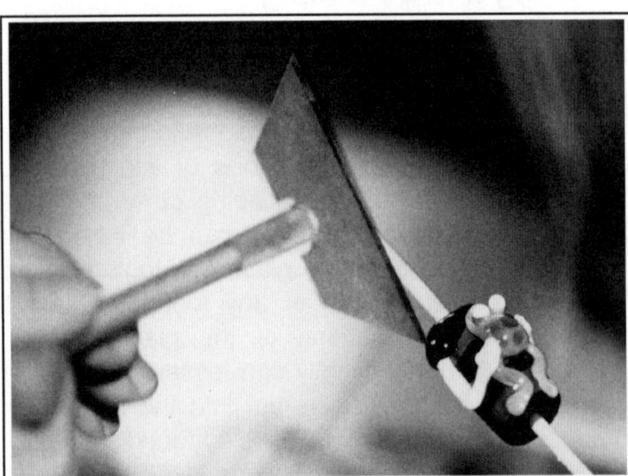
Figure 165. Sharon Peters sculpting some Beanie Boy bead features using a utility knife shaper.

Applying constructions

Your bead surfaces can also be decorated with constructions or images that are made ahead time and are applied while making the bead. To practice your flameworking skills, you have already made a number of constructions such as canes, latticino, ribbons, and murrine. Let's now discuss how these constructions can be applied onto your wound beads.

Canes

When applying canes to the surface of a bead, you have to be careful how much heat you expose them to. Because of their smaller diameter, canes heat up much faster than rods. Therefore, you want to work them in a smaller flame or at the edge of your flame with just enough heat to soften them up, as is being done in Figure 166. When applying canes and other constructions, you need to make sure that both the bead attachment surface and the construction attachment surface are tacky hot as you bring them together. After attaching, check to see that you do not have any undercuts at the attachment point. If you do, you may have to reheat the joint with a sharp flame to ensure that the cane will not break off. Do this by gently heating them up in the outer reaches of your flame to completely attach them to the bead.

Figure 166. Tom Holland applying a cane to a bead. Photo by: Sage.

Canes can be applied to a bead in a number of ways. They can be applied circumferentially, looped, lengthwise, spiraled, or swirled onto it. A number of these orientations are illustrated in Figure 167. Once applied, they may be left raised or marvered into the bead surface. When working canes and constructions into the bead surface, the effect that you achieve is greatly dependent upon the applied heat. If you work the raised decoration hot on the glass, it will melt and spread out over the surface of the bead. If instead, you heat it and the bead but slightly chill the decoration by the touch of a tool before working it into the bead surface, you will get narrower and crisper lines.

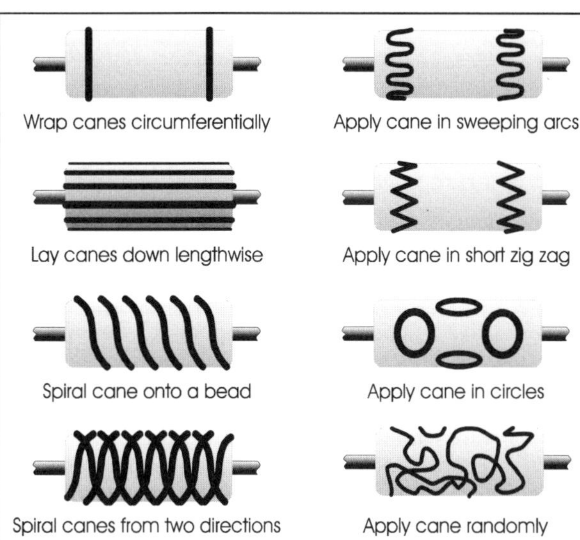

Figure 167. Possible orientation in which cane may be applied.

Applied cane can be modified by surface distortions like raking, furrowing, or twisting. Examples of what these techniques can do have already been illustrated previously. They can also be ruffled or moved around with tweezers to give them a wavy appearance. This is obviously easier to do prior to being melted into the bead surface.

Stringer painting

By working fine canes or stringers a little hotter as you apply them to the bead surface, you can almost paint images onto the surface of your bead. This stringer painting technique is how artist Pati Walton applies some of the fish images into her beads. These images are then later stretched and worked into the desired shape through the use of tools like tungsten picks. This technique can also be used to apply other kinds of decorations, such as the word shown in Figure 168.

Figure 168. An example of stringer painting on a bead.
Artist: Lisa Niven
Size: 1¼"L x 1"Dia

Latticino

Applying latticino to a bead is very similar to applying cane. They are also small in diameter and can easily be overheated. They are usually applied through the edges of a flame with the bead slightly below the flame. The flame is positioned to heat the surface of the bead and the side of the latticino. As you attach the latticino to the bead surface, you will give it a counterclockwise twist that not only tightens the spiral on the latticino a little tighter for an enhanced effect, but it also brings the two preheated surfaces together. You can reheat the bead afterwards to get whatever final surface texture you want for the latticino. I think latticino look especially nice with some relief to them, so many times I will only lightly reheat them to get beads with a raised pattern, as in Figure 169. I also like the look of beads like this where the whole surface is covered in latticino.

Figure 169. Bead with heavy raised latticino application.
Artist: Donna Nova
Size: ¾" Dia x 1 ½"L
Photo by: John Zalusky

Some beadmakers tell me that they don't spiral their latticino during construction. Instead, they just pull it out straight as is done for compatibility testing. Then, they spiral the latticino as they apply it to the bead. They claim that this technique gives them more control over the tightness of their spirals. Try it and decide for yourself which technique you prefer.

Latticino is often added circumferentially on the ends of a bead for a decorative finish. It also looks good when applied as spiral wraps on the face of the bead. Latticino once applied can be distorted by raking down the middle for a nice effect, as was illustrated in Figure 156. If you are going to distort them, you may want to marver them into the surface of the bead first.

Ribbed cane floral decorations

Ribbed cane can be used in a number of ways to form floral decorations for your beads, and many artists use this to good effect because it gives more natural color variation. To see examples of this, look at the floral decorations on the beads of Leah Fairbanks and Sharon Bates.

Figure 170. Ribbed cane slice flowers.
Artist: Al Janelle
Size: 1¼"H*1"W* ½"T

Since ribbed cane

already looks like a flower in cross section, it can be used and applied like murrine, as will be explained shortly. Al Janelle uses some this way in his bouquet beads as seen in Figure 170. You can also get the cross sectional image of a ribbed cane by applying it hot. For small diameter ribbed cane, you can prewarm the cane and the area to which it is to be applied, touch the cane to the surface of the bead, let it cool slightly, and then wiggle it back and forth to break it off at the surface of the bead. Then, heat it to soften its edges. This will display the cross sectional image of the cane.

Ribbed cane can also be applied hot in a number of other ways to take advantage of its color variation when viewed from the side, as shown in Figure 171. The first way to do this is to get it hot, touch the surface of the bead, swirl the cane, burn it off, and marver it to a slightly raised bump on the surface. This gives an appearance of something like a rose.

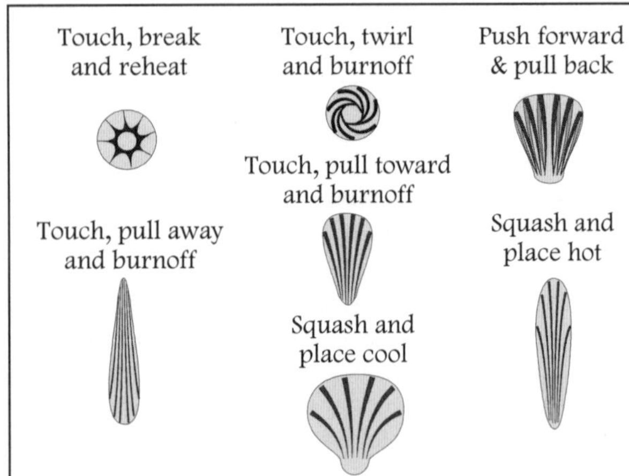

Figure 171. Hot application techniques of ribbed cane.

Second, you can heat the end of the cane to form a small gather, touch the surface of the bead, and immediately push forward and pull back. This will give the appearance of a shell-like effect. The third technique is to again form a small gather, then touch the area that will be the center of the flower, pull outward and burn off the excess cane. This creates a flower with a pointed petal. Alternatively, if you touch the gather to what is the outside of the flower, pull inward and burn off the excess cane, you will form a flower with lightly rounded outer petals like a daisy.

You can also make floral leaves by applying cane warm instead of hot. Here, instead of applying the gather right away, squash it first to form a wide petal and then apply it relatively cool to the bead surface with the cane end to the center. Burn off any excess cane. This can be used to construct a wide petaled flower like a tulip. If the squashed gather is applied hot, it can be used to form a more elongated rounded petal. If you want to make it more leaf-like, grab the top of the applied petal and pull it to a point.

In all cases, the floral applications described above are then heated and either marvered into the bead surface or sculpted as desired. Then green foliage is added as needed. This foliage could also be made with ribbed cane, although cased cane looks just as good. For more information on using ribbed cane to make floral decorations on the surfaces of beads see my booklet on Leah Fairbanks from the beadmaker series.

Figure 172. Sharon Peters applying ribbon.

Ribbons

Ribbons can be applied in a number of ways. One way is to attach it on end onto a bead, stretched out, and shaped like flower petals or cornhusks as is being done in Figure 172. Ribbon can also be used in making sculptural beads, like the fish beads that is illustrated in Figure 201. There you heat up the end of the ribbon and the attachment point on the bead. Next press the two together forming a slight bulge. Then gently pull on the ribbon to form a nice smooth joint with no undercuts. Heat up the end of the section to pull it out and shape it.

Figure 173. Clown bead
Artist: Jim Kervin
Size: 1"H x 3/4"Dia

Another way to attach ribbon to a bead is along

one edge of the ribbon. This looks especially nice if you spiral the ribbon down the bead as you apply it. When doing this, you heat up the ribbon and the areas of attachment as you go. At the same time, you have to heat up the bulk of the ribbon to be able to bend it to conform to the surface of the bead. Work it a little at a time and make sure that the joint between the ribbon and the bead surface is good, or you may find the ribbon rolling some on you as you proceed down the length of the bead. At the ends of the bead pull the ribbon down to a point at the surface. After you are finished, you might consider ruffling it up with some tweezers as was done for the collar of the clown in Figure 173. This is done by first twisting one way and then the other.

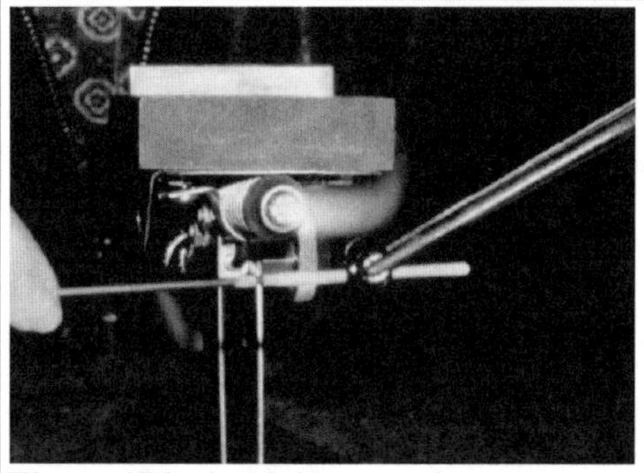
Figure 174. Applying murrina to a bead.

These two techniques are the most common ways of applying ribbon but if you use your imagination you can probably think of many others. You could make loops or twists, for example. These will be more fragile but in the right thickness and with the proper annealing they should be okay.

Murrine

Before you apply millefiori or mosaic cane to a bead, it has to be sliced or nipped into short murrine slices about one eighth of an inch in length. Next preheat each murrina slightly before applying it to a bead. This can be done by holding them with your tweezers out in the flame, by putting them in an annealing kiln on a steel plate (which is referred to as a ferro), or by keeping them on a heated marver. At the same time, preheat the bead until the application area is nice and soft.

Then, apply the murrina and push it into the surface of the bead. You can apply the pressure to do this in a number of ways: by pushing the murrina into the bead with tweezers, by pushing the bead down on a marver over the murrina, or by squeezing the murrina and the opposite side of the bead between the jaws of your tweezers as seen in Figure 174. Try to push the murrina at least ¾ of the way into the bead surface. Then, you need to gradually work to get it flush with the surface of the bead by gently heating and marvering the sides of the murrina down. Once it is firmly marvered into the bead surface, you do not have to be quite so gentle with the heating.

Many murrine tend to bubble or scuzz up when heated. This is caused by rough-cut surfaces or air trapped at the pattern interfaces. This problem can be reduced if you apply a casing of clear glass to the top of the murrina before heating it up too much. Then, reheat the area and marver it into the bead surface as desired. You may want to leave the clear dot raised so that it acts as a lens that magnifies the murrina pattern for enhanced viewing, as seen in Figure 175. Work slowly and not too hot or you may smear the murrina. You may have to reapply heat a couple of times to get it worked in right. Also, as was described before for ribbed cane, it may help to chill the murrina for just a second before applying pressure to it.

Figure 175. Bead with lens-like casing to magnify murrine.
Artist: James Allen Jones
Size: 1" Dia x ¾" L

For murrine or mosaic cane slices that are semi transparent and will be cased with clear for viewing through them, you may want to polish them well before applying them. Use diamond belts, as well as felt and cork wheels to make sure that you remove any scratches on the surface that can trap bubbles or distort the image.

Some kinds of latticino-like constructions can also be applied like murrine and when melted in look like little spiraled dots. To make a sample of this kind of latticino, make a big gather in the middle of a rod about a half-inch in diameter and about an inch long. Draw a few stripes down the side. Thin stringers or cane may be used to get very fine lines. Then heat it all up and pull it out slowly while twisting it a lot. Making the construction larger and then pulling it out allows you to get much finer lines in your spirals. Pull it slowly to get a fairly thick cane on the order of just under a normal Effetre rod thickness (about 3/16"). Try to twist it a lot to get a really tight spiral. Cut it up into about quarter inch lengths. Apply it like murrine, but do not push it more than about half way into the bead surface. When you reheat it to fully attach it, the cane shrinks up on itself to look like a dot of the base color with a spiral on top of it, similar to Figure 176 that was not twisted.

Figure 176. Latticino as a murrina.
Artist: Don Schneider
Size: ¾" Dia x ¼" L
Photo: Bill Breslar

Casing constructions

Many times after you have applied decorative constructions to the surface of a bead, as with murrine, you may decide that you want to cover or case part of or all of the bead in a transparent colored glass without distorting the image too much. This magnifies and enhances the image. The secret is to keep the bead barely warm enough for the casing to adhere while adding the casing glass as hot as possible so as not to trap air. To do this, make sure that the bead that you are casing is kept well below the flame.

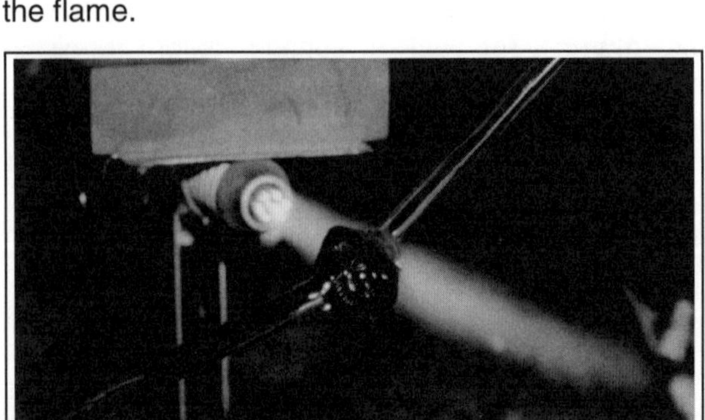
Figure 177. Dabbing a clear casing onto a bead.

Apply the casing rod hot through the flame, pushing down slightly to squeeze out the air at the bead surface, slightly twisting the casing rod back and forth or rotating it to evenly heat it during application. When casing delicate images that you want to be sure not to smear, it helps to just dab on a little glass at a time with small gathers, as is being done in Figure 177.

On the other hand, if you are casing a large area with delicate features you can wrap the glass as we did in casing rods or use the lollipop technique as shown in Figure 178. Here you make a large gather, flatten it into a lollipop-like shape with your mashers, reheat it, wrap the whole thing at once around the bead, and work it into the surface. After you are done, heat the bead thoroughly and lightly marver the surface as desired. Try not to trap any bubbles in your casing. Sometimes, if you have a few bubbles on the surface of a casing and your casing is relatively thick, you may be able to reheat that section and pull the bubbles out of the casing, but you risk distorting any constructions beneath it.

If you look closely at your casings, you will notice that they will almost always have some minute bubbles in them. I am not talking about bubbles of trapped air from not applying the casing hot enough or with insufficient pressure. Instead, I am talking about the fine bubbles that often scum up the surface of a bead. These fine bubbles are caused by scratches and imperfections in the surface of the clear rods that are a result of handling damage during its manufacture and distribution. Clear is especially susceptible to this damage because it is soft and scratches easily. These scratches can be seen quite easily if you heat the rod to a glowing orange state. These scratches are also why packaged murrine from Effetre, especially the transparent ones, tend to form scum when applied.

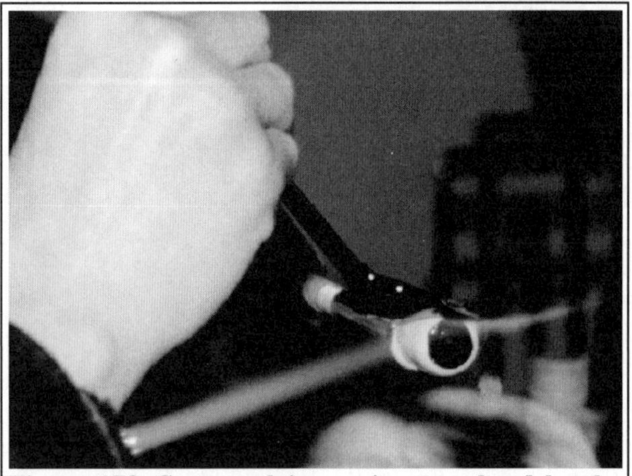
Figure 178. Sage applying casing to a bead by the lollipop technique.

One way to get around this problem is to get a crucible kiln and make up a pot of clear glass. Then you can get a gather of the bubble-free clear glass and use it to case your bead, as is being done for the marble in Figure 179. But unless you are going to be casing a lot of beads, making up a crucible full of clear glass may be more trouble than you want to deal with.

So is there anything that we can do to get bubble free casings at the torch? One labor intensive answer would be to polish the outside of the clear glass rods prior to use, but this may or may not be successful depending upon your perseverance. A

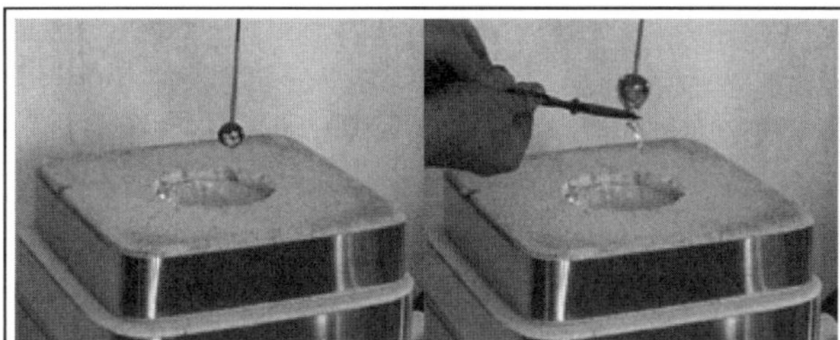

Figure 179. Casing a marble using a crucible kiln. Courtesy of Sundance Art Glass

reasonable alternative is to peel off the outside surface of the glass rod to remove the scratches. This is easier to do on larger diameter clear rods, which have a larger volume to surface ratio. You skim off the scratched surfaces by heating up the rod, grabbing a section of its outside surface with your tweezers or pliers and peeling it off like a banana as shown in Figure 180. Safely dispose of this skin in a container of water. This also serves to cool the tool so that it does not stick to the glass. After stripping the skin off of a rod, the remaining inner core will be bubble and scum free. If used for casing, it will be optically pure.

Other techniques for reducing the number of bubbles that you get in your casings include:

- Polishing your glass rods ahead of time using something like a piece of leather.
- Etching the rods with etching creams or liquids and cleaning them off before using them in the flame.
- Working in a cooler flame.

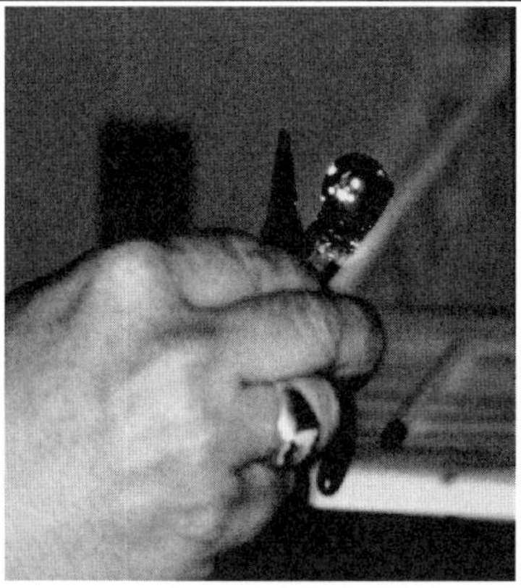

Figure 180. Pealing a clear rod.

Inclusions

Besides glass constructions, you can also add some forms of non-glass inclusions to your beads. These are usually completely encased in the interior of beads made primarily from transparent glass. If the inclusion ends up being very big then the beads will need to be well annealed to prevent them from cracking. Some of the things that you can use as inclusions are metal foils or leaf, mica chips, cubic zirconia (in Bullseye), quartz in (borosilicate), and wire or screen.

Foil and leaf

Foil and leaf are usually added to a bead as a background or for a splash of color. They are available in a number of different metals: gold, silver, platinum, palladium, etc. Foils are easier to handle than leaf because they are thicker, less likely to fly away on you, and more resistant to burning off right away. Leafs and foils come packaged in small booklets of tissue like those seen in Figure 181. The tissue pages protect them from damage and make them easier to handle.

Figure 181. Packages of gold leaf.

Silver is one of the better foils to start with because it is reasonably priced, looks good, and stands up reasonably well under the torch. It does react somewhat differently with the different colors of glass — sometimes remaining silvery, sometimes diffusing into the glass to give it a yellow tint. This is what silver stain was all about after all. Gold and platinum don't have this problem but are a lot more expensive. Platinum is hard to find and appears to only be available in the states as a dental foil. It stays nice and silver colored. Palladium can take on many different colors from silver to blue, depending upon how you heat it up in the flame. You can try practicing with copper foil but it rapidly oxidizes and turns an ugly brown or rust color.

To use foil or leaf, start by cutting it to the size needed for the bead. If you are encasing the whole bead in foil, you may want to make more than one wrap around bead for richer color. Cutting leaf can be a little tricky as you cannot touch it or it will just tear. It is almost best not to remove it from the tissue paper that it comes on. In fact you may want to add a second piece of tissue over the top of the leaf to make a leaf sandwich when cutting it into the smaller pieces.

Transfer the cut piece of leaf to your marver for picking up onto the bead. Do this by removing the top piece of tissue and putting leaf side down onto the marver with the other piece of tissue on top of it. Leave that piece of tissue on top to help keep the leaf from blowing away. Misting work surface will help hold leaf in place. Moving the tissue slightly, so that it is at a slight angle to the leaf, makes it easier to remove when you are in a hurry to apply it.

If your cut pieces of leaf blow away, don't bother to try and pick them up with your fingers. You will just tear the leaf to smithereens. Instead, run a comb through your hair and use the static electricity on the comb to pick up the leaf. Then, tease it off the comb and back onto the marver with a small soft brush.

Figure 182. Janice Peacock picking up leaf.

If you do a lot of leaf work and have a problem with it blowing all over the place, here is the solution that I observed when I visited a glassblowing studio. You can imagine how hard it must be to keep leaf from blowing around there, where the airflow is much greater to handle all the combustion gases. They had a solution for this problem that I though was really neat. They made a box with a screen on the top and a fan blowing out the bottom. They could then lay out their gold leaf on top of the screen and the air being sucked through by the fan held the leaf down on the screen.

Of course, we don't use quite as much leaf (sheets) at one time so the idea would have to be miniaturized for our needs. This could be done using a small box and a fan like those used in computers. You might even be able to lay a whole sheet on the screen, score out the section that you want to use, pick it up on your bead, and leave the rest on the screen. One of the things you might have to work with is how you exhaust the fan so that it does not blow things around on the table. I can envision a double bottom box for this. The upper section has the fan on the bottom blowing down into the bottom section of the box. This section could have a slot opening on the back to exhaust the air away from your work area.

Now that you have the leaf laid out for application, you need to get ready to apply it. Start by shaping your bead and getting the surface smoothed out really well. If you are making flat bead surfaces, be sure to remove any chill marks. To apply the foil or leaf, heat the bead to tacky hot. Remove the tissue off of the foil or leaf and roll the bead on it to pick it up, as shown in Figure 182. Burnish the foil or leaf onto the bead with your tweezers by rubbing them back and forth across the bead. If you don't burnish it well enough, the leaf may burn off as soon as you hit it with the torch flame in the regions where it does not make good contact with the bead. Even if you do have it well burnished, you can still burn it off if you are not very careful, especially with leaf. Keep moving the bead in and out of the flame to slowly heat it up and melt it into the surface of the bead.

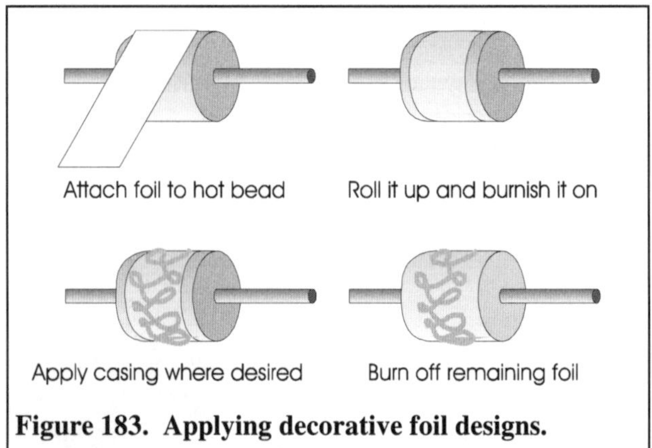

Figure 183. Applying decorative foil designs.

At this point, the foil or leaf should be attached to the surface of the bead well enough that it will wear fairly well. But you may want to case it with a transparent glass casing for increased durability or to allow you to selectively burn off sections of the foil. To avoid burning off the foil or leaf, reheat the bead slowly. You have to reheat the bead or the casing glass will not stick. Apply a casing overcoat to those areas where you want the foil to remain when you are done, all the while keeping the bead out of the direct flame. You can use the casing to provide decorative foil regions by applying it in the form of dots, lines, spirals, or all over the whole bead. The overcoat should be as hot as possible when it is applied so as not to trap any air next to the foil.

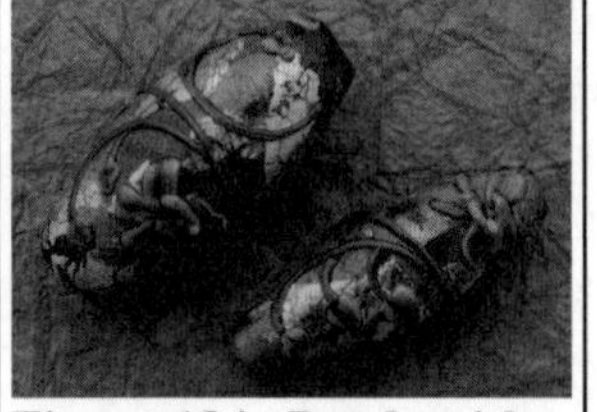

Figure 184. Beads with pattern from foil
Artist: Leah Fairbanks
Size: 1½"L x ¾" Dia
Photo by: George Post

After you have applied whatever decorative casing you want reheating the bead to burn off the exposed foil. Whenever burning metal off of a bead, you should always make sure that you have proper ventilation so as not to be breathing any fumes. Gold especially can sometimes have mercury and other impurities in it that can be bad for your health. Finish by adding whatever other decorations you desire to the bead or finish casing it for a uniform surface. This whole process is illustrated in Figure 183. If you just lightly melt the foil or leaf you can get it to form a rough interrupted metal surface.

Figure 185. Bead with foil leaf
Artist: JoElla Johnson
Size: 1 ½"L x 1"W x ¼"T

You can also create other special effects by adding additional layers of the same leaf or different metal leaf to get more color variation or increased depth of color. By working the surface of the bead after casing the leaf, you can get it to break up into many small pieces of leaf for another interesting effect. like that seen in Figure 184. You can also change the appearance of the metal by casing it in different transparent colored glasses. Effetre transparent light rose looks really impressive over silver leaf; it appears almost golden. Also some of the higher melting temperature foils like palladium don't really have to be cased. Just make sure that you secure the edges of the foil with some glass to prevent it from unraveling. But, be a little careful when doing this because the palladium foil may change to silver color if overworked in the flame.

Another interesting technique that I have not seen used much is to cut shapes out of foil that you then embed in a bead. JoElla Johnson does some beads like the one seen in Figure 185. She cuts leaf shapes from copper or silver foil, which she puts into beads. Since her beads tend to be fairly large and the foil to be fairly thick, she at times has problems with a bead cracking. She has to anneal her beads fairly extensively. This technique works best with the more heat resistive foils like palladium. It also helps to stick to small simple shapes but it does show some promise.

Figure 186. Punched foil shapes can be used in beads.
Artist: Sharon Peters
Size: ¾" Diameter x 1½" L

One way you can get simple shapes is to punch them from foil or leaf. Crafts stores will have punches in a number of shapes like hearts, stars, suns, circles, etc. Punched pieces can be picked up off your marver with a hot bead and worked into the surface. Figure 186 shows a couple of punches, stars and suns along with beads that incorporate some of these punched sun shapes.

Mica

Colored mica available for fusing can also be used successfully for decorating beads. It is usually applied by getting the bead tacky and rolling it on some mica that has been spread out on your marver. You should then gently marver the mica into the surface of the bead. If you decide to reheat at this point, be careful because the color on the mica burns off even faster than do foils. You should case the mica in transparent glass as soon as possible, again trying to avoid heating the bead.

Powdered colored mica is also available. It is sold under the trade name of "Pixie Dust". It is applied by getting your bead tacky hot and rolling it in the pixie dust that you have in some sort of vial, as Janice Peacock demonstrates in Figure 187. I like using one of those kitchen scoops that I talked about for frits and enamels for this purpose. If this is your last step in making your bead, the pixie dust does not need to be cased. Excess material will rub off of your bead but enough should remain to give the desired "pearl-like" finish. Overheating pixie dust should also be avoided or you can burn out some of the color.

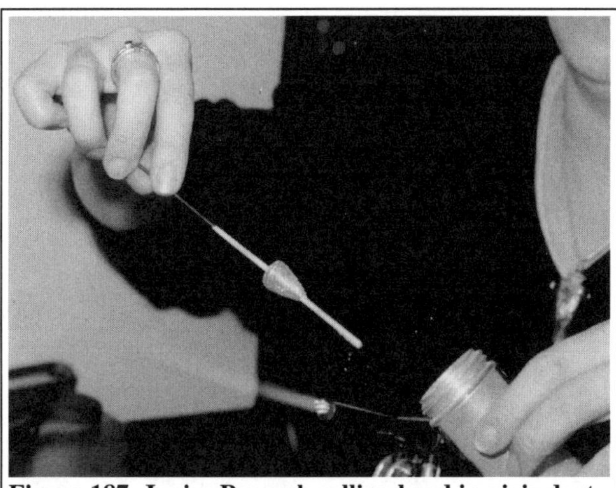

Figure 187. Janice Peacock rolling bead in pixie dust.

Wires and screen

Wires and screens can also be used as inclusions in your transparent beads. They should be of a very fine gauge so as to be easily deformed by the glass and not to exert much stress on it. They are applied to a hot tacky surface and should be cased if you expect them to stick and remain whole.

Figure 188. Silver dot bead. Artist: Stevi Belle Size: 2 ½" L x 1 ¼" Dia Photo by: Jerry Anthony

But this may not be the effect that you are trying to achieve. By putting fine silver wire on the surface of a bead and reheating it, you can get the wire to break up into a series of dots, as seen in Figure 188. You could also apply the wire like glass from a rod to make regular dots on the surface of a bead by melting the tip of the wire and touching it to the hot surface of a bead. Be careful though, because if the dots get too big, they can break off the surface.

Tubing

Even metal inclusions as large as tubing can be successfully embedded in a bead. This usually works best if the tubing is used to form the core of the bead. Copper seems to be more compatible than most other metals and is ideal for this technique, which was first shown to me by Mary Klotz, who uses it to form small spacer beads like those shown in Figure 189. She has lots of short pieces of copper tubing for sale if you are interested in pursuing this technique. They can be a little tricky to cut and to debur the ends. Deburring is done by reaming or filing to avoid blocking the hole.

Figure 189. Assorted copper tubing core beads. Artist: Mary Klotz Size: ½" to 1" L up to ¾" Dia. Photo by: Mary Klotz

To use these short pieces of tubing, jam one on the end of a mandrel that is slightly smaller in diameter than the hole in the tubing. The mandrel can be modified to have a slight flat about half an inch from the end of the mandrel to bind the tubing in place. Then, heat up the tube until it is glowing and apply glass to it as if it were a mandrel. The glass used with this technique is usually transparent so that you can pick up the reddish color of the fire scale on the copper tubing. I have also seen this technique used with multicolored enamel chunks with interesting results.

Dichroic coatings

The use of dichroic glass can add wonderful color effects to your beads. Its use is a little tricky and requires some discussion. First of all, as mentioned previously, the compatibility of any dichroic glass is dictated by the base glass on which the coating was applied. Since most of the high temperature dichroic is still made for fusing and is therefore on COE 90 compatible glass, you may decide to work with that as your palette. Dichroic coated Effetre glass has become more readily available but is often in limited supply. Remember also to make sure that the dichroic coating is high temperature compatible. Otherwise, you may see it burn off in the torch. Even if high temperature compatible, you still have to treat dichroic coatings right or you will ruin them.

As you apply and work the coated glass, don't be surprised to see the coating break up, crack or wrinkle as in Figure 190. This happens as you stretch and move the base glass around as the dichroic coating is very thin and does not flow as well as the base glass. You can enhance the variation of color even more by using a dichroic-coated ripple glass rather than flat glass because it will have considerable variation in the coating thickness. This variation is caused by the coating having a constant amount of coating material per viewing area. If the surface of the glass is on

Figure 190. Dichroic bead with checking in coating. Artist: Patti Frantz Size: 1"L x ½"W x ¼"T

a slant, the area coated is greater but since the coating amount is constant, the coating has to get thinner. The main disadvantage with using ripple glass is its much greater thickness, which results in a thicker layer of clear glass on the bead. Although, as we shall see, much of this extra glass can be removed if desired.

The first thing that you will have to learn when working with dichroic glass is that you want to avoid applying your flame directly onto the dichroic coating. If the coating hits the flame, you will very likely fry it or burn it off. What happens in this kind of situation is that the coating material will burn to form a scum on the glass, as seen in Figure 191. This can also happen if you get the bead too hot and the dichroic surface has not been firmly affixed to the glass beneath it or has air bubbles trapped at that interface. This is more of a problem when using a propane-oxygen torch where much more heat is available.

Figure 191. Edge scum seen on dichroic glass that was improperly applied.

The coatings prefer a cooler flame, so when working dichroic glass, turn down the oxygen on your flame and heat the dichroic glass on the glass side, not the coating side. This can be facilitated by preheating the dichroic strip before picking it up to apply it. A good way to do this is by having it sit on a pastarelle, a heated metal plate.

If you are adding dichroic glass that has an opaque base, you have to apply this with the dichroic coating side up if it is to be visible. To do this, keep your bead just below the flame and add your dichroic glass by preheating the bottom of the dichroic glass as you feed it onto the bead. Be careful when doing this because it is easy to burn yourself this way. In this process, you are rotating the top of the bead away from you as you normally do and adding the glass to the top of the bead. Marver it in as best you can after application. To marver it, heat it up way out in the end of your flame and do not get it too hot.

If you are going to work on the bead some more, then you need to protect the coating. The way to do this is to case it in clear glass. As in most situations, you want to keep the bead relatively cool as you case it. The casing glass should be hot and fluid as you add it. Press down as usual to try to avoid trapping air. Then reheat the bead and marver it into shape.

If your dichroic coating is on a clear base glass, you will usually apply it coating side down. It will usually be applied over a solid opaque colored core for contrast. A dark color like black is ideal. As before, you want to heat the non-coated side. You can keep your bead below the flame and feed the dichroic through the flame with the dichroic surface facing away from you onto the bottom of the bead, as shown in Figure 192. An even better way is to have the bead above the flame and feed the glass up through the flame.

This technique is better for two reasons. First, when you are feeding strips of glass down through the flame it tends to deflect enough of the rising hot air onto your hand to make holding the glass very uncomfortable. Second, feeding from below allows you to just attach the strip to the bead and then let it hang by itself. This frees your feed hand to use tools like your tweezers. Use gravity to help wind it up.

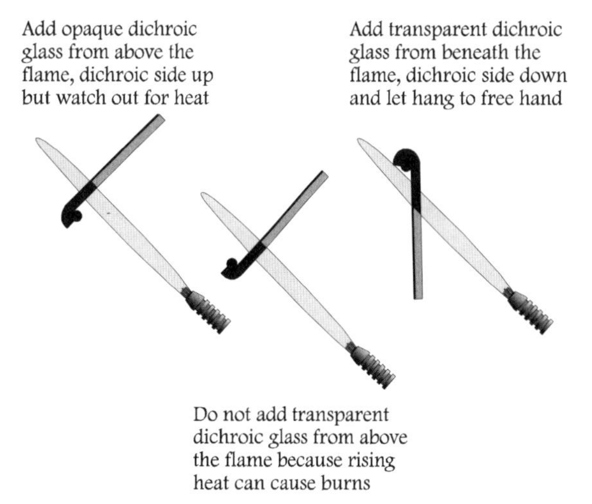

Figure 192. Proper way to apply dichroic sheet glass.

You need your tweezers to firmly attach the dichroic-coated side of the glass along its complete length to the bead surface. You have to pay special attention to the edges to prevent them from rolling up and exposing some of the coating to the flame. Use your tweezers to squeeze down on those edges and get a little of the clear glass to flow over the edge and attach itself to the glass beneath. Avoid trapping air beneath the dichroic coating as you apply it, to prevent forming scum at this interface or as a bubble rises to the surface. Smoothing out the surface of the bead before adding more dichroic glass can help minimize trapping air. This will remove any dents in the bead that could trap air. Applying the glass hot enough to stretch and shape it to the surface of the bead also helps to avoid trapping air.

After completing a full wrap on the bead, pull off any extra dichroic glass and lightly heat the bead in the end of the flame. If the end of your wrap was not firmly attached, you will find that it may try to roll up and expose some of the coating to fry. To avoid this, lightly heat the glass and marver it out to squish down the edges of clear base glass to get them to spread out and seal in the coating. If it is not convenient to marver the edges down, then pinch them down with your tweezers or pliers as shown in Figure 193. In fact, Pati Frantz, a dichro expert, finds this to be much more convenient to do and her motto is "If you can mash don't marver."

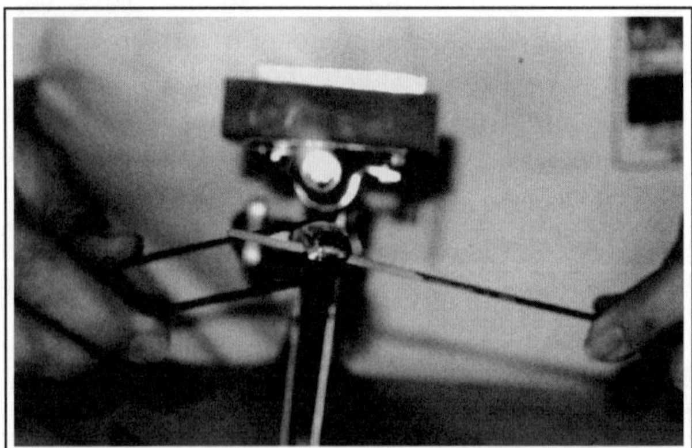

Figure 193. Pinch down edges of applied dichroic.

She says that a big issue when she first started selling dichroic beads was the visibility of the beginning and ending of the dichroic wrap. Customers kept thinking that they were seeing cracks in her beads and accused her of selling inferior beads. She learned to overcome this issue by disguising the edges of the dichroic coating. This can be done by either applying constructions like cane over the ends or by feathering them. Cane application is more appropriate when you are just adding small pieces of dichroic glass and you can trace around each of them with cane.

Feathering is primarily done for complete dichroic wraps. This has to be done both at the start and end of the wrap. To feather it, you grab a little bit of the hot glass and stretch it out. Pull it either in the direction of wrap or against it to make the end of the coating indistinguishable. You should pull a little of the clear glass off each time. Then move over a little bit and stretch the next section in the opposite direction. At the start of the wrap it also helps to pull some of the clear glass off, so that when the coating at the end of the wrap comes around, it is closer to the same depth in the bead as the coating at the start.

Unless your dichroic glass is thin glass, you may find that you have a thicker clear glass coating than you really want. This is especially the case if your dichroic glass was ripple glass or if you are mashing your dichroic beads to form tableau beads. This is also more of a problem with dichroic Effetre glass because that tends to be a thicker sheet glass.

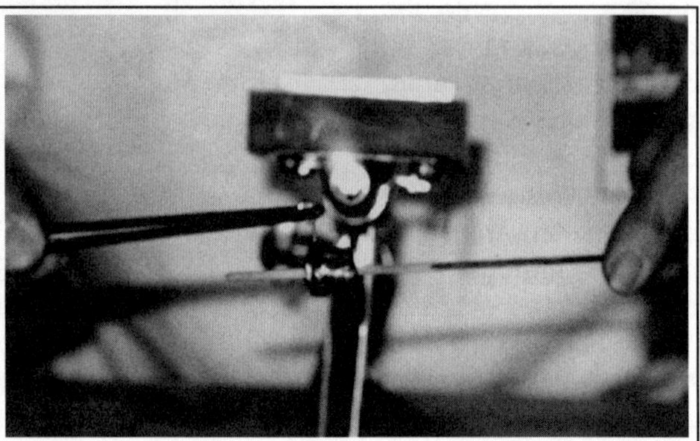

Figure 194. Pinching clear glass off a dichroic bead.

If you have this problem, you can remove some of the offending clear glass by heating a spot, pinching it with your tweezers as seen in Figure 194, chilling it, reheating the pinched area, pulling it off, and tossing it into a glass of water. Try to keep the bulk of the bead cooler as you pull off the glass to avoid disturbing the dichroic coating beneath. If you are removing a big wad of glass, you may find it useful to double pinch it before pulling the wad off. The second pinch is done at right angles to the first. Continue removing clear glass until you are satisfied with the result.

To get more depth and variation of dichroic color, you may want to add additional layers of dichroic glass to your beads. If you decide to add more than one layer of dichroic glass, do not try to put the coated side of one against the coated side of the other. They just don't want to stick that way. The only way you can get it to work is if there are enough cracks or holes through the bottom coating to expose sufficient glass to form a bond. Also remember to smooth out the bead before adding the second layer so as not to trap air. Other than this, treat the second layer like the first. For greater color variation, you may not want each dichroic layer to be a complete wrap.

Besides making dichroic beads, you can also make dichroic stringers with which to decorate your beads. Do this by building up multiple layers of dichroic glass on a clear or colored glass core and then pull it out into stringers. This is an excellent way to use up your small dichroic scraps.

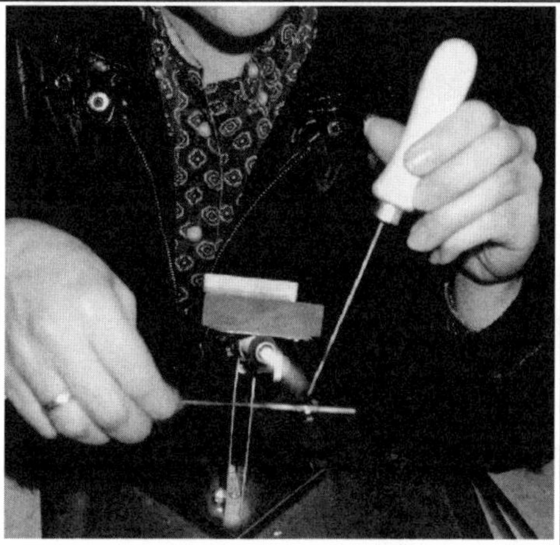

Figure 195. Poking bubble pit into bead.

One last thing that you should be aware of is that Pati Frantz also reports that she finds dichroic beads much more susceptible to thermal shock and recommends that they go directly into an annealing kiln rather than trusting them to heated vermiculite and annealing at a later time.

Bubbles and cracks

Sometimes you just want to break all the rules and put bubbles or cracks into a bead for effect, for example to create bubbles coming from a fish's mouth in an aquarium bead. Bubbles can be put into a bead in a number of ways. Very fine bubbles can be simulated by rolling a bead in a light dusting of sand or silica flour on your marver and then casing it in a transparent color. Because of its crystalline properties, these inclusions will look like fine bubbles.

To add larger bubbles into a bead, you can try distorting the bead surface to create depressions and then casing these depressions with a transparent color to trap air. To distort the surface, you can shape the bead on things like files, flower arranging frogs or wire brushes which will leave indentations on the bead surface, or you can just poke holes in it with a sharp pointed tool as shown in Figure 195. If making multiple depressions with the same tool, be sure to chill it between applications in water so that the glass will not stick to it. Lastly, reheat the bead lightly and case the depression with a transparent color.

When putting bubbles into your work, there are two things that you have to watch out for. If the bead is too cool, the trapped air may expand more than desired upon reheating. The other is that if the casing glass is too hot, it may fill in some of the depression. After placing and casing all of your depressions, you may want to strongly reheat the bead. Doing so will give the glass and the air enough mobility to reform into their lowest surface energy interface configuration, a sphere. When doing this, be aware that large bubbles may try to migrate to the hottest or least viscous portion of the bead, which is usually the surface. To avoid this, heat the bead slowly in the outer region of the flame and repeatedly chill the outer surface by gently rolling the bead on a marver. For information on how to make a tool to put multiple indentations in a bead at one time, see the article on "Bubbles and Droplets" from Glass Line that is listed at the end of this chapter.

Another rule that you may want to break occasionally is to introduce cracks into your beads. To do this, get your bead really hot and then dip it into some water. You will get a lot of cracks, as seen in Figure 196. Reintroduce the bead into the flame to fuse the outer surface of the bead. You may want to try multiple dips and degrees of reheat to play with this effect. It should be obvious that these beads will not be as strong as a normal bead.

Figure 196. Crackle glass bead.
Atrist: Jim Kervin
Size: ¾"L x 3/8" in diameter.

Playing with this technique will also give you a feel for how heat penetrates into a bead as you watch the cracks vanish upon reheat. When you do this, you will not be able to marver the bead to make it longer because the water washes away much of the exposed separator compound. For this same reason, putting cracks into a bead should be one of the last steps in making the bead.

Examples of more complex wound beads

There are an infinite number of bead variations possible using the decorative skills to which you have been exposed in this chapter. We have already addressed some possible examples as these skills were introduced. But, to pique your interest a little more, let's look a few examples of beads that you can make to give you ideas of what can be achieved with practice and that you might otherwise not try. For more detailed step-by-step beadmaking instructions see any of the booklets in my beadmaker series.

Tableau beads

The first bead we will discuss is a tableau bead. This is a simple flat disk-shaped bead, which will usually incorporate a picture of some sort, as in Figure 197. It works very well as a central pendant on a string of beads. The flat surface helps make the bead lie with the intended image facing in the desired direction. The basic bead is constructed by winding an ellipsoidal shaped glob onto the mandrel. You flatten this gather by pressing it between your marver and your paddle or by squashing it with a set of mashing pliers, you will get a circular disk. When you squash the bead, do not make it thinner than about three times the mandrel thickness or it may crack along the mandrel.

Figure 197. Tableau bead Artist: Kathy Johnson Size: 1¼"H x 1"W x 3/8"T

For this example, we will apply the image of an eye to the face of a tableau bead. Start by applying a fairly large dot of black to the center of the flat side of the bead. Flatten it out with your marver. Add a white dot on top of the black dot and marver both into the surface of the bead.

Pull a small black point to use as a tool. Heat up one side of the circle and stretch it out into an eye shape by raking a short distance with your glass tool right at the junction of the white and the black dot, outward down the axis of the bead. The surface of the glass should not be so hot enough that you affect too wide an area as you rake out the eye shape. Remember to stop at the end of the rake, blow on the end of the point, and break it off. Next, heat up the other side of the black circle. Stretch it out as was done with the first side in the opposite direction to complete the basic eye shape. Again break off the tool, reheat the bead and marver the surface flat. Add a black dot to the center of the white to serve as the iris of the eye.

You can decorate the eye further if you want by raking eyelashes from the top and the bottom of the outer black ring of the eye. Here you would heat these areas with a small sharp flame before raking. Further decorations can be added to the bead in the form of latticino on the edges, looping circles around the eye, or whatever else you may come up with. There is also no reason that a tableau bead has to be round. You can make them from any shape—single cones, bicones etc.

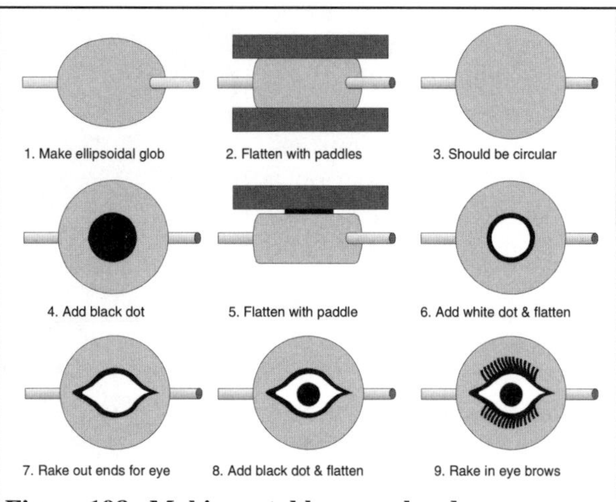

Figure 198. Making a tableau eye bead.

Hollow wound beads

One form of wound bead that many artists are not aware that they can make are hollow beads. This allows making much larger beads without greatly increasing their weight.

This bead is constructed similarly to the technique used for making those clay bowls that you may have learned about when you were younger. That consists of building up the shape of the bowl from coils. You start by making two small thin disk shaped beads as far apart on the mandrel as the bead is to be wide. From there, you build up the

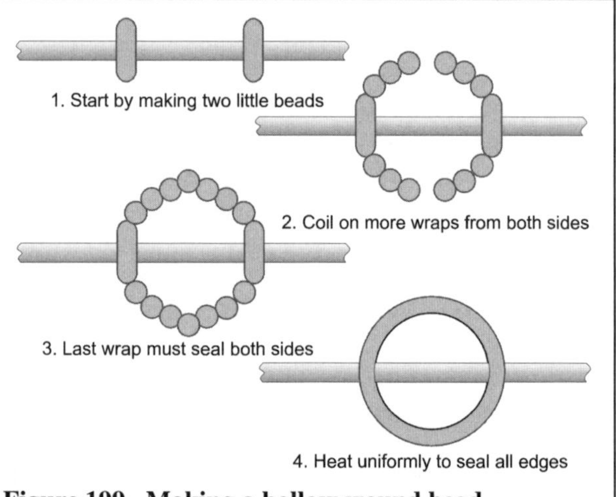

Figure 199. Making a hollow wound bead.

shape of the hollow bead by wrapping coils of glass around the two original beads as shown in Figure 199.

It is easiest to coil a little at a time on each end, switching back and forth from one end to the other as you go. This allows you to be able to build up the bead without having to try to lay a coil inside of the last coil. This also helps to prevent thermal shocking the bead because you worked entirely on one side and the other side has cooled before you can get back to it. The secret of success with this type of bead is not to break the seal of the separator compound underneath the small beads and to make sure that each wrap is completely attached to the one beneath it as you build up the bead. This is especially critical on the last wrap where you have to ensure that the wrap seals onto both of the hollow cups that you have constructed.

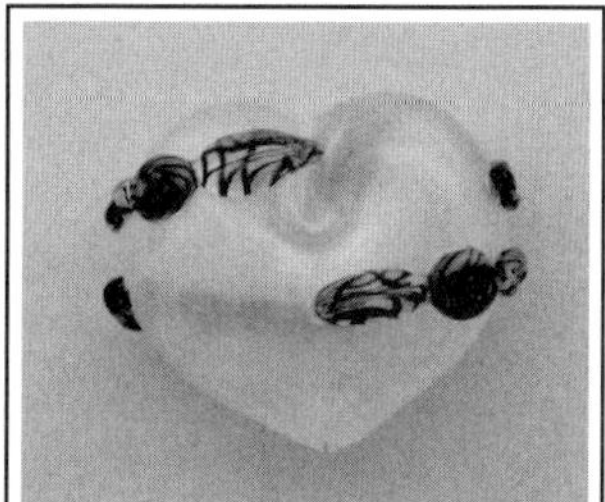

Figure 200. Heart Bead. Artist: Matt Marchand Size: 1"L x 1¼"W x ½"T

After you have completed all the wraps, heat up the bead uniformly to seal all the edges. If you did not get a good joint between some of your coils, they may separate at this time and start to collapse. If this starts to happen, try to patch the hole with a little dab of glass and heat it up again. If you did get a good seal between the wraps, the bead will start to inflate as you heat it from the air expanding inside the bead. As you continue to heat the bead, the glass will flow and even out the wall of the bead. Some artists will not heat up the glass to the flow point and instead prefer the look of the coils. This gives the bead much more texture.

Some people find winding a spiraling layer of wraps hard to do. Sharon Peters tells me she prefers to make her hollow wound beads by making two large disk beads and then shaping them with a paddle until they touch each other. She then adds one wrap of glass at the joint between them and she is done.

Using this technique, it is also possible to do things like making a hollow bead around another bead, which can then roll around inside the hollow bead. With practice, you will be able to shape the hollow bead. The shaping can be something as simple as rolling or pressing the bead hot on a paddle, to as complex as pulling points out from the surface of the glass or raking it. For an example of a shaped hollow bead, see Matt Marchand's heart bead in Figure 200. You can also decorate the surface of the hollow beads with color or constructions. Pam Dugger can stretch out sections for her hollow fish beads by heating up a section of the bead and then spinning the mandrel really fast to spin it out by centrifugal force. She uses this technique to form the snout and tail sections of her fish.

One difficulty with hollow wound beads is cleaning out the separator compound. As you pull the bead off of the mandrel, the separator compound cracks and gets trapped inside the bead. I find it best to try and blow this out dry. I try not to get the bead wet until I have most of the separator out of the bead or I'll never be able to get it out. Blowing air through the bead will definitely help with this. If you do get the separator wet and it sticks, I have been told that using vinegar will help make it light and fluffy again so that it can be blown out or there is always the old water pick. Another trick that some artists use to get around this problem is to build the hollow bead upon a small cylindrical core. That way they don't have to worry about the separator compound.

Sculptural beads (fish, heads)

As a beginning sculptural bead that also uses many of the decorative techniques that have already been discussed, let's fabricate some tropical fish beads. The first step is to choose the rough color scheme that you want for your bead. You can make your fish with the color scheme of a real fish or be creative and make up one of your own. Next, in preparation for making your bead, you need to make some ribbon with the color scheme that you propose for the fins. With that completed, you are ready to start

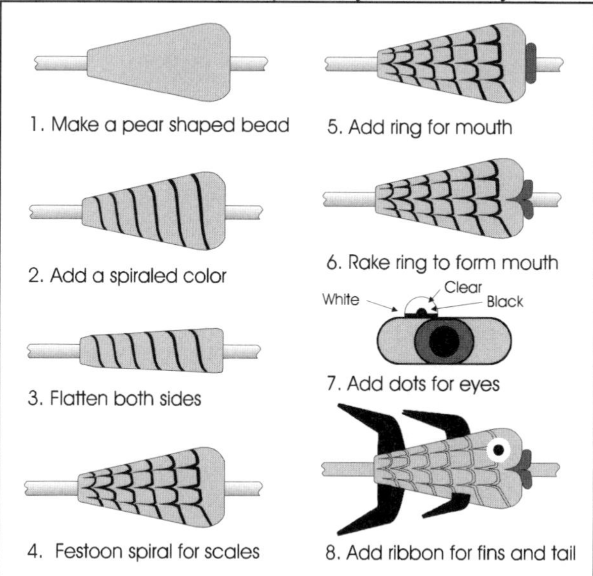

Figure 201. The steps in making a sculptural bead.

construction of the bead proper.

You start, as illustrated in Figure 201, by making a pear shaped bead of the base color for the body. Then, you trail on a spiral of a contrasting color over that. After thoroughly heating up the bead, flatten it as shown in the figure. Use a point drawn from the same color as spiral, to festoon each side of the bead by raking a number of times in the same direction (head to tail) to give the appearance of scales.

Now, you are ready to start adding features to the fish. To make the mouth, add a ring of red to the head of the bead and then rake it back. For the eyes, start out with a dot of white and flatten it out. Then, add a small dot of black to the center of the eye. Finally, for that bulgy fish eye look, overcoat it all with a thick clear dot as illustrated in the figure.

Lastly, you have the sculptural portions of this bead to finish, the addition of the fins. These fins are made from the ribbon that was constructed ahead of time. Proceed by working your way from the larger fins to the smaller ones. Start with the tail fins. Heat the attachment point of the ribbon and the body. Get a good attachment by pressing them together so they bulge lightly and then pull them out slightly to get a nice smooth joint. Apply a little heat to shape and draw out the tip of the fin as desired. Repeat this procedure next with the other tail fin, then the dorsal fin, and finally the two belly fins. If you do not want to use ribbon to make your fins, you can add big bulgy dots of glass to the outside of the bead and pinch them into fins with your pliers.

Fish beads are very popular with many artists because they make beautiful beads with bright colors. Fish beads are also nice beads because they lay really well for pendants as well as necklaces. They are also easy to make. Sharon Peters says that she never really starts out trying to make a fish bead. Instead, when a bead is not behaving well, she squishes it and makes it into a fish. Figure 202 is an example of one of these misbehaving beads from early in Sharon Peters' beadmaking career.

Figure 202. Spotted fish bead
Artist: Sharon Peters
Size: 1½"L x 1¼"H x ¾"T

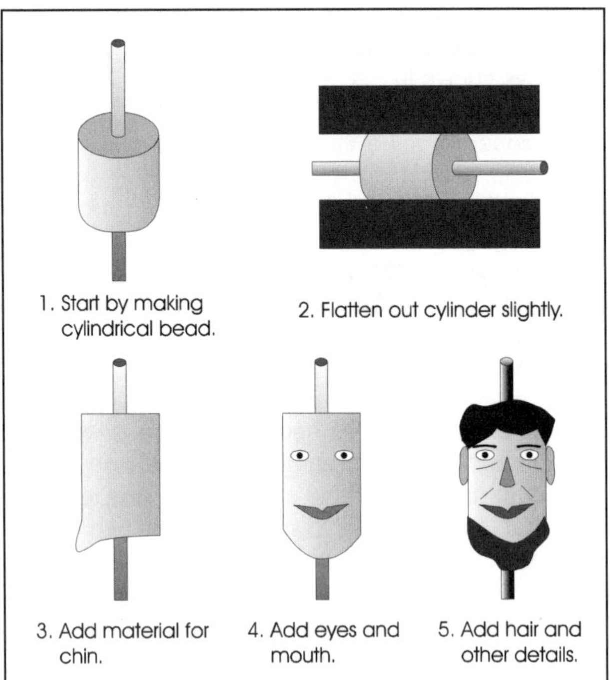

Figure 203. Making a sculptural head bead.

Another example of a sculptural bead is a head bead, as illustrated in Figure 203. Start by making an ordinary cylindrical bead. Flatten the bead slightly, then add extra material onto one end to form the chin. Shape the flattened cylinder into a head shape. Next, add two small black dots to the surface of the bead to form the outline of the eyes. These two dots will probably not be the same size but that does not really matter because you are going to shape them to the same size before fusing them into the face.

You do this by gently heating only the dots and then marvering them out to the desired size that you want even though that may result in slightly different thicknesses. Then you heat up the dots to sink them into the surface of the bead. Next, add a white dot inside each of the black dots and repeat the heating, pressing to size, and melting it in. Be sure to leave as thin and equal a lip of black all the way around the white as you can. Heat up the eye and pull slightly at either end with a tungsten pick to get the basic eye shape.

Next, move on to the mouth. Add a thin line of black or white for the color between the lips. Don't worry if it is just a little bit too big because you can make it appear narrower by covering it with the red of the lips. Do this now by adding a thin line of red to the top and the bottom of the mouth. Shape them into the general lip shape by pinching the ends and pulling down the center of the top lip with a fine set of tweezers. Stretch out the corners of the mouth with your pick.

Now, sculpt any depressions into the face. One of the best tools for this is a tungsten pick with a curved point. Push the corners of the mouth into the surface of the bead slightly. Push in laugh lines at either end of the mouth by rolling the hook pick on the U of the hook on either side of the mouth. Push up under the lower lips to raise them slightly and create the upper part of the chin. Make the groove between the lips. Push in on either side of the place where the nose will be to form the shallow between the nose and the cheeks. Roll the hook around the edge of the eyes to inset them and form the edge of the eye socket.

Figure 204. Lady with a hat bead.
Artist: Loren Stump
Size: 1½"L x 1"W x ¾"T.

The last step is to add any raised finish details. Add eyebrows by touching a dot to the brow over the inside of the eye and immediately lift up and stretch it out along the area over the eye to form a tapered eyebrow. Burn off any remaining stringer and marver it into place. Add a small dot to the eye for the iris and another for the pupil of the eye. Add glass for the nose and shape it with your hook. Add a little blob for an ear and shape it. Add hair and/or beards. Sculpt them with a pick or use a razor blade to add fine lines or waves to the hair. With that the bead is done and placed into the annealer. With practice you should be able to make a face like one of Loren Stump's as seen in Figure 204 or at the very least one like my crazy clown beads shown in Figure 173.

Part of the secret in making sculptural beads is to always plan out the order that you will build it.

- First, sculpt the general shape of the piece.
- Next, paint on the larger features that are worked flush into the surface.
- Then, do all inward sculpting since valleys are less vulnerable to heat than protrusions.
- After that, add the more vulnerable protruding features. Go from smaller to larger or area to area so that the previous ones do not get melted while doing work on subsequent features.
- Lastly, add the finishing features and detail sculpting. Attempt to work in different sections of your bead at a time while at the same time going back occasionally to keep it all warm.

These are just a simple start into the many possibilities available in sculptural beads. You can move on to any of a number of things: animals, flowers, people, etc. For further examples, you may want to see Louis Wilson's or Al Janelle's videos on sculptural beads and glass sculpture, or my book on Sharon Peters, which is part of my beadmaker series.

Suggested further reading

Beadle, The Venerable AKA Murray Bloom. ***"Bubbles and Droplets"*** in **Glass Line** Vol. 9 No. 5 (February/March), 1996

Jenkins, Cindy. **Making Glass Beads**, 1st ed., Lark Books, 1997

Kervin, Jim, **The Wild and Wonderful World Of Sharon Peters And Her Silly Sculptural Shapes**, GlassWear Studios, 2001

Kervin, Jim, **The Fanciful Floral Beads Of Leah Fairbanks And Her Gardens Of Glass**, GlassWear Studios, 2002

Kervin, Jim, **The Classic Bead Shapes Of Jim Smircich And His Amazing Control Of Heat**, GlassWear Studios, 2002

Kervin, Jim, **The Enamel And Electroform Decorated Beads Of Kate Fowle Meleney**, GlassWear Studios, 2002

Mickelsen, Robert A. ***"Flame On! The Soft Touch Part Two: Beadmaking"***, in **Glass Line** Vol. 5 No. 6 (April/May), 1992

Reynolds, Gil. "***What's Hot? -- Glass Beads"*** in **Glass Art** Vol. 8 No. 1 (November/December), 1992

Tettinger, Corina, **Passing the Flame, *A Beadmakers Guide to Detail & Design***, Bonzo Bucks Book Publishing, 2003

Tourtillott, Suzanne, **Making Beautiful Beads, Glass, Metal, Polymer Clay, Fiber**, Lark Books, 2002

Waggoner, Shawn. ***"Beadmaking II: The Wound Bead Artist"*** in **Glass Art** Vol. 8 No. 2 (January /February), 1993

Mosaic Cane

Rose with Leaves
Artist: Loren Stump
Size: ½" Diameter
Date 1997
Photo: Jim Kervin

American Indian
Artist: Loren Stump
Size: ¾" H x ½" W
Date 1997
Photo: Jim Kervin

Robin Hood
Artist: Loren Stump
Size: ¾" H x ½" W
Date: 1997
Photo: Jim Kervin

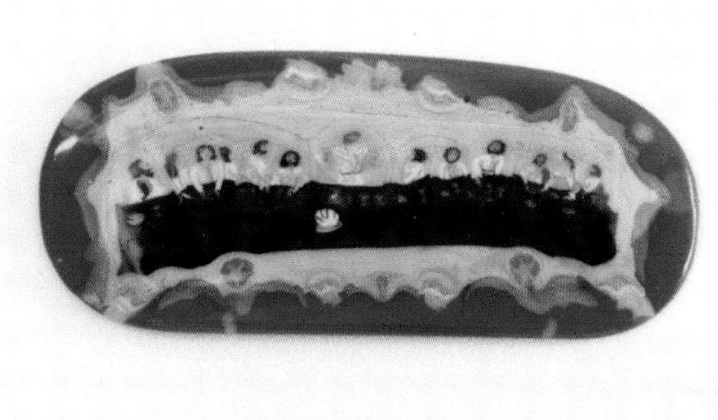

The Last Supper
Artist: Loren Stump
Size: 1" H x 2½" W
Date: 1997
Photo: Jim Kervin

Assorted Canes
Artist: Heather Trimlett
Size: Various
Date: 1998
Photo: Melinda Holden

Egyptian Male
Artist: Loren Stump
Size: ¾" H x ½" W
Date 1997
Photo: Jim Kervin

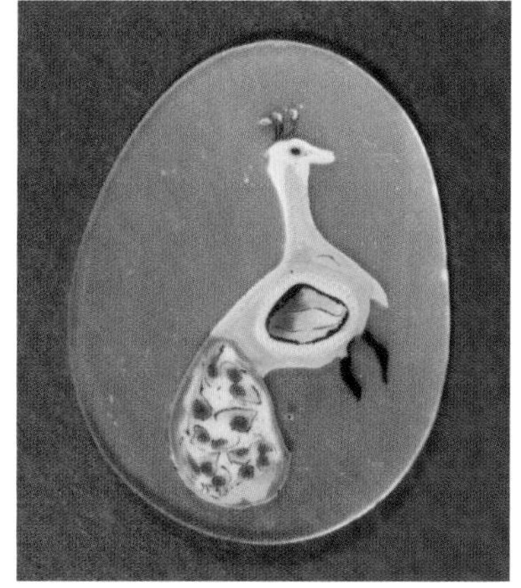

Peacock
Artist: Janice Peacock
Size: ½" W x ¾" H
Date: 1999
Photo: Jim Kervin

Face, Queen & Peacock
Artist: Jim Weurfel
Size: Various
Date: 1999
Photo: Jim Kervin

Dot Beads

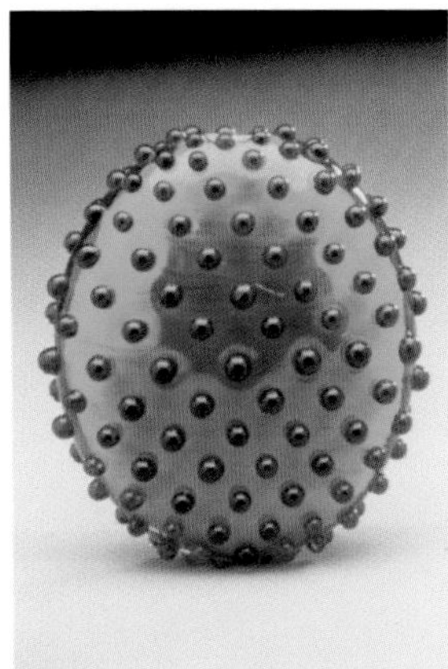

Raised Dot Bead
Artist: Kristina Logan
Size: 1¼" W x 1½" L
Date: 1996
Photo: Dean Powell

Spotted Ivory Bead
Artist: Kristina Logan
Size: 1½" Dia x ½" T
Date: 1997
Photo: Dean Powell

Raised Dot Beads
Artist: Seydoux & Zumkeller
Size: ½" Dia x ½" L
Date 1997
Photo: Robert K. Liu

White Core Dots
Artist: Jana Burnham
Size: ¾" Dia x 1¾" L
Date: 1996
Photo: Jim Kervin

Raised & Inlaid Dot Bead
Artist: Andrea Guarino
Size: 1¼" Dia x ¾" L
Date: 1997
Photo: Jim Kervin

Saturn Ring Grouping
Artist: Brad Pearson
Size: 1" Dia x ¼" L
Date: 2002
Photo: Taylor Dabney

Enameled State Ambit
Artist: Susan Breen Silvy
Size: 1¾" Dia x ½" L
Date: 2002
Photo: Jeffrey O'Dell

Space Station Bead
Artist: Gina Lambert
Size: ½" Dia x 1¼" L
Date 1998
Photo: Jim Kervin

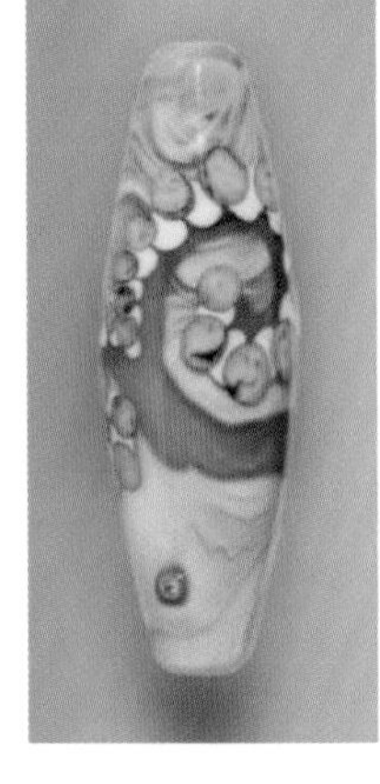

Paisley on Amber
Artist: Rob Eaton
Size: ½" Dia x 1¾" L
Date: 2003
Photo: the artist

Raked Dot Bead
Artist: Patti-Cahill-Howard
Size: ¾" Dia x ½" L
Date: 1997
Photo: Jim Kervin

Hollow Dot Bead
Artist: Bernadette Fuentes
Size: 1" Dia x ½" L
Date: 1997
Photo: George Post

Modified Dot Beads

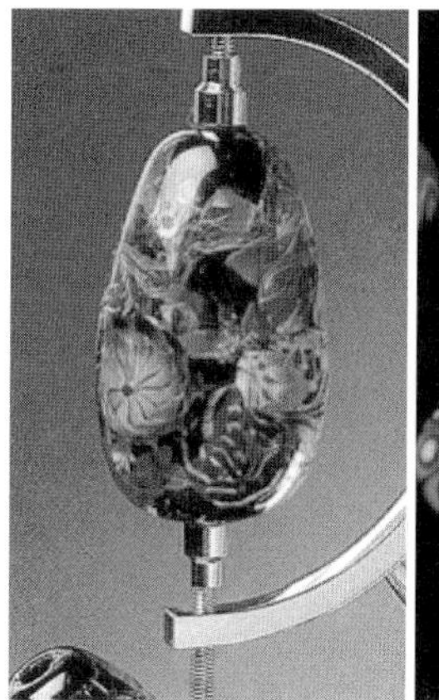
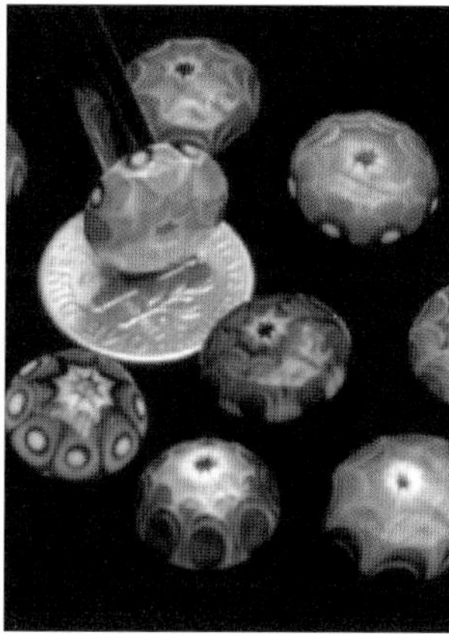

Seaform Bead & Gismo Components
Artist: Budd Mellichamp
Size: ¾" Dia x 1¼" L
Date: 1996 / 1997
Photo: Robert Overton & the artist

Assorted Dot Beads
Artist: April Zilber
Size: Various
Date: 1997
Photo: Janice Peacock

Southwest Star Bead
Artist: Lisa Walsh
Size: 1¾" Dia x ½" L
Date: 2002
Photo: Greg Walsh

Liberty Edition Grouping
Artist: Brad Pearson
Size: Various
Date: 2002
Photo: Taylor Dabney

Layered Dot Bead
Artist: Kim Wertz
Size: ½" Dia x 1" L
Date: 1997
Photo: Greg Galardy

Twisted Dot Bead
Artist: Lani Ching
Size: ¾" Dia x 1¼" L
Date: 2000
Photo: Jim Kervin

Fritter Bead
Artist: Gerg Galardy
Size: ¾" Dia 1¼" L
Date: 2002
Photo: the artist

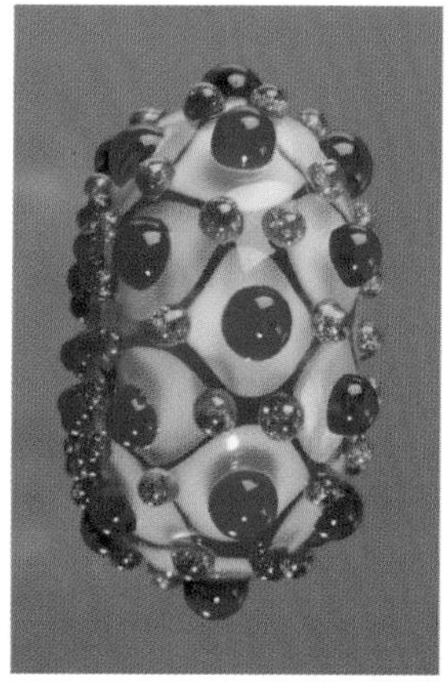

Byzantine Bead
Artist: Larry Scott
Size: ¾" Dia x 1" L
Date: 2002
Photo: Roger Schreiber

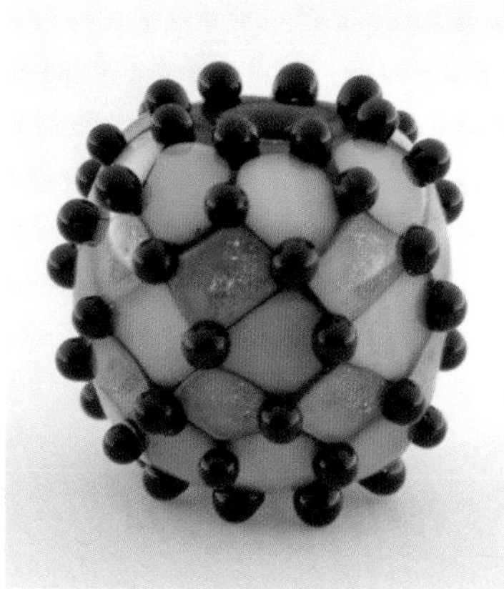

Spider Web Bead
Artist: Maud Mekalanos
Size: ¾" Dia x ¾" L
Date: 1997
Photo: Jim Kervin

Warring States & Horned Eye Beads

Warring Stated Bead
Artist: Larry Brickman
Size: 1½" Dia x 1" L
Date: 1999
Photo: Jim Kervin

Warring Stated Bead
Artist: Larry Brickman
Size: 1¼" Dia x 1" L
Date: 1997
Photo: Jim Kervin

Warring Stated Bead
Artist: Kim Wertz
Size: 1¼" Dia x ¾" L
Date: 1997
Photo: Greg Galardy

Horned Eye Bead
Artist: Bob Rubanowice
Size: 1¼" Dia x 1¼" L
Date: 1998
Photo: Jim Kervin

Warring States Bead
Artist: Tom Boylan
Size: 1" Dia x 1¼" L
Date: 1997
Photo: the artist

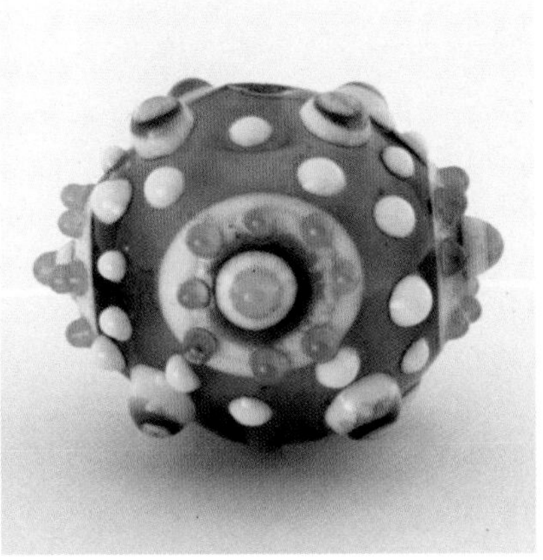

Warring States Bead
Artist: Jim Kervin
Size: 1¼" Dia x 1" L
Date: 1998
Photo: the artist

Horned Eye Bead
Artist: Tom Holand
Size: 1¼" Dia x 1½" L
Date: 1995
Photo: the artist

Warring Stated Bead
Artist: Tom Holland
Size: ¾" Dia x ½" L
Date: 1998
Photo: Jim Kervin

Warring States Bead
Artists: Seydoux & Zumkeller
Size: 1¼" Dia x 1¼" L
Date: 1998
Photo: Robert K. Liu

Classic Shaped Beads

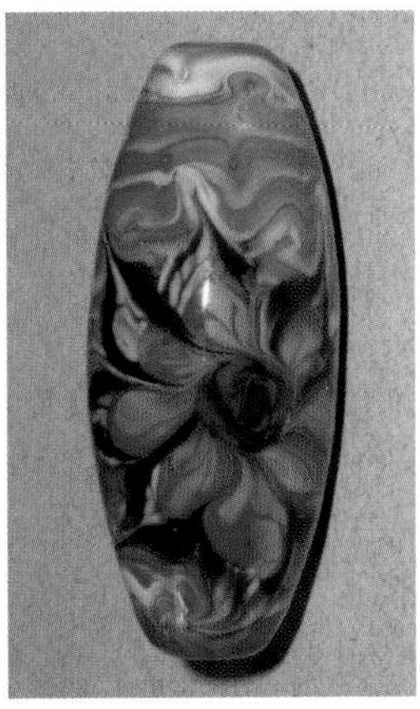

Van Gogh Bead
Artist: Jim Smircich
Size: ¾" Dia x 1¾" L
Date: 1996
Photo: Jim Kervin

Black Web Bead
Artist: Jim Smircich
Size: ¾" Dia x 1½" L
Date: 2002
Photo: Jim Kervin

Shield Pendant
Artist: Jim Smircich
Size: 1¼" W x ½" T x 1½" H
Date: 1999
Photo: the artist

Silver Bicone
Artist: Bernadette Fuentes
Size: ¾" Da x 1½" L
Date: 1998
Photo: Tommy Elder

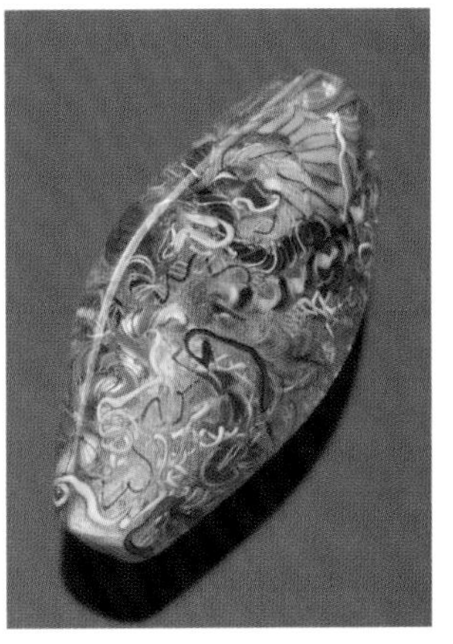

Mardi Gra Bicone
Artist: Michele Waldren
Size: 1" Dia x 2" L
Date: 1997
Photo: Chris Arend

Black Kimona
Artist: Alex Shapiro
Size: ¾" Dia x 1¾" L
Date: 2002
Photo: the artist

White Temari
Artist: Emiko Sawamoto
Size: 1" Dia
Date: 1998
Photo: the artist

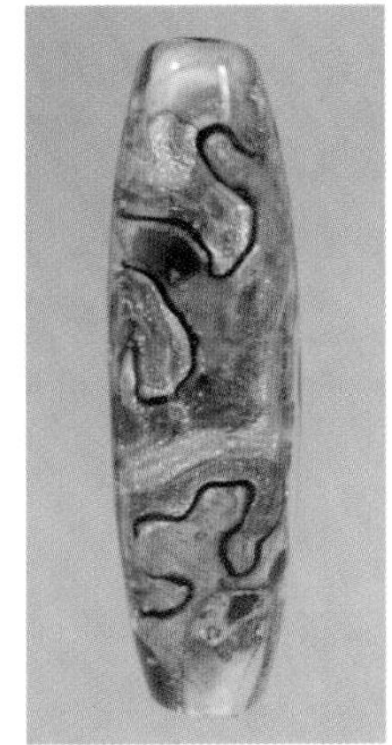

Patchwork
Artist: Allison Lindquist
Size: ½" Dia x 1¾" L
Date: 2002
Photo: Jim Kervin

Squiggle Bead
Artist: Lisa St. Martin
Size: ¾" Dia x ¾" L
Date: 1998
Photo: Jim Kervin

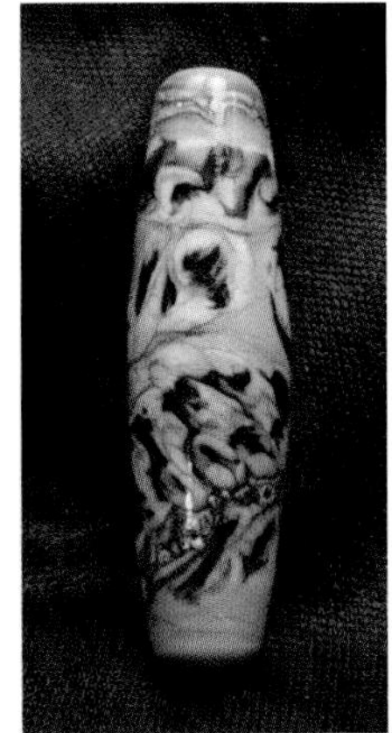

Patterns Series
Artist: Amy Smith
Size: ½" Dia x 1½" L
Date: 2002
Photo: the artist

Stargate
Artist: Jill Symons
Size: ½" Dia x 1¾" L
Date: 2002
Photo: the artist

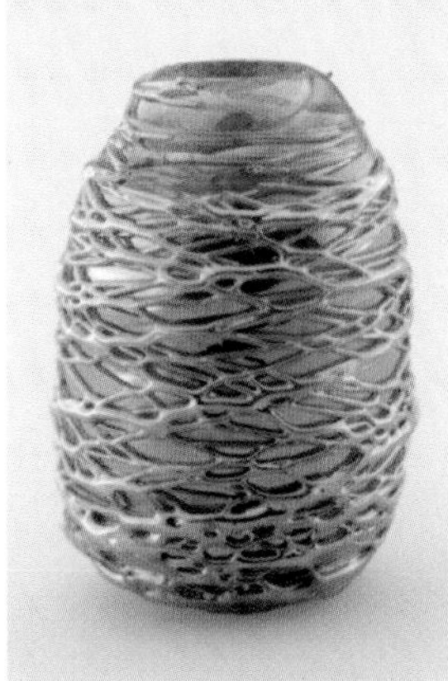

Ocal Irridized Spider
Artist: John Curtis
Size: ¾" Dia x 1" L
Date: 1997
Photo: Jim Kervin

Dichroic Beads

Dotted Dichroic Core
Artist: Patricia Frantz
Size: 1" Dia x 1½" L
Date: 1997
Photo: Jim Kervin

Goldstone Laced
Artist: Patricia Frantz
Size: ¾" Dia x 1¼" L
Date: 1997
Photo: Jim Kervin

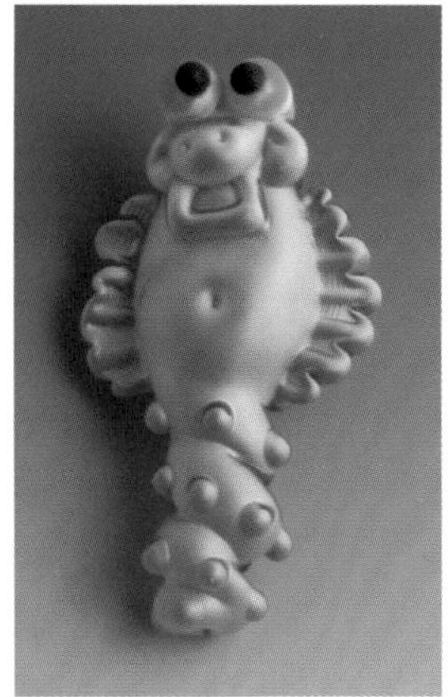

Banana Slug
Artist: Sharon Peters
Size: 1¼" W x ¾" T x 2" L
Date: 2002
Photo: Janice Peacock

Dichroic Bamboo Beads
Artist: Carol Fonda
Size: ½" Dia x ¾" L
Date: 1998
Photo: Jim Kervin

Patterned Dichroic Beads
Artist: Cay Dickey
Size: Various
Date: 1993
Photo: Robert K. Liu

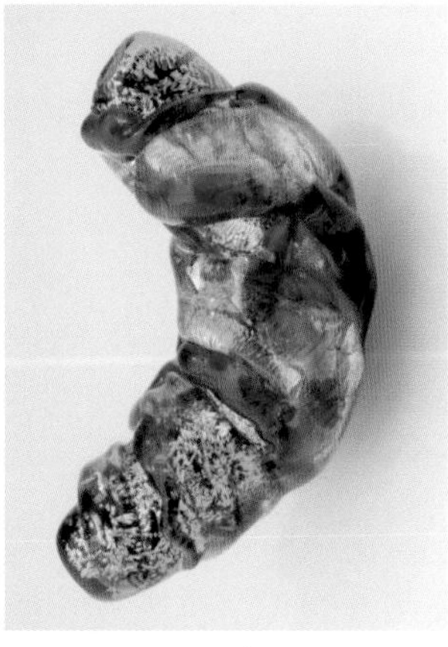

Curved Dichroic Bead
Artist: Cay Dickey
Size: ½" Dia 1½" L
Date: 1999
Photo: Carl Tamura

Amorphous Dichroic Beads
Artist: Cay Dickey
Size: Various
Date: 1993
Photo: Robert K. Liu

Dichroic Pendant
Artist: Stevi Belle
Size: 1½" Dia x 3" L
Date: 1996
Photo: Jerry Anthony

Amorphous Dichroic Bead
Artist: Lisa St. Martin
Size: 1½" W x ½" T x 2" L
Date: 1999
Photo: Jerry Anthony

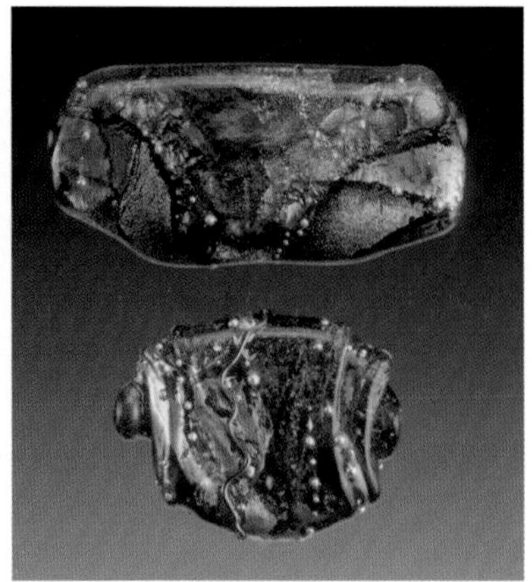

Dichroic Beads
Artist: Stevi Belle
Size: 2" to 3¼" W
Date: 1996
Photo: Jerry Anthony

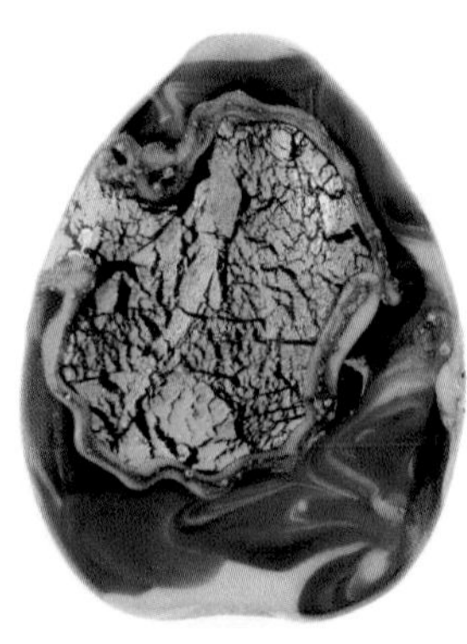

Boulder Opal Bead
Artist: Marie Claude Chapman
Size: 1¼" W x ½" T x 2" L
Date: 2002
Photo: the artist

Murrini Beads

Yuzen Bead
Artist: Emiko Sawamoto
Size: 1" Dia x 1½" L
Date: 2002
Photo: Rich Images

Egyptian Lotus Bead
Artist: Emiko Sawamoto
Size: ¾" Dia x 1¾" L
Date: 2002
Photo: Rich Images

Red Lady Bead
Artist: Pati Walton
Size: 1" W x ½" T x 1¼" L
Date: 2002
Photo: the artist

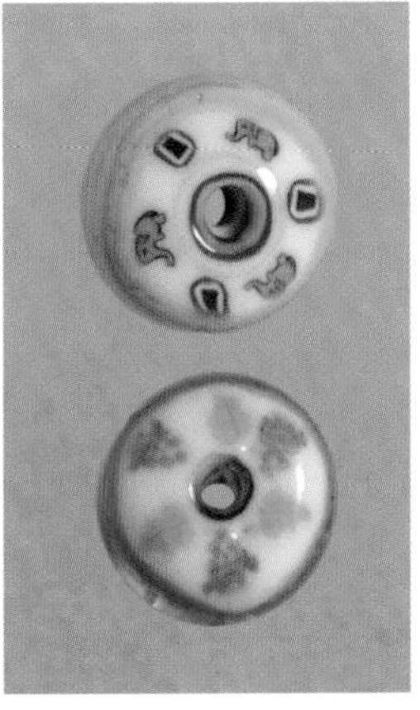

Murrini Endcaps
Artist: Allison Lindquist
Size: ¾" Dia x ½" T
Date: 2002
Photo: Jim Kervin

Self-Winding Pocketwatch
Artist: Loren Stump
Size: 1¼" W x ½" T x 1½" H
Date: 1996
Photo: David Telfner

Car 54 Where Are You?
Artist: Loren Stump
Size: 1" W x 1" H x 1½" L
Date: 1997
Photo: Jim Kervin

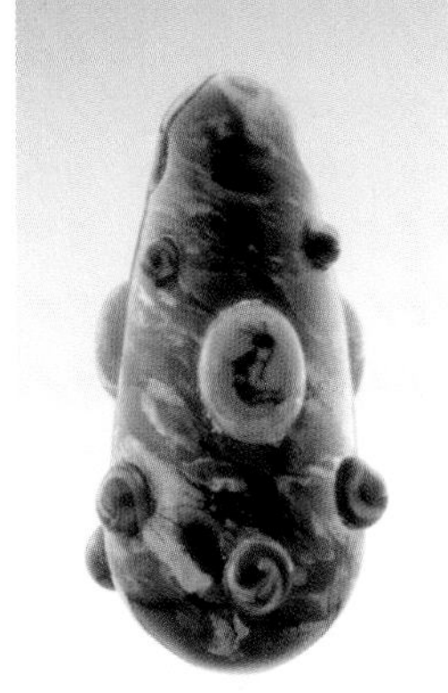

Kokapeli Pendant
Artist: Bernadette Fuentes
Size: ¾" Dia x 1¼" L
Date: 1997
Photo: Jim Kervin

Three Swirl Beads
Artist: Alex Shapiro
Size: Various
Date: 2002
Photo: the artist

Fused Murrini End Cap Bead
Artist: James Allen Jones
Size: 1" W x ½" T x 1" L
Date: 2001
Photo: Jim Kervin

Fumed Twisted Beads
Artist: Greg Galardy
Size: Various
Date: 2002
Photo: the artist

Heart Beads

Hollow Gold Leaf Heart
Artist: Matt Marchand
Size: 1¼" W x ½" T x ½" L
Date: 1997
Photo: Laura Liska

Clear Floral Heart Bead
Artist: Jackie Mixon
Size: 1¼" W x ½" T x 1¼" L
Date: 1999
Photo: Jim Kervin

Floral Heart Bead
Artist: Lezlie Levitt
Size: 1¼" W x ½" T x 1" L
Date: 1998
Photo: Jim Kervin

Gold Leaf with Grapes
Artist: Becky Cooper
Size: 1¼" W x ½" T x 1½" L
Date: 1999
Photo: Jim Kervin

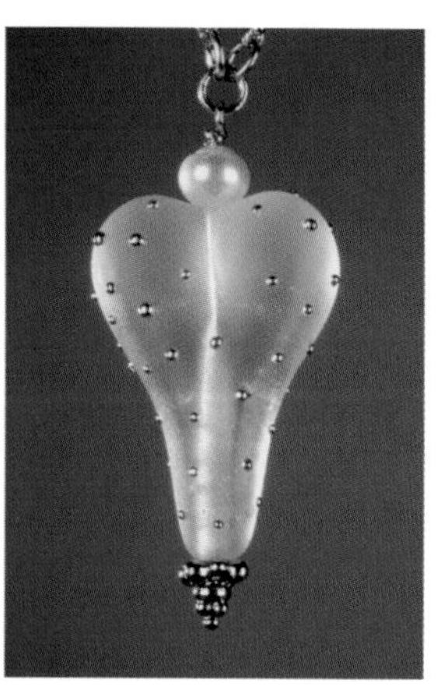

Frosted Heart of Gold
Artist: Beth Williams
Size: 1" W x ½" T x 1½" L
Date: 1998
Photo: Lynn Swigart

Frosted Heart Bead
Artist: Keri Madera
Size: 1¼" W x ½" T x 1" L
Date: 1997
Photo: the artist

Inside Out Heart Bead
Artist: Chad Pits
Size: 1" W x ½" T x 1¼" L
Date: 2003
Photo: the artist

Heart in Hand Bead
Artist: Kim Wertz
Size: 1" W x ½" T x 1" L
Date: 1998
Photo: Greg Galardy

Pixie Dust Heart Bead
Artist: Peggy Prielozny
Size: 1" W x ½" T x 1" L
Date: 1999
Photo: Jim Kervin

Tableau Beads

Silver Leaf Tableau
Artist: JoElla Johnson
Size: 1¼" W x 1½" H
Date: 1998
Photo: Rich Images

Western Tableau
Artist: Kathy Johnson
Size: 1" W x ¼" T x 1½" H
Date: 1997
Photo: Jim Kervin

Earth Tab
Artist: Sandra Seaman
Size: 1" W x ¼" T x 2" L
Date: 2002
Photo: Lib Saylor

Untitled
Artist: Mag Alef
Size: 1¼" W x ½" T x 1½" L
Date: 2002
Photo: the artist

Tuxedo Bead
Artist: Cindy Brown
Size: ¾" W x ¼" T x ¾" L
Date: 2003
Photo: the artist

Autumn Tableau
Artist: Jill Symons
Size: 1½" W x ½" T x 1¼" L
Date: 2002
Photo: the artist

Painted Face Tableau
Artist: Bob Rubanowice
Size: ¾" W x ¼" T x ¾" L
Date: 1998
Photo: Jim Kervin

Amber Bug Bead
Artist: Tom Hanks
Size: 1" W x ½" T x 1½" L
Date: 1997
Photo: Jim Kervin

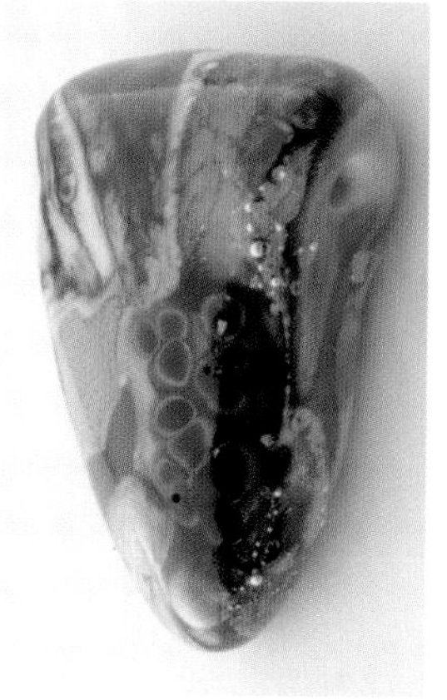

Ancient Tooth Bead
Artist: Angie Graham
Size: 1¼" W x ¾" T x 2" L
Date: 1998
Photo: Jim Kervin

Star Bead
Artist: Lisa Walsh
Size: ¾" Dia x ¼" T
Date: 2002
Photo: Jerry Anthony

Red Dot Bead
Artist: Kathy Perras
Size: 1" W x ¼" T x 2" L
Date: 2000
Photo: Jerry Anthony

Floral Beads

Fuchsias Urn Bead
Artist: Leah Fairbanks
Size: 1" Dia x 2¼" L
Date: 1999
Photo: George Post

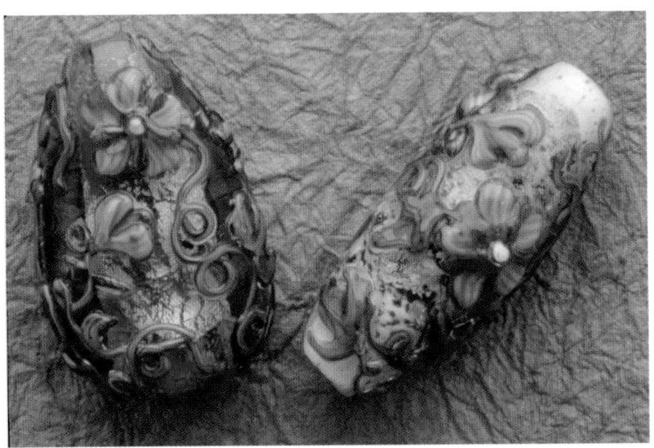

Morning Glory Beads
Artist: Leah Fairbanks
Size: 1" & 1½" Dia x 2" L
Date: 1996
Photo: George Post

Azalea Bonzai Vessel
Artist: Leah Fairbanks
Size: 1¼" Dia x 2" L
Date: 2001
Photo: George Post

Grape Cluster Bead
Artist: Elizabeth Blood
Size: ¾" Dia x 1½" L
Date: 1998
Photo: Jim Kervin

Layered Floral Bead
Artist: Kristen Frantzen Orr
Size: ¾" Dia x 1¼" L
Date: 1997
Photo: Jim Kervin

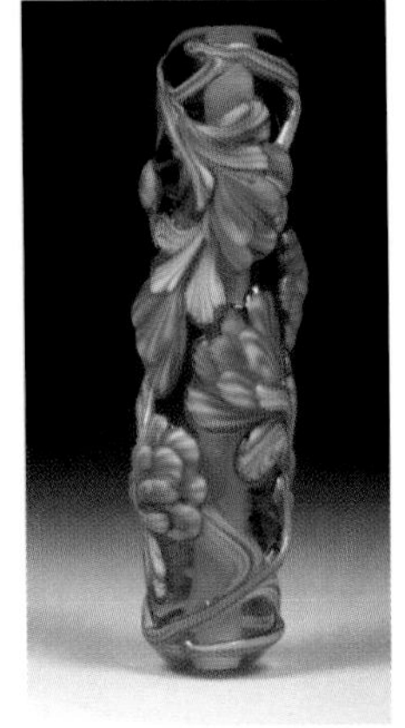

Layered Floral Bead
Artist: Kristen Frantzen Orr
Size: ½" Dia x 2¼" L
Date: 2002
Photo: David Orr

Poppy & Lupin Bead
Artist: Sharon Lang
Size: 1½" Dia x 2" L
Date: 1997
Photo: the artist

Cased Floral Bead
Artist: Kim Wertz
Size: 1" Dia x 1½" L
Date: 1997
Photo: Greg Galardy

Six Window Floral
Artist: Kim Wertz
Size: 1" Dia x 1½" L
Date: 2002
Photo: Greg Galardy

Enchanted Garden
Artist: Dolly Ahers
Size: 1½" Dia x 1¼" L
Date: 2003
Photo: Jeff Scovil

Fantesy Flower Beads
Artist: Shirley Green
Size: 1" Dia x 1¼" L
Date: 1997
Photo: the artist

Floral Beads

Two Orchids
Artists: Glen & Cynthia Taylor
Size: ¾" Dia x 2" L
Date: 2002
Photo: Jeri Pankey

Christmas Holly Bicone
Artists: Lisa Walsh
Size: ½" Dia x 1¼" L
Date: 2000
Photo: Greg Walsh

Iris and Daffodil Beads
Artist: Lee Lynn Thompson
Size: 2" to 2½" L
Date: 2003
Photo: Ingrid Hein

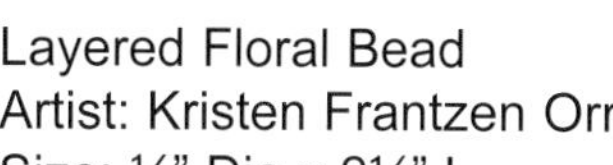

Layered Floral Bead
Artist: Kristen Frantzen Orr
Size: ½" Dia x 2¼" L
Date: 2002
Photo: David Orr

Lotus Beads
Artist: Kilm Miles
Size: 1¼" Dia x 1" L
Date: 2001
Photo: Jerry Downs

Temari Daisy Bead
Artist: Emiko Sawamoto
Size: 1" Dia
Date: 2002
Photo: Rich Images

Blooming Affair
Artist: Marna Hartjen
Size: 1" Dia x 1½" L
Date: 2003
Photo: the artist

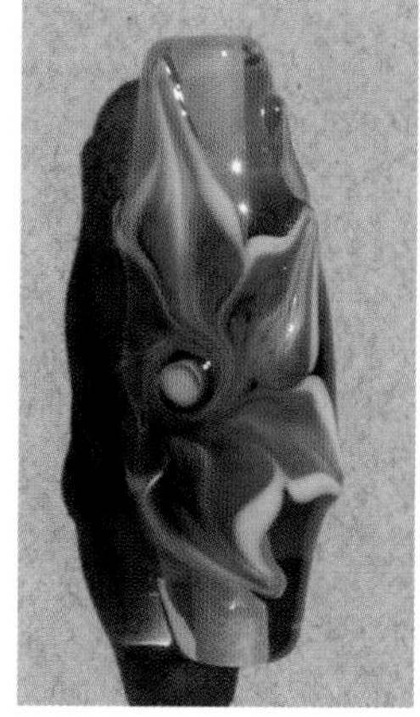

Van Gogh Flower
Artist: Jim Smircich
Size: ¾" Dia x 2" L
Date: 2002
Photo: Jim Kervin

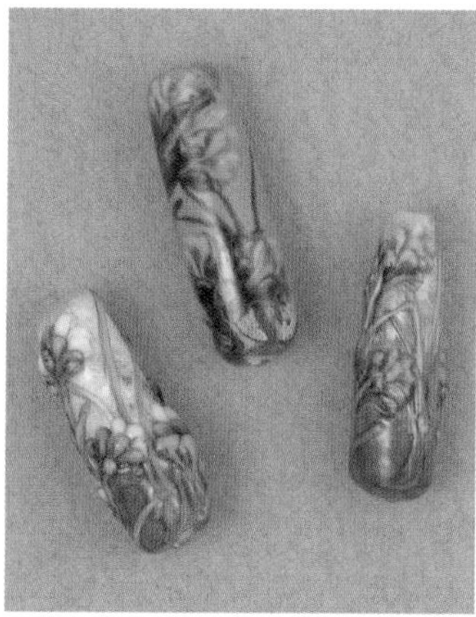

Le Fiore Vive Series
Artist: Lisa Kan
Size: 1¼" to 1½" L
Date: 2003
Photo: the artist

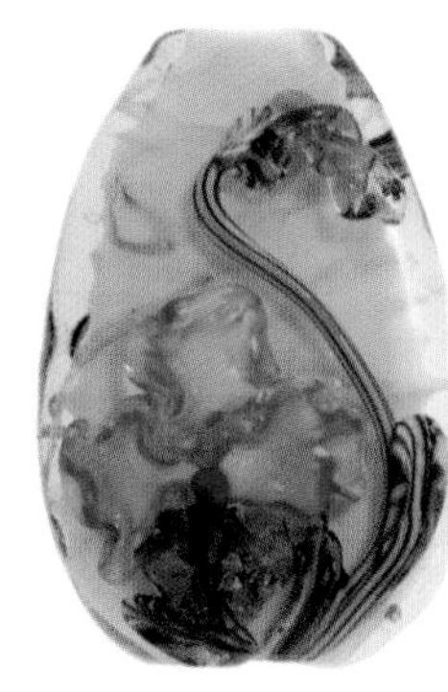

Floral Bead
Artist: Marie-Claude Chapman
Size: 1" W x ½" T x 2" L
Date: 2002
Photo: the artist

Landscape Beads

Tiger Bead
Artist: Pati Walton
Size: 1¼" W x ¾" T x 1" H
Date: 2002
Photo: the artist

Desert Stream Bead
Artist: Pati Walton
Size: 1" Dia x 1¼" L
Date: 1998
Photo: Michael Bush

Timberwolf Bead
Artist: Pati Walton
Size: 1¼" W x ¾" T x 1" H
Date: 2002
Photo: the artist

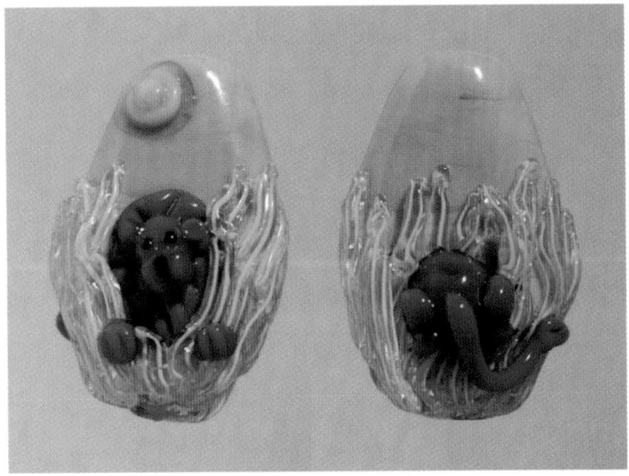

Lion in the Grass
Artist: Sharon Peters
Size: 1" W x ¾" T x 1½" L
Date: 2002
Photo: Jim Kervin

Flower Gardin Bead
Artist: Sharon Bates
Size: 1" Dia x 2" L
Date: 1998
Photo: Jim Kervin

Tree Bead
Artist: Kate Drew-Wilkinson
Size: 1" W x ½" T x 1" L
Date: 1997
Photo: Jim Kervin

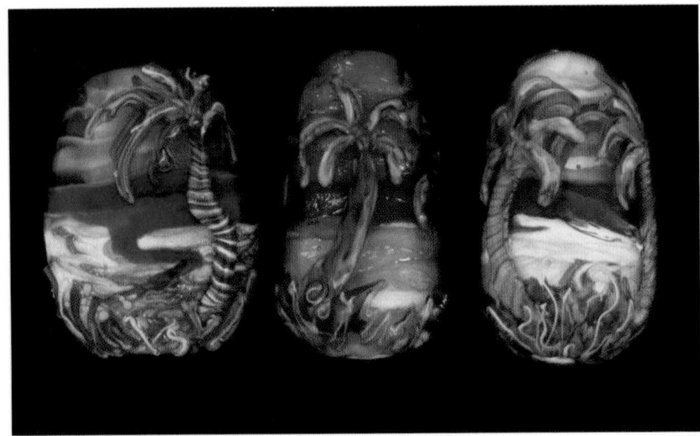

Three Tropical Paradise Beads
Artist: Terre Beasley
Size: ¾" W x ½" T x 1¼" L
Date: 2002
Photo: the artist

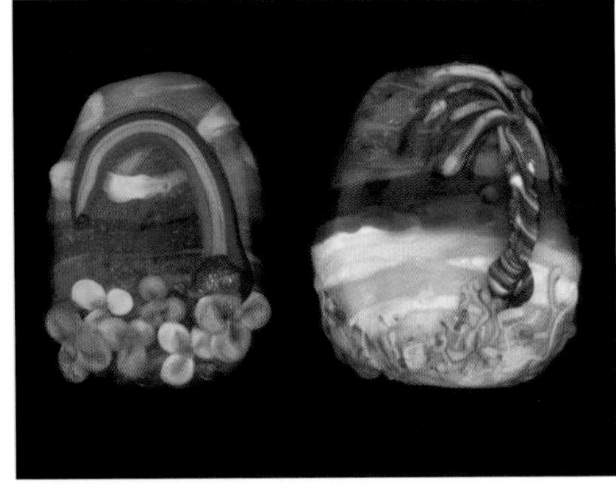

Over the Rainbow & Tropical Paradise Beads
Artist: Terre Beasley
Size: ¾" W x ½" T x 1¼" L
Date: 2002
Photo: the artist

Aquarium Beads

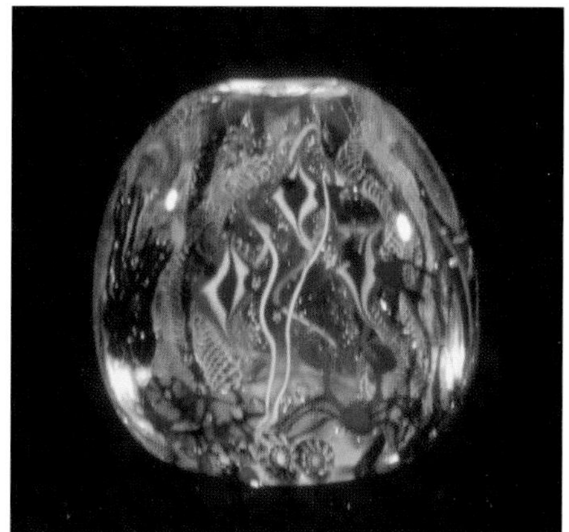

Aquarium Bead
Artist: Pati Walton
Size: 1½" W x ¾" T x 1½" L
Date: 1997
Photo: AZAD

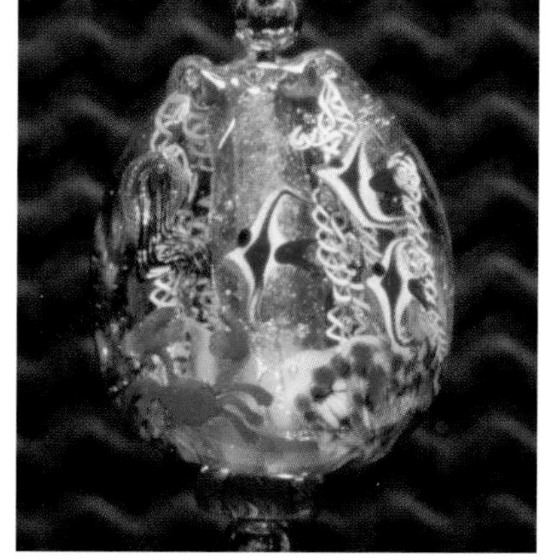

Aquarium Bead
Artist: Pati Walton
Size: 1¼" Dia x 1½" L
Date: 1997
Photo: AZAD

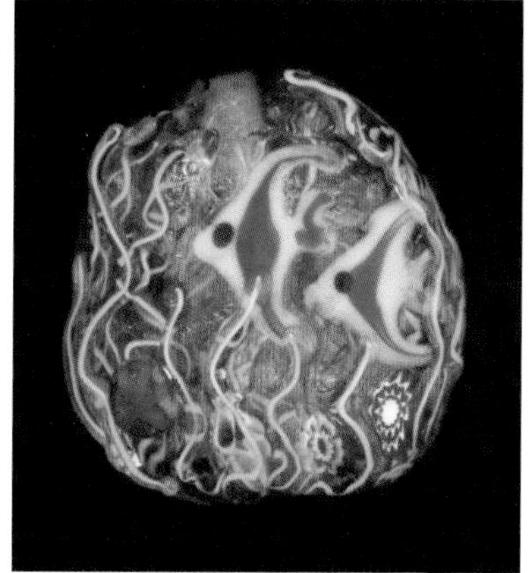

Aquarium Bead
Artist: Terre Beasley
Size: 1" W x ½" T x 1" L
Date: 2002
Photo: the artist

Kitty Dreams
Artist: Juanita Dunn
Size: 1" Dia x 1½" L
Date: 1997
Photo: Jim Kervin

Painted Aquarium Bead
Artist: Kathy Johnson
Size: 1" Dia x 1" L
Date: 1997
Photo: Jim Kervin

Painted Aquarium Bead
Artist: Bernadette Fuentes
Size: 1¼" Dia x 1" L
Date: 1998
Photo: Tommy Elder

Fused Aquarium Bead
Artist: Mary Kennedy
Size: 1½" W x ¼" T x 2" H
Date: 1998
Photo: Don Kimrey

Fused Aquarium Bead
Artist: Mary Kennedy
Size: 2" W x ¼" T x 1½" H
Date: 1998
Photo: Don Kimrey

Fantasia Bead
Artist: Catharine Weaver
Size: 1" Dia x 1" L
Date: 2003
Photo: the artist

Head Beads

Marboro Cowboy
Artist: Loren Stump
Size: 1½" W x 1" T x 1½" H
Date: 1998
Photo: Jim Kervin

Kaboki Face
Artist: Loren Stump
Size: 2" W x 1" T x 2" H
Date: 1997
Photo: David Telfner

Long Haired Lady
Artist: Loren Stump
Size: 1¼" W x 1" T x 1½" H
Date: 1998
Photo: Jim Kervin

Mildred
Artist: MaryAnn Moenck
Size: ¾" W x ¾" T x 1" H
Date: 1999
Photo: Jim Kervin

Famous Star Faces
Artist: Emiko Sawamoto
Size: 1¼" W x 1" T x 1½" H
Date: 1996
Photo: the artist

Noh Theater Devil Mask
Artist: Emiko Sawamoto
Size: 1½" W x 1" T x 2" H
Date: 1998
Photo: Rich Images

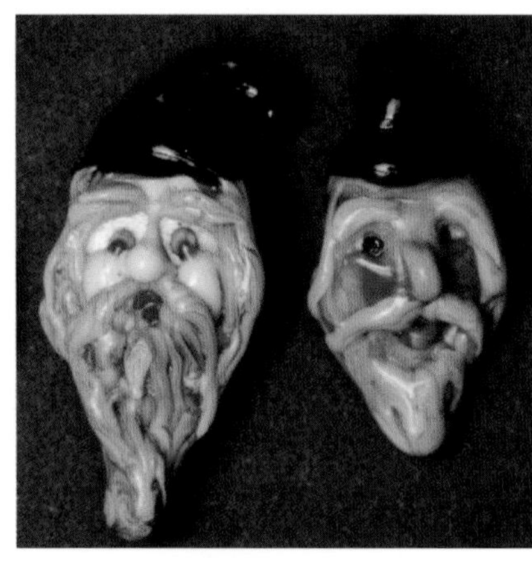

Gargoyle Face
Artist: Donna Nova
Size: 1¼" W x ½" T x 1 ¼" H
Date: 1998
Photo: Jim Kervin

Clown Bead
Artist: Jim Kervin
Size: ¾" W x ¾" T x 1¼" H
Date: 1997
Photo: the artst

Santa Beads
Artist: Mary Klotz
Size: ¾" W x ½" T x 1" H
Date: 1997
Photo: Marshall Dupuis

Head Beads

African Mask
Artist: Patricia Sage
Size: ¾" W x ¼" T x 2" H
Date: 1999
Photo: Jim Kervin

Gollum Heads
Artist: Sharon Peters
Size: Various
Date: 2002
Photo: Janice Peacock

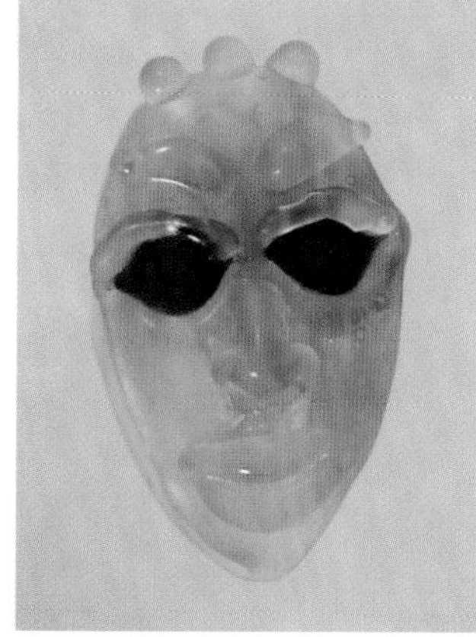

Dichro Head
Artist: Janice Peacock
Size: ¾" W x ¾" T x 1¼" H
Date: 2002
Photo: Jim Kervin

Green Eyed Lady Bead
Artist: Lezlie Levitt
Size: 1¼" W x ¾" T x 1½" H
Date: 2000
Photo: Jim Kervin

Good Morning Sun Swine
Artist: Sharon Peters
Size: 1¼" Dia x ¾" H
Date: 2001
Photo: Jim Kervin

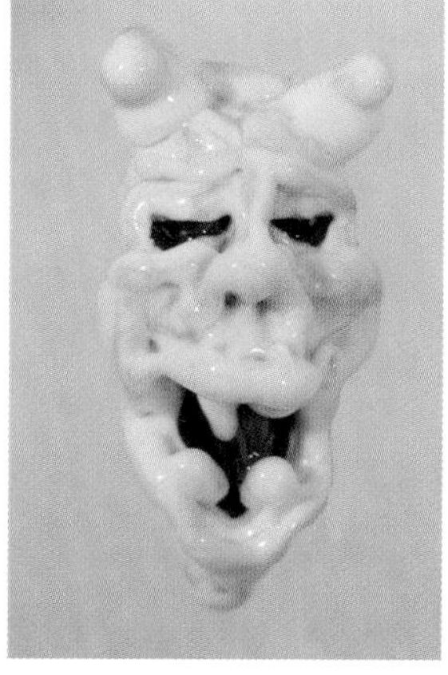

Devil Bead
Artist: Sheryll Hubbard
Size: ¾" W x ¾" T x 1½" H
Date: 2002
Photo: Jim Kervin

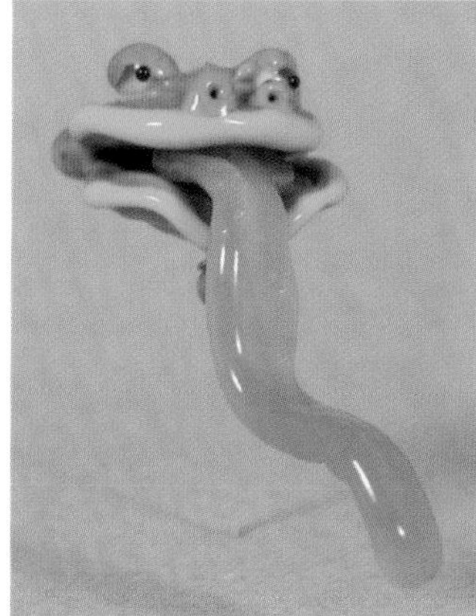

Frog Head
Artist: Ralph McCaskey
Size: ¾" Dia x 2" H
Date: 2002
Photo: Jim Kervin

Horse Head Bead
Artist: Kathy Johnson
Size: 1½" W x ½" T x 1½" H
Date: 1996
Photo: the artist

Lady in Pink
Artist: Loren Stump
Size: 1¼" W x 1" T x 1¾" H
Date: 1996
Photo: Jim Kervin

Animal Beads

Elephant Bead
Artist: Al Janelle
Size: 2¼" W x 1" T x 1¾" L
Date: 1998
Photo: the artist

Hen Bead
Artist: Al Janelle
Size: 1¼" W x ½" T x 1" L
Date: 1997
Photo:Jim Kervin

Monkey Bead
Artist: Al Janelle
Size: 1½" W x ¾" T x 1½" L
Date: 1998
Photo: the artist

Tiger Head
Artist: Loren Stump
Size: 1½" W x ¾" T x 1¾" L
Date: 1996
Photo: Robert K. Liu

Beconing Cat
Artist: Emiko Sawamoto
Size: ¾" W x ½" T x 1¼" L
Date: 1997
Photo: Jim Kervin

Cow in Moomoo, Cat in Sundress & Reba
Artist: Sharon Peters
Size: 1¼" Dia x 2" L
Date: 1998
Photo: Janice Peacock

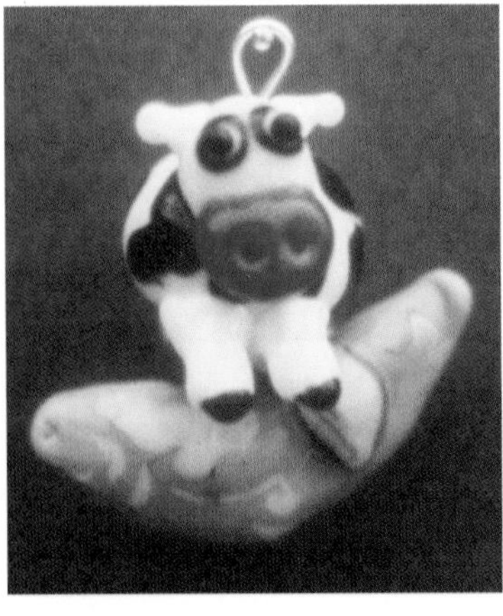

Cow Jumped Over The Moon
Artist: Jennifer Lue Zitkov
Size: 1½" W x ¾" T x 1¾" L
Date: 1999
Photo: the artist

Ant Urn Bead
Artist: Barbara Becker Simon
Size: 1" Dia x 1¼" L
Date: 2001
Photo: Rob Stegmann

Butterfly Bead
Artist: Audrie Wiesenfelder
Size: 1½" W x ½" T x 1" L
Date: 1998
Photo: Jim Kervin

Animal Beads

Lizardo's de CAPrio
Artist: Sharon Peters
Size: Various
Date: 2002
Photo: Janice Peacock

Cat's on Top
Artist: Sharon Peters
Size: 3" W x 1" T x 2" H
Date: 2002
Photo: Janice Peacock

Dog Beads
Artist: Kathy Perras
Size: 1" Dia x 1¾" H
Date: 2000
Photo: Jerry Anthony

Parrot
Artist: Pam Dugger
Size: 3" H
Date: 2002
Photo: Jeffrey O'Dell

Proud Peacock
Artist: Emiko Sawamoto
Size: 1¼" W x ¼" T x 1¼"H
Date: 2002
Photo: Rich Images

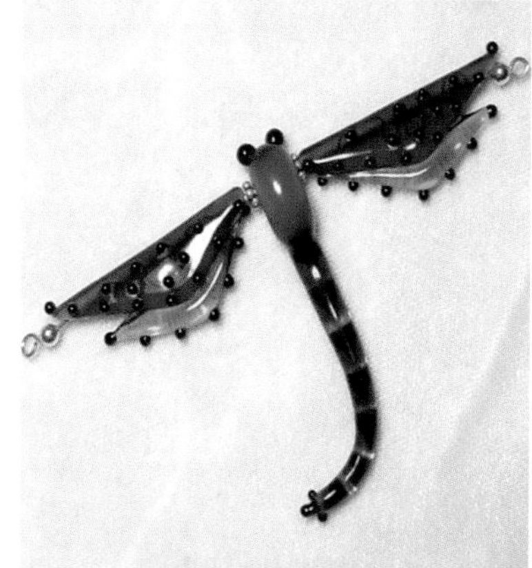

Dragon Fly
Artist: Kim Wertz
Size: 3" W x 3" L
Date: 2002
Photo: Greg Galardy

Christmas Dove
Artist: Linda Edmunds
Size: 1½" Dia x 2" H
Date: 2002
Photo: the artist

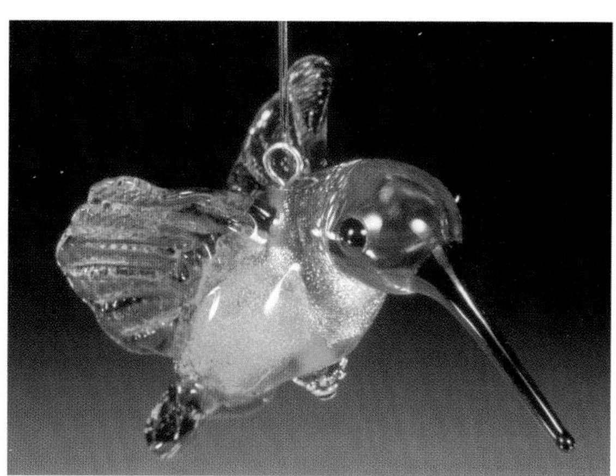

Dichro Hummingbird
Artist: Patricia Stoll
Size: 2½" L
Date: 2002
Photo: David Orr

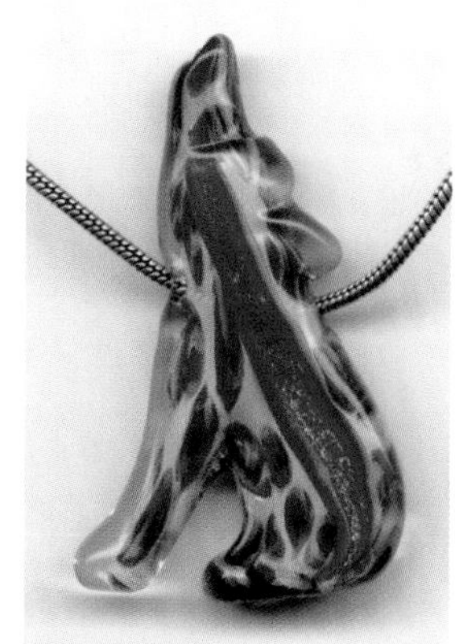

Red Wolf
Artist: Chad Pitts
Size: 1¼" W x ¼" T 2" H
Date: 2003
Photo: the artist

Fish & Seaform Beads

Blue-Girdled Angelfish
Artist: Pam dugger
Size: 2½" W x 1¼" T x 1½" L
Date: 2002
Photo: Jeffrey O'Dell

Tiger Fish
Artist: Pam Dugger
Size: 1¾" W x ¾" T x 1½" L
Date: 2003
Photo: the artist

Stratified Dot Fish Bead
Artist: Patricia Sage
Size: 1¼" W x ½" T x 1¾" L
Date: 1996
Photo: Tom Holandt

Sunken Dot Fish Bead
Artist: Deanna Griffin Dove
Size: 1¼" W x ¾" T x 1¾" L
Date: 1999
Photo: Robin Campo

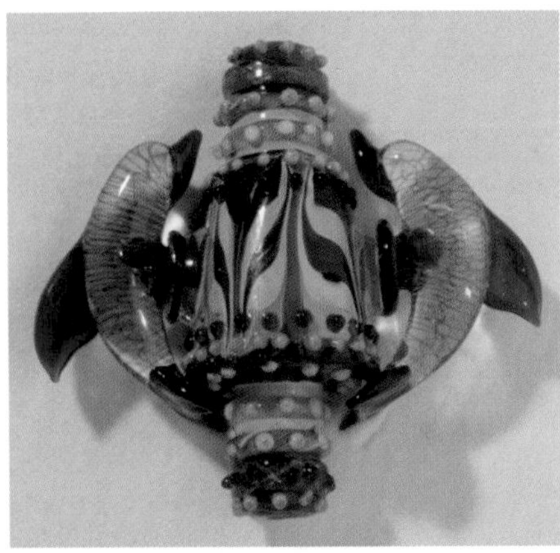

Twin Dolphin Bead
Artist: Lewis Wilson
Size: 2" W x 1¼" T x 2" L
Date: 1998
Photo: Tom Tennies

Blue Fusiform Bead
Artist: Patti Dougherty
Size: 1" W x ½" T x 1½" L
Date: 1998
Photo: the artist

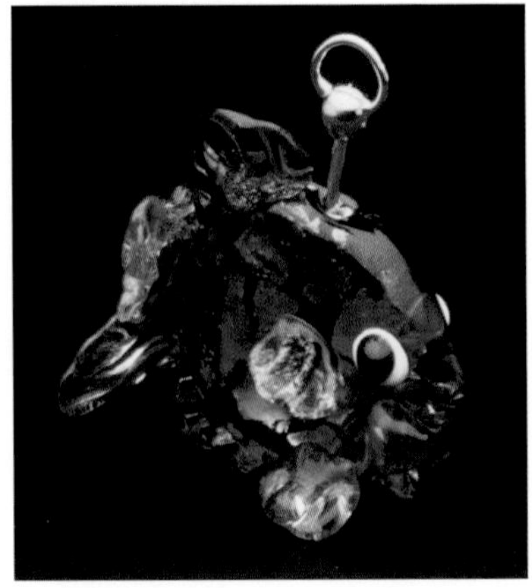

Transparent Fish Bead
Artist: Paula Radke
Size: 1½" W x ½" T x 1¼" L
Date: 1997
Photo: the artist

Fish & Seaform Beads

Blue Trigger Fish
Artist: Wayne Robbins
Size: 1¾" W x ¾" T x 1½" L
Date: 1997
Photo: the artist

Trigger Fish
Artist: Brad Pearson
Size: 1½" H x ¾" T x 1½" L
Date: 2002
Photo: Taylor Dabney

Fish with Attitude
Artist: Ofilia Cinta
Size: 1¾" W x 1" T x 1½" L
Date: 2002
Photo: Rich Images

Bass Fishing Blues
Artist: Chad Pitts
Size: ¾" W x ½" T x 1¾" L
Date: 2002
Photo: the artist

Fish with Attitude
Artist: Ofilia Cinta
Size: 2" W x 1" T x 1¾" L
Date: 2002
Photo: Rich Images

Dichro Fish
Artist: Barbara Becker Simon
Size: 2" W x ¾" T x 2" L
Date: 2002
Photo: Rob Stegmann

Octopus
Artist: Tracy Bascom
Size: 1" W x ¾" T x ¾" H
Date: 2001
Photo: Jim Kervin

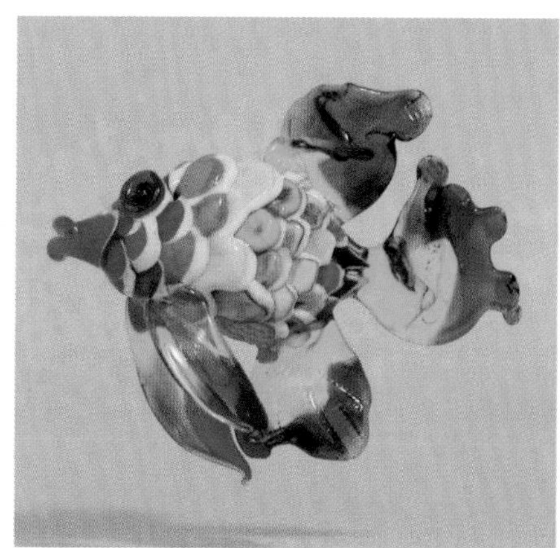

Stratified Dot Fish
Artist: Patrise Mecuro
Size: 2" W x 1" T x 1¾" L
Date: 2001
Photo: Jim Kervin

Other Sculptural Work

Collection of Cars
Artist: Loren Stump
Size: Various
Date: 1997
Photo: David Telfner

Bubble Gum Machine & Lightbulb
Artist: Al Janelle
Size: ¾" Dia x 1¼" L
Date: 1998
Photo: the artist

Gollum Bead
Artist: Sharon Peters
Size: 2" W x 1" T x 2½" L
Date: 2002
Photo: Janice Peacock

Carosel Hourse
Artist: Patti Genack
Size: 2¼" W x ¾" T x 1¾" H
Date: 2001
Photo: Jim Kervin

Lady with Hat
Artist: Stevi Belle
Size: 1¼" W x ¾" T x 2¼" L
Date: 2001
Photo: Jim Kervin

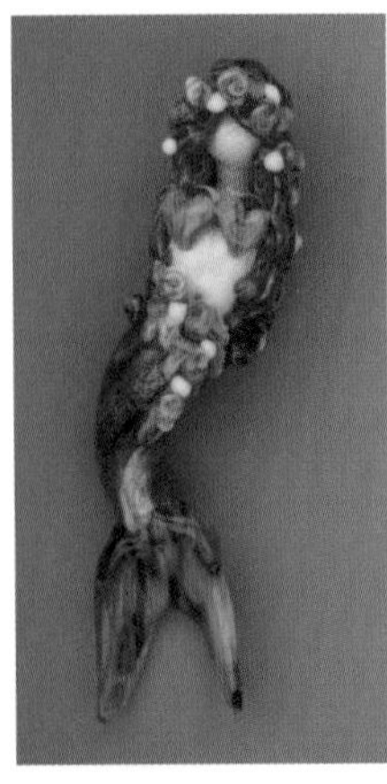

Mermaid
Artist: Pat Hoyt
Size: 2½" L
Date: 2002
Photo: Rich Images

Blue House Bead
Artist: Shanon Kindle
Size: ¾" Dia x 1¾" H
Date: 1998
Photo: Jim Kervin

Cat in Basket
Artist: Emiko Sawamoto
Size: ¾" W x 1" T x 1¼" H
Date: 1996
Photo: Jim Kervin

Mugwamp Bead
Artist: Angie Graham
Size: ¾" W x 1" T x 1¼" L
Date: 1998
Photo: Jim Kervin

Stone-Like Beads

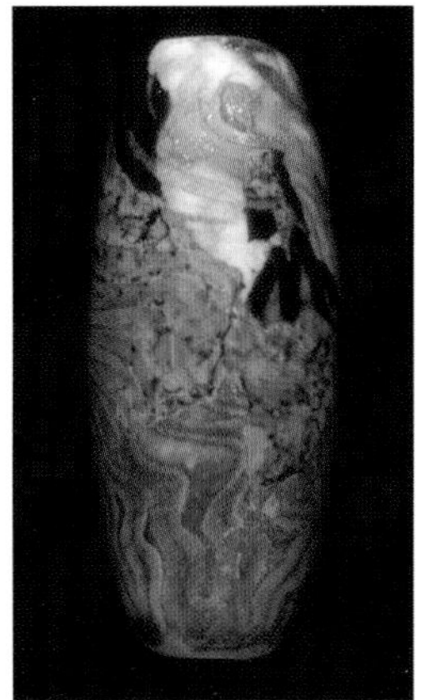

Aerial View
Artist: René Roberts
Size: ¾" Dia x 2" L
Date: 1998
Photo: George Post

Cobalt Donut
Artist: René Roberts
Size: 1¼" Dia x ½" T
Date: 2002
Photo: the artist

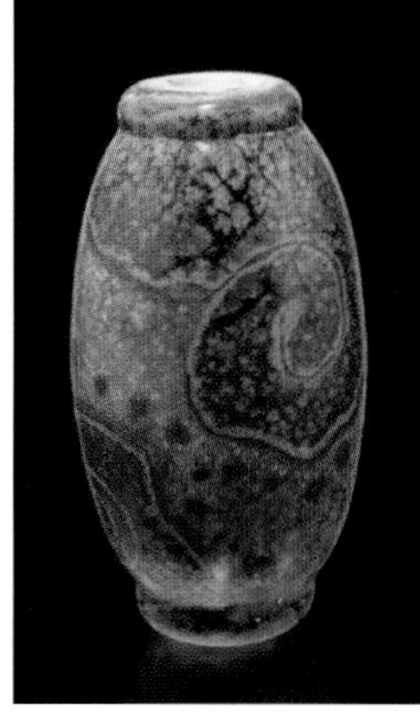

Stonework Bead
Artist: René Roberts
Size: ¾" Dia x 1½" L
Date: 2001
Photo: Hap Sakwa

Black Lagoon
Artist: René Roberts
Size: 1" W x 1½" L
Date: 1998
Photo: the artist

Blue Batik
Artist: Diana Dugina
Size: 1" W x ½" T x 1" L
Date: 2002
Photo: the artist

Treasure Rocks
Artist: Andrea Guarino
Size: Various
Date: 2003
Photo: the artist

Jade
Artist: Nanette Nelson
Size: ¾" W x ½" T x 1" L
Date: 2003
Photo: the artist

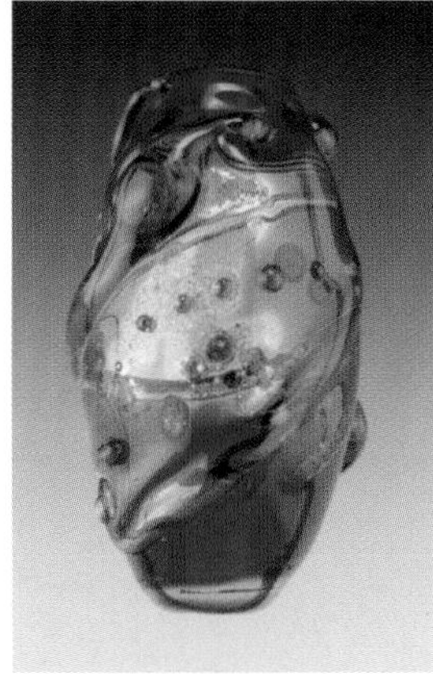

Red & Silver Bead
Artist: Nancy Herrington
Size: ¾" Dia x 1¾" L
Date: 2002
Photo: the artist

Bronze Age Bead
Artist: Shirley Cook
Size: ¾" Dia x 1¾" L
Date: 2002
Photo: the artist

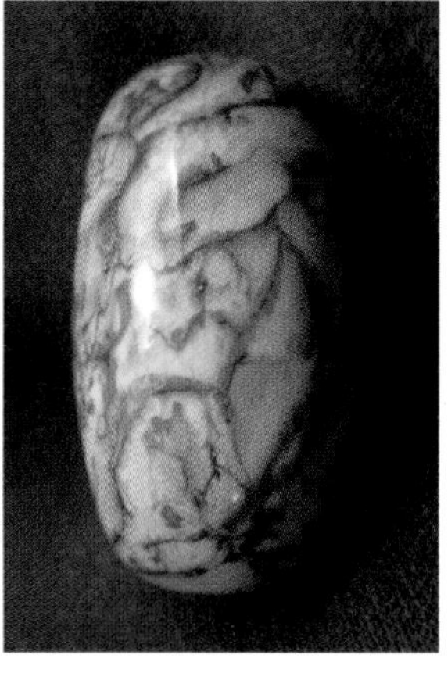

Marble Bead
Artist: Amy Smith
Size: ¾" Dia x 1½" L
Date: 2002
Photo: the artist

Raku Bead
Artist: James Allen Jones
Size: 1" Dia x ¾" L
Date: 1997
Photo: Jim Kervin

Borosilicate Beads

Blue Boro Eclectics
Artist: Lauri Copeland
Size: ¾" Dia x ½" L
Date: 2002
Photo: the artist

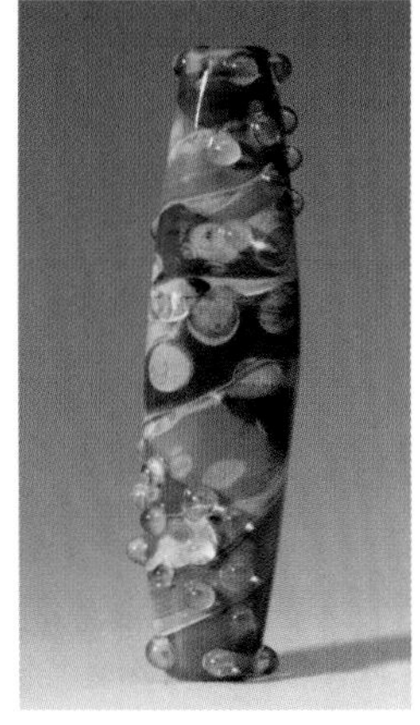

Teal Firestorm
Artist: Nancy Tobey
Size: ½" Dia x 2" L
Date: 2002
Photo: Steve Gyurina

Milano Leaf
Artist: Nancy Tobey
Size: 1" W x ¼" T x 2¼" L
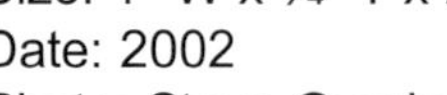
Date: 2002
Photo: Steve Gyurina

Staff Bead
Artist: Nancy Tobey
Size: ¾" W x ¼" T x 2¼" L
Date: 1999
Photo: Jim Kervin

Walk in Two Worlds
Artist: Keith Kreitter
Size: ¾" W x ½" T x 1" L
Date: 1997
Photo: Jim Kervin

Octopus' Garden
Artist: Michael Barley
Size: 1½" W x ¾" T x 1½" L
Date: 2002
Photo: Jim Kervin

Anemone Series
Artist: Gail Crossman-Moore
Size: Various
Date: 2002
Photo: Charley Frieberg

Incredible Inside Out Bead
Artist: John Olson
Size: 1¼" Dia x 1¼" L
Date: 2003
Photo: the artist

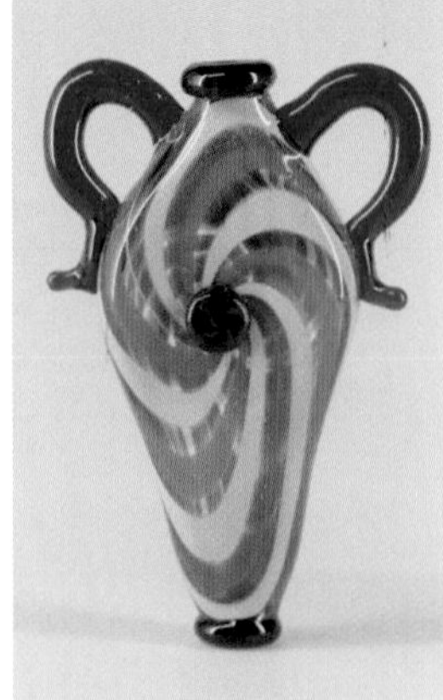

Montage Vessel
Artist: Doni Hatz
Size: 1¼"W x ½"Tx 1½"L
Date: 1997
Photo: Jim Kervin

Blown Boro Bead
Artist: Tom Boylan
Size: 1" Dia x 1¼" L
Date: 1997
Photo: Jim Kervin

Inside Out Twist
Artist: Chad Pitts
Size: ¾" Dia x 1¾" L
Date: 2003
Photo: the artist

Wound Borosilicate Beads

Patina Forest Series
Artist: CarolAnne Bouchles
Size: 1¼" Dia x 3" L
Date: 2003
Photo: Robert Diamante

Abstract Boro Bead Series
Artist: Eloise Cotton
Size: Various
Date: 2002
Photo: Hap Sakwa

Anemone Bead
Artist: Gail Crossman-Moore
Size: 1" Dia x 1" L
Date: 1999
Photo: Jim Kervin

Anemone Bead
Artist: Gail Crossman-Moore
Size: 1¼" Dia x 1¼" L
Date: 1999
Photo: Jim Kervin

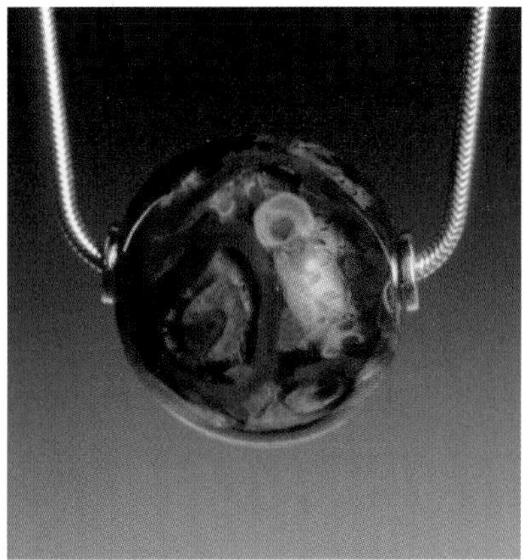

Abstract Boro Pendant
Artist: Eloise Cotton
Size: 1¼" Dia x 1¼" L
Date: 1995
Photo: Marcia Lieberman

Dot Bead
Artist: David Martin
Size: 1" Dia x ½" T
Date: 2001
Photo: Jim Kervin

Sunset Bead
Artist: Jay Shuster
Size: ¾" W x ¼" T x 2" L
Date: 2002
Photo: Jim Kervin

Eye Bead
Artist: Jesse Taj
Size: ¾" Dia x 1¾" L
Date: 2002
Photo: Jim Kervin

Raked Layer Bead
Artist: Robert Jennik
Size: ¾" Dia x 2¼" L
Date: 2000
Photo: Jim Kervin

Hollow Wound &Tube Beads

Devil Lion Fish
Artist: Pam Dugger
Size: 2½" W x 1¼" T x 1¾" H
Date: 1998
Photo: Jim Kervin

Hollow Wound Balls
Artist: Helga Seimel
Size: 1¼" Dia x 1¼" L
Date: 1996
Photo: Shari Maxson Hopper

Hollow Pixie Heart Bead
Artist: Matt Marchand
Size: 1¼" W x ½" T x 1" L
Date: 1997
Photo: Jim Kervin

Flying Saucer Beads
Artist: Heather Trimlet
Size: Various
Date: 1998
Photo: Melinda Holden

Ancient X Bead
Artist: Karen Ovington
Size: ¾" W x ½" T x 1¼" L
Date: 1998
Photo: Tom an Enyde

Pink Tube Bead
Artist: Don Schneider
Size: ¾" Dia x 2" L
Date: 1996
Photo: Bill Bresler

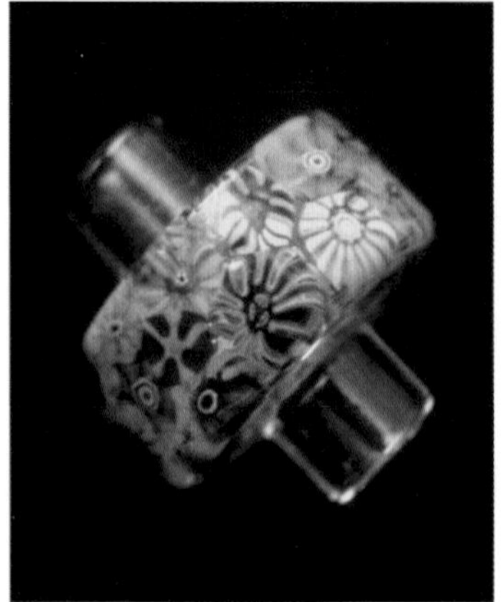

Disk Tube Bead
Artist: Don Schneider
Size: 1" Dia x 1" L
Date: 1996
Photo: Bill Bresler

Raised Murrini Bead
Artist: Don Schneider
Size: ¾" Dia x 1½" L
Date: 1995
Photo: Bill Bresler

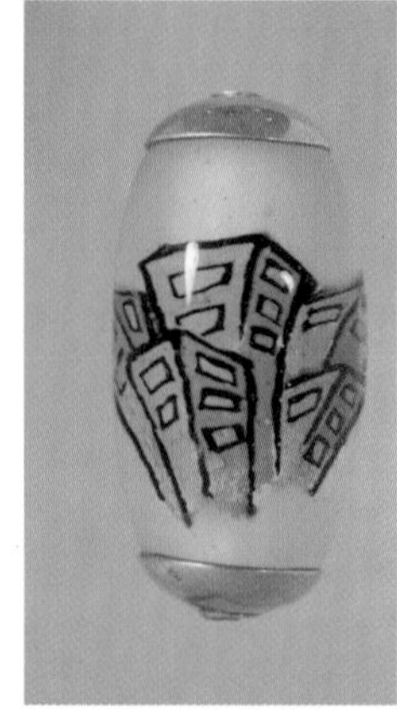

Reverse Painted Bead
Artist: Bronwen Heilman
Size: ¾" Dia x 2" L
Date: 2002
Photo: Jim Kervin

Enameled, Electroformed & Etched Beads

Ruins Bead
Artist: Diana East
Size: 1"W x ½"T x 1½"L
Date: 2002
Photo: Jim Kervin

Aladin's Palice Bead
Artist: Diana East
Size: 1"W x ½"T x 1½"L
Date: 2002
Photo: Jim Kervin

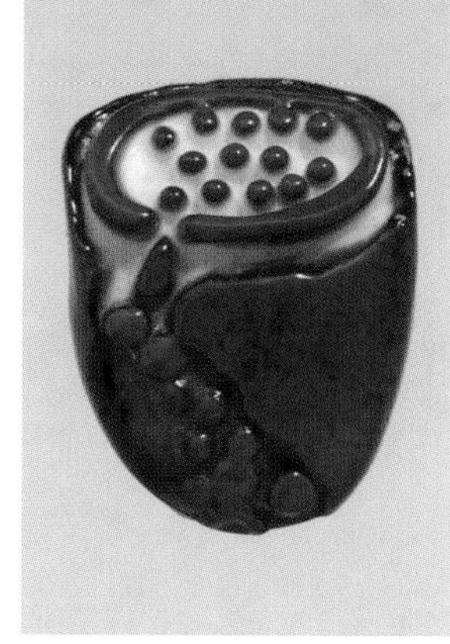

Carved Tableau
Artist: Bronwen Heilman
Size: 1¼"W x ½"T x 1¾"H
Date: 2000
Photo: Jim Kervin

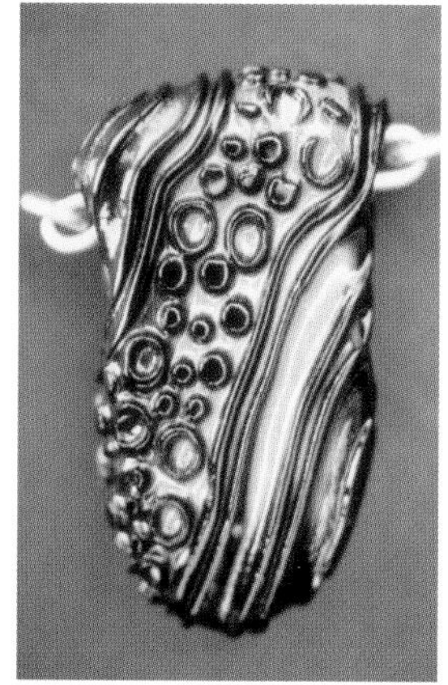

Sandblasted Tableau
Artist: Bronwen Heilman
Size: 1½"W x ½"T x 2¾"L
Date: 1998
Photo: the artist

Baking Soda Bead
Artist: Karen Ovington
Size: 1¼" Dia x 1" L
Date: 1999
Photo: Jim Kervin

Petroglyph Bead
Artist: Kate Fowle Meleney
Size: ½" W x ¼" T x 1" L
Date: 2002
Photo: Jim Kervin

Anthromorph & Goddess Beads
Artist: Kate Fowle Meleney
Size: Various
Date: 2001
Photo: Jerry Anthony

Pods
Artist: Marjorie Burr
Size: Various
Date: 2002
Photo: the artist

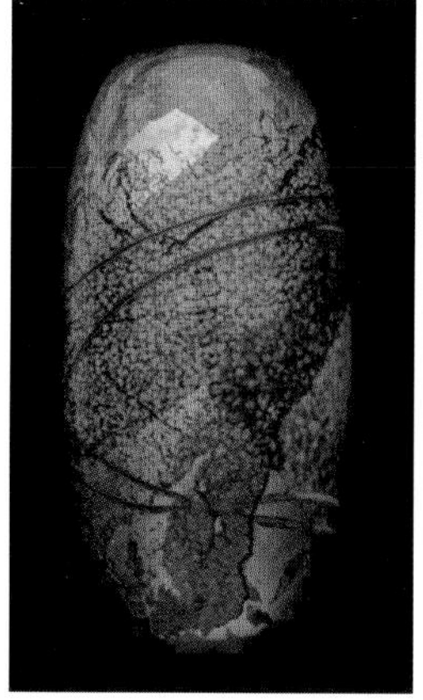

Seamoss
Artist: René Roberts
Size: ¾" Dia x 2" L
Date: 1997
Photo: George Post

Etched Beads
Artist: Caitlin Hyde
Size: ½" to ¾" Dia x 2" L
Date: 1999
Photo: Jim Kervin

Freeform Beads

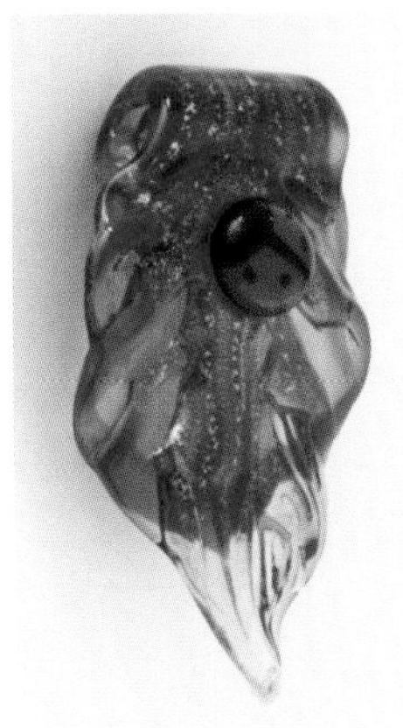

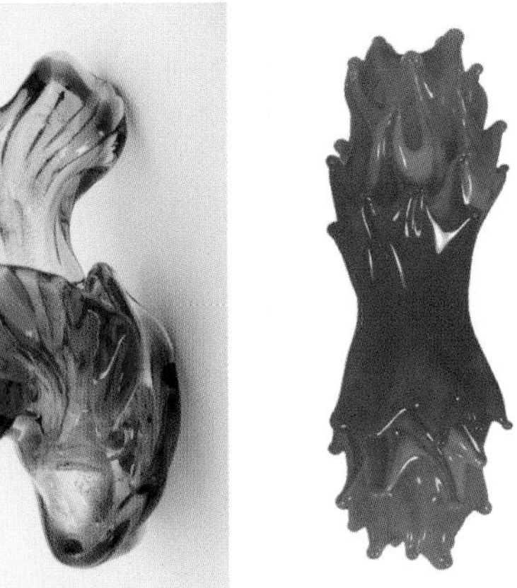

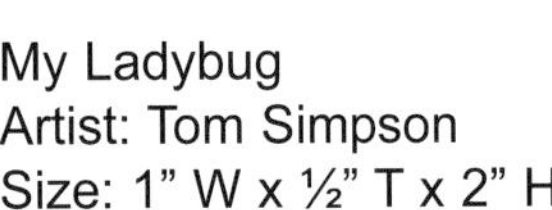

My Ladybug
Artist: Tom Simpson
Size: 1" W x ½" T x 2" H
Date: 1999
Photo: Jim Kervin

Left: Lola Bead Right: Floral Bead
Artist: Monty Clark & Carol Fonda
Size: 1½" W x ¾" T x 1" H
Date: 1998
Photo: Jim Kervin

Flame Bead
Artist: Chrissy Nixon
Size: ½" Dia x 1½" L
Date: 2002
Photo: Jim Kervin

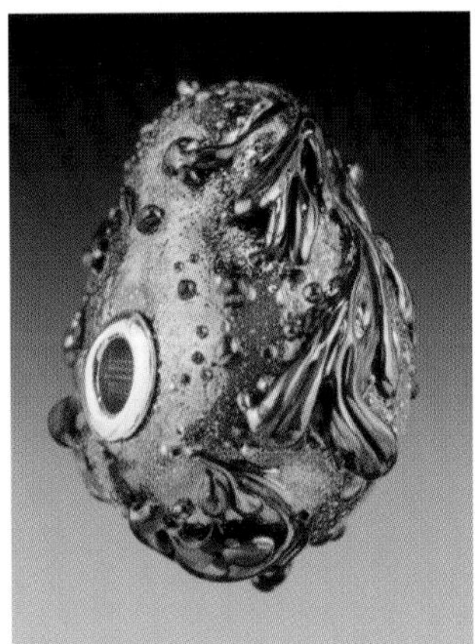

Brocade Bead
Artist: Susan Breen Silvy
Size: 1" T x 1" L x 1½" H
Date: 2002
Photo: Jerry Anthony

Left: Violet Swirl Right: Red Floral
Artist: Ann Scherm Baldwin
Size: Various
Date: 2002
Photo: Jerry Anthony

Flame Bead
Artist: Alex Shapiro
Size: 2" Dia x 1½" L
Date: 2001
Photo: Jim Kervin

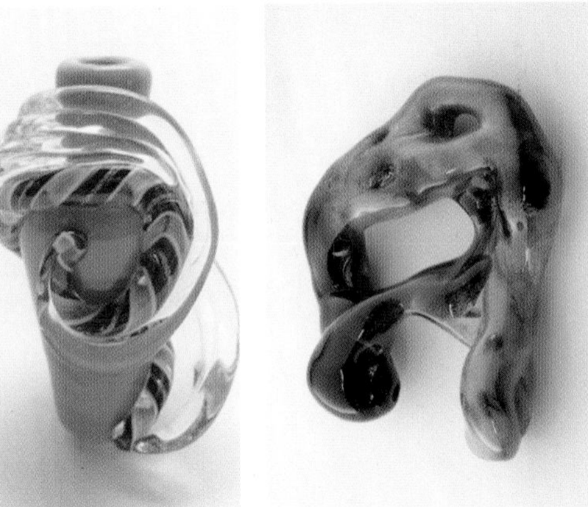

Triple Fold Bead
Artist: Tom Holland
Size: ¾" Dia x ½" L
Date: 1998
Photo: Jim Kervin

Blue Allure, Caramel Delight & Gray Grace
Artist: Marna Hartjen
Size: 3", 2" & 1½" L
Date: 2003, 2003 & 2002
Photos: the artist

Freeform Bullseye
Artist: Mimi Abers
Size: 1½" W x ½" T x 2" H
Date: 1998
Photo: Jim Kervin

Chevron & Coldworked Beads

Carapace Bead
Artist: Larry Scott
Size: ¾" W x ½" Tx 1¾" L
Date: 2002
Photo: Roger Schreiber

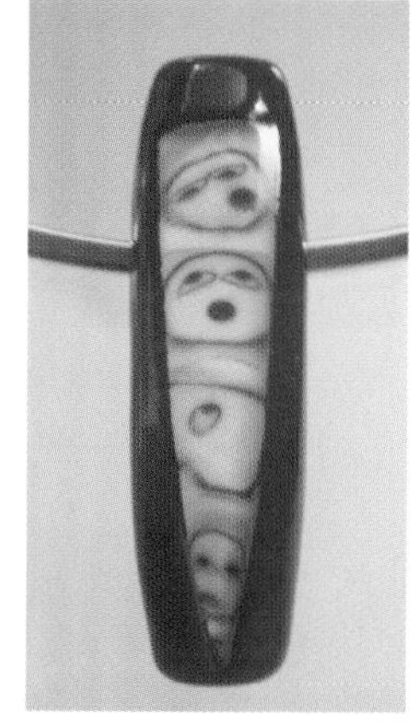

Faces Pendant
Artist: Diana East
Size: ½" Dia x 2" L
Date: 2002
Photo: the artist

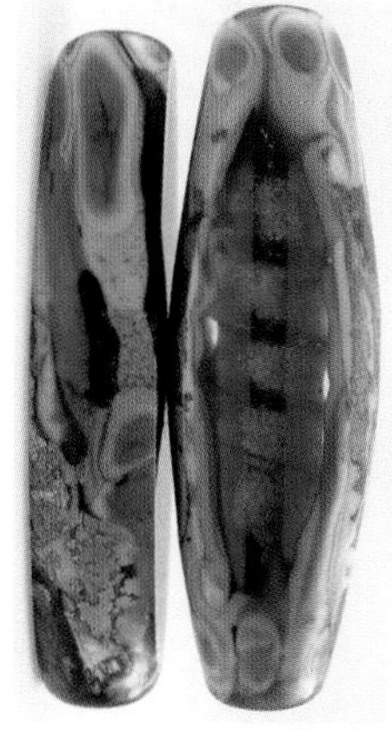

Silkstone Beads
Artist: Lauri Copeland
Size: ½" Dia x 2" L
Date: 2002
Photo: the artist

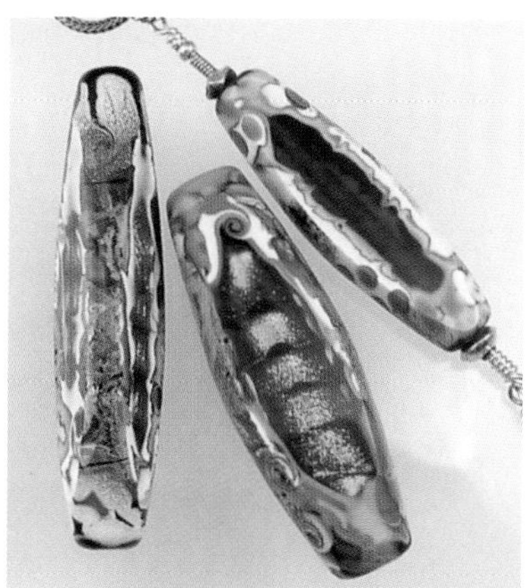

Silkstone Beads
Artist: Lauri Copeland
Size: ½" Dia x 2" L
Date: 2002
Photo: the artist

Faceted Chevrons
Artist: Greg Galardy
Size: ¾" Dia x 1¾" L
Date: 2002
Photo: the artist

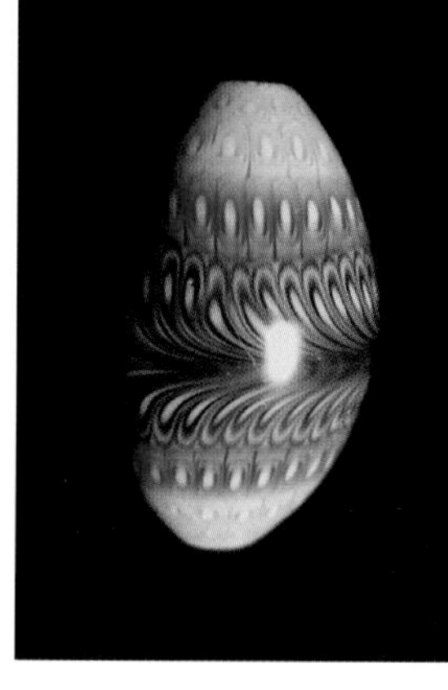

Faceted Chevron
Artist: Greg Galardy
Size: ¾" Dia x 1¾" L
Date: 2002
Photo: the artist

Assorted Polished Cane Beads
Artist: Tom Holland, Sage & Beau Anderson
Size: Various
Date: 1997
Photo: Tom Holland

Assorted Chevron Beads
Artist: Mary Mullaney & Ralph Mossman
Size: Various
Date: 1995
Photo: Robert K. Liu

Assorted Chevron Beads
Artist: Mary Mullaney & Ralph Mossman
Size: Various
Date: 1995
Photo: Jake Schmeers

Fused Beads

Painted Enamel Landscapes
Artist: Bruce St. John Maher
Size: 1" W x ¼" T x 2½" H
Date: 1998
Photo: Janice Peacock

Dichroic Pyramid Pendant
Artist: Bruce St. John Maher
Size: 1" W x ¾" T x 1¼" H
Date: 1999
Photo: Jim Kervin

Painted Enamel Silhouettes
Artist: Bruce St. John Maher
Size: ¾" W x ¼" T x 1½" H
Date: 1996
Photo: the artist

Cone Beads
Artist: Molly Vaughan Haskins
Size: 1¼" Dia x ¾" T
Date: 1994
Photo: Robert K. Liu

Disk Beads
Artist: Molly Vaughan Haskins
Size: 1¼" Dia x ¼" T
Date: 1994
Photo: Robert K. Liu

Fused Bead
Artist: Malcom Potek
Size: 1" W x ¼" T x 2¼" H
Date: 1997
Photo: the artist

Fused Bead
Artist: Malcom Potek
Size: 1"W x ½"T x 2¼" H
Date: 1998
Photo: Jim Kervin

Morning Blues
Artist: Kara van Wyk
Size: 1½" W x ¼" T x 2" H
Date: 1998
Photo: Malcom Potek

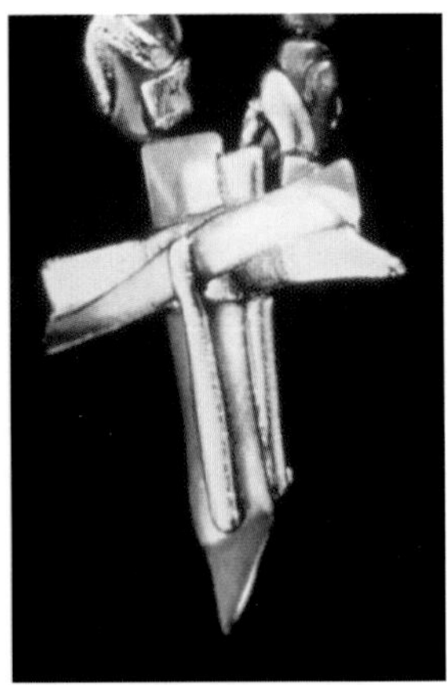

Dichroic Cross
Artist: Paula Radke
Size: 1½" W x ¼" T x 2" H
Date: 1997
Photo: the artist

Fused Beads

Cosmic Crater Pendant
Artist: Nancy Goodenough
Size: 1" W x ¼" T x 2" H
Date: 1997
Photo: George Post

Cosmic Crater Pendant
Artist: Nancy Goodenough
Size: 2½" W x ¼" T x 1½" H
Date: 1996
Photo: George Post

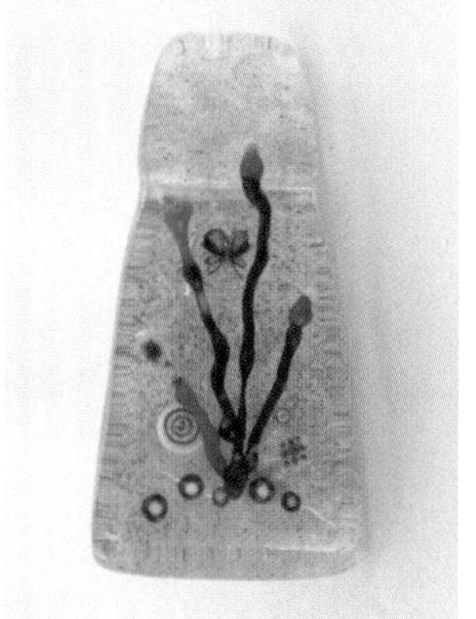

Floral Pendant
Artist: Jim Wuerfel
Size: 1" W x ¼" T x 2" H
Date: 1999
Photo: Jim Kervin

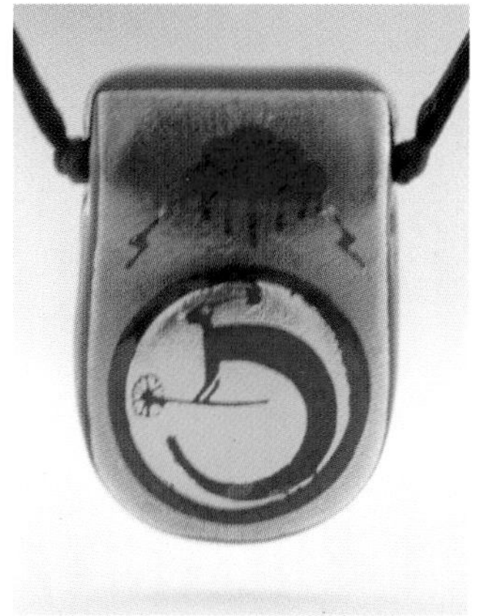

Rabbit with Flowers & Rain
Artist: Sara Creekmore
Size: 1" W x ¼" T x1½" H
Date: 1997
Photo: Jim Kervin

Dill Pendant
Artist: Cay Dickey & Scott Omori
Size: 2" W x ¼" T x 1¾" H
Date: 1997
Photo: Carl Tamuri

Coldworked Fused Frit
Artist: Bob Aurelius
Size: 1½" W x ¼" T x 1¾" H
Date: 1998
Photo: Jim Kervin

Cloak Bead
Artist: Monty Clark & Carol Fonda
Size: 1" W x ½" T x 3" H
Date: 1998
Photo: Jim Kervin

Assorted Fused Beads
Artist: Monty Clark & Carol Fonda
Size: Various
Date: 1998
Photo: Monty Clark

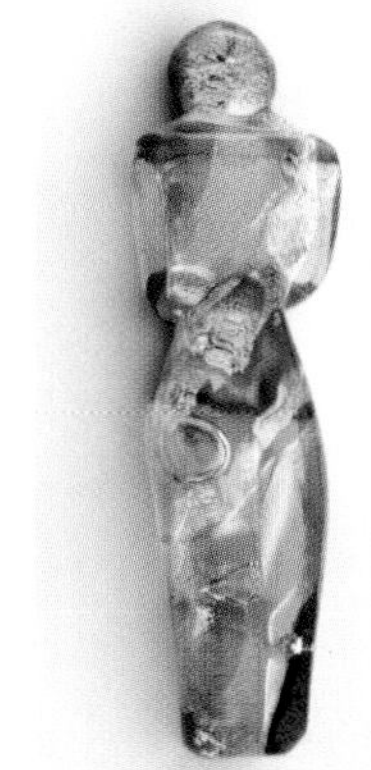

Goddess Bead
Artist: Monty Clark & Carol Fonda
Size: ¾" W x ½" T x 2¼" H
Date: 1998
Photo: Jim Kervin

Blown Beads

Decaled Blown Beads
Artist: Shari Maxson Hopper
Size: ¾" Dia x 1½" L
Date: 1998
Photo: the artist

Enamel Painted Blown Bead
Artist: Shari Maxson Hopper
Size: 1¾" Dia x 2" L
Date: 1998
Photo: the artist

Beads With Various Treatments
Artist: Shari Maxson Hopper
Size: Various
Date: 1998
Photo: the artist

Twisted Blown Bead
Artist: Tom Boylan
Size: ¾" Dia x 1½" L
Date: 1998
Photo: Jim Kervin

Raked Blown Bead
Artist: Tom Boylan
Size: ¾" Dia x 1½" L
Date: 1998
Photo: Jim Kervin

Powder & Frit Decorated
Artist: Don Schneider
Size: 1¼" Dia x 2" L
Date: 1995
Photo: Bill Bresler

Montage Bead
Artist: Doni Hatz
Size: 1" W x ¾" T x 1" L
Date: 1997
Photo: Trevor Hart

Blown Effetre Montage Bead
Artist: Brett Pierce
Size: 1¼" Dia x 2" L
Date: 1999
Photo: Jim Kervin

Various Blown Beads
Artist: Doni Hatz
Size: Various
Date: 1997
Photo: Trevor Hart

Pâte de Verre & Kiln Cast Beads

Floral Bead
Artist: Donna Milliron
Size: 1½" Dia x ½" T
Date: 1998
Photo: Jim Kervin

Cast & Faceted Bead
Artist: Bruce St. John Maher
Size: ¾" W x ¾" H x 1" L
Date: 2002
Photo: Jim Kervin

Floral Bead
Artist: Donna Milliron
Size: 1½" Dia x ½" T
Date: 1998
Photo: Jim Kervin

Fabric of Life Pendant
Artist: Donna Milliron
Size: 2" W x ¾" T x 1½" H
Date: 19988
Photo: Christopher Marchetti

Floral Bead
Artist: Donna Milliron
Size: ¾" W x ½" T x 2" L
Date: 1998
Photo: Jim Kervin

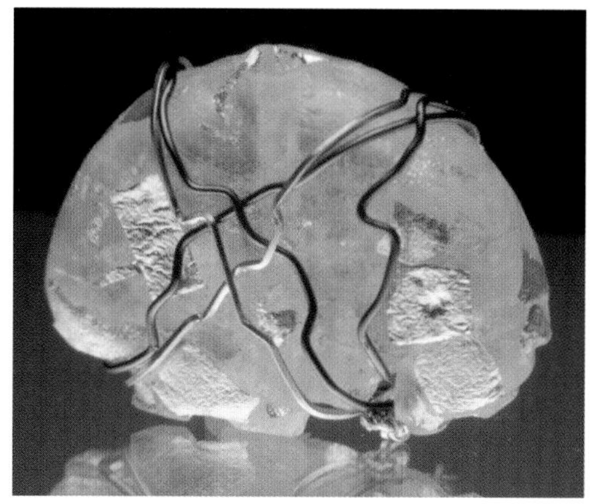

Fariy Basket Bead
Artist: Donna Milliron
Size: 1¾" W x ¾" T x 1¼" L
Date: 1998
Photo: Christopher Marchetti

Red Eye Pendant
Artist: Jim Kervin
Size: 1½" Dia x ½" T
Date: 1996
Photo: the artist

Happy Face Pendant
Artist: Jim Kervin
Size: 1½" W x 1¾" H x ½" T
Date: 1997
Photo: the artist

Greek Statues
Artist: Mary Klotz
Size: ¾" W x ½" T x 1¼"
Date: 1997
Photo: Marshall Dupuis

Sculptural Work

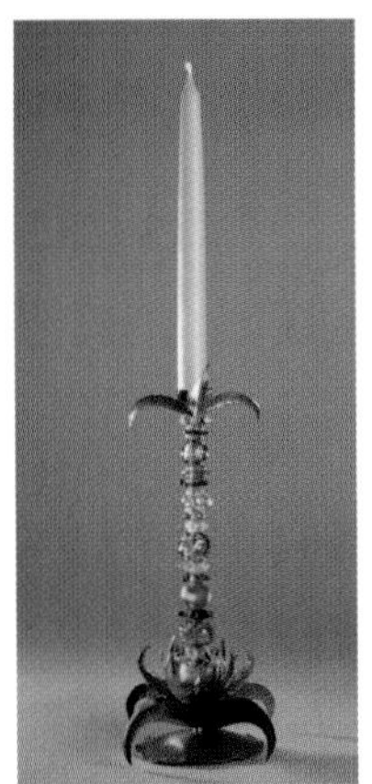

Beaded Candlestick
Artist: Beth Williams
Size: 4" Dia x 10" H
Date: 2002
Photo: Lynn Swigart

Bead Bowl
Artist: Kathryn Wardill
Size: 3½" Dia x 4" H
Date: 2001
Photo: the artist

Sea Turtle
Artist: Catherine Weaver
Size: 3" H
Date: 2002
Photo: the artist

Do Do That Poo Do
Artist: Sharon Peters
Size: 1¼" Dia x 2" H
Date: 2001
Photo: Janice Peacock

Red Angel
Artist: Pat Hoyt
Size: 2¾" H
Date: 2002
Photo: Rich Images

Bead Mobile
Artist: Beth Williams
Size: 14" W x 19" H
Date: 2002
Photo: Lynn Swigart

Purple Fairy
Artist: Mavis Smith
Size: 2½" H
Date: 2003
Photo: the artist

Blue Nympyh
Artist: Lee Lynn Thompson
Size: 2½" H
Date: 2002
Photo: Ingrid Hein

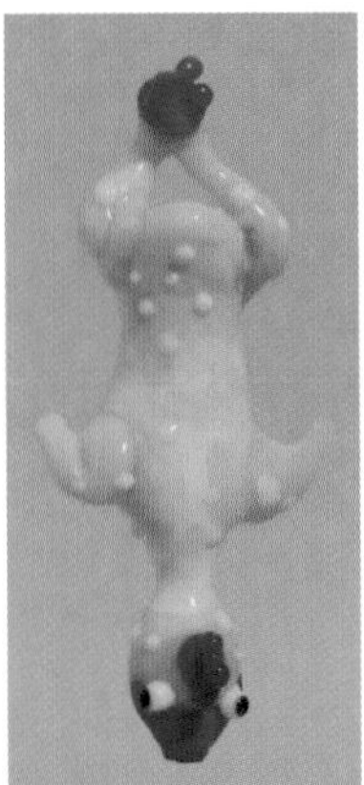

Rubber Chicken
Artist: Greg Fuchs
Size: 1" W x 2" L
Date: 2000
Photo: Jim Kervin

Clown Trio
Artist: Bobby Pedersen
Size: 1" Dia x 3" H
Date: 2002
Photo: the artist

Kabuki Dancer of White Lion
Artist: Emiko Sawamoto
Size: 2½" H
Date: 2002
Photo: Rich Images

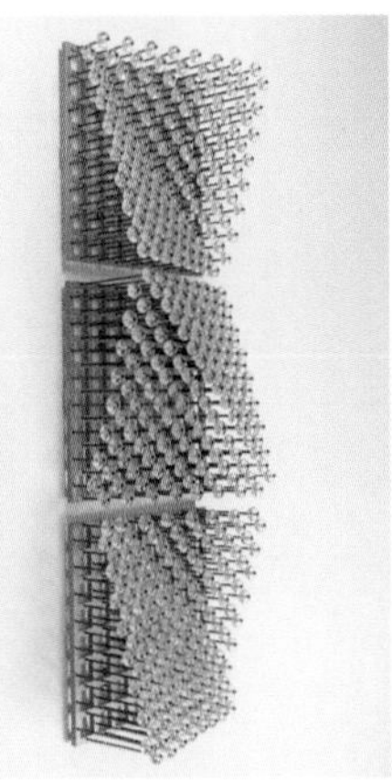

Wall Sculpture
Artists: Carol Bugarin
& Jacob Kulin
Size: 37" x 12" 2002
Photo: Eric Kulin

Vessels

Teapot
Artist: Heather Trimlett
Size: 1¼" W x ½" T x 1½" L
Date: 1996
Photo: Melinda Holden

Turtle & Dolphin Vessels
Artists: Dave & Rebecca Jurgens
Size: 1"W x ½"T x 1½"L
Date: 2002
Photo: the artists

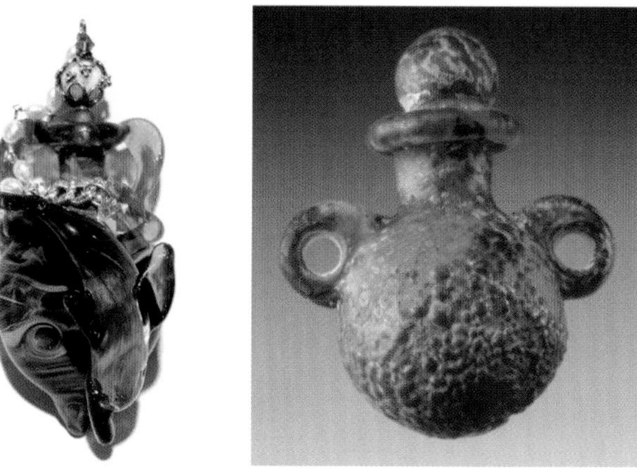

Ancient Vessel
Artist: Stevi Belle
Size: 1¼" W x 1" T x 1½" L
Date: 1997
Photo: Jerry Anthony

Flower Vase
Artist: Teresa Pinto
Size: 1" Dia x 2¼" L
Date: 1998
Photo: Jim Kervin

Blown Vessel
Artist: Leroy Goetz
Size: 1 ½" W x ½" T x 2¼" H
Date: 1997
Photo: Jim Kervin

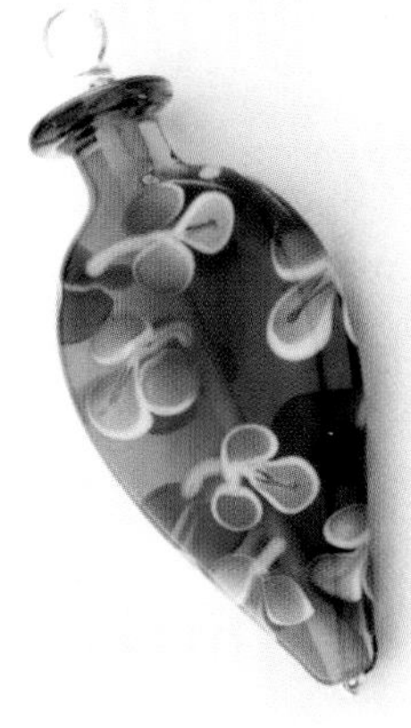

Flowered Vase
Artist: Carol Bugarin
Size: 1¼" W x ¼" T x 2¼" L
Date: 1998
Photo: Jim Kervin

Silver Red Vessel
Artist: Mitra Totten
Size: 1" Dia x 2" L
Date: 2002
Photo: the artist

Question Amphora
Artist: Janice Peacock
Size: 1¼" W x ½" T x 1¾" L
Date: 1998
Photo: the artist

Raked Blown Vessel
Artist: Doni Hatz
Size: 1" W x ¼" T x 2¼"L
Date: 1998
Photo: Jim Kervin

Genie Bottle
Artist: Beth Williams
Size: 1" Dia x 1½" L
Date: 1997
Photo: Jim Kervin

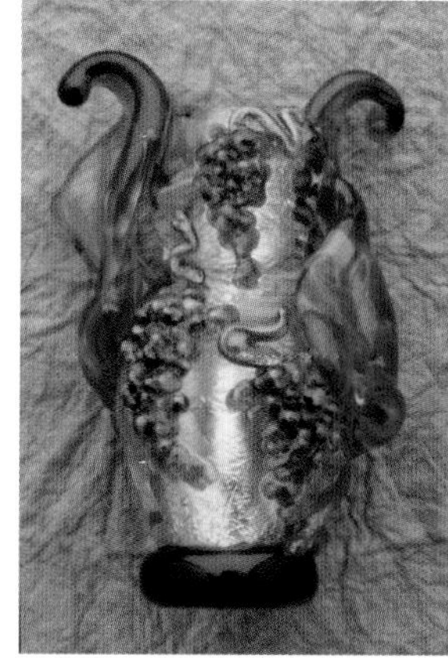

Grape Urn
Artist: Leah Fairbanks
Size: 1½" W x ¾" T x 2" L
Date: 1996
Photo: George Post

Vessels

Earthly Elements Amphora
Artist: Dolly Ahers
Size: ¾" Dia x 2" H
Date: 2002
Photo: David Orr

Duck Pond Vessel
Artist: Mavis Smith
Size: 3½" H
Date: 2002
Photo: the artist

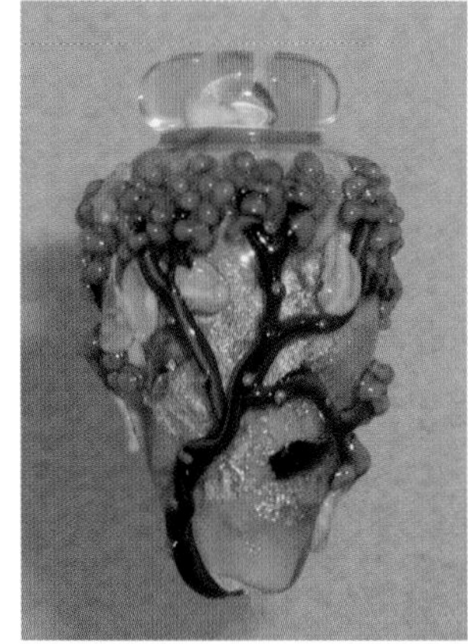

Azalea Bonzai Vessel
Artist: Leah Fairbanks
Size: 1" Dia x 2" L
Date: 2002
Photo: Jim Kervin

Earthly Elements Pendant
Artist: Dolly Ahers
Size: ¾" Dia x 1¾" L
Date: 2002
Photo: David Orr

Electroformed Vessel
Artist: Ann Davis
Size: ½" Dia x 2" H
Date: 2002
Photo: Jim Kervin

Etched Amphora
Artist: Barbara Becker Simon
Size: 1¼" Dia x 2" L
Date: 2000
Photo: Jim Kervin

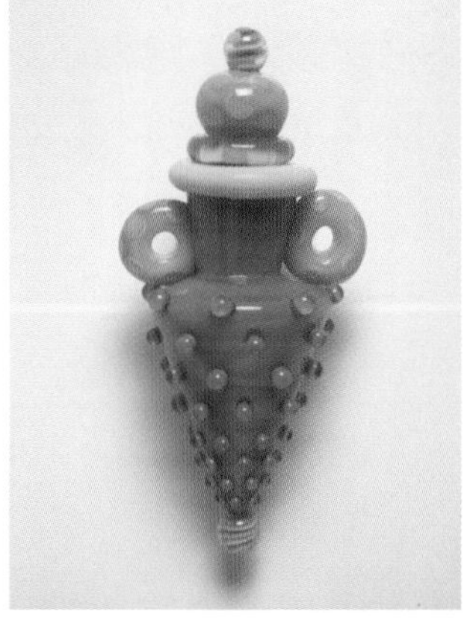

Hollow Vessel
Artist: Heather Trimlett
Size: 1½" Dia x 3" H
Date: 2002
Photo: Melinda Holden

Boro Vessel Bead
Artist: Gail Crossman-Moore
Size: ½" Dia x 2" L
Date: 2002
Photo: the artist

Mistress of the Heat
Artist: Mona Gollan
Size: 2½" W x 5" H
Date: 2002
Photo: the artist

Earthen Vessel
Artist: Bobby Pedersen
Size: 1"W x ½" T x 1¼" H
Date: 2002
Photo: the artist

Black Vessel
Artist: Bobby Pedersen
Size: 1¼" W x ¾" T x 2" H
Date: 2002
Photo: the artist

Dichroic Amphora
Artist: Ginny Sycuro
Size: 2½" H
Date: 2002
Photo: Jerry Downs

Jewelry

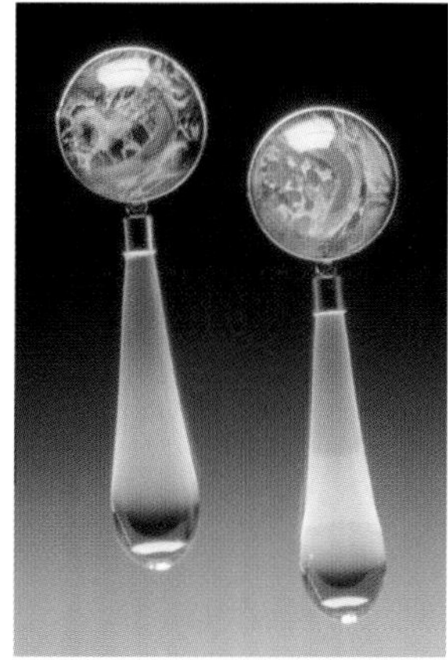

Cabochon Drop Earrings
Artist: Eloise Cotton
Size: ¾" W x ½" T x 2½" L
Date: 1997
Photo: Hap Sakwa

Fused & Kiln Cast Bracelets
Artist: Molly Vaughan Haskins
Size: 1¼" H x 2½" Dia
Date: 1997
Photo: Patty Hulet

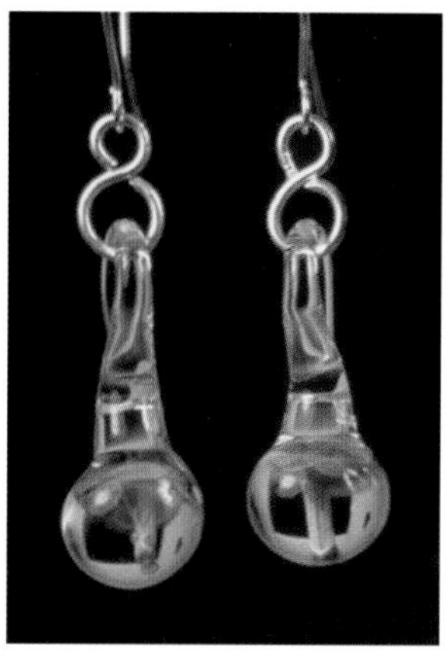

Mushroom Earrings
Artist: Barbara Burgess
Size: 1¼" L x ½" Dia
Date: 1998
Photo: Barbara Burgess

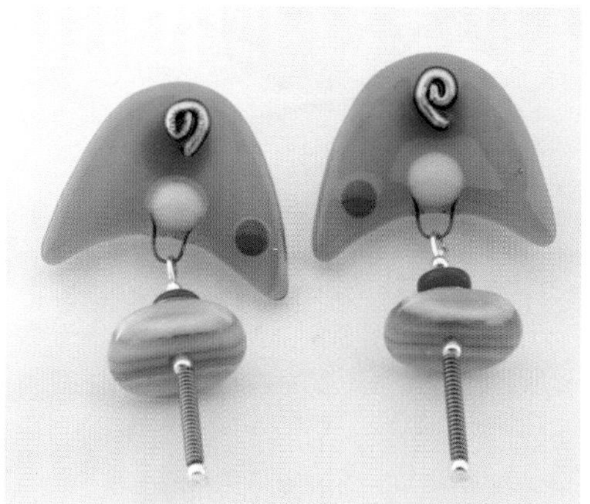

Fused Earrings
Artist: Bernadette Mahfood
Size: 1¼" W x ½" T x 2" L
Date: 1998
Photo: Jim Kervin

Happy Life Bracelet
Artist: Susan Breen Silvy
Size: 7" L x ¾" Dia
Date: 2002
Photo: Jeffrey O'Dell

Azurite Ring
Artist: Mitra Totten
Size: ¼" Dia Marble
Date: 2002
Photo: the artist

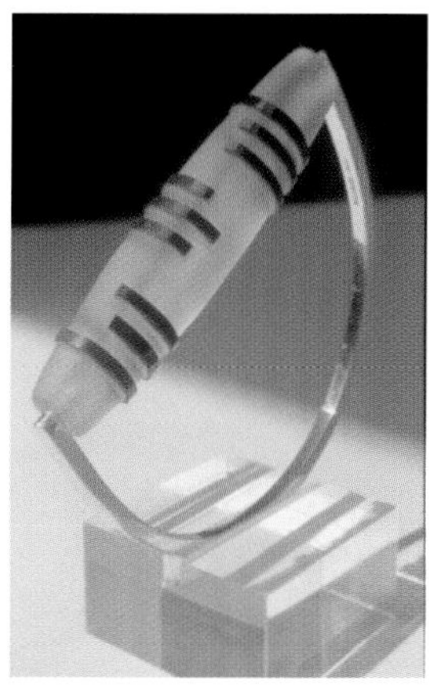

Sandblasted Bracelet
Artist: Diana East
Size: ½" Dia x 2½" L
Date: 2002
Photo: the artist

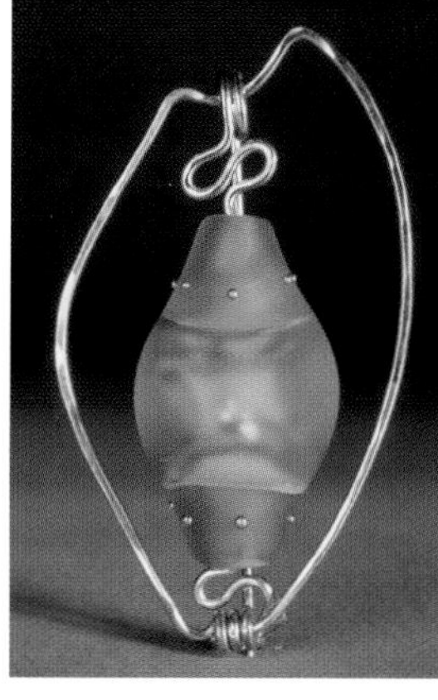

Etched Broach
Artist: Beth Williams
Size: ¾" Dia x 1¾" L
Date: 2002
Photo: Lynn Swigart

Hollow Hairpins
Artist: Kathryn Wardill
Size: ¾" Dia x 7¼" L
Date: 2002
Photo: the artist

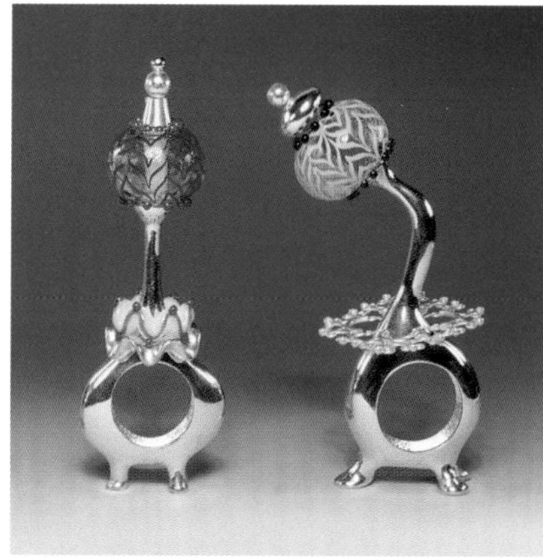

Standing Out Series
Artist: Kathryn Wardill
Size: 4" H
Date: 2001
Photo: the artist

Necklaces

Cool Stixs Necklace
Artist: Barbara Becker Simon
Size: 12" Hang
Date: 2001
Photo: Rob Stegman

Frosted Twists Necklace
Artist: Beth Williams
Size: 12" Hang
Date: 2002
Photo: Steve Gyurina

Spring Leaves Necklace
Artist: Donna Nova
Size: 18" Hang
Date: 2002
Photo: Wilbur Norman

Fantasy Flower Faces
Artist: Nancy Pilgrim
Size: 16" Hang
Date: 2002
Photo: Jeff Scovil

Choker
Artist: René Roberts
Size: 7" Diameter
Date: 2002
Photo: Hap Sakwa

Dichroic Ribbon Necklace
Artist: Nancy Pilgrim
Size: 16" Hang
Date: 2002
Photo: Ralph Gabringer

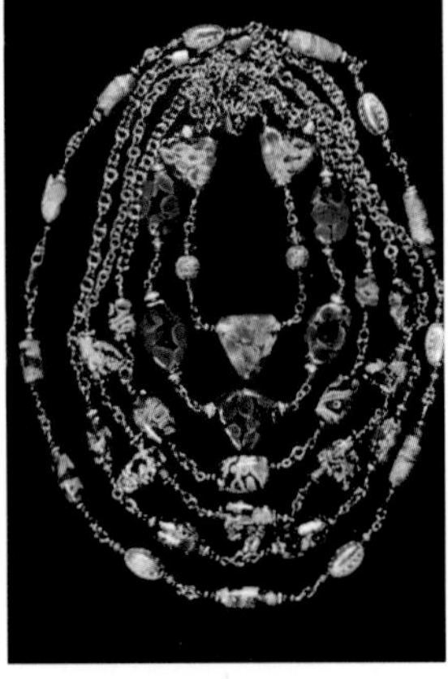

Spotted Necklace
Artist: Barbara Wright
Size: 18" Hang
Date: 1999
Photo: Alon Picker

Fused Tiger Necklace
Artist: Malcom Potek
Size: 14" Hang
Date: 1998
Photo: Malcom Potek

Southwestern Choker
Artist: Bronwen Heilman
Size: 18" Hang
Date: 1997
Photo: Bronwein Heilman

Graduated Dot Necklace
Artist: Paula Radke
Size: 18" Hang
Date: 1997
Photo: Paula Radke

Other Lampworked Glass Objects

As a way to further develop our lampworking skills, I am going to discuss a number of other glass objects that we can make at the torch besides glass beads. Like glass beads, some of these may also be used for jewelry purposes. The first glass objects consist of cabochons, marbles, pendants, buttons, and paperweights. They all have something in common about their manufacture; they are all made using molds of some kind. Then we'll finish the chapter with a discussion of how to make two types of vessels —core vessels and blown vessels.

Cabochons

The easiest of the glass objects that we'll learn how to make are cabochons. Some examples of faceted cabochons can be seen in Figure 205. They look something like a slice off of a marble, with a front surface that is usually spherical and a back surface that is flat. They are usually thinner than half of a sphere. They are made in marble molds or something similar.

Figure 205. Some typical examples of cabochons.

Marble molds, as discussed earlier, are made from either graphite or a dense fruitwood. If made out of graphite it will usually be a rectangular chunk of graphite with a handle, that has one or more hemispherical cavities cut into it. If made from a dense fruitwood, such as cherry wood, it will usually be a short cylindrical piece with a handle that has a single hemispherical cavity cut into one face. Wood molds have to be kept wet and when forming the cabochon the glass actually rides on a film of water turned to steam in the cavity. If wood molds are not kept wet, they will char and burn. If you want some detailed information on making your own marble molds, check out the article from Glass Line on this topic listed in the reading list at the end of this chapter.

Figure 206. Pushing a gather into a shaping mold.

A cabochon is formed by getting a gather on the end of a rod and pushing it into the cavity in a marble mold that is a little larger than the gather. This step is shown in Figure 206. Once the front face of the cabochon is formed, the back is smoothed out or left unfinished. If it is to be smoothed out, a small non-removable punty is attached to the front surface and the rest of the original rod is burned off the back. This is then heated up, mainly in the center to avoid distorting the front surface of the cabochon, and flattened out by pressing it down on a graphite paddle. Glass can be added to the back to fill it in as necessary.

Once the back is completed, a removable punty is usually attached to it and the other punty is burned off the front of the cabochon. The front surface may be lightly decorated at this time. If the final shape is desired to be smooth, the front surface is reheated and smoothed in the mold.

As was seen for mashing, whenever we smooth a surface by pressing it into a mold, we will usually introduce some slight chill marks. Preheating the molds can minimize these chill marks, although this only works for graphite molds. Any marks put into the cabochon can be softened by reheating the spherical surface in the flame and letting it air cool a bit before breaking it off of the punty into a piece of fiber blanket or the marble mold. The small punty break point can be smoothed out by heating it up with the flame while holding it in the mold or with tweezers. Then, deposit the finished cabochon into your annealer.

Cabochons can be used in a number of ways. They include:

- Mounting them into findings. Depending upon the finding this may allow them to be used as a pendant, a pin, a button, a bolo tie, a button cover, etc.
- Add glass attachments to the back and use it as a button. We will discuss that more later.
- Pierce it with a tungsten pick to make it into a pendant with a hole perpendicular to its face.
- Put a loop on the top to hang it from.

Since the main focus of this book is making glass objects for jewelry, let's look at these last two options in greater detail with two examples.

For our first cabochon, we are going to make one with a commercial murrina mounted on a plain colored background. This is then cased with clear glass to magnify the murrina's image. Start by forming a gather on the end of a colored rod. Then flatten the gather out into a "maria," as shown in Figure 207. A maria is a flat disk on the end of a glass rod, made by pushing a gather straight down onto a graphite paddle. For this cabochon, it would be nice to have the maria be about three quarters of an inch in diameter. Soften the chill marks on the maria by reheating it lightly in the torch. The maria will form the back of the cabochon.

Next embed a murrina into the front surface of the maria. You do not want it raised more than about an eighth of an inch. Do this by getting the area where

Figure 207. Pressing a gather to form a maria.

you will insert the murrina glowing hot and soft. At the same time, preheat the murrina out in the end of your flame holding it with your tweezers. Then press it into the center of the maria as shown in Figure 208. If it does not go in far enough on the first attempt, then you will have to push it in further. Do this by first heating around the edge of the murrina. Next slightly chill the top surface of the murrina by touching it lightly with your paddle and then push it down hard, forcing it deeper into the maria. That first light touch of the paddle helps prevent the murrina from distorting as you push it in.

Now lightly reheat around the edge of the murrina and smooth it out with your paddle. Try not to get the murrina too hot at this point. This is because the surfaces of bare murrine tend to scum up and from lots of tiny bubbles if overheated before they are cased.

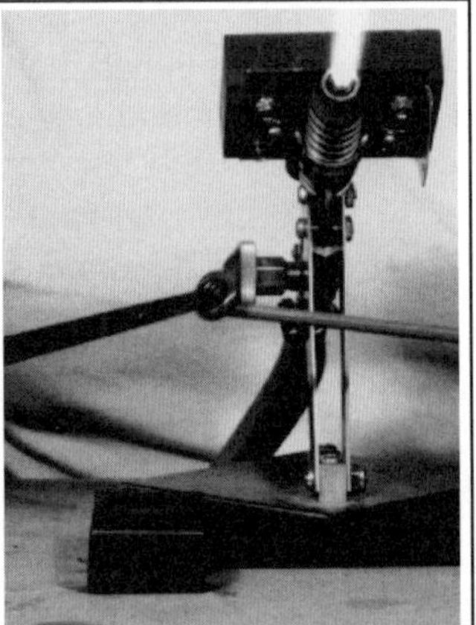

Figure 208. Applying a murrina onto a maria.

To case the murrina, develop a large gather on a clear rod. Then push the hot gather down onto the surface of the warm maria. Burn off the clear rod, leaving enough glass to form the rounded clear surface of the cabochon. If you did not cover the entire surface the first time, make another gather and add some more glass. Have it mound up on the surface so that you will be able to develop a nice smooth surface. Heat up the clear glass and try to have it gather in on itself. When it has smoothed out some, shape it in a marble mold as shown in Figure 209 to finish the job. Use a paddle to smooth up the back edges that you can reach.

Next, we want to pierce the cabochon to get it ready for hanging. Do this by warming it as well as getting your straight tungsten pick white-hot. Then push the pick into the front surface of the cabochon out near one edge. If it does not go all the way through, then stop, reheat them both, and push the pick through from the backside this time. Continuing to push just from the front can cause the edge to fold over.

After you get through, smooth the hole with the pick as necessary. If needed, reheat the cabochon pendant and refresh its shape by rolling it in the shaping mold. Finally, melt off the punty and smooth out the back as described previously. Then put it into the annealer to cool.

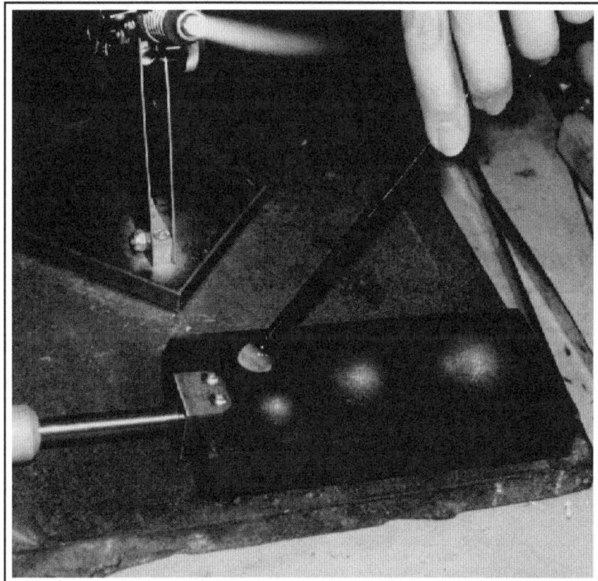

Figure 209. Smoothing cabochon in a marble mold.

The other cabochon pendant that I want to describe is a shield pendant like that in Figure 210, which was first shown to me by Jim Smircich. I call it shield-shaped because it has a hollowed out back similar to that of a shield. This results in a much lighter piece.

To make one, start with a nice hot gather. Push it straight down onto your marver to form a large maria. Reheat short sections of its rim and pinch them out with mashers to spread it. Do this a little bit at a time to squeeze it all out. You may have to go around more than once to make it big enough. Square faced mashers work better than round ones for this because they allow you to get up against the rod. If you decide to make a bunch of these pieces, you may want to purchase or modify a set of mashers by cutting one face shorter than the other. Jim has done this to a set of disk mashers and says they work great for this purpose. It smoothes up the front face better as you mash it.

Figure 210. Shield pendant.
Artist: Jim Smircich
Size: 1½" Dia x ¼" T
Photo: Jim Smircich

After mashing the maria into a big disk, you have two choices in how to shape it. One is to heat it to low red heat and shape it in a marble mold, as is seen in Figure 211. The other is to heat it and marver it into the shield shape with a graphite paddle.

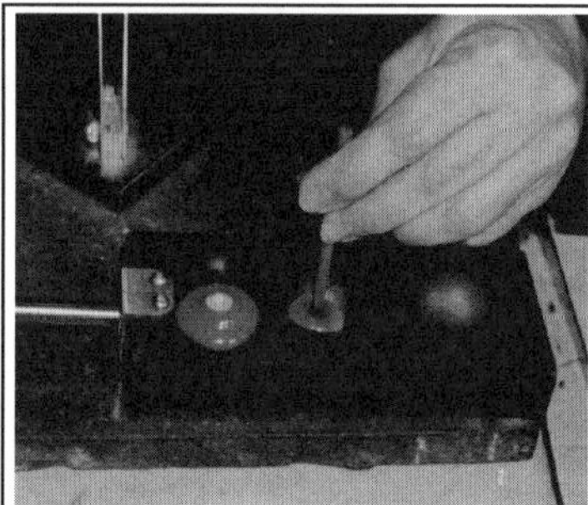

Figure 211. Shaping disk in a mold to form the shield.

Next, you can add surface decoration to the front of the pendant. In this case, I just added a series of dots on dots in the center, one on top of the other and spread them out each time by pushing the glass lightly back into the mold. Don't get the whole pendant too hot or you may lose its shape. Instead, reheat it just enough that it doesn't thermal shock.

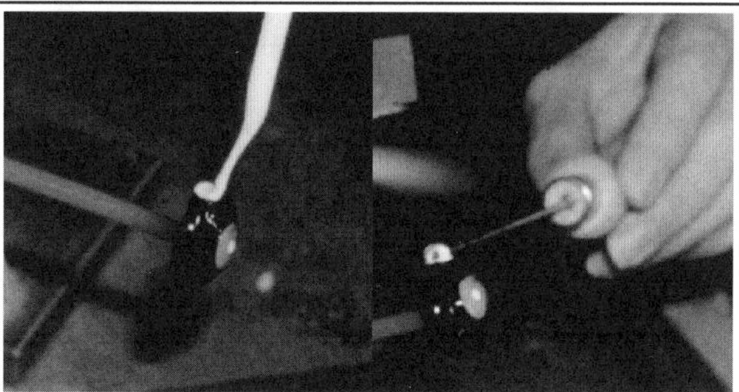

Figure 212. Adding loop to hang shield pendant.

Now we need to add the loop to the edge of the cabochon so that it can be used as a pendant. To do this, make a small gather and push it down on the edge of the piece. As you pull away, leave a small round ball behind. Shape the ball of glass into a saddle shape by pushing a tool like a pick or a clean mandrel down onto the center of the ball, with the tool parallel to the edge of the shield. This forms the bottom of the loop.

To make the top of the loop, reheat the front of the saddle and form a gather of the same color. Attach them together as in the left of Figure 212, taking care to form a good smooth attachment with no undercuts. Then pull some of the gather out into a short fat stringer. Burn off the top of the stringer from the rod. Warm it slightly and use a set of fine tweezers to bend it down onto the other side of the saddle to form a loop. Reheat the end of the stringer and that edge of the saddle. Use your tweezers to push them together to form a good attachment. Cool the tweezers in some water if you think that they are getting too hot. Adjust the shape of the loop with tweezers or a pick, as shown in the right side of Figure 212.

Now finish the pendant by burning off the original rod and smoothing the hollow backside of the pendant. You can either use tweezers to hold onto the loop as you do this, or hot fingers to hold on to the edge of the shield. Afterward, reheat the pendant slightly and stick it into your annealer to cool. Jim says that he has not had much luck cooling them in vermiculite

Marbles

You might think that making marbles would be pretty similar to making cabochons, except that we end up with a completely round object. It really isn't. For cabochons, we used the bottom of the cavity to form the finished front surface. For marbles, we usually use the bottom of the cavity only for rough shaping. We use the top edge of the cavity for final shaping. Brass rings or a graphite tool like that seen in Figure 213 can also be used for final shaping.

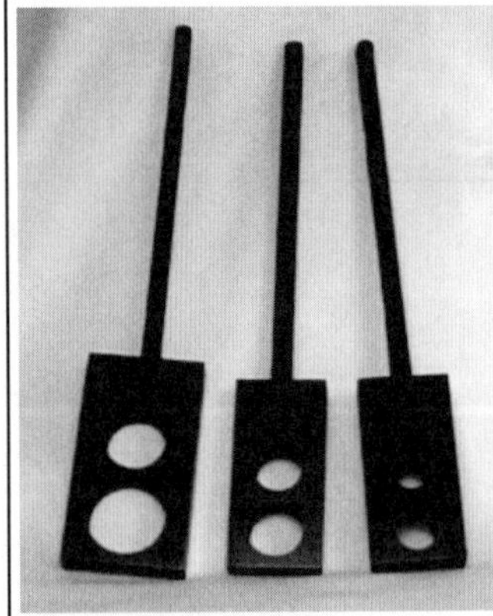

Figure 213. Marble paddles Courtesy of Sundance Glass

In making marbles, you can proceed one of two ways. You can make one-of-a-kind marbles where each one is made and decorated separately. Alternately, you could choose to go into mass production of similar looking marbles. You do this by making a large piece of marble stock, such as a big complex latticino, and then pinch off a number of individual marbles from it.

Single marble manufacture

To make single one-of-a-kind marbles, you basically create a marble from a gather on a rod. You then decorate that marble with the techniques that you learned about for decorating wound glass beads. I will discuss how to make a relatively simple marble using some constructions that we have already learned to make, latticinos. We'll discuss what I call a wormhole marble. It gets this name because I watch way too much Science Fiction and it looks like how I imagine wormholes in space might look.

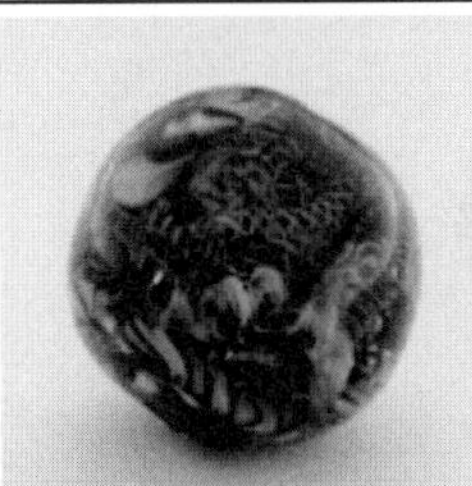

Figure 214. Marble Artist: Jim Kervin Size: 1¼" Diameter

For this kind of marble, I first make a lot of latticino both of the twisted filigrana and the white core type. These represent my wormholes. For this, you might want to get some of the new colors of filigrana that are being imported. You might also want to make yourself some good strong cased aventurine. The kind you can buy is usually too wimpy to even bother with. Once you have a good pile of these components, you are almost ready to begin. You also need to get together and clean a couple of clear, light and dark transparent blue rods.

I start by making a quarter inch diameter gather on the end of a dark transparent blue rod. I like to use a deep blue for the center, but you might like a lighter one. Now randomly lay down the latticino and cane all over the front half to two thirds of the gather. Turn down the flame on your torch to a small one and heat the interface between the gather and the latticino as you apply it. Just squiggle it on using a number of different latticino pieces as seen in Figure 215.

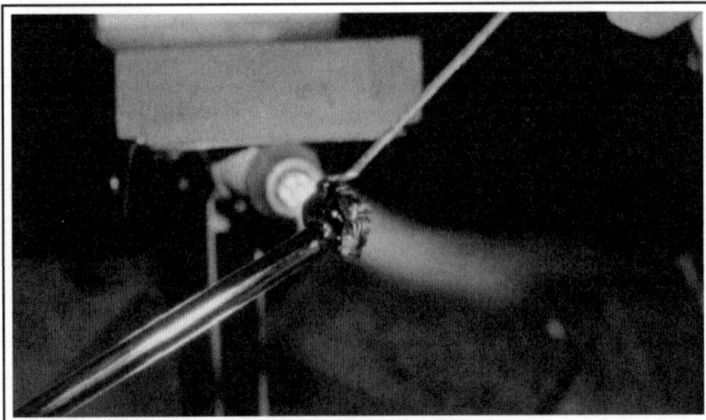

Figure 215. Wrapping the marble's wormhole core.

Both the gather and the latticino have to be hot as they come together or they will not bond. You have to heat the latticino gently as you lay it onto the surface because its small diameter allows it to heat up very quickly. It also helps to twist the latticino counterclockwise as you apply it, to bring its hot surface down to the hot surface of the gather. You should also push down on it as you apply it so that it will fill the voids between the different pieces.

When you have a good uniform layer of latticino and cane all over the front half of the gather, turn up the flame on your torch and gently heat it all so that everything sticks well. Heat it slowly in the outer edge of the flame, moving it out of the flame occasionally to let the heat sink into the core and allow the outer surface to harden. Now that you are getting everything fairly hot, you will have to rotate the gather so it does not droop.

Next we want to case this half. Move the marble way out into the outer reaches of the flame. Make a hot gather on the end of a clear or light transparent blue rod, then paint it over the latticino and cane on the front half of the marble. You might find that you have to dab it into the grooves between them as seen in Figure 216. Fill it all in; any voids can serve as a crack initiation point. Don't get the latticino or cane too hot or you may distort them. Build up another gather and paint on more. Stop every once in a while and heat up the whole thing to allow the outer surface to smooth out.

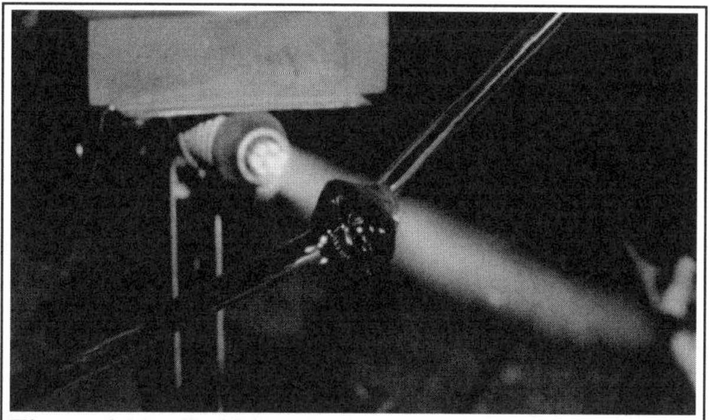

Figure 216. Dabbing casing onto wormhole marble.

Build up the thickness of the outer casing to the point where the marble will be a little over an inch thick. Get the clear uniformly hot by heating it in the outer reaches of you flame and then stick the whole thing into the smallest cavity in the marble mold that it will all fit into. Twist it all around to help round this half. If it is way too small for the cavity, you can paint on a little more casing glass onto the outer surface. Don't put so much on though that it will not fit into the cavity or you may form folds in the casing. Once you have this end smooth, we switch to the other side.

Make a small gather onto the finished end of a casing rod and use it to make a strong punty on the cased end of the marble. Burn off the dark transparent blue rod on the other end as close to the central gather as you can. Smooth out the surface of the blue gather using the heat of the flame. Then squiggle latticino and cane on this end of the gather. Try to use the same color scheme on this end as on the other end so that it will look uniform.

After you have this end of the marble covered with cane and latticino, case everything as you did on the other side. Try to case it as evenly as you can so that the casing is of uniform thickness all the way around the marble. Then stick it into the same cavity of the marble mold and roll it around to round it up. Again don't get it so thick that it will not fit into the cavity of the mold or it will form folds as you roll it.

If it does not get perfectly round at this point, then move on to the next smaller cavity and round it out by rolling it on the top edge of the cavity, as shown in Figure 217. Don't overheat it or push on it too hard. Rolling it should make it nice and smooth. Using the upper edge is necessary when using graphite molds to prevent forming chill marks on the outer surface of your marbles. Since with hardwood molds the marble actually rides on a layer of steam, this is not strictly required when sizing them.

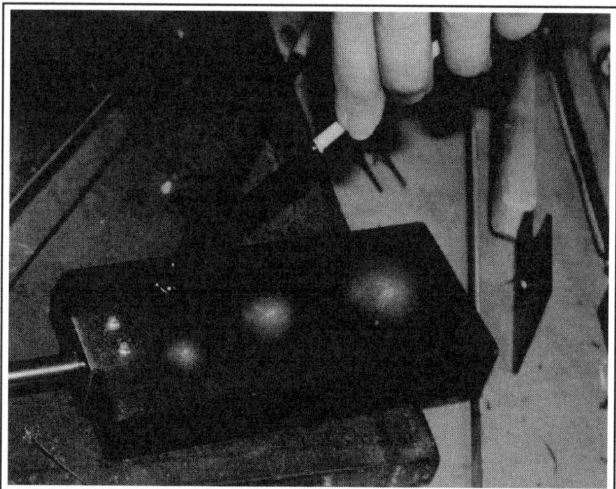

Figure 217. Shaping marble on upper edge of mold.

Lightly attach a new punty to the smoothed surface. Do this by attaching a hot gather on a casing rod to the cool surface of the marble. To help keep this final attachment small, it might help to sharpen the casing rod by rolling it at an angle on your marver first and only getting the tip hot before applying it. Then, burn the well-attached punty off the other end. Heat up that end of the marble and smooth it out on the top edge of the marble mold cavity.

Allow the marble to cool and harden enough that you can grab it with a set of hot fingers or alternately drop it into the shaping mold. Break off the weakly attached punty while holding the marble in the hot fingers or the mold. Then, lightly heat up the attachment point on the surface of the marble to smooth it out. Allow it to cool slightly and then roll it into the annealer. When making marbles, I will often put a layer of fiber blanket on the bottom of the annealer so that the marbles do not end up rolling around.

Multiple marble manufacture

In making marble multiples, we form a number of nearly identical marbles from a piece of marble stock. This marble stock can be made by making large decorative latticinos or by fusing stacks of sheet glass in a kiln. In either case you will have to ensure that the marble stock is well annealed before getting started.

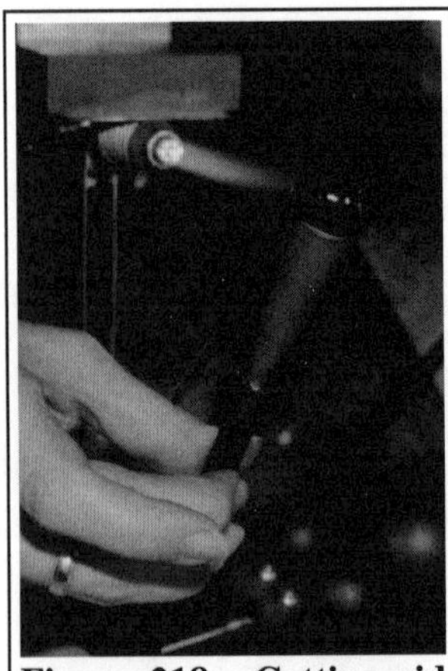
Figure 218. Getting rid of final punty mark.

We have previously discussed how to make very fancy latticino and bundled cane at the torch. Either of these, although not mentioned at the time, could be used as marble stock. But, since it is new, let's discuss how to make marble stock by fusing stacks of sheet glass. If you have ever done much fusing, you may have learned a similar technique as a means of making millefiori for kilnworking. When I first learned the technique, we used small glory holes to shape the stacks. I suggest that you consider doing it this way because it is much faster than doing it in a torch.

Anyway, let's get started. What we are going to do is make stacks of glass in the kiln of whatever size you want to work with. I suggest making stacks about 1½" high by 1½" wide and 3 inches long. Each of these stacks will have a simple image that we construct in its cross section. The images are forced to be simple because of the large thickness of the glass compared to the thickness of the stack. Obviously, all the glass in any one stack should be self-compatible. Not so obviously, it also helps if the glass used has two smooth sides. This minimizes trapping of air bubbles between pieces.

Figure 219 shows a single stack set up in the kiln ready for fusing. For multiple stacks, lay them out on the kiln shelf. Since you do not want to chance having them stick to any kiln wash, you should use some fiber paper underneath them—especially if you do not have a good kiln controller. To prevent the stacks from falling over, you want to support them from the sides with firebrick or kiln furniture.

Figure 219. Stacked sheet glass in the kiln.

So let's start laying up some stacks. Start with a firebrick either kilnwashed or covered with fiber paper or both on the side that will touch the glass stack. Next, set up your stack using the firebrick to stabilize it. I usually plan out my stacks on graph paper first. Then I cut out all the pieces and stack them on my worktable. At this point, I transfer the stacks into the kiln. If this is to be your only stack, then you would finish on the other end with more fiber paper and another firebrick. If you are going to make multiple stacks, you will want to separate each one from the next with fiber paper so that they do not stick to each other when they are tack fused. Lastly, finish up the last end with another firebrick treated like the first one.

Now, slowly bring the kiln up to tack fusing (1300 to 1400°F) and let it soak there for 10 to 15 minutes so that the stack will fuse together. Then, drop the kiln temperature to the glass annealing temperature (~1000°F). We do this so that the stacks do not get accidentally stuck together as we remove them one by one.

Next, fire up your torch or glory hole. When ready, get yourself a long punty of either pyrex or stainless steel. Wrap a cone of glass on one end with the base outward and about the same size as the end of the stack. Use your paddles or marver to shape the cone. Get the base of the cone real hot, turn off the power to the kiln so you do not electrocute yourself, reach into it, stab the end of one of the stacks, close the kiln, turn the kiln back on, and shape the stack. As you start doing this, you may find it helpful to get someone to act as a kiln door jockey for you so you do not have to do so many things at once.

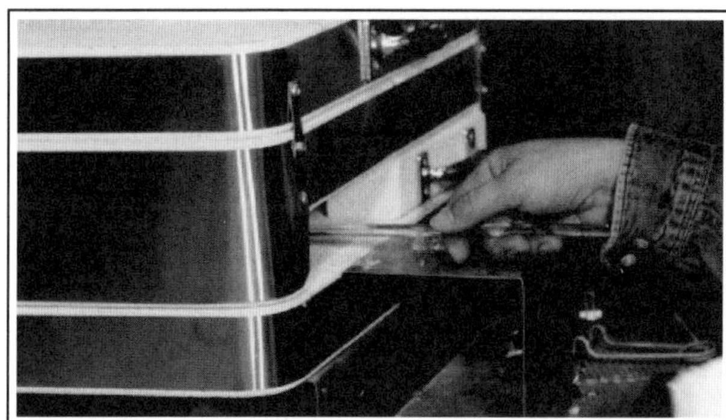

Figure 220. Stabbing fused stack with shaped punty.

It should be fairly obvious that what you really want to do to your marble stock is give it a cylindrical cross section. So your next step will be to work the stack on your marver to change it from a rectangular to a circular cross section. To do this, you are going to get it hot in either the glory hole or the torch and marver it round, as was discussed for mosaic cane construction. When you get it hot, the stack will soften and start to droop. Therefore, as usual, you will have to rotate it to counteract this.

Once you have the stack shaped the way that you want it, you have a choice to make. You can either start making marbles or you can cut the stack off the punty and set it back in the kiln. Then you could form all the rest of the sheet glass stacks into marble stock before getting started, or you could anneal them and wait for another day to make marbles. Just make sure that if you put them back into the kiln that they do not touch each other, or they may stick together. This problem is aggravated if you forgot to lower the kiln temperature to annealing after tack fusing the stacks.

When you have built up some marble stock and are ready to start making marbles, you need to get the marble stock hot and onto a punty. If working at a torch, you will want to use at least a six to eight inch punty because this makes it easier to handle the heavy piece of marble stock. You will want an even longer punty if working at a glory hole because of the heat it puts out. If you are doing this work from a glassblowing bench, you will want the punty long enough to reach from one arm of the bench to the other. You will also want to get your annealer going and set up with a punty rest, as shown in Figure 221. This gives you a place to set the marble stock down as you shape each individual marble.

When you have the marble stock under control on the punty, the first thing you are going to want to do is bring the pattern on the free end of the marble stock down to a point. This usually only has to be done for the first marble on a piece of stock. You do this using a set of jacks, glassblowing tweezers with blades like a scissors that you have to squeeze to close. You can get a similar effect using a set of scissors. The scissors that are best for this use are thin bladed ones, like those used for cutting hair. Using a little beeswax on the blades will help to prevent the glass from sticking. Save these scissors for use only as jacks, as they will lose most of their temper.

To bring the pattern to a point, you basically cut a short piece off the end of the marble stock. You do this in such a way that you pull the whole cross section down into a point. To start, heat the end of the marble stock to get it soft. As always, once the marble stock starts to get hot, you will have to keep it rotating to prevent it from drooping.

Now roll the last quarter inch of stock on the open V of the scissors to form a slight groove all the way around. This is easier done if working off a glassblowing bench or a set of lampworking rollers. Most of you will not have either of these, but you can make a rack that essentially serves the same purpose, as shown in Figure 222. Here you roll the punty on two sets of crossed nails hammered into a short section of 4" x 4". This allows you to easily handle the punty and frees up your other hand to work with the jacks. As you roll the marble stock on the jacks and the groove is fully formed, you can start to gently squeeze more on the scissors to push the groove in a little deeper. Do not squeeze too fast or you will get a flat cut and the marble stock will not want to roll on the jacks anymore. Do it slow and keep the stock rolling on the V of the scissors as shown in Figure 223.

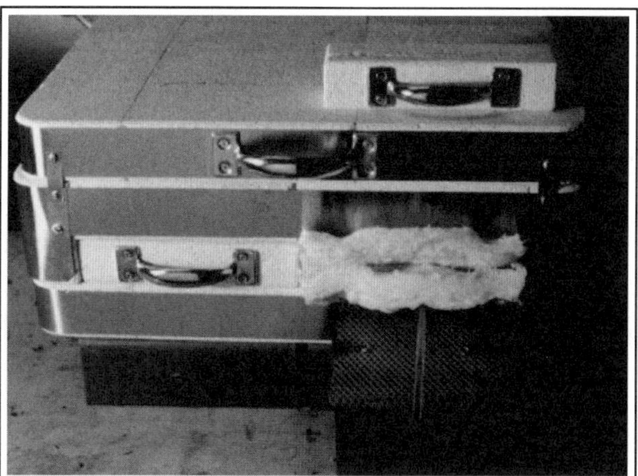

Figure 221. Annealer set up with a punty rest.

Figure 222. Using a homemade stabilizing rack.

As the marble stock starts to cool, you can squeeze more and more on the scissors just as you could push harder when marvering. You are trying to get the groove to proceed at an equal depth all the way around the piece until it comes to a point. If you can't get it there all at once, just lightly reheat it a little and cut some more. Have a can of water available on your table into which to cut the end so it will not take a bad bounce and end up in your lap. In fact, when making marbles it helps to have a lip on the table so that a hot marble cannot drop off of your punty and roll into your lap.

Heat up the cut end of a marble stock in your torch and round it out in the marble mold cavity that is just slightly larger in diameter than the marble stock. Note which hole this is. Heat up the marble stock about one diameter from its end. Stick it back into the mold at about a forty-five degree angle and gently roll it on the edge of the mold to form a crease. This will show you how much material you will need to form a marble of this size. Heat this crease area up in the flame. Use your scissors to work the crease deeper as before but stop ¼ to 3/8" in diameter short of cutting this piece off.

Figure 223. Cutting off end of marble stock.

Heat up the front half of the jacked down portion. Form its shape by rolling it on the edge of the next smallest cavity as was done for the one-of-a-kind marble. After you have that shaped, jack down the crease a little more and try to form the back half of the marble as much as possible. This is made easier if you use one of Jim Smircich's new marble molds, as shown in Figure 224, because it is easier to work into the crease. Be careful with them though because the edges of this tool are pretty fragile. Check out your work to see how round it is. Continue to work it as necessary. Look to see if the surface is smooth. If it has chill marks or ripples in the surface, gently reheat the area to smooth them out. Continue rotating to prevent droop of the jacked connection, which is thinner than the rest of the marblestock. Then jack down the crease a little more, to where it just barely stays in place without flopping around.

Figure 224. Jim Smircich using one of his marble shaping tools.

Now lightly attach a small punty to the finished end of the marble by touching a small, hot gather to the cooler marble. The glass that the punty is made from should be compatible to that of the marble because you may not get it all off afterward. Clear glass is preferable because if some gets left behind it will not be as visible. Lastly you can minimize the area of the attachment by marvering the punty rod to a point prior to attaching it.

Remove the marble from the rest of the stock by focusing the torch flame on the last bit holding them together, as shown in Figure 225. Pull them slightly apart, allow the joint to cool, and then again focus the flame on the thinned area just as we did to flame-cut a rod. Try to distort the pattern as little as possible when doing this. When you get the marble cut off, set the marble stock aside in your annealer, keeping the handle outside so that you will not burn yourself later as you pick it back up.

The rest of this procedure is pretty much identical to what was discussed for one-of-a-kind marbles. Reheat the flame cut half of the marble and smooth it out on the rim of the smaller marble cavity until you finish up the shape. Allow it to cool to the point where its outer surface gets hard. Then you either break the marble off the punty into the mold punty end up, or grab it with some hot fingers and break the punty off. If it will not break off, nip it off. Then flame polish the attachment area. Allow the marble to cool just to the point where the surface is hard and put it into the annealer.

Figure 225. Flame cut the marble from marble stock.

Then grab the marble stock and make some more marbles. You should be able to make four to five marbles from each stack. Watch out as you grab the punty in case the handle got too hot while in the annealer.

Looped pendants

Next we are going to learn to make looped pendant beads like the one seen in Figure 226. A looped pendant bead is a bead that, instead of having a hole through it, has a loop at the top like the one that was suggested for use with the perfect latticino. These beads are usually teardrop shaped and are hung from the loop.

Figure 226. Mushroom pendant
Artist: Jim Kervin
Size: ¾" Dia x 1 ¼" L

To demonstrate this technique, I will discuss how to make a hanging mushroom pendant like the ones that you may have seen at a local bead store. They seem to sell well and with a little practice yours can be more elaborate than any you will typically see. The steps to make one of these pendants are shown in Figure 227.

Start by planning out your mushroom color scheme. Pull out a short section of cane of your chosen stem color, and get the exterior cap colors ready. Next take a clear glass rod and make about a ¼ to ½ inch diameter gather on the end. Remember to keep the rod rotating to keep the gather on center. You might also find it easier to handle by tilting the rod up at about a 45° angle to the horizontal as you gather. The size gather that you can handle will depend both on your skill level and the diameter of the rod. Large gathers are easier to handle on larger diameter rods.

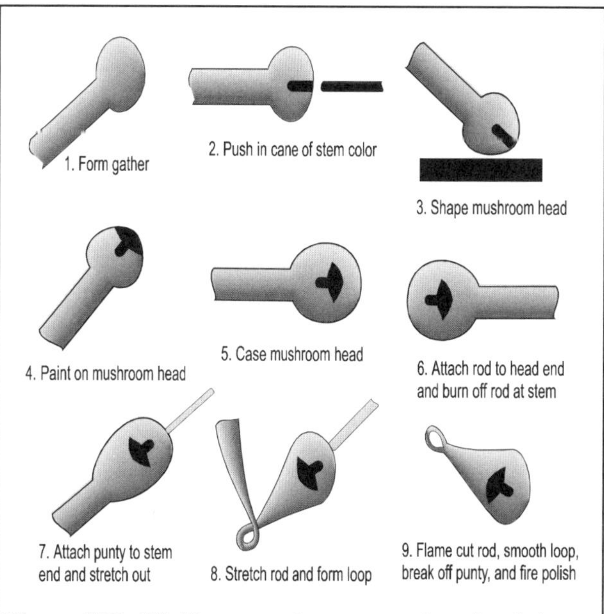

Figure 227. Making a mushroom pendant beads/

Get the gather hot and soft, then plunge a short section of the mushroom stem cane down into the end of the gather opposite the rod. Push it down into the center of the gather. Burn off any of the cane that remains outside the gather. Shape the gather into a slight taper using a graphite paddle. Do this by holding the gather at a slight angle to the paddle and rolling it back and forth lightly across the surface of the paddle. Allow the gather to just roll lightly at first. As the gather starts to harden, you can push a little harder against the paddle as you roll. The taper should have the stem running down its center to a rounded tip.

Now case the last quarter inch of the tip with the color that you have chosen for the cap of the mushroom. You may want to do this in two steps, first is for the underside of the cap and second for the outside color. Reheat the tip and marver it smooth on the paddle to the shape you want for the mushroom. Decorate the exterior of the cap as desired. You can add dots, stringer paintings, or enamels to get whatever effect you are looking for. Case the cap of the mushroom with clear glass. Add enough to form the gather into a sphere about ½ to ¾ inch in diameter with the cap of the mushroom closer to the rod end. Let the gather chill slightly and then attach a hot gather on another clear rod of about the same diameter to the top end of the gather.

Reheat the joint between the original rod and the gather until it gets soft. Burn off the first clear rod from the gather. Reheat it and smooth that end of the gather. You can do this by heating the gather up and allowing it to pull in on itself or you can use your marble mold to shape it. Do this by pushing the bottom of the gather down into the smallest cavity into which the whole gather will fit. Then reheat the gather and roll it on the rim of the next smallest cavity to shape it as we discussed for marbles.

Remove it from the flame and allow it to cool just slightly. Now attach a punty to the bottom of the gather but attach it to a cool gather so that it will be easy to break off later. Next heat up the other end of the gather where it connects to the rod and draw out the gather and the top of the ball to form a nice smooth teardrop shape.

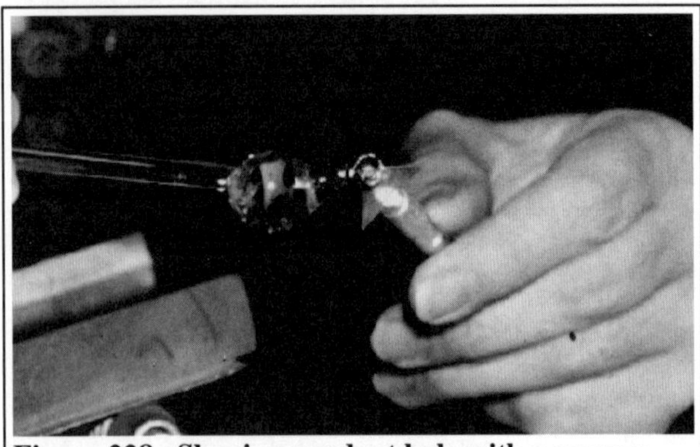
Figure 228. Shaping pendant hole with a reamer.

We are now ready to form the loop. Heat the section of the second rod at the top of the teardrop and pull it out to a point. Quickly loop the point around on itself to form the loop from which the pendant will hang. Burn off any excess rod from the loop and shape it in the edge of the flame with a reamer or tweezers as shown in Figure 228. Lightly reheat the whole bead except for the punty joint. Break the pendant off the punty, grab the loop end with your tweezers, and fire polish the punty joint area. Then stick the pendant into the annealer.

You might want to practice loop making using borosilicate glass. With borosilicate you don't have to concentrate as much on keeping the glass hot so that it does not crack. Using borosilicate also makes it easier because larger diameter rods are available that you can use. Another variation of a looped pendant suggested by the "Beadle" (see reference) would work well when you are practicing with borosilicate. It consists of just inserting a tiny bit of color into an otherwise clear pendant. The steps for this are illustrated in Figure 229.

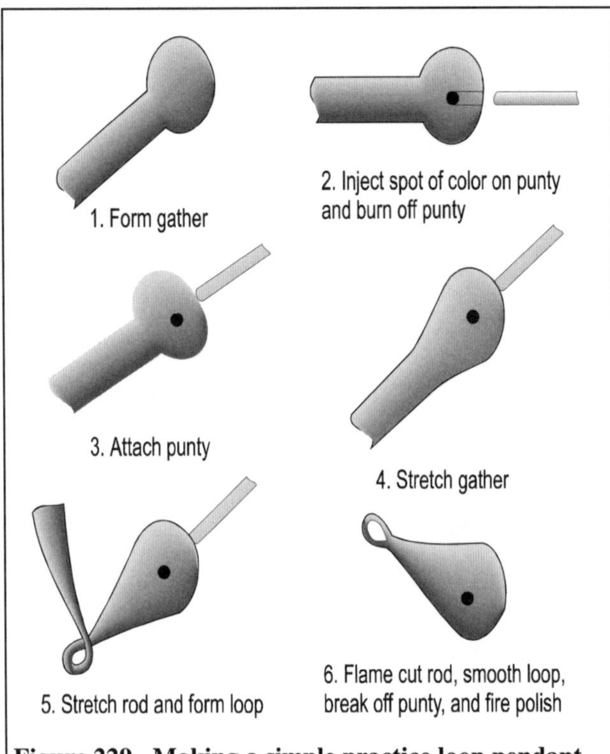

Figure 229. Making a simple practice loop pendant.

The steps for this pendant are pretty similar to the previous one. You start out with your gather, and then you put a small bit of color on the end of a cane drawn from a second clear rod and push it into the interior of the gather. To push it in you have to reheat the gather to the point where you can just barely keep it on the end of the rod before pushing the cane into it. Then again burn off the cane at the surface of the gather and reheat the gather to regain a uniform shape before continuing.

Buttons

A variation of loop addition that can be used to make button shanks was presented by Lewis Wilson in the reference at the end of this chapter. Start by making a nice cabochon as discussed in the beginning of this chapter. Get the front smoothed up and then the back by attaching the front lightly to a punty. Attach a medium diameter cane to the back of the button about one third of the way across the back as shown in Figure 230. Next flame cut off most of the

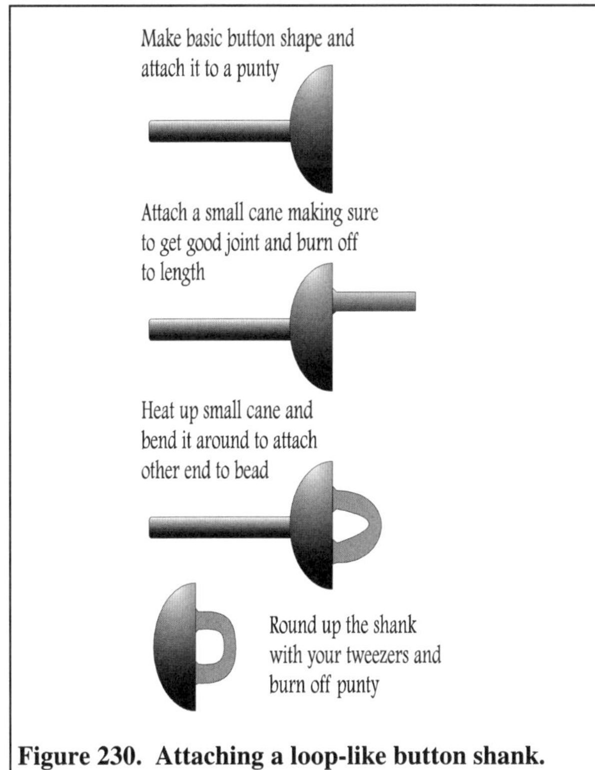

Figure 230. Attaching a loop-like button shank.

rest of the cane leaving about three-quarters to an inch behind.

Then, heat up the short section of cane, use your tweezers to bend it over, and attach it to the back. You attach it to a position on the back of the button one half the distance to the opposite side. This will divide the back into three equal parts. Make sure that you get a good connection to the cabochon by pushing the hot end of the cane down onto a warmed spot and then gently pulling slightly up on it to form a nice smooth joint. Finish by heating the button loop and shaping it as necessary with a reamer. The best reamer for this job is a sharpened graphite rod.

I have also seen artists make buttons like this a little differently. Instead of attaching a straight cane to the back of the button and then bending it over to form the loop, they prebend a short loop and then attach both ends to the back of the button at once. I suggest you use whatever process works best for you.

Another easy raised button shank can be made by adding a small dab of hot glass to the back of the button-to-be and pinching it lightly to form a fairly thick shank, as shown in the left side of Figure 232. Then put a hole through the shank, using your tungsten pick to drill a hole from both sides of the shank. Tilt the holes down and join them in the center as we did for the murrine pendant cabochon. Use the tungsten pick as a reamer to finish up the look of the shank. This is the technique that was used to make the buttons seen in Figure 231.

Figure 231. Pyrex dot buttons. Artist: Gail Crossman-Moore Size ¾" Diameter x ½" T

Many times you don't want a raised button shank, you want a button that will lie close to your blouse or shirt. For this situation there is a variation of the previous technique that can be used to construct a recessed button shank. Instead of adding a glob of glass and pinching it to form a raised shank, you push your tweezers into the back of the cabochon and pinch slightly to form a recessed shank as shown in the right side of Figure 232. You will probably have to come in from the left and right side to get the recessed pinched-shank to look right. Once you have the grooves established, you can then use your tungsten pick as before to drill the hole through the recessed shank from both sides, as shown in the right side of the figure.

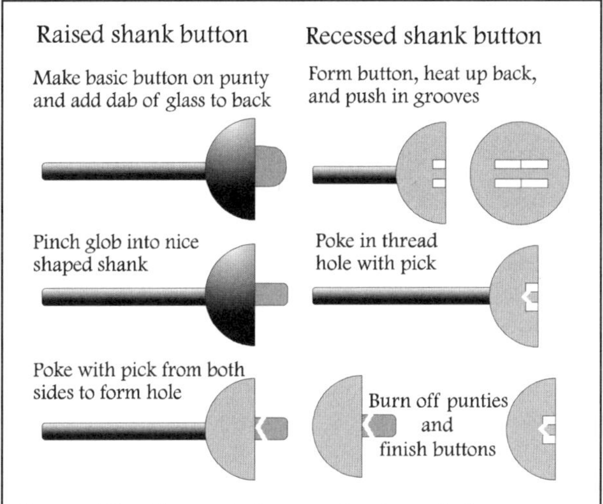

Figure 232. Alternate button shank techniques.

Another interesting way that I have seen a raised button shank constructed is to use a small bead for the shank. This will serve as an alternate method for those of you who may have trouble drilling holes with a tungsten pick. For this technique, you start off by making a small bead on a mandrel and setting it aside in your annealer, which is set at the annealing temperature. Make sure to shield the end of the mandrel so that it does not get too hot to grab.

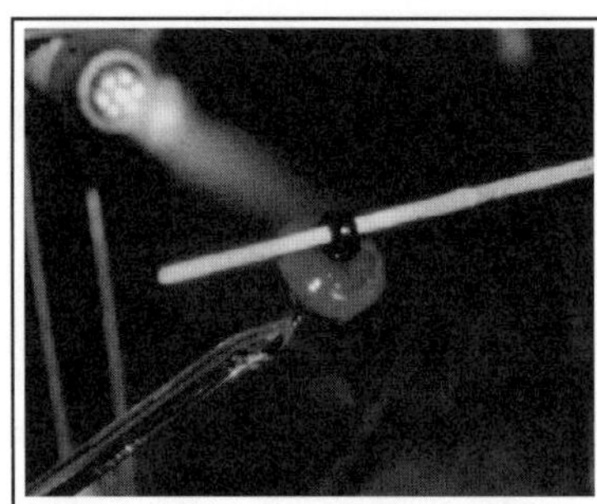
Figure 233. Putting together a bead shanked button.

Then, construct a cabochon. Once you make it, transfer it to a punty on the front face and smooth up the back face. Now, remove the bead from the annealer. Get the center of the back of the cabochon and one side of the bead hot and push them together as shown in Figure 233 to form the raised shank button. Just make sure that if you have a top and bottom to the design on the cabochon that you push them together such that the button hangs correctly.

All of the previous discussions have focused on glass-shanked buttons. It is also possible to put a metal shank on your buttons. This could be desirable because some people might not trust glass-shanked buttons or they may not want the bulk of glass in the shank. Metal-shanked buttons are made using wire bent in the form of a U embedded in the glass to make the shank.

I have seen wire made from a number of metals used for this purpose. They include copper, stainless steel and nichrome. Copper is probably the most compatible with the glass but I do not like how it forms fire scale in the flame. It looks discolored and dirty to me. Stainless steel works well but it can be hard to find. Keith Kreitter says that he cuts up stainless steel cotter keys for this purpose, that he got from someone who was rebuilding an aircraft engine. They worked well but may be a little hard to find. The last choice is the nichrome wire that we discussed earlier. This can be obtained from a ceramic supply store in the form of either kiln staples or stamen wire.

To install the metal shank, you first bend some of the wire in the form of a U, and trim the U to length. I find one quarter of an inch to be about right. Then heat up the top one eighth of an inch of the two ends of the U until it is glowing. At the same time, be preheating the back of a cabochon to soften it. You will probably have the cabochon attached to a punty on its front surface during this operation. Stick the U into the back and hold it steady until the glass hardens. Burn off the punty on the front while holding the protruding portion of the U with your tweezers. Smooth up the front of the button and it is ready to go.

All of the previous techniques produced a button that has a smooth front face with no thread showing. There are times, though, when you may want the thread to show because it will be part of the design. The easiest alternative for this situation is to wind a flat disk button on one of the button mandrels shown in the chapter on tools. Make sure that you have a thick enough coating of mandrel release to allow for any out-of-straightness of the folded over mandrel.

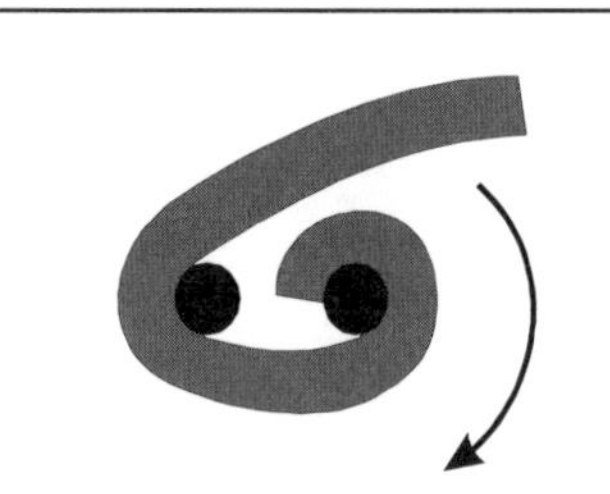
Figure 234. Winding button on a button mandrel.

I wind this kind of button by starting on the inside of one of the two mandrels and then continue around to the outside, as shown in Figure 234. I continue around the central section and around the other mandrel and back to the center to finish it off. This first center portion of the bead can be fairly plain because it will be partially obscured by the thread.

Smooth out the inner disk and then add a fancier decorative section around it. This can be of twisted cane, latticino or whatever. This could finish the button or you may want to distort the decorative edge into a ruffle using your tweezers. Start by pinching one area and twisting it about 45°. Then pinch right next to it and twist 45° in the opposite direction. Continue this all the way around the button and it will make a nice ruffle.

Paperweights

In making paperweights, you construct small lampworked glass items like flowers that you case all at once in a large gather of clear glass. The casing is then picked up and shaped. Paperweights are most commonly shaped into globes because this shape acts as a lens to magnify the image inside the globe.

To make paperweights, it is a great help to have a crucible kiln. Without one, it is very difficult to come up with enough hot glass at one time to quickly case the small lampworked objects. If you case them too slowly, the lampworked constructions will deform from the heat. It also helps to have at least a small glory hole because of the larger bulk of glass that you have to heat up each time you go to shape the paperweight.

An essential element in paperweight manufacture is a casing mold. These are used to suck the glass down around the lampworked items fast enough so that you do not trap bubbles. A small simple version of a casing mold to start with is the "Stump Sucker," so called because Loren Stump designed it. This mold, as was described earlier, is one that is essentially a small cup of graphite. It is used to case a glass construction by pulling a glob of molten glass, which is added to the top of the cup, down around the lampworked constructions using human supplied suction.

Let's walk our way through the construction of a simple paperweight. The simple paperweight that we will discuss is made in the millefiori style using slices of commercial murrine. Instead of using precut pieces, it would be nicer if you would buy some pieces of cane so that you will be able to snip and polish them all to the same length. Alternatively you could snip them to various lengths to establish a texture to surface of the pattern inside your paperweight.

Figure 235. Setting up murrini in the casing mold.

Lay out a pattern of murrine chips that fill the bottom of your graphite casing mold, as shown in Figure 235. Warm the mold and the pattern of murrine chips on a hot plate but be careful that you do not melt the attached hose by letting it touch the hot plate. Take a gather of clear glass from your crucible kiln, or prepare a really large gather on the end of a rod, and drip it into the casing mold as shown in Figure 236. To make a large enough gather at the torch you want to work off of about at least ½" diameter rod or three normal ones taped together. As the glass drips down into the mold, suck on the hose really hard. Don't worry, you will not suck any glass up the hose.

Now take a hot clear glass rod and touch it to the top surface of the glass in the mold to act as a punty. As the glass hardens, pull the paperweight out of the casing mold and keep it hot in the outer reaches of your flame. Be very careful, and make sure that the casing mold does not start to lift up. It will be really hot and you could burn yourself badly if you come into contact with it. You could just finish up the shape at this point but I find small paperweights look better with a colored back.

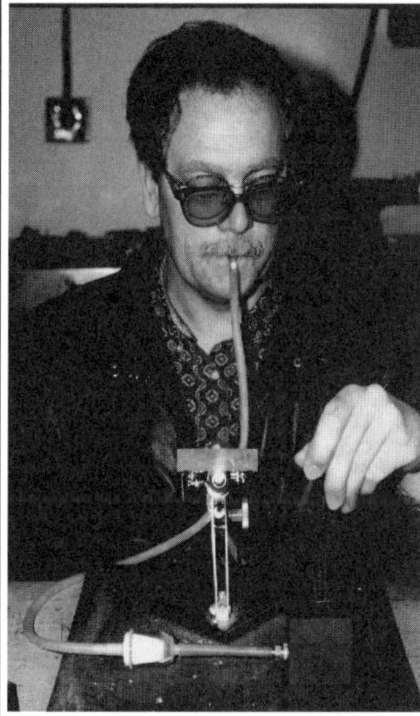

Figure 236. Adding molten glass into casing mold.

To add color onto the back, form a gather on the end of an opaque rod. Then, paint the glass onto the bottom of the paperweight and smooth it out. Lightly attach a punty rod of the same color to the bottom. Burn off the clear punty on the other end and heat up the paperweight in either a torch or glory hole. Shape the paperweight in a graphite mold as shown in Figure 237. If you want a bigger paperweight, add another gather of clear glass over the whole thing and then shape that into a bigger paperweight using a larger shaping mold. Use your largest marble mold or a folded bundle of very wet newspaper to shape this paperweight.

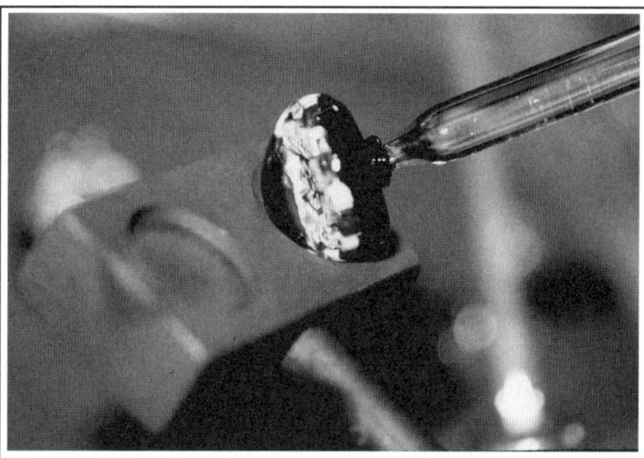

Figure 237. Shaping paperweight in graphite mold.

After final shaping of the paperweight, allow the outer surface to chill. Then, snip off the punty on the back before tucking the paperweight away into the annealer to cool. Afterward, you can cold work the back of the paperweight to give it a smoothed finished look. You could also facet the front surface for effect.

For those of you looking for information on making paperweights, there are a number of books and videos available on the subject. Some of these are listed in the suggested reading section at the end of this chapter.

Vessels

There may come a time when you want to make a small vessel to hold a liquid like a perfume. You may think that this is beyond your capabilities, but if you can do most of the things that we have already discussed then you have sufficient skills to make small vessels. I am going to present two very different techniques for doing this. The first is based on the skills you learned for winding beads and the second is based upon those you will learn for blown beads, which are discussed in the next chapter. In fact, it may help to read that chapter before trying to make one of the blown vessels discussed here.

Core vessels

The earliest glass vessels made by man were core vessels. First developed by the Egyptians, they are glass vessels that are wound around a central core. Figure 238 shows an example of an ancient core vessel. The core is removed afterwards to form the hollow in the center of the vessel. The core cannot be too hard or you will not be able to remove it from vessels with smaller necks than bodies. Historically, these cores were made of concoctions of things like crushed rock or sand held together by binders like dung or clay that was wrapped around a metal rod. The clay and dung were the binders that held the core together while the sand and the straw acted as materials that weaken the core so that it could be broken apart easily when it was time to remove it. These days, I don't know many beadmakers that like to work with dung so we form our cores out of other materials.

Figure 238. Egyptian core-formed vessel. circa 1400-1300 BC Height: 14 cm Courtesy of the Corning Museum of Glass

Some artists use high tech materials like those reported on by The Venerable Beadle. In some of his articles, he discussed two different materials with which he had experimented to form cores for winding vessels and hollow beads. The first of these is Foamglas. It is an insulative material that can be found in some hardware stores. It is used to make sanding blocks for wood workers because of its abrasive properties. For making core vessels, it is used with a good coat of separator compound. Because its coefficient of expansion is 86 x 10-7, it is not suitable for work with many of the glasses that we beadmakers are accustomed to working with. Borosilicate glass works well with it because the core will shrink away from the vessel. The core can then be removed by breaking it into small pieces.

Another core material that the Venerable Beedle has found to be fairly compatible with the glasses we use is the metal aluminum; be it in the form of wire, foils, expanded metals. The form, which he liked best, was Duocel, a foamed form made by ERG Materials & Aerospace Corporation of Oakland California. The only problem with using aluminum is its low melting temperature 1220°F. If not handled carefully, it will melt on you and you will lose the shape of the core. For that reason, you have to make sure that you coat it with a good layer of separator compound. Then, when the vessel is finished, the core can be etched out using muriatic acid from swimming pool suppliers.

Most beadmakers want to work with more common materials to make their cores. The material that most tend to choose is fine steel wool. I use 0000 steel wool that I tightly wrap around an old mandrel as shown in Figure 239. It helps to roughen up the surface of the mandrel with a grinder as well as to bend the core area of it into a zig zag, as can be seen in Figure 243. Both of these give the mandrel a little more tooth for the steel wool to cling to.

To make a core, unfold the steel wool and flatten it out, then, wind it tightly around the mandrel. It helps if you can anchor the mandrel down as you wrap the steel wool. I use a vise, but Brian Kerkvliet uses a brick. Any loose fibers that poke out as you wrap up the wool can be folded under the next wrap to hold it down. When you have it all wrapped up on the mandrel, roll it between your hands to finish shaping it. You may want to wear leather gloves when you are shaping it tp protect your hands.

After you have finished shaping the core to your satisfaction, dip it into separator compound to give it a fairly strong bead release coating as shown in Figure 240. Smooth out the release coating and let it completely air dry. At this point, I typically add a large pin vise handle onto the mandrel because core vessels can get pretty heavy and it hurts my hands to try to hold them on a normal mandrel.

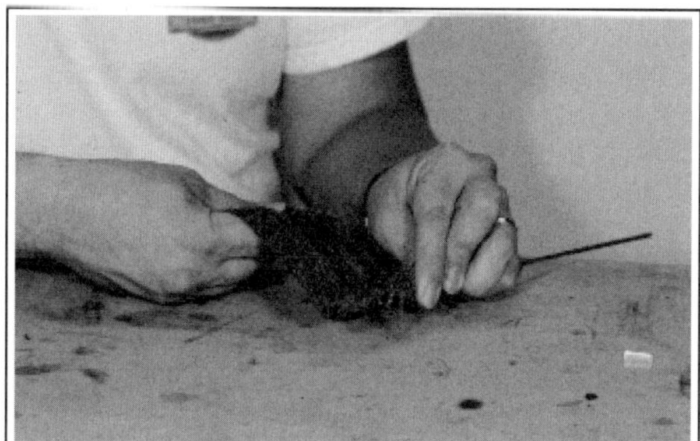

Figure 239. Forming a steel wool core.

To ready the finished core for wrapping, you have to heat it up in the flame to fully mature the separator coating. Heat it up slowly in the outer reaches of the flame. Burn off any errant hairs of steel wool. You may see some smoke coming off of the core as you heat it up. Just keep heating it slowly until the smoking stop and the separator coating completely changes color. Try not to overheat the core though or you can get the steel wool to start burning and the core will collapse.

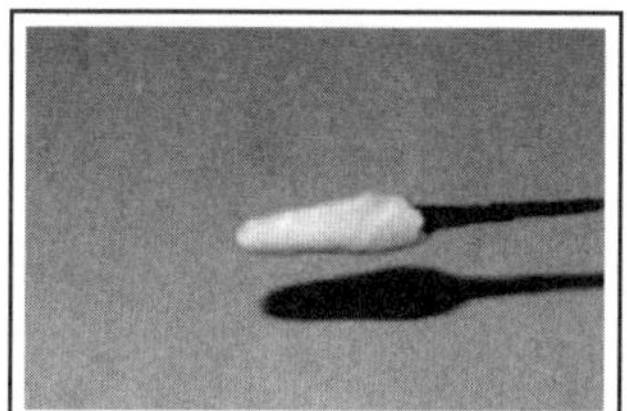

Figure 240. Finished core on mandrel holder.

Next, you want to apply a thin layer of the base colored glass of the vessel to the core. Start with the wrap that will define the lip of the vessel. As in making a bead, you want this first wrap to be nice and uniform because this defines the start of the vessel and it will be very visible in the final piece. You don't want this opening to be too small in diameter because you are going to have to remove the core through it. This can especially be a problem if the zig zag bends in your mandrel are too large.

Continue to wrap on more base glass until you have a nice uniform coating over the whole core. To prevent overheating the core as you apply this layer, it might help to use glass that has been preheated on a pastorelli or in your kiln. This will allow it to heat up faster. You can prevent overheating by keeping the core beneath the flame. Apply the wraps of glass close together so that they overlap slightly and no core material is showing.

If you get any bubbling coming up through the glass, you may not have completely worked all the moisture out of the core. If so, reheat it again in the outer reaches of the flame and work out any bubbles before continuing to finish the base layer of glass.

After the first layer is applied, smooth it out and then apply a second layer. This will give the vessel a little more strength, as well as make it less vulnerable to thermal shock. This will also give some depth to the walls, allowing you to distort them later by raking or twisting. Since some of the second layer may be visible in the finished piece, you may not want all of it to be one color. Make sure that the upper lip of the vessel has a nice rounded edge by adding extra glass so it is not too sharp. You might also want to make the glass at the bottom of the vessel a little thicker than that at the top to lower the center of gravity and make it more stable.

Because of the large size and variations in contours you may encounter in making core vessels, you may find yourself using some different shaping tools than usual, for instance very large diameter graphite rods. I use them, as is being done in Figure 241, to shape the necks and handles of the vessels.

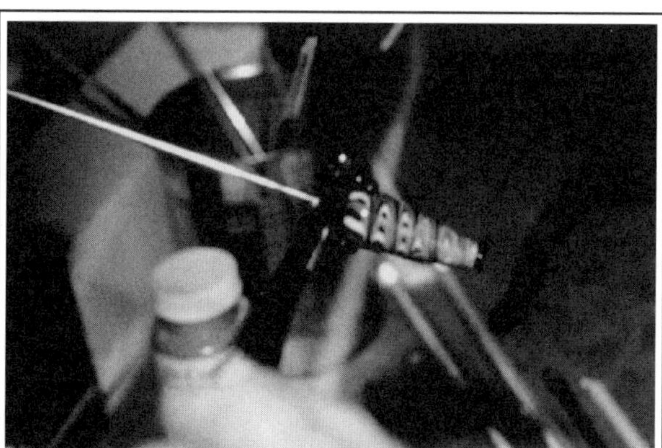

Figure 241. Using large graphite rod on core vessel.

Now you can decorate the outside surface of the core vessel with any of the techniques that we have discussed for decorating wound beads. You just have to be aware of how hot the whole vessel is.

Don't let any one section get too cold, so every once in a while as you are decorating, you want to stop and lightly heat the whole piece in the outer part of the flame.

Add detail to the body of the vessel first as it is easier to keep these areas evenly heated. Then go on and add the more delicate parts like handles and a base. Handles are made from attached and shaped rods or canes. Bases are wound from coils like the sides of a hollow wound bead. Work out the seams between the coils since they can act as initiation sites for cracks. Push the vessel down on your marver to adjust the bottom and insure the vessel stands correctly. Add the most delicate features last.

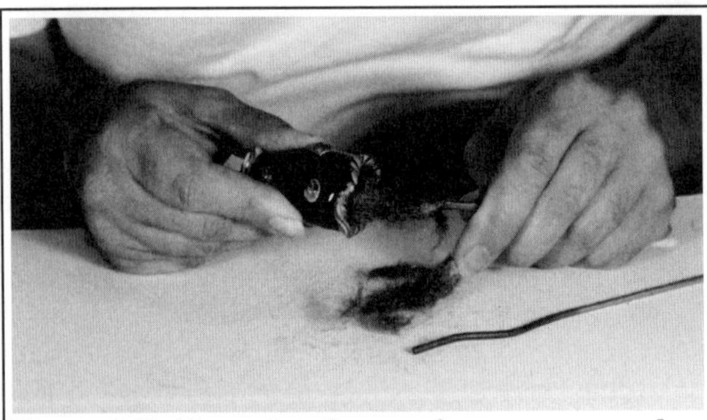

Figure 243. Removing the core from a core vessel.

After all decoration is complete, uniformly heat up the whole vessel in your torch to flame anneal it. Let it cool enough to harden, remove the handle from your mandrel, and stick the core vessel directly into your annealer, which is at or just below the annealing temperature. Because of their size and complex shape, I do not recommend trying to cool core vessels in vermiculite.

Figure 242. Quasi-core vessel
Artist: Teresa Pinto
Size: 1½" W x 1" T x 2" L

After annealing and cooling a core vessel safely down to room temperature, it is time to remove the core. Pull the core out slowly with your tweezers, taking out a little bit of steel wool out at a time. You may want to do this wet so that you do not have to put up with a lot of powder from the bead release. Take your time, and don't be in a hurry because it would be a shame to break the vessel at this point. After removing the core, you have to clean the separator out of the vessel. I don't know of any easy way to do this, but recommend grinding it out with diamond tools.

Many bead artists now make what might be thought of as quasi-core formed vessels by using large diameter mandrels or plugged stainless steel tubing to form the core. They then give shape to the vessel by varying the thickness of the glass that they wind on the "core". Clean up is a lot easier with one of these vessels because they only have a straight bore to clean the separator out of. A good example of this type of "core" vessel can be seen in Figure 242.

Blown vessels

As I mentioned earlier, the techniques for making blown vessels that I will present are based upon skills that are described in the discussions on making blown beads in the next chapter. It might help to read that chapter before trying to make the blown vessel described here. To make one of these vessels, you will use borosilicate tubing both as a blowpipe and to form part of our vessel. Borosilicate is a good place to start because its greater viscosity makes it easier to control. Figure 244 shows an example of a nice blown borosilicate vessel.

> **Safety Note**: Working borosilicate glass requires greater eye protection than soda-lime glass. See eye protection in safety chapter.

Figure 244. Blown vessel
Artist: Suellen Fowler
Size: 1½" Dia x 3 " L

To make such a vessel, start off with a section of ½" diameter medium wall borosilicate tubing at least eighteen inches long. If both ends are rough, then fire polish one of them to act as a blowing mouthpiece. Allow this end to cool before starting, unless you want a nickname of hot lips.

Now, we want to form a bubble on the other end of our blowpipe. To do this, we first gather this end of the tube in the flame using the tennis racket grip, until we get the tube to close up on itself like a test tube. This maneuver requires keeping a steady rotation of the tubing as you heat the end in the flame. You can speed it up some if by pinching the end of the tubing together using your tweezers.

Now that you have a closed end, you could heat this up and blow it out but all you would end up with is a thin fragile bubble. To make a reasonably thick walled vessel, we need to add multiple wraps of additional glass to the section of our blowpipe that we will eventually blow out into the body of the vessel. How long a section you add glass to depends upon how large a vessel you want to try to make. How large a size you can work with will be limited both by the size of flame your torch can project as well as how skilled you are. Things get more difficult as they get bigger, so start out small, say with 19 mm heavy wall tubing.

Therefore, I suggest that you start off working on a section of tubing about 1½" long. After you have closed off the end of your piece of tubing, wrap glass down the last 1½" to form your gather. You could add colored glass in this first layer of wraps, but because of the higher cost of colored borosilicate, you may want to wait until the second wrap. Of course, you could also wrap colored glass on this layer and clear glass on the second layer. After all, you are in charge here.

Figure 245. Wrapping first layer on the blowpipe.

To add glass to this section, take solid borosilicate rod about 5mm in diameter and case the last 1½" of the outside of the tubing with it. Do this by first warming this region of the blowpipe in the flame. Then coil on the rod starting 1½" from the end as shown in Figure 245. These pictures are of Suellen Fowler from a demonstration she gave at a Gathering of the Society of Glass Beadmakers. Keep the flame mainly on the rod as you add it to the tubing so that the tubing will not get so hot that it becomes hard to handle. Apply the rod as we discussed previously for cane, and keep the wraps close to each other. Go slowly and be sure to heat the rod enough so that you do not have to force it. Wrap on extra glass all the way to the rounded end of the tube.

Now, take that first wrap of glass and melt it into a uniform mass. Melt a small section at a time and work it on your marver. You will find that you really have to push borosilicate glass around a lot more than you are used to with soft glass. When the total mass is fused, heat it up until it appears whitish-pink. Then take the gather out of the flame and allow it to hang down for a few seconds. Next, gently blow it out into a bubble roughly the final size of the vessel, or in this case about 1½" in diameter, as shown in Figure 246. Allow this bubble to cool while hanging down until it sets up.

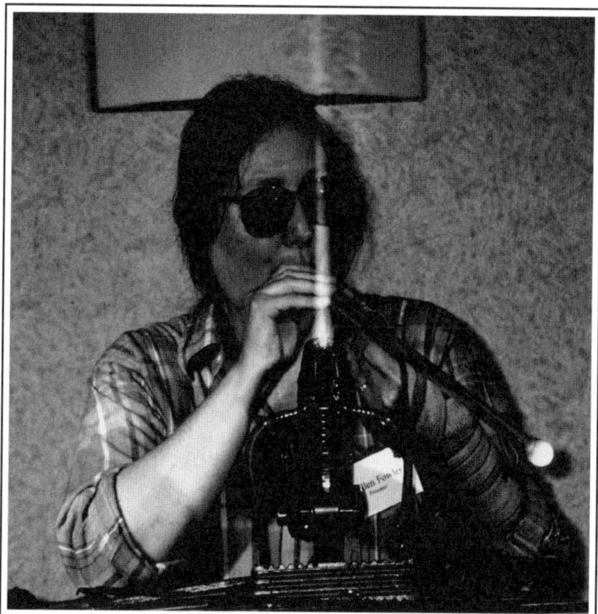

Figure 246. Blowing initial bubble roughly to size.

At this point, it may help to reinforce the neck of the vessel. Do this by winding on more glass or wiping on some short axial stripes of clear glass about ½" long onto the tubing just up from the bubble. Apply these stripes relatively hot and push them down onto the tubing. Allow these to cool slightly before continuing.

Once it is cooled to where the bubble does not flop around, it is time to add a layer of color. Coil it on just as we added the first layer of clear glass, starting up on the reinforcing stripes. Make sure that you overlap the coils slightly so that the color will be uniform. You usually wait until after blowing out the initial bubble before adding color, to avoid color variation caused by thinning of the color layer as you blow it out. At this point, you should add any color decorations onto the surface that you will want melted into the surface of the vessel.

Any distortion or combing of the applied patterns should also be done at this time while the walls of the vessels are thick and before completely melting them into the surface. When combing or distorting a pattern, just heat up a small section of the bubble at a time and use a tool made from a colored rod of the decoration color. When done, fuse all the wraps into the surface of the bubble, keeping the whole bubble rotating so that it will not droop.

Puff out the bubble slightly as necessary to restore its shape. Then, allow the bubble to hang straight down to allow the neck to stretch a bit. If it does not stretch to your satisfaction, reheat the bubble at the point one-third of the way from the top of the bubble to the bottom. Hold the bubble pointed down at about a 45° angle, as this will allow gravity to help stretch the neck. When the neck starts to stretch, stop and return to hanging it straight up and down as shown in Figure 247.

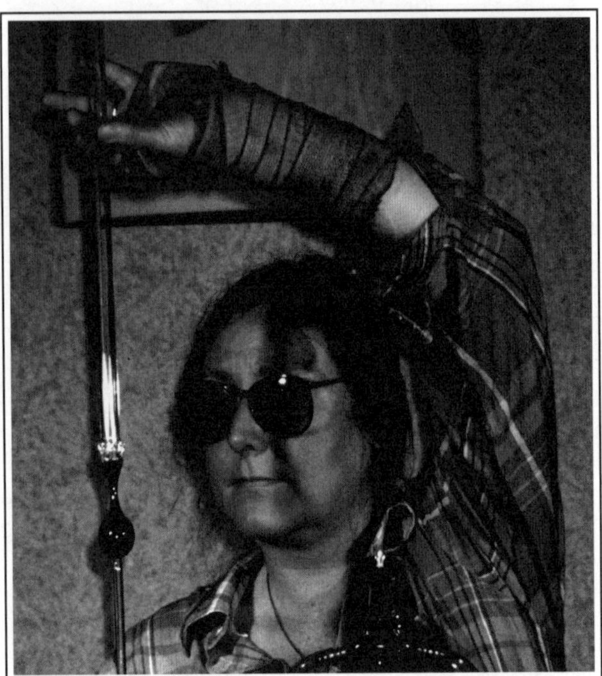

Figure 247. Stretching out the neck of the vessel.

Now reheat the bubble and blow it out a little as desired. Then, while hanging it straight up and down, slowly set it on the marver to give it a flat bottom. If you don't get it right the first time, then reheat the bottom quarter of the bubble and again set it down on the marver.

If you want your vessel to have handles now is the right time to add them. Take a colored rod, heat the end of it and place it on the bottle where you want to attach it. Touch them together hot and then pull out gently on the rod to get a nice smooth joint. Heat the rod and bend it around in a loop to the next point of attachment. Heat and attach here also. Burn off any extra rod. Reheat the handle and shape it with a graphite rod. Attach a second handle if desired.

Figure 248. Reaming the vessel opening to shape.

If you have a set of large hot fingers, allow the bubble and handles to become firm and then preheat the hot fingers and use them to grab the bottom of the vessel. Heat up around the neck of the blowpipe at the point where you want the top of the vessel to be. Thin out the junction between the vessel and the blowpipe by gently pulling on it.

Remove the vessel from the flame and break off the thin glass. Reheat the lip area and smooth it out. Remove any glass needed to get the top uniform by heating up the area and pinching or shearing it off. Flare out the neck slightly using a reamer. Do this by reheating the area and gently inserting the reamer into the opening while rotating, as shown in Figure 248. Try tilting the reamer around to form fancier lips on the top of the vessel. After flaring the neck, you may want to slightly shape the mouth of the vessel by pressing it against the surface of the marver. You might also want to consider adding a decorative lip wrap.

Figure 249. Pulling out the stopper.

At this point, you could be done or you might want to make a stopper for the vessel. To do this, make a gather at the end of a ½" diameter rod. If you want some color on the stopper, you could wrap the last little bit of the rod with color before gathering this end into a ball. When gathered to your satisfaction, take it out of the flame and hang it straight down.

Now, attach a small diameter temporary punty to the end of the gather. Hang it to allow the punty to center itself. Heat up the main rod at the point where it attaches to the gather. When hot and soft, hang it vertically with the punty down. Pull gently on the punty to draw the attachment point of the rod out to form a tail for the stopper, as shown in Figure 249. When the tail is pulled out to your satisfaction, stop and let it harden.

Distort the ball of the stopper if you want by flattening, twisting or whatever. Then, allow the stopper to harden and break the punty off of the gather. Fire polish the top surface of the stopper. Take it out of the flame and let it harden hanging vertically downward so the tail will stay straight. Grab the top of the stopper with some hot fingers or tweezers and burn off the tail from the rod where you want. Round off the end of the tail to a nice end in the flame. Pull it out and let it harden. Anneal the vessel and the stopper.

After they are cooled, try out the fit of the stopper in the top of the vessel. If you want to make them fit a little better, you can make a little paste of some medium grit grinding compound with water and apply it to the point of the stopper tail where it makes contact with the top of the vessel. Work this interface to grind it to fit better adding more grit or water as necessary. Take it easy so that you do not break the stopper.

Getting the right fit can be made easier by making a reamer with a positive stop on it so that you flare out the neck of the vessel to a consistent size. The tail of the stopper can be contoured to match by gently heating the spot where it contacts the opening of the vessel and pushing it into a hole in a paddle that has been cut to match the reamer. This will make the stopper and the vessel opening match better. Finish grinding them to fit will then be much easier.

Figure 250. Different steps in making a vessel.

Suggested further reading

"Beadle, The Venerable" AKA Murray Bloom, ***The Bead Column-Pendant Beads***", Glass Line Vol. 7 No. 6 (April/May) 1994

"Beadle, The Venerable" AKA Murray Bloom, ***The Bead Column-Hollow Wound Beads Part 2***", **Glass Line** Vol. 8 No. 2 (February/March) 1995

Coleman, Gerry, **The Basics of Making Marbles**, Video by Killer Beads

Dietz, Ulysses Grant, ***Paul J. Stankard, Homage to Nature,*** Harry N. Abrams, Inc., 1996

Fowler, Suellen, ***Flamework: An Intimate Art,*** video by Marcie Davis 2001

"Fritts, Drew" AKA Murray Bloom, "***Bullseye Marbles***", Glass Line Vol. 12 No. 5 (February/March) 1999

"Fritts, Drew" AKA Murray Bloom ***"Make Your Own Cherry Wood Marble Molds***", Glass Line Vol. 12 No. 4 (December/January) 1998/1999

Kerkvliet, Brian, ***"The Bead Gets Bigger"***, from **Glass Art** Vol. 10 No. 6 (September/October) 1995

Kerkvliet, Brian, "***Marbvelous Marbles***", from **Glass Art** Vol. 11 No. 3 (March/April) 1996

Reilly, Pat, ***Paperweights***, Courage Books, 1994

Miller, Bonnie J., **Why Not? The Art of Ginny Ruffner**, Tacoma Art Museum, 1995

Wilson, Lewis. "***Venetian Paperweight Buttons***" Bead and Button No. 3 (June) 1994

Wilson, Lewis "**Paperweight making**", video by Crystal Myths

Blown beads

As was discussed earlier, solid beads can become prohibitively heavy, as they get larger. One way of getting around this problem is to wind hollow beads, but a better way to make light hollow beads is probably to blow them. Beads can be blown either on a blowpipe or from tubing. The more common technique and the one most easily accessible to the beginning lampworker is to blow their beads from tubing.

You may find this technique to be a little harder than winding because you don't have the solid mandrel to help stabilize your work. The glass of choice for blown beads, as it was for small blown vessels, is borosilicate glass or pyrex. It is nice to work with because its low coefficient of thermal expansion does not require the entire bead be kept hot all the time. It even allows you to put down the bead while you are working, let it cool off, then pick it up, and start working again. This is something that is almost impossible to do with soda-lime glass.

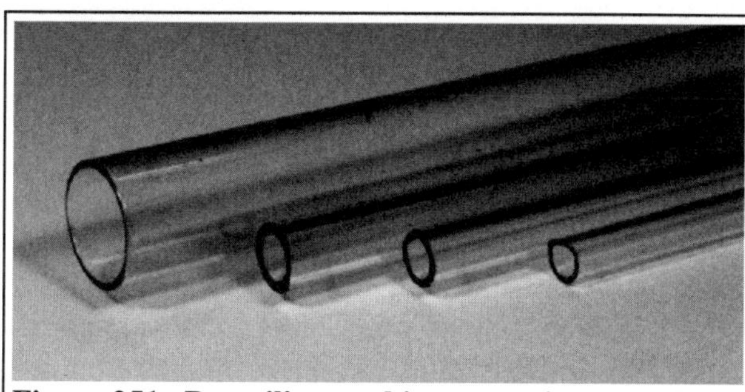

Figure 251. Borosilicate tubing comes in many sizes.

The price that you pay for this benefit is the higher temperature and heat input required to work borosilicate glass. For borosilicate glass, you definitely need a fuel-oxygen system. Even a minor bench burner is barely adequate for this work. Other disadvantages of working with borosilicate glass are that its higher viscosity requires more effort to shape it and its color selection is limited as well as costly.

Tubing skills

Before we get into making blown glass beads from tubing, let's discuss how manipulation of tubing differs from the flameworking skills that we discussed for winding beads with glass rods. Glass tubing is a little harder to work than glass rod, because it is hollow. This gives it less mass, causing it to heat up and lose heat faster than you might initially expect. It can also buckle and collapse if not kept constantly moving. You have to develop a whole new feel to work with it.

Tubing, like rods, is usually referred to by its diameter, in particular its outside diameter (O. D.). Since it is not solid, its complete specification requires an additional descriptor; either inside diameter or wall thickness. Of the two, specification

Table 18. Common glass tubing sizes.

Standard Wall		Medium Wall		Heavy Wall	
O. D. (mm)	Wall (mm)	O. D. (mm)	Wall (mm)	O. D. (mm)	Wall (mm)
2	.5	6.3	1.2	9.5	2.0
3	.6	12.7	1.6	12.7	2.4
4	.8	15.9	1.6	15.9	2.4
5	.8	19.0	1.6	19.0	3.2
6	1.0	25.4	2.4	22.2	3.2
7	1.0	31.7	2.4	25.4	4.0
8	1.0	38.1	2.4	31.7	4.0
9	1.0	44.4	2.4	38.1	4.0
10	1.0	50.8	3.2	44.4	4.0
11	1.0			50.8	4.8
12	1.0				
13	1.2				
14	1.2				
15	1.2				
16	1.2				
17	1.2				
18	1.2				
19	1.2				
20	1.2				

of wall thickness is the more common. Wall thickness may be specified by an actual dimension or a qualifier such as standard wall, medium wall, or heavy wall. Table 18 lists some common sizes of standard, medium, and heavy wall tubing.

In working with tubing, the heavier the wall thickness, the easier it is to control the glass when the tubing starts to get soft. Increasing the wall thickness also increases the period over which the glass will remain soft once heated. Doubling the thickness more than doubles the working time. Heavier walled tubing also tends to be more uniform in wall thickness.

Cutting tubing

Cutting small diameter tubing up to about 30 mm in diameter is done exactly as it was done with rods—by using a glass knife to score it and then breaking it by hand. However, as the tubing gets larger, it is harder to break uniformly by hand. In this case, score it and propagate a crack around the circumference of a tube. Propagation is facilitated by the judicious use of heat.

To do this, make a score with your glass knife all the way around the outside diameter of the tube. Next apply a little saliva to part of the score. Then bring that portion of the cold tube up under the flame and just barely touch it to the edge of the flame. This should initiate a crack at the base of the score, which you can lead around the tube with more heat (rotating the cracked edge toward you) or by pulling lengthwise on the tube. If you cannot get the crack to initiate right away, it is often better to move to a new spot around the circumference of the tube and start over. Continued application of heat at one spot will just cause the crack at the bottom of the score to blunt.

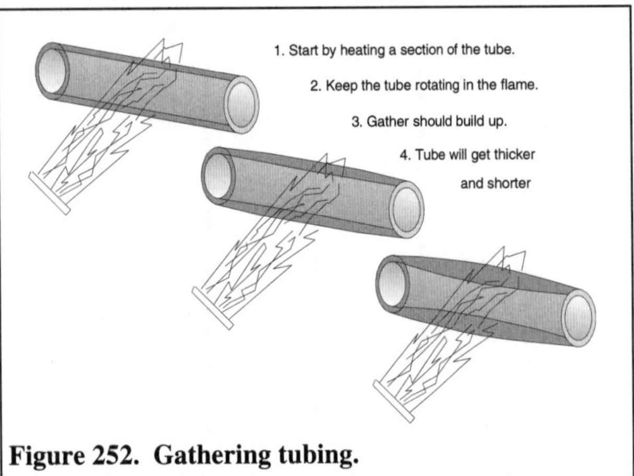

Figure 252. Gathering tubing.

An alternate technique of applying heat to run a crack is to make a single wrap of resistance wire around the circumference of the tube over the score and to run electrical current through it. This heats up a narrow region of glass in the vicinity of the score all the way around the tube. After heating it up, the current is turned off and a damp cloth is applied to the score to initiate a crack by thermal shock. Then pull on the tubing to run the crack around the circumference of the tube.

Gathering or shrinking tubing

In the case of tubing, what we mean by gathering is heating up the tubing in such a way that the tubing starts to shrink in diameter and increase in wall thickness from surface tension of the glass, as seen in Figure 252. This can be continued, if desired, all the way until the tubing completely closes up. This is exactly what is done to get a round closed end on the end of some tubing for something like a test tube.

Figure 253. Robert Mickelson shows positioning of your hands when gathering large tubing.

Developing a gather on a tube is done very similar to the way that we did a gather on a rod. You introduce the tubing into a medium flame at the place you want to make the gather (end or interior) by waving it through the flame as before. Be careful in doing this because tubing tends to be more sensitive to thermal shock than solid rods. But since the tubing is borosilicate glass, it is not as sensitive as it would be if it were soda-lime glass.

Once in the flame, you rotate the tube with a steady regular motion. Use a double tennis racket grip or the upside down tennis grip, as shown in Figure 253, when gathering in the center of a tube. This applies the heat uniformly all the way around the tubing, which may be larger than the flame, and prevents it from drooping. If you get tired of rotating it in one direction all the time, you can vary by rotating it back and forth.

To get a feel for how the glass is heating up, peek over the top of your glasses to check out the color of the flame. As the tubing starts to get hot, the flame will become more intensely yellow. Peking at the color of the flame as you spin the tube can help you tell if you are heating it uniformly. The important thing in getting the glass to thicken and draw down uniformly is to apply your heat evenly around the tubing. To facilitate this process, it helps to use a softer flame. As with solid glass rods, if your gather droops just rotate the tube and it will straighten itself out.

Safety Note: The higher working temperature of borosilicate glass requires more protective glasses than when working soda-lime glass. See section on eye protection in safety chapter.

When you first start making gathers in tubing, you may find it hard to keep the cross section of your gathered tubing uniform and circular. As you make your gather, you may lose control and have it twist out of shape. For gathers at the end of a tube, this is usually the result of not heating uniformly around the exterior circumference of the tube.

For gathers away from the end of the tube, you have to hold both ends of the tube. Here, non-uniform gathers are usually the result of not rotating the tubing at the same speed on both sides of the gather or not keeping them in line. One hand may just be slower than the other. If you have this problem, notice that it does not happen until the glass gets quite soft. This points out the secret to successfully working with tubing, don't let it get too hot. Working a little slower at a cooler temperature accomplishes the same objective while keeping the glass stiffer so that it is easier to handle.

Pulling points

When making blown glass beads, you will need a way to hold the bead as you are working on it. This is usually done by pulling points at the ends of the section of the tube that you are working, as shown in Figure 254, and using them as handles. The process for pulling points on tubing is illustrated in Figure 255. As before, when you pulled points or cane from rod, you first have to make a gather in the center of the tube, which you subsequently pull out

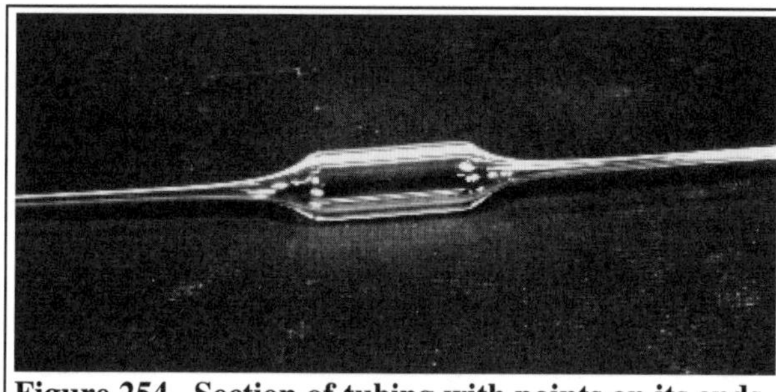

Figure 254. Section of tubing with points on its ends.

into a point. The difference here is that the point will be hollow.

So, start by making a gather a couple inches in from the end of a piece of tubing and about an inch and a half long. Keep both ends of the tube rotating it evenly and remove it from the flame. Begin to draw it out while simultaneously bending the main part of the tubing down at a slight angle and continuing to rotate until you pull it out about 12 inches long and about $^1/_8{}^{th}$ inch in diameter. Then, straighten out the tube, pull it straight, and hold it taut.

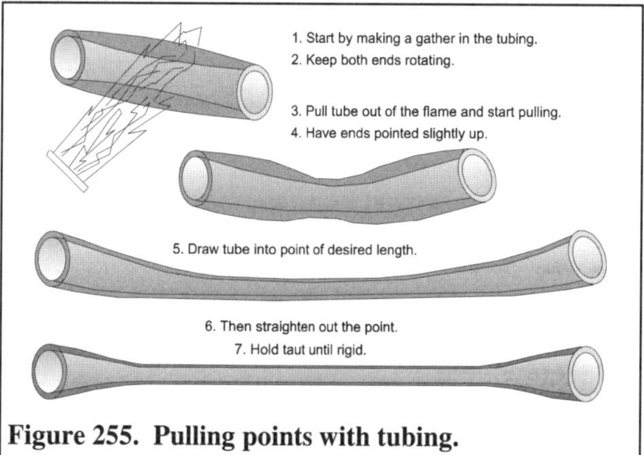

Figure 255. Pulling points with tubing.

Once it stops moving, continue to hold it in tension for a few more seconds to allow it to solidify. Make sure that the glass has completely set up before you release the tension on the point, otherwise it can bend on you. With practice, this process becomes one smooth easy rhythm. The tricky part is to keep the point on center relative to the tubing. Some people find holding the tubing vertically in the last step helpful in getting the points aligned. If you are going to be making blown beads, you should practice gathering and pulling points a number of times until you get the hang of it.

You can separate the point at its center by reheating a short section of the center. Because of its smaller size, it will heat much faster. Heat the short section of the point and pull it out in the flame to allow it to separate. You may find it easier to do this final flame cut if you pull out a small section of the point a second time first.

Points can also be pulled from the end of a tube. To do this, start by closing off the end of the tube with a gather. Use pliers if you have to on larger tubing to help close off the end. Then attach a punty to the center of the closed off end, as shown in Figure 256. Next reheat the gather in a little from the end until it starts to close in on itself (remembering to rotate all the time of course) and pull it out into a point.

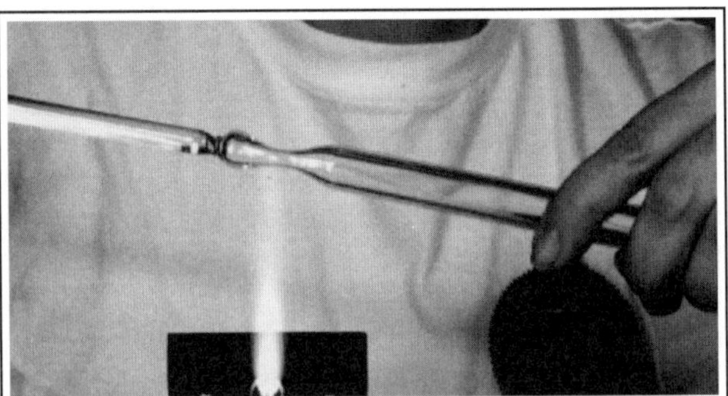

Figure 256. Pulling a point from the end of a tube.

The tapered end of a well-made point will be circular in cross section and in perfect alignment with the center of the tubing. If you roll it between your thumb and forefinger, the central tubing section will run true. If your points are not centered, and they probably won't be when you start, they can be adjusted enough to work. To accomplish this, apply a small flame to the region where the tube narrows down into the point. Gather this region in slightly by continuing rotation while heating and possibly pushing the point back into the tube slightly. Then remove it from the flame and slightly pull on the point to straighten it out.

You may also find that your points are not as circular in cross section as you would like. This is usually the result of not heating the gather uniformly around its circumference before pulling. The cooler side does not pull out as well and therefore will be flatter. The cure for this is simple, keep the tube rotating evenly whenever in the flame.

Inflation/reinflation

One skill that you have not practiced up until now in working on beads is inflation of a bead by blowing into it. With blown beads, you may shrink and reinflate a bead a number of times until you get the shape right. Usually all you will have to do is to give a slight puff into the bead via a hollow point to reinflate it. If you do not like the result, you can just slowly heat the bead up out in the end of the flame, let it gather back in on itself, and try again.

To practice this, start by pulling two points on a short section of tubing. One point should be open and one should be closed. Now, heat up the center of the tube to gather it in on itself and shrink it down. One of the ways to tell when the tube is hot enough for inflating is when it becomes hard to keep it on center and it wants to droop on you. Pull it out of the flame while continuing to rotate. Put the open point into your mouth while still rotating. Then, gently inflate the tube as seen in Figure 257. You may find that you may have to blow a little harder initially to get the glass moving. You can then ease up some as it starts to move and finally you have to blow harder again as the glass chills. A common mistake of beginners is to blow too hard and too soon—resulting up in a paper-thin bubble. So take it easy.

Blowing it out

Sometimes you want to create a hole in the side of a blown bead, as illustrated in Figure 258. The easiest way to do this is to chill the bead slightly, use a sharp flame to spot heat the area where you want the hole, and then blow into the point. This will cause the heated portion of the wall to pooch out like a balloon until it breaks. Heat up the jagged edges and use a small tungsten rod to pick off the extra glass. Use a graphite or brass reamer to get a nice uniform hole.

Figure 257. Inflating a section of heated tubing.

If you want to make multiple holes in the bead, then blow out each one but don't pop them right away. Get them all blown out and then break them out. Once one blows out, you cannot blow out any more unless you plug the hole.

Blowing out holes can also be used as another way to cut tubing. In this method, we heat a narrow area all the way around the tube and pull it into two pieces by pulling a point and breaking the two pieces apart. Gather the point to close up the end of the tube. Then heat the very end of the constant cross section area on the closed end, take it out of the flame, and blow it out. Break the paper-thin glass

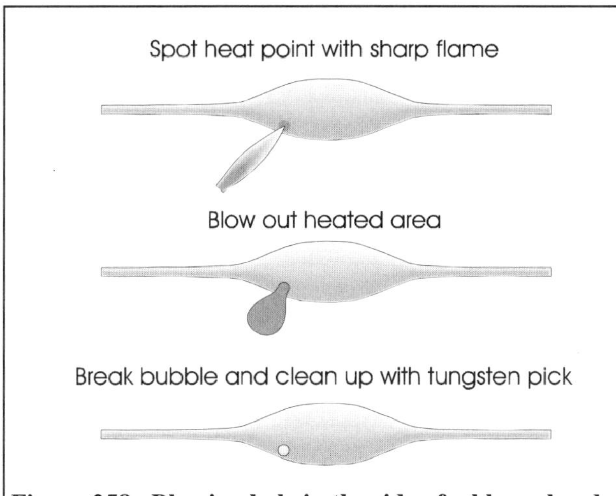

Figure 258. Blowing hole in the side of a blown bead.

off the end of the tube. Then smooth out the edges of the hole with your pick as above and you are ready to go.

I should mention at this point that if you want to continue working strictly with Effetre, you can blow your own tubing. Brett Pierce did this for his blown bead in the color plates. To do this, build up about a three-quarter inch diameter gather of Effetre on the end of some $^3/_8$ or ½ inch diameter heavy wall pyrex or stainless steel tubing. Blow out the gather into a small bubble and then stretch it out into tubing.

Brett finds that if he does not let the wall thickness get more than about $^1/_{16}{}^{th}$ of an inch thick, he does not have problems with thermal shock and can almost handle it like borosilicate glass. He does have to be a little more care reheating this tubing than he does with borosilicate tubing. He uses the soft flame of a Bunsen burner to preheat Effetre components as he assembles them. Also, the glass is so soft that he finds that he can reinflate a point without having the other end sealed shut.

Borosilicate tube beads

Figure 259. Tube bead.
Artist: Don Schneider
Size: ½" Diameter x 1½" L
Photo: Bill Bresler

As a way of practicing a few of the tubing skills that I have discussed, let's talk about how to make borosilicate tubing beads like those by Don Schneider. An example of one of these beads can be seen in Figure 259. To make a tube bead, he starts with some medium-wall borosilicate tubing 6 to 10 mm in diameter. He then cuts it into workable lengths of one to one and a half feet and fire polishes the ends.

After preheating the last couple inches of one of these pieces to a temperature just slightly below where it starts to show any color, he cases most of the outside of this section of tubing in a solid rod of colored glass. A number of manufacturers now make colored borosilicate glass. It tends to be quite expensive in comparison to soda-lime glass, and for this reason, it is usually used sparingly. This is the situation here, where it is applied as a thin casing to the clear tubing, rather than making the whole body of the bead from colored borosilicate.

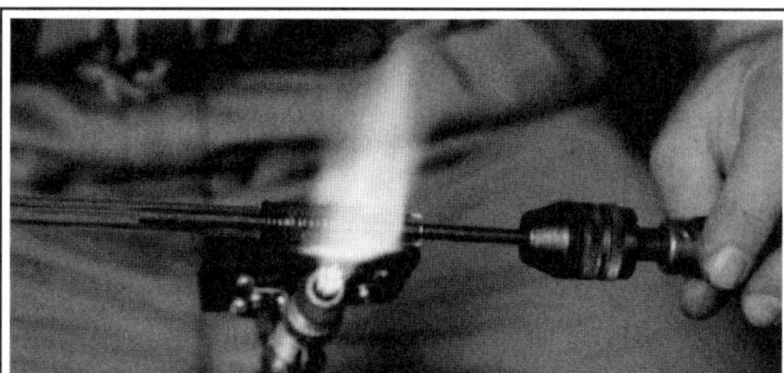

Figure 260. Using graphite rod to keep tubing shape. Photo Bill Bresler.

After winding on the colored casing, Don works it into the surface of the tube by heating it and rolling it smooth on the marver. To assist in maintaining its tubular shape while marvering, Don uses a graphite rod down the center of the tube, as shown in Figure 260. You need this because borosilicate's much higher viscosity requires that he push on it to get the glass to flow. With out the graphite rod, this would flatten the tube. The graphite rod should be mounted in a handle to keep from burning yourself and getting your hands dirty. He uses a pin vise to hold his, but you could also used doweling.

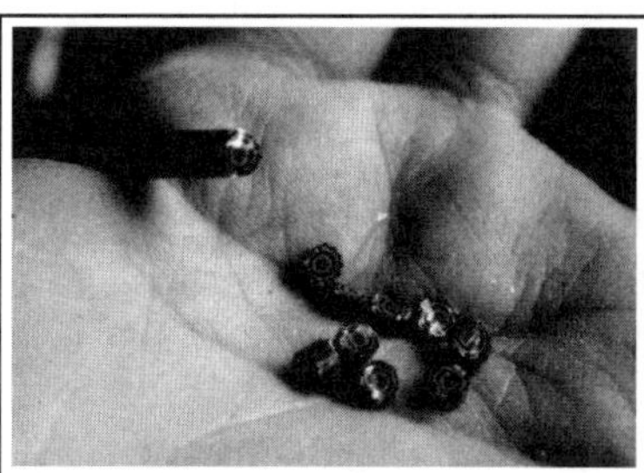

Figure 261. Borosilicate murrine
Artist: Don Schneider
Size: ¼" Diameter
Photo: Bill Bresler

To decorate his beads, Don adds murrine pieces that he cuts from hand-made millefiori like those in Figure 261. He makes them out of borosilicate glass using similar techniques to those described previously. He also uses latticino. You could actually use many of the bead decorating

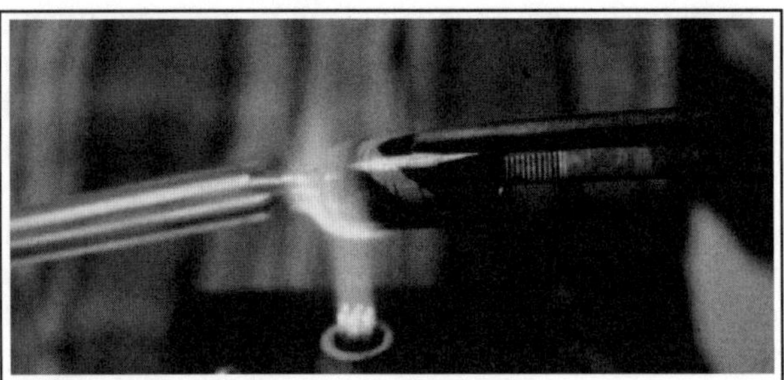
Figure 262. Pulling bead off of tube. Photo: Bill Bresler.

methods that we have talked about like frit, dots, cane, etc. The only thing that you have to remember is that you are working with borosilicate glass and have to work it slightly hotter than soda-lime glass.

After you are done decorating a bead, you are ready to flame cut it off the end of the tube. To do this, turn your flame down to a pinpoint, then quickly heat a thin ring around the tube where you want the end of the bead to be. When hot and soft remove the tube from the flame and grab the other end of the bead with your tweezers, as seen in Figure 262. Pull out this ring into a thin thread and break it free from the tubing. While holding the bead with your tweezers, break off any shards of glass and use a flat file to smooth up the end of the bead. Then shape the end of the bead on your marver, as shown in Figure 263 for the first end.

Figure 263. Smoothing up end of cut tube bead. Photo: Bill Bresler.

These edges should then be fire polished in the flame by holding the bead with a hot fingers tool rather than your tweezers to allow you to roll it in your hand as you heat the tube in the flame. If it needs a little more shaping, you can slide it back onto your graphite rod and use your graphite paddle to marver it. Afterward, the bead ends can be squared on the face of your marver.

Figure 264. Scarf slide
Artist Don Schneider
Size: ¾"H x 1¼"L x ½"T

If you want more free form shapes, you can evenly heat up the bead in the final shaping step on the graphite rod and let gravity start to stretch it. Once it starts to stretch, the process can be encouraged and modified by inserting a second graphite rod into the center hole and using the rod to further stretch open the hole, possibly even inserting twists. This method can be used to turn your tubular bead into bolo tie beads or scarf slides, like the one seen in Figure 264.

Blowing beads

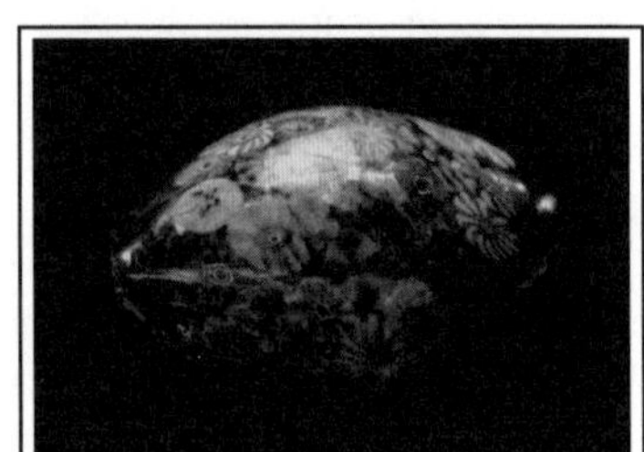
Figure 265. Blown beads
Artist: Don Schneider
Size: ¾" Diameter x 1½" L
Photo: Bill Bresler

With the basic tube working skills behind us and with the practice you got in making tube beads, we are now ready to discuss how to make a blown bead like that shown in Figure 265.

Basic blown bead

For blowing beads, ¾ to 1 inch in diameter (20 or 25mm) heavy wall tubing works as a good starting material. If you don't want to waste any of the tubing, close off one end with a gather and then pull it out into a point with a punty as discussed previously. Then go in from the end of the straight section of the tubing about 2 inches, make another gather, and pull another point. The amount you move inward depends on the size of the bead that you want to make.

Break off the tube section in the middle of the second point. You can use your glass knife to score the point if you want to avoid jagged edges. You should now have a tube section that looks like the first step in Figure 266. If you did not care about wasting a little glass in trade for slightly increased speed, this same thing could have been made from two internal gathers on the tube.

You want to be sure that one of the two points is closed off at its end. Otherwise, when you blow into the bead to reinflate it nothing will happen. If they

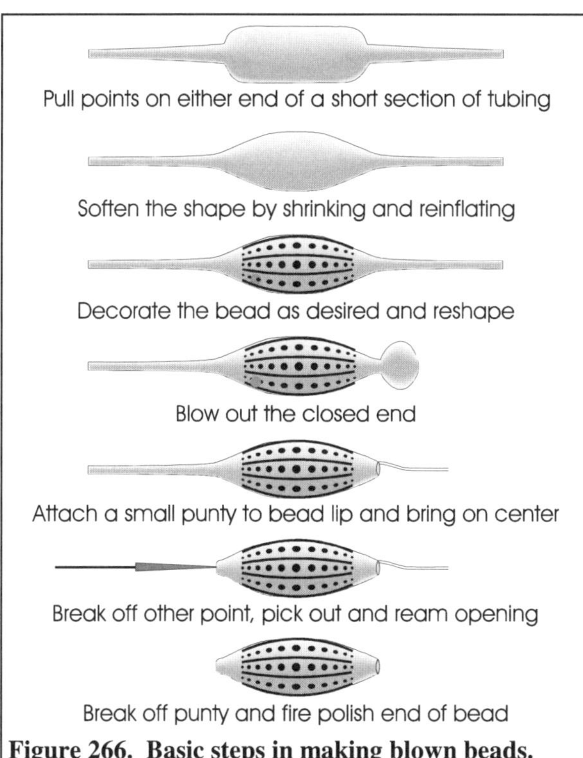

Figure 266. Basic steps in making blown beads.

are both open, heat one end up and pinch it closed. Now, add any decorations that you want to the bead (more on this in the next section). After you have the bead decorated to your satisfaction, shrink the bead down to the desired shape through a series of operations consisting of uniformly heating it followed as necessary by reinflation. You can also roll or push it on a marver as shown in Figure 268, or use tools like mashing pliers to get your shape.

It is important to work slowly and not to blow too hard. Remember to keep the bead spinning to prevent it from sagging or buckling and to keep your points centered. If a point should go off center, all that is usually necessary to get it back onto center is to lightly heat the bent area and give it a slight tug. Sagging can also be handled by removing the bead from the flame, hanging it straight down, and using gravity to bring it back into shape. Doing this outside of the flame allows more control over the process. Buckling of a point can be corrected with a slight reinflation but is often indicative of a different problem—uneven wall thickness from pulling your points incorrectly.

Figure 268. Flattening a blown bead on a marver.

After you are done shrinking the bead down to about half of its original size and increasing wall thickness to about twice its original thickness, shape the bead. When you get the desired shape for your blown bead, melt off the closed point at the edge of the bead. Then, heat up the melted end, blow it open, pick off any glass shards, and use a reamer to properly shape the opening, as shown in Figure 267. A reamer is used for this purpose by inserting it into the hole as you heat it and spinning the reamer or the bead to get the desired shape. You may have to reheat the hole a few times before you get it right.

Now, slightly chill the bead to stabilize it. Spot heat a small section of the bead lip that you just finished and attach a small punty. Heat the punty and bend it onto center so that you can work the other side of the bead. As an alternative, you could use a set of hot fingers to hold the bead on the completed end while you finish the other end. Next, burn off the other point and pick it open. Use the reamer to shape the hole. Chill slightly and use a tweezers to grab the bead by this newly formed end. Break off the punty (if you used one) and touch up the punty mark with the flame. Then bury the bead in the heated vermiculite or put it into your annealer.

Figure 267. Picking open the end of a blown bead.

Shaping blown beads

Blown beads can be shaped in a number of different ways, some of which are identical to those discussed for wound beads. Generally though, blown beads tend to be simple in shape (spheres, ellipsoids and such), relying on their clear colors and translucence for their beauty. But if you do want to shape one, you have a number of options open to you. You can roll it or press it on your marver to shape it. You can decoratively distort it by pinching,

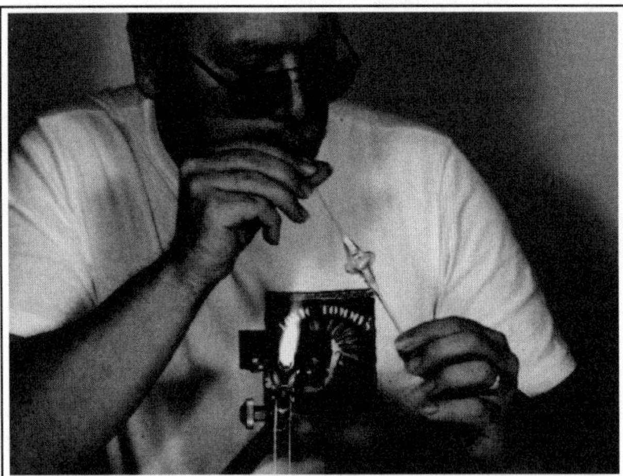

Figure 269. Decoratively distorting a blown bead.

pulling out or poking in sections of the bead with tools like pliers or picks. Figure 269 shows an example in which I am blowing out a portion of a bead.

Since you are making a blown bead, you might also want to try some of the shaping ideas that can only be practiced in that medium. Some of these are illustrated in Figure 270. You can you use your flame to shrink down sections so that it is smaller in diameter at this point and thicker in other sections. Conversely, you can blow out sections to make them thinner but larger in diameter. You can also pull out sections of the bead like points to make the bead long and slender for dangles for earrings. You can twist your beads to make them collapse into spirals.

For something even more interesting, you might want to try making a small mold from wood or graphite with a unique shape and blowing the bead into the mold. If you use wood, you will have to use the molds wet, as you do for marble molds. With this technique, you can make beads with all sorts of interesting shapes from simple rectangular solids and bipyramidic solids to complex non-regular shapes like birds and simple animals.

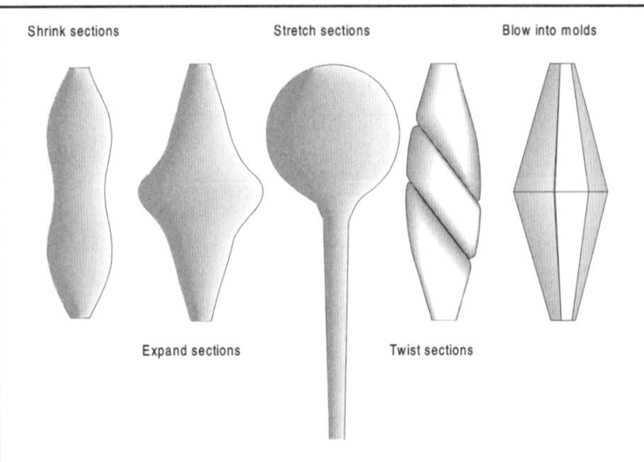

Figure 270. Shaping ideas for blown beads.

Decorating blown beads

Many of the decorating techniques discussed for use with wound beads also work well with blown beads. Figure 271 shows Don Schneider laying canes onto a blown bead. You can also decorate them by:

- rolling them in frit or enamels
- painting them with paints or enamels
- using glass decals
- adding dots
- trailing on color or stringer painting
- surface distortion in the form of twists or pokes
- applying canes, latticino, murrine or ribbons
- adding inclusions like wires or screens
- using sculptural lampworking techniques.

We have not talked too much about sculptural techniques for borosilicate glass. To find out more about this, I suggest either Lewis Wilson's sculptural lampworking video series or Homer Hoyt's book.

Figure 271. Decorating a blown bead.
Photo: Bill Bresler

One of the tricks in adding decorations to blown beads is to have the pieces that you are adding be hotter than the bead. This is because the bead tends to heat up fast and can get out of control if you are not careful. You want to keep the bead just warm enough to make a good joint between the decoration and the bead. If not, your decoration could fall off later. You accomplish this by feeding your decorating rod though the flame onto the bead while applying slight pressure down onto the bead. If applying cane, try to keep the rod rotating slightly as you apply it to heat the glass uniformly. If you find this hard to do, try twisting it back and forth instead.

One way to make sure that your decorations are properly fused onto the surface of the bead is by slightly gathering the bead and reinflating it after applying all your decorations. Another thing to be aware of when applying decorations to blown beads is that areas with large changes in wall thickness can be locations of localized stress that will need flame annealing to prevent cracking.

When trying to decorate blown beads, you should know that not all the techniques that you have learned for use with wound beads work as well for blown beads. This is the result of not having the stabilizing influence of the mandrel and the much higher viscosity of borosilicate glass. One of the most notable of these techniques that does not work very well is raking. To rake properly you have to get the surface of the bead really hot to some depth. Blown beads are generally too thin to do this properly, and attempts to do so can result in major distortion or tears to the bead surface. Raking is possible though once you develop a good feel for working with blown beads, but don't expect this any time soon.

To get an effect similar to raking, you instead can take advantage of one of the shaping techniques available for blown beads, twisting. This process is illustrated in Figure 272. Start decorating the bead by applying longitudinal stripes down the axis of the bead. Spot heat one circumferential section of the body of the bead, being sure to keep it rotating quickly to prevent it from drooping. When hot, twist one end of the bead one direction and the other end in the opposite direction as if you were winding a latticino. This will produce a spiral like effect.

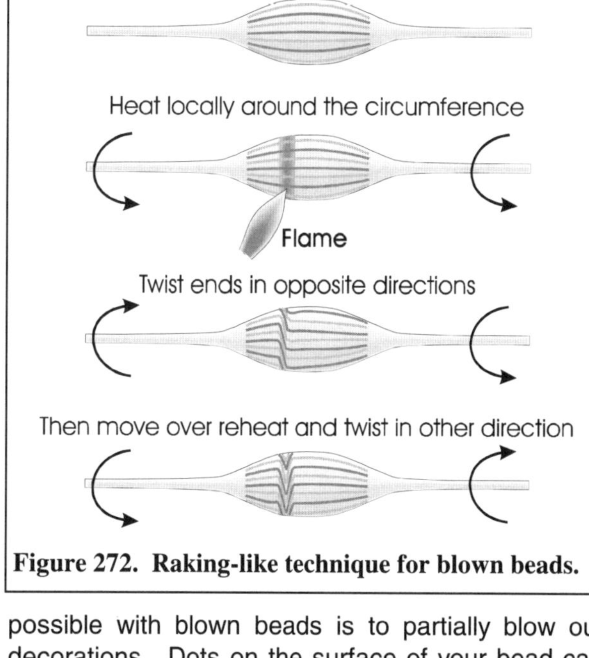

Figure 272. Raking-like technique for blown beads.

Next spot heat the circumferential section of the bead next to this spiral and then twist in the opposite directions to get a spiral in the opposite direction. Back-to-back, these two steps will result in an effect similar to circumferential raking. If you do a number of these in the same direction but slightly separated, then you will get an effect similar to festooning. If you switch directions every time, you will get an effect something like feathering. The only thing that you need to be aware of is that this process gets harder to do near the ends of the bead where the wall is thicker.

Figure 273. Painted blown bead
Artist: Shari Maxson Hopper
Size: 1" Diameter
Photo by: Shari Maxson Hopper

Another technique that is only possible with blown beads is to partially blow out decorations. Dots on the surface of your bead can be heated up and blown out a little so that they become hollow. You can also gather and blow out some circumferential decorative rings. If you wanted, you could also go all the way and blow a hole out of the side of a bead. This would be good for a necklace to which you want to add a pendant. If more than one additional hole out of the bead is desired, do not break any of the bubbles until all of them are formed.

Surface decorations that can done with clear borosilicate blown beads to give them color include decorating them with compatible enamels or lusters, as was done for the bead in Figure 273. You can mix up some lower temperature enamels with a liquid binder such as Thompson's Klyr-fire, paint them on and fire them in the kiln. To decorate a bead with high temperature enamels at the torch, roll them in the enamel and then uniformly heat the bead to a light cherry red to fire the enamel.

Alternatively, paint lusters onto your beads. Let them air dry and fire them in the kiln. Try all four types of lusters: metallics, iridescents, halos, and colored to get a feel for how to work with them. Be sure to have adequate ventilation when working with these materials because some of the vapors released in firing can be toxic.

Another nice decorative technique to use with blown beads is to mirror the inside of the bead, as has been done to those in Figure 274. Silvering is not too difficult a process and can easily be done by an small studio artist. To silver the inside of a bead, you first clean the glass if it is not fresh. Next, you sensitize the glass surface by pretreating it with a tinning solution. The silvering which is done next is a three-step process. First, the silver solution is applied. Next, the silver surface is activated and then reduced. Finally, all chemicals are rinsed out of the bead. For more information on silvering see either of the references listed at the end of this chapter: "The Independent Glassblower" or Homer Hoyt's book.

Figure 274. Internally mirrored blown beads.
Artist: Shari Maxson Hopper
Size: ¾" Diameter x 1½" L
Photo by: Shari Maxson Hopper

Another process, which you might want to try on your borosilicate blown beads, is to irridize them. Irridizing a glass surface can be achieved by spraying a metallic solution on the glass surface while it is hot (1100°F to 1150°F). This forms a thin layer of lustrous color. The most successful of the solutions to use is 1 part by volume stannous chloride with 1 part muriatic acid and 2 to 4 parts of water. This is the solution that Bullseye Glass Company uses to irridize their glass.

The solution can be sprayed after heating the bead either in the torch or in the kiln. The solution is very toxic so this must be done with adequate safety measures both to protect you from the fumes as well as the solution. A plastic or glass siphon sprayer is necessary for application, as the acid will attack metal. The solution should be sprayed in a hood, which is then washed down and neutralized afterward. After spraying, put the bead into an annealer. For more information see Boyce Lundstrom's article from Glass Line.

There is also a Mother of Pearl thermoluster manufactured by Engelhard that gives an irridizing effect similar to that of stannous chloride. It uses 1,1,1-trichloroethane tetraisopropyl titanate as its active ingredient. It is supposed to be much less toxic, although more flammable, than the stannous chloride solution reported on above and its use requires good ventilation and protection from contact with your eyes and skin, much less ingestion. Use of a paint hood is suggested. It is the same chemical that Spectrum Glass Company and Armstrong Glass Company use to irridize their glass. It is non-corrosive to metals but I would not advise using an expensive airbrush to apply it. Your bead should be warm, over 800°F, but not hot when applying this product, as shown in Figure 275. This should be the last step in making your bead because the thermoluster will burn off if you heat the bead over 1200°F. Be sure to ask for an Material Safety Data Sheet (MSDS) with it.

Another idea might be to combine different surface treatments. You could first add flameworked decorations and then apply lusters, iridizing or mirroring. It might also be interesting to paint multi-colored luster patterns like on those small Murano bottles and vases, and then mirror the inside.

One thing that you might want to consider trying when making hollow blown beads is to fill them. Shari Hopper uses this idea with some of her blown beads. You can fill them with many different things, for instance dried foods. You could make a dried bean necklace and fill each bead with a different type of dried bean. You can also make a grain necklace and put in things like rice, wheat, oats, etc. How about flowers that you then let dry inside the bead. Small figurines might also be an interesting idea. Or how would a ship inside a bead sound.

Doni Hatz makes lampworked borosilicate flowers

Figure 275. Spraying thermoluster onto a hot bead.

that she puts in her beads, like the one in Figure 276. Sharon Peters is using hollow beads to form the globes of space helmets for some of her alien beads.

I am sure that with a little imagination you will be able to come up a lot of ideas of things to put inside of your beads—some practical and some not so practical. How about real aquarium beads! Could you imagine the looks that you would get if you had real fish swimming around inside of a bead. You would want some kind of small fish that likes to be alone like Siamese fighting fish and of course you would have to be real careful when bending over or the fish could flop out.

Figure 276. Blown bead around flameworked flowers.
Artist: Doni Hatz
Size: 1½" Diameter x 2" High
Photo by: Trevor Hart

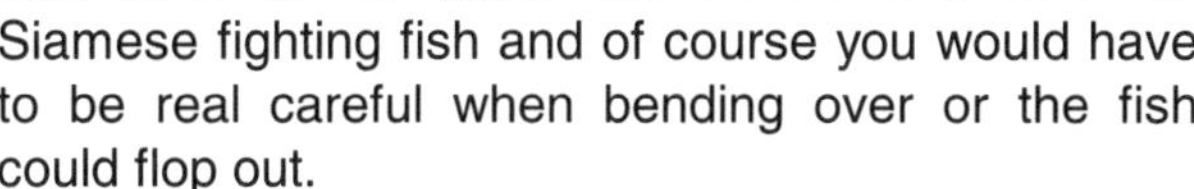

Play with this idea and let your mind run wild. There are lots of things that would work. How about an ant farm bead or a terrarium bead? You could even grow bonsai trees in your beads. How about tiny stuffed animals? The possibilities are endless.

Another idea might be memory necklaces with treasured keepsakes in them from loved ones.

Of course, you are wondering how to get all those different things into a bead, as. I did the first time I saw this technique used. The trick is to put them into the bead while it is still a tube, after pulling the first point but before pulling the second point, you still have a relatively large opening. If the object is large, you may have to inflate the tubing and cut the inflated section in half to have a big enough opening. Then after inserting the object into the inflated section, you join them back together. Once you have an object in the tubing, gather the bead in some on the end and pull it to a point. Try to work a lot cooler than usual if you put something really delicate or flammable in your bead.

Suggested further reading

Carberry, Edward. **Glassblowing, An Introduction to Artistic and Scientific Flameworking**, Second Edition, MGLS Publishing 1994

Gruenig, David. "***Silvering Glass***" **The Independent Glassblower** Issue # 26 (June/July/August) 1992

Hasluck, Paul N. **Traditional Glassworking Techniques**, The Corning Museum of Glass, 1988

Hoyt, Homer L. **Glassblowing An Introduction to Solid and Blown Glass Sculpturing**, Crafts & Arts Publishing Co. Inc., 1989

Lunstrom, Boyce. "***Iridizing Pyrex Glass At The*** *Bench*" **Glass Line** Vol. 4 No. 5 (February/March) 1991

Remschneider, Douglas J., ***Blown Beads***, video by Remschneider Glass 2001

Schneider, Don. "***Lampworked Beads***" **Glass Studio** No 35 (repeated and updated in **Glass Line** Vol. 7 No. 4 December/January 1994)

Wilson, Lewis, ***Sculptural Glassworking***, video by Crystal Myths™, Inc

Drawn beads

Drawn beads, like those seen in Figure 277, are made from a gather on the end of a blowpipe. The gather is blown into a small bubble, which is decorated with layers and stripes of color. The bubble is then blown out, an assistant attaches a punty to its end, and it is drawn out into tubing. After cooling down, the tube is cut into short sections and the ends are smoothed out to form the finished bead. Let's examine the draw bead process in greater detail.

Figure 277. Assorted drawn beads.

Preparation

Manufacture of drawn beads is not really practical by lampworking on a torch. If you try doing it this way, you will be doing it on a very small scale or you will need a much larger torch than a minor bench burner.

There are a number of different levels to which you can make drawn beads, depending upon the type of equipment you have available. Ideally, you would have a complete hot glass studio with a multiple crucible furnace, a good-sized glory hole, marver, hot bench, and tools. But it is possible to work with combinations of equipment less extensive than this. I will present what can be done with a number of different equipment inventories.

To make drawn beads, you need at least two new tools in addition to those we have already discussed: a blowpipe and a punty. Like the mandrels used for making wound glass beads, you want your blowpipe and punty, or at least the tip of them, to be made from stainless steel. As you may remember, the reason for this is that stainless steel is a poor conductor of heat. This allows you to use a relatively short piece of pipe or rod, which is glowing cherry red on one end but is cool enough to handle on the other end.

The size of the blowpipe and punty that you use depends upon the size of the flame and the equipment that you are working with. An artist with a complete hot shop will use blowpipes that are about 4' long and ¾" in diameter. His punties will be 4' long and about $^{3}/_{8}$" in diameter.

If you were working on a minor bench burner, your tools will be a lot smaller, say on the order of a quarter-inch diameter blowpipe and one-eighth-inch diameter rod for your punty. Ed Hoy's carries a cute little blowpipe that can be used for this purpose or you can use small diameter stainless steel tubing. This tubing is sold for winding beads with larger holes. The small blowpipe can be seen in the bottom of Figure 278. If you want, you can also use

Figure 278. Small blowpipes and punty.

pyrex tubing for your blowpipe when working at a torch. Just be sure that you remove all the pyrex from the bead before you are done or you will get cracking from compatibility mismatch.

If you have a small glory hole, you can work with equipment sized somewhere between the two that we have already discussed, a blowpipe of about a half-inch diameter and a punty about one quarter inch in diameter which are also seen in Figure 278. Tools of this size are available from a number of glassblowing suppliers.

Always work with the largest diameter tubing or blowpipe possible because this requires more air be blown into the tube to pressurize and shape the bubble. This increase in air gives you greater control and feel when blowing out the bubble.

The other very important thing to have if you are getting into larger equipment is more protective eyewear than that needed for lampworking. The IR irradiance received from a glory hole can range anywhere from about 30 to 100 mW/cm^2 depending upon how far your eyes are from the heat. This is much greater than anything you receive while lampworking and is considerably greater than the 10-mW/cm^2 threshold limit value that is recommended for an 8 hour/day worker. If you are going to be working with this equipment, you should be wearing at least a #3 or #4 welder's shade and AUR 186 glasses.

Forming the bubble

As stated earlier, the method that you use for this work will depend upon what type of equipment you have available.

If you have a complete hot glass studio, you would gather on your blowpipe directly from a crucible of molten glass in your furnace and go from there. With the recent appearance of **small crucible kilns** on the market this kind of work is also feasible in small studios.

If you have this kind of equipment, start by preparing the glass melt in your crucible kiln or glass furnace as was described in the chapter on kilns. Heat up the end of your blowpipe to a dull red in a glory hole. If the blowpipe is not warm enough, the glass may not stick or might chill so quickly over the end that you will not be able to get a bubble started. Now make a gather by propping the blowpipe on the edge of the crucible kiln with the hot end sticking out over the crucible. Tip the pipe so that the last ¾" just touches the surface of the glass in the crucible and roll the pipe in position to gather the glass. It helps to roll the pipe into the edge of a corner so that the blowpipe does not roll around and get out of control.

Usually, only one or two full rotations will be necessary to get a good gather. The faster you rotate the blowpipe, the larger the gather will be. The size of gather you use depends upon how large a central clear core you want in your bead. When you have as much glass as you want on the blowpipe, tilt the end up out of the crucible while continuing to rotate. This will roll up any stringers of glass clinging to the gather, so that you will not trail them out onto your equipment as you leave the crucible kiln. Hot glass is really corrosive to firebrick and will shorten the life of your kiln.

Figure 279. Gathering glass from a crucible kiln.
Courtesy of Sundance Glass

If your crucible kiln does not have a good lip to roll on or a corner to roll into, there is always the straight dip option as shown in Figure 279. Here you hold the blowpipe vertically and dip the business end straight down into the crucible for about an inch. Then pull the blowpipe out and turn it horizontally over the opening of the crucible, switching to a two-handed grip with your forward hand under the blowpipe and your rear hand above it. Keep the gather centered over the crucible because it will be trailing off stringers of glass. Rotate the pipe to bring the stringers under control.

As you know by now, this gather will be soft and will want to run off the end of your blowpipe. You will have to keep rotating the blowpipe just as you rotate a bead on a mandrel to keep it from drooping off.

Close the furnace or crucible kiln while keeping the pipe rotating and let the gather skin over slightly. Then quickly move over to your marver. Roll the gather on the marver to further chill the outer skin of the gather and to shape it. What you are trying to achieve is sort of a cylinder or teardrop shape on the end of the blowpipe, with about two thirds of the gather off the end of the pipe. Roll the gather on the marver by cradling the back end of the blowpipe in your back hand and applying light pressure on the blowpipe with your forward hand. Roll from one edge of the marver to the other to form a nice symmetric shape. If your gather folds as you are doing this, then you are working it too hard and too soft. Allow it to skin over a little more before moving to the marver. Not too much though or it will be too hard to work. It is always best to work the gather as hot as you feel comfortable controlling it. Being right handed, I turn my left side slightly to the marver or your right side if you are left handed, as the artist in Figure 280.

Figure 280. Working a large gather at the marver.

Control the shape of the gather by tilting the blowpipe as you roll it on the marver. Start by tilting the cool end down to taper the gather away from the blowpipe and push the glass off the end of the blowpipe. It may help to move the glass outward by pulling gently on the blowpipe during this step. You may also use the far edge of the marver to help pull more of the gather out onto the end of the blowpipe. Then shift the blowpipe so that it is parallel to the floor to make the bulk of the gather into a cylinder. Lastly tilt the cool end of the blowpipe up to marver a bullet-like shape on the end of the gather.

Don't take too long in shaping the gather or your glass will be too cool to introduce a bubble down the center. If this happens, you will have to reheat the gather in the glory hole and lightly chill the surface again to form a skin before you can start blowing the bubble.

Introduce the small bubble into the gather by blowing into the pipe and capping it with your thumb while still under pressure. If you just keep on blowing or if the outer skin of your gather is not properly chilled, your bubble will get too big and go out of control. You just want a small bubble on the pipe at this point, as seen in Figure 281. Too large a bubble in the initial gather will result in a thin skin around the bubble. The thin skin will be unstable when you reheat it for decoration or further blowing.

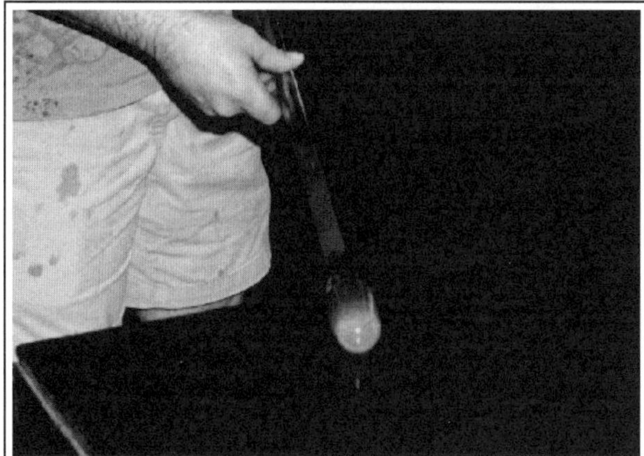

Figure 281. A small starter bubble in a gather.

If you want to maximize the amount of the bubble that you can draw out into beadstock, you may want to further neck down its connection to the blowpipe. This is done by moving to a hot glass bench — a bench with two slightly downward sloping arms of something like angle iron that are above the height of your lap and extend well out in front of the bench. The arms will have pins on the end to prevent the blowpipe from accidentally rolling off the front end. There will also usually be a table on one end or the other to hold your tools. Which side will depend upon whether you are right handed or left handed.

Sit down at the table end of the bench while continuing to rotate the blowpipe. Once seated, continue to rotate the pipe by rolling it back and forth on the arms of the bench using your non-dominant hand (your left if right handed) and pick up a set of jacks in the other. Jacks are tweezers-like tools that have smooth, often rounded, inside working edges.

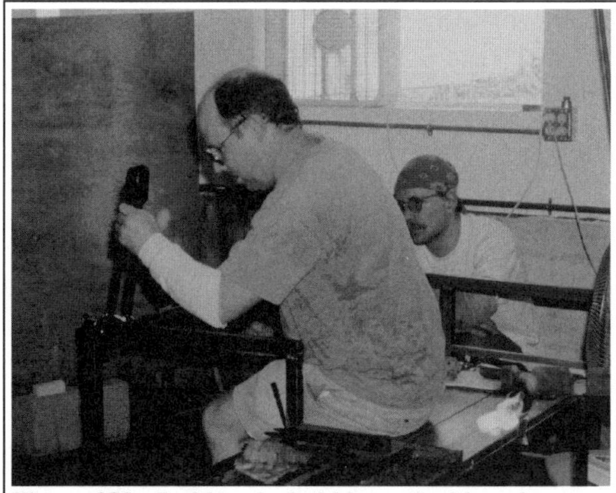

Figure 282. Jacking the bubble on the blowpipe.

They are used like reamers to shape the glass. Gently squeeze in on the glass with the jacks just beyond the end of the blowpipe while at the same time rotating the pipe, as seen in Figure 282. Go lightly at first to get a ring all the way around the bubble and then harder as the glass chills.

For a smaller studio without a furnace or crucible kiln, a couple of other bubble forming techniques can be used. First, **if you only have a glory hole** or have made a fire bucket with your torch, you can cut strips of compatible sheet glass and wrap them around the end of a smaller blowpipe to form the bubble sort of as if you were making wound beads and the blowpipe was your mandrel. Obviously you will be working out at the end of your blowpipe and will be wrapping most of the glass strip out past the end.

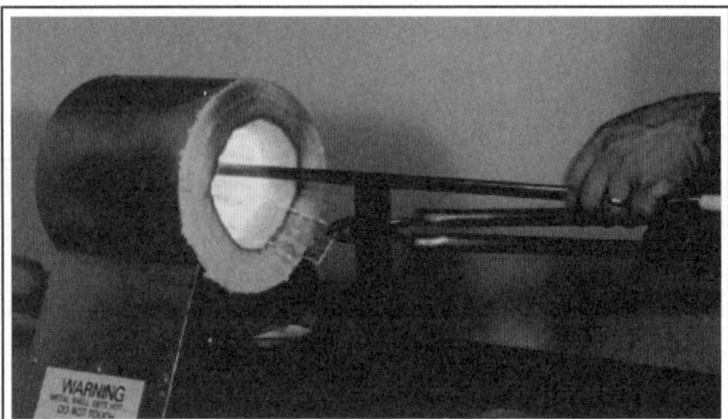

Figure 283. Sneaking sheet glass into the glory hole.

To use this technique, it helps to have an assistant, and you will probably also want one when you start drawing out the tube. The assistant's job is, as shown in Figure 283, to heat up the sheet glass for blowing by slowly sneaking it into the glory hole. This is done using long handled (one to two feet) pliers so that you do not burn your fingers. These pliers can be made by crimping a section of pipe over the handles of ordinary pliers.

The sheet glass is heated up in stages. Start by holding it off to the side, outside the mouth of the glory hole. Then slowly sneak it into the flame as it heats up. Try to look for changes in color or rounding of the edges to use as indicators of how fast to feed the glass into the flame. Be careful not to introduce it too quickly or pieces will break off and fall onto your glory hole liner. Hot glass is very corrosive to ceramic fiber liners and can eat their way though them if allowed to.

Once the sheet glass starts drooping, pull it out and wrap this hot section around the end of your blowpipe, which has been kept warm by moving it in and out of the glory hole as necessary. Stick the glass onto the blowpipe as shown in Figure 284 so that a third of it is on your blowpipe and two-thirds hangs out into space beyond the end of the pipe. The glass will wrap only part way around the blowpipe at this point because a lot of it is still hard.

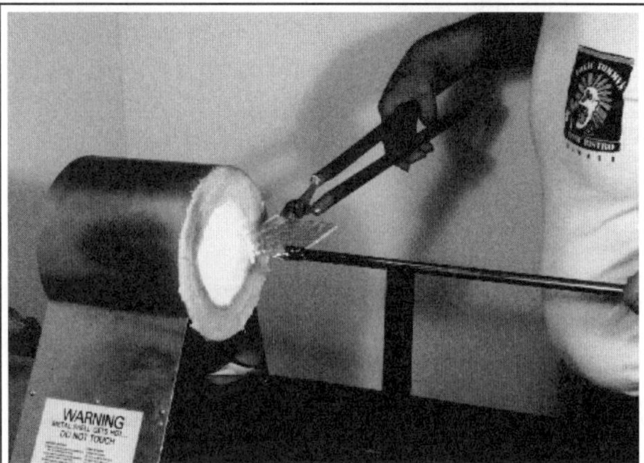

Figure 284. Wrapping sheet glass onto a blowpipe.

To complete the wrap, stick the blowpipe back into the mouth of the glory hole such that the transition of the region of the wrapped section to the flat section is up and the flat is parallel to the floor. Allow the heat of the glory hole and the force of gravity to help pull the unattached glass down and complete the wrap. Use the marver as needed to help close the wrap and complete the "gather".

A bubble will be started naturally as the glass out past the end of the pipe folds over and closes off the end of the cylinder. If it starts to collapse, you can blow it out slightly to inflate it. Shape the gather on your marver to make the bubble more symmetric. Add more glass if necessary to make a good-sized bubble.

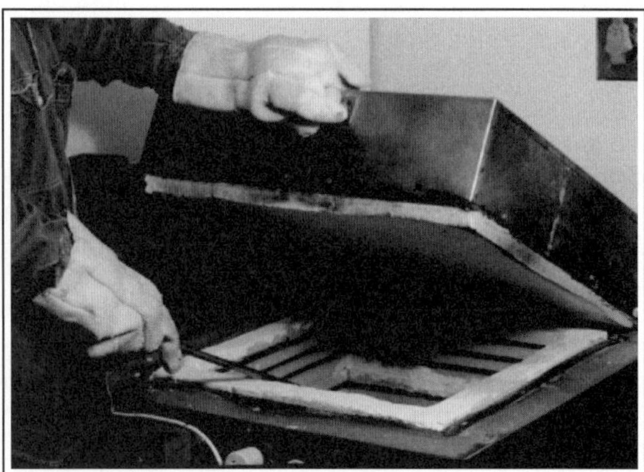
Figure 285. Gathering glass from a kiln.

If you have a kiln and a glory hole, you may choose instead to pick up glass sheet or rods out of the kiln. Bring them to a temperature where the glass starts to become soft and pliable, about 1100°F, but not so hot that you pick up kiln wash on the glass. You can prevent pickup of kiln wash by laying down a sheet of prefired ceramic fiber paper on top of the shelf. Get the end of your blowpipe red hot and roll it over the glass to gather it onto the pipe as shown in Figure 285. If you have the luxury of an assistant to act as kiln jockey, hold the pipe as was described for marvering when picking up the glass otherwise just use one hand as seen in the figure.

In your initial attempts, you will want to use a single color of glass so that if it does not wrap perfectly around the pipe you will have not messed up any pattern you are trying to achieve. As you get practice wrapping hot sheet glass around your blowpipe, you will come to realize exactly how much glass to lay out in the kiln so that it will wrap completely around the pipe. For the first wrap the length should be about 3¼ times the blowpipe outer diameter or slightly more, depending on the thickness of the glass.

The width of the sheet glass you lay up for the first wrap is controlled by the size of the bubble you want and can handle. About 3" is a good place to start—one inch on the pipe and two inches off the end. As you get better, you might want to consider laying out patterns of glass on the kiln shelf that will then be contained in the final beads.

The dimensions of pieces for subsequent wraps will increase in both length and width. For each additional wrap of glass you have to make the length of the piece about 6½ x (the glass thickness) longer or about 1½" longer than the previous one. The width of subsequent wraps increases by twice the thickness of the glass or about ½" wider than each previous one.

For those of you working with only a torch and glass rods, take a few wraps around the end of a miniature pipe for attachment. Then wrap more and more glass onto this to form a nice attachment point. As you get enough on the blowpipe, start building it up off the end of the blowpipe like one half of a hollow wound bead, as discussed in the wound bead chapter and shown in Figure 287. Next roll over

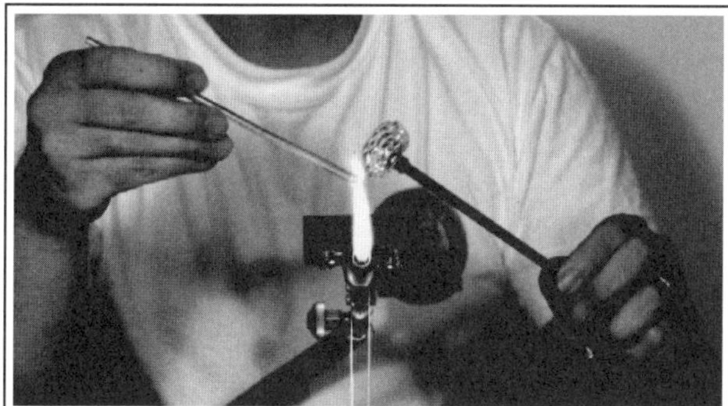

Figure 287. Wrapping glass onto a small blowpipe.

the free edge of the wound glass to build up a "gather" hanging on the end of the pipe. By keeping the gather cooler, you will be able to wind on more and more glass until it reaches the desired shape. If you work the gather too hot, it may get out of control.

Blow into the pipe to introduce a small air bubble into the center of the glass, and then continue to wrap on more glass, making sure that you do not let your bubble collapse. This is prevented by working a bubble a little cooler. As you add glass to the bubble, you want to keep it pear shaped with most of the glass off the end of the blowpipe. This is because only the glass off the end of the pipe can be drawn out into tubing.

Decorating the bubble

Once you have a fairly thick, good-sized starting bubble by whatever method you use, you can decorate it however you want. You can add a layer of color over the whole surface or in discrete locations. You can pick up decorations on the outside of your bubble. You can shape it into a cross section other than round, as those in Figure 286. You can also distort the surface to change any pattern you may have developed in the bubble's cross-section. Let's look at each of these ideas in turn and see how they might be accomplished.

Figure 286. Drawn beads from non-spherical bubble. Artist: Lark Dalton Size: ½" W x ½" L

Adding a layer of color

The easiest way to add color to the outside of the entire surface of a bubble is by **using a second crucible with molten glass** of a different color in which to dip the slightly chilled bubble. You would gather glass from this crucible over the bubble just as you did from the first. Here you dip the blowpipe so that the new glass layer just comes up to the end of the blowpipe, since anything left on the end of the pipe afterwards is wasted. Usually the second gather of colored glass is made thinner than the first, so you only want to make a single rotation and go a little slower as you make this second gather. Then chill and shape the gather either on the marver or with a hardwood block at the bench.

Another easy way to add a layer of color is to reheat just the outer surface of the bubble and **rolling it in frit or enamels**, as shown in Figure 288. If you reheat more than the outer surface, the bubble will be hard to manage and will want to flop around. If you also heat the surface on which you lay out the frit, the frit will be easier to pick up. A metal marver on a hot plate works well for this purpose. After picking up frit, roll the bubble on a marver to work the frit into the surface of the bubble.

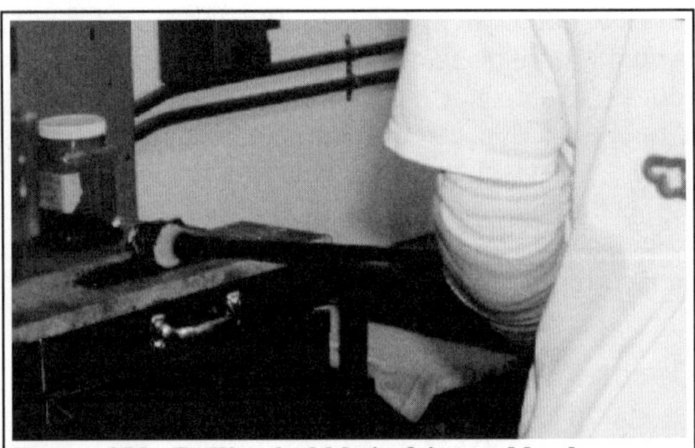

Figure 288. Rolling bubble in frit to add color.

Before putting the bubble back into the glory hole, tap the blowpipe near the bubble on a hard object like the edge of your marver. This will help to dislodge any loose frit that might fall off the gather when exposed to the heat of the glory hole. Reheat the outer surface of your bubble to smooth it out and if desired pick up more frit on its surface. You will get a more uniform color layer by picking up a multiple layers of frit, especially if the frit is a fine one. You might also use a coarse incomplete color layer as a design element, which will stretch out to form striations in color on your bead. Stop occasionally to smooth out the surface of the bubble on the marver and check to see how uniform the color coating is. This will also suck some of the heat out of the bubble, so when you stick it back into the glory hole the core will not get too hot.

Another way to get a uniform layer of color on the outside of a bubble is to **pick up colored sheet glass out of the kiln**. Ideally, the piece will be long enough to wrap all the way around the bubble so that you do not get a gap in the color. Gaps or overlaps in color can be worked out to some extent on the marver. The piece of glass could be a fused sheet of glass of multiple colors, but don't count on keeping too much of the image in the final beads, because the bubble stretches as you draw it out. Usually linear or long striped line patterns applied down the length of the glass works best. They get stretched finer and finer as you draw the glass bubble out into beadstock, making them look even better.

Of course, you don't have to pick up the sheet glass out of a kiln. You can have an assistant apply sheet glass **using a glory hole** and apply it to the bubble, as was described earlier for starting a bubble that way. The trick here is in not letting the bubble get so hot that it flops around. Prevent that by frequently going to the marver and chilling the bubble but not the sheet glass that is not yet conforming to it. With patience you will get the sheet glass to wrap all the way around the bubble. One benefit of this technique over picking glass up from the kiln is that if you do not get the piece to go all the way around the bubble it is easier to add more glass to discrete locations, as shown in Figure 289. In fact it might be a lot easier to apply the coating as a number of small pieces rather than one big one.

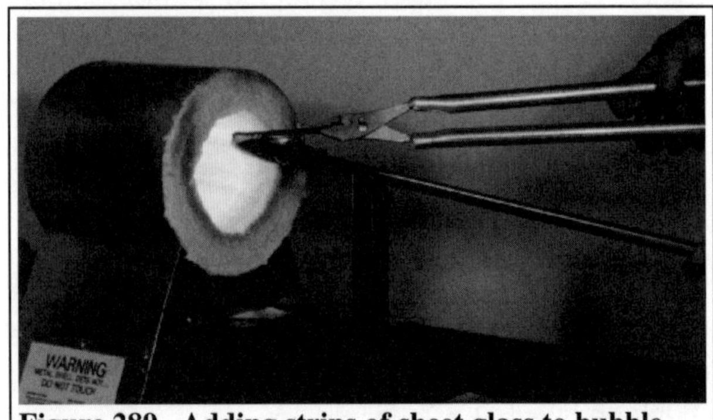

Figure 289. Adding strips of sheet glass to bubble.

If you are **working at the torch**, you can just paint on the color as we did when casing rods. Lay a stripe down the length and paddle it smooth. Ensure that you keep the whole bubble as well as the joint to the blowpipe warm, so that it does not thermal shock. But again, keep from getting the bubble so hot that it ends up flopping around. Keep laying the color on stripe by stripe until you get a nice even coating.

When adding layers of colored glass, you may want to **vary the thickness of added colored glass** around the bubble. When doing this you have a couple of options open to you. You could add the glass directly with varying thickness or you can add it uniformly to your bubble and then distort it.

Figure 290. Pushing grooves into bubble with an optic mold. Photo courtesy of Heron Glass.

There are a number of ways to distort the bubble. The first would be to rake it as you did for wound beads, but here the idea is to leave creases running down the length of the bubble. This can be hard to control, both in the depth of the creases and in how uniformly spaced they are around the bubble. It is probably a lot simpler to just press into the side of the bubble in a number of places with a sharp object like a knife. By just locally heating these areas, you will be able to introduce some sharp creases.

A second choice is to use a marver with a series of parallel grooves cut into it to put in the creases. Rolling the bubble on this marver will result in uniform grooves, but the problem with this technique is that if you do it on successive layers, you will find that the ridges will not line up from one layer to the next. First, because it is hard to line up the starting point from one layer to the next. Second, because the angle subtended by a constant-length circular arc gets smaller as the radius or size of the bubble gets larger.

To form distortions of constant angular orientation, optic molds are usually used. Optic molds, as explained earlier, are conical molds with interior variations of a given shape. The shape is constant but of decreasing size as you go deeper into the mold, which prevents undercuts that could trap the glass in the mold. Common cross-sectional shapes include triangles, squares and multi-pointed stars. The ones being manufactured for lampworkers by Steiner are too small for the purpose of distorting large bubbles.

A simple optic mold for shop use can be constructed as was illustrated in the chapter on mosaic cane, by drawing equal angled arcs on the top of a piece of wood. Finishing nails are then driven into the block of wood at the marked locations. The nails should be driven in a slight angle leaning away from the center of the circle to avoid trapping the glass. For uniform distortion, you must try to control the angle at which you drive the nails in so it does not change. With this type of mold, you have to be careful that you do not let the glass wrap around the nails or you will not be able to remove the bubble after distorting it.

With an optic mold as shown in Figure 290, the number and angular orientation between the grooves in the glass are constant from layer to layer because they are controlled by the mold. All you have to be concerned with is aligning the bubble as you push it into the mold and how deeply you insert it. These techniques will allow you to draw the bubble out to make multi-colored chevron beads (also known as Star or Rosetta beads). Of course, you will have to backfill the distorted areas to get the cross section back to a circular one.

If you look at a lot of drawn beads, you will notice that many will have **stripes down their length**. You may want to add similar stripes to your beads. We have already discussed one way of doing this, by picking up a striped sheet of glass out of the kiln. You could also paint them on at the torch, or you could lay decorations out on your marver and pick them up by rolling the bubble across them, as shown in Figure 291. One of the graphite marvers with grooves cut into it would work well for this, but you may have the same problem of consistent alignment between layers that you had with rolling the bubble

Figure 291. Picking up canes from marver. Photo courtesy of Heron Glass.

on the marver to add creases. It is also hard to keep the spacing between the first and the last line the same as the rest. After rolling the bubble all the way around you may have overlapping stripes or gaps in the pattern that you have to adjust.

Alternately, you can pick up cane that is arranged around the inside of a bucket. This technique handles the angular spacing well but suffers from the problem that the rods can move around on you. This problem can be mitigated by putting holes in the bottom of the bucket for one end of the rod and notches at the top of the bucket for the other. After picking up these additions onto the outside of your glass, they can either be heated up and marvered into your bubble or they can be just lightly heated to retain texture. This can be done either in your glory hole or with a large torch.

Sometimes you also want your drawn beads to have **cross sectional shapes other than circular**. To achieve this, the bubble can be shaped on the marver with a paddle into a triangle, square or some other cross section. It can also be blown into or pressed into an optic mold of the desired shape. By being careful as you draw out the tube, this shape can be retained in the final bead. If you add more glass to one side than the other, you can force the hole in the bead to be off center for a different effect.

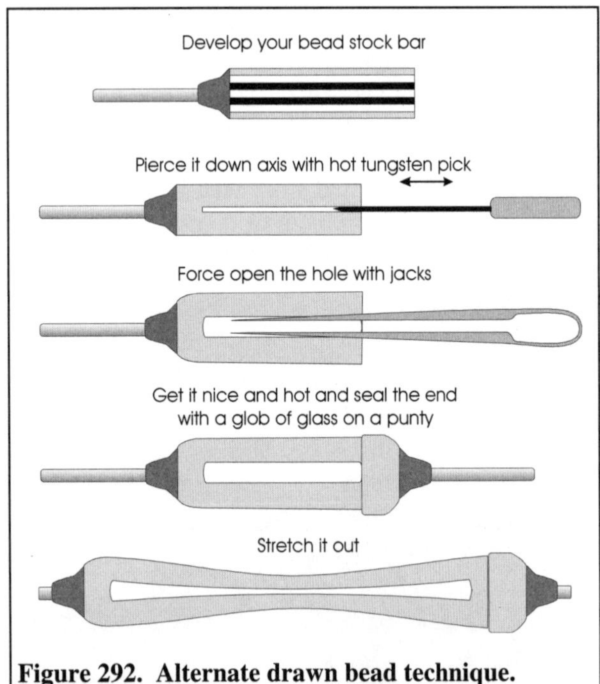

Figure 292. Alternate drawn bead technique.

An entirely different method of forming a decorated bubble, which can be drawn out into tubing, is illustrated in Figure 292. This can be used with pieces formed using the kilnforming methods that we discussed for manufacture of mosaic cane or for multiple marble manufacture. You start by making a cylinder a few inches in diameter and in length. Attach a punty on one end. Then work the cylinder in a glory hole to get it hot and poke a hole down its center with a long tungsten pick or glassblowing jacks. Smooth up the hole and enlarge it as necessary with glassblowing jacks.

Size the hole that you put into the cylinder with the knowledge that as you pull tubing out of any bubble the wall thickness to hole diameter ratio will remain approximately constant. Attach a second punty with a small gather of glass over the open hole, trapping a bubble down the center of the cylinder. Then draw out the cylinder as described in the next section. This is another good way to try to make patterned beads without using a crucible kiln.

Another variation for making the bubble while working at a torch was presented by Larry Scott in a series of articles in Lapidary Journal. These references are listed at the end of this chapter. Instead of forming a bubble on a blowpipe, he winds a tube on a borosilicate maria or flat on the end of a rod. The tube is wound as was described for a hollow mandrel wound bead. He suggests starting with a clear wrap of Effetre glass around the maria and then building up the colored tube from there.

Once he has the colored tubing wound for some distance onto the end of the maria, he smoothes it out on his marver using a graphite rod down the center, as was described for making one of Don Schneider's tube beads in the last chapter. Next he decorates the tube as desired with stripes or whatever. You could melt the decorations into the side of the tubing or keep them raised. Melt them in by reheating the tube and marvering it again using the graphite rod down the center to stabilize it. Then attach another maria at the other end to trap the air down the center of the tube. Now it is ready to be drawn out slightly to whatever diameter you want. It should be obvious that you will only get short, small diameter beads with this technique.

Blowing out the bubble

As was just discussed, your bubble needs to have fairly thick walls to have thicker beads. Also the size of the air pocket that you put into your bubble depends on how far you are going to draw it out. The further that you draw out the bubble into tubing, the larger the air pocket you will need to get the appropriate size hole down the middle for your bead. Again, the ratio of the wall to hole size is important.

To better understand this principle, let's discuss a concrete example. Let's say that you are trying to create a bead that is one half inch in diameter with a one eighth inch in diameter hole down the center. There are at least two ways to think of how you want to size your bubble. The first is by diameter ratios. The final hole-to-outside diameter ratio that you are looking for is $^{1}/_{8}$"/½" or ¼. Therefore one way to size the bubble would be to say that you want the center hole diameter to be about ¼ that of the outside diameter.

The other would be to compare the wall thickness to the air pocket diameter. Here, the finished bead wall thickness is (½"-$^{1}/_{8}$")/2 or $^{3}/_{16}$". The hole-to-wall-thickness ratio is then $^{1}/_{8}$"/$^{3}/_{16}$" or $^{2}/_{3}$. Therefore you want the air pocket diameter to be about $^{2}/_{3}$rds that of your wall thickness. Use whichever of these methods you find easier to relate to.

At this point, you also want to extend the bubble out further into the gather, rather than just blowing it up like a balloon. To prevent the bubble from blowing up uncontrollably instead of traveling down into the gather, you lightly chill the sides of the bubble on a marver or paddle. This makes the sides more viscous than the center and the air will go down the center toward the end as you blow it out. It might also help to open the end of the bubble up and adjust its size manually, as shown in Figure 294. Mary Mullaney and Ralph Mossman of Heron Glass

Figure 294. Adjusting hole in a bubble prior to draw Photo courtesy of Heron Glass.

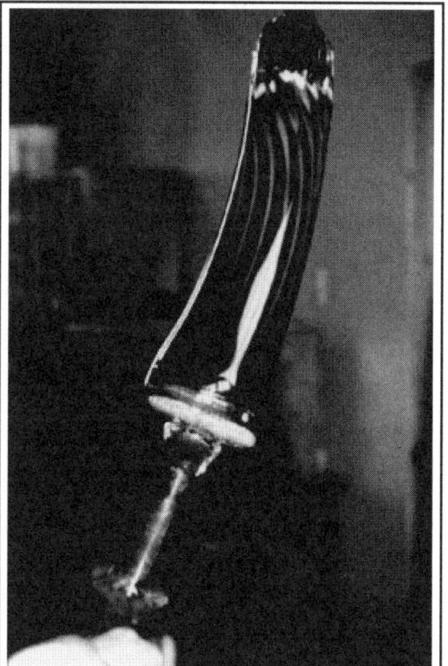

Figure 293. Attaching punty to bubble for drawing. Photo courtesy of Heron Glass.

say that this was one of the important "tricks" that they learned for making their great drawn chevron beads.

Drawing out tubing

As you prepare to draw the bubble out into a tube, there are a few things that you need to remember. The first is that you want to draw out the whole cross section of the bubble. Therefore, you will want to keep the punty attachment about the size of the full cross section of the bubble. This attachment is made by getting a small gather of glass on the end of a punty and forming it into a cone. The base of the cone is at the end of the rod and the point of the cone is pointing toward your hand. The base should just barely cover the end of the punty as seen in Figure 293. If the base gets out too far from the end of the punty, it becomes hard to control and will stretch during pulling.

Second, as in drawing out cane or points, the drawn diameter as well as thickness of the drawn beadstock is a function of the how fast you draw out the bubble into a tube and the initial temperature of the bubble. The slower you draw it out, the larger and thicker the resultant beads. If you want, you can also twist your tube as you draw it out. This will cause the decorations on the bubble surface to spiral up the length of the bead. Twisting can also create an interesting effect if your bead has a non-circular cross section. These twists will have to be fairly tight though, to appear in the length of a single bead. So twist it rapidly as you pull it out.

As in pulling out any other construction, always wait a few moments after your last reheat before you start drawing the bubble out into tubing or invariably it will end up too small in diameter. Either air cool or lightly marver it to slightly chill the outside. Then start your pull. At the end of the pull when you can draw no more from the bubble, pause for a second and hold the tube taut before putting it down.

Once you have the tubing pulled to the desired size, you have to cool it down. Depending upon how small a diameter you pulled, you will need to either immediately cut it up into manageable sections and put them into your annealer or leave it suspended off the floor on slats to air cool. I usually take the breakpoint between these two choices to be about the diameter of a pencil. Anything over the size of a pencil should be kiln annealed. For tubing smaller than this diameter, annealing is optional. But as always, long-term results are more assured if you do anneal.

Finishing the bead

After your drawn tube has cooled, you cut your beads from it. The beads can be cut by any of a number of techniques. You can use the same techniques that we have already discussed for cutting rods (scribe and break, nipping, etc.) Another method is to use any of the many commercially available diamond saws (wire, band and cut-off.) Lastly tungsten chipping hammers and anvils can be used to chip off beads. These are some of the subjects that will be discussed in the chapter on finishing beads. That chapter will also discuss mechanical grinding and polishing of the ends of your beads.

Instead of grinding and polishing, the beads could also be fire polished in the torch flame or a kiln. To fire polish beads in a torch, you have to first heat them back up in your annealer. Then, reach in with your tweezers, pull out a bead, and heat the end of the bead in the flame until the edges start to smooth out. Flip it end-for-end and do the same thing to the other end. Then, put the bead back into the annealer and cool it down slowly.

Another idea, that of fire polishing your beads in a kiln, can be a little tricky, as it requires precise temperature control. What you want to do here is to set the bead up on a coated ceramic bead rack and bring the temperature just to the point where the surface of the bead glosses over. Too hot and the bead will stretch and stick to the separator. Too cold and the edges will still be fairly sharp and will not round. Of the two techniques, I prefer the results from flame polishing.

Suggested further reading

Scott, Larry. ***"Torch-Drawn Moretti Tube Beads, Part 1"*** **Lapidary Journal** Vol. 53 No. 3 (June) 1999

Scott, Larry. ***"Torch-Drawn Moretti Tube Beads, Part 2"*** **Lapidary Journal** Vol. 53 No. 4 (July) 1999

Waggoner, Shawn. "***The Talismanic Glass Jewel Techniques of Blown and Fused Jewelry***" **Glass Art** Vol. 4 No. 4 (May/June), 1989

Waggoner, Shawn. "***The Drawn Glass Bead***" **Glass Art** Vol. 8 No. 3 (March/April), 1993

Press Molded Beads

Let me start this chapter off with the admission that I don't know a lot about press molded beads, like those seen in Figure 295. This is because I have never worked with them, nor have I observed them being made. What I do know about them comes by way of reading and some excellent lectures presented by and subsequent discussions with Shari Hopper. She has traveled to Czechoslovakia where the making of press molded beads is still a surviving cottage industry. She has since edited her film clips into a short video that you can purchase if interested. I am also indebted to Andy Magisano and George Darveaux of Gypsy Dragon Bead Company, who let me examine some of the vintage tools that they bought in Eastern Europe. A book on the subject by Waltraud Nurwirth has also become available that helps to further shed light on the subject.

Figure 295. Assortment of press molded beads.

Modern development of the press molding process came from a desire to satisfy the costume jewelry industry's need for cheap, gem-like stones with which to decorate clothing. This led to development of some simple pliers-like tools to make cabochons, shaped pieces of glass with one flat side. The flat side is made for easy attachment to a metal backing that is then sewn to the fabric. This process is easily extended to two sided jewels, which can be enclosed by a ring of metal. But, as we will see, it took some ingenuity of design to develop tooling that would put in holes for stringing these glass jewels.

Basic technique of press molded beadmaking

Basically, the process of press molding consists of heating up a glass rod to a semi molten state using a small furnace, kiln, or glory hole. The molten glass is then fed into a pliers-like press similar to that seen in Figure 296, where two jaws with dies on them are squeezed together to form the exterior shape of the bead. Because of the repetitive squeezing operation, the workers who molded the beads came to be known as squeezers. At the same time, a needle is pushed through the molten glass to form the hole in the bead. The needle can be pushed through either perpendicular to or parallel to the jewel faces. The molten glob on the rod is usually large enough to make a couple of beads before having to be reheated.

Figure 296. Press molding beads. Photo: Shari Maxson Hopper.

The beads are rough at this point and have some flashing on them. These are thin sections of glass formed by excess glass squeezing out into the area where the jaw molds of the pliers meet. The beads are fed down a funnel into a collection can where they await post processing. The can may be kept

Figure 297. Old tumbler for polishing beads.
Photo Shari Maxson Hopper

warm, but generally no real effort is made to have it hot enough to anneal the beads. In general, Shari says most East European beads are not annealed.

Post processing of press molded beads typically consists of breaking them apart at the flashing and screening the results to separate the beads from the flashing. The beads are then rough polished on a wheel to get rid of the flashing marks and to smooth them out. Afterwards, they may be further polished by tumbling them in a tumbler like that seen in Figure 297 with finer and finer size grit compounds or by fire polishing. Alternatively, rough faceted surfaces of the bead may be polished by cold working the bead as seen in Figure 299 to make polished faceted beads.

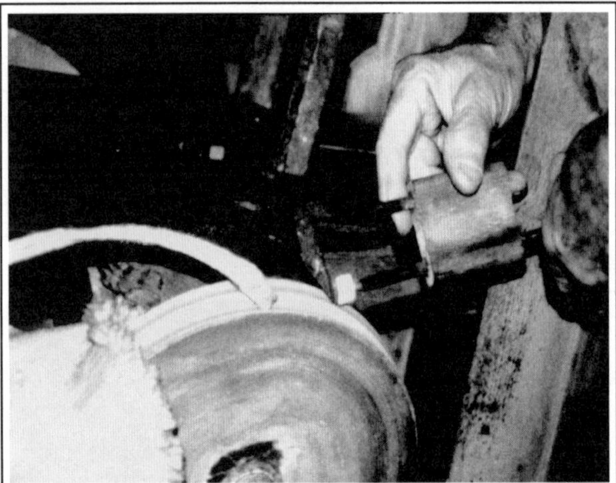

Figure 299. Polishing up a faceted bead.
Photo Shari Maxson Hopper.

Press molding equipment

As mentioned earlier, the equipment for press molding beads was derived from tools that look like a big set of pliers. They are very similar to some of the shaping or mashing pliers that you may use in beadmaking to put texture, like leaf ridges, into the glass, but press mold pliers are meant to make stand alone objects. Figure 298 illustrates what one of these devices looks like. The basic construction of the tool is from steel for strength and durability.

The patterned dies on the jaws may be fixed to the tool or they may be removable to allow for interchangeability with other dies of different patterns. Figure 300 shows a bead press with some of its interchangeable dies. To use them, you just stick a blob of glass between the dies and push down on the tool to make the jewel. Bringing the dies together shapes and chills the glass at the same time. The handles may be spring loaded to quickly open the jaws for the next jewel. This allows one-handed or one-footed (if hooked up to a pedal) operation of the tool. With this tool, you can quickly turn out jewels or cabochons. The next question is how do we put in holes to turn them into beads?

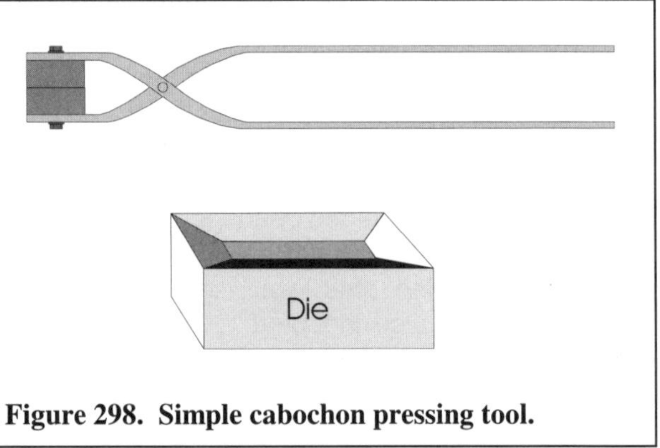

Figure 298. Simple cabochon pressing tool.

The earliest solution to this problem was probably just to turn it into a two-person operation, one person to feed the glass and squeeze the mold, and the other to pierce the bead with a needle to form the hole. This required a considerable amount of practice for the piercer to be able to judge when the glass was at just the right temperature for the piercing operation. To help the piercer to hit the right spot on the bead, there was usually a feature in the mold like a funnel to guide the needle into position.

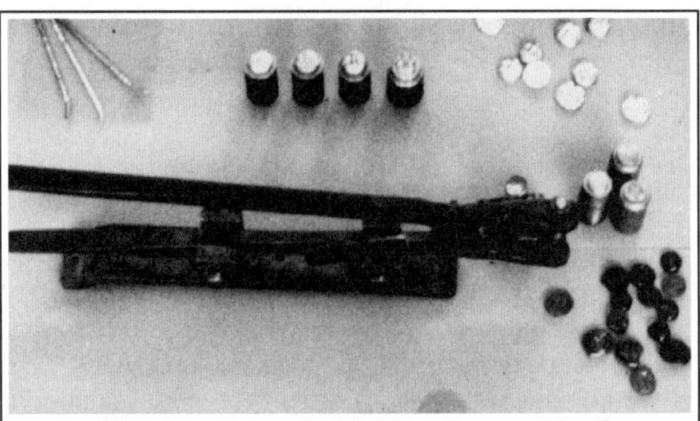

Figure 300. Bead press with interchangeable dies.
Photo Shari Maxson Hopper

This type of operation took a lot of coordination and limited how many beads could be squeezed out in a day. Thus, it was not long before some smart individuals developed ways to mechanize the piercing operation so that it became one with the press molding. In retrospect, there are many ways to achieve this objective, as seen by the many illustrations of piercing press molds in Neuwirth's book. I will explain how this can be done based upon the operation of the two mechanisms that I was lucky enough to examine.

The easier to understand of the two examples that I will present is the case where you want a hole pierced into a bead parallel to the face of the jaws of the die. Before I explain how this tool works, let's discuss some of the requirements that it must have. It must first establish the rough shape of the jewel. Second, the relative fragility of the needle that puts the hole in the bead requires that it plunge straight in and out to prevent it from becoming jammed in the hole or bent. In addition this must happen at just the right moment in the chilling process to prevent trapping the needle. This is what the device illustrated in Figure 301 does.

In this tool, linkage *a,* which consists of the bottom handle and the top die is held stationary. First of all, you can see from our previous discussion how the basic shape of the bead is established by pressing the jaw dies together. Here tension of the spring on top of the tool initially restricts any downward motion of the end of the top handle (linkage *c*). This causes closure of the dies by clockwise rotation of linkage *b* about pivot point #1 to occur first.

Then after the dies have closed, further motion about pivot point #1 is no longer possible. This means all further downward motion of the top handle has to results in motion of the T shaped linkage *c* about pivot point #2. This motion pushes linkage *d* forward on the guide rod through motion of pivot point #3 on the bottom of linkage c. (Note that linkage d is not attached at pivot #1.) Since the pin block is restrained by the guide rod to move parallel to the face of the bottom die, the pin moves straight into and out of the bead. The pin is forced through a slot in the face of the bottom die and the glob of rapidly chilling molten glass forming the hole.

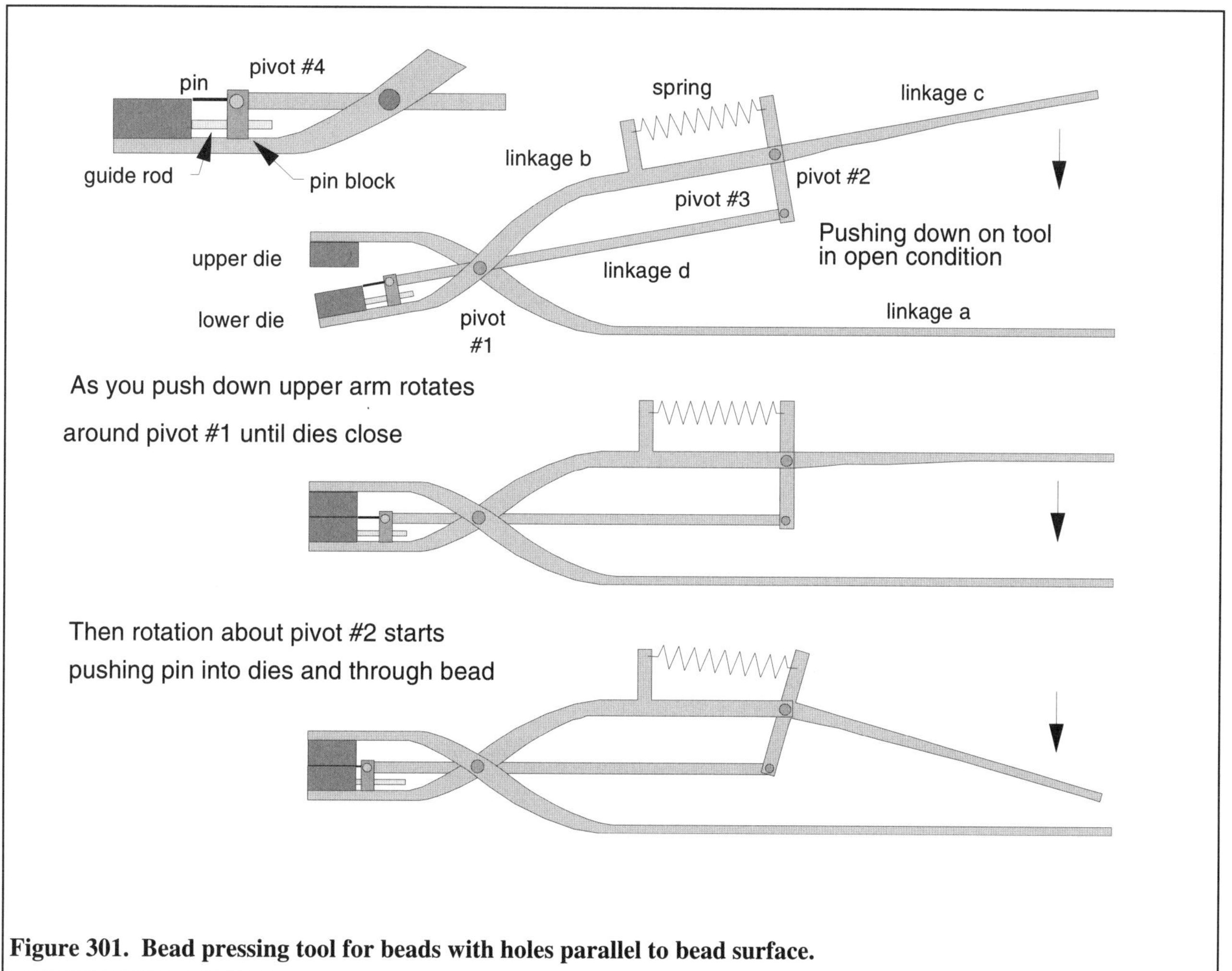

Figure 301. Bead pressing tool for beads with holes parallel to bead surface.

As pressure on the upper handle is released, the spring pulling on the top of linkage *c* first causes the pin to be withdrawn from the bead through counterclockwise motion of linkage *c* and resultant pulling on linkage *d*. As more pressure is released the weight of the lower jaw causes the dies to come apart exposing the finished bead. Then the feed rod is pushed further into the jaw, pushing out the finished bead and supplying more molten glass for the next cycle. The cycle can be accomplished a few times before the feed rod has to be reheated.

Hopefully now that you understand the operation of the first press mold beadmaking tool, it will make the next one easier to understand. This one makes holes in the bead perpendicular to the face plane of the dies. It is illustrated in Figure 302. As before, linkage *a* is fixed to a base. In this tool as you press down on the handle of linkage *b* both the dies are pressed together and the pin gets pushed through the dies simultaneously.

The dies close as before by clockwise rotation of linkage *b* about pivot point #1. At the same time, this causes sliding pivot point #2 to push down upon linkage *c*. This in turn causes rotation of linkage *c* about pivot point #3 and drives sliding pivot point #4 downward, which results in pushing the pin block along the guide rod. This sliding pushes the pin through a hole in the top die, the rapidly cooling molten glass, and another hole in the bottom die. Pulling up on the handle on linkage b causes the pin to withdraw and the dies to open for more glass to be fed in. This final release could be made easier by adding a compression spring between linkages *a* and *b* to the right of pivot point #3. This spring would help force the linkages apart on the return stroke.

Linkage *c* and the sliding pin block are slotted at sliding pivot points #2 and #4 respectively, because the pivot point pins move relative to each of these components. Sliding pivot point #2 moves backward

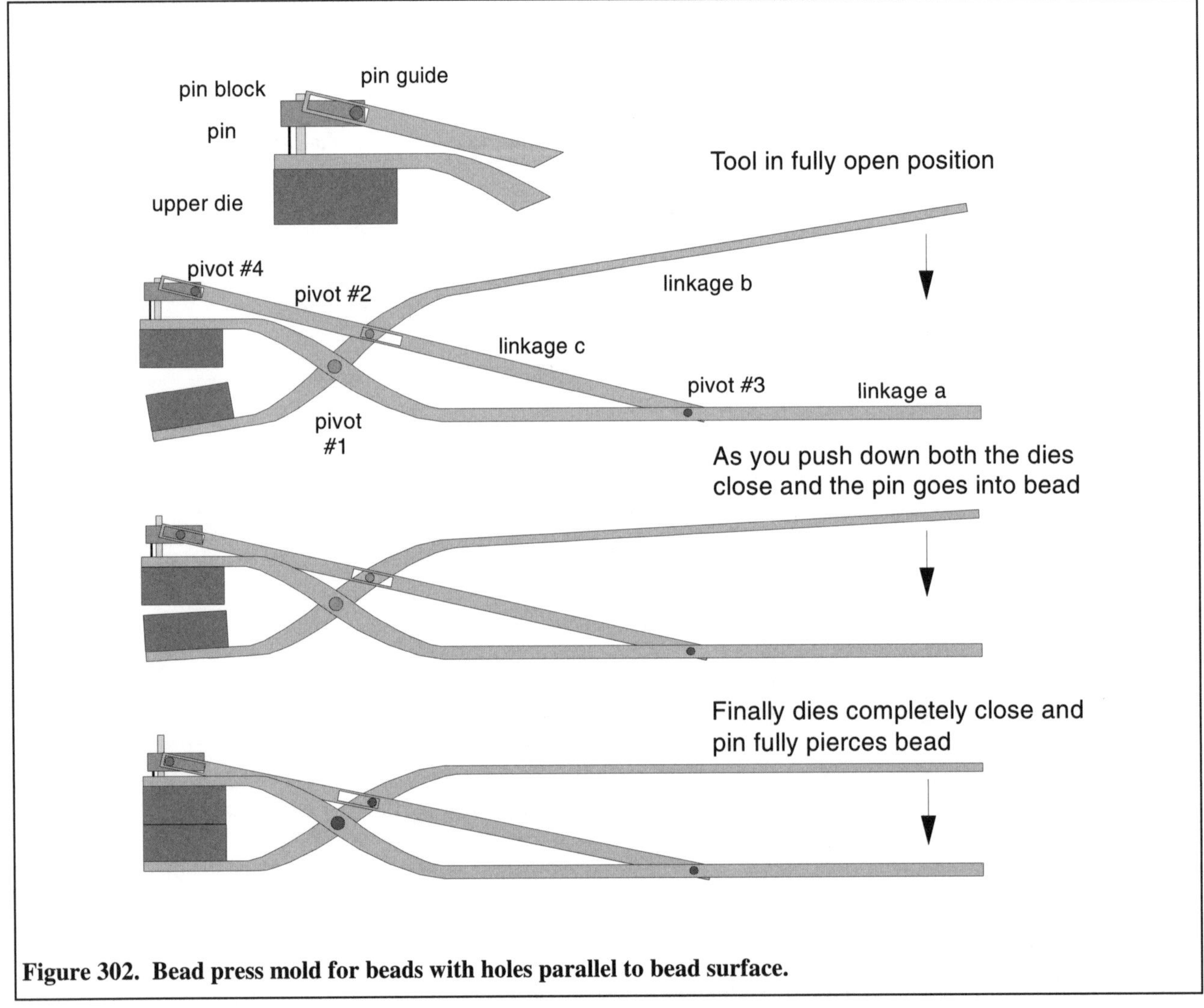

Figure 302. Bead press mold for beads with holes parallel to bead surface.

toward the handle end of the slot as the jaws close, while sliding pivot point #4 moves towards the end of the jaws as they close.

I hope that you were able to follow the explanations on how both of these tools work because they are really quite interesting. As I mentioned before, there are many variations in tooling designs to accomplish each of these themes, each with its own geometry and linkage organization. Some of these themes have also been mechanized to turn out many beads a second. With this explanation of how the tooling works and a little engineering know how, it would be possible for you, if you really wanted to, to build one of these tools on your own.

To separate the beads apart from the flashing, little rollers like those seen in Figure 303 were used to apart the flashing between the beads.

Figure 303. Hand-powered tool to break beads apart.
Photo Shari Maxson Hopper.

Decorating pressed and pierced beads

As you can probably guess after reading the explanation of how these tools work, there is not a lot that you can do to decorate beads that are made this way. Once they are done, they are done. There is not much that you can do in hot working these beads. About the only thing that you can do would be to color them with something like enamels, paints or lusters. You can also change the shape of the beads by changing the dies on the jaws. Of course, this is not something that you will be able to do on the fly because the dies, besides having to be rugged and made out steel, they also have to be rigidly attached to the linkages. You would have to go to a machine shop to get new dies made. Figure 304 shows some of the many die mold patterns available for press mold beadmakers in Gablonz.

The other thing that you can do to introduce variations into press molded beads is to play with the glass that you feed into the tool. Shari tells me that the glass used for this purpose often has variations in color that go through it much like those in commercially available stained glass. These color variations act as accents within the bead.

You could also mix or layer glass colors before or as you feed it into the tool. Shari points out that as there is no real mixing of the glass in the pressing operation, the beads that you get from the molds will have whatever accents and striations that were in the feedstock. This is further assisted by the fact that the glass doesn't have to be as hot to press a bead as in winding one. This means that colors and patterns in the feedstock will not diffuse as much and complex patterns could possibly be fed into it. Because of the rapid chilling, some chill marks are often put into the bead that could serve as decorative accents.

Another possibility for decorating these beads is that they could be cold worked. They can be carved, polished, plated, etc. By making beads of multiple colored layers they could be carved to have cameo like images. I am sure that if you think about it, you could come up with more ideas on how to decorate pressed and pierced beads.

Figure 304. Some of the many die patterns used to make press mold dies.
Photo Shari Maxson Hopper.

Suggested further reading

Neuwrith, Waltraud, **Beads from Gablonz**, Printed by Druckhaus Graal, Bad Vöslau, Vienna Austria, 1994

Hopper, Shari Maxson, **Bohemian Beadmaking,** 2000

Fused Beads

Fusing is a kilnworking process where layers or pieces of glass are heated up together in a kiln to high enough temperatures that their surfaces become soft and flow together to form permanent fused pieces. The degree to which the glass layers fuse together depends upon the temperature to which they are taken. Examples of the extent of flow for the typical degrees of fusing (tack, full and flat) are illustrated in Figure 305. They include:

- **Tack fusing** occurs when the glass is heated only to the lower end of the fusing range. Here the glass layers will stick together but there will be very little change in the shape of the layers. The glass edges will be just slightly rounded.
- **Full fusing** occurs when the glass is heated to a slightly higher temperature. Here the glass layers will start to sink into each other. The edges will become a lot softer and start to flow from one piece to the other in smooth transitions.
- **Flat fusing** occurs by heating to a higher temperature still. Here the layers collapse down into one another to form one flat fused mass of uniform thickness.

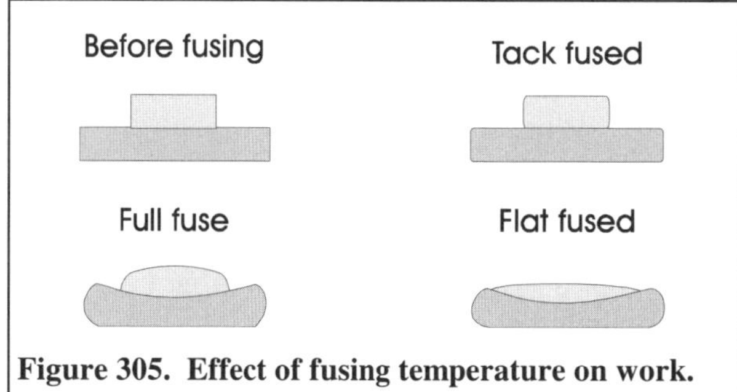

Figure 305. Effect of fusing temperature on work.

I find that the different temperatures for these fusing regimes are for most soda-lime glasses about 100°F apart. Bullseye glass, for example, tack fuses at about 1350°F, full fuses at about 1450°F, and flat fuses at about 1550° F. These temperatures will be slightly different for glasses from other manufacturers depending upon their formulation. The glasses that flow at higher temperatures are said to be harder while the ones that flow at lower temperatures are said to be softer.

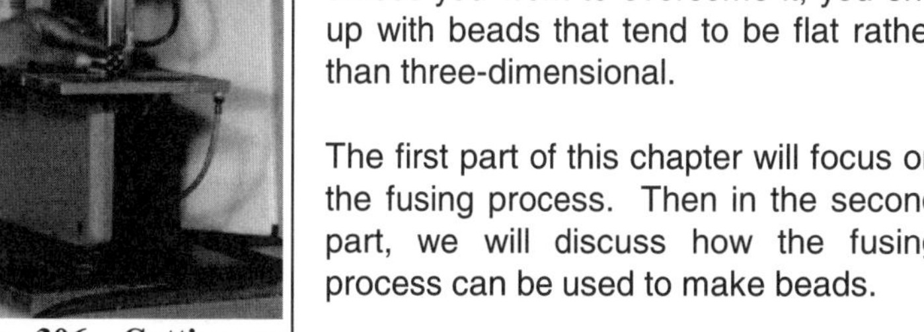
Figure 306. Cutting up fused beadstock.

You will also find that the flow temperature may also vary with glass color. For example, black glass will tend to flow at lower temperatures than clear glass even if they are both glass from the same manufacturer. This is because darker colored glass will absorb radiant heat from the kiln much quicker than lighter colors. Thus, they heat up to kiln temperature faster. The consequence of these differences may be changes to the pattern, which you have set up with your glass components during fusing. The darker colors will get soft first and can flow into any gaps between pieces before the rest of the glass gets very soft.

When making fused glass beads, you have two options. The first is to make each of the beads as individual fused pieces. The second is to make larger fused pieces, or beadstock, that you later cut apart into individual beads on a diamond saw, as in Figure 306. Then you can finish them either by fire or grit polishing. In either case, unless you work to overcome it, you end up with beads that tend to be flat rather than three-dimensional.

The first part of this chapter will focus on the fusing process. Then in the second part, we will discuss how the fusing process can be used to make beads.

Choosing your glass

The first step when you begin fusing is, as usual, choosing your glass palette. As you can guess, the glass in your palette has to be compatible. As we discussed previously, this means that they must all have nearly the same coefficient of expansion throughout the processing temperature range and approximately the same annealing point. Glass is commercially available for fusing that has been factory tested to ensure its compatibility. This saves you the problem of having to try to determine if the glass is compatible or not on your own.

Bullseye Glass Company has maintained a good, continuous testing program to guarantee the compatibility of its fusing glass. Other companies have also started doing this and some have developed formulations that are compatible with Bullseye. Wasser and Uroburos are examples of these.

Spectrum glass company, on the other hand, has started up a glass fusing line with a coefficient different than that of Bullseye that is becoming better with time. Uroburos is also making some glass that is compatible with this line.

Similarly, pretty much all Effetre glass is compatible to itself (some of the alabasters may be an exception) and could be used for fusing within its own line of glass. Effetre is now also making flat glass that can be fused to the rods or factory made millefiori slices as well as any lampworked objects you may make.

We have discussed how to do a glass compatibility test for lampworking by pulling threads and watching how they bend. This will work fine for small handmade wound beads but is not necessarily good enough for larger fused pieces. The reason for this is that the thread test is not sensitive enough in measuring compatibility between two glasses. It can not ensure that induced stress in two pieces of glass that pass the test will be low enough to prevent larger pieces from cracking. This lower accuracy results from differences in flow characteristics of the two glasses, as well as your proficiency in testing.

Measuring glass compatibility for fusing

The most accurate way to ensure that two glasses are compatible is to run a fusing test strip. To run a test strip requires a clear compatible base glass against which to test. What you are really doing is testing the compatibility of each of the two test glasses against this clear base glass. Then by using the Transitive Property of Glass Fusing (i.e. if A is compatible to B and C is compatible to B then A must be compatible to C) we can presume their compatibility.

To run a fusing compatibility test strip, you start by cutting a strip of the clear base glass about 1½ inches wide and about 1½ inches long for each specimen that you are going to test. Thus, if you are going to test 6 specimens, the strip should be at least 9 inches long and 1½ inches wide.

Next cut out ½ by ½ inch square specimens from each of the different glasses that you want to test for compatibility. Then wash, clean, and dry the glass carefully to prevent any contamination from biasing your results. Space the specimens on the strip of clear base approximately ½ inch from all edges and 1 inch from each other.

Keep track of which glass is which since sometimes they may change color during firing. It helps to mark both the original glass sheet and the test strip by the square specimen to ensure no mix-ups. Marking pens that have metallic-based inks are available that will fire into the glass surface and are readable afterward. Steel Paint marking pens made by the Alton Company are one brand you can buy. When you are ready, the test strip will look something like Figure 307.

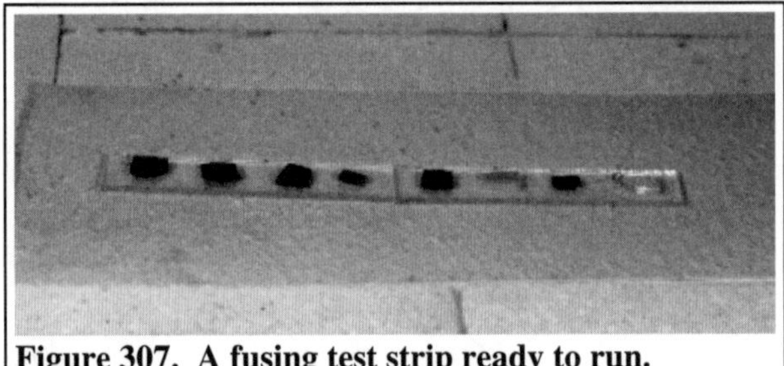

Figure 307. A fusing test strip ready to run.

Now fire the test strip, as will be described, to a flat fuse. This will require heating the glass to a processing temperature somewhere in the range of 1450 to 1650°F, depending on the hardness of the glass. After this firing, the thickness of the strip will be almost constant all the way down the strip and it will have shrunk in on itself somewhat.

Once you have fired the test strip, you can examine it for signs of incompatibility by checking it for stress. To do this, we use polarizing filters like those on expensive sunglasses. You will need two of these filters to conduct the test. (I got my filters from Edmund Scientific.) These filters have fine parallel assemblages of crystals that only let light through that is vibrating in one direction, say left and right.

If you rotate these filters relative to each other over a light table, you will see that they will get dark and light periodically. They are darkest when the filter on the bottom only lets light vibrating left-to-right through and the second filter only lets light vibrating top-to-bottom through. From this point, if you rotate the top filter 90° relative to the bottom filter, the crystals in both are now aligned such that they both now only allow light that is vibrating left-to-right through. This orientation allows the maximum amount of light through. As you turn the top filter further, they will again get darker until after another 90° rotation the light passing through the filters is again at a minimum.

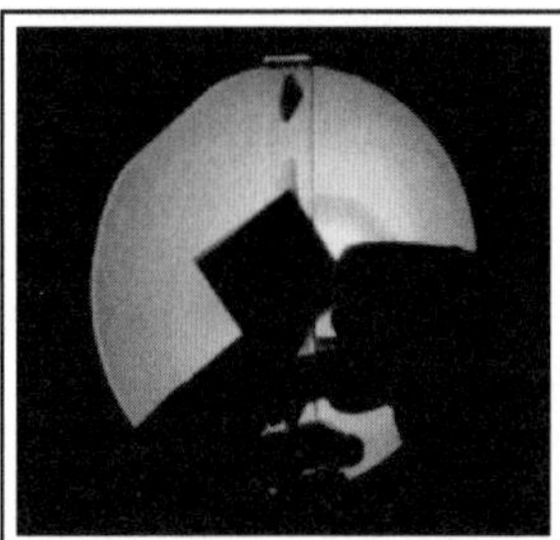

Figure 308. Reading a stress test.

You are probably wondering how these filters can be used to measure stress in glass. To understand how this works, you have to know that light, which passes through stressed glass, is twisted so that the direction of its vibration changes while light that passes through unstressed glass is not twisted. With this in mind, put one filter below the test strip on the light table (or over a light bulb) and the other filter on the top of the glass, as in Figure 308.

Rotate the top filter to the position that lets through the minimum amount of light. Any signs of incompatibility that exists in the test strip will be visible as a halo of light around the test specimens where the light has been twisted by stress in the glass.

Figure 309 illustrates what this will look like for varying amounts of stress in the glass. The bigger the halo, the greater the amount of stress. The only exception to this rule is for strips that have cracked. Stress will be relieved in the vicinity of a crack. Of course, developing cracks should also give you a clue that something is wrong. Specimens that show only what is labeled as slight stress or less are compatible enough with each other for fusing.

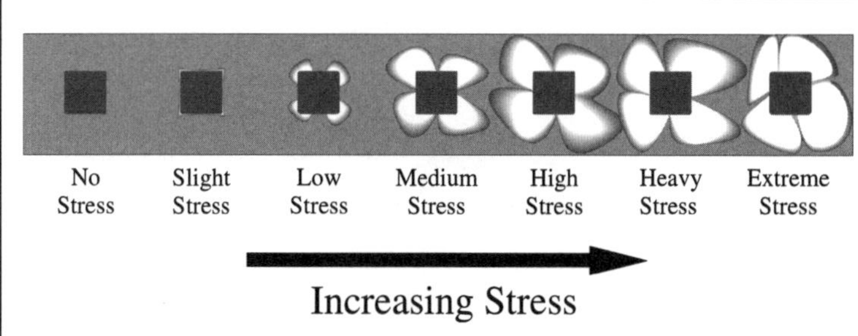

Figure 309. Interpreting results from a compatibility test strip.

Color stability

Another thing to be aware of when choosing and mixing glass in projects is that some glasses will change color when they are fired. This is caused by the metal oxides changing their oxidation state from the atmosphere inside the kiln. It is usually better to steer away from using such glass.

Also, some colors seem to interact with each other and form a third color along their common boundary. This could be used as a design element but it is best avoided. These are things that you will only become aware of as you work with fusing different types and colors of glass.

Fusing glass with your kiln

We have already discussed kiln construction, how they work, how to maintain them, and some basic kiln safety rules. Let's now discuss the procedures for using a kiln to fuse glass.

Preparing for a firing

Before firing glass in a kiln, you have to prepare a kiln shelf to put your work on. Kiln shelves are made from clay or mullite and are designed to withstand the high temperatures inside a kiln, but they must be treated to prevent your glass beads from sticking to them just as your mandrels had to be treated. For this reason, a kiln shelf needs to be coated with kiln wash as you did to the bottom of your kiln when you tempered it.

If there is any residual kiln wash on the shelf from prior use, you will have to scrape it off with a paint scraper to get a more uniform coating. Do this over newspaper so that you can fold it up and capture the dust afterward. Kiln wash dust is an irritant so make sure that you wear a dust mask or respirator during dusty operations like this. If the kiln shelf is scratched, you may also want to sand out some of the scratches with sandpaper in order to get a nice smooth shelf surface. Any imperfections will be picked up on the back of your work. The shelf is now ready to coat with kiln wash. If your shelves are new, it is always a good idea to temper them as you did the kiln.

Commercial kiln wash mixtures are available from most glass or ceramics stores. If you cannot find some, you can make your own from a 50/50 by weight, dry mixture of aluminum hydrate and kaolin clay. Mix a small amount of the dry mixture with water until you get a thin watery solution; about three parts of water to one part of dry mix.

Figure 310. Kiln washing your shelves.

Use a soft brush to paint several thin coats onto the shelf applying each coat perpendicular to the previous one, as seen in Figure 310. There should be no visible streaks as you brush it on. Let the wash air dry overnight, as this seems to form a stronger coating possibly through chemical reactions. If you are impatient to get started, you can put the coated shelf directly into your kiln and heat it up slowly to 200°F. After it is dry and cool, you can further smooth the surface of the kiln wash layer by rubbing your hand across it. If not overfired, the coating should last a number of firings. Once it starts to develop bare spots, it should be replaced.

Next, clean your glass. Any dust or body oils can cause spotting of the glass during firing. I use Windex, and isopropyl alcohol is also a good choice. Handle the glass by the edges once it is clean. Cover it with a clean paper towel to keep the dust off. Lay out your work on the "washed" kiln shelf. The different fusing projects should be positioned on the shelf so that they are not touching each other, otherwise they might become fused together.

Find three or four 2" or longer ceramic posts from your collection of kiln furniture and place them on the bottom of the kiln in the locations where the corners of your shelf will be. These posts will raise the kiln shelf off the bottom of the kiln for more even heating. Place your thermocouple through the hole in the peephole plug into the kiln. It should end up just above (within a couple of inches) your project on the kiln shelf. You are now ready to go.

Some glasses have a tendency to crystallize or devitrify on their surface through loss of fluxing agents when heated in a kiln. This is a tendency that you will only learn about from experience in using each type of glass. Sometimes you may only get a touch of it on the first firing cycle but it gets progressively worse with each subsequent firing. Other glasses don't seem to be susceptible to devitrification.

There are a couple of ways to deal the problem of devitrification without having to restrict work to glasses that are immune to it. The first is to live with it. I know some artists who like the look and actually try to find ways of inducing it. Personally I don't like the look of it. Once it has developed, you can sandblast or acid etch it off and fire the glass again to restore surface luster. The other technique to control devitrification is prevention.

Devitrification develops from reactions at the surface of the glass and not in the bulk of the glass. So one way to deal with the problem is to cover that surface up. The way that this is usually done is, as Dan Fenton would say, to spray it with your favorite "devit medicine" prior to firing, as is being done in Figure 311. The "devit medicines" that he is referring to are clear overglazes or enamels.

These overglazes are mixtures of micron sized particles of low melting-temperature glass. They were actually formulated as additives for enamels that serve to modify both their firing temperature and their expansion coefficient, but work well for our purposes. They are not cure-alls though, because they can interact with agents used in iridizing glass or lusters. Overglazes could be used to selectively remove a portion of an iridized surface or to try to selectively fire-polish just a portion of a sandblasted surface. Another problem with overglazes is that they stick tenaciously to kiln wash, which you now have to figure out how to remove.

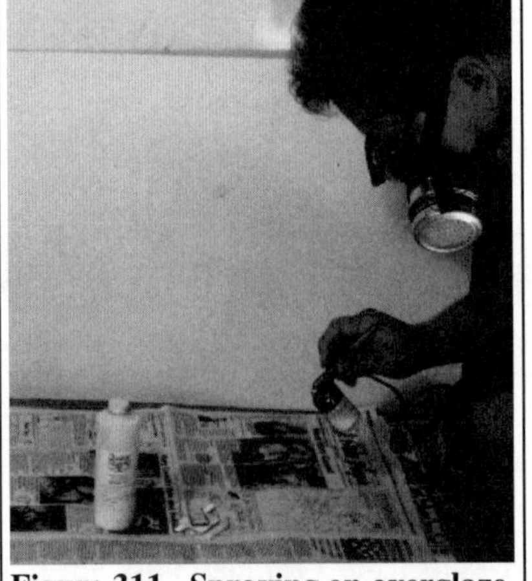
Figure 311. Spraying on overglaze.

When choosing which overglaze to use, there

are a few factors that you should take into consideration. These include:

- how hot you want to heat the glass in your next step (you may want to keep the temperature low to avoid glass flow)
- their lead content (are you going to eat off of or drink out of the glass)
- its compatibility to your glass (does it have the right coefficient of expansion)

There are fluxes available commercially that match the Bullseye expansion 90 family ("Spray A", "Super Spray" and "Standard Ceramics Flux-92") and some for borosilicate glass (Reusche & Co. 32). Lead free fluxes generally require firing to higher temperatures (1300°F) than high lead ones (1100°F).

Most overglazes come as dry powders, which you mix with a 50/50 mixture of alcohol and distilled water. You apply this slurry by either painting it or by spraying it onto the surface of the glass. To spray it use nice even strokes with a small airbrush from a distance of about 6 to 10 inches, trying to get the edges also.

It is important to get a nice uniform coating that is not too thick because thick coatings will fire hazy. Coatings that are too thin, on the other hand, may look blotchy. The difficulty with getting just the right amount on has led some fused-glass bead artists to swear off all use of overglazes entirely.

If you only want the overglaze on one part of a stack up, spray that part individually, allow it to dry, and then move it over to the kiln shelf by handling it on the edges. Because of the tendency of overglazes to stick to your kiln wash, I prefer to spray the project on some newspaper spread out on my worktable. After it dries, I then transfer it to my washed kiln shelf. Put the pieces together carefully though, as you do not want to smear the overglaze. Since the overglazes are usually finely ground, high-lead glasses, you should wear a respirator or better yet spray it on in a paint hood. When I am done, I fold up the newspaper to get rid of any overspray.

If you are having problems with overglaze sticking to the kiln wash on your shelf, try covering the shelf with a non-rigidized ceramic fiber paper such as Fiberfrax™ 970-J. This is a paper made from alumina fibers that have been woven together and are held together using organic binders. **Ceramic fiber papers should be prefired to burn out the organic binders, which can leave unsightly residues on your beads.**

Overglazes can also be used to shine up the edges of beads cut from a larger fired piece. Here you cut the beads off and grind the edges flat. Apply the overglaze to the bead and fire it to a temperature that correctly matures it but does not allow any glass flow.

The overglaze that you choose for your work will depend on the effect you are trying to achieve. If you want nice sharp corners, then you will choose a low-fire one. If you want more rounded corners, then you will choose a high-fire one. If you are trying to fire both ends of the bead at once, you will have to suspend it on a ceramic bead rack and use a low fire overglaze to prevent slumping the bead.

To lay-up glass to make simple fused glass beads you have to use a hole former in the space where you want the bead hole to be. We sandwich a piece of whatever material we use for this between two layers of glass, as shown in Figure 312. Then when we fire the bead the glass slumps around the hole former, which we clean out later to reveal the bead holes.

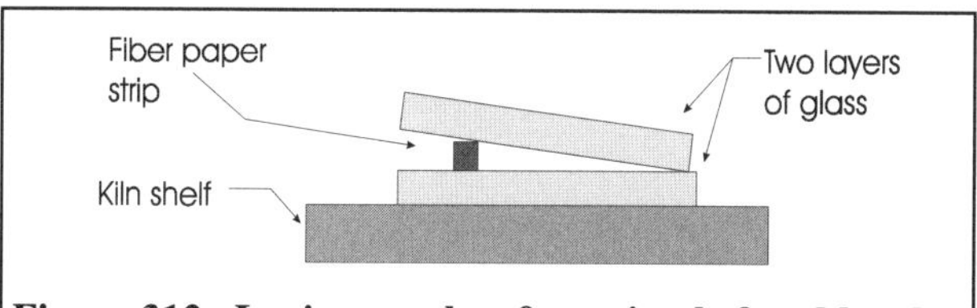

Figure 312. Laying up glass for a simple fused bead.

One of the best materials to use as a hole former for making beads is ceramic fiber paper that is cut into strips or made into cord. You can use the paper as it comes from the manufacturer or you can prefire it. If you use unfired ceramic fiber you will get burnout fumes from the organic binder that holds the fiber together, which can discolor the glass. If you choose to prefire the fiber paper, it should be rigidized before use to give it some strength. The yarn or paper is rigidized by soaking unfired paper in a hardening solution of 15% colloidal silica followed by air drying and firing it in a kiln to about 1300°F. If your beadmaking process is a multi step one with cutting and grinding steps between firings, you may find that you will need to replace the fiber paper between firings.

A way to get round holes in your beads is to use sections of mandrels coated with separator compound. You can also try coating bamboo sticks or copper wire with a thick coating of separator compound. The bamboo sticks will burn out but the separator will remain behind and should have enough strength to keep the hole from collapsing. Copper wire can be stretched, which causes it to narrow, and easily be pulled out of short beads.

Before starting a firing, you should take a second to reflect on the size and thickness of the piece that you are working on. This will influence the rate at which you can change temperature and the amount of time required to soak at process temperature. You should also reflect on what processes you are doing to decide whether you will have to vent the kiln as you heat it up.

If you are applying overglazes or lusters, then you will need to vent the kiln during the heating phase to remove any fumes that are given off during those processes. Many times you may want to vent the kiln just to let moisture escape. With these considerations in mind, you are now ready to start to plan out your kiln-firing schedule. A basic kiln fusing cycle is illustrated in Figure 313. It consists of three main phases: the heating phase, the process or fusing phase and the cooling phase.

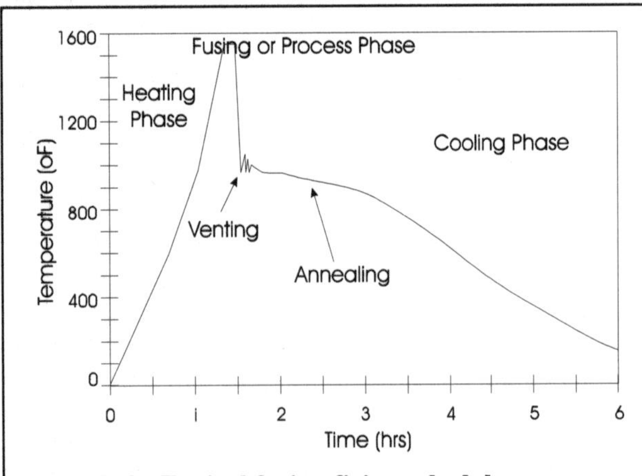

Figure 313. Typical fusing firing schedule.

Plan out your run on a worksheet like that shown on the next page. Then as you fire the kiln, record the actual run measurements as you go along so that you have a record of what you did. This will allow you to keep track of what works well and what doesn't. In the long run, this can save you a lot of time and money.

Phase one of the firing cycle: heating

In the heating phase of the firing, what you are doing is raising the temperature in the kiln from room temperature to the process temperature. The rate at which you do this it is expressed in degrees per minute. So, if you are going to fire from room temperature or 70°F to a low-temperature overglaze polish temperature of about 1100°F in one hour, you will be heating the glass at a rate of (1100°F-70°F)/60min or 17.2°F/min.

That is actually a pretty fast heating rate for most projects unless your pieces are very small. The maximum rate at which you can increase the temperature is a physical limitation of your kiln. It will depend upon its power capacity and its construction. But the maximum rate at which you should heat a fusing project depends upon the size and thickness of the project.

The larger or thicker the project, the slower that you should to raise the kiln temperature. You have to go slower because you can develop larger temperature differences through the glass cross section or across a piece. The areas that are hotter expand more quickly than the cooler areas. The distribution of this expansion stresses the bonds between the atoms in the glass, and if this stress becomes too large, the bonds will break, leading to cracks in the glass. This is not much of a problem with beads but may be a problem with larger projects.

The glass is most sensitive to thermal shock during the first 700°F of temperature rise because this is in its brittle solid regime. You can heat faster as you get past this and move into the non-brittle solid regime. Table 19 gives some suggested heating rates to be used with fusing projects of different thicknesses in both of these regimes. If the length or width of your project is of the same order of magnitude as the thickness, you can probably double these rates without any problems.

Table 19. Suggested heating rates.

	Side Fired Kiln		Top-Fired Kiln	
Glass Thickness (in)	Brittle Zone (°F/min)	Non-Brittle (°F/min)	Brittle Zone (°F/min)	Non-Brittle (°F/min)
1/8	7.5	11	8	12
1/4	6.5	9.5	7	10
3/8	4.5	7.5	5	8
1/2	2.5	5.5	3	6
1	1.5	2.5	2	3

Knowing how fast you should heat the glass, how do you determine how to adjust the controls to achieve this heating rate? If you do not have a kiln controller, you will have to practice with your kiln and keep good records using record sheets such as those suggested earlier to develop an understanding of your kiln's physical limitations. In doing this, you will learn how quickly it heats up when it is set at different infinite range switch settings. To test for this, start with your kiln at room temperature and set your infinity switches to a given setting (say 50%) and time when it reaches various temperatures.

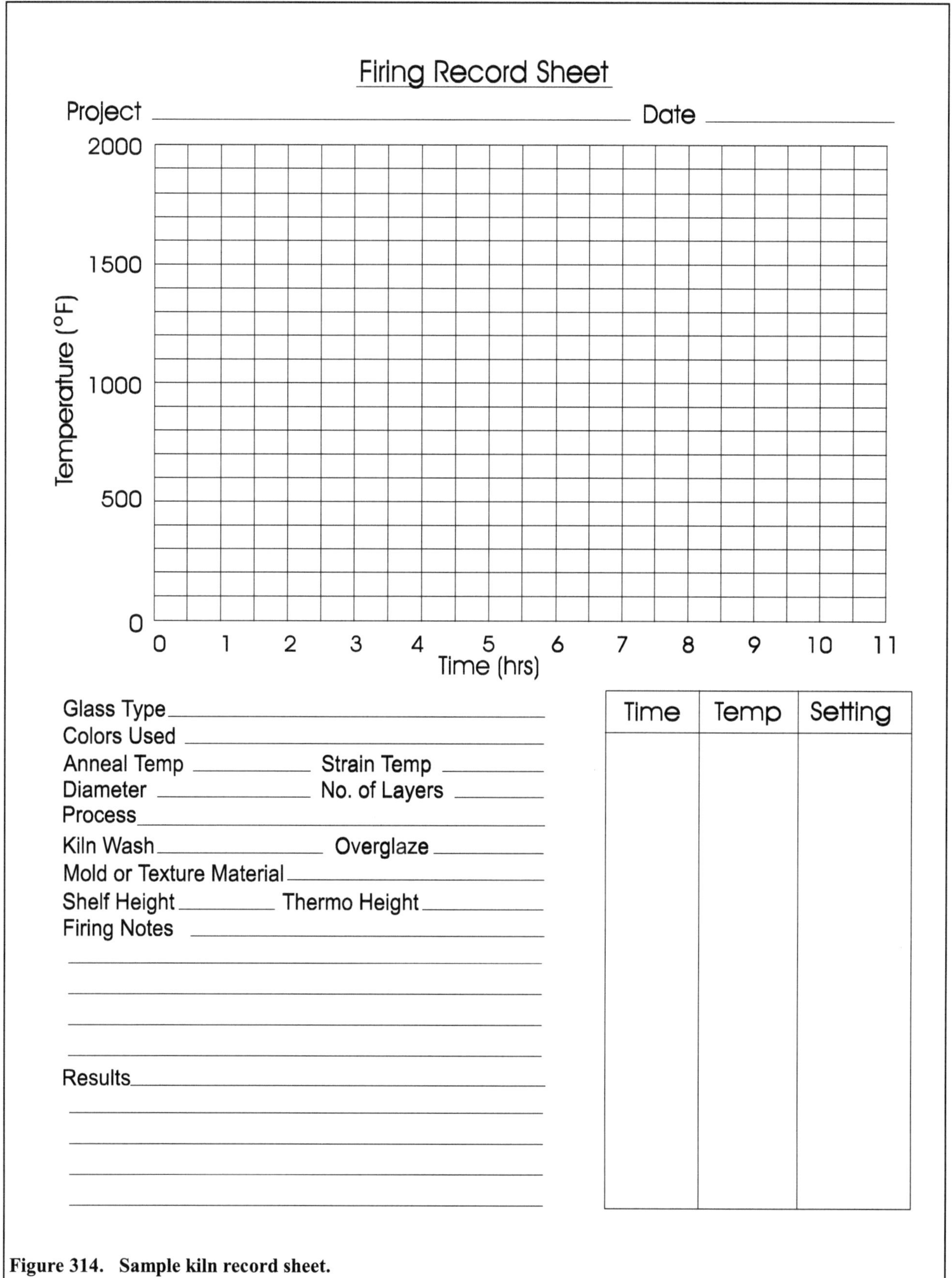

Figure 314. Sample kiln record sheet.

If you graph this data, you will get a chart like that in Figure 315. Notice that it is not a straight line but instead the kiln heats faster at low temperatures than at higher temperatures. This happens for a number of reasons, one of which is that more energy is lost through the kiln walls at higher temperatures. Once you have this data, you can use it to determine the control settings required to get different heating rates. With data on a couple of different infinity control settings, you will be able to interpolate between them for heating rates at other switch settings.

Be aware that heating rates vary depending upon how full the kiln is. So you will want to do this testing with at least one kiln shelf present in the kiln, or better yet with a project similar to what you normally fuse. You might want to combine these runs with tests to see what happens to stacks of glass taken to different processing temperatures. For example, try taking stacks of Bullseye glass to 1350, 1450, and 1550°F to see the difference between tack fusing, full fusing, and flat fusing. Alternately you could distribute cones around the kiln and check for its uniformity of heating.

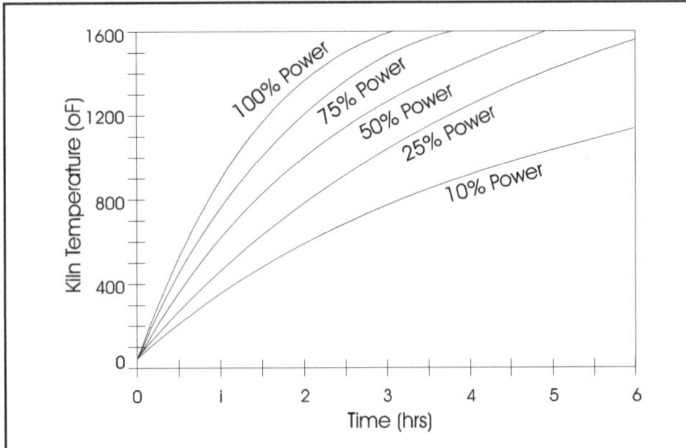

Figure 315. Plots of temperature versus time for a Cress C-20-H.

Phase two of the firing cycle: process

The results obtained in the next phase of a firing, the process or fusing phase, are a function of the process you are doing. Different processes require raising the kiln to different temperatures and holding there for different lengths of time. As an example, for fusing you will raise the temperature to that which will give the degree of fusing that you want and hold it there for about 15 to 30 minutes. For pâte de verre you have to hold the kiln at temperatures for much longer time periods to allow the heat to penetrate into the mold and for the glass to flow.

As I discussed earlier, because of their different hardnesses, the temperature at which different soda-lime glasses fuse will vary somewhat. Likewise, this temperature is also a function of the color of the glass. Darker colors absorb radiant energy more efficiently and thus will get hotter faster and at slightly lower kiln temperatures when ramping up. Therefore, a black Bullseye glass, which is nominally a harder glass, will soften at similar temperatures to that of a light colored Wasser glass, which is normally considered to be a lot softer.

During the fusing phase, you want to hold the temperature as steady as possible to accomplish the process without overfiring. It requires a little time for the glass to flow. Unfortunately it is sometimes hard to tell if the desired result has been achieved by peeking into the kiln because it is so bright and your glasses are very dark to protect your eyes. You just have to trust your pyrometer and records from previous runs to guide you. Table 20 should give you a feeling for temperatures required in fusing different types of art glass.

Glass flow increases with higher temperature. So for better control of what is happening, you can usually trade off a little lower temperature for a little more time at that temperature to achieve the same amount of heat work. This may be the desired way to go for you because overfiring can ruin many decorative effects from glass flow and it can happen very quickly if you are not careful. Holding the temperature slightly lower is also a good way to keep your project from sticking to the kiln wash.

Holding your kiln steady at a particular temperature requires much less heat input than was involved in the heating phase. This is because only enough heat needs to be added to make up for that lost through the walls of the kiln. Hopefully this is not too much. Because of this, you will find that you may have to turn your infinity switch way down to prevent further rise in temperature and need to keep closer tabs on the kiln in phase two.

A good tool for maintaining a constant temperature is a set point controller. It is an electronic device that automatically holds a kiln temperature constant. It does this by using a thermocouple to measure the kiln temperature and cuts off power when the kiln temperature rises over the set temperature and turns the power back on when the temperature falls back down a certain preset amount.

Phase three of the firing cycle: cooling

The last phase of a typical fusing cycle is the cooling phase. Here we try to get our fused piece back from the high process temperatures in the least stressed condition possible. **The first part of the cooling phase usually consists of venting the kiln to rapidly lower its temperature to about 1000°F.** Venting is done to minimize time in the flexible regime. Spending time there is not desired because it can result in crystallization of the glass. This crystallization appears as a dull haze on the surface of the glass. This condition, as we have already discussed, is commonly known as devitrification. It can occur when soda-lime glass is held for long periods of time in the temperature range of 1300 to 1400°F.

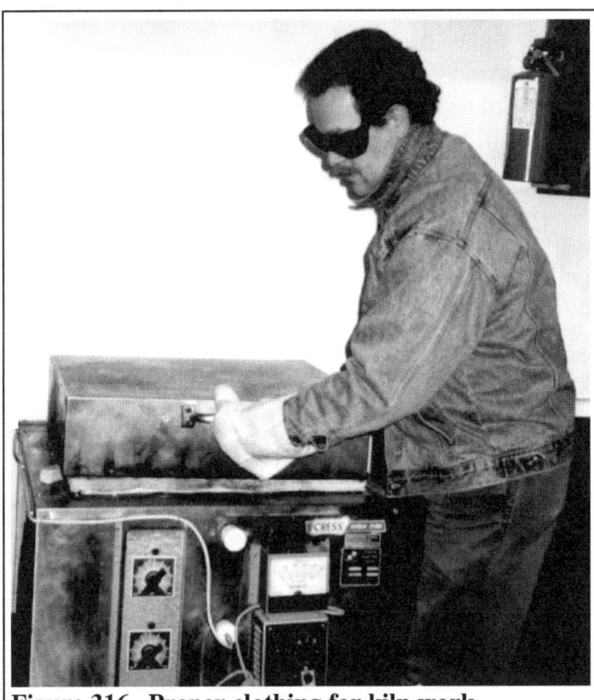

Figure 316. Proper clothing for kiln work.

Before venting the kiln, first don your dark protective glasses and your heavy non-asbestos gloves, then open the kiln door slightly, as seen in Figure 316. Keep track of the kiln temperature on the pyrometer. As soon as it drops down to about 1000°F, close the door and allow the inside of the kiln to regain equilibrium. You may need to vent the kiln a number of times to get it steady in the right temperature range.

Be careful during venting that temperatures in parts of the kiln do not drop so low that you thermal shock your project. Better to take it easy and vent a number of times than to crack your work. Some people advise that any further venting after the first vent be done by propping the door open about 1" until the kiln equilibrates to the proper temperature. This is fine, unless you are like me and always doing three things at once, causing you to lose track of what is happening in the kiln. For those of you like me, stick around and hold the kiln open or set a kitchen timer to remind you to close it back up.

The next portion of the cooling phase, the slow cooling or annealing portion, is where you must cool the kiln fairly slowly through what is known as the annealing range. This must be done to allow any stress that may have just been frozen into the glass during the venting to flow out.

The annealing range for a glass occurs in its non-brittle solid regime. This, as was discussed earlier, is in the range of 800 to 1000°F for soda-lime glasses. It is bounded at the top by the annealing point and at the bottom by the strain point. The annealing range temperatures for some common art glasses are given in the first portion of Table 20.

In the annealing range, glass is a solid but its atoms are still mobile enough that they can twist and stretch around one another to relieve any stress. It is important that you go through this range at a slow enough rate that all the stress in your glass can be removed and that no new stress develops. If you cool too quickly, you will have to reheat the glass to remove the stress that this will induce. The slow cooling process is commonly referred to as annealing, but it is really just controlled cooling of your glass. This is discussed in much greater detail in the chapter on annealing since it is something that should be done to finish all lampworked beads.

Before starting the slow cooling cycle, first soak the project at the annealing point for a short period of

Table 20. Fusing process temperatures for different fusing glasses.

Glass Type	Strain Point (°F)	Annealing Point (°F)	Slumping Temp (°F)	Tack Fusing (°F)	Partial Fusing (°F)	Full Fusing (°F)
Bullseye	820	990	1050	1250	1350	1450
GNA	800	960	1200	1350	1450	1550
Effetre	680	970	—	—	—	—
Pyrex	950	1040	—	—	—	—
Spectrum	700	950	1100	1200	1300	1400
Wasser	650	950	1000	1150	1250	1350

time to allow it to equilibrate after crash venting. Then slowly cool it down to the strain point. This is the temperature at which atomic motion is now so much slower that stress cannot be released in a reasonable amount of time. For similar reasons, new stress can also no longer be trapped in the piece after this point so we can speed up our cooling at this point. After this, you cool from the strain point to room temperature at a rate that is just slow enough so the bead will not thermal shock, without any worry of trapping stress.

The time that you should soak at the annealing temperature and rates at which you should cool both through the annealing range and then to room temperature is controlled mostly by the thickness of the glass in your project. Suggested values of these rates for Bullseye and other 90 coefficient of expansion glass fusing projects of different thickness are given in Table 21. Here the annealing range is 990 to 820°F ad the final cooling range is from 820°F to room temperature. Ramp times are the time to traverse the temperature range at the suggested cooling rate.

Table 21. Annealing schedule times and ramps for Bullseye glass.

Glass Stackup Thickness (in)	Number of Glass Sheets	Anneal Soak (min)	Annealing Cooling Rate (°F/hr)	Final Cooling Rate (°F/hr)	Annealing Cooling Ramp (hr)	Final Cooling Ramp (hr)
0.125	1	15	267	800	0.9	0.9
0.25	2	20	67	200	3.5	3.4
0.375	3	30	30	89	7.8	7.7
0.5	4	45	17	50	13.8	13.6
0.625	5	55	11	32	21.6	21.3
0.75	6	80	7	22	31.1	30.6
0.875	7	100	5	16	42.3	41.7
1.0	8	120	4	12	55.2	54.4

Values for annealing of Effetre and other glass beads are given in the chapter on annealing beads. That chapter will also discuss how to calculate cooling rates for other glasses. Note that those cooling rates will be lower because it is assumed that fusing projects lie flat on the shelf and are larger in the flat dimension.

Fusing considerations

There are a number of things to consider in making fused beads that differ from other beadmaking techniques. They must be understood to maintain control while making fused beads and to use these different techniques in shaping your fused glass projects.

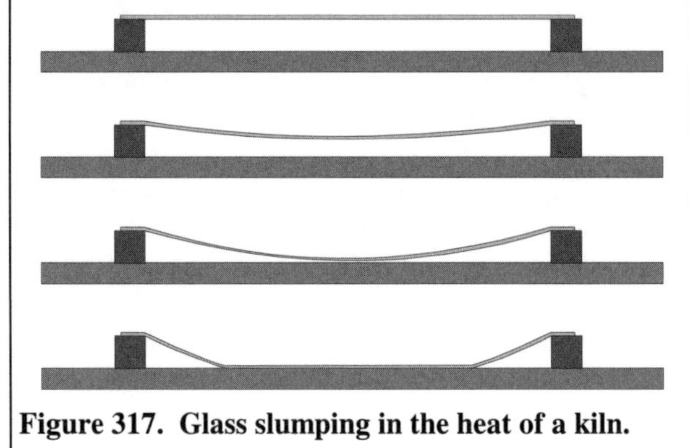

Figure 317. Glass slumping in the heat of a kiln.

Slumping

As you heat glass in the kiln above its softening point, if it is not completely supported it will start to sag and stretch under the effect of gravity, as illustrated in Figure 317. This can be used to your advantage to shape the glass to your liking. Molds of many shapes are available on which to shape glass, and you can also make your own. They can be made from a number of different materials such as ceramics, ceramic fiber paper, stainless steel, or plaster.

We will discuss how to make plaster molds for pâte de verre beads in the next chapter. This same process could also be employed for making small slumping molds for beads. If you want to know more about making your own slumping molds,

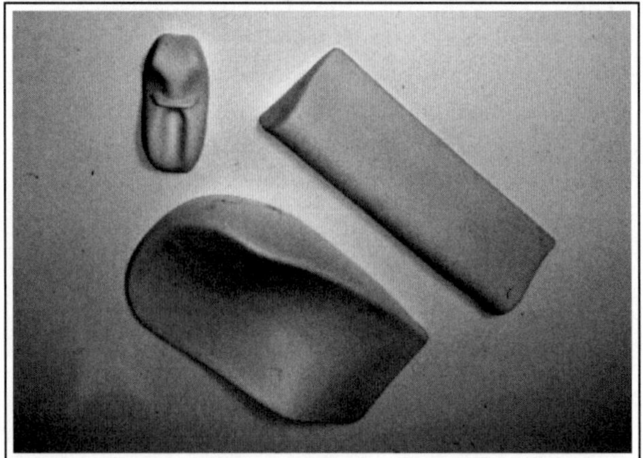

Figure 318. Commercially available slumping molds.

check out one of the general fusing references at the end of this chapter or the next. There are also a number of small commercially available ceramic molds such as those shown in Figure 318 that can be used for making small glass jewelry. They can also be used in making beads.

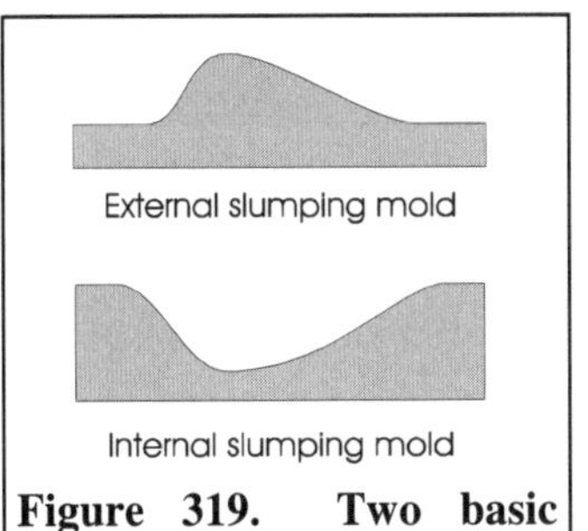

Figure 319. Two basic kinds of slumping molds.

There are two basic types of slumping molds: external and internal. Before the age of politically correct speech, these molds were referred to as male and female molds respectively. **External molds** are used to drape objects over the mold and support the glass in the center while the glass slumps down around this point. **Internal molds,** on the other hand, support the glass on the edges of the piece and the glass slumps down into the center of the mold. In either case, the mold has to be coated with a layer of kiln wash before use to prevent the glass from sticking to it.

The glass also has to be cut so that it fits on the mold correctly and does not drape over the edges. This would cause the glass to crack from pinching down on the mold as it cools. For this reason, external molds with extreme slumps are made from stainless steel. The COE of stainless steel is higher than glass and molds made from steel will actually shrink away from the glass during cooling. For a similar reason, internal molds are usually made from ceramic materials. These materials have a lower COE than glass, allowing the glass to shrink away from the mold as it cools.

If you use internal molds, you will find that they will usually have air holes in the bottom. This allows air to escape as the glass slumps down into the mold. These holes have to be kept clean of kiln wash and the mold has to be raised slightly off the kiln shelf, as in Figure 320, to ensure air egress through the hole and out from under the bottom rim of the mold. If not, trapped air can form uprisings as the glass gets soft. The holes are cleaned by pushing a pin or a wire through the holes after application of the kiln wash.

When slumping large pieces, you have to heat up the kiln more slowly then if you were fusing the same amount of glass on a kiln shelf, especially during the early stages of the firing. This is to

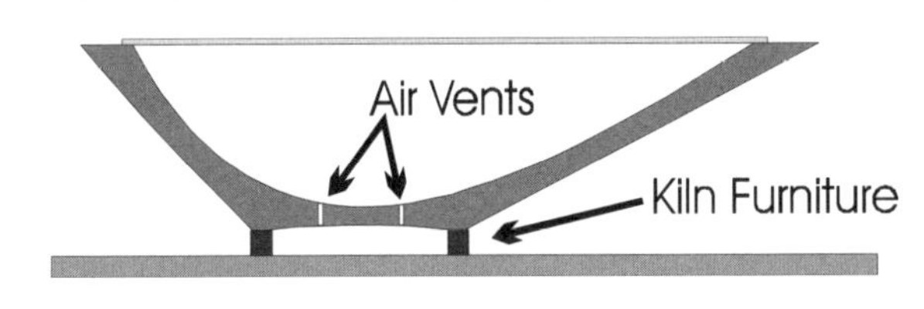

Figure 320. Setting up an internal mold for slumping.

ensure that the glass is heating up evenly. Unsupported portions of the glass do not have the mass of the mold beneath them to slow their temperature rise as the other sections do. Also on external molds you are actually heating from both sides of the glass, except in the area where the glass is touching the mold.

Both of these effects can lead to higher thermal gradients in the glass prior to slumping than are encountered in fusing. Once the glass has been heated up beyond the strain point however, there is usually no longer any real concern about thermal shock. Rates during cooling after slumping are not as much of a concern as during heating (beyond normal annealing concerns) because the glass will now be in full contact with the mold, causing it to cool more uniformly.

Slumping will begin at temperatures just above the glass's annealing temperature and will mature quickly at temperatures about 50°F below the tack fuse temperature for a particular glass. So as you heat past the annealing point, you will start to see the glass slowly sag. As the temperature increases, the glass will stretch faster and soon come in contact with the rest of the mold. At the upper end of the slumping temperature region, it will begin to pick up fine detail from the mold.

Figure 321. Glass set on slumping molds to make light-weight ear rings.

Don't expect too much detail though. If you proceed higher in temperature, the glass will start to flow and those portions over raised sections of the mold will start to thin. If you reach this point, you have overfired the slumping run. After slumping, anneal and cool the glass as if it were a fusing run.

Slumping can be used to introduce shape and texture into a fused piece without having to increase the thickness of the glass too much. This is a good idea to use when you are making earrings. They can be very uncomfortable to wear if they are too heavy.

Figure 322. A piece with cooling cracks.

Volume control

When you fuse glass at high temperatures, it will change its shape and volume as it seeks its ideal thickness. This ideal thickness is dictated by the glass's surface tension and is about a quarter of an inch or just slightly over the thickness of two standard sheets of glass. Therefore if you are fusing layers thinner than this, they will pull in on themselves attempting to achieve this ideal thickness. This will occur first at the edges and then in the interior of the piece.

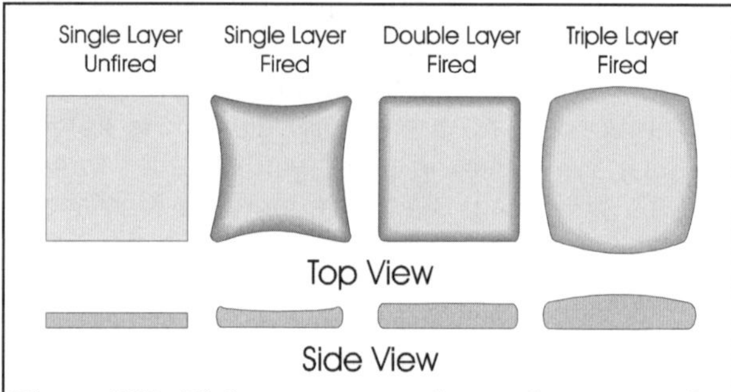

Figure 323. Firing squares to show volume control.

This result of this flow is illustrated for a series of flat fused squares of varying numbers of initial layers in Figure 323. Although this effect can be controlled somewhat by firing at lower temperatures for a longer amount of time, you can never completely get rid of it. By doing a little advanced planning ahead of time, you can get around this effect. Do this by trying to layer the correct amount of glass to get one-quarter inch in thickness.

The existence of this effect leads to a couple of design concepts that you need to consider whenever you are developing ideas for fused projects. They are:

- lay up a two layer thickness of glass for objects that you are going to fully fuse to avoid distortion.
- try to keep the largest mass of design additions of glass away from the edges of the piece as this will generally lead to variations in the border.
- to keep your fused objects thinner than the typical ¼" will require restricting your work to tack fusing.

You will eventually develop a feeling for these details with experience.

What happened

Sometimes even though you think that you did everything right, your fused bead project will turn out to be a disaster. Here are some of the most common problems experienced in fusing.

Cracking

Cracking is most likely due to thermal shock. Thermal shock results from heating or cooling your work too fast. In heating, the outer edge of the glass is trying to grow faster than the inner volume. In cooling, the outside is trying to shrink faster than the inside. In either case, if there are large temperature gradients in the project, there will be a large amount of stress present.

If your projects are small, they may be able to accommodate the stress because its magnitude will be smaller. But if you try to do larger projects with the same firing schedule, you may run into trouble. Use the rates that are given in this chapter as a guide for larger projects. They are probably slightly conservative, but if you have a lot of money or time involved in a fusing project (and doesn't time really equate to money anyway), you might want to be conservative.

If you get cracking in a piece, you can determine when the cracking occurred during the firing cycle by carefully examining the cracks.

- Soft, partially re-fused cracks will have occurred during the heating phase.
- Sharp cracks will have occurred during the cooling phase.

The logic behind this is based on the fact that any sharp edges will get rounded at fusing temperatures.

Therefore, any sharp cracks remaining after a fusing run will not have seen fusing temperatures. Thus, the cracks in the piece in Figure 322 occurred in the cooling phase of the firing.

There are other possible sources of cracking besides thermal stress. One of these is from a piece being restrained somehow during the cooling phase as it tries to shrink. There are a number of ways that this can occur. One of the most common is when you are trying to slump your bead or bead stock over a ceramic mold of some kind and the project is larger than the mold. In this case, the project will fold a little over the edges of the mold. Then as you cool down, the glass squeezes around the mold, because of its higher COE. In this situation, the mold always wins and breaks apart the glass.

Glass can also become restrained by sticking to something. One way that this can happen is if you place your projects too close together on the kiln self where they can spread during the fusing process and stick together.

Another common cause of cracking initiated by sticking is from breaks in the wash on the kiln self. This allows the glass to become restrained by sticking to the shelf during the fusing process. Make sure that you have a good uniform coating of kiln wash on your shelves before each firing and that the coating is thick enough.

Figure 324. Bubbles trapped in a piece from glass texture.

Bubbles

When making fused glass beads, you may at times discover bubbles in your work. If they are small this may not really be a problem, except aesthetically, and maybe not even then. You may like the look of the bubbles and may even try to introduce them at times. Some artists use bubbles as a design element. Carol Fonda tells me that sometimes when she gets a bubble in her work, she will drill it out. She uses the hollow spot as a place to mount a small gem like an opal.

Bubbles may come from air trapped between the glass layers, the glass itself, or other sources. Air between the glass layers in a fused piece, as in Figure 324, is often the result of texture on the glass surface trapping air during fusing. This becomes more of a problem the larger your project is. There are three things that can be done to try to eliminate this problem. The first is easy, just use glass without texture. The reason that this in not always possible is that much of the glass that is made as the standard of the industry for fusing (i.e. Bullseye) is textured. Dan Fenton suggested that a way to get around this is to prefire the glass, sandblast the backside clean, and look mom – no texture.

The last technique to prevent trapping air between glass layers may probably not eliminate the problem but will certainly help reduce it. Air gets trapped inside a piece when the edges of the piece fuse sooner than the center. To try to prevent this, raise the top piece off of the bottom piece slightly by inserting a couple of small pieces of glass underneath the top piece at its periphery. Heating slowly will then allow center of the piece to slump and make contact before the edges. This will allow the air at the center to get out before the edges get fused. If you routinely get air bubbles in your work, I advise you not proceeding higher than the flat fuse temperature or they may rise to the surface. If this happens, you may get bubbles thin enough at the surface that the glass over them can chip.

If you do not want bubbles in your beads, look closely at the glass that you are using. Many art glasses contain bubbles as a decorative feature to help break up light and to give it an antique look. These bubbles are called seed bubbles and cannot be removed easily by kilnforming. You do not get the glass hot enough to reduce the viscosity to the point at which they will rise to the surface and pop. This process in glass preparation for blowing is called fining and requires temperatures in the neighborhood of about 2150°F for soda-lime glasses. So be selective in choosing your glass to avoid this source of bubbles.

The last common source of bubbles comes from moisture getting trapped beneath your glass. The most common source of this moisture is kiln wash that has not been dried properly. In this situation, the bubbles can be very large—up to inches across, and they will often break through the piece. This problem can be overcome by proper drying of shelves before use or by using ceramic fiber paper on top of the shelf instead of kiln wash.

Shelf marks and kiln wash sticking

Figure 325. Shelf marks.

When fusing glass on a kiln shelf, you may sometimes get a lot of unwanted texture on the bottom of a piece or kiln wash sticking to the bottom of your project, like that shown to the right in Figure 325. Besides being undesired, it can be a nuisance trying to clean the kiln wash off the back of such a project.

There is really not too much that you can do to prevent getting a little texture on the back of your fused project, because the whole idea of fusing after all is to get the glass soft enough to stick together, flow, and develop smooth edges. It is normal that the piece will pick up whatever texture exists on top of the kiln shelf that is underneath it. So the only thing that you can do is to make that texture as smooth as possible. If the wash has areas of pull out from previous firings, scrape it off and replace it.

If there are too many "pebbles" on the surface of the wash, think about looking for a new source of wash. Washes formulated specifically for glass rather than ceramics should be ground so that they have finer particles. Unfortunately, this makes the kiln wash more of an inhalation hazard. Check the surface of the washed shelf for proper adhesion before reusing it, by running your hand over the surface. If you still don't like the feel of the surface that you get using kiln wash, you can try firing over prefired unrigidized fiber paper. This will be really soft though and will have to be replaced quite often. Hey, if you have the bucks go for it.

The other factor that can increase the texture that you see on the bottom of the glass and causes the kiln wash to stick is overfiring. If you take the kiln temperature higher than it really needs to be, then the glass gets softer than it needs to be. This causes it to stick to whatever it is sitting on – kiln wash or fiber paper. This also results in developing sharp edges around the bottom of your piece like those in Figure 326. The mechanism by which these sharp edges form is that the glass is sticking somewhat to the kiln wash on the shelf while at the same time trying to contract in volume. Thus the glass that is sticking along the edges gets thinned out.

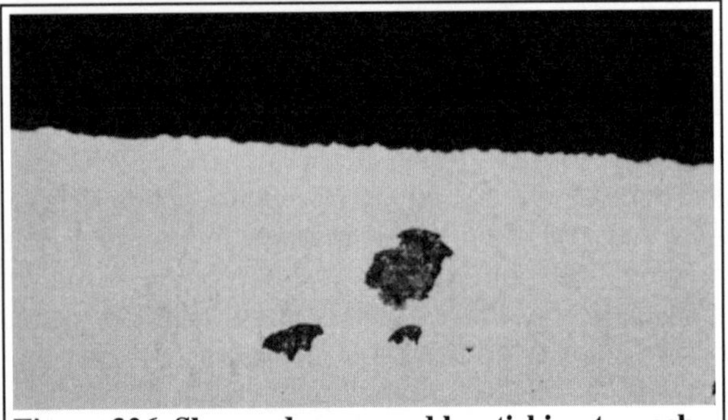

Figure 326. Sharp edges caused by sticking to wash.

The way to alleviate this is not to go to as high a temperature in your firing. If you really need that much heat work, get it by spending extra time at a lower temperature. Think of glass as maple syrup. When hot, it is really runny and will get all over the place making a big mess. When slightly cooler, it will still pour but it will pour slower so that you have more control over where it goes.

Figure 327. Simple layered bead
Artist: Kara van Wyk
Size: 1"W x 1"H x $^{3}/_{8}$"T

Making fused beads

Now that we have discussed the fusing process in a fair amount of detail, let's focus on how it can be applied to making beads.

Simple layered beads

You have already seen how you can make a simple bead by layering two pieces of glass with a piece of ceramic fiber paper between them. As you heat this glass sandwich, the top piece of glass slumps over the fiber paper and fuses to the piece below it. Since you used two full layers of glass, it will more or less retain its shape and not shrink much. This type of bead will have one good face that you can decorate as you see fit using any of the techniques that we will discuss shortly such as glass paints. An example can be seen in Figure 327.

The other possibility for making fused beads is to fuse loops of metal into the glass to attach them together. Here you just position the wire loop such that the portion that you want to embed into the glass is between the top and bottom piece. Any part that is sticking out will then be available for attachments. For this you want a high temperature wire that will not be melted or highly oxidized in the kiln.

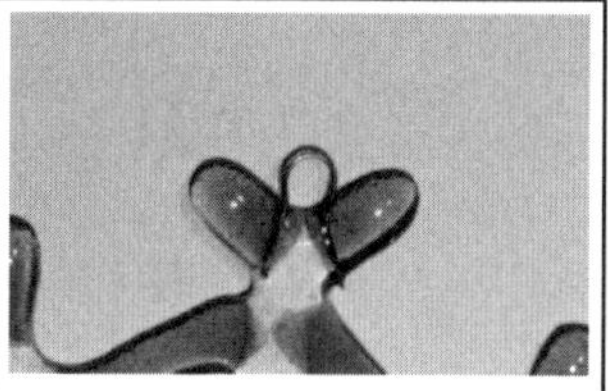

Figure 328. Wire hanger.

The ideal is nichrome, the same wire that your kiln elements are made of. You can get some from a ceramic supply store in the form of kiln "staples", 2" long pieces bent in the shape of a U, or on a small spool. You might also find it called stamen wire in ceramic supply stores where they use it for making things like Christmas ornaments. I take a piece ¾ to 1" in length and either bend it in a capital Omega shape (Ω) or a U where I keep on bending until the top crosses. Either of these are positioned during fusing so only the loop hangs out, as in Figure 305. These work better than a straight U shape because it gives the glass something to hang on to.

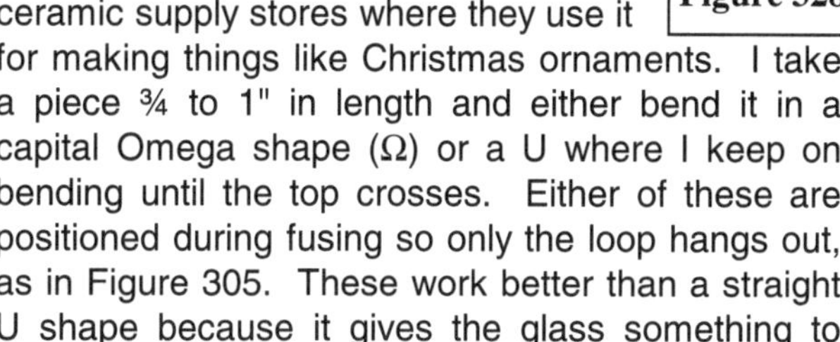

There are many variations possible with simple fused bead techniques. The first is the shape of the bead. They can be circles, ellipses, squares, rectangles, triangles, etc. With computer-aided machine tools these days, you could get production runs cut on water jet cutters to whatever shapes you want. The second variation is that both pieces of glass do not have to be the same size. As shown in Figure 329 for beads using hole formers, you get a different effect if you put a larger piece on top of a smaller piece than you do for the reverse.

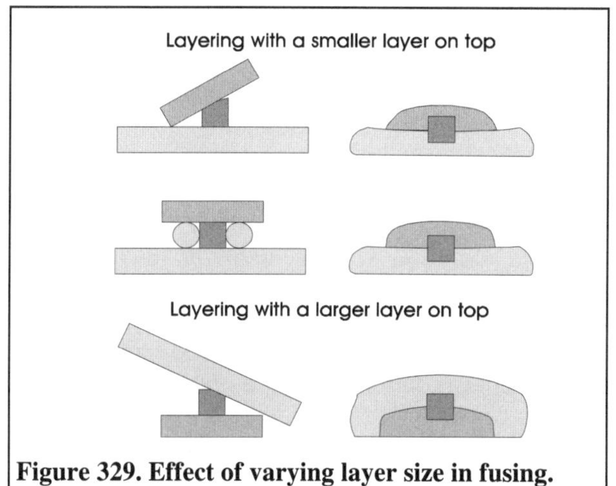

Figure 329. Effect of varying layer size in fusing.

Placing a smaller piece on top, as seen in the top half of the figure, allows you to see a decorative background piece beneath it. But by just balancing the top piece of glass on the hole former, the portion over the hole former may get too thin. Adding some glass under the top piece on either side of the ceramic fiber paper helps balance the smaller piece over the hole former so that it does not move. It also assists a little in volume control by helping to minimize thinning of the upper layer over the hole.

The other lay-up orientation, that of putting the larger piece over the smaller, allows the larger piece to wrap around the smaller piece with one uniform color. This is nice for those cases where the side of the glass is a different color than the top of the glass (as is the case for Wasser glass), because this way the side will usually roll under the piece onto the kiln shelf. When a smaller piece is placed on a larger piece, the side of the glass will usually show up as a ring around the top piece.

As an alternative to sheet glass, the top or bottom layers could be made of frit or small glass particles sprinkled in place. We will discuss using and making frit in much more detail in the next chapter on sculptural Pâte de Verre beads. Basically, using frit rather than sheet glass allows a number of additional design choices and painterly placement of color. It allows developing a gradation of color through the bead.

You can develop a gradation of color by using a mixture of two colors of frit and changing the ratio of the two frits over the length of the bead. Then when the frit fuses, the bead will have sort of a granite-like appearance where the ratio of the colors varies. I like the effect that this achieves when using transparent colors. Another interesting effect that you can achieve with frit is to tack fuse it together, giving the bead an interesting pebbly texture. This option is shown to the left in Figure 330. The other

Figure 330. Some options available fusing with frit.

piece to the right is fully fused frit.

With simple fused beads, you have the option of varying the fusing process temperature that you use. As discussed earlier, if you only tack fuse your glass, you will barely round its edges. At flat fuse, on the other hand, it makes one flat bead. You can adjust the process time and temperature to get anything in between these two options, as was illustrated back in Figure 305. Also, why have just one hole or a straight hole? You can have more holes or different effects by changing how you lay out your fiber paper. Bolo tie beads anyone?

You can also lay up larger fused bead stock pieces in a sheet orientation, which have a pattern running across them and a bead hole along one edge. I like this technique for jewelry, because after fusing the piece, you can cut the sheet up into strips perpendicular to the hole to make a dangling bead necklace where the pattern flows from one long dangling bead to the next. These beads, as will be discussed later, could be refired to fire polish the edges or be smoothed by tumble polishing.

Decorating simple fused beads

You can decorate your kiln-made beads with many of the same design elements that we used in making lampworked beads: murrine, canes, frit, latticino, inclusions, etc. The only difference is that here the elements are placed on the stackup of glass cold and are fused into the glass in the kiln. This change has its benefits and its problems. It is beneficial in that it allows for more precise placement of the design element. If you don't like the position of the decoration, you can move it, as long as you have not fired the piece.

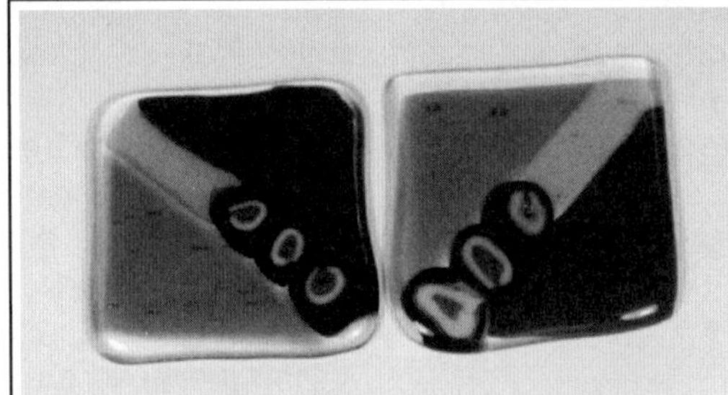

Figure 331. Effect of what layer is decorated.

The problem with placing decorations for a fused piece is that, unless you have a light touch, you can move them when you don't want to. This is especially a problem when moving the kiln self, set up with your project, from the worktable into the kiln. Some people try to get around this problem by working with the shelf already in the kiln but I find that this gives me backaches. The other option is to try to hold the decorations in place as you move the kiln shelf into the kiln.

The most common way used to hold pieces in place during assembly is by the use of glues. A glue typically suggested for this purpose is Elmer's white glue. It is applied sparingly with a toothpick and will burn off during firing of the piece. There are also other commercially available formulations like Thompson's Klyr-fire that are made to be used in a kiln and burn off clean without any residues. If you are gluing down fairly large decorations, it is suggested that you apply the glue near the edges because it can cause bubbles during firing if trapped in the center of a piece of glass. Be aware that glued decorations may move as the adhesive burns off during the firing process if not well supported.

Using glue allows decorations to be arranged in many variations. They can be stacked or draped over one another. Then, by controlling the fusing temperature, you can have them blend into one another or just tack fuse and retain their individuality. You can use frit and canes to "paint" images on your glass beads. These could use lampworked elements like those of Jim and Nevi Wuerfel. To really get a feel for the possibilities available to you, look at one of the suggested fusing references that have a lot of pictures.

If you are adding inclusions like screens, wires, foils, etc. to your fusing projects, these are usually not placed on the upper surface of the glass, because they can burn off or get badly oxidized. It is better to place them between layers of glass to protect them from the oxidative effects of high temperature air.

Another thing to be aware of during firing lay-up is that decorations on the top layer tend to spread out as they are fired to full fuse and beyond. This causes them to lose some of the crispness of their images. Therefore, if that is important to you, it helps to cover the image with a thin layer of glass. This will keep the image in place and sharp rather than soft and mushy. As an example of this, examine the difference between the two coasters seen in Figure 331. The one at the left had the design on top, while the one on the right had it on the bottom. Otherwise, they are identical. Look at how straight the lines at the right are in comparison to the ones on the left.

There are also many other processes and materials that can be done to decorate the surfaces of kilnworked glass. They include lusters, paints, enamels, and decals. I am going to declare these beyond the scope of this work and am listing some suggested references at the end of this chapter to find out more about these topics.

Making tubular bead stock

If you want your fused beads to have patterns on all sides, you will have to use a slightly different technique from those we have talked about to this point. You will have to use molds to form beadstock, which is patterned on all sides, which you then cut up into individual beads. The bead stock can have many cross sectional shapes: squares, triangles, circles, etc. For this discussion, I will illustrate how to do the easiest cross section type, squares. For illustrations in how to manufacture circular cross sectional beads, see the article on Molly Vaughan Haskins' work from Ornament Magazine listed at the end of this chapter.

Prior to starting the fabrication of fused glass beadstock, you can make or develop molds in which to fuse them. They can be made from many of the same materials that slumping molds are made from. For making square cross sectional beadstock, I used rigidized fiber paper formed in the shape of a U that I then supported along the sides with slices taken off of an old kiln shelf, as in Figure 333.

Figure 333. Square beadstock fusing set up.

For triangular beads, a V shaped trough could be similarly constructed. For her circular cross section beads, Molly Vaughan Haskins used mullite kiln stilts, which had been manufactured with a circular hole down the center. She cut them in half down their length to make two beadstock molds. These molds have to be well kilnwashed to prevent the glass from sticking to them.

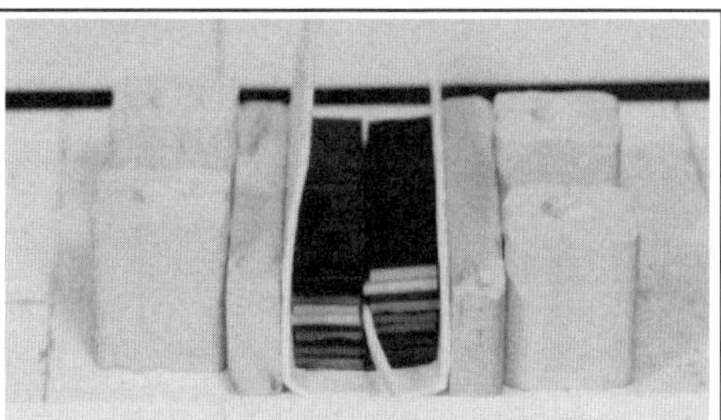

Figure 334. Lay up of glass for beadstock destined to be cut into disk beads.

Next, depending on what you are trying to achieve in your fused beads, you may want to prepare patterned or decorated sheet glass for the outside surface of your beads. Molly used mainly Wasser glass in making her fused beadstock

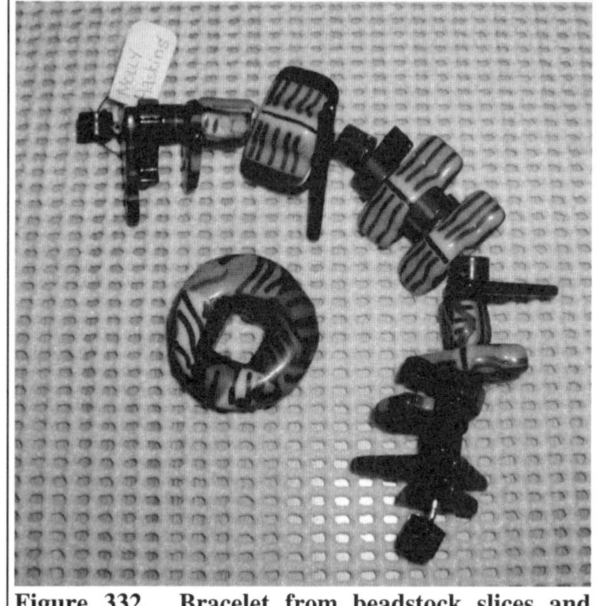

Figure 332. Bracelet from beadstock slices and simple fused beads
Artist: Molly Haskins.

because all the different colors and patterns are about the same hardness. In other words, their viscosity curves are about the same, resulting in the fact that they soften and fuse at about the same temperature and rate.

This is not true with most other glass manufacturer lines. They will vary in hardness from one color to the next. Wasser was a very soft glass, meaning its viscosity tends to be lower at any given temperature allowing it to flow at lower temperatures. It seems to match the properties of Bullseye's black. For your beads, you may want to fuse stripes, dots, latticino, etc. onto the sheet glass prior to cutting it up to make strips to lay in the molds. What I have done in the figure is use some old multicolored Wasser for the edges of the beadstock and Bullseye black for the center.

Now you are ready to start stacking the glass and the hole former into the mold. What you do here depends it upon whether you are after disk shaped beads or longer beads. The difference is whether you only decorate the outside of the beadstock or you also try to decorate throughout the thickness. For disk beads, since more of the inside of the beadstock slice shows than the outside, you want to have lots of color and decorations coming up through the beadstock, as seen in Figure 334.

For longer beads, you may want the inside to be a uniform color. Black seems to be a good color for that purpose. Usually the cross sectional dimension for the different cases will be different also. For disk beads, you will tend to have beadstock cross sectional dimensions that are larger than for normal longer beads. So start cutting up strips and laying them into the mold. Use one of the glues that I talked about in the last section to help hold things in place if needed. Don't forget to position the hole former down the center of the stack.

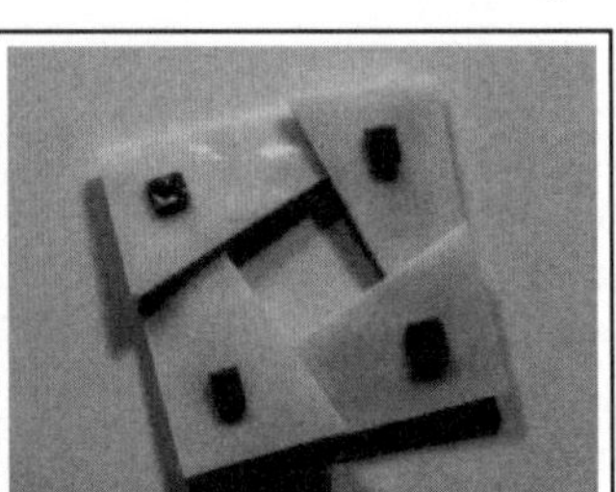

Figure 335. Setup for an individually fused bead.

Now fire the stack, like any other fusing project, paying particular attention to the ramp rates and annealing to avoid thermal shock as well as to keep the final stress in the beads low. You will want to keep your process temperature down in the low full fuse region to prevent too much flow. Let time at temperature do some of the work for you. Some cross sectional shapes may require multiple firings with rotation of the beadstock bar between firings to get the cross sectional shape to look right. This appears to be especially true with circular cross sections. Castings of this cross section can be facilitated by use of a mold top that settles down on the stackup to shape the top portion of the beadstock bar as it gets hot.

After the final firing run, your beadstock is ready to cut to length for the desired bead shape. Then you can either grind and fire polish the cut surfaces or tumble polish the whole bead. We have already discussed the use of low melting-temperature glazes for fire polishing. The procedures for slicing the beadstock and tumble polishing the slices are discussed in the chapter on finishing of beads since they are applicable to a number of beadmaking techniques.

Individual mold beads

If you want beads of shapes other than disks or tubes, you have to resort to use of a different type of mold. One type that we have already discussed is slumping. Here, you can take a simple flat fused bead as seen in Figure 332 and as set up in Figure 335 or use a thin slice from a beadstock bar as discussed above. Then slump them into an internal mold or onto an external mold to shape it. Alternatively, you can cast beads individually in molds that you purchase or make. This technique is described in the next chapter on pâte de verre beads, where instead of frit you use small pieces of glass.

Suggested further reading

Anderson, Harriette, **Kiln-Fired Glass**, 2nd ed., Self-published, 1997

Cummings, Keith, **Techniques of Kiln Formed Glass**, A & C Black 1997

Elskus, Albinas. **The Art of Painting on Glass**, Chas. Scribber and Sons 1980

Fenton, Dan. "***Luscious Lusters***", **Professional Stained Glass magazine**, Vol. 8 No. 4 (November) 1988

Lundstrom, Boyce and Schwoerer, Daniel. **Glass Fusing Book One**, Vitreous Publications, 1983

Moorman, Shar. **Warm Glass - Kiln-fired Glass Forming Techniques**, CKE Publications

Reynolds, Gil. **The Fused Glass Handbook**, Hidden Valley Books

Ross, Anne L. "***Kiln Formed Glass Beadmaking***", **Ornament Magazine**, Vol. 18 No. 1 (Winter) 1994

Schuler, Fredrick & Lilli, **Glassforming, Glassmaking for the Craftsman**, Chilton Book Company, 1970

Walker, Brad, **Contemporary Warm Glass**, Four Corners International Inc, 2000

Pâte de Verre Beads

Pâte de Verre, which is French for paste of glass, is a kilnworking technique where a paste of powdered glass is packed into a refractory mold and fired until the glass is fused. Different colors of glass are combined together to achieve pleasing effects. By varying the firing temperature, you can manipulate the degree to which the individual grains fuse together from a full density bead to a sugary texture as in African powder beads. After annealing, the beads are removed from the mold.

Using Pâte de Verre techniques, you can make intricate one-of-a-kind beads, which have an alabaster like quality, like that seen in Figure 336. You can also make production line reproductions of simpler beads depending on where your interest lies. Multiples of complex shapes are possible using lost wax casting techniques. In this section, you will learn the basics of this process.

If you would like to learn more about the process of making multiples, I suggest that you consult one of the books on the subject, such as "Pâte de Verre and Kiln Casting of Glass" by Dan Fenton and myself, "The Technique of Glass Forming" by Keith Cummings or "Glass Casting and Moldmaking - Glass Fusing Book Three" by Boyce Lundstrom.

To get started in Pâte de Verre beadmaking, you will need a few items.

- The first is a kiln. You may already have a kiln to anneal all the lampworked beads that we have been discussing throughout most of this book. Unfortunately, you may need a larger kiln with a more complex controller to do much in the way of Pâte de Verre beadmaking.
- The next item, a palette of compatible glass, is another thing that you may have from your other beadmaking techniques.
- Refractory mold making materials are a new requirement that is unique to Pâte de Verre beadmaking. We will discuss two materials here; firebrick and plaster based refractories.

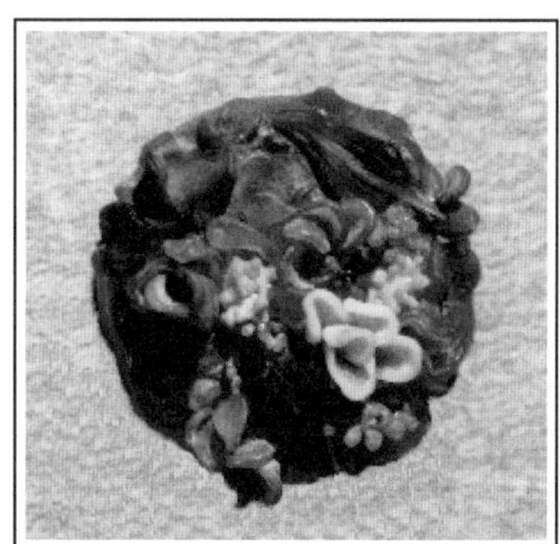

Figure 336. Pâte de Verre bead.
Artist: Donna Milliron
Size: 1½" Diameter x ½" Thick

For simple bead shapes, you may also be able to purchase molds from a fusing or ceramics supply store. You could also make them from many of the materials that are usually used for constructing slumping molds, such as rigidized fiber paper, clay, refractory mixes, etc. These reusable types of molds will have to be kilnwashed prior to use.

Lastly, you will need material to act as a hole former for the beads. These can be made from ceramic fiber strips as was discussed for fused beads. Metal wires coated with separator compound or wood for low temperature beads is also possible.

Frit preparation

Fully fused Pâte de Verre work has a unique alabaster appearance that results from microscopic air bubbles trapped between the fused grains of glass. This leads us into a discussion of the first step of the process, making glass frit. Frit is a name given to small granules of glass. You can make your own frit or buy prepared frit like that in Figure 338.

There are a number of ways that you can make frit. The easiest is just to put on a pair of safety glasses, grab a hammer and bash away. The problem with this technique is that glass ends up flying everywhere. It can be controlled somewhat by wrapping the glass in newspaper first. I put small pieces of glass in a paint or coffee can and beat on them with something long like a capped piece of pipe, as in Figure 337. A nice side benefit of mechanical frit production is that you get a chance to work out all your frustrations without making any enemies, but it is very time consuming. This technique produces a wide variety of frit sizes, from fine to fairly large chunks.

You can sift out the size range that you are most interested in and continue to mash any large chunks until you are satisfied with the final result. If you are trying to make castings of beads from patterned glass as Molly Haskins did, you may want to keep your chunks fairly large or you will lose all of the pattern.

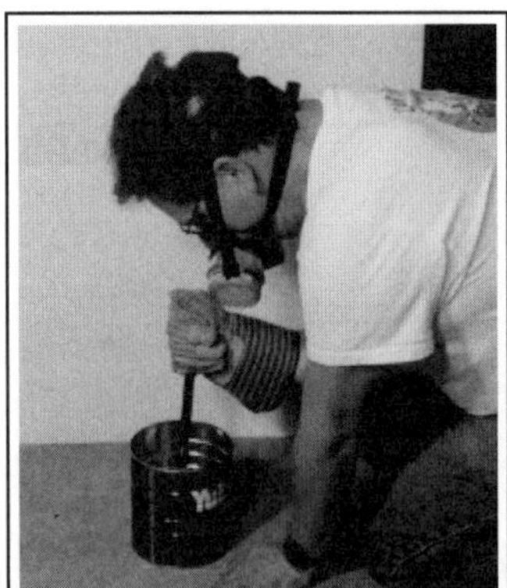
Figure 337. Beating scrap glass in coffee can to frit it

A second method that produces a nice roundish frit slightly larger in size than most mechanical impact methods is to heat glass in the torch and then chill it in water. In fact, you have probably already made a bunch of frit without even realizing it in your attempts to make lampworked beads. How many times have you introduced a glass rod into the flame only to have it thermal shock into small pieces? Hey, save those pieces and use them. To do this a little more purposefully, you can heat up your glass strips or rods and stick them into a cup of water. This quick chill results in tremendous thermal stresses throughout the glass that literally tears it apart.

To speed up this process, you can use your kiln to heat up glass in bulk. Then turn off the kiln, reach in using heat resistant gloves and tongs, pull some of the glass out, and immerse it in a bucket of water. If your buckets are made of plastic, keep your glass pieces small, and hold the glass up off of the bottom of the bucket until it cools (which it is doing as it cracks up). Standing unexpectedly in a puddle of water is not a smart thing to do when standing next to a powered electric kiln. It can prove to be quite a shocking experience.

If you are heating multiple colors of glass in one kiln run, it makes it easier to sort the frit afterward if you frit each color into a separate bucket. To make the kiln fritting process a little faster, you might want to take the kiln all the way up to tack fuse before you shut it off so that the glass can be picked up as lightly fused lumps rather than individual pieces.

The hotter the glass is when put it into the water, the smaller will be the resulting frit. If you have a crucible kiln, you can pour molten glass from the crucible directly into the bucket (slowly though so as not to melt the bucket). Your can use fireplace tongs to grab the crucible. You may have to remove a baffle at the top of the crucible on some kilns to do this (this should be done while the kiln is cold before the run). If your frit is not small enough for you, the thermal treatment makes it easy to mechanically break it up into smaller frit.

In determining what size frit to use, you have to decide what you want your final project to look like. The finer the frit, the more air that gets trapped in the Pâte de Verre process and the more opaque the resulting bead. Donna Milliron tells me that she likes to use a #2 Bullseye frit because it yields the translucency and density that she likes in her beads.

Figure 338. Commercially available Bullseye frit.

Bead mold construction

Next we have to discuss how to make molds in which to cast our pâte de verre beads. The size and intricacy of your bead will dictate how much work you have to put into making your mold. In this book I will discuss two methods for making molds: carving them from firebrick and casting with plaster based investments.

Simple brick molds

The easiest bead mold is one for columnar beads as used in antiquity and as continues to be used to make powdered glass beads. These beads were traditionally made in Africa using clay molds, round pancake affairs with multiple bead holes. The bead holes are made by poking sticks into the wet clay and making a smaller hole in the bottom to center the hole former. These molds are then dried and fired.

You can make a simple bead mold using firebrick to try the same technique. Just take a brick and drill holes part way down into it. You can make them all the same size or of many different sizes. Then in the bottom of the hole, you drill a slightly smaller sized hole to hold your hole former. For the low temperature fired African beads, leaf stems are used as the hole former. For higher temperature fired beads, other materials need to be substituted.

The depth to which you make the holes in the mold depends upon two factors. The first is fairly obvious; you can make longer beads with deeper holes. The second is not quite so obvious. For low temperature beads with a texture like sugar, the bead is pretty much the same size after firing as it was before firing. For beads fired to higher temperatures, a lot of shrinkage occurs.

This shrinkage occurs primarily in the length of the bead as the individual frit pieces get soft and settle down deeper into the mold. In going to a full density glass bead made from frit, you will get about 30% shrinkage in volume. This equates to a 30% shrinkage in length for constant cross section molds. Thus, if you want a final full density bead about 3/4" long, the hole that you fill with frit will have to be about an inch deep.

You also have to kilnwash firebrick molds prior to use to prevent the glass from sticking to them. This allows the possibility of reusing them. When cutting the shapes into the mold, you might want to consider having a shallow draft or taper in them, as seen in the second hole of Figure 339. This makes removal of the bead easier after firing. Also avoid having any undercuts in the mold or it will have to be sacrificed to remove the bead.

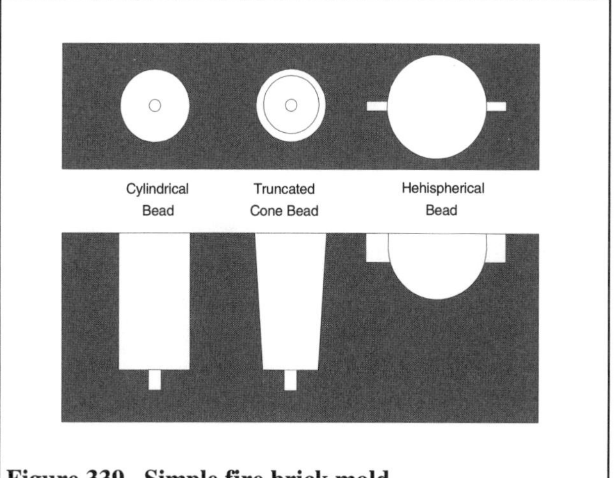

Figure 339. Simple fire brick mold.

Plaster based molds

Firebrick is fine for very simple beads. For beads more complicated in shape than the ones you can carve into firebrick, you will need to learn to make soft sacrificial molds. These molds are made from plaster-based mixtures using the techniques that are illustrated in Figure 340.

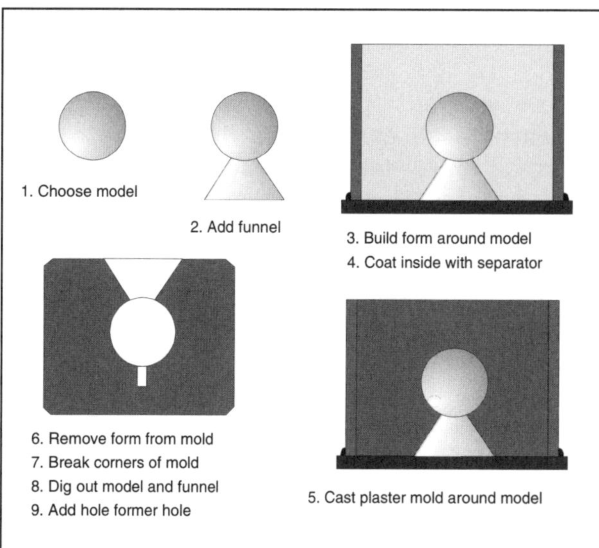

Figure 340. Basic steps to plaster mold making.

To start, make a model for the bead. There are many materials from which an original bead model can be made. The traditional material used for Pâte de Verre models is wax. The beauty of wax is that it is easily removed after casting the mold by melting it out over a pan of hot water in the kiln.

Alternatively, your model could be made from any object that is combustible, like a nut. In this case, the object is burned out of the mold during the cure cycle and the ashes cleaned out before casting your bead. Other combustible materials, which can also be used as bead models, include plastic, wood, vegetables, etc.

Lastly, your model could be made of clay. This is an excellent choice if you are making flat beads like medallions with a minimum of undercuts. After investing the mold around the clay, it can just be pulled out from the back and the mold cleaned well with water to remove any clay residues. Once you have your bead design, you are ready to start thinking about making the mold.

Because your mold is no longer simple as with the fire brick mold, you want to make sure that it gets completely filled. As we now know, whatever glass we stick in the mold will shrink in volume during the firing. Therefore, it may be a good idea to add a reservoir onto the bottom of your model, as shown in Figure 336. For this, mount a small funnel of wax or clay about 1" long. The small end of the funnel should be at least 3/8th" in diameter and the large end about 1" in diameter. It does not need to be very big for beads. This will serve as a place to put extra glass that will flow into the mold and completely fill the designated bead volume.

Because your sacrificial molds are plaster based, they have to be cast in something. These are known as mold frames. They are constructed around your model with a bottom and sides. I find making round frames to be easiest.

To construct round mold frames, I use old strips of linoleum for the sides, as seen in Figure 341. Remnants can usually be obtained cheaply, if not for free, from a flooring contractor. Good sizes to prepare ahead of time are strips varying in width between 1 to 3 inches and in lengths ranging from 8 to 24 inches. I use the longer pieces when I make molds for casting multiple beads at once. When needed, these strips are coiled to size with the ends held in place by duct tape or rubber bands.

Figure 341. Coddles made from strips of linoleum.

When planning the size of a mold frame you need, make sure that you plan for sufficient thickness of the mold. Leave about a inch separation between models and about a half-inch between each model and the side of the mold. Also leave at least a half-inch between the top of the model and the top of the frame.

Figure 342. Hot gluing linoleum coddle to base.

The bottom of the mold frame is usually made from cardboard. I also make mine from glass since it is reusable and I tend to have a lot around. Cut the base so that you have at least one half inch all around the outside of the frame. The bottom edge of the coddle is then hot glued down to the base as seen in Figure 342.

As you plan out your bead mold, you have to consider how you will get the hole in your bead. If you are making a flat medallion, the hole former will run parallel to the mold surface and will be set into slots cut into the mold. For this situation, you can mount your model down flat onto the cardboard bottom of the coddle. Next, the mold is cast around it leaving the backside open.

After the mold is cast, you cut two slots a little deeper than half the thickness of the model and about a quarter of an inch long on either side of the model impression. Into these slots, you will lay your hole former so that it lies across the model volume. Then use a little prefired fiber paper to fill in the top part of the slot above the hole former to prevent glass from filling this area. The right bead hole in Figure 339 is set up for this technique.

For other bead shapes, you will want the hole former to extend vertically down the funnel, which you build into the mold for adding the glass frit. To do this, you have to orient the model with the hole running up and down in the mold. You mount it to the funnel at one end and have the other end where you want the bead hole pointing up. When

Figure 343. Filled bead mold with vertical hole former.

you later install the hole former into the mold you can prevent it from sliding over during the firing by using some copper wire to hold it up, as seen in Figure 343. It also helps to drill a small hole in the bottom of the bead cavity as was done for the firebrick mold. This hole will anchor the bottom of the hole former.

To make the mold easy to remove, you can coat the inside of the mold frame with a separator compound. Products such as liquid dish washing detergents, cooking pan coating (Pam) or light machine oil (WD-40) are suggested. It is easiest if this coating can be applied as a spray.

Depending on what you used for your original model and how you plan to remove it from the mold, you may also want to coat the model with separator compound. For materials that you are going to burn or melt out, this is not necessary. If you do use the separator on the original model, be aware that some surface detail can be lost – so apply it sparingly.

It is now time to mix the plaster-based mold material. I recommend a mold made of a 50/50 solids mix of Hydrocal plaster and 200-mesh silica flour. Silica flour is finely ground flint and is a respiratory hazard. It can cause a disease called silicosis, a disease very similar to asbestosis, so I suggest that you wear a respirator whenever handling it and work to keep the dust down. Mixing plaster can sometimes be a little tricky. Don't expect to necessarily get it right the first time. With a little practice though, you will soon become a pro.

> **Safety Note**: Always use a respirator when working with silica flour.

Mix enough to completely fill your mold in one pour. This will make the strongest possible mold. If this is not possible, allow the previous batch of plaster to set up before adding the next batch. In mixing any plaster-based material, there are a number of suggested rules that should be followed to achieve best results:

1. Always use cool, about 70°F, clean water for your mix. Likewise, keep your mixing bucket and tools clean. The presence of old hardened plaster will cause the new plaster to set up faster, by as much as half the expected setup time.
2. Add the dry plaster-based mixture to the water, not water to the plaster. Slowly sift it out onto the surface of the water. The plaster mix will absorb water and sink. Keep sifting mix onto the water until it no longer sinks and the surface stays slightly dry. This indicates a good plaster to water ratio. As a way to gauge how much water to start with, realize that your finished mix will have approximately twice the volume of the original water.
3. Next, allow the mixture to sit undisturbed and rest for about 3 minutes. This time can be varied from as short as one minute to as long as 10 minutes. It is called "slaking" and is necessary for the plaster to set properly. During this time, the plaster is starting to chemically absorb water and grow crystals.
4. Now stir the plaster-based mix, trying to avoid whipping any air into it. Stir from the bottom to the top to allow any air to rise to the top. The mold mixture should appear to be creamy at this point, not thin and watery, but sort of opaque on the stirrer. Do not overstir because this will cause the plaster to set faster.
5. After mixing, apply the plaster to the model by slowly pouring it into the mold frame. Try not to trap bubbles. It works best if you pour the plaster into an empty corner of the mold frame and allow it to flow around your models. Afterward, gently vibrate the mold by tapping on the edge of the frame or shaking the worktable to free any trapped air and allow it to rise to the surface.
6. Finish by cleaning your plaster-coated tools and bucket in water right away. Start by pouring off any extra plaster mix into some disposable trash container such as a cardboard box or a plastic bag.

Do not clean your equipment in your sink or any other plumbing fixtures (i.e. toilet.) The mold mix particles will settle out in your pipes, and since plaster can set up underwater, will eventually set up and harden. This practice could lead to a complete blockage of your plumbing. Instead always wash your tools off in another large container of water. Let the heavier plaster particles sink to the bottom of the bucket. Then dispose of the water on top in some appropriate manner, like giving a tree a drink. Put the plaster sludge at the bottom into a plastic bag for disposal.

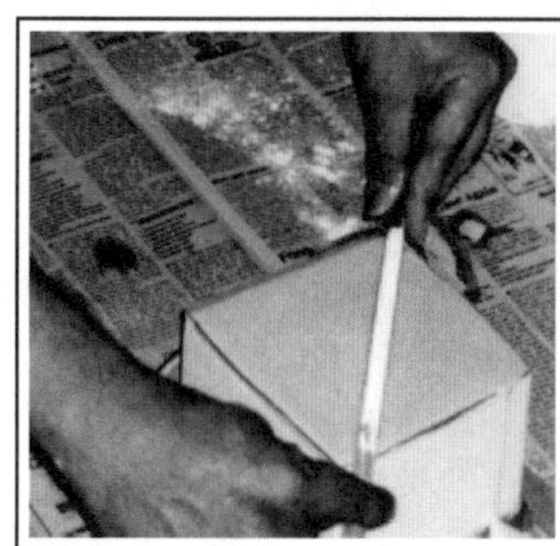

Figure 344. Screeding bottom of the mold.

When first poured, the plaster will look shiny and have a slight water film. As the shine goes away and the plaster starts to get mushy, you will want to draw a flat instrument like a glass rod across the top of your pour, as shown in Figure 344. This will form a nice flat bottom for your mold to sit on the kiln shelf. This should be done in a number of light passes to avoid ripping up the smooth plaster surface, and is complete when your mold is flush with the top of your box. Cleaning the plaster off your screeding instrument after each pass helps to avoid ripping the plaster.

Your mold should start to harden in about 20 to 30 minutes. If not, you may have gotten a bad batch of plaster or have somehow done something drastically wrong. Setup for plaster-based molds generally take about two hours to develop the proper interconnective chemical bonding. Once the plaster has set up, remove the frame from around the mold along with any hot glue.

Next you should scrape all the edges of the mold with a sharp knife trying to remove any sharp edges or divots along the edge. These may serve as points for cracks to initiate as the mold dries and is cured.

After your mold has completely cured, it is time to remove your models. Since plaster mixes expand upon curing, this should be easy. (Assuming that you don't have a lot of undercuts in your models.) You may be able pry the model out with a sharp tool. Injecting compressed air under your model is also helpful in breaking the suction between it and the mold.

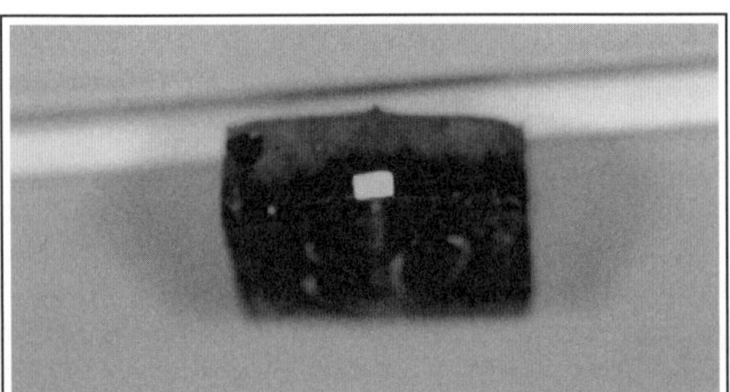

Figure 345. Square hole in pâte de verre bead from fiber paper strips.

If you used something like clay, you can carve out the bulk of it from the mold and wash out any residual clay with warm water. All residual clay must be removed or it will contaminate your final work.

If you used wax, you can melt it out over a pan of water in your kiln after you dry your mold. (Don't let all the water evaporate out of the pan or you may start a fire.) After you have melted out all the wax you think possible, you will have to burn out the rest during curing of the mold in the next step.

For best results, a mold should be well air dried before putting it in the kiln for casting. Drying reduces the amount of water in the mold so that it does not turn into steam when heated in the kiln. The expansion of water as it changes into steam will crack the plaster

If you used wax or organic models, you should burn all organic residues out of the mold after drying. If not, you can cure the mold during the frit-casting step. To burn out a mold, place it in your kiln with the funnel opening up. Slowly heat the mold to drive out any remaining water, but not too fast or steam could be produced.

Of course slowly is a relative thing. It is relative to how much time you have already put into this mold and how willing you are to take chances. You can use an initial temperature rise rate in the range of 100°F per hour per inch thickness of the mold. Soak the mold for about an hour per inch of thickness, first at 225°F to remove physically adsorbed water and again at 350°F to remove any chemically bound water. Then continue to slowly heat the mold up to 1200°F to burn out any residual organic materials. Here the heating ramp rate should again be in the range of 100°F/hr. The slower you go, the stronger the mold will remain.

At about 900°F, the mold will start to turn black and will smoke as the organics begin to burn out. For your protection, keep the kiln well ventilated. As it gets near 1200°F, the mold will turn white again because all the carbon will have been burned out. After this has occurred, slowly cool the mold back down to room temperature.

Filling your mold

The first step in filling a bead mold for casting is the insertion of a hole former into the mold. The type of material you choose for a hole former depends upon how dense you want to fuse the bead.

If you are looking for a lightly fused, sugar-like bead, then you are going to do a low-temperature fusing run. In such a situation, the frit does not move around much and just fuses in the spots where the pieces are touching each other, without filling in the voids between them. In such a case, a material that burns away like the leaf stems that the Africans use is adequate. A more up-to-date material might be something like kiln washed bamboo. Be aware though that the carbon from any of these may stain your beads.

When you want a full-density bead where the frit will pack in and fills voids, you have to use a hole former that can survive the high temperatures of the full-fuse firing cycle. In this case there are a number of high-temperature hole former options available. You could use short sections of kiln-washed mandrel and pieces of rigidized Fiberfrax® alumina yarn (available in $^{3}/_{32}{}^{nd}$ and $^{1}/_{8}{}^{th}$ inch diameters) or fiber paper strips.

Most bead artists use fiber paper strips rather than yarn because it is cheaper and easier to find. Because of this they end up with beads with square holes as in Figure 345. It is best to rigidize and prefire the paper to give it strength during the firing process. The yarn or paper can be rigidized by soaking it in a hardening solution of 15% colloidal silica followed by air drying and firing in a kiln to about 1300°F. The hole formers may or may not then be coated with separator compound. As I said before, let the hole former stick up out of the funnel for easy removal after firing. For medallion flat molds, fill in the top parts of the slots with unrigidized fiber paper as was also discussed earlier.

Now slowly pour the frit into the mold. You can use one single color, layers of color, mixtures of colors, or pack different colors into specific locations, as was done for the pendant in Figure 346. Try not to bend the hole former or it may be hard to remove after firing. When using large patterned glass chunks instead of frit in simple-shaped, reusable molds, you may find that use of a little glue helpful in holding the pattern together in the desired orientations as you pack the mold.

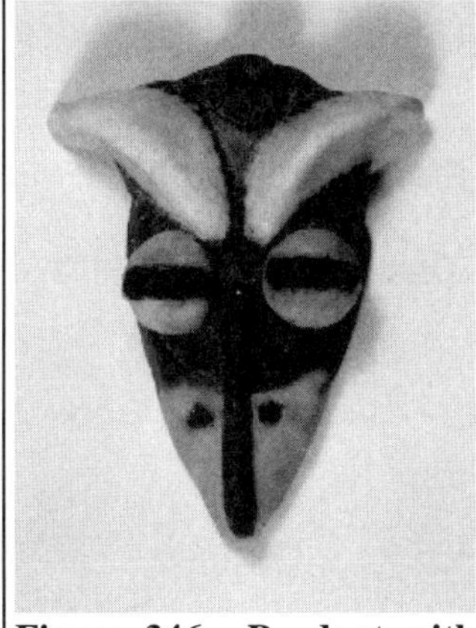

Figure 346. Pendant with color discretely placed. Artist: Jim Kervin Size: 1" W x 2" L x ½" T

Firing your bead

The bottom of the mold that you screed with the ruler should sit flat on the kiln shelf. In addition, check to see that your kiln shelf is level. Otherwise, whatever you are making will vary in final thickness. This may not be apparent on small beads, but it certainly can be on larger medallions. Use sand to level under your mold if you have a problem with this.

Once your mold is filled and in the kiln, it is time to cook. The basic firing schedule is sketched out in Figure 347. Slowly bring the mold up to the Pâte de Verre temperature for your glass (about 1300°F for Bullseye.) Ramp rates have to be controlled in order to prevent thermal shocking your mold and should be in the range of 100°F/hour/inch of plaster thickness.

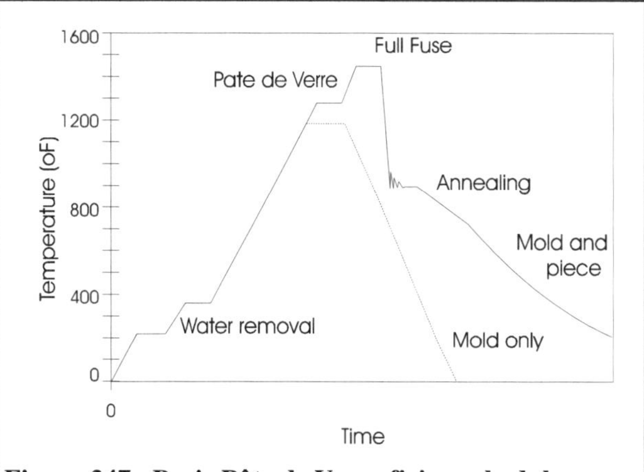

Figure 347. Basic Pâte de Verre firing schedule

If you have not prefired your mold ahead of time, you will have to go slower and dwell at both 225 and 350°F for at least an hour per inch of mold thickness to remove water bound in the plaster, as was described earlier. It is during this rise to process temperature that your mold is most likely to crack, if at all. Here your glass is still fairly rigid and your mold starts to shrink fairly quickly once it reaches about 1200°F.

Upon reaching Pâte de Verre temperature for your glass, you will need to hold the kiln at that temperature until you are sure that your glass has equilibrated inside the mold. The mold insulates the glass, causing its temperature to lag behind that of the kiln. Hold longer if you heated faster. You will have to hold the temperature at the control point for 1 to 2 hours per inch of thickness of the mold, depending on how fast you heated up the mold. You will then want to continue on up to full fuse point and hold for another hour per inch of mold thickness to get full fuse. Check to see if you need to add more frit as it consolidates itself.

After you have finished your hold at process temperature, vent the kiln to rapidly drop its temperature down to the annealing point as was done for fusing. Remember we are doing this to avoid devitrification. Then, close your kiln. You will have to hold at this temperature to allow the glass to equilibrate again for the same 1 to 2 hours per inch of mold thickness. You will now slowly lower the work from the annealing point to the strain point for your glass over a time period of 4-8 hours per inch thickness of casting.

To finish you want to slowly cool your casting to room temperature. You should do this at a rate of about 100°F per inch of mold thickness. Then, allow the mold to remain undisturbed at room temperature for a few hours before you even think of demolding. After it is completely cooled off, slowly break away the mold from the glass. Use a small hammer and chisel if necessary to slowly break plaster molds apart. (For properly constructed firebrick molds, you should just be able to slide the bead out of the mold.) If it starts to feel hot, stop and let it cool some more. After you have the casting free from the mold, don't stick it in water right away to wash off any remaining mold material. Let it sit for a couple more hours before you clean it. The key to the whole firing process is patience.

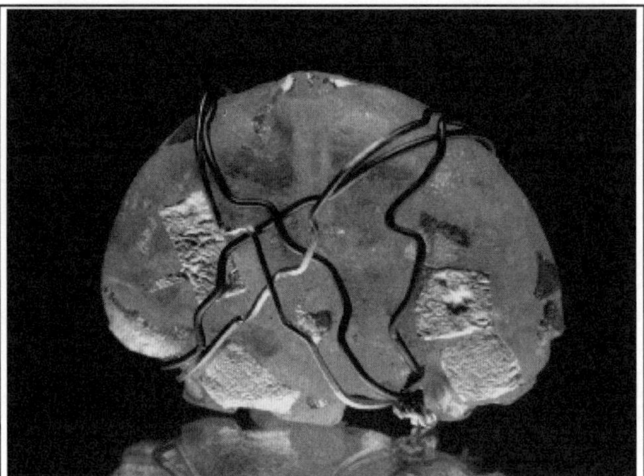

Figure 348. Finished pâte de verre bead all shined up.
"Fairy Basket Bead" Artist: Donna Milliron
Size: 1½" Diameter x ½" Thick
Photo by: Christopher Marchetti

Most artists find that some cold work of the beads is required after firing to clean them up and polish them. This is usually done using sanding belts, grinding wheels and polishing felts before you get them as shiny as the one in Figure 348. Final polishing can then be done by tumbling as will be described in the next chapter.

Suggested further reading

Cummings, Keith. **The Technique of Glass Forming**, A & C Black., 1997

DeCamp, Lane. ***Inspired Beads, Artistry at Arrow Springs***, **Bead & Button Magazine** Num. 8 (April) 1995

Fenton, Dan and Kervin, Jim. **Pâte de Verre and Kiln Casting of Glass**, GlassWear Studios, 2001

Francis, Peter Jr. ***West African Powder Glass Beads***, **Ornament Magazine** Vol. 16 Num. 4 (Summer), 1993

Kohler, Lucartha. **Glass An Artist's Medium**, 1st ed., Krause Publications, 1999

Lundstrom, Boyce. **Advanced Fusing Techniques - Glass Fusing Book Two**, Vitreous Publications, Inc., 1989

Lundstrom, Boyce. **Glass Casting and Moldmaking - Glass Fusing Book Three**, Vitreous Publications, Inc., 1989

Schuler, Frederic and Lilli. **Glassforming**, 1st ed., Chilton Book Company, 1970

Tokyo Glass Art Institute**, The Art and Technique of Pâte de Verre**, 1st ed., Tokyo Glass Art Institute, 1998

Annealing Beads

In this chapter we will discuss final annealing of your lampworked beads or objects so that they will withstand the test of time. I cannot emphasize the importance of this step enough. If you do not anneal your beads there is no guarantee that they will not break at some time in the future. This is especially important for those of you that intend to sell your work. Nothing will sully your name and that of the whole beadmaking profession as having a bead that someone has paid good money for spontaneously self-destructing. Now if you were selling cheap mass-produced beads from a third-world country, people would expect and be forgiving of some breakage. I know that I have seen a lot of these beads broken when cruising the bins of the local bead store.

As an example of what can happen, let's discuss Prince Rupert's drops. These drops look like little tadpoles of glass that are both tough and fragile at the same time. The drops are named for a 17th century prince, who after seeing them demonstrated in a Bavarian glass factory, used them to impress and amaze England's King Charles the second.

The drops are a crude form of tempered glass made by dropping a glob of molten glass into a cup of water. The quick quench cools the exterior into a solid. As the interior cools and shrinks, it pulls on the exterior of the drop putting it into compression and giving its strength. If you look at the drop between two polarizing filters as we discussed in the chapter on fused beads you will see all the stress in them. You can beat on the head of the drop with a hammer with no damage, but if you even scratch the tail you will set off an explosive chain reaction that results in glass shards flying everywhere. Similarly, if your beads have stress in them, they may seem strong but could fall apart when insulted at some time in the future.

From our earlier discussion on the properties of glass, you can understand that a lot of stress still remains in your beads after cooling them in vermiculite. Even though you may flame anneal a bead as well as you can, the temperature on the outside of the bead drops too rapidly in any uncontrolled cooling situation relative to the inside of the bead to allow it to remain stress free. The inevitable result of this is significant residual stress.

The larger the bead, the more stress will be contained inside after uncontrolled cooling. You may be able to get by without annealing small beads but you can never be sure. This uncertainty is compounded if you add inclusions or dichroic glass to your beads. Another area for concern is with sculptural beads, which have widely varying cross sections at different locations in the bead and corresponding cooling rates. Therefore, it is best to kiln anneal all beads to remove as much stress as possible.

Source of stress

Where does all this stress come from? As you remember, glass expands when heated and contracts when cooled, so any temperature gradients in the glass result in differences in length of adjacent portions of the glass. These differences in lengths of nearby sections are commonly referred to as strain. They can, in the limit, be thought of as differences in distances between adjacent glass atoms.

Atoms in any material stay together because they are attracted to each other and these attractive forces can be thought of as rubber bands. So as you stretch (strain) the rubber bands, they build up forces (stress) in them that want to push or pull the atoms back to their optimal position. For rubber bands, if you hold them stretched for long periods of time, they start to grow in length and loose much of the force on them. For glass, this can happen at higher temperatures where the attractive forces become weaker but not at lower temperatures.

In cooling a bead, the glass cools from the outside surface. This sets up temperature gradients in the glass such that the outside is cooler than the inside. The optimum distance between glass atoms increases with temperature as seen by the fact that glass has a positive COE. So the temperature gradient sets up a density gradient, which causes the adjacent atoms to yank and pull on each other.

At high temperatures, where the atoms are still relatively mobile, they will flow around to relieve this stress just as a rubber band stretches with time. Thus they will move into an area where the rubber bands, or forces, between the atoms are stretched or are in tension. Likewise they will flow out of an area where they have been squeezed together, commonly known as compression. So in the high temperature fluid and flexible regimes, you don't have problems with stress. The glass just flows to relieve it.

At low temperatures in the brittle solid regime, bonds between the atoms are rigid and cannot stretch much relative to each other. So when temperature gradients cause stress in this temperature regime by differential heating or cooling, they are stuck with it. But the stress state in this situation is temporary and goes away as soon as the temperature gradients go away and all the rubber bands again become the same length again.

The situation, where you run into trouble and develop permanent stress is in cooling your beads from high temperature when the outside becomes cool enough that the atoms cannot move much but the inside is still hot enough that the atoms are free to move. As the hard outside squeezes on the soft inside, the atoms on the inside move around to push back evenly on the outside like air pushes on the sides of a balloon. Then as the inside cools a little more, these atoms get locked into position based upon the existing temperature gradient.

As the bead continues to cool and the temperature gradient reduces, the atoms in the center of the glass find themselves farther apart than the desired spacing on which the atoms on the outside of the glass are located. Thus they will be in tension, pulling against the surrounding glass with a residual stress, while the outside will be in compression, trying push back against the inside.

If the glass on the outside or the inside is not strong enough, the glass cracks apart. This may happen immediately upon returning to room temperature or, if just barely strong enough, as with the Prince Rupert drops, it can occur at a later time when subjected to a stressful environment. This can be in the form of a thermal variation or an insignificant physical impact.

Terms relevant to annealing

Before you can start annealing, you have to know the annealing temperature range for your glass. As we have discussed, there are three commonly defined points that are important in defining the annealing range — the softening point, the annealing point and the strain point.

The **softening point** marks the transition between the flexible solid temperature regime and the non-brittle solid temperature regime for a given glass. It is the lowest temperature at which a rod or strip of glass will slump over an extended heat soak of a reasonable length of time (an hour.)

The **annealing point** is that temperature at which the atoms are mobile enough to allow all stress to quickly flow out of the glass but is below the softening point so that the glass is not so mobile that the bulk glass will flow.

The **strain point** is the temperature at which the atoms are no longer mobile enough to allow the stress to flow out of a piece in a reasonable length of time. This, as was mentioned earlier, serves as the boundary between the brittle solid and the non-brittle solid temperature regimes.

The region in which you have to be careful during cooling is the **annealing region**. It goes from the annealing point down to the strain point. The softening point is important because it is an easily measurable temperature that can serve as an approximate signpost that you are approaching the location of the other two points.

Allowable temperature changes

With these basics behind us let's next discuss how to calculate the stress that changing temperature can cause in glass. It should be relatively intuitive that the faster you change the surface temperature of a piece, or its rate of change, the more stress and strain that you will have in the glass. The actual magnitude of stress will depend upon a number of factors. These include:

- The rate of surface temperature change.
- The thermal conductivity of the glass.
- A material property call the elastic modulus, which relates the stress and strain in the glass. (Essentially the spring constant of the glass.)
- The coefficient of expansion of the glass.
- The geometry of the piece of glass, which for simplicity we will mainly look at flat glass sheets of thickness, t.
- How the heat is being applied, say from one side or two.

When changing the surface temperature of a flat sheet of glass, the center of the sheet will always lag behind. If one were to solve the heat transfer equations for this situation, you would find that the relationship between the temperature at the surface of the glass and that at the center is a parabolic one of the form:

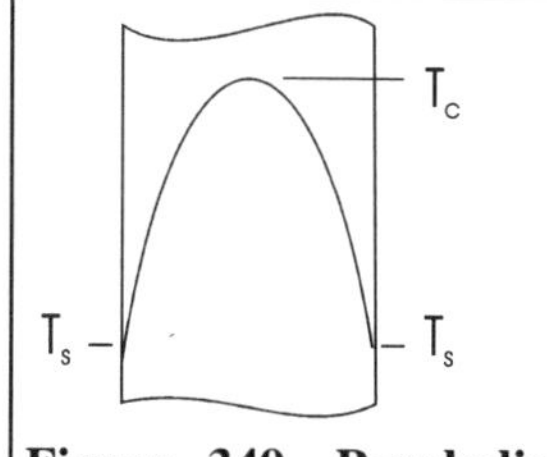

Figure 349. Parabolic thermal distribution

$$\Delta T = T_s - T_c = t^2 R / (8 K)$$

where:

ΔT — is the difference in temperature between the surface and the center of the sheet in °C,
T_s — is the temperature at the surface of the sheet in °C,
T_c — is the temperature at the center of the sheet in °C,
t — is the thickness of the sheet of glass,
R — is the rate of temperature change at the surface of the sheet in °C/sec, and
K — is the thermal conductivity of the glass.

Thermal gradients occur during heating or cooling because as we change the external temperature of the bead, heat has to flow into or out of it until it reaches equilibrium with its environment. Until then, the temperature across the cross section of the bead will vary just like the temperature in the center of a roast lags behind when you cool it. Again we don't care as long as we do not cook it too fast and char the outside of the roast as well as wait the appropriate amount of time for the center to reach the proper temperature. So we need to know how fast heat sinks into the bead.

The above equation describes a temperature distribution that is in the glass, which looks like the one pictured in Figure 349. This temperature distribution will set up strain in the glass because the atoms at the surface of the sheet will want to be a different distance apart than those at the center of the sheet. The strain (ε) between the surface and the center is equal to the ratio of the distance between atoms at the surface to that in the center of the sheet. This is expressed as:

$$\varepsilon = \alpha L (T_s - T_c) / L = \alpha \Delta T$$

where:

ε — is the strain in the glass in in/in (inches/inch),
α — is the coefficient of thermal expansion of the glass in in/in/°C, and
L — is the distance between atoms in inches.

This strain or stretching of the distance between atoms will be opposed by stress trying to maintain the desired distance between all of the atoms in the sheet of glass. The equation that relates the stress (σ) and the strain is called Hook's law and is of the form:

$$\sigma = E \varepsilon / (1 - \upsilon)$$

where:

σ — is the stress in the glass in lb/in^2 or psi,
E — is the Young's modulus of the material in lb/in^2 or psi, and
υ — is Poisson's ratio, which is dimensionless .

The factor $(1 - \upsilon)$ is a correction to account for the fact that when you pull on a material in one direction that it tends to shrink in the directions perpendicular to it. Try pulling on a rubber band and see what I am talking about.

We can now combine these three equations by replacing the ε in the third equation with its equivalent ($\alpha \Delta T$) from the second equation. Then we replace the ΔT that we just brought in with its equivalent ($t^2 R / (8 K)$) from the first equation. When you do all that you get an equation that calculates the maximum stress in the glass as a function of the rate of temperature change.

$$\sigma = [E \alpha t^2 / (8 K (1 - \upsilon))] R$$

or since what we really want is an allowed rate of temperature change for a given maximum acceptable stress in the glass, we can rearrange the equation to the form

$$R = [8 K (1 - \upsilon) / E \alpha t^2] \sigma$$

Now you may not believe it but this is really a pretty simplistic derivation because we have assumed that all of the material properties of the glass are constant. That is not true but it is close enough to being true for our work.

Let's simplify this equation a little bit more by replacing some of the letters representing the glass's material properties with representative approximate values. The ones that we will use are:

υ — a Poisson's ratio of ~ 0.22,
E — a Young's modulus of ~ 10^7 lb/in^2,
K — a thermal conductivity of 0.0013 in^2/sec, and
α — replace the coefficient of thermal expansion with ~ 2.4 x 10^{-7} COE in in/in/°C.

The 2.4 is a fudge factor to account for the fact that a glass's COE changes considerably at the higher temperatures we will be considering.

Putting all these into the last equation gives the approximate relationship

$$R \approx \sigma / (\, 100 \text{ COE } t^2 \,)$$

While you weren't looking I also compensated for the fact that part of the glass is in compression and part of it is in tension and because what we are really interested in is the maximum tensile stress. If this gets too large then the glass can crack. This change threw in a factor of three into consideration. It will also sometimes throw another factor of two into consideration depending on whether we are heating or cooling that I will discuss later. For thickness in inches, COE of integers (actually in 10^{-7} in/in/°C) and stress in psi, this equation will give rates in °C/sec.

If you would rather calculate your rates in °F/min then the equation becomes

$$R \approx 1.08\, \sigma / (\, \text{COE } t^2 \,)$$

Since this equation is only an approximation and the fact that our beads will already have a lot of stress in them before we start, the allowable stresses that we will choose to stay beneath are ones considerably below the actual lowest expected tensile breaking stress of about 4000 lb/ in^2 (psi). I would suggest having at least a factor of safety of 4 and use an allowable stress of 1000 psi in your calculations of allowable temperature rate changes.

As I mentioned going into this discussion, we will be considering the case of a sheet of glass on which both the top and the bottom surface are having their temperature changed at the same time. In most cases we usually have a piece laying on a kiln shelf with only one surface exposed to the kiln elements. In this case the kiln shelf acts like the other half of the sheet and we have to treat the glass as if it were twice as thick. Thus if you have a fused piece that is the usual one quarter of inch in thickness, you have to anneal it on a schedule as if it were one-half-inch thick. (If you were to go back to the fusing section and calculate those rates, you would find that I was even more conservative in my allowable stress there to attempt to compensate for the much lower COE of the kiln shelf that the glass is sitting on and may be lightly attached to by way of the kiln wash.)

Similar reasoning can also be applied to larger blown beads where the outside is exposed to the kiln elements while the inside is exposed to the inside wall opposite to it. So here if you have a blown bead with an eighth of an inch wall thickness, you have to anneal it as if it were one quarter of an inch thick piece of glass.

The next question that probably comes to mind is what if you do not have a quasi-flat object. What if instead you are talking about a round bead?

Effect of geometry on annealing

I ran a number of heat transfer calculations to explore the effect of different shapes and sizes on cooling rates of glass objects. What I wanted to do was demonstrate how the temperature distributions vary as the geometry was changed.

I looked at how temperature variations develop in three basic glass configurations: large flat sheets, long cylinders, and spheres. I calculated how the different shapes affect how fast the center of the glass cools down during an instantaneous crash cooling from 1400°F to 1000°F. To approximate this for the calculation, the outside surface of the piece is assumed to be instantaneously reduced to 1000°F.

Of course, the outside surface does really not instantaneously change temperature like that in real

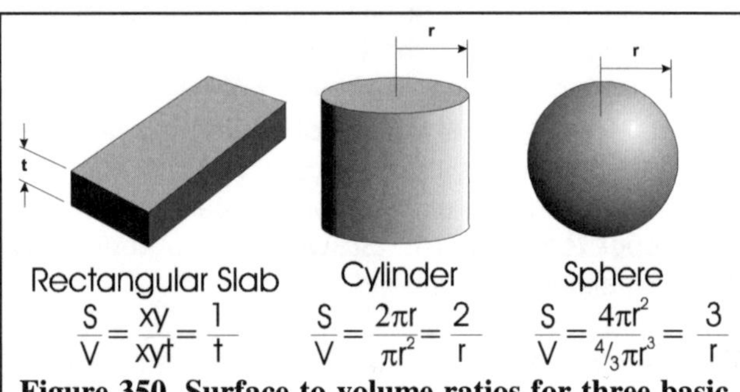

Figure 350. Surface to volume ratios for three basic shapes studied.

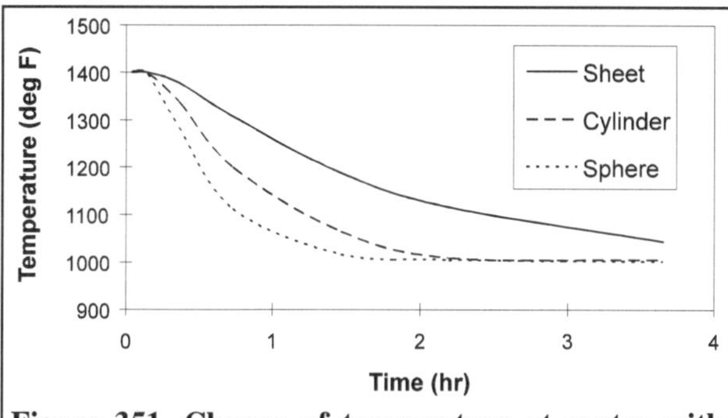

Figure 351. Change of temperature at center with time for different shapes.

life. Instead, the outside surface cools by air convection and radiation. This would slow down the cooling process, and therefore the actual cooling times would be longer than those estimated here.

As you might expect, each of these shapes cools somewhat differently. This is because the surface to volume ratio increases as you go from a rectangular slab to a long cylinder and then on to a sphere. These ratios, which are given in Figure 350, go from 1/t to 2/r to 3/r. Since cooling occurs from the surface, the higher the surface to volume ratio; the faster the object will cool. Thus a sphere transfers heat out of it three times faster than a rectangular slab and one and a half times faster than a cylinder.

Figure 351 illustrates how these different heat transfer capabilities affect how fast the center of each shape will cool with the step change in temperature of the outside of the shape. It plots the temperature of the center of the glass for each of these three different shapes: a 6" thick sheet (cooled from both sides), a 6" diameter cylinder, and a 6" diameter sphere. In this graph, we see that the temperature variations in large sheets are more than about twice those in spheres and one and a half those in long cylinders for fairly long time periods.

Thus, if you wanted it is allowable to change the temperature of spheres twice as fast or cylinders one and a half times as fast as sheets to get the same temperature gradient. I ignore this factor when I calculate my rates of allowable temperature change.

Typical annealing cycle

The basic idea behind the annealing process is as follows. You lay out your beads on a kiln shelf as shown in the right side of Figure 352. You heat the beads up to the point where the atoms are mobile enough to move around and relieve any strain, but

Figure 352. Beads laid out for annealing.

not so mobile that the beads slump and lose their shape. Then, you cool the beads back to room temperature at a slow enough rate that any temperature variation, and thus shrinkage of the bead, is uniform enough that large stresses are not introduced.

Figure 353 illustrates a typical complete annealing cycle. It consists of five phases: a heating phase, an annealing phase, a slow cooling phase, an equilibrium phase, and a final cooling phase. If you are sticking your beads directly into a hot kiln as you make them, then your heating phase will be minimal. Your kiln will already be at or just below the annealing point. Let's look at each of these phases in greater detail

Heating phase

In the heating phase the main objective is to heat up the bead to the annealing temperature without breaking the bead. We are not worried if we are stressing the bead because that stress will all flow out of the bead during the annealing phase. If we break the bead, this is something that is much

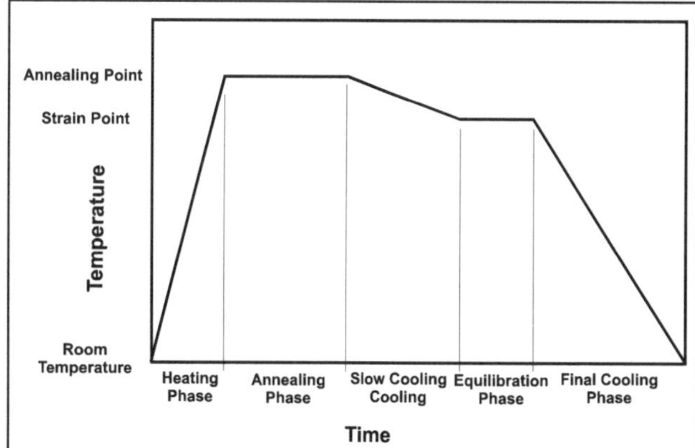

Figure 353. Typical kiln temperature cycle during an annealing run.

harder to fix. So the question is how fast can you heat the bead without breaking it?

To understand that, we have to review how thermal gradients stress a bead. As you heat a bead, its outside will be hotter than the inside. Along with that, the outside will be trying to grow larger relative to the inside from thermal expansion. This will cause a stress tug-of-war between the inside and outside of the bead, and as long as the rope doesn't break we're happy. But if it does, then the bead breaks and we are sad.

In this situation, the inside of the bead is trying to hold the outside of the bead back. This means that the inside is in tension and that it is the portion of the bead that we have to be concerned about crack initiation. The outside of the bead on the other hand is in compression. Here the atoms are pushing against each other trying to expand as much as the higher temperature requires them to. There is very little concern about a crack initiating here.

To better understand what is happening inside the bead, let's examine its average temperature. Figure 354 shows the temperature distribution in a sheet of glass as it is heating. The outside of the sheet is at T_s and the center of the sheet is at T_c. Somewhere in between these two points is a position at temperature T_a, the average temperature of the sheet. The shaded areas of the temperature distribution above and below this temperature, as seen by the horizontal line, have to be the same. It just so happens that T_a is one third of the way between T_c and T_s. This is that factor of three that I corrected for earlier.

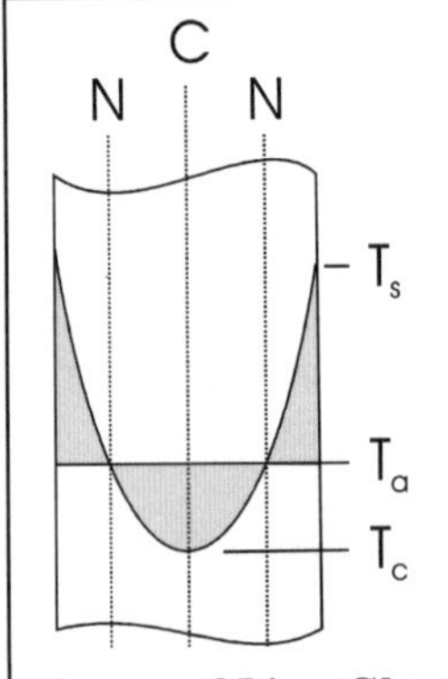

Figure 354. Glass sheet thermal distribution when being heated

If we imagine planes in the sheet of glass stacked up parallel to the surface, like cards in a deck, the ones that go through the average temperature point are the planes marked N, for neutral planes, in the figure. Since these planes are at the average temperature, there is no stress in them. During a constant rate temperature change, any portion of the glass where the temperature of the glass is lower than the average temperature will be in tension. This is the volume between the two N planes in the center of the sheet. In addition, the magnitude of the maximum tensile stress is proportional to the difference between the average temperature and the coolest temperature in the volume, which in this case is at the center of the sheet. This difference

$$(T_a - T_c) = {}^1/_3 (T_s - T_c)$$

Likewise, any portion of the glass at higher temperature than the average temperature will be in compression and the maximum compressive stress will be proportional to the difference between the highest temperature in that region, which in this case is at the surface of the sheet, and the average temperature. This difference

$$(T_s - T_a) = {}^2/_3 (T_s - T_c)$$

This is the factor of two that I ignored earlier and which we can ignore in this case because that portion of the glass is in compression.

Thus to calculate our allowed heating rate, we determine the appropriate thickness (t) of the glass, its coefficient of expansion (COE), and choose an appropriate allowable stress. As an example, I will consider a ½ inch diameter Effetre glass (COE=104) bead and will hold it to the same 1,000 psi maximum stress that we discussed earlier. Plugging these values into our allowable rate equation, yields the following allowable heating rate

$$R = 1.08 (1000)/ (104 [½]^2) = 41.5 \text{ °F/min}$$

Annealing phase

The temperature to which you will heat the beads should be well below that for which you will see any slumping over the time that you will soak them there. But, at the same time, it should be high enough that stress will flow. This temperature is commonly called the annealing point. You will soak the beads at this temperature, for about a half an hour to allow all the stress to flow out of them.

Table 22 lists annealing temperatures for some common beadmaking glasses. Realistically you don't need to be exactly at the glass's annealing temperature. Looking at the table, you see that the annealing temperature for any of the first four glasses is about 1000°F. This temperature is not that much higher than any of these listed annealing temperatures and thus using it for the annealing point for any of them would not cause a problem unless you were to dwell there for long periods of time. If you did, the beads may slump on you.

The amount of time that you soak your beads at the annealing temperature partially depends upon the cycle that you are doing. If your kiln has been hanging at the annealing temperature, then you only need to allow enough time for the stress to flow out of the bead. This occurs in about 15 minutes at temperature. So a one half-hour dwell should be more than enough for any of the pieces that we deal with in beadmaking.

If you try to use this rule-of-thumb for much larger work, you might run into a little trouble. Looking back at Figure 351, we see that the temperature difference in a six-inch-thick sheet only drops about one fifth of the crash temperature difference in one half hour. For this case you would want to let the glass equilibrate for probably 10 hours. (Note I threw in a factor of two here to account for the fact that I am usually heating projects this thick from only one side.)

To allow time for the center of the bead to catch up with the surface we have to estimate how long it takes for the temperature to penetrate to the core of the bead after going through the heating cycle. For this, I would recommend an annealing point soak based on the following formula

For d < 1" $t = 30$ min
For d ≥ 1" $t = 30 + 4\,d^2$ min

Thus for our ½" diameter bead we would soak for 30 minutes and for our 6" thick slab (treating it as double the thickness) we would soak for 606 minutes.

Slow cooling phase

After soaking at the annealing temperature, you next have to slowly lower the kiln temperature down through the rest of the annealing zone. This zone is where stress's ability to flow changes rapidly. It is bounded above by the annealing point and below by the strain point. This is the lowest temperature at which stress can flow in any appreciable time, hours. Strain points for several common beadmaking glasses are also listed in Table 22. Where ones are not present use a safe value like 650°F. It is during cooling through this zone where stress can be trapped. So you have to go slowly.

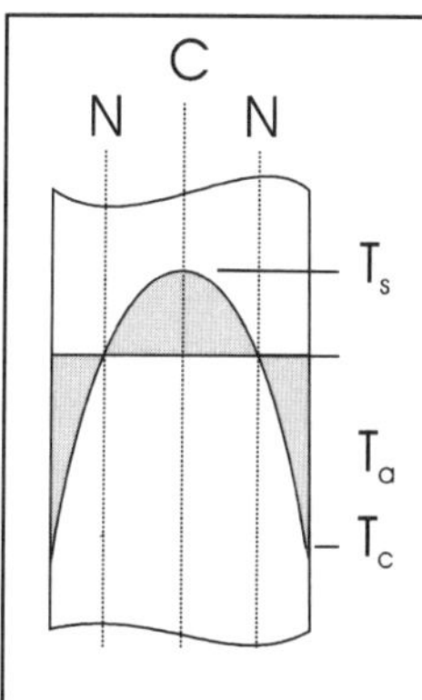

Figure 355. Glass sheet thermal distribution when being cooled

Table 22. Annealing zone temperatures for common glasses.

Glass Manufacturer	Strain Point (°F)	Annealing Point (°F)	COE
Wasser	650	950	90
Spectrum	700	950	96
Effetre	680	970	104
Bullseye	750	980	90
Satake	—	870	113-120
Lauscha	—	900	95-105
Pyrex	950	1058	32
Window	850	1150	—

In cooling we reverse the temperature distribution that we saw in heating. Figure 355 shows what this looks like. In this distribution the average temperature is again one-third of the way between T_c and T_s. This time though the center of the sheet is at a higher temperature. It is the surface of the sheet, which is at the lower temperature than the average temperature and will be in tension as it tries to compress around the warmer core. Since

$$(T_s - T_a) = {}^2\!/_3\,(T_s - T_c)$$

that factor of two will now come into play in calculating the tensile stress in the sheet and the allowable rate of temperature change for cooling has to be reduced by a facto of two to account for this fact. It becomes

$$R \approx 0.54\,\sigma / (\,\mathrm{COE}\ t^2\,)$$

In addition, since the stress that is put into the glass during the slow cooling phase will remain trapped in the glass, we want to have a much lower value for the allowable stress in this phase than in the heating phase. I suggest reducing it by another factor of four down to 250 psi. If you are going to be real abusive to the bead afterwards such as by grinding it or sandblasting it, you may want to reduce the allowable stress even further. As an example, plate glass companies try to keep the residual stress in their glass below 100 psi so that it will cut controllably.

Thus in going back to our example of the ½ inch diameter Effetre bead, which we now want keep its residual stress below 250 psi. Plugging these values into the allowable cooling rate equation gives:

$$R = 0.54\,(250) / (104\,[\,½\,]^2\,) = 5.2°\mathrm{F/min}$$

Equilibrium phase

You lower the kiln temperature at this rate until it reaches at least the strain point, which for Effetre is about 670°F. I will often cool at this reduced rate to about 20°F lower than this to allow time for the center of the bead to drop below the strain point. For thicker work, you should probably dwell at the strain point temperature for about one half of the amount of time that you did at the annealing point to again let the center of the work catch up with the outside. The equations for this soak time are

For $d < 1"$ $t = 15$ min
For $d \geq 1"$ $t = 15 + 2\,d^2$ min

This dwell does not need to be as long as the one at the annealing temperature because you have been changing the temperature much slower in the slow cooling phase than you were in the heating phase.

Final cooling phase

Lastly, you have to bring the beads back down to room temperature. Here you are cooling through the brittle solid zone. You cannot trap any stress in the beads by cooling too fast, but it is still possible to go so fast that the glass can crack. What I have just described is basic annealing temperature cycle illustrated in Figure 353.

The orientation of the temperature and stress distributions in this phase are the same as in the slow cooling phase, but any stress introduced during cooling in this phase is only temporary as it was in the heating phase. The allowable cooling rate equation is again

$$R \approx 0.54\,\sigma / (\,COE\ \ t^2\,)$$

but in this phase we can allow a higher temporary stress. You might choose to again use 1000 psi as the allowable stress but I am a little more conservative and use 750 psi. My reasoning for this is that I already have 250 psi of residual stress trapped in the piece from the slow cooling phase of the annealing cycle. Therefore to keep the tensile stress at the surface below a maximum of 1000 psi, I can only allow an additional 750 psi of temporary stress in the piece.

So once again for our ½" diameter Effetre bead example we can calculate an allowable final cooling rate by plugging 750 psi into the allowable cooling rate equation as follows

$$R = 0.54\,(750) / (\,104\,[\,\tfrac{1}{2}\,]^2\,) = 15.6°F/min$$

For those of you with firebrick kilns, which retain heat better, this may simply mean that at this point, or shortly thereafter, you simply shut the door, turn off the kiln, and let it cool naturally. You may want to try this ahead of time and watch how fast your kiln cools to see how fast it cools when you turn it off.

At this point, I imagine some of you have had your eyes glazing over, thinking that you will never be able to apply all these equations. For those of you, I have provided tables at the end of this chapter that cover many of the main glass types that you may use in beadmaking.

When you use these tables, make sure that you are using the right one for your glass since each one is constructed for a different coefficient of expansion. Also make sure that you are using a table for the correct set of units as I have included tables for both English and metric units. Once you have determined the correct table follow down the left column for thickness to reach a value about the size of your largest bead diameter.

Then you go across the row to determine your allowable temperature change rates and dwell times. As an assistance in programming some kiln controllers I have included the time to heat from room temperature (RT) to the annealing point (AP) at the allowable heating rate, the time to slow cool from the annealing point (AP) to the strain point (SP) at the allowable slow cooling rate, and the time to cool from the strain point (SP) back down to room temperature (RT) at the allowable final cooling rate. With this data you should be able to quickly sketch out an annealing cycle for your work.

Choosing an appropriate diameter

The one factor that can still throw you off is in deciding upon the proper diameter or thickness to use in determining your annealing parameters. So let's review a few rules that you should use in determining the value to use for the diameter, d.

The first rule is to use the smallest dimension across the largest cross section of your bead. Thus for a torpedo bead which is 2" long, 1" in diameter at the waist and ¼" in diameter at the ends, you should use 1" as the value for d in determining you annealing parameters. This point of the bead was the largest cross section of the bead.

The second rule is that if the glass object is sitting flat on the kiln shelf, then you should use a value for d equal to twice the thickness of the portion sitting on the kiln shelf.

Lastly, if you have a hollow bead then you should treat the bead as if it were twice the wall thickness of the bead.

With this you now have everything that you need to anneal your beads perfectly each time. Doing so will ensure that every bead that you make may potentially outlive you and be around for future generations to enjoy.

Suggested further reading

Billeci, Andre G. ***"Annealing Glasses"***, **Glass Studio** No. 5

Dunham, Bandhu Scott. **Contemporary Lampworking A Practical Guide to Shaping Glass in the Flame**, Salusa Glassworks 1997

Fenton, Dan. ***"Annealing fused work or how to be cool",*** **Professional Stained Glass magazine**, Vol. 8 No. 3 (April) 1988

Lillie, H. R., ***"Basic Principles of Glass Annealing,"*** **The Glass Industry** Volume 31, Number 7, July 1950 Page 355-382

Narayanaswamy, O. S. "***Annealing of Glass***" **in Glass Science and Technology** Volume 3 Viscosity and Relaxation Edited by D. R. Uhlmann and N. J. Kreidl, Academic Press Inc. 1986

Pincus, Alexis G. and Holmes, Thomas R., **Annealing And Strengthening in the Glass Industry**, Ashlee Publishing Co., Inc. 1987

Platt, Karl. ***"Revealing Annealing"***, **Glass Art magazine**, Vol. 5 No. 5 (July/August) 1990

Scholes, Samuel R. and Greene, Charles H. **Modern Glass Practice**, Ceramic Book and Literature Service (CBLS), 1993

Stone, Graham, **Firing Schedules for Glass *The Kiln Companion***, 1996

Table 23. Annealing tables for beads of borosilicate glass with a COE of 32, an annealing point of 1058°F (570°C), and a strain point of 950°F (510°C)

English units

Diameter (in)	Heating (°F/min)	Time (min) RT to AP	Annealing dwell (min)	Slow Cool (°F/min)	Time (min) AP to SP	Equilibrium dwell (min)	Final cool (°F/min)	Time (min) SP to RT
0.3	375.0	2.6	30	46.88	2.3	15	140.6	6.3
0.4	210.9	4.7	30	26.37	4.1	15	79.1	11.1
0.5	135.0	7.3	30	16.88	6.4	15	50.6	17.4
0.6	93.8	10.5	30	11.72	9.2	15	35.2	25.0
0.7	68.9	14.3	30	8.61	12.5	15	25.8	34.1
0.8	52.7	18.7	30	6.59	16.4	15	19.8	44.5
0.9	41.7	23.7	30	5.21	20.7	15	15.6	56.3
1.0	33.8	29.3	34	4.22	25.6	17	12.7	69.5
1.1	27.9	35.4	35	3.49	31.0	17	10.5	84.1
1.2	23.4	42.2	36	2.93	36.9	18	8.8	100.1
1.3	20.0	49.5	37	2.50	43.3	18	7.5	117.5
1.4	17.2	57.4	38	2.15	50.2	19	6.5	136.3
1.5	15.0	65.9	39	1.88	57.6	20	5.6	156.4
1.6	13.2	74.9	40	1.65	65.5	20	4.9	178.0
1.7	11.7	84.6	42	1.46	74.0	21	4.4	200.9
1.8	10.4	94.8	43	1.30	82.9	21	3.9	225.3
1.9	9.3	105.7	44	1.17	92.4	22	3.5	251.0
2.0	8.4	117.1	46	1.05	102.4	23	3.2	278.1

Metric Units

Diameter (mm)	Heating (°C/min)	Time (min) RT to AP	Annealing dwell (min)	Slow Cool (°C/min)	Time (min) AP to SP	Equilibrium dwell (min)	Final cool (°C/min)	Time (min) SP to RT
6.0	336.0	2.1	30	42.00	1.4	15	126.0	3.9
8.0	189.0	3.7	30	23.63	2.5	15	70.9	6.9
10.0	121.0	5.8	30	15.12	4.0	15	45.4	10.8
12.0	84.0	8.4	30	10.50	5.7	15	31.5	15.5
14.0	61.7	11.4	30	7.71	7.8	15	23.1	21.1
16.0	47.3	14.9	30	5.91	10.2	15	17.7	27.6
18.0	37.3	18.9	30	4.67	12.9	15	14.0	34.9
20.0	30.2	23.3	30	3.78	15.9	15	11.3	43.1
22.0	25.0	28.2	30	3.12	19.2	15	9.4	52.2
24.0	21.0	33.6	30	2.63	22.9	15	7.9	62.1
26.0	17.9	39.4	34	2.24	26.8	17	6.7	72.9
28.0	15.4	45.7	35	1.93	31.1	17	5.8	84.5
30.0	13.4	52.5	36	1.68	35.7	18	5.0	97.0
32.0	11.8	59.7	36	1.48	40.6	18	4.4	110.4
34.0	10.5	67.4	37	1.31	45.9	19	3.9	124.6
36.0	9.3	75.6	38	1.17	51.4	19	3.5	139.7
38.0	8.4	84.2	39	1.05	57.3	19	3.1	155.6
40.0	7.6	93.3	40	0.95	63.5	20	2.8	172.4
42.0	6.9	102.9	41	0.86	70.0	20	2.6	190.1
44.0	6.2	112.9	42	0.78	76.8	21	2.3	208.6
46.0	5.7	123.4	43	0.71	84.0	22	2.1	228.0
48.0	5.3	134.4	44	0.66	91.4	22	2.0	248.3
50.0	4.8	145.8	46	0.60	99.2	23	1.8	269.4

Table 24. Annealing tables for beads of Bullseye glass with a COE of 90, an annealing point of 980°F (527°C), and a strain point of 750°F (399°C)

English units

Diameter (in)	Heating (°F/min)	Time (min) RT to AP	Annealing dwell (min)	Slow Cool (°F/min)	Time (min) AP to SP	Equilibrium dwell (min)	Final cool (°F/min)	Time (min) SP to RT
0.3	133.3	6.8	30	16.67	13.8	15	50.0	13.6
0.4	75.0	12.1	30	9.38	24.5	15	28.1	24.2
0.5	48.0	19.0	30	6.00	38.3	15	18.0	37.8
0.6	33.3	27.3	30	4.17	55.2	15	12.5	54.4
0.7	24.5	37.2	30	3.06	75.1	15	9.2	74.0
0.8	18.8	48.5	30	2.34	98.1	15	7.0	96.7
0.9	14.8	61.4	30	1.85	124.2	15	5.6	122.4
1.0	12.0	75.8	34	1.50	153.3	17	4.5	151.1
1.1	9.9	91.8	35	1.24	185.5	17	3.7	182.8
1.2	8.3	109.2	36	1.04	220.8	18	3.1	217.6
1.3	7.1	128.2	37	0.89	259.1	18	2.7	255.4
1.4	6.1	148.6	38	0.77	300.5	19	2.3	296.2
1.5	5.3	170.6	39	0.67	345.0	20	2.0	340.0
1.6	4.7	194.1	40	0.59	392.5	20	1.8	386.8
1.7	4.2	219.2	42	0.52	443.1	21	1.6	436.7
1.8	3.7	245.7	43	0.46	496.8	21	1.4	489.6
1.9	3.3	273.8	44	0.42	553.5	22	1.2	545.5
2.0	3.0	303.3	46	0.38	613.3	23	1.1	604.4

Metric Units

Diameter (mm)	Heating (°C/min)	Time (min) RT to AP	Annealing dwell (min)	Slow Cool (°C/min)	Time (min) AP to SP	Equilibrium dwell (min)	Final cool (°C/min)	Time (min) SP to RT
6.0	119.5	5.4	30	14.93	8.6	15	44.8	8.4
8.0	67.2	9.7	30	8.40	15.2	15	25.2	15.0
10.0	43.0	15.1	30	5.38	23.8	15	16.1	23.4
12.0	29.9	21.8	30	3.73	34.2	15	11.2	33.7
14.0	21.9	29.6	30	2.74	46.6	15	8.2	45.9
16.0	16.8	38.7	30	2.10	60.8	15	6.3	60.0
18.0	13.3	49.0	30	1.66	77.0	15	5.0	75.9
20.0	10.8	60.5	30	1.34	95.1	15	4.0	93.7
22.0	8.9	73.1	30	1.11	115.0	15	3.3	113.4
24.0	7.5	87.0	30	0.93	136.9	15	2.8	134.9
26.0	6.4	102.2	34	0.80	160.7	17	2.4	158.3
28.0	5.5	118.5	35	0.69	186.3	17	2.1	183.6
30.0	4.8	136.0	36	0.60	213.9	18	1.8	210.8
32.0	4.2	154.8	36	0.53	243.4	18	1.6	239.8
34.0	3.7	174.7	37	0.47	274.7	19	1.4	270.8
36.0	3.3	195.9	38	0.41	308.0	19	1.2	303.6
38.0	3.0	218.2	39	0.37	343.2	19	1.1	338.2
40.0	2.7	241.8	40	0.34	380.3	20	1.0	374.8
42.0	2.4	266.6	41	0.30	419.2	20	0.9	413.2
44.0	2.2	292.6	42	0.28	460.1	21	0.8	453.5
46.0	2.0	319.8	43	0.25	502.9	22	0.8	495.6
48.0	1.9	348.2	44	0.23	547.6	22	0.7	539.6
50.0	1.7	377.8	46	0.22	594.2	23	0.6	585.6

Table 25. Annealing tables for beads of Spectrum glass with a COE of 96, an annealing point of 950°F (510°C), and a strain point of 700°F (371°C)

English units

Diameter (in)	Heating (°F/min)	Time (min) RT to AP	Annealing dwell (min)	Slow Cool (°F/min)	Time (min) AP to SP	Equilibrium dwell (min)	Final cool (°F/min)	Time (min) SP to RT
0.3	125.0	7.0	30	15.63	16.0	15	46.9	13.4
0.4	70.3	12.5	30	8.79	28.4	15	26.4	23.9
0.5	45.0	19.6	30	5.63	44.4	15	16.9	37.3
0.6	31.3	28.2	30	3.91	64.0	15	11.7	53.8
0.7	23.0	38.3	30	2.87	87.1	15	8.6	73.2
0.8	17.6	50.1	30	2.20	113.8	15	6.6	95.6
0.9	13.9	63.4	30	1.74	144.0	15	5.2	121.0
1.0	11.3	78.2	34	1.41	177.8	17	4.2	149.3
1.1	9.3	94.6	35	1.16	215.1	17	3.5	180.7
1.2	7.8	112.6	36	0.98	256.0	18	2.9	215.0
1.3	6.7	132.2	37	0.83	300.4	18	2.5	252.4
1.4	5.7	153.3	38	0.72	348.4	19	2.2	292.7
1.5	5.0	176.0	39	0.63	400.0	20	1.9	336.0
1.6	4.4	200.2	40	0.55	455.1	20	1.6	382.3
1.7	3.9	226.1	42	0.49	513.8	21	1.5	431.6
1.8	3.5	253.4	43	0.43	576.0	21	1.3	483.8
1.9	3.1	282.4	44	0.39	641.8	22	1.2	539.1
2.0	2.8	312.9	46	0.35	711.1	23	1.1	597.3

Metric Units

Diameter (mm)	Heating (°C/min)	Time (min) RT to AP	Annealing dwell (min)	Slow Cool (°C/min)	Time (min) AP to SP	Equilibrium dwell (min)	Final cool (°C/min)	Time (min) SP to RT
6.0	112.0	5.6	30	14.00	9.9	15	42.0	8.3
8.0	63.0	10.0	30	7.88	17.6	15	23.6	14.8
10.0	40.3	15.6	30	5.04	27.6	15	15.1	23.1
12.0	28.0	22.4	30	3.50	39.7	15	10.5	33.3
14.0	20.6	30.6	30	2.57	54.0	15	7.7	45.4
16.0	15.8	39.9	30	1.97	70.5	15	5.9	59.3
18.0	12.4	50.5	30	1.56	89.3	15	4.7	75.0
20.0	10.1	62.4	30	1.26	110.2	15	3.8	92.6
22.0	8.3	75.4	30	1.04	133.4	15	3.1	112.0
24.0	7.0	89.8	30	0.88	158.7	15	2.6	133.3
26.0	6.0	105.4	34	0.75	186.3	17	2.2	156.5
28.0	5.1	122.2	35	0.64	216.0	17	1.9	181.5
30.0	4.5	140.3	36	0.56	248.0	18	1.7	208.3
32.0	3.9	159.6	36	0.49	282.2	18	1.5	237.0
34.0	3.5	180.2	37	0.44	318.5	19	1.3	267.6
36.0	3.1	202.0	38	0.39	357.1	19	1.2	300.0
38.0	2.8	225.1	39	0.35	397.9	19	1.0	334.2
40.0	2.5	249.4	40	0.32	440.9	20	0.9	370.3
42.0	2.3	275.0	41	0.29	486.1	20	0.9	408.3
44.0	2.1	301.8	42	0.26	533.5	21	0.8	448.1
46.0	1.9	329.9	43	0.24	583.1	22	0.7	489.8
48.0	1.8	359.2	44	0.22	634.9	22	0.7	533.3
50.0	1.6	389.7	46	0.20	688.9	23	0.6	578.7

Table 26. Annealing tables for beads of Effetre glass with a COE of 104 an annealing point of 970°F (521°C), and a strain point of 680°F (360°C)

English units

Diameter (in)	Heating (°F/min)	Time (min) RT to AP	Annealing dwell (min)	Slow Cool (°F/min)	Time (min) AP to SP	Equilibrium dwell (min)	Final cool (°F/min)	Time (min) SP to RT
0.3	115.4	7.8	30	14.42	20.1	15	43.3	14.1
0.4	64.9	13.9	30	8.11	35.7	15	24.3	25.1
0.5	41.5	21.7	30	5.19	55.9	15	15.6	39.2
0.6	28.8	31.2	30	3.61	80.4	15	10.8	56.4
0.7	21.2	42.5	30	2.65	109.5	15	7.9	76.8
0.8	16.2	55.5	30	2.03	143.0	15	6.1	100.3
0.9	12.8	70.2	30	1.60	181.0	15	4.8	126.9
1.0	10.4	86.7	34	1.30	223.4	17	3.9	156.6
1.1	8.6	104.9	35	1.07	270.3	17	3.2	189.5
1.2	7.2	124.8	36	0.90	321.7	18	2.7	225.6
1.3	6.1	146.5	37	0.77	377.6	18	2.3	264.7
1.4	5.3	169.9	38	0.66	437.9	19	2.0	307.0
1.5	4.6	195.0	39	0.58	502.7	20	1.7	352.4
1.6	4.1	221.9	40	0.51	571.9	20	1.5	401.0
1.7	3.6	250.5	42	0.45	645.6	21	1.3	452.7
1.8	3.2	280.8	43	0.40	723.8	21	1.2	507.5
1.9	2.9	312.9	44	0.36	806.5	22	1.1	565.5
2.0	2.6	346.7	46	0.32	893.6	23	1.0	626.6

Metric Units

Diameter (mm)	Heating (°C/min)	Time (min) RT to AP	Annealing dwell (min)	Slow Cool (°C/min)	Time (min) AP to SP	Equilibrium dwell (min)	Final cool (°C/min)	Time (min) SP to RT
6.0	103.4	6.2	30	12.92	12.5	15	38.8	8.7
8.0	58.2	11.1	30	7.27	22.2	15	21.8	15.5
10.0	37.2	17.3	30	4.65	34.6	15	14.0	24.3
12.0	25.8	24.9	30	3.23	49.9	15	9.7	35.0
14.0	19.0	33.9	30	2.37	67.9	15	7.1	47.6
16.0	14.5	44.2	30	1.82	88.6	15	5.5	62.2
18.0	11.5	56.0	30	1.44	112.2	15	4.3	78.7
20.0	9.3	69.1	30	1.16	138.5	15	3.5	97.1
22.0	7.7	83.6	30	0.96	167.6	15	2.9	117.5
24.0	6.5	99.5	30	0.81	199.5	15	2.4	139.9
26.0	5.5	116.8	34	0.69	234.1	17	2.1	164.1
28.0	4.7	135.4	35	0.59	271.5	17	1.8	190.4
30.0	4.1	155.4	36	0.52	311.7	18	1.6	218.5
32.0	3.6	176.9	36	0.45	354.6	18	1.4	248.6
34.0	3.2	199.7	37	0.40	400.3	19	1.2	280.7
36.0	2.9	223.8	38	0.36	448.8	19	1.1	314.7
38.0	2.6	249.4	39	0.32	500.0	19	1.0	350.6
40.0	2.3	276.3	40	0.29	554.1	20	0.9	388.5
42.0	2.1	304.7	41	0.26	610.8	20	0.8	428.3
44.0	1.9	334.4	42	0.24	670.4	21	0.7	470.1
46.0	1.8	365.5	43	0.22	732.7	22	0.7	513.8
48.0	1.6	397.9	44	0.20	797.8	22	0.6	559.4
50.0	1.5	431.8	46	0.19	865.7	23	0.6	607.0

Finishing Beads

After completing the hot glass manufacturing steps for making your beads or beadstock, there are often some finishing steps that need to be done to complete them or to enhance their beauty. Each type of bead will have different needs.

- Fused or drawn beads may need to be cut to length. The cut edges of these beads will then need to be smoothed and polished.
- Wound beads may need the ends ground slightly to take sharp edges off.
- Pâte de Verre beads may need to be polished to make them shine.

Some artists also like to etch their finished beads to give them a matte finish. Others like to carve them by sandblasting. Some like to add electro-formed metal coatings. This chapter will discuss some of these processes and how to achieve them or will try to point you to other sources for this information.

Cutting beads to length

There are a few different ways to cut beads to length. These techniques vary in speed, accuracy and cost of equipment. We will discuss them in order of increasing expense.

Chipping hammer and anvil

The simplest and cheapest method to cut long kiln cast or drawn beads to length is unfortunately also the least controllable. It is to use a chipping hammer and anvil similar to that used in Dale de Verre. That is the form of stained glass where the thick slabs of glass are set into concrete.

- The anvil is a piece of steel bar with a 45° angle cut on the top surface. It is usually fastened to a working surface like a sawhorse.
- The chipping hammer is more commonly known as a tile setter's hammer. Its head has a square shaped face on one side and the other side comes to a sharp edge like on the anvil.

The glass is cut by placing it on top of the anvil a d aligning it so that the position where you want the cut is placed along the sharp edge, as in Figure 334. Then, strike the glass with the sharp end of the hammer just a little toward you from the sharp edge of the anvil. The process works best if you try to swing the hammer past the end of the anvil as you chip the glass. The tools will also last longer and cut better if they have tungsten-cutting surfaces, but this will make them more expensive.

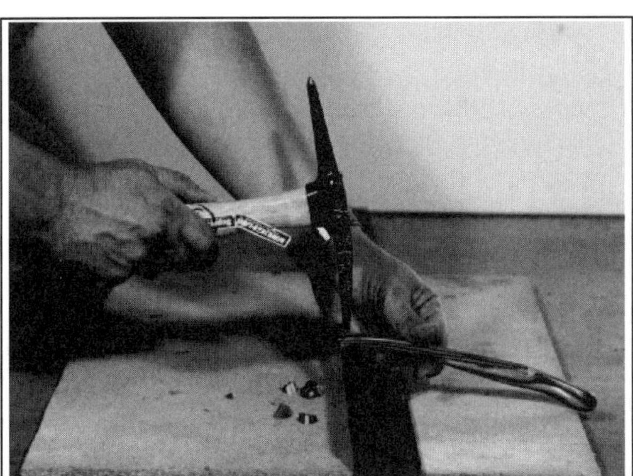

Figure 356. Cutting beadstock with a chipping hammer and anvil.

For obvious safety reasons, you should wear goggles to protect your eyes from any flying debris and gloves to prevent getting cut if the bead stock breaks in an unexpected manner. Watch those edges. They will be really sharp.

Glass knives or nippers

Small-diameter, round bead stock can be cut into beads using tungsten glass rod knifes. This is done as you do for glass rods, by scoring a groove around the circumference and breaking it with your fingers. Likewise, you could use tile or mosaic nippers to cut the bead stock to length. These techniques were described in greater detail in the tools section of this book. They will not work well though if the thickness of the glass gets too great. Then you will have to turn to another method, such as sawing.

Sawing to length

The most accurate way to cut bead stock to length is to saw it with a glass saw. Glass saws use diamond embedded blades to grind their way through a piece of glass. They come in three main configurations: band or wire saws, cutoff saws and table saws. In all cases, the saw will use a cutting fluid to keep glass dust out of the air and to keep the blade cool so that the diamonds are not melted out of the blade's binding matrix.

A band saw has a blade made of a continuous loop of metal banding or wire that runs between two drive pulleys through a table that has a slot in it. A guide to react against the force of the glass pushing against it supports the back of the blade. Water is fed onto the blade from a reservoir above the blade or by passing the blade through a water-filled reservoir.

- If water is fed from above, you will have to be sure that the feed reservoir is full and the feed valve is adjusted properly.
- If the blade picks the water up from a reservoir below, then you just need to make sure that the reservoir is filled to the proper level.

To cut the glass, slowly push it up against the front of the blade and feed it in as the glass gets ground away. One of the disadvantages of a band or wire saw is that the blade tends to wander a little as it cuts through the bead stock, leaving a rougher surface than that achieved with the other types of saws.

A cutoff saw has a configuration similar to that of a radial arm saw. With this saw, you pull the spinning disk shaped saw blade toward you and it cuts off a slice of the glass bead stock that is being held on the table. Cutting fluid will be fed either from above or from below by the blade picking it up from the reservoir. The same cutting lubricant adjustment requirements as for the band saws apply.

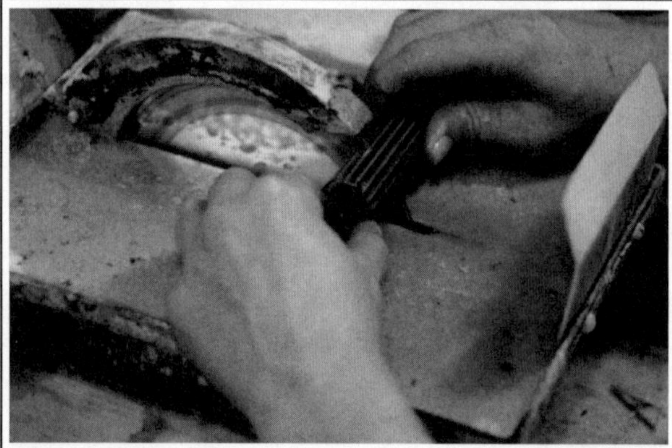

Figure 357. Using a table saw to cut up bead stock. Courtesy of Heron Glass.

A table saw, like the one seen in Figure 357, has a configuration where the spindle of the blade is mounted below the table. Cutting fluid is picked up by the blade from a reservoir below the table. To cut beadstock, you push it up against the spinning blade.

The table for all three of these saw configurations will usually have a guide to hold the beadstock and feed it at the desired angle into the blade. You may not always want to have the ends of the bead perpendicular to the axis of symmetry of the bead (i.e. its hole). You may want to cut circular cross sections at an angle in order to get elliptical beads. Alternatively, you may want to give your beads trapezoidal shapes by cutting the beadstock at an angle, then flipping it over and cutting it again at the same angle. Figure 358 illustrates some of the possibilities for cutting bead stock.

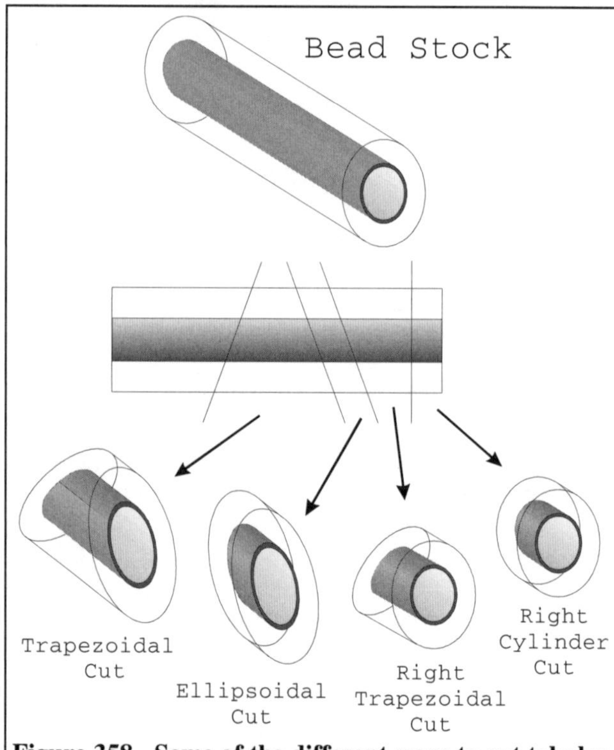

Figure 358. Some of the different ways to cut tabular bead stock into beads.

Even though the cutting fluid helps keep glass dust down when sawing, it is recommended that you

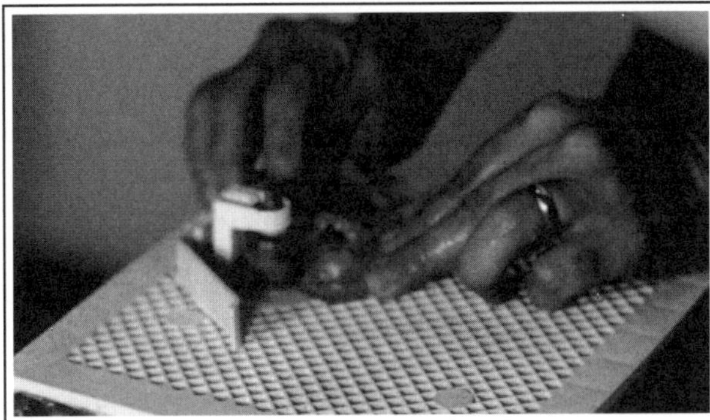
Figure 359. Grinding kiln-made beads.

wear a respirator with a mist cartridge or at the very least a dust filter when using any glass cutting or grinding equipment. This is because small cutting fluid droplets with glass dust are thrown into the air and can be inhaled. For the same reason, you should also wear goggles to keep glass out of your eyes. Be sure to read the equipment instruction manuals for more complete details.

Grinding and shaping beads

After cutting drawn beads to length or sometimes after making wound beads, you may have a sharp edge or a rough surface that you want to grind off. For this job, grinders are suggested. They use diamond embedded tools like the saws, and come in a number of configurations: cylinders, wheels or flat disks. You may even have some of these if you worked previously with stained glass.

In all cases, grinders should be lubricated with cutting fluid as was discussed previously for saws. Basically, all you do is hold the surface of the bead that you want to smooth up against the lubricated cutting surface, and the diamond will cut away at the edge and smooth it. Whenever using grinders always wear goggles just like when sawing, and you may also want to consider wearing a respirator. Be sure to read your instruction manuals so that you understand how to operate your equipment correctly.

Tumble polishing beads

The final polishing of cut bead edges has been traditionally done by tumbling. This technique allows polishing many beads at one time and is much less labor intensive than doing each one individually.

You can tell if a bead has been tumble polished by looking at its edges.

- If they are rounded, then there is a good chance that the bead has been tumble polished.
- If instead of being rounded, the edges are sharp then your bead has most likely been polished on a lap or wheel.

We will now briefly discuss tumble polishing. If you want to learn about lapping, I suggest you consult a reference on beveling like the one by Isenberg or my Pâte de Verre book with Dan Fenton listed at the end of this chapter.

The theory behind tumble polishing

Nature has been practicing tumble polishing for eons. You have only to go to the beach, look at all the smooth pebbles and know that at one time each of these was probably a sharp, jagged rock to realize the scale on which she has been practicing this art. The soothing sound of waves breaking on the beach is the sound of her tumbler in action.

Tumble polishing of beads was traditionally done by putting the beads in a pear shaped barrel of beaten iron filled with a mixture of charcoal and clay or sand. The drum was suspended over a fire and rotated by an apprentice. The charcoal mixture would pack the inside of the bead holes preventing them from collapsing. It also kept the beads from adhering to each other as the heat softened their surfaces. The mixture, combined with the friction of the beads hitting one another, rounded their edges and smoothed their surfaces.

These days apprentices want a lot more for their timeas well as more challenging work, so we grind our beads cold in electric-driven lapidary tumblers. The type of tumbler that you are most likely to buy is a drum tumbler like the one seen in Figure 360. It consists of a simple drum that lies on its side on a pair of rollers. One of the sets of rollers is powered by an electric motor and the other runs free. The motors are one speed and have been set by design

Figure 360. A drum tumbler.

to run at the right speed for tumbling gems.

The drum will most likely be of molded plastic and round in cross section. The inside wall of the drum will have low ridges that cause the load to circulate inside the tumbler as it rotates. The lid will either screw on or be fastened with nuts or clips.

You can get tumblers in either single or multiple barrel designs like the one in the figure. In the multiple barrel designs, the barrels just hook on to one another end-to-end and ride on multiple rollers. This allows you to have beads in the different stages of polishing going at all times.

The size of the barrels you want depends upon your bead throughput and their size. A one and a half inch long bead is too big for a quart barrel and when you run a batch, the barrel should be ²/₃ to ¾ full of beads. Since each step in the grinding process takes about a week, use these factors to gage how large a tumbler you need. If you produce about ½ gallon of beads a week, you could get either a triple ½ gallon tumbler or a single 1-gallon unit. One feature that I like about the tumbler in Figure 360 is that it will accommodate two sizes of barrels, either quart or gallon.

Figure 361. Typical vibro-tumbler.

Generally speaking, the larger the barrel the more efficient it will be, but I prefer a smaller multiple barrel tumbler because I can use a different barrel for each different grit. This makes it less likely to contaminate a fine grit tumble run with coarse grit from a previous run.

Another type of tumbler that is very good for beads is a vibro-tumbler such as that in Figure 361. They have a plastic drum that polish beads by a vibrating action instead of a rotating one. The operation of this type of tumbler is very similar to that which I will describe for the drum tumbler, but the times may be slightly different.

The vibratory action is accomplished by mounting the container on a spring base and driving the base with a rotating unbalanced weight. This causes the base to vibrate back and forth just like an unbalanced fan. This vibration grinds the beads using the relative motion of the fluid and the beads. This type of tumbler costs about the same as a rotating tumbler but is felt by some to work faster and to reduce breakage of delicate beads.

The grit that is used in tumbling is the same that you may already use for sandblasting, silicon carbide. It is the material of choice because it is one of the hardest materials known. It has the property that when a silicon carbide crystal breaks, it forms another sharp fracture edge regardless of particle size. Thus, the grit continues to stay sharp as it breaks down. These two properties combine to make it an excellent grinding agent, second only to diamonds.

In theory, you could just load up your tumbler with the glass beads and a coarse grit, walk away for a long, long time and return to find your beads all polished. But since most of us want to get our beads off to market as soon as possible, we choose instead to tumble in a number of stages, proceeding to finer and finer grit in each stage.

Grits are graded according to their size. This is measured by passing the particles through wire mesh or screens. The number of openings per inch it has defines the mesh size of the screen. The larger the mesh number the finer the grit.

Your first tumbling run will use a coarse grit of about 80 mesh. This would be followed by a run with a medium grit of about 220 mesh, then by one with a fine grit of about 400 mesh and lastly a polishing run using cerium oxide polishing compound. Some artists prefer using finer grit in the 500 to 600 mesh range before moving on to polishing.

The practice of tumble polishing

After cutting your drawn or kiln-made beads into sections, flatten them out just a little on a roughing wheel or grinder like that seen in Figure 359, if you have one. Now you are ready to ready to start tumble polishing the sharp edges. If you know anything about tumble polishing, treat the beads as if they were soft rocks or Apache tears.

Open up the barrel and fill it between ½ and ²/₃ full with glass beads. If the beads are kiln-made, don't worry about removing the fiber paper before the first tumbling but do so before the next. If you do not have quite enough beads to fill the barrel, cut up some sheet glass or glass rods to about the same size and give them an equivalent smoothing as you gave the beads. It also helps to make things run smoother if you mix a number of different sized beads in a run.

Next, add your coarse grit (if you have done a good job smoothing your bead on a flat grinder with an 80 grit, you can possibly proceed directly to a medium grit). In a quart tumbler, you would add 3-4 oz of grit and in a gallon one, you would add 8-10 oz. You may already see here what I meant about a larger barrel being more efficient.

Lastly, add plastic pellets to fill the barrel $^{2}/_{3}$ to ¾ full (about 10 to 20% pellets). These pellets slow down the action inside the barrel so as not to crack or chip the beads. You can buy plastic pellets from lapidary shops. You can also slow down the action more, if necessary, by adding sugar to the water, but this gets everything sticky.

Next, cover it all with water but leave at least an $^{1}/_{8}{}^{th}$ of the barrel empty for air space. Now put the lid back on, making sure that the joint is absolutely clean, so that you get a good seal and do not scratch the joint surface.

Figure 362. Bead after first tumbling run.

Once you put the barrel back on the tumbler and get it sealed, start it tumbling. Check it at least every day to see how things are progressing. When you open the lid, carefully point it away from you. This is because I have been warned that gas pressure tends to build up when grinding some materials and can cause the grinding sludge to spray out. I have not had this happen to me but it has to other people that I know.

After about 24 hours, you will start to be able to see the effect of grinding. The sharp edges will start to be blunted and the shiny surface of the glass will start to dull. Continue on for as many days as it takes to get the edges rounded to the shape that you want them. Also check the cut surface to see if it has smoothed out to your satisfaction. Never stop tumbling for more than about an hour or the grinding slurry can harden up from hydraulic compaction. If this happens, try to break up the sludge by hand before you start tumbling again or you are courting disaster. After the first tumbler step, you will get a bead that looks like the one in Figure 362.

Once the first grinding step has been completed to your satisfaction, it is time to proceed on to the next grit. Start by removing all the beads and cleaning out the sludge from the barrel. Be careful in loading and unloading the beads so that you do not crack or chip them. You want to drain all the sludge into a bucket because if poured it down the sink or your toilet, it will collect in your pipes and harden, leading to some expensive plumbing bills.

Rinse out the barrel and pour the rinse water into the bucket also. Rinse the beads and plastic pellets in a large bowl and pour that water into the bucket. After the sludge has settled in the bucket you can pour off the clear water on top into your flower garden and scrape out the thickened sludge into some newspaper and dispose of it in the garbage.

Clean the beads and pellets again under running tap water in a strainer to get rid of any last remains of the previous grit. You have to get it all out or it can keep putting larger scratches into the beads during the next step, where it will be very visible. Cleaning the grit out of the bead holes is the hardest part. Try using pipe cleaners in the holes. Using an ultrasonic cleaner and some detergent also helps. Weed out any chipped or cracked beads as they can scratch your other beads.

Then clean the barrel well. The barrel is harder to clean, especially if it has been used for a while. That is why I suggest a separate barrel for each grit size, especially the cerium oxide. If you do this, make sure that you mark each one and its lid with which grit is used in it. The plastic pellets can get grit embedded in them too so you may want to set these aside for your next coarse grind and use new ones in the next step. Save them in marked plastic zip lock bags.

Now, replace the beads and plastic pellets in the barrel, add the next grit, water and you are ready to roll. If for any reason you now have less than $^{2}/_{3}$ of a barrel of beads, you need to fill up the void somehow with glass that has been ground a similar amount of time. If not, the sharp edges of the added glass can scratch the beads you have already spent so much time on. That is why I suggest that you start out the first grind with the barrel about ¾ full and save graded material from previous runs for filler as needed. Adding more plastic pellets is not as desirable because they will cause the grind to take a lot longer, but they will work.

The medium grinding step should not take more than a week at most. The way to tell when the beads are ready to move on to the next grit size is to take a bead out of the barrel, clean it off and look at it under a magnifying glass. Look to see if the pits in the surface of the glass left by the grit appear pretty uniform and that the larger ones from the previous step have been wiped out. It may help to save completed samples from each step so that you have something to compare to.

In addition, realize that you don't have to polish the beads back to a complete shine if you don't want to. The matte finish of a partially polished bead also looks good and many artists acid etch their beads, as we will talk about shortly, just to obtain that type of look.

After the medium grit step repeat the cleaning and refilling procedure in preparation for the fine grinding step. The fine grinding step will also take about a week. When you think that you have ground the beads enough, take one out of the barrel and try seeing if it will polish up with a little cerium oxide and water on some felt. You will have to rub it for a minute or two. If you have a buffing wheel with cerium oxide, this should only take a few seconds. The beads are done if the surface has the same shiny finish wet or dry. If so, you are done with the fine grind and ready for the final polish stage.

After the fine grind, try to clean the beads, the pellets, and the barrel even better than before if possible. Then, replace the beads and pellets into the barrel, add water, and a tablespoon of dry laundry detergent. Tumble this mixture for a couple of hours. This will help to work out any last remains of grit. Clean the beads, the pellets, and the tumbler again and rinse them out well.

Now reload the tumbler, only this time using cerium oxide and a pinch of detergent to act as a wetting agent. It also helps to add some more pellets or some other soft filler material to further cushion the tumbling of the beads this time. The most common filler material used is sawdust or wood chips. You should be able to get a good polish in about two days.

The polishing of your beads is now complete. But, because of the high cost of cerium oxide, you may want to save this slurry in order to use it again. It is probably good for three or four polishing sessions. After separating out the beads and cleaning them, do another detergent wash step to clean off the last remains of cerium oxide and to give them a brilliant shine. They will look so good that you won't be able to keep them on the shelf.

Surface treatments

There are a number of surface treatments that can be applied to a bead after the heat work is done. We shall discuss a few of them, and how they will further enhance the look and feel of your beads.

Mirroring

Mirroring or silvering is not too difficult a process and can easily be done by an individual artist. It works best with blown beads where you can apply it to the inside of the bead. To silver the surface of a bead, you must first clean the glass if it is not fresh.

Next, sensitize the glass surface by pretreating it with a tinning solution. The silvering is a three-step process. First, the silver solution is applied. Next, the silver surface is activated and then reduced. Finally, all chemicals are rinsed off the glass. For more information see either of the references listed at the end of the chapter, from "The Independent Glassblower" or Homer Hoyt's book.

Etching

As mentioned earlier, many bead artists like to etch the surface of their beads to give them a matte finish like those in Figure 363. This is especially attractive with transparent colors. Traditionally, this was done with hydrofluoric acid, but the corrosive fluorine ions that it uses to etch glass are also very damaging, as

Figure 363. Chemically etched bead
Artist: Caitlin Hyde Size: 1¼ " L x ¼" Dia

they can penetrate your skin and attack your bones. Proper description of its use is fairly rare in the literature and you should think carefully before deciding to use it in you work. If you are interested, one of the better references that I have come across is an old article from Glass Studio Magazine that is listed at the end of this chapter.

Because of the dangers associated with its use, most bead artists do not like to work with hydrofluoric acid, turning instead to etching creams and etching solutions like Dip N Etch.

Instead of hydrofluoric acid (HF), these etching solutions are based upon sodium bifluoride salt. The active ingredient when dissolved in water is still fluoride ions, but they are less mobile and not all available at the same time. This makes them much less dangerous than hydrofluoric acid but they should still be treated with plenty of respect. A single spoonful of etching cream has actually killed a grown man when ingested, so keep these materials away from children. Because they are less active, they do not etch as well or as fast as hydrofluoric acid. You can not do any deep etching with them.

Etching creams are nice because they are thick and stay where you put them. You can paint them on with a brush to get a patterned etch. The down side to this is that they may not supply as many ions to the glass as you might like because there is not a continual resupply of ions to the glass surface. They may require multiple applications to get the desired depth of etch.

Etching liquids will provide a continuous supply of ions to the glass, and therefore provide a more uniform etch than creams. But because they are liquid, they will attack the whole exposed surface of the immersed bead. Therefore, if there are parts of the bead that you do not want to etch, you will have to mask them off. There are two general ways to do this.

- The first is to paint a masking material onto the areas that you want masked. You use this technique when you have large etched areas between smaller unetched areas. For this a material like fingernail polish works well.
- The other is to cover the whole bead with masking material and then just scrape away the mask in areas that you want to etch. This technique is good for putting in fine etched details. For this technique, I dip the beads in hot wax and scrape it away with clay working tools.

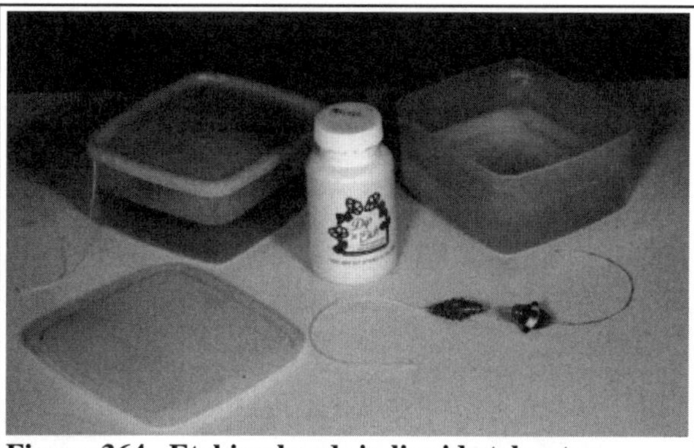

Figure 364. Etching beads in liquid etchant.

When using liquid etchants, I pour them out of their container into small plastic Tupperware containers that I reserve for this purpose. I use these instead of something like plastic cups because I don't want small children to think that it might be water or soda and drink it.

Then I string whatever masked or unmasked beads I want to etch on plastic fishing line and hang them into the solution as seen in Figure 364. I always put on the lid to keep it away from little hands. I check on the beads after whatever time is recommended by the manufacturer, removing them from the liquid by lifting the fishing line and rinsing by dunking them into water. I then dry them off and look at them to decide if they need further etching.

When done with the etching solution, pour it back into its container using a plastic funnel. Then rinse all instruments and containers well with water. Do not use metal instruments as these can get corroded.

When handling any of these materials, you should take some safety precautions. Even though etching creams and liquids are not as dangerous as hydrofluoric acid that does not mean there is no danger in their use. Avoid any ingestion, inhalation or contact with your skin. Wear rubber gloves whenever handling any of these materials. When handling liquid versions, you should wear splash goggles to avoid contact with your eyes.

Sandblasting

If you want to etch deeply into the surface of a bead then an etching cream is not the way to go. They are just too slow. You could do it with hydrofluoric acid, but that stuff is just too dangerous for my liking. One safe option remains, sandblasting.

Figure 365 Aladdin's Palace Bead
Artist: Diana East?
Size: ¾" W x ¼" T x 1½" H
Photo: Diana East

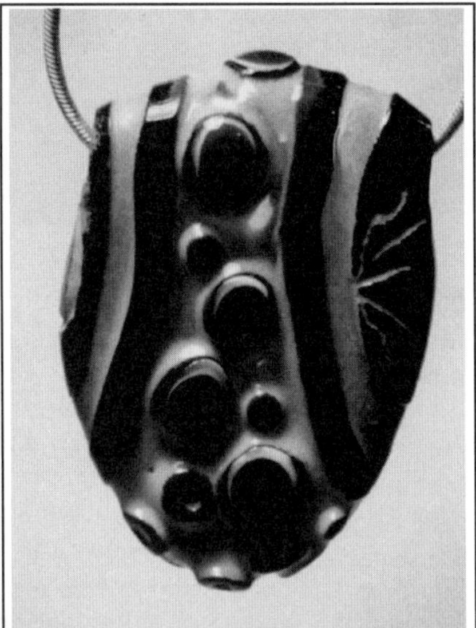

Figure 366. Deeply carved bead.
Artist: Bronwen Heilman
Size: 1" W x ¼" T x 1½" H
Photo: Bronwen Heilman

There are only a few beadmakers that currently use the process of sandblasting in their work. Diana East from the United Kingdom uses a light surface sandblasting to carve mystical images into the surface of some of her beads. Figure 356 shows one of her Aladdin beads. It is an image of an Arabian palace that has been carved through a light enamel coating into the base bead of a contrasting color beneath the enamel.

Bronwen Heilman, on the other hand, performs deep sandblasts carving to produce designs with considerable surface relief. Deep carving allows her to establish bold, multiple-colored beads if she wants by carving through multiple enamel layers of contrasting colors, as she did for the bead in Figure 366. This can be a little tricky if your layers are thin because in the heat of blasting you can go through them in the blink of an eye.

The process

Sandblasting carves away glass from the surface of a bead using a high-speed stream of abrasive grit. The abrasive is thrown against the glass by entrapping it in a high-speed stream of air. The usual abrasive used is the same silicon carbide grit that we used in tumble polishing. We use it for the same reasons that we used it there, because it is so much harder than glass and because it retains a sharp and effective abrasive as it wears. Instead of rounding with wear its grains fracture to form new sharp cutting surfaces.

To create interest in the carved pattern the base bead is often made with multiple layers of colors the thickness of which may dictate how deeply you carve into the bead. With multiple thin enamel layers you have to carve very lightly or you will blast through multiple layers without intending to do so. If you want to have deep carving, then you will most likely paint thicker layers of glass onto the beads in the flame.

Control of what part of a bead gets etched is achieved by masking the portions that you do not want etched just as we did for acid etching. You can use a number of materials to mask off sections of the bead. These include glues like Elmer's or hot melt glues, as well as adhesive-coated vinyl resists similar to shelf paper.

Equipment

The main pieces of equipment that you will need to sandblast are a compressor, a sandblaster, and a sandblasting cabinet. These can be bought together as a system or individually to meet your needs. How big a system you get depends upon where you think you may go with the process. For only doing beads you do not need a large cabinet because the pieces are so small and if you are only going to do light etching you do not need a very robust system, a small abrasive pen system would do.

There are two main types of sandblasting systems, siphon and pressure. A siphon system is the cheapest but less efficient of the two. Basically it consists of a hopper, which feeds abrasive to the gun by way of a hose on the barrel, as seen in the left photo in Figure 367. When the trigger is pulled on the gun, high-pressure air from the compressor rushes through the gun. As it passes over the feed hose connection in the barrel, it pulls abrasive into the air stream and shoots it out the nozzle at the work piece. In order to be effective the air pressure to the gun has to be on the order of 80 to 110 psi at about 12 CFM.

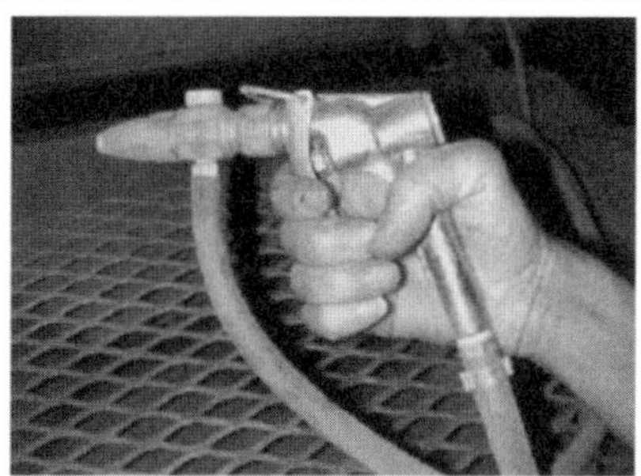
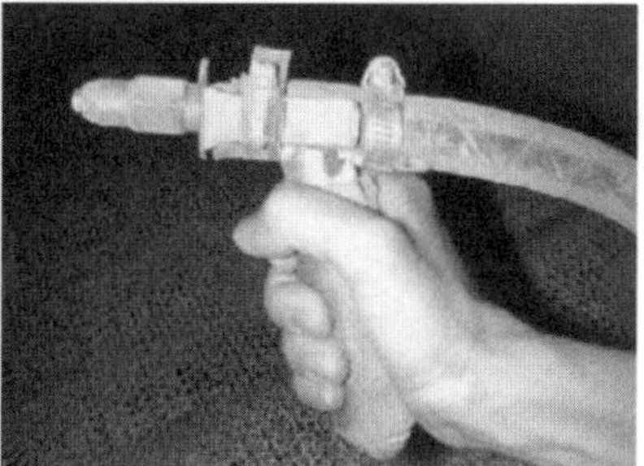

Figure 367. Guns for three different sandblasing systems; siphon, pressure pot, and pen Photos by Bronwen Heilman

A pressure system on the other hand is more sophisticated and expensive but much more efficient system. Its hopper is under pressure from the compressor to push the abrasive out and the pressurized sandblasting mixture is fed to the gun by way of a single hose, as seen by the center photo in Figure 367. The requirement of a thick, welded steel hopper explains the increased expense of this kind of system. The increase in efficiency comes from being able to get more abrasive into the air stream at lower airflows. In fact you have to throttle back the abrasive flow and add extra air by way of a mixing valve at the bottom of the hopper to get an optimum abrasive mix. You can typically blast much faster with a pressure system at 40 psi and at 6 CFM than you can with a siphon system at 100 psi. This allows use of a smaller air compressor or lower loads on a larger one.

Both of these systems require an air compressor but the size and cost of the one for a siphon system is large enough that it covers the difference in price of the two systems. You may already have an air compressor that you could also use for this purpose if you are using an oxygen generator. If not, then consider whether you might go that way in the future and buy a compressor that will be applicable for that purpose also.

Besides the larger guns, many jewelry sandblasting kits also come with smaller pen-like guns like the one in the right photo in Figure 367. The guns although easy to handle do not allow controllability of the grit/air ratio and suffer from frequent clogging of the orifice

If you are only going to do light blasting you might want to start out with an inexpensive system like the Badger abrasive gun. It is a small siphon system that looks like an airbrush. It only costs about $30 but it allows you to try out the process to see if you like the results. Realize though that you get what you pay for it and don't expect the system to be too robust. I would like to stress that if you work with one of these that you still need to figure out some way to deal with the dust. Either collect it by using a small fume or paint hood or that you use the principle of dilution by working outside blowing the dust away from you. This system uses very little in the way of compressed air and you can get by with about a 1/12th hp system that puts out about 22.5 l/min at low pressure.

To round out your sandblasting setup you should get a blasting cabinet like the one seen in Figure 368. It will contain the abrasive grit so that it can be reused as well as catch any fine silica powder that is generated in the process. The powder is collected

Figure 368. Small table-top sandblasting cabinet. Photo by: Bronwen Heilman.

in a hopper at the bottom of the cabinet. For small objects like beads a small desktop cabinet is all that you need. You can find a number of these systems, many with simple siphon blasting systems built into them that sell for about $150. For about $100 more you can find some systems that will come with a small dust collector that will help keep your vision clear. Because these are siphon systems they will require a compressor with a capacity of about 5CFM at 100 psi. Check out the recommendation for the system that you decide to buy.

Safety Note: ***Silica dust generated while sandblasting can cause silicosis, a condition similar to asbestosis, and should be handled appropriately. Contain it and wear a HEPA filter respirator whenever you expose yourself to it.***

If you decide to move on to blasting larger objects than beads say like mirrors, be prepared for sticker shock. Larger systems typically cost a couple thousand dollars.

Choosing a masking material

You can use any of a number of materials to mask the area of the beads that you do not want sandblasted, but they should have three main properties:

- They should stick well to the glass while at the same time be easily removable after you are done.
- They need to be strong enough to resist the abrasive action of the sandblaster.
- They should be easily applied and modified as needed for the design.

This is usually achieved by the application of glue or a resist material like shelf paper to the bead.

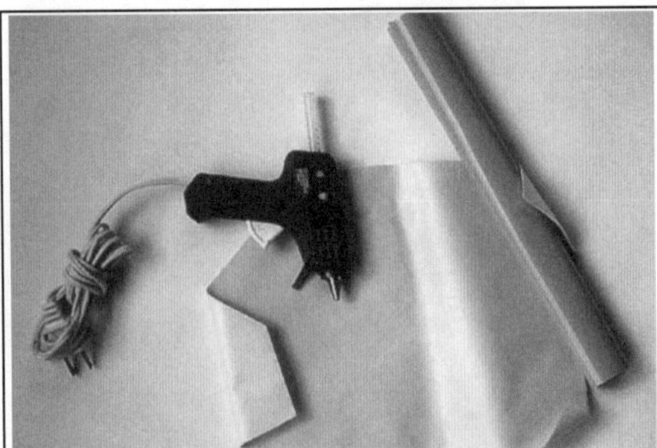

Figure 369. Resist materials: glues and films
Photo by Bronwen Heilman

Glues

The two main types of glues that you can use for resists are casein-based glues like Elmers or hot melt glues. Either of the two glues can be trimmed with a sharp stencil blade but it is just a little harder with hot glue.

Of the two, casein-based glues are easier to work with because they can be painted onto the bead into a pattern. This does entail the problem of preventing flow of the glue over the curved surface into adjacent areas where you did not want it as well as applying it thick enough to be able to resist deep blasting.

Hot glues on the other hand can only be squiggled onto your bead using your hot glue gun. Control of where you apply the hot glue is problematic and those trailing threads of glue are really annoying. On top of all this, I always end up burning myself a little bit whenever I use hot glue guns.

Film resists

A film resist consists of two parts; the plastic film and the adhesive the hold it onto the glass. The adhesive has to stick well to the glass. You may have to clean the bead ahead of time to ensure that it does so. The toughness of the plastic film is what determines how well it will resist the abrasive action of the grit. This is a function of the film thickness and composition — the thicker it is the tougher it is. Material-wise rubber is the strongest material but also the most expensive and is usually reserved for deep etching. Most of the time you will use a vinyl-based film a few mils (thousandths of an inch) thick.

When using resists on beads you have three options: you can apply the resist as small sections, you can apply it as a large piece that may have small sections cut out or from which you cut out sections, or a combination of the two. Which one you choose will often depend on whether you want most of the surface etched or unetched. When applying larger pieces of resist to a bead is that it is often difficult to get a large piece of resist to conform to the shape of the bead. So if you wrap a large piece of resist on, at least the section near where you cut must be well attached and wrinkle free. Areas further from the cut can be allowed to wrinkle. When wrapping all the way around the bead be sure to have an area of overlap.

In developing your design it is often easier to draw on and cut your resist while it is flat before applying it to the bead. If nothing else your razor blade will not be sliding off of the hard curved surface of the bead. Because the designs are usually so small, I sketch out the design and draw them directly onto the resist. Then I cut it out using an exacto stencil knife. When you do this, make sure that you cut all the way through the resist to avoid ragged ends or corners. If you use short strokes, I find that ensuring the blade is starting in a previous portion of the cut helps keep it clean and crisp.

Figure 370. Large sandblasting cabinet vacuum and dust collector
Photo by: Bronwen Heilman

The process of sandblasting

The first step is making a bead that you want to sandblast. This usually means making a bead with one or more layers of color to blast through either using enamels or application of thin layers of glass. The bead should be well annealed so that the stress induced during blasting will not cause it to break. The bead should probably be left on the mandrel to allow easy handling during blasting. Most of the separator could be broken off to avoid contaminating the grit. Lastly we clean the bead with alcohol so that the resist will adhere to it.

Next we need to develop the pattern and transfer it to the resist. This transfer can be done by drawing the sketch directly onto the resist, by using carbon paper, or by gluing the sketch to the resist. Now we either cut pieces out of the patterns and apply them to the bead or we apply the resist and cut out pieces to expose sections of the bead. In either case, make sure that the resist is firmly attached to the bead especially at the exposed edges.

At this point we are ready to blast. Transfer the bead to your cabinet. Adjust your lighting so that you can see what you are doing. Lighting is very important because once the blaster is going it can be hard to judge how things are progressing. Turn on the power to the compressor and let it build up pressure. If needed, adjust any throttle valves and you are ready to go.

When you blast, it helps to start off to one side of the bead, make a pass over the bead and release the trigger after you move off of the bead all the while aiming the gun perpendicular to the surface. This will give you a nice uniform etch. You typically do not want to sit and dwell at one location.

Safety in sandblasting

First, as already mentioned, you do not want to inhale the dust that you create when sandblasting. That is why we try to capture it inside of a cabinet or dust collector and dispose of it. Larger systems may have an integral vacuum and dust collector as seen in Figure 370. When you have to clean out the cabinet and the dust collector, it is absolutely necessary that you wear a HEPA filter respirator to avoid inhaling the dust.

The other safety item that you may need is ear protection. Sandblasters tend to be very loud and the noise can permanently damage your hearing. At the very least, wear some of the soft foam rubber earplugs that you squish up and stick in your ears. If you start doing sandblasting on a regular basis, you should consider investing in some of the protective earmuffs. They offer better protection and I find them more convenient.

Sandblasting demos

To better understand the sandblasting process, let's step through two quick demonstrations by Bronwen Hielman and Diana East. For both artists, the first step in the process is the construction of a bead blank with multiple layers of color. In Bronwen's example, this consists of a white base bead with a thick blue glass casing and a thinner red enamel one. The blue layer was painted on by hand in the torch as seen in the first photo in this series, while the red layer was applied by rolling the hot blue-cased bead in enamel. She then sagged and paddled the bead into a tableau shape.

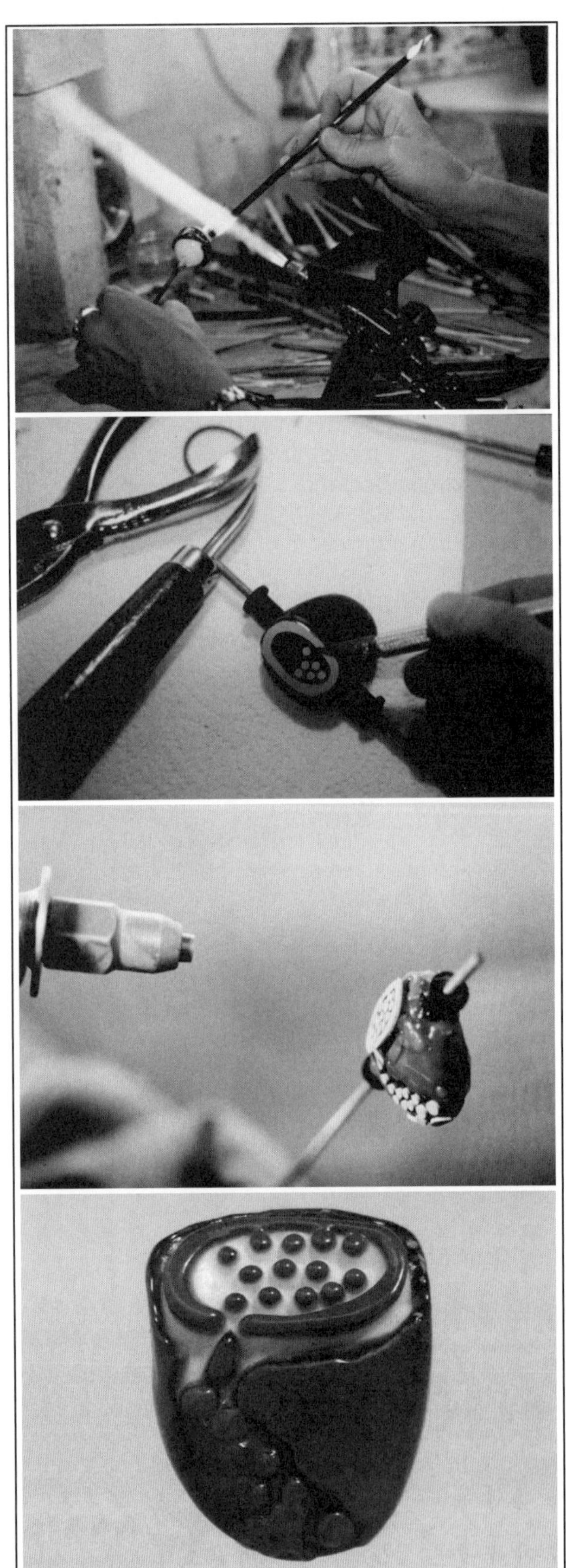

Figure 371, Bronwen Heilman bead demo
Photos by: Bronwen Heilman

Next Bronwen places her masking elements cut from a film resist onto the bead surface as seen in the second photo. She cuts the elements separately and then places them onto the bead because each element is very small and she wants the shapes to be precisely cut and placed. She uses a hole punch to get the neatly cut circles. If you want to have other shapes, you can also fine punches at crafts stores that will make stars, moon, and other shapes to lighten your trimming task.

With all the resist in place, Bronwen now sandblasts the bead as seen in the next photo. The little rubber stopper that she has slid onto the mandrel at both ends of the bead helps to hold it in place and keep it from flapping in the breeze as she blasts away. Notice how she holds the bead fairly close to the gun as she blasts. This allows her to better direct the grit locally where she wants on the bead. After sandblasting, she cleans up the bead and removes the resist to reveal the finished bead seen in the last picture of this series.

Some of the beads by Diana East are similar to those of Bronwen but Diana also makes some mystical landscape beads that are really inspiring. We have already seen one of her "Aladdin's Palace" beads in Figure 365. In the demo presented here, she will briefly illustrate how she makes one of her "Moon Lit Ruins" beads. She got the inspiration for this bead from an illustration by Edmund Dulac.

For this bead she makes a base bead of dark transparent blue with some internal dichroic highlights and a deeper layer of trees under over which she applies a fairly thick coating of white enamel that she applies using a small sieve followed by a light coating of blue enamel. Onto this background, she paints on vegetation, both ground cover and trees using glass stringers to get the base bead seen in the photo. For the leaves she uses reduction frit. Lastly she fumes on a thin layer of gold. The thin layer of gold causes the reduction frit to turn green and the white enamel to turn pinkish.

Next Diana applies a film resist onto the bottom half of the front and back of the bead. Onto this she draws the skyline of the ruins that she wants to capture on the bead and cuts off the excess resist with a sharp artist's knife to get the masked bead that we see in the next photo. Note how she has added windows and some cut outs for tree trunks. She then burnishes the resist onto the bead well, especially concentrating around the raised tree trunks to ensure that it bonds to the bead.

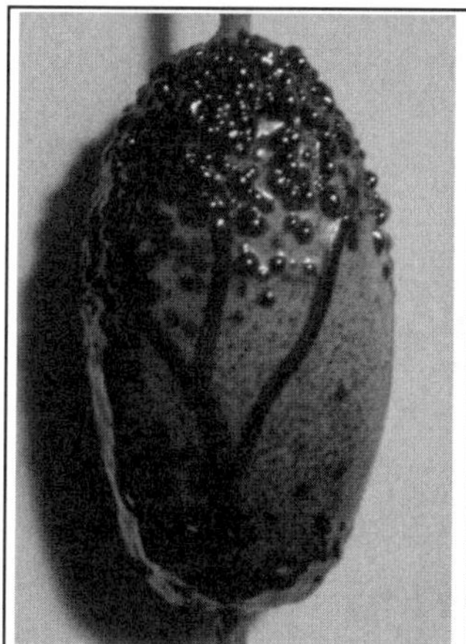
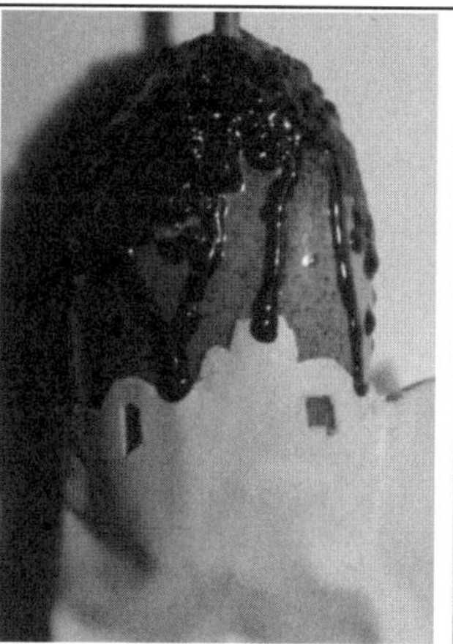
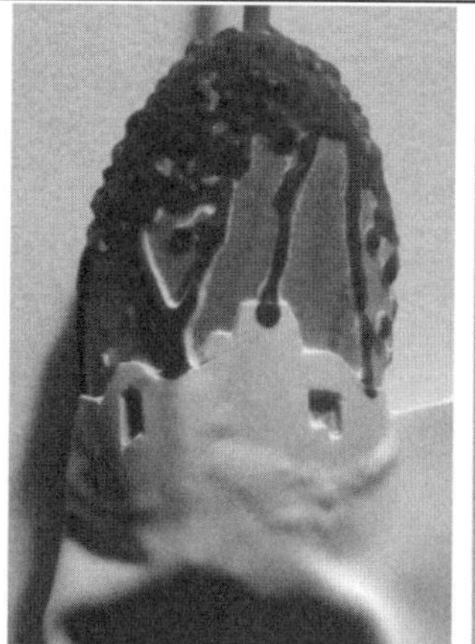

Figure 372. Diana East demo bead **Photos by Diana East**

Now she is ready to blast. Diana lightly etches down between the tree trunks and above the resist until she get through the white enamel layer as seen in the next photo. She has to be careful in doing this that she does not blast away the tree trunks. You can see remains of the white enamel layer on either side if the tree trunks.

Then she removes the resist and masks some of the gold with a painted on etchant resist. She lightly etches the exposed surface to remove unwanted gold and finishes by applying a light coating of oil to shine up the bead.

Electroplating and electroforming

Electroplatingis the addition of thin metal layers by similar electrolytic means. These can be of other metals of contrasting colors such as stainless steel, titanium, nickel, silver, gold, or rhodium. These thin coatings can then be patinaed to get different colors. Figure 356 shows an example of an electroplated bead. It is actually made from a silver-plating bath.

Figure 373. Electroplated bead.
Artist: Ralf Koslow
Size: ¾" Diameter

Electroforming, on the other hand, is the addition of a relatively thick metal layers formed onto a conductive or a non-conductive surface. This layer is made by building up layer after layer of atoms using an electrolytic cell, usually an acid-based copper plating one. These layers are thick enough that they could be, if desired, made self-supporting structures by removing the core onto which the electroformed layer was added. For an example of this, see Kate Fowle Meleney's vessel bead in Figure 374. She also helped provide me with a lot of the information for this section of the book.

The process

Electrolytic deposition is carried out by using an electric current to move atoms of the material being plated from an anode to the object we want to plate. These atoms, which travel in the form of positively charged ions, move through a solution charged with these ions. The anode, which is made from the metal being plated, is also positively charged which allows the metal ions to dissolve off of it into the solution. The ions are then pushed or pulled through the solution by the attraction of electric forces. The solution has materials added to it that help make the plating more uniform. When they reach the object, the ions plate out as atoms onto its surface, completing the electric circuit.

Figure 374. Vessel bead with electroformed copper
Artist:Kate Fowle Meleney
Size: 1¾" L x ¾" W x ¼" T

Most artists tend to work mainly with copper plating for a number of reasons. First, copper is a lot less expensive than a lot of other materials. Second, its baths are easier to maintain. They are also less toxic because they do not contain cyanide. For this reason, I will restrict my discussion to electro-forming with copper. If you want to add a flash of silver or gold over this you can usually find an electroplater in the Yellow Pages to do it for you.

Equipment

The basic components of an electroplating system can be seen in Figure 376. They consist of a rectifier/power supply, an anode, an electrolytic bath, lead wires, and various connectors. Ultimately, the type and size of equipment that you need depends upon the degree into which you want to get into this process. But let's go over what each of these basic components are and what they do.

A **rectifier** is a power source that supplies direct current (DC) power to the system. It converts the standard alternating current (AC) power from your wall socket into DC power, the same as you get from a battery. The rectifier should allow for control of both the voltage and the current of the DC power. The voltage should be controllable over a range of 0 to 15 volts and the current over 0 to 10 amps. This is important because the character of the applied metal coating changes with these parameters. It helps if you have gauges on the rectifier so that you can measure the input.

The **anode** for the system should be a relatively heavy piece of the material being plated. It also has to have a fair amount of area to allow better transfer of material from the anode to the solution. Since most of our plating is usually of copper, I suggest using two pieces of heavy solid copper sheet of at least 20 gauge. For a larger bath, you may want to have more anodes spread around the bath to get more uniform platings. Cut out your two rectangles from the copper sheet, about one inch wide by four inches long. Make sure that they are clean or they will not work. Scour them down with Scotch Brite pads if you have to.

The **plating bath** should be put in a non-conducting container such as plastic or glass. For beads, it does not have to be too big. In fact, the bigger the container the more plating bath that you will need, so it helps to keep the bath as small as possible. A 600-ml beaker or a large Tupperware container is about the right size for this purpose. The solution can be saved and reused many times. Filter it out through two coffee filters damped with distilled water to get any particulate that may brake off of the copper anode during the run before returning it to its original bottle.

Your rectifier will most likely already come with **wires** and **connectors** attached. You will use one to connect the positive (+) terminal to the copper anode and a second to connect the negative (-) terminal to the wire cathode system from which you hang your bead. You will also want a couple of feet of bare 18 gauge and 8 gauge copper wire to form the suspension framing for your bath.

Preparing your beads for plating

The electroplating process is usually used to add metal layers onto other metal objects. In fact, the surface of the object to be plated has to be conductive for this process to work. Since our beads are made out of glass, the first step has to be to make the surface of the bead to be plated conductive. To do this, we add a layer of conductive paint to the bead, as in Figure 375. You can get conductive paint from either Safer Solutions or Rio Grande. If you have sharp edges in the area that you are trying to plate, they will tend to receive thicker plating because the current density will be higher there.

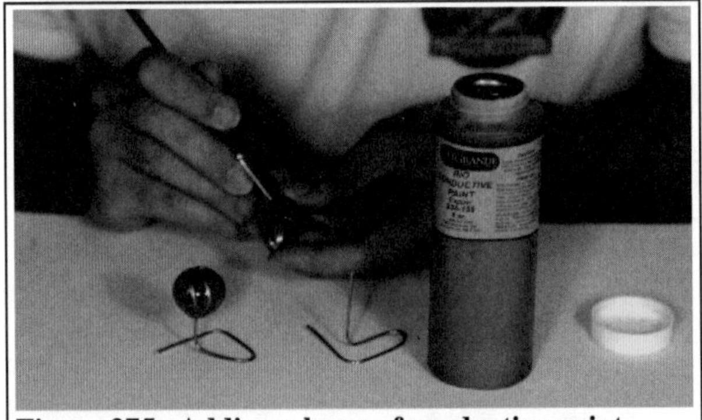

Figure 375. Adding a layer of conductive paint.

The first thing to do is to clean your bead well so that the paint will stick. Then paint the portion of the bead surface that you want to plate with the conductive paint. Since the copper skin won't permanently adhere to the glass, you have to be sure that the paint is applied in a shape that wraps completely around the bead so that it is well anchored to the bead and will not peel or slide off. The paint also has to form a continuous coating or the whole surface will not get plated. Make sure that you apply the paint uniformly and completely, but not too thick. If you are having a hard time getting the paint to stick, you might try lightly etching the bead first. For reasons that you will see later, it also helps if one end of the bead does not get plated.

Allow the conductive paint to dry. This may take anywhere from 2 to 12 hours depending upon which kind of paint you are using. Water-based paints take longer to dry and do not stick as well as organic solvent paints. Prop the bead up as the paint is drying so that it does not touch anything. After it is dry, do not handle the bead by the painted portion or oils from your hand may interfere with the deposition of the plating.

Setting up system

Now let's set up the plating system. Start by filling the bath container with electroforming solution to within an inch or two of the top of the beaker. Then take about a foot of 8-gauge copper wire and bend it into a big U that you will place on the top of the bath container. You want to bend it so that the sides of the U are just inside the rim of the container and the bottom of the U extends at least an inch over the edge of the bath. This will form the framing for the anode system.

Next, we have to hang the anodes from this frame. Attach them by bending them over the sides of the U so that they are suspended just off the bath, as seen in Figure 376. Crimp the anodes tightly onto the 8-gauge wire so that they make good electrical contact. Rebend the 8-gauge wire as necessary to make sure that the anodes hang near the edge of the bath, leaving plenty of room for the bead in the middle.

Cut another length of 8-gauge wire such that it hangs about an inch over the sides of the container. This will be used to hang your bead. Before you start up the system always make sure that this wire is not touching the U. Now suspend your bead, which is the cathode for this system, from this wire.

Do this by feeding a short length of the 18-gauge wire through the hole in the bead and bending it up so that touches the conductive paint. Wrap the other end around the cathode wire so that the painted portion of the bead is hanging in the bath and the unpainted portion of the bead is out of the bath. This is so the bead does not get trapped on the wire by plating on both ends. This is why we try not to apply conductive paint to both ends of the bead if we can help it. But if you must, you will have to use a smaller gauge of sheathed wire that you leave the insulation on in the area where it goes through the bead, or paint insulative masking on the wire in this area with fingernail polish. Crimp the wire onto the 18-gauge cathode wire so that it makes good contact, and hang the bead so that it is suspended midway between the two anodes.

Attach the leads from your rectifier to the 8 gauge hanger wires: the + lead to the U and the - lead to the bead hanger. Make one last check to ensure that your 8-gauge wires do not touch each other or you may end up blowing the fuse in your rectifier. I use short pieces of plastic tubing to space the wires apart, by slicing the pieces of tubing open down their length and fitting them over the edge of the beaker. You may find taping them in place is easier for you. Just make sure that the 8-gage wires cannot get bumped together during the plating run.

The electroforming run

Now comes the moment of truth. Turn on power to your rectifier and slowly dial up the voltage to just under one volt. Check to see that your voltage and amperage gauges are registering. If not, then nothing is happening and you have some sort of problem. There are a number of possibilities:

- your rectifier may not be working. The fuse might be blown or maybe it is not plugged in.
- your bath solution may be depleted and needs to be replaced.
- your leads may not be clipped well. Clean them up if necessary.
- you may have copper salts built up somewhere on the wiring, preventing the flow of current. Again clean them up.

Don't turn your voltage up too high or you will form bubbles. These are undesirable because they keep the solution away from the bead, thus blocking any

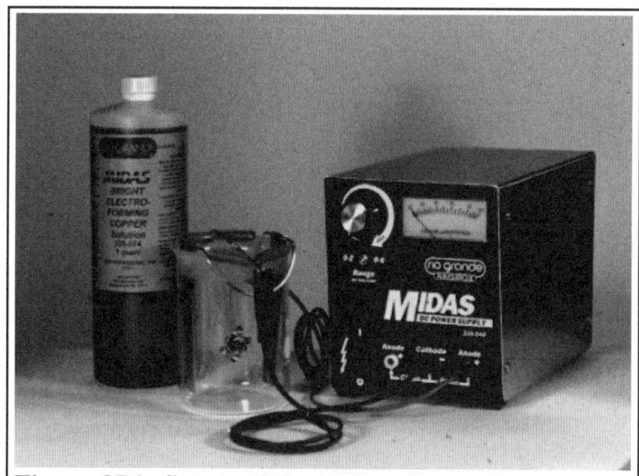

Figure 376. Set up of electroforming system.

deposition. If this happens, swing the bead back and forth in the solution to get them off the piece. Ideally, your bath should have some sort of agitation system in it to help disperse the bubbles. If not, be satisfied with turning down the voltage and going slower.

If your bath is good, you should start to see copper plating on the piece within about 5 minutes. But, to get a nice thick plating, the bead will need to stay in the bath for a number of hours. Anywhere from one to eighteen hours will be required, depending upon what kind of thickness you are trying to achieve. If you are trying to get a shiny plating, then you may find that you have to replenish the solutions with brighteners after a while.

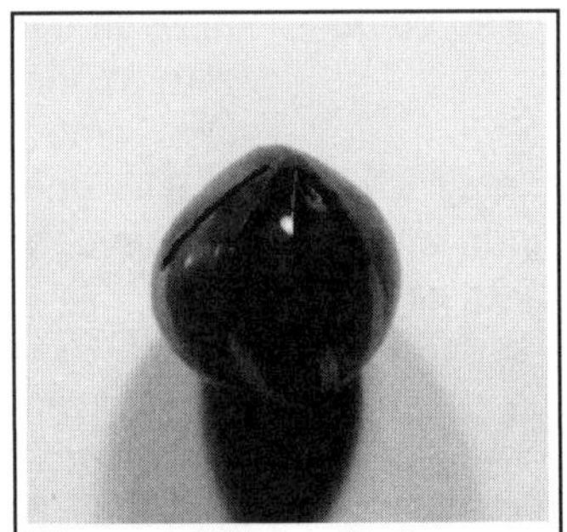

Figure 377. Patina on electroformed copper.

During the electroforming run, you should move the cathode wire point of contact occasionally. If you don't, you will find that this area has not been plated very well. Move it at least three or four times during the run. As you do this the first couple of times, make sure that the wire does not scratch through the conductive paint. If it has and you really want that area plated, then you will have to pull the bead out of the bath, rinse it off, dry it and repaint that area. The paint will then have to dry before it can be returned to the bath.

Check the piece periodically to make sure that you are getting a good plating. When you are satisfied with it, remove the bead from the bath and rinse it off. At this point, you will find that the coating will probably have a matte pink color. To brighten it up, brush the surface with a brush dipped in liquid detergent. After you are done, clean this off.

If the final finish you are looking for is a bright copper, you will have to seal the bead with a light coating of spray acrylic or lacquer. Otherwise, the plating will quickly oxidize and get dull. Alternatively, you might like to patina the bead. You could use some of your old stained glass patinas or get one of the many other colors available from jewelry suppliers. Figure 377 shows how the copper darkens on the top half of an electroformed bead looks where it goes from a bright to a patinaed finish.

Safety in electroforming

In electroplating and electroforming, you will be using solutions that are both toxic and corrosive. These materials will require special handling. like those used for acid etching. They are dangerous to ingest, touch, or breathe. You will have to protect yourself from entry of these materials into your body by any of these methods. Let's cover each of these topics in turn.

The first, ingestion, is pretty easy to protect against. You just have to avoid getting any of this material inside of you. Do this by not eating or smoking in your studio. Make sure that you clean up every day before you go home.

The next concern, touch, is handled by wearing protective clothing. This means gloves, aprons, splash goggles, and face shields. Its best if this clothing is rubberized, as you want to keep the chemicals off your skin. You can find out more about these in the next chapter.

The last concern, inhalation, is handled by providing you and your workers with adequate ventilation. You should get good local ventilation for your studio, if nothing else a good fan to pull the vapors out of your studio. We also discuss the making of such systems in the next chapter. In addition to ventilation you may need to get yourself a respirator that is rated for acid fumes and wear it when you are working.

Suggested further reading

Anonymous. **Midas™ Plating Guide**, Rio Grande Albuquerque 1994

Croasdale, Martha. **Glass & Metal, The Art and Technique of Electroforming onto Glass**, Whitehouse Books.Com 1998

Dobbins, Norm & Ruth, **Etched Glass Techniques & Designs**, Hand Books Press, 1998

Drobbins, Norm & Debra Felberg Oxley, **Glass Etching Surface Techniques and Designs**, CKE publications, 1988

Dunham, Bandhu Scott. **Contemporary Lampworking A Practical Guide to Shaping Glass in the Flame**, Salusa Glassworks 1997

Fowle, Kate. ***"Electroforming on Beads",*** **The Bead Release** Vol. V Issue 3

Gilchrist, Paige & Diana Light, **Etching Glass**, Lark Books, 2000

Gruenig, David. "***Silvering Glass***", **The Independent Glassblower** Issue # 26 (June/July/August) 1992

Hoyt, Homer L. **Glassblowing An Introduction to Solid and Blown Glass Sculpturing**, Crafts & Arts Publishing Co. Inc., 1989

Isenberg, Anita & Seymour. **How to Work in Beveled Glass**, Chilton Book Company 1982

Kohler, Lucartha, **Glass An Artist's Medium**, Krause Publications, 1999

Oxley, Debra Felberg & Norm Drobbins, **Glass Etching II Carving Techniques and Designs**, CKE publications, 1993

Watson, L. S., **Sand Carving Glass, A Beginner's Guide**, Tab Books Inc., 1986

Wexler, Jerome. **How to Tumble Polish Gemstones and Make Tumbled Gem Jewelry**, Gem Guides Book Co., 1987

Safety

Your safety should be your number one priority while beadmaking, even above producing a quality product. The best way to stay out of trouble is to understand what you are doing and why. For this reason, I have gone to great pains to try to explain how your equipment works and its safe use. This understanding will allow you to realize that something wrong is occurring and to take immediate action to correct it. In this chapter, I will remind you of many of the hazards associated with the equipment you are using and provide you general safety rules.

Fires

In working with any of the high temperature processes discussed in this book, a number of general rules should be followed in order to avoid starting fires. Fires usually start because you have improperly located your equipment or have failed to maintain it properly. So check it out occasionally.

Positioning your equipment to avoid fires

1) Position your hot equipment at least 2 feet away from sheet rock walls and 3 feet from exposed wood.

2) Have a non-flammable floor surface underneath your equipment. Concrete is best, ceramic tile or brick is second best and some sort of non-asbestos fire-resistant board is the minimum requirement.

3) Use a non-flammable work surface on your worktable. Sheet metal is acceptable but may conduct heat to locations where you are not expecting it to be hot and cause burns. Some other non-asbestos, fire-resistant surfaces are better.

4) If possible equipment like kilns and glory holes should be mounted on stands to allow air circulation around them.

5) Large industrial glassworking setups or equipment may require a different type of building construction. Check into this before you expand your shop.

6) Check to see that no flammable liquids are stored near your equipment. If some are stored in the same room, provide sufficient ventilation to prevent build up of vapors and store them in a flammable liquid storage cabinet.

7) Check all natural gas and propane sources to make sure that you have no leaks. Do this by painting all the joints in your gas system with a soapy water solution and looking for bubbles.

8) If you work out of your garage, back your car out before you start working so that there are no gasoline fumes around.

9) Always keep at least one ABC rated fire extinguisher nearby. Position it so you will not have to reach over a fire to get to it – preferably near an exit.

10) Keep a clear exit from your work space at all times through which to escape in case of a fire.

Proper operation of your equipment to avoid fires

1) Never let children play around your equipment.

2) Do not allow consumables to build up in your work area.

3) Read and follow the manufacturer instructions for your equipment.

4) Never leave your equipment unattended. The only exception for this might be a kiln where you can pop in and out to check on it. If you are the forgetful type, I suggest using an interval timer to remind you to check up on it.

Pressurized gas equipment

We have already discussed the hazards and most of the operational considerations for use with pressurized cylinders. But since they pose one of the biggest risks that you will be dealing with in most beadmaking situations, I believe it is prudent to list them again in this section, where they will be easy to locate for later reference. These general rules include:

1) Build a storage rack fixed to the wall for all your extra oxygen tanks and chain them into it when not in use. Have a similar rack near your workbench in which to chain your working tanks.

2) Avoid storing extra tanks anywhere near sources of heat and keep them out of the sun.

3) Use the protective covers on tank valves when not in use.

4) Make sure propane tanks are not overfilled.

5) Never use any grease or oils on an oxygen regulator or connection.

6) Make sure that all connections are leak tight and that your equipment is turned off when not in use. Never use leaky equipment. Keep heat, flame and sparks away from your hoses, regulators and cylinders.

7) Be sure to use flashback arrestors or at the very least check valves on your system.

8) Stand to one side of your oxygen regulator as you open the cylinder valve and be sure to open the valve slowly.

9) Always light the fuel gas before opening the oxygen on your torch.

What to do in case of a fire

Besides taking the safety precautions listed above, you need to learn to be able to extinguish any fire as soon as possible after it starts. This will prevent it from getting a chance to take hold and from getting near your pressurized gas equipment. To do this, you must have the right kind of fire extinguisher. For our work, this will be an ABC dry chemical extinguisher often referred to as a tri-class dry chemical fire extinguisher, such as seen in Figure 378.

Figure 378. Dry chemical fire extinguisher.

These extinguishers use nonconducting chemicals (good for use around kilns) that effectively suppress the three main types of fires. These types as you may know are:

(A) fires involving combustible materials like paper, wood, cardboard, cloth or other similar materials;
(B) fires involving oils, gasoline, chemicals, paints, or other flammable liquids; and
(C) fires involving live electrical equipment, such as kilns, crock pots, etc.

These ABC fire extinguishers are available in easy-to-store wall mounted units weighing 2 ½ to 30 pounds.

You should read over the instructions that come with your fire extinguisher and ensure that you understand how to use it. General rules for the operation and use of fire extinguishers are:

1) You should hold them upright so that the dry chemical feeds properly.

2) Most have a safety pin that you have to pull first to be able to start operation.

3) Don't get too close to the fire. Stand about 8 feet away.

4) Aim the extinguisher at the base of the fire and squeeze the handle to spray the dry chemical.

5) Sweep the chemical spray from side to side to completely cover the fire.

6) In order to ensure the proper functionality of your extinguisher when you need it, you should inspect it periodically, monthly or more often. They will usually have a pressure gauge, which should read in the proper marked range.

7) If you have to use your extinguisher for any reason, you should have it recharged and checked out by an authorized distributor since they are more prone to leakage after once being used.

8) After use, clean off all surfaces coated with the dry chemical because it is fairly corrosive.

If a fire gets near your pressurized gas tanks, evacuate the building and the nearby area. Notify the fire department and be sure to warn them about the presence of pressurized gases.

Burns

Burns can be caused by exposure to caustic chemicals, electricity, radiation or heat. In beadmaking your main concern will be heat, although we may occasionally use chemicals or be exposed to electricity. Burns, as you probably know, are classified by their severity into first-, second-, or third-degree burns as follows:

- **First-degree burns** are usually characterized by reddening of the skin and pain. This type of burn, although painful, will heal fairly quickly.
- **Second-degree burns** are characterized by the development of blisters and swelling. They heal a little slower but are usually not serious enough to seek medical attention.
- **Third-degree burns** involve damage to deeper skin layers and may have a charred appearance. They are often not very painful because the nerve endings in the skin may have been damaged.

You should usually seek medical attention after a third degree burn because of the damage it does to the body's protective layer against infection.

In beadmaking, burns are usually a result of inappropriate attire or not paying proper attention to what you are doing. Here are some general purpose rules to help avoid receiving burns.

What to wear to avoid thermal burns

1) When working, always wear natural fibers like cotton or wool, not synthetics like nylon or rayon. Synthetics will melt and shrink when exposed to heat.

2) Wear long pants when working, so if you drop a hot object, it will not immediately land on your skin. Avoid pants with cuffs or open pockets that might catch hot items.

3) Do not wear sandals when doing any flameworking.

4) When working around very hot equipment like kilns and glory holes, protect your body parts from the heat by using gloves, long sleeve shirts, light jackets, etc.

Proper equipment operation to avoid thermal burns

1) Never reach across an open flame to grab something. Turn off the torch when not in use to reduce chances of burns.

2) Always position the hot ends of your tools and glass away from you so that you will not grab the hot end. You do this because you can not see which end is hot.

3) Put down your hot rods in such a position so that they will not roll off your workbench onto your lap. A rack, as shown in Figure 379, helps prevent this from happening.

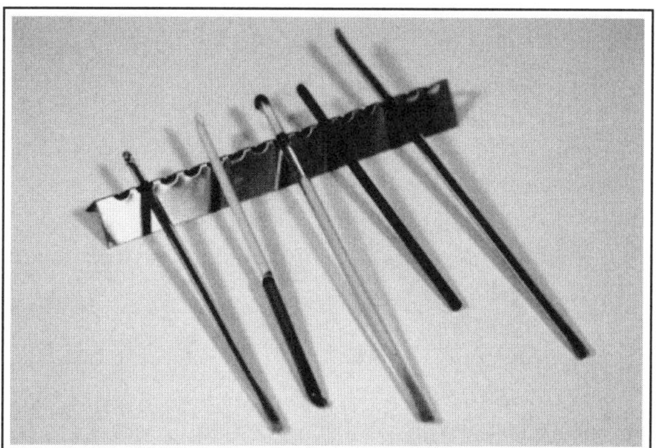

Figure 379. Racks for resting your hot glass rods.

4) Position a dark background behind any open flames so that they are more visible.

5) Turn off a kiln before you reach into it.

6) Sit in a chair that offers a quick escape in case you drop a hot tool or piece of glass. I do not think that one of those ergodynamically correct chairs that you kneel on is appropriate.

7) Be aware of where you have set down hot objects on your bench so that you will not touch these areas until they have cooled.

8) Mount your torch to your workbench so that it cannot be accidentally pulled into your lap.

What to wear to avoid chemical burns

Whenever you are handling caustic materials, you need to wear special equipment to prevent chemical burns. The following is a suggested list in case you decide to work with acids, especially hydrofluoric acid. Of course how much of this you wear depends in part on how much of the material you are handling. I would consider splash goggles, gloves, and a rubber apron the minimal protection necessary. More complete protection would consist of:

1) Splash goggles that seal to your face.
2) A face shield to wear over the goggles to protect the rest of your face.
3) Gloves appropriate for the material being used.
   - Natural rubber is good for dilute acids, alkalis, and alcohols.
   - Neoprene rubber is good for dilute acids, alkalis, alcohols, and ketones.
   - Butyl rubber is good for acids, alkalis, alcohols, ketones, esters, and many other solvents.
   - Nitrile rubber is good for dilute acids, alkalis, petroleum solvents, oils, greases, and amino acids.

   You may also want to get the gloves long enough to roll the top down to make a cuff to prevent solvents from running down your arm
4) A rubberized laboratory apron.
5) Full length rubber overalls that fit down over your boots.
6) Rubber shirts.
7) Rubber hats.
8) Rubber boots.
9) Respirator with an acid cartridge.

What to do if you get a burn

Treatment for a burn will depend on the type of burn and its severity. In the case of very severe burns, you may also have the complication of shock. The body goes into shock as a means to reduce the demands it places on its component systems. Things that may contribute significantly to causing shock include loss of blood or chemical balance, extreme pain, or traumatic experiences.

In the case of shock, you should try to lie the victim down to allow better blood circulation and cover them with a blanket to preserve body heat. If requested, administer fluids in the form of sips of water or water mixed with baking soda to the ratio of ½ teaspoon to a quart of water. Then seek medical attention immediately.

Let's now look at the first aid treatment for the different types of burns.

Thermal burns

First-degree burns should be treated by cooling off the affected area with cold running water. Then if necessary apply a dry compress to protect the area.

Second-degree burns can also be immersed under water for up to a couple hours. Then, if desired, use cold compresses. After you are done cooling it, blot the burn dry and cover it with a sterile compress. Do not apply antiseptic preparations, ointments, or sprays if the burn is severe. Also never pop blisters or intentionally remove skin. For large burns, you may also want to elevate the affected limb to reduce swelling.

Third-degree burns are usually just stabilized and then medical attention is sought. Do not clean the burn, or try to remove attached clothing or other materials. Cover the burned area with a clean compress of freshly laundered material covered possibly by a clean plastic bag. Elevate the affected limb. Have the person sit down and not walk if possible. Be wary of the possibility of shock. Seek medical attention.

Chemical burns

If the burn is to the skin, wash away the chemical as much as possible with large amounts of water using a shower or hose as quickly as possible for at least 5 minutes. Remove any articles of clothing from the affected area. Do not scrub the area. If any directions for treatment of burns are present on the chemical container, follow them. Apply a bandage and get medical attention. Notify them what material you were working with. Better yet, bring the container.

If the burn is to the eyes, again wash with large volumes of water as quickly as possible for at least 5 minutes for acid burns and 15 minutes for alkali burns. (Alkali burns are trickier because the eye might appear at first to be only slightly injured but eye injuries can progress to develop deep inflammation and tissue damage.) While washing out the eye, ensure that the face and eyelids get washed also since they probably have been affected. If only one eye is affected, have that eye down and wash from the nose outward when rinsing so that you are not rinsing material into the other eye.

For acid burns to the eyes, if a weak solution of 1 teaspoon of baking soda in 1 quart of water can be made quickly rinse with this solution after the water rinse. For alkali burns, check the eye for any loose particles of dry chemical and remove them with a sterile gauze or a clean handkerchief. Rinse some more, then cover the eye with dry pad or protective dressing. Try to have the victim not rub their eyes. Seek immediate medical attention.

Electrical burns

Electrical burns are treated essentially like thermal burns. The only difference is that you need to be aware that shock and CPR treatment may be necessary. In order to be ready for such an emergency you should consider getting CPR training from the Red Cross.

Toxic materials

The first step in evaluating what type of material toxicity plan you need for your studio is to examine the materials that you are or will be using in your work. What are they? What is in them? Is it hazardous? How hazardous is it? What form does it take? How might it enter my body? The more informed you are about these materials the better you will be able to evaluate what you need to do to protect yourself, your employees, and your family.

For example, if you decide to make any Pâte de Verre beads, the mold materials tend to be respiratory irritants at the very least. As an example, look at free silica that is used as a refractory additive in many mold formulations. Silica dust in your lungs can lead to a disease of a progressive nature called silicosis after heavy exposures even of only a few months duration. Of course we are talking of pretty heavy industrial exposures here, but the same thing can happen from low-level exposures, it just takes more of them over a longer period of time. Thus, it is important that you observe good hygiene practices whenever working with molds and mold making materials.

If you mix any of your own colored glass, be aware that many of the colorants are toxic materials. They are usually heavy metals like lead or cadmium that not only are poisonous but also are not easily eliminated from the body. Operations like scraping kiln shelves or grinding creates silica-containing dust.

Other bad actors include: fiber paper that has been fired to high temperatures, overglazes since they are frequently high lead glasses, enamels and paints since they contain lead and other heavy metals, very fine frits, plaster, cements, etc. Even things that seem innocuous like vermiculite can pose a health hazard. Its chronic inhalation may cause asbestosis or cancer and its ingestion may cause cancer.

There are a number of different designations for toxins based on how this toxin works on the body. They include:

- Poisons are toxins that interfere with chemical processes in the body. These toxins may be cumulative or noncumulative depending on how fast they are eliminated by the body.
- Mutagens are toxins that cause changes in our genetic blueprints.
- Teratogens are toxins, which affect how the genes in a developing fetus become expressed by changing the background chemistry of the environment.
- Allergens are toxins that react with the body's immune system. These reactions may vary from the sniffles and watery eyes to anaphylactic shock.

The degree of toxicity of a material describes its capability to hurt you. Highly toxic materials may only need a little bit to cause problems, so you cannot always judge danger by how much material you are using. You have to also consider other factors like how often you use the material. Long-term usage of lesser toxic materials might also lead to health consequences. This is partly attributed to the fact that previous exposures may sensitize you to the material. As an example, cancer is now suspected to be a result of chronic exposures to low levels of many chemicals called carcinogens. In fact, it is not understood if there are any safe exposure limits for carcinogens.

Toxicity of materials is primarily measured by testing with animals. A material is fed to animals in increasing doses until a dose is determined that will kill one half of all the animals. This lethal dose, know as the LD 50, can be used to rank relative toxicity of different materials for ingestion. A similar type of testing is done for inhalation hazards called the LC 50 test. Because of the expense, these types of experiments have not been done for a lot of the common materials that we deal with.

Based on these tests and some known levels of toxicity for certain materials in humans, threshold limit values (TLVs) can be established for safe exposures. The American Conference of Government Industrial Hygienists publishes tables of these values. They give a safe time-weighted-average (TWA) for chronic 8-hour workday exposures to many materials. You can use these values in two ways. First, you can use them to decide which of a number of similar materials to use for a process based on their toxicity. Second, if you do not have a choice of materials available to you, you can use the TLV-TWAs to determine how careful you have to be with this material.

The best practice is to minimize all possible exposures to toxic materials. To do that, you have to understand how toxic materials can get into your body. There are three main routes of entry into the body: skin contact, ingestion, and inhalation. We have already discussed how to avoid skin contact with toxic materials when we discussed what to wear to avoid chemical burns. Restricting eating and smoking from the work place can avoid ingestion of toxins. Inhalation is harder to control because we cannot restrict breathing. Let's look at what you can do to avoid problems with toxic materials in your workspace.

Pregnancy & beadmaking

An extra level of caution should be present in doing anything out of the ordinary when pregnant because a developing baby is much more sensitive to toxins than you or I, especially during the 10 weeks of development. This is because it is going through a tremendous amount of cell growth and specialization. Toxins can cause mutations or abnormal development of limbs and organs.

First and foremost let me encourage you to discuss the issue of beadmaking with your OB-GYN. Unfortunately, unless she or he is a beadmaker, they will not be cognizant of the materials that you will be working with or the care with which you already handle them. They should be able to make you aware of some of the issues.

Since your baby is already putting a strain on your body, you have to take extra care of yourself and get more rest. Try to take more frequent breaks and be sure to drink plenty of fluids. Cut back on your torch time.

Because of the increased risk, two things are definitely recommended during pregnancy over and above all others. First avoid handling or using toxic materials like enamels, glass paints, metals, metal oxides, fine frits, etc. Just handling them carries the risk of stirring them into your breathing air, so clean up your work area early on using wet swipes and mops. Later after having the baby, get into the habit of ritually washing your hands after lampworking so that you do not carry any toxins in on them. This will help block the ingestion route into your body and the baby's.

My other major concern is to ensure that you have proper ventilation so that you block the inhalation route into your body. This will protect you from combustion gases and any trace metals that might be released as you melt colored glass. If you feel you must add a second layer of protection by using a respirator with fume or HEPA filter cartridge do so but I am not sure it is worth it because it will not protect you against carbon dioxide and it will tire you out. A better plan would be to increase the ventilation of your workspace.

Good work practices to avoid toxicity problems

One of the best ways to avoid problems with material toxicity is to develop good work practices that incorporate a high degree of cleanliness. Unfortunately this is not a virtue a lot of artists are known for. Examples of good work practices when dealing with powdered toxic materials are as follows:

1) Isolate a work area for mixing these materials so the dust does not get spread all around your studio. If you do not have a space to dedicate to a mixing process, create one temporarily when mixing the materials and then clean up the area right after you are done working with them. This does not in any way mean that you should not keep an isolated work area clean. Your work area should have adequate ventilation to help remove dust from the air without at the same time tending to create it.

2) Consider using restricted volumes in which to contain handling of the materials. You could mix chemicals in a small homemade glovebox like that illustrated in Figure 380 or confine all spray painting to a paint hood.
3) If you have two processes using the same toxic material, try to arrange them so they do not get spread all around the work place. Organize

your work processes so that both operations are done in the same area.

4) Clean your work place regularly by either wet mopping or using a HEPA vacuum cleaner. Other methods such as sweeping or using an ordinary shop vacuum will just spread the dust around into your breathing air.

5) Store all materials in covered containers to prevent dust from being spread around. This also helps in preventing some of these materials, like plasters, from absorbing water from the environment.

6) Make sure that all the materials are properly labeled as to what they are and what hazards they present.

7) Obtain and keep on file Material Safety Data Sheets, MSDS, for all toxic materials that you use in your work.

8) Whenever you have the choice between using one of two materials, use the least toxic. Examples are using non-asbestos gloves in kiln work or cleaning with alcohol rather than acetone.

9) Have a training program for both you and your employees so that you are sure they understand the hazards of these materials and proper work practices.

10) When working with toxic materials, you should wear a respirator rated for the type of material and process you are engaged in. Make sure that your respirator fits and that you are wearing it properly. Respirators are not 100% effective and should not be used as a substitute for proper ventilation

11) Acquire and have on hand at all times the proper safety clothing and equipment for handling corrosive materials that we have talked about previously. These may include the following: face shield or goggles, gloves, aprons, and safety shoes.

12) Do not eat, drink, or smoke in your studio. You shouldn't smoke anyway but don't compound the problem by having that habit result in ingesting other unintended materials at the same time.

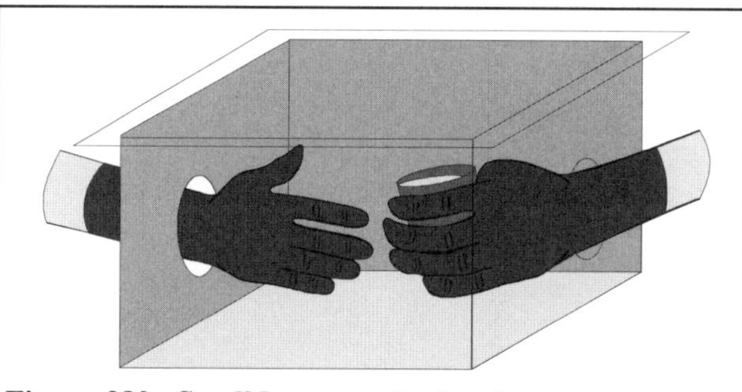

Figure 380. Small home-made glovebox..

13) Don't take your studio home with you. Wash your hands as you leave the shop or as you arrive home. (Please not in the kitchen sink.) Change your clothes before leaving the shop, or at the very least wear a long shop coat over your normal clothes that you then leave in the shop. Wash and dry work clothes separately from family clothes.

14) Dispose of all chemicals properly to avoid exposing your friends and neighbors.

Ventilation

As I discussed, the route into the body that is probably hardest to guard against is inhalation. Whenever materials are heated to their melting point and above, a mixture of particulate matter and gases is released that may be toxic. The worst of these are probably metal fumes.

Inhaling large amounts of metal fumes can cause both immediate and long-term effects. Acute, high level exposures can cause flu-like symptoms within about 6 hours that last for up to 24 hours. Chronic low-level exposures to metals such as lead can cause permanent neurological damage and reduced brain function. Lead fumes are released during high temperature processes, such as using low melting temperature lead glasses and fluxes. Some of these fumes are heavier than air, so you should consider ventilating your workspace both high and low. You may also need to ventilate your kilns. Especially effective for this are the kiln ventilation systems that draw air out through a hole in the bottom of your kiln.

Before we discuss how to guard against inhalation problems, let's devote a little time to understand what we are guarding against. Inhalation hazards can come in a number of different forms: gases, vapors, fumes, mists, and dusts. Do you know the

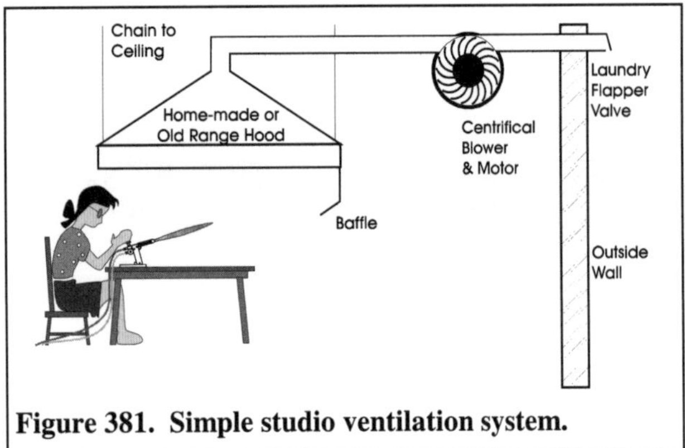

Figure 381. Simple studio ventilation system.

difference between them? They are defined as follows:

- **Gases** are materials in the air that we breath that do not have a solid or liquid form at normal pressures and temperatures.
- **Vapors** are gaseous forms of solid or liquid substances that may or may not be the result of increased temperature such as steam or propane vapors.
- **Fumes** are extremely small solid particles created by heating metals to above their melting point or by chemical reactions.
- **Mists** are small droplets of liquid, which are released into the air by mechanical actions such as spray, splashing, or bubbling.
- **Dusts** are solid particles of many sizes and shapes that are generated by mechanical actions such as grinding, crushing, or sanding.

The smaller or more gaseous the material, the easier it is for the material to penetrate deep into your lungs and be absorbed by your body.

Ventilation works to solve the problem caused by these materials by either of two methods:

- **Dilution ventilation** where the objective is to try and reduce the concentration of toxic materials in the air we breathe by mixing it with large volumes of fresh air. This is accomplished by exhausting large volumes of air and replacing it with new air. This does not mean just installing a room air conditioner in a shop window. They do not exchange anywhere near the amount of air that we are talking about.
- **Local ventilation** where the attempt is made to remove toxic materials from the workplace at their source by sucking them out at the point where they are generated. This type in most cases is the better ventilation solution. A simplified ventilation system that you can make for your studio would look something like that illustrated in Figure 381.

When considering ventilation plans here are some general principles to consider:

1) Try to remove contaminated air at its source. Pull it away from you and your employees as shown in the figure.

2) Use a baffle to catch the jet of torch gases and roll them into the ventilation hood.

3) Exhaust the air outside of the shop as far from air intakes as possible.

4) Exhaust systems are more efficient if they minimize the distance and number of bends through which they have to move the air. Also airflow resistance is minimized by using circular ducting.

5) Airflow is more controllable if you avoid unwanted cross drafts and add sufficient supply make-up air through a planned intake system.

6) It is easier to control contaminated air by pulling it out of your workspace rather than by trying to push it out. Otherwise if your ducting leaks, the contaminated air will be pushed back out into your studio.

7) Discharge your effluent air in a responsible manner. Do not pollute someone else's air.

If you are really interested in installing a ventilation system, I suggest that you contact an industrial ventilation specialist or get one of the references on this subject listed at the end of this chapter.

Ventilation is something that you should definitely consider having in your studio. Recent studies of torch effluents found a significant amount of NOX is being released. This can lead to headaches and respiratory problems. You know you are getting too much exposure when you get that metallic taste in your mouth or when your spouse complains about it when they come out to your studio for a visit.

Be sure to reevaluate your ventilation system whenever your working conditions change. One beadmaker I know got carbon monoxide poisoning after upgrading to a larger torch. It seems that the larger faster jet from the new torch bounced off the back wall of her hood and rolled back around to her face. Repositioning the torch and adding a baffle to break up the jet solved the problem. This just shows you how simple things can change everything.

Carbon monoxide detectors

Carbon monoxide is a poisonous gas produced by incomplete combustion of any torch fuel and is more prevalent in torches that provide a reducing environment like the handheld torches. It is an invisible, odorless and tasteless gas that kills thousands each year.

Carbon monoxide inhaled into our lungs gets dissolved into our blood. There it competes with oxygen for the hemoglobin in our red blood cells and usually wins. Once there, it clings on to the hemoglobin much more efficiently than oxygen and it takes a long period of time to get out of your system. This substantially reduces the amount of oxygen that your blood can carry to your vital organs. As the concentration of carbon monoxide increases in our blood, the symptoms as listed in Table 27 get progressively more severe. The speed with which carbon monoxide gets absorbed and its final levels in our blood depend upon its concentration in the air we breathe. At high enough concentrations, it can kill in minutes.

Table 27. Symptoms of carbon monoxide poisoning.

Symptom	CO blood level
Slight headache	15%
Severe headache	20%
Drowsiness, fatigue	30%
Nausea, vomiting	40%
Death	50%

Carbon monoxide can be removed by properly functioning ventilation systems like those just described. But since we know that it can be an ever present by-product of our flameworking, it seems only prudent to try to determine if dangerous levels may be building up in our studios. Since we cannot see, smell or taste it, we have to rely on sensors to warn us of its presence.

Home alarms like those in Figure 382 are available from First Alert and Lab Safety and Supply. They cost about $40 and although not calibrated to the OSHA standard limits of 35ppm for a constant 8 hour workday exposure, they have been demonstrated by Underwriter Laboratories to provide detection capability of a wide variety of dangerous exposures listed in Table 28. OSHA level alarms are available but are more expensive. As an example, the alarmed version from Lab Safety and Supply sells for about $511.

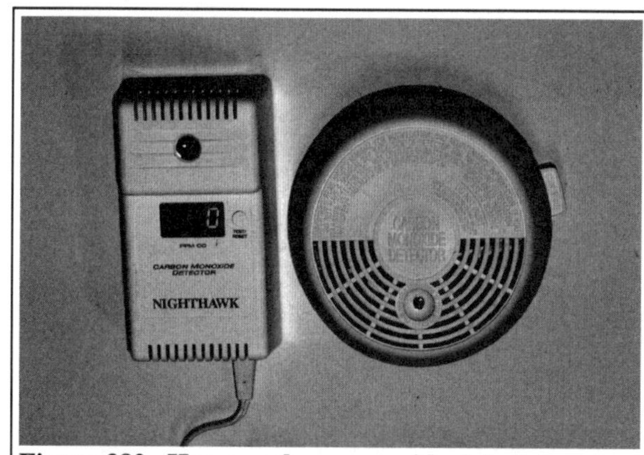

Figure 382. Home carbon monoxide detectors.

Carbon monoxide poisoning is a real danger in poorly ventilated lampworking studios so seriously consider getting a carbon monoxide detector. Mount it at your breathing level (since carbon monoxide is lighter than air) and as near to your workspace as possible.

Table 28. New UL standards for carbon monoxide detectors.

Time	Carbon monoxide concentration (ppm)
15 minutes	400
35 minutes	200
90 minutes	100
30 days	15

Respirators

Sometimes when doing especially dirty operations or when doing temporary dirty operations in a general workspace, you may want more protection than is offered by your ventilation system. This is the time to use a respirator. It should be stressed that respirators are usually considered temporary measures. They should only be used as the primary protective device when no other means is possible or the contaminant is so toxic that a single control measure is not felt to be sufficient. You primary means of inhalation protection should always be your ventilation system.

If you are an employer and decide that your employees need to periodically use respirators, you should be aware that OSHA requires a written plan for their use. This plan is to acquaint your employees with respirator use and selection. It should also include medical screening to look for proper respiratory system function, fit check of the respirator, training in the use of respirators as well as their limitations, and setting up procedures for their maintenance.

Choosing a respirator

In choosing a respirator, you need to consider first what is the form of the airborne toxic material from which you are trying to protect yourself. Is it a dust, mist, fume, vapor or gas? Next you should consider how long you might be working in that atmosphere. Longer times require larger canisters. How toxic is the material? Lastly you need to look at how they fit. They should be comfortable, leak proof, easy breathing, and non-interfering with vision. Some of these questions may be difficult for you to answer. If so, you should consult a reputable respirator consultant.

The style of respirator that most artists will use is a quarter mask respirator that covers only the mouth and nose or a half mask respirator like that in Figure 383 that covers the mouth, nose and chin. There are also full mask respirators that cover the whole face and whole head repirators to add protection for your eyes.

Check your respirator's fit by first holding your hands over the ends of the filters and sucking in. You should feel the mask pull against your face and hold there until you exhale. Next check the fit by exhaling while holding your hand over the exhalation valve. This should cause the respirator to lift off of your face. Both of these checks should be done every time you don the respirator. In addition, with some chemical filters in place, try fanning some strong smelling chemical vapors like ammonia for which the cartridges are rated near your face and see if you can smell them. Be careful not to splash anything into your face. You may want to wear some splash goggles when doing this to protect your eyes.

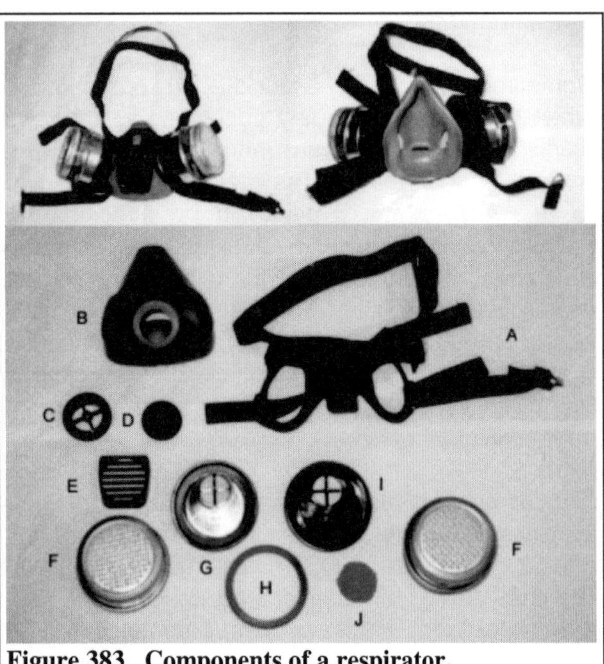

Figure 383. Components of a respirator.

If all of those tests are successful, you should have a good seal. You guys with beards, long mustaches, and/or long side burns should be aware that there is no way that you are going to get a good seal and that the respirator will not be completely effective for you. No facial hair should be touching the sealing surface under the respirator. Guys with heavy five-o'clock shadows will probably have to shave every day to ensure a continued fit. The fit of your respirator should be checked periodically to ensure that physical changes such as weight loss or gain have not altered it.

Once you have a good fit on your respirator, you need to choose what type of filters you will use. As should be obvious, this is a function of the materials with which you are working. Dusts and fumes usually just require mechanical filtration of the air. A filter made of folded felt or paper has this capability. Mists, vapors, and gases will require cartridges incorporating chemicals that purify the air by trapping the materials. Some examples for which chemical cartridges are available include acid gases, organic vapors, paints, and ammonia.

Care of a respirator

Like any piece of safety equipment, respirators require periodic maintenance to ensure their operation when you need them. After each use, they should be cleaned and checked for worn or broken components. Cleaning should consist of disassembling it, washing the rubber components periodically with warm, soapy water, and air-drying them before reassembly. Look for deteriorating plastic surfaces, rusting metal, and cracked glass. If okay they should be stored in plastic bags.

The plastic bags ensure that chemical filters are not being exposed to atmospheric vapors when not in use. Not doing this can greatly reduce the useful lifetime of a respirator cartridge because they become saturated with use. For the same reason, careful records should be maintained of the amount of time that chemical cartridges have been used. In storage, they should be kept in a place that is out of the way but at the same time is easily accessible in the event of an emergency. This location should also protect them from sunlight and temperature extremes. You should always keep replacement cartridges and filters on hand and they should be stored similarly.

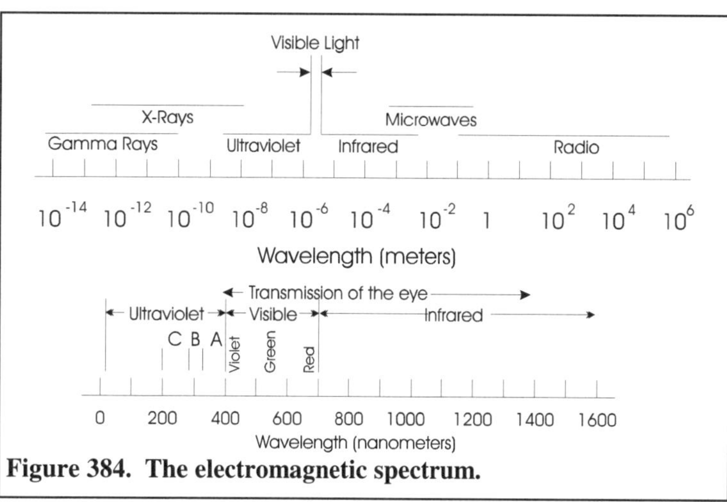

Figure 384. The electromagnetic spectrum.

You can usually tell when filter cartridges are starting to reach the end of their useful life because they start to get harder to breathe through as they get clogged up. Chemical filter life is not so easy to judge. They just stop absorbing the chemical agents without any warning. This can be aggravated by rough handling of the respirator, which can cause the chemical absorbents to pack up and air to leak past. You might be able to test using aromatic but less toxic chemical agents, but sometimes not.

For this reason, chemical filters are considered to be consumed after 8 hours of use or two weeks after being unpacked. Even if never removed from the package, some chemical cartridges may become ineffective over time. Such cartridges will usually come stamped with an expiration date. Also respirators are designed to be effective for what are considered normal exposures and will just not be effective enough against very high concentrations of contaminants. They will not be able to absorb all the material and will wear out quickly.

Optical considerations

In beadmaking or any process involving objects at high temperature, you also have to worry about more esoteric things like exposure to non-ionizing electromagnetic radiation. This radiation has properties of both particles and waves. Its particle nature dictates that it travels as a discrete particle, called a photon, in straight lines at a fixed speed. Its wave nature dictates that the energy of each photon is inversely proportional to its wavelength (i.e. as a photon's energy increases, its wavelength gets smaller).

The electromagnetic radiation with which we are most familiar is caused by electrons that have been thermally excited to higher energy states and subsequently fall back down to lower energy states. Each transition from a higher energy level to a lower energy level results in the release of a photon with an energy equal to that of the difference between the two energy levels. This cycle is repeated as long as application of heat continues to the glowing material.

Electromagnetic spectrum

The electromagnetic spectrum is just what its name implies, a complete spectrum of radiation with wavelengths, which as illustrated in Figure 384, go from angstroms to meters. The area of the electromagnetic spectrum of general consideration is that from about 200 to 2000 nanometers. A nanometer, abbreviated as nm, is 1/1,000,000,000th of a meter (10^{-9}). The lower cutoff is 200 nm because radiation with wavelengths shorter than this is usually absorbed by air.

It is convenient to label or give names to portions of this spectrum, which are usually based on some combination of properties such as wavelength, common use, or biological activity. Thus the spectrum is considered to be broken up into:

- **Visible light** is the range of the spectrum that humans have evolved to use for sight. This familiar span ranges from the shortest wavelength of 400 nm for violet to about 700 nm for red. The exact range visible to each person varies somewhat.
- **Infrared radiation (IR)** is that radiation which has wavelengths longer than the visible range. It is usually associated with heat energy.
- **Ultraviolet radiation (UV)** is that radiation with wavelengths shorter than the visible range.

The ultraviolet region of the spectrum is usually further subdivided into smaller bands on the basis of phenomenological effects. Because these effects do not have sharp wavelength cutoffs, the effects may carry over somewhat between bands.

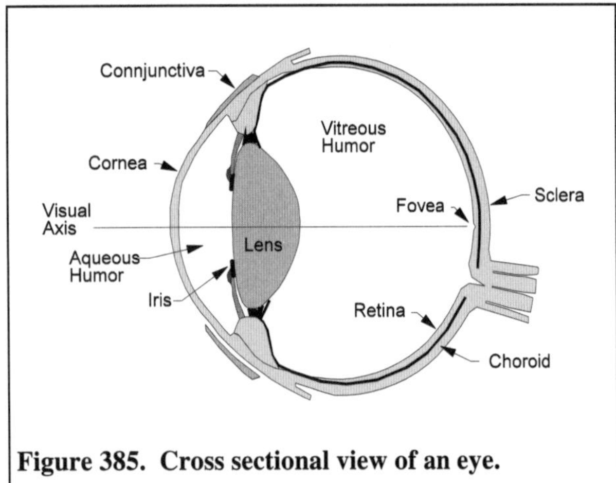

Figure 385. Cross sectional view of an eye.

- **UV-A** is the band from 320 nm to 400 nm. It is that spectral region that was used in the 60's to excite those fluorescent posters.
- **UV-B** is the band from 290 nm to 320 nm. It is that band of radiation usually known for causing sunburns.
- **UV-C** (200 to 290 nm) is the lowest band. It is not present in great quantity in nature because it is readily absorbed by earth's atmosphere.

Electromagnetic radiation damage

When the electromagnetic energy in a photon is absorbed by tissue, all of that energy is transferred to the absorbing atom or molecule. This energy puts the atom or molecule into an excited state. The mode of the excitation depends upon the wavelength of the photon. The shorter the wavelength, which as you may remember equates to higher energy of the photon, the more energetic the result.

In increasing order of energetics, the following may occur: molecular rotations, atomic vibrations in the molecule, changes in electronic energy state, or expulsions of electrons. This highest energy result is also known as ionization and takes more energy than is available from the region of the spectrum with which we are concerned. That is why I originally said we are dealing with non-ionizing radiation.

Infrared radiation may induce rotational and vibrational states in a molecule. Visible and ultraviolet radiation may induce higher vibrational states or electronic excitations. Vision and photosynthesis are two beneficial results of such interactions. Once molecules within a cell absorb the energy, any of a number of results are possible. The energy could be dissipated as heat. The molecule may be structurally altered or even break apart. The molecule may react with another molecules. The overall result to the cell from these changes may vary from changes in cell function to death. The question is how does all this relate to the eye.

The eye, as illustrated in Figure 385, is essentially a near-spherical organ with a transparent window on the front called the cornea. The cornea is part of the exterior sheath of the eye called the sclera. The eye is sheltered from the outside by the brow and the eyelids of which the conjunctiva is part. The iris divides the eye into two chambers filled with clear fluids or humors. It also serves to regulate how much light enters the eye. Rays of light enter the eye and are focused first by the shape of the cornea and second by the lens onto the retina. This is where the chemical reactions that the brain interprets as sight occur. Electromagnetic radiation of different wavelengths interacts differently with the eye. Let's examine how each of these different spectrum ranges interact with the eye to cause damage.

<u>UV-C</u> is essentially totally absorbed in the cornea. Its effects are cumulative over about a daylong exposure because of the fast rate of growth of corneal cells. Acute effects of absorption by the cornea are essentially pain and inflammation. It may feel as if you got sand in your eyes. This is usually felt sometime between 30 minutes to 24 hours after the exposure depending on the degree of the exposure. Higher exposures are felt sooner. The worst of the symptoms are usually over after about 6 to 24 hours and rarely last longer than 48 hours, again because of the rapid cell growth rate. Very rarely does permanent damage result. Unlike skin, the cornea does not develop increased tolerance with repeated exposure. One type of permanent damage that can result to the cornea is through the growth of a pterygium over the surface of the eye with some resultant loss in sphericity of the eye.

<u>UV-B</u> is partially absorbed by the cornea (about 40%) and partially by the aqueous humor (about 10%.) This has similar effects on the cornea as UV-C. The rest of the photons (about 50%) are absorbed by the lens. The primary effect of repeated exposures of the lens is decreased transmission or increased scattering of visible light. The basic mechanisms or fundamental changes that result in this phenomenon, called cataract formation, are poorly understood. They are thought to be due to changes in cell structure, fluid imbalances,

mineral buildups or protein aggregation. The damage is cumulative and permanent.

UV-A has less and less absorption by the cornea and aqueous humor as the wavelength increases toward visible light. So more and more is absorbed by the lens until, as the wavelength approaches visible light, the lens too starts to become transparent. This can lead to accelerated aging of the retina, but far and away the primary damage again occurs to the lens as with UV-B.

Visible light can also cause damage to the eye and this will primarily occur in the retina. Because of the eye's sensitivity to visible light, protective reactions such as iris constriction, squinting or closing of the eye will generally protect it. If you persist in viewing the bright visible light, you can suffer photochemical retinal injuries that can reduce the eye's ability to detect light up to complete blindness.

Near infrared (700 to 1400 nm) is generally considered more dangerous than UV because a good portion of it penetrates through the various ocular media and is actually focused onto the retina. This leads to heat buildup that can not be felt because there are no pain sensors there. The buildup of heat leads to denaturation of the biomolecules in the retina. In addition, absorption in the other features such as the lens and the iris can also result. Here the lens is primarily damaged by tissue peeling of the posterior surface of the lens. Damage to the iris is usually in the form of hemorrhages and inflammation.

Far infrared (1400 nm to 100 µm) is primarily absorbed in the cornea. Delivered at low power, it can again lead to itchy sore eyes. At moderate power, opacification caused by protein coagulation can result but pain felt on the skin usually causes you to close your eyes first.

You have to understand that damage is actually done by ambient levels of UV, visible and IR light all the time, but that this level is such that the natural on-going cellular renewal process is able to keep up with it. Something that upsets this balance by decreasing the body's recuperative powers can only make the situation worse. Chemicals that make the eye tissue more photosensitive can do this. Tetracyline, a common antibiotic, is an example of a common drug that is a photosensitizer. You may be interested to know that individual or racial features do not seem to play as important a role in eye sensitivity to light exposure as they do for the skin.

There are a number of factors that dictate the severity of an optical exposure that you receive. They include: the temperature of the object, its size and the distance from your eyes.

The hotter an object is, the more light that it emits and the wider the spectrum of the emitted light. Both of these factors are a result of the electrons being raised to higher energy levels. This allows them to either have more small energy transitions as they fall to their ground state or have larger ones. More transitions mean more photons, although of longer wavelengths. Larger energy transitions mean more energetic photons of shorter wavelengths.

The size of the hot object defines the amount of material that is heated to high temperature. This translates directly to more electrons getting excited and thus more photons released. **Therefore you get a much larger dose of optical radiation from a kiln than you do from a torch at the same temperature.**

The last factor that affects an exposure is your distance from it. The light from a kiln seems much brighter from 3 feet away than it does from across the room. This is because the distance between photons gets greater or their density gets lower as you get further from the light source. Thus the farther away you are, the fewer photons that hit your eye. Unfortunately, knowing all this does not necessarily help all that much because you may not be able to do much about controlling these factors. You still have to get the glass to a certain temperature to work it, you want a reasonable sized bead, and your arms are only so long.

Threshold limit value (TLV) standards have been set for UV, visible and IR light exposures by the American Conference of Governmental Industrial Hygienists (ACGIH). These standards give recommended limits and they are published as part of the ACGIH annual booklet on TLV's for chemical materials in the workplace. These limits have been established to avoid injuries to the eye of the type listed from chronic workplace exposures of 8 hours a day. To determine whether the exposure you are receiving is bad or not, you have to first evaluate the frequency distribution of that exposure. This is weighted by the eye's sensitivity to that spectrum and these products are then summed over all three spectral regions. Of course if at all possible, you should always operate by the ALARA principle. Keep your exposures As Low As Reasonably Achievable.

Eye protection

There are two basic types of protection from electromagnetic radiation: absorbing and reflecting filters. One type of absorbing filter that you may already be aware of is welding filters. They are characterized by shade numbers where the higher the shade number the darker they are. The problem with using them for beadmaking is that it becomes difficult to distinguish colors when wearing them; everything looks green.

Heat absorbing glass is one way to reduce the IR without losing color. Two millimeters of Schott™ KG5 or Hoya 165 glass will reduce the IR content by a factor of about 1000 with little appreciable color loss. Reflecting filters form the other type of eye protection and usually consist of a thin layer of gold or aluminum on the outer surface of your glasses. This layer reflects much of the incident radiation. This type of protective glasses suffers from a number of problems. First they can scratch easily if not handled delicately and second they change the apparent colors of your bead, although not as badly as welders shades.

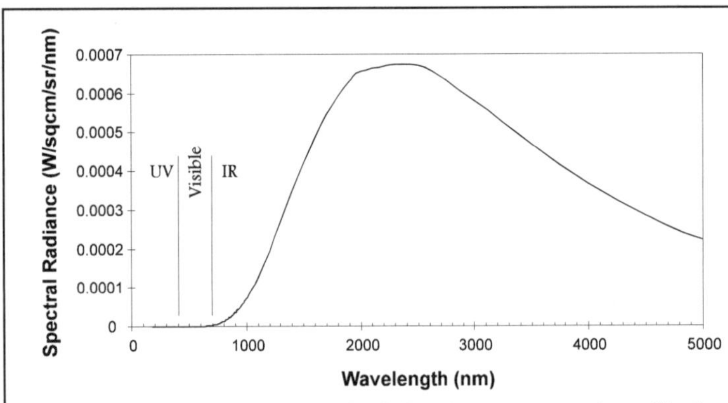

Figure 386. Blackbody model of the electromagnetic radiation from hot glass

In order to investigate the risks of exposure to electromagnetic radiation and decide which form of protection makes sense, I developed a spreadsheet that first calculated an approximation of the electromagnetic radiation that is emitted by a hot glass object. This was done by modeling it as a blackbody radiator with an emmittance of one. From spectral measurements of glass irradiance that I have seen in the literature, this is not a bad assumption. It tends to under represent the UV exposure slightly, as well as the visible sodium flare, while at the same time overestimating slightly the IR portion of the spectrum. The chart in Figure 386, depicts the black body spectral distribution for an object at 1700°F, it is seen that almost all of the radiation given off by such an object lies in the infrared portion of the spectrum. So the visible light that we see is a small part of what is actually emitted.

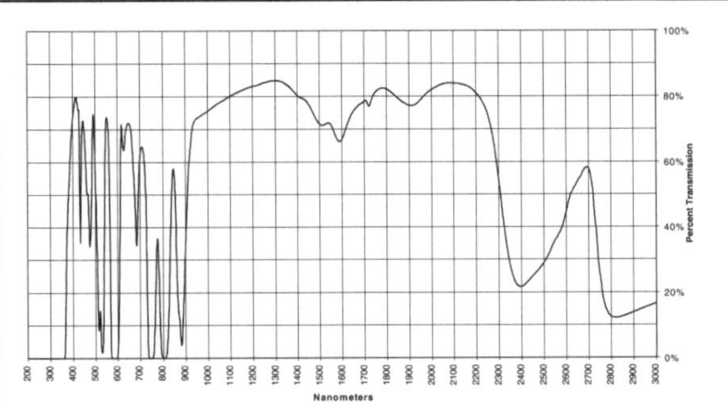

Figure 387. Transmission curve for AUR-92™ glasses©. Courtesy of AURA Lens Products

The next step was to determine how much radiation passes through various different types of glasses. Bob Aurelius of Aura Lens Products™, Inc. provided me with transmission curves in the UV, visible and near IR for a variety of common glasses such as the one in Figure 387. But as you can see from the figure, this is only a small part of the spectrum that we need to protect against. He also made me aware of Gary Meyers' study from Fusion magazine that discusses absorption over the entire IR region. Using these and other sources I found by searching through technical libraries, I was able to estimate transmittance for various different glasses across the relevant portion of the IR spectrum (out to 5000 nm). So now I could calculate what was impinging on the eyeball.

In order to decide if the exposure was harmful or not, I compared it to the threshold limit values published by the ACGIH as discussed earlier. From this study I learned a number of things. First UV and visible light exposure do not seem to be a problem for any situation that you are likely to get into while making glass beads. Second, for the beadmaker making wound soda-lime glass beads on a handheld torch, rose didymium glasses are probably sufficient. This may not be true when working on a mixed gas torch.

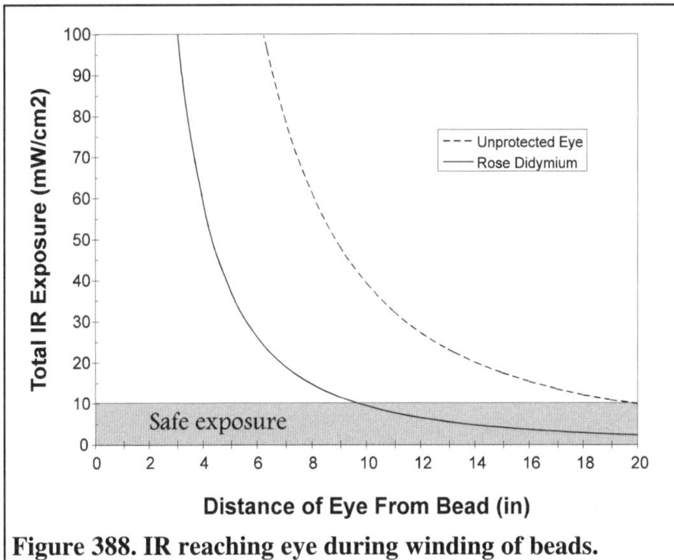

Figure 388. IR reaching eye during winding of beads.

Figure 388 illustrates how your total IR exposure from a 2 in^2 bead (or 1.6" in diameter) heated to 1700°F changes with the distance that you hold it from your eyes. The threshold limit exposure of 10 mW/cm^2 represents the upper edge of the safe exposure zone in the figure. From the figure, you can see that if you were to always work with your arms outstretched to 20 inches or greater you would not even need protective glasses. Wearing protective didymium glasses allows you to safelywork with the bead as close as 10 inches, but if you tend to hold your beads closer than 10 inches, your glasses will not provide you with enough protection.

Some people are more sensitive than others and may find they have to hold the bead further away to avoid that burning itching feeling that you get when you have overdone things. Alternatively, they may want to wear glasses that can provide more protection than rose didymium.

From examining the transmission curves that I have been provided, it appears that the AUR-92™ lens and the CBS™ Fleury lens provide a little extra protection over rose didymium. For more even more protection, you might also want to consider using a lens that includes some heat (IR) absorbing glass such as the AGW-186™. I also know that 15 nm of gold coating would provide enough reflectance to protect your eyes but do not know how much is on the glasses currently on the market. All of these glasses are more expensive than ordinary didymiums though. You could also consider using a medium welder's shade such as a #3 or #4 but you will lose your ability to see the true colors and will not be able to see beyond the sodium flare.

If you are making borosilicate beads, the temperatures at which you are working are hotter. Also if you are blowing hollow borosilicate beads, you tend to bring the bead up toward your face to inflate them. These factors all work to increase your exposure. So in this case you will want to invest in glasses with a little more protection than rose didymium. The suggested protection for working borosilicate by Mike Aurelius of Aura Lens Products™, Inc are as follows"

- Clear Boro: AGW-186 or equivelent
- Small beads (under 1 inch): AGW-200 Shade 4 or 5
- Large Beads (over 1 inch): AGW-286 Shade 4
- Sculptures, Fuming, lots of color: AGW-286 Shade 5

You can approximate the protection of AGW-200 lens by using a plastic green welding clip-ons over your didymium or AUR-92 glasses. The plastic welding clips run about $30.00. Keep in mind that this is not a long-term solution. The dyes used in making these clip-ons were not designed for long-term high temperature usage and will start to fade. They should probably be replaced every 4 to 6 months to ensure the required protection levels.

If you are making drawn glass beads, where you are working in front of a furnace and glory hole, you would be advised to read the report by Dave Gruenig on a NIOSH inspection of the Louie Glass Company, Inc. of Weston, West Virginia that was published in The Independent Glassblower. An operation such as this will expose you to considerable IR radiation, both from the glass that you are handling as well as from the hot equipment.

Their findings and my calculations agree that for such an operation as this didymiums are not even close to being adequate, you require heavy-duty protection such as a dark welder's shade. The problem is that to be adequate for this purpose the shade should transmit only about 1% of the incident IR radiation (about a number 5 shade). This allows your face to feel hot about the same time as your eyes are starting to receive dangerous amounts of radiation. The problem with this is that these shades are so dark that it is hard to see what you are doing.

Dave presents some good ideas on how to compromise in a way to satisfy both of these requirements. He suggests that for the general work around the shop you wear a shade that provides a good amount of protection but still allows you to see what you are doing. He suggests wearing about a #1 or 2 welder's shade for this (the AGW-99™ would also be a good choice and would allow good color visibility.)

Then when you make a gather or reheat your work, you can flip down a darker shade like a #3 or 4 that you have mounted on a plastic face shield over the lighter glasses. This shield should be trimmed to expose your face because if your face becomes unbearably hot, then that is an indication that you are probably getting a larger IR dose than even the shades can compensate for. Another option for getting additional protection from radiation coming off hot equipment is to permanently mount supplemental shades in front of the equipment.

During the making of kilnworked beads, you are not exposed to hot glass for long periods of time, but the physical size of the hot open kiln allows a lot of electromagnetic radiation to be emitted. For such a case, you should probably again wear at least a number 3 welder's shade and try not to peek into the kiln too much.

Even if you decide that you do not need eye protection from the electromagnetic radiation, you need to wear some sort of protective glasses to protect your eyes from flying glass shards that come off of glass rods when they thermal shock.

Skin protection

Besides our eyes, we all know that electromagnetic radiation can also affect our skin. We are painfully reminded of that fact anytime we stay in the sun too long without protection. The question is can the light or radiation from our torch do the same thing. The conventional wisdom says no.

The part of the solar spectrum that damages our skin is the UV rays. As discussed earlier, the UV portion of the spectrum is generally broken up into UV-C, UV-B and UV-A. Most all of the UV-C is absorbed by ozone in the atmosphere and very little reaches the earth's surface. It is the UV-B that damages our skin, causing sunburn, skin aging, cancers, ad tanning. It is primarily absorbed in the surface of skin. UV-A can go deeper but is less damaging because it is less energetic. This is why this portion of the spectrum is used for tanning salons. But be aware that less damaging does not mean no damage and similar judgments can probably be made for visible and infrared light.

UV rays damage our skin through altered biochemistry of DNA, cell membrane disorders, effects on enzymes and other proteins and amino acids partly through the production of free radicals. These damage products are released and cause our body to go into defensive reactions and bring blood into the affected area by dilating skin capillaries leading to the characteristic redness of the skin. Cells irreparably damaged shrivel up and die.

Short of death other long-term effects can also occur from excessive sun exposure. These effects include wrinkling, coarsening, sagging, and spotting of our skin as it ages. These visible changes are indicative of invisible microscopic changes that occur as our thin, straight, elastic fibers thicken, tangle, and eventually degrade into an inelastic clump. Using sun tan lotion and taking antioxidants can help avoid some of this damage.

As you go up the spectrum from UV to the visible and infrared portion of the spectrum, the energy contained in each photon decreases making them less damaging but again not completely without damage. Have you ever noticed how your dental hygienists hide when you get an x-ray. That is because an infrequent exposure as you are receiving is not likely to cause damage but repeated exposures like they could receive would increase the likelihood that damage could occur. Similar logic can be applied to visible and UV light exposures.
As you can see in Figure 386, the bulk of the radiation released from our torch flame is in the form of visible and infrared radiation. IR radiation is generally considered to be non-damaging to the skin and is used medically for deep heating massage. The main result of such an exposure being warming of the area and increased blood flow to it. This is because you are essentially cooking yourself on low heat and your body is trying to cool you down. If you choose to ignore it, you can end up cooking yourself. So if you feel hot, deal with it by donning some protective cotton clothing to mitigate the effect.

In summary, it is still unclear whether exposure to the radiation released by your torch is harmful beyond chance burns. There is very little UV present in it so that is probably not an issue, but it could not hurt to religiously use protective suntan lotion when you work, the higher the sun protection factor the better. I am not sure if this really does much to protect against IR, so I would suggest that if you can feel the heat on your skin that you shield it with a long-sleeved cotton shirt.

Hearing risks

We beadmakers are subjected to certain low level noise sources that are on almost constantly during our work. These sources include the sound of our torch, the whir of the ventilation system, the pumping of an oxygen concentrator, etc. We all now recognize the danger to our hearing of loud noises such as those at a typical rock concert, but few of us recognize the danger from day-to-day low level sound sources.

Ricky Charles Dodson brought this danger to my attention because he became aware of it the hard way. He went in for a checkup and his doctor pointed out that he had a significant hearing loss in the high frequency range. His doctor asked him if he was exposed to a lot of loud noises in his work. When Ricky said no, the doctor next queried him about constant low-level sound exposures of some type. Ricky again could not identify anything, at least not until later when he got back to his studio and started working. He then realized that he was constantly surrounded by low-level sound.

Sound is produced when something causes vibration waves in air. These sound waves spread out from the noise source getting weaker as they go. The measure of loudness used for sound is the bel – named after Alexander Graham Bell. The term

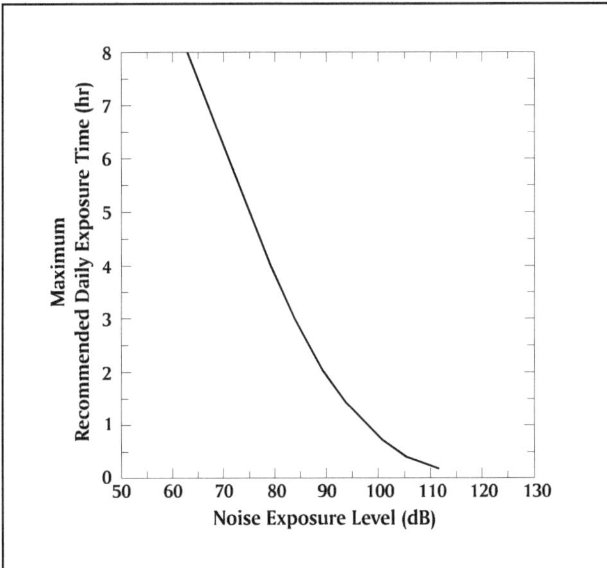

Figure 390. Maximum recommended sound exposure levels.

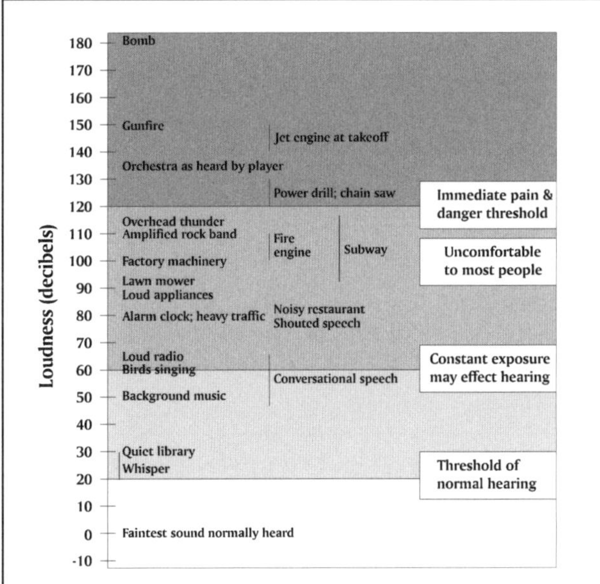

Figure 389. Loudness of common sounds.

you are probably familiar with is the decibel (dB) or one tenth of a bel. Bels and decibels are logarithmic values (do not worry about what this means) of the actual loudness value such that for every 10 dB or 1 bel the sound is actually 10 times louder. For 20 dB it is 100 time louder and so on. As an example, Figure 389 illustrates the loudness levels of many common day-to-day sound conditions.

People have a responsive hearing range from about 20 to 20,000 vibration cycles per second (known as hertz or Hz) but usually can discern sounds from about 500 to 4000 Hz. The range of typical speech sounds is from 500 to 2000 Hz. It is the upper range of about 4000 Hz that is usually lost from age or constant exposure to noise. Why does exposure to constant noise deaden your hearing? You might think that you would get accustomed to higher noise levels with repeated exposures, just like you get stronger with exercise. Unfortunately not, instead these high levels of noise damage the delicate nerves of the ear.

So how loud do noises have to be to damage the ear? We already alluded to this in Figure 389 with the captions in the boxes to the right, but let's define it a little better. Figure 390 gives us a little better answer to this question. It gives accepted threshold limit values for daily exposures of different noise loudness levels that will not result in hearing problems as published by the ACGIH.

If you ignore these recommendations and expose yourself to noise every day for eight hours a day,

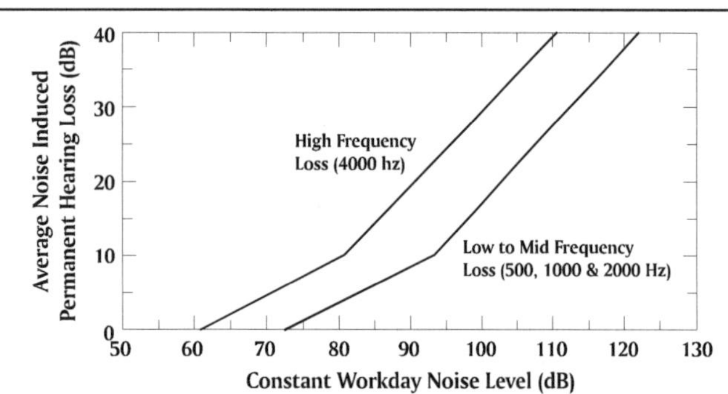

Figure 391. Expected hearing loss from working noise exposures.

what level of hearing loss can you expect over your working lifetime (assumed to be 50 years). The answer to this question is illustrated in Figure 391. Here we see that in conditions as low 80 dB or equivalent to that of a noisy restaurant we can expect to lose 10 dB of our high frequency hearing capability. This means that a sound has to be 10 times louder before we will hear it. Similarly a 90 dB work environment, equivalent to mowing the lawn, would result in a 20 dB hearing loss. Here a sound would have to be 100 time louder before we would hear it. Note that these values from Kryter are even lower than those recommended by the ACGIH.

So a word to the wise, you should assess your studio situation to decide if wearing some soft sponge ear plugs or those hard plastic ear muffs might not make sense to block out some of this noise. I would especially recommend it for Hot Head® torch users. You may even find yourself more peaceful and those of you who want to can still listen to the radio or television while wearing them.

The sponge ear protectors are inexpensive, only about a quarter a pair when bought in bulk quantities. You just wad them up and stick them into your ear. Don't keep wearing the same pair over and over though because this can lead to developing external ear infections, besides that they lose their resiliency and are less effective after a few wearings. So toss them out and use a new pair.

Ergonomic risks

As with almost any activity, there are ergonomic risks associated with glass beadmaking. They include strains, sprains and cumulative trauma disorders. These afflictions are the result of exceeding the normal physical capabilities of the body. The body has a way of letting us know when this has happened through pain or soreness in body parts. You need to listen to these warnings and analyze what you are doing to cause this injury. The goal is then to determine how to modify what you do to accomplish the task in a way that matches your capabilities. Also by learning more about risk factors, you may be able to modify your work practices to reduce risk of injury.

Risk factors

One of the biggest ergonomic problem areas in the general population is back injury. Eighty percent of us will suffer lower back pain caused by one of a number of reasons: poor posture (yes, your mother was right), improper lifting, or bad physical conditioning. What can you do to avoid problems? Here are some suggestions:

- First make sure that whatever chair you use at your bench provides proper support for your back.
- Try to observe how you do things to ensure that you are not doing them in a way that put you in awkward positions for any period of time.
- Try not to bend forward, sideways, or twist when lifting objects.
- Try to develop a mechanical means of lifting heavy objects whenever possible.
- When lifting heavy objects, keep them close to your body. Lift from your knees whenever possible and try to have objects raised about 30" off of the floor before lifting them. Get someone to help you with heavy objects.
- Keep yourself in good physical condition, especially your stomach muscles, which actually supply much of the support for your back.

A common complaint with beadmakers is of sore and tired shoulders. This is largely a result of improper positioning of the arms. Any posture where the arms are held extended at angles more than 45° from the body in any direction puts strain on your shoulders. This problem is aggravated by holding this posture for long periods of time or by lifting loads on the order of as little as 10 pounds.

For beadmakers, the primary problem with their shoulders comes from how they hold their arms. If they hold them pointed outward for long periods of times this will strain the shoulders. To alleviate this problem, it is suggested that you develop a means to rest your elbows on some surface during your time at the bench. This can be in the form of rests on your workbench or your chair. Also make sure that your bench is at a height such that you are comfortable when your elbows are resting on the rests. Jim Smircich is marketing some armrests to support them at torch level for people that like to work at that height.

One area that does not appear to be too much of a problem with beadmakers is the elbow. One does not usually get tennis elbow from beadmaking. Elbow problems are usually the result of forearm rotations or of arm extensions with weights at the end of your arms. These types of motions are not common in beadmaking.

An area of increasing concern is in the hand and the wrist. Motions of the hand which take the wrist near the ends of its motion (more than about 45° off of straight) causes compression on nerves to the hand by tendons, bones and ligaments. You need to try to hold your hands in such a manner as to keep the wrists straight when working at your bench to avoid this pitfall. The type of grasp that you use in your work also affects the stress on your wrists. Making tools with larger handles or grips up to about 1 1/4" makes them easier to handle. Padding tool grips and making them higher friction also makes it easier to work with them.

Cumulative trauma disorders

Many repetitions of an injurious body motion can increase the damaging effect of any of the above problems. You know if repetitive motions are injurious if you wake up with them still being sore the next day. Cumulative damage is increased when cold, vibratio,n or mechanical stress accompanies the motions. Cold limits your feelings, which in turn inhibits your ability to feel the natural body feedback mechanism. Vibration requires stronger gripping forces that squeeze the underlying nerves more. Mechanical stress results from any pressure on the nerves. This can be from something as simple as resting your arms against your forearms or wrists instead of on your elbows. This can obstruct blood flow and again put pressure on underlying nerves.

The most widely known of these disorders is carpal tunnel syndrome. It is the loss of feeling and dexterity to the hands and is caused by pressure on the median nerve by tendons, bones or carpal ligaments in the wrist. Repeated insults on this nerve lead to inflammation of the surrounding tissue as well as prolonged and debilitating pain. To avoid this problem, you need to keep your wrists as straight as possible while you work, avoid leaning on your forearms or wrists, take frequent rests and make sure that your tools are as comfortable as possible to handle.

Suggested further reading

American Conference of Governmental Industrial Hygienists (ACGIH), **Threshold Limit Values for Chemical Substances and Physical Agents and Biological Exposure Indices**, 6500 Glenway Ave., Bldg. D-7, Cincinnati, OH 45211-4438, Tel (513)661-7881

ACGIH. **Industrial Ventilation**, 1982

The American Red Cross. **Standard First Aid and Personal Safety**, Doubleday & Company, Inc. 1973

Clark, Nancy; Cutter, Thomas, and McGrane, Jean-Ann. **Ventilation - A Practical Guide for Artists**, Craftspeople, and Others in the Arts, Lyons & Burford, 1984

Grandolfo, M. Rindi, A and Sliney, D. H., **Light, Lasers, and Synchrotron Radiation A Health Risk Assessment**, NATO ASI Series, 1989

Gruenig, David. "**Eye Protection for Furnace Glassblower**", The Independent Glassblower, Issue No. 18, (August/September), 1990

Kryter, Karl D. **The Effects of Noise on Man**, Academic Press, Inc, 1985

McCann, Michael. **Health Hazards Manual for Artists**, Nick Lyons Books, 1985

McCloskey, E. S. "**Lets Make an Exhaust Hood**", Glass Line, Volume 9 Number 1, (June/July), 1995

Myers, Gary E. "**Optical Radiation Hazards in Glassblowing**", Fusion August 1976

Rossol, Monona. **The Artist's Complete Health and Safety Guide**, Allworth Press, 1990

Spielholz, Peregrin. **Identifying and Controlling Ergonomic Risks in Glassblowing**, 1993 Journal of the Glass Art Society

Afterward

In this chapter, I would like to speak about some topics that don't really fall in with those which came before. How does one get better? How does one go about developing your own style? How to go about marketing your work? How should you price your work? These are all tough questions to which all new beadmakers want answers.

Getting better

Okay, now you know a little bit about how to make beads, but how do you go about getting better at it? Well there is really only one answer to this question. Practice or as any beadmaker will tell you — TOT, time-on-torch. Of course, the time needed to get better is reduced if you don't have to make all the mistakes yourself. You have already helped yourself some by reading this book. You can further reduce the time needed by watching other beadmakers work. I cannot show you the rhythm of the work in a book.

Watch how other beadmakers manipulate the glass. See where they hold the bead and the glass relative to the flame. When do they enter the flame? An excellent way to do this is to take a class. How do you find out about classes? Check your suppliers. Read glass magazines. Join the International Society of Glass Beadmakers or visit their web site, www.isgb.org. If you still cannot find a good class, then consider buying a video.

Keep working at it.

Developing your own style

As a beginning beadmaker, you will probably find yourself faced with this predicament. You are new to the bead world and have not realized the vast potential of ideas and styles that are possible. You have taken a class from a beadmaker with a unique style that is well recognized in the bead world and that you would like to emulate.

You could just copy the style directly, but try to avoid this. Not only will your savvy customers recognize that style but also the word will spread around. Soon other glass beadmakers will know it also and you will find your image diminished in their eyes instead of improved. So how can you use what you've learned without turning out copies or nearly so of that teachers work?

The answer is work with it. Spend time at the torch practicing this new style but throw variations into it. Try different things. Try out different colors and arrangements of objects. As you do this, you will find yourself making choices about design elements that do or do not work for you. The choices that you make will help form your own style and will help distinguish your work from that of your teacher.

So the only answer is you have to work with it. Try many variations:

- If her beads were round, try making yours tear drop shaped.
- If hers were bright colors, try making yours with muted ones.
- If hers had a precise pattern, make yours more random.
- If hers were small, make yours larger.
- If hers had multiple straight lines, make yours with wavy lines.
- If hers had a few well-defined elements, add more elements in yours.

You may not get all of these ideas to work out initially but keep at it. Realize also that part of your dissatisfaction just might be because you are always mentally comparing your work to that of your teacher and that no matter what you do, you don't feel that it measures up. This is not true. Realize that your teacher may have been making beads for years to get where she is. Don't expect your style to instantly be as good.

Some things will be inevitable; there are only so many ways to make dot beads. So, if you are making them, you have to expect your work to look a little like some other beadmaker's and vice versa. Don't worry about this, but don't go out there trying to make yours look like someone else's. Work with a technique until you find your own voice.

Another thing that can help you to develop your own style is to make yourself more aware of all the design choices that you have available to you. You can achieve this by widening your exposure to the bead world. Study a multitude of artists' work and decide what makes each one tick. Make a list of these features. Pick one randomly and try to include it in your work—not the whole idea, but just one feature. Another thing that I like to do is try to figure out how they made a certain bead. This may give you ideas of things to try in your work.

Another place to look for ideas is in nature. Eric Seyoux and Nichol Zumkeller tell the story of how one evening when they were preparing dinner, they were struck by the beauty of the striations in color of red onion slices. They took this idea and used it to develop a new look for some of their beads. You can do the same.

By going through this process to develop your own style, your work will not just be a copy of someone else's. It will be one all your own that you can be proud of and may someday be recognizable by collectors throughout the country.

Marketing your glass beads

Making glass beads is such a seductive pastime that it can quickly become the endpoint of your work and interest. After all, glass beads are works of art and things of great beauty. But, if you are like many beadmakers, it would be nice to make some money off them.

Unfortunately, not everyone knows what to do with loose beads. They think of them as being unfinished pieces of jewelry. Therefore, you should also think about learning to mount your beads into pieces of jewelry. Learn to make them into necklaces, earrings, pins, key chains, etc. Try to find new niches for their use.

Figure 391. Rosaries by Bonnie Blincoe.

Bonnie Blincoe has come up with such an idea. By making a few different sized and shaped beads, she is able to make collector rosaries. A collection of these is seen in Figure 391 and close up of one of the crosses is seen in the color plates. The cross takes a fair amount of shaping but she says that the real tricky part of making rosaries is the three-holed bead for the junction of the loop and the single strand hanging from it.

So this is one idea that someone came up with, what other things might you try. How about lines of beads for some special occasions, like the one in Figure 392? You could make hearts with arrows for Valentine's day, cakes with candles for birthdays, or presents with ribbons for Christmas, filled Champagne glasses for New Years, pumpkins for Halloween, etc. And who could resist a wedding cake for their sweetheart on that special day.

Figure 392. A simple special occasion bead.

Special beads don't have to be complex. Mary Kloetz says the wedding anniversary beads that she makes are pretty simple but still sell well. They are basically round spotted beads. The trick is that the number of dots signifies the anniversary year.

Another thing that you have to decide is how you are going to sell your beads. Are you going to sell them retail or wholesale? Before you make a choice, ask yourself the following questions:

- how do you feel about making the same bead over and over versus making one-of-a-kind-beads?
- do you enjoy a steady income?
- are you willing to accept lower prices for your beads?

- do you enjoy going out to meet the public?
- do you prefer staying at home?

Think about these things and use your answers to help decide which marketing method you prefer.

Once you decide which it will be, you will need some information on how to bring it about. You will need information on things such as shows, galleries, and marketing. You can get a lot of this information by connecting to other beadmakers or by taking business classes at the annual Gathering of the International Society of Glass Beadmakers. Another source is the magazine, "The Crafts Report." It offers lists of upcoming shows all over the country. Each month, it also features profiles on a couple of different galleries and articles on different topics of interest to crafts people. So, I suggest that you subscribe to this magazine.

Figure 393. Hand-made glass bead necklace
Artist: Barbara Wright
Photo by: Alon Picker

Pricing your work

Pricing your work is not an easy thing. It has to pay for itself. You don't want to give your work away. To do this, you need to account for all your costs and make sure that they are covered whenever you sell your beads. So what types of things go into calculating your costs for a month:

- your lampworking tools.
- your glass rods.
- your torch gases.
- your rent.
- your time.
- your utility bills

Your time is a hard thing to calculate. It is not just the time you spend making the bead. It also includes: the time that you spend packaging and marketing your work, the time you spend going to the retail shows, the time you spend learning new techniques, and the time you spend designing new product. Once you have all these hours totaled up, then you have to multiply them by a price-per-hour that you think your time is worth. This is a value that will change over time as you get better but you should start out at least at minimum wage.

Now, add all of these things up and add about 25% more to cover any contingencies that you may not have thought about. Take the sum of all these costs and divide it by your total production time for the month. That is how much you have to make an hour to break even. So, if a bead takes a whole hour, your hourly rate is how much you will have to charge to break even. If it only takes half an hour to make, then you only need to charge half of this.

This value should be your wholesale price. This is price that you will give to buyers for stores or which you will expect from galleries. With that, you will have to decide the dollar amount of the minimum sale for which you will accept for wholesale sales. How many depends a lot on the value of your pieces but should be anywhere from six to a dozen items. The more inexpensive your work, the larger the required number of pieces.

Your retail price is then about twice that. This is the price that you charge customers that you sell to at shows or fairs. Hold to this price. If you sell cheaper than this, you are undercutting the people that resell your work. If they find out about it, they will feel cheated and may soon stop carrying your work. They have purchased your work assuming that you were not going to go into unfair competition with them. If your work is worth that much in a store, then it is also worth that much when you go out and sell it yourself.

At this point, there is one last thing you should do. Go out and compare these prices to what you see selling at shows, in stores, and in galleries. Check out the quality of the work. Is yours as good as this? Are they in the same ballpark. If your beads are as good and your prices are a lot lower, consider raising them some. If you are new, you may want your prices to be a little lower to make them attractive. But if they are too low, people will wonder what is wrong with your goods.

On the other hand if your price is too high, then you have to figure out how to trim your costs. Maybe you have to be willing to accept less an hour. Maybe you have to trim some of your overhead costs, like spending time in classes or dreaming up new product, and instead start spending more time making it.

Or maybe you just will not be able to support yourself selling beads. I hate to be a naysayer, but it may not be for everyone. Many of us have to have a regular job in addition to our beadmaking. Be sure you can make it financially before letting go the safety of your parachute. Talk to others that have tried it and see what they have to say. But if you work out the numbers and they look okay, your work is good, and it sells well; then go for it.

Suggested further reading

Crawford, Tad. **Business and Legal Forms for Fine Artists**, Allworth Press, 1990

Long, Steve and Cindy. **You Can Make Money From Your Arts And Crafts**, Mark Publishing, Inc. 1988

Rosen, Wendy. **Crafting as a Business**, The Rosen Group, Inc. 1998

Appendixes

Suppliers and manufacturer sources

AIM Kilns
350 SW Wake Robin Ave.
Corvallis OR 97333
Tel (800) 222-5456 (541) 758-8133
Fax (541) 758-8051
Web Page: www.aimkilns.com
Manufacturer of kilns and annealers.

Alpha Supply, Inc.
1408 Fourth Ave. 2nd Floor
Seattle, WA 98101
Tel (800) 257-4211 Fax (800) 257-4244
Web Page: www.alpha-supply.com
Wholesale distributor of lapidary & jewelry supplies. Includes tumblers, saws, laps, cleaners, etc.

Allen Graff
3823 E. Anaheim Street
Long Beach, CA 90804
Tel & Fax (310) 494-3823
Manufacturer of dichroic glass. Send for free catalog.

Arrow Springs
4301 A Product Dr.
Shingle Springs, CA 95682
Tel (800) 899-0689
Fax (530) 677-1600
Web Page: www.arrowsprings.com
Supplier of beadmaking equipment and supplies. Includes torches, supplies, tools, holding fingers, molds, kilns, sludge, etc.

ABR Imagery Inc
3415 South Knightridge Rd.
Bloomington, IN 47401
Tel (866) 342-4764 Fax: (812) 339-8947
Web Page: www.dichroicimagery.com
Manufacturer of dichroic glass with images.

Art Glass House
3650 N. US Highway 1
Cocoa, FL 32929
Tel (800) 525-8009 Fax (321) 631-9565
Web Page: www.artglasshouse.com
Distributor of borosilicate glass.

Aura Lens Products
51 8th Street North
Sauk Rapids, MN 56369
Tel (320) 253-0919 (800) 281-2872
Fax (320) 253-1239
Web Page: www.auralens.com
Manufacturer of protective glasses including rose didymium, AUR-92™, AGW-99™, AGW-186™, and combinations of the same.
*™ * of Aura Lens Products*

Bethlehem Apparatus Co., Inc.
890 Front St., P.O. Box Y
Hellertown, PA 18055 USA
Tel (610) 838-7034 Fax (610) 838-6333
Web Page: www.bethlehemburners.com
Manufacturer of Bethleham torches.

Bullseye Glass
3722 SE 21st
Portland, OR 97202
Tel (503) 232-8887 Fax (503) 238-9963
Web Page: www.bullseye-glass.com
Manufacturer of CE 90 fusing and beadmaking glass.

C & R Loo, Inc.
1085 Essex Ave.
Richmond, CA 94801-2112
Tel (800) 227-1780 (510) 232-0276
Fax (800) 996-3939 (510) 232-7810
Web page: www.crloo.com
Distributor of stained glass, fusible glass, dichroic glass, hot glass tools, frits, powders (Kugler Zimmermann, etc.), and glass for casting.

Carlisle Machine Works, Inc.
P.O. Box 746 - Millville, N.J. 08332
Tel (800) 922-1167 Fax: (856) 825-5510
Web Page: www.carlislemachine.com
Manufacturer of Carlisle torches.

Covington Engineering Corp.
P.O. Box 35
Redlands, CA 92373
Tel (877) 793-6636 Fax (909) 793-7641
Web Page: www.covington-engineering.com
Manufacturer and distributor of lapidary and cold glassworking equipment and supplies. Includes tumblers, belts, laps etc.

Crystal Myths, Inc.
3806 Cherokee Rd. N.E.
Albuquerque, NM 87110
Tel (505) 883-9295 Fax (505) 889-9556
Web Page: www.crystalmyths,com
Videotapes on glass beadmaking and sculptured glass school of lampworking. Sponsors bead shows.

Denver Glass Machinery, Inc.
2800 South Shoshone
Englewood, CO 80110
Tel (303) 781-0980 Fax (303) 781-9067
Web Page: www.denverglass.com
Manufacture of annealers, kiln, furnaces, glory holes, and diamond equipment.

D & L Stained Glass
4919 N. Broadway
Boulder, CO 80302
Tel (303) 449-8727 (800) 525-0940
Fax (303- 442-3429
Web Page: www.dlstainedglass.com
Distributor of borosilicate glass.

Glass Torch Technology
1988 Herbert Ave.
Hellertown, PA 18055-1739
Tel (610) 838-2446
Manufacturer of the new triple mix torches of which the Lynx is the entry-level torch.

Ed Hoy's International
27625 Diehl Rd.
Warrenville, IL 60555-3838
Tel (630) 836-1353 (800) 323-5668
Fax (708) 416-0448
Web page: www.edhoy.com
Wholesale distributor of complete hot and cold glassworking equipment and supplies. Includes torches, regulators, tools, glass etc. $50 minimum order from the hot glass catalog.

Frantz Art Glass & Supply
130 West Corporate Road
Shelton, WA 98584
Tel (360) 426-6712 (800) 839-6712
Fax (360) 427-5866
Web Page: www.frantzartglass.com
Distributor of beadmaking equipment and supplies. Includes torches, regulators, safety glasses, tools, Moretti glass, gold leaf, millefiori, etc.

Fusion Headquarters
15500 NE Kincaid Rd.
Newberg, OR 97132
Tel (503) 538-5281 Fax (503) 538-6527
Web Page: www.fusionheadquarters.com
Distributor of hot glass equipment and supplies. Include Murphy Fire Bucket, Fuse Master Products, books, videos, molds, Bullseye pattern *bars, kilns, etc.*

Glass Alchemy, Ltd.
6539 NE 59th Place
Portland, OR 97218
Tel (503) 460-0545 Fax (503) 460-0546
Web Page: www.glassalchemyarts.com
Manufacturer of colored borosilicate glass.

Glasscraft Inc.
626 Moss St.
Golden, CO 80401-4047
Tel (303) 278-4670 (888) 272-3830
Fax (303) 278-4672
Web Page: www.glasscraftinc.com
Distributor of flameworking and beadmaking supplies. Includes torches, regulators, safety glasses, tools, borosilicate and Moretti glass, etc.

Jalapa Gas and Chemical Corp.
7223 Decker Dr.
Baytown, TX 77520
Tel (800) 776-1485 Houston (281) 424-8787
Fax (281) 424-9349 E-mail JalapaGas@aol.com
Web Site: www.chemtane2.com
Manufacturer and distributor of Chemtane 2.

Jen-Ken Kilns
Centre De Verre
18 Bartlett St.
Allenstown, NH 03275
Tel (800) 958-5319 (603)485-8644
Fax (603) 485-4867
Web page www.cdvkiln.com
Manufacturer of kilns and annealers.

Losoya Glassworks
207 Beckers Lane
Manitou Springs, CO 80829
Tel (719) 685-4071 Fax (719) 685-4064
Web Page: www.glasssupply.com
Distributor of beadmaking equipment and supplies.

Nortel Manufacturing Ltd.
2040 Ellesmere Rd., Bldg 18
Toronto, ONT M1H 3B6 Canada
Tel (416) 438-3325 Fax (416) 438-3325
Manufacturer of Minor, Mid-range and Major bench burners.

Northstar Glassworks, Inc.
9450 SW Tigard St.
Tigard, OR 97223
Tel (503) 684-6986 (866) 684-6986
Fax (503) 670-0978
Web Page: www.northstarglass.com
Manufacturer of colored borosilicate glass.

Pacific Art Glass
125 W. 157th St.
Gardena, CA 90248
Tel (310) 516-7828 Fax (310) 516-0335
Wholesale distributor of stained glass, fusing and beadmaking supplies.

Paragon Industries, Inc.
2011 South Town East Blvd.
Mesquite, TX 75149-1122
Tel (800) 876-4218 (972) 288-7557
Fax (888) 222-6450
Web Page: www.paragonweb.com
Manufacturer of kilns and annealers.

Reusche & Company of T.W.S. Inc
1299 H Street
Greenley, CO 80631
Phone (970) 346-8577
Fax (970) 346-8575
Manufacturer glass enamel both high-fire and low-fire

Rio Grande
7500 Bluewater Rd. NW
Albuqeque, NM87121-1962
Tel (800) 545-6566 (505) 839-3300
Fax (800)648-3499
Web page www.riogrande.com
Distributor of jewelry tools andsource for electroforming and electroplating supplies.

Spruce Pine Batch
PO Box 159
Spruce Pine, NC 28777
Tel (828) 765-9876 Fax: (828) 765-9888
Web Page: www.sprucepinebatch.com
Wholesale distributor of batching materials including colored glass powders like Kugler, Zimmermann, etc.

Steinert Industries, Inc.
1507 Franklin Ave.
Kent OH 44240
Tel (330) 678-0028 (800) 727-7473
Fax (330) 678-8238
Web Page: www.steinertindustries.com
Manufacturer of glass blowing supplies many of which, like specialized marvers and optic molds which can be used in beadmaking.

Sundance Art Glass Distributers
179 Stierlin Rd.
Mountain View, CA 94043
Tel (650) 965-2266 (800) 9hotglass
Fax (650) 965-9542
Web page www.artglass1.com
Manufacturer of kilns and tools for art glass industries. Distributor of beadmaking supplies.

Thompson Enamels
650 Colfax Avenue
Bellevue, KY 41073
Tel (859) 291-3800 Fax: (859) 291-1849
Web Page: www.thompsonenamel.com
Manufacturer of Moretti and borosilicate compatible enamels for beadmaking.

Wale Apparatus Co.
400 Front St.
P.O. Box D
Hellertown, PA 18055
Tel (610) 838-7047 (800) 334-9253
Fax (610) 838-7440 (888) 334-9253
Web Page: www.waleapparatus.com
Distributor of beadmaking equipment and supplies. Includes torches, regulators, safety glasses, tools, glass, gold leaf, millefiori, etc.

Whitehouse-Books.com
60 East Market Street
Corning, NY 14830
Tel (800) 935-8536 (607) 936-8536
Fax 607-936-2465
Web Page: www.whitehouse-books.com
One-stop shopping for all your books and videos on glass and glassworking techniques.

Related periodicals and resources

Bead & Button
Published by Kalmbach Publishing Co.
21027 Crossroads Circle
P.O. Box 1612
Waukesha, WI 53187-1612
Customer Service Tel (800) 533-6644
Editorial office (262) 796-8776
Web page www.beadandbutton.com
Bimonthly magazine devoted to the use of beads and buttons with occasional articles on bead artists and techniques.

Bullseye Connection
1308 NW Everett Street
Portland, OR 97209
Tel (888) 220-3002 (503) 227-3002 (local)
Fax (503) 227-3130
Web Page: www.bullseyeconnection.com
Glassworking Resource Center whose vision of bringing artist and user closer together as we develop and explore the mysteries of colored glass and the myriad ways it can be re-formed into fine craft, art and architecture.

Fusion Journal
Published by American Scientific Glassblowers Society
302 Red Bud Rd
Thomasville, NC 27360
Tel (336) 882-0174 Fax (336) 882-0172
E-mail asgs@nr.infi.net
A quarterly journal on topics of interest in scientific glassblowing.

Glass Art Magazine
Published by Travin Inc.
P.O. Box 260377
Highlands Ranch, CO 80126-0377
Tel (303) 791-8998 FAX (303) 791-7739
Bimonthly magazine on many aspects of glassworking.

Glass Art Society
1305 4th Avenue, Suite 711
Seattle, WA 98101-2401
Tel (206) 382-1305 Fax (206) 382-2630
E-mail glassartsoc@earthlink.net
Web page www.glassart.org
International nonprofit organization to advance appreciation, understanding and development of the glass arts worldwide. They have an annual convention and publish minutes of the convention.

Glass Craftsman Magazine
Formerly Professional Stained Glass Magazine
Published by Arts & Media Inc.
P. O. Box 678
Richboro, PA 18954-0678
Tel (215) 860-9947 Fax (215) 860-1812
Web page www.glasscraftsman.com
Bimonthly magazine on many aspects of glassworking.

Glass Line Newsletter
120 South Kroeger Street
Anaheim, CA 92805-4011
Tel (714) 520-0121 FAX (714) 520-4370
Web Page http://www.hotglass.com
Bimonthly newsletter for lampworkers including beadmaking. It has a column on beadmaking. Also has an on-line bulletin board system.

Glass Talk Radio
Tel (714) 894-7879
Web Page: www.glasstalkradio.com
Weekly web radio show on glass with frequent discussions on flameworking

Glass Patterns Quarterly, Inc.
8300 Hidden Valley Road
Westport, KY 40077
Tel (502) 222 5631 Fax (520) 222-4527
E-mail gpqmag@aol.com
Web page www.glasspatterns.com
Quarterly magazine with how to projects. Occasional articles on beads.

Lampworkers Lounge
Web Page: www.lampworkerslounge.com
On-line magazine on lampworking with forum & chat room. Primarily for borosilicate lampworkers.

Lapidary Journal
Published by Lapidary Journal Inc.
Devon Office Center, Suite 201
60 Chestnut Avenue
Devon, PA 19333-1312
Tel (610) 293-1112 Fax (610)293-1717
E-mail ljmagazine@ao;.com
Web page www.lapidaryjournal.com
Monthly magazine devoted to gemstones and jewelry making. Frequent articles on glass beadmakers and beadmaking techniques. Good source for information on lapidary equipment. Yearly bead issue.

Ornament Magazine
Published by Ornament Inc.
P.O. Box 2349
San Marcos, CA 92079-2349
Tel (800) 888-8950 (760) 599-0222
Fax (760) 599-0228
E-mail ornament@cts.com
Occasional articles on beadmaking and bead happenings with lots of color advertisements of other artists' work.

The Bead Release
Quarterly newsletter for the International Society of Glass Beadmakers.
International Society of Glass Beadmakers
1120 Chester Ave #470
Cleveland, OH 44114
Web page: www.isgb.org
Web page has a forum, which is a good place to get information on glass beadmaking

The Flow, a glassworker's journal
713 WSW Loop 323 #101
Tyler, TX 75701
Magazine on lampworking

The Crafts Report Publishing Co., Inc.
300 Water St., Box 1992
Wilmington, DE 19899
Tel (302)656-2209 (800) 777-7098
Fax (302)656-4894
Web page www.craftsreport.com
Publisher of The Crafts Report a magazine for all crafts people. A subscription currently costs $29 a year. It offers information on all kinds of topics.

The Bead Museum
5754 W. Glenn Dr.
Glendale, AR 85301
Tel (623) 931-2737
Display of contemporary beads and beads from around the world.

Corning Glass Center
home of The Corning Museum of Glass
One museum Way
Corning, NY 14831
Tel (607)974-8271
A great place to visit and learn more about glass.

Warm Glass
4140 Clemmons Road, #320
Clemmons, NC 27012
Web Page: www.warmglass.com
On-line tutorial and forum on glass fusing.

Wet Canvas, Cyber Living for Artists
Web Page: www.wetcanvas.com
On-line forums on a number of topics one of which is glass art and beadmaking.

Contributing Artists

Abers, Mimi; Berkeley, CA; XXVI
Ahers, Dolly; Mesa, AZ; X, XXXIV
Alef, Mag; Two Rivers, WI; IX
Aurelius, Bob; Sauk Rapids, MN; XXIX
Baldwin, Ann Scherm, Virginia Beach, VA; XXVI
Barley, Michael; Sequin, WA; XXII
Bascom, Tracy; Boulder, CO; XIX
Bates, Sharon; Morgan Hill, CA; XII
Beasley, Terre; Cocoa, FL; XII, XIII
Belle, Stevi; Raton, NM; FC, 136, 152, VI, XX, XXXIII
Blincoe, Bonnie; Louisville, KY; 143, 288
Blood, Elizabeth; Albany, GA; X
Bouchles, CarolAnne; Greene, ME XXIII
Boylan, Tom; Mendocino, CA; IV, XXII, XXX
Brickman, Larry; Bremerton, WA; IV
Brown, Cindy; Arvada, CO; IX
Bugarin, Carol; Boston, MA; XXXII, XXXIII
Burgess, Barbara; El Cerrito, CA; XXXV
Burnham, Jana; Springfield, IL; II
Burr, Marjorie; Everette, WA; XXV
Cahill-Howard, Patti, Asville, NC; II
Chapman, Marie Claude; Beecroft Australia; VI, XI
Ching, Lani; Portland, OR; III
Cinta, Ofilia; Elmhurst, IL; XIX
Clark, Monty; Auburn, CA; XXVI, XXIX
Cook, Shirley; Fremont, CA; XXI
Cooper, Becky; Redwood City, CA; VIII
Copeland, Lauri; Overland Park, KS; XXII, XXVII
Cotton, Eloise; Martinez, CA; XXIII, XXXV
Creekmore, Sara; Magdelena NM; XXIX
Crossman-Moore; Gail, Orange, MA;171, XXII, XXIII, XXXIV
Curtis, John; Sheboygan, WI; V
Dalton, Lark; Lopez Island, WA; 197
Davis, Ann; Springfield, VA; XXXIV
Dickey, Cay, Oceanside, CA; BC, VI, XXIX
Dougherty, Patti, Elkins Park, PA;XVIII
Dove, Deanna Griffin, ; XVII
Drew-Wilkinson, Kate; Bisbee, AZ; XI
Dugger, Pamela; Hollywood, FL; XVII, XVIII, XXIV
Dugina, Diana; Pittsburgh, PA; XXI
Dunn, Juanita; Phoenix, AZ; XIIII
East, Diana; Leicester, England; 256, XXV, XXVII, XXXV
Eaton, Rob; San Jose, CA; II
Edmunds, Linda; Atlanta, GA; XVII
Fairbanks, Leah; Willets, CA; FC, 156, X, XXXIII, XXXIV
Fonda, Carol; Auburn, CA; VI, XXVI, XXIX
Fowler, Suellen; Berkeley, CA; 176
Frantz, Patricia; Shelton, WA; 152, VI
Fuchs, Greg; Richwood, OH; XXXII
Fuentes, Bernadette; Arlington, TX;II, V, VII, XIII
Galardy, Greg; Arcata, CA;III, VII, XXVII
Genack, Patti; Beulah, CO; XX
Goetz, Leroy; Portland, OR; XXXIII
Gollan, Mona; Rapid City, SD; XXXIV
Goodenough, Nancy; Monte Rio, CA; XXIX
Graham, Angie; Stephenville, TX; IX, XX
Green, Shirley; Oakland, CA; X
Guarino, Andrea; Port Townsend, WA; II, XXI
Hanks, Tom; Cullowhee, NC; IX
Hartjen, Marna; Escondido, CA; XI, XXVI
Haskins, Molly Vaughan; Eureka, CA; 225, XXVIII, XXXV
Hatz, Doni; Loveland, OH; 191, XXII, XXX, XXXIII
Heilman, Bronwen Tucson, TX; 256, XXIV, XXV, XXXVI
Herrington, Nancy; Vashon Island, WA; XXI
Holland, Tom, Fox, AR; IV, 138, 141, XXVI, XXVI
Hopper, Shari Maxson, Paradise, CA, 189, 190, XXX
Hoyt, Pat; Baker, MT; FC, XX, XXXII
Hubbard, Sheryll; XV
Hyde, Caitlin; Carbondale, IL; 254, XXV
Janelle, Al; Austin, TX; FC, 105, 145, XVI, XX
Jennik, Robert, Milwaukee, WI; XXIII
Johnson, JoElla; Sacramento, CA; 151, IX
Johnson, Kathy, Seattle, WA; 156, IX, XIII, XV
Jones, James Allen, Portland, OR; 147, VII, XXI
Jurgens, Dave & Rebecca; Mililani, HI; XXXIII
Kan, Lisa; San Marino, CA; XI
Kennedy, Mary; Waialua, HI; 114, XIII
Kervin, Jim; Livermore, CA; 146, 155, 164, 169, 223, 288, IV, XIV, XXXI
Kindle, Shannon; Mt. View, CA; XX
Klotz, Mary; Woodboro, MD; 152, XIV, XXXI
Koslow, Rolf; Edgewater, NJ; 261
Kreitter, Keith, Sante Fe, NM; XXII
Kulin, Jacob; Boston, MA; XXXII
Lambert, Gina; Chicago, IL; II
Lang, Sharon; Navato, CA; X
Levitt, Lezlie; Thornhill, Ontario; VIII, XV
Lindquist, Allison; Oakland, CA; V, VII
Logan, Kristina; Portsmouth, NH; II
Madera, Keri; Chico, CA; VIII
Maher, Bruce St. John; Monte Rio, CA; XXVIII, XXXI
Mahfood, Bernadette; Winona, MN; FC, XXXV
Marchand, Matt; Willets, CA; VIII, 157, XXIV
Martin, David; MontgomeryCtr., VT; XXIII
McCaskey, Ralph; San Pablo, CA; XV
Mecuro, Patrise; XIX
Mekalanos, Maud; Charlestown, MA; III
Meleney, Kate Fowle; Saunderstown, RI; 137, 261, XXV
Mellichamp, Budd;, Tallahassee, FL;III
Miles, Kim; Ranchos de Taos, NM; XI
Milliron, Donna; Shingle Spring, CA; 227, 234, XXXI
Mixon, Jackie; Saugus, CA; VIII
Moenck, MaryAnn; Maplewood, MN; XIV
Mossman, Ralph; Driggs, ID; XXVII

Photography Credits

Alef, Mag	IX
An Enyde, Tom	XXIV
Anthony, Jerry	FC, 136, 152, VI, IX, XVII, XXV, XXVI, XXXIII
Arend, Chris	V
AZAD	XIII
Beasley, Terre	XII, XIII
Boyland, Tom	IV
Bresler, Bill	148, 185, 186, 188, XXIV, XXX
Brown, Cindy	IX
Burgess, Barbara	XXXV
Burr, Marjorie	XXV
Bush, Michael	XII
Campo, Robin	XVIII
Chapman, Marie Claude	IV, XI
Clark, Monty	XXIX
Cook, Shirley	XXI
Copeland, Lauri	XXII, XXVII
Corning Museum of Glass	7, 111, 174
Crossman-Moore, Gail	XXXIV
Dabney, Taylor	II, III, XIX
Diamante, Robert	XXIII
Dougherty, Patti	XVIII
Downs, Gerry	XI, XXXIV
Dugger, Pamela	XVIII
Dugina, Diana	XXI
Dupuis, Marshall	XIV, XXXI
East, Diana	256, 261, XXVII, XXXV
Edmunds, Linda	XVII
Elder, Tommy	V, XIII
Friebergy Charley	XXII
Gabringer, Ralph	XXXVI
Galardy, Greg	III, IV, VII, VIII, X, XVII, XXVII
Gollan, Mona	XXXIV
Green, Shirley	X
Guarino, Andrea	XXI
Gyurina, Steve	XXII, XXXVI
Hart Trevor	191, XXX
Hartjen, Marna	XI, XXVI
Heilman, Bronwen	256, 257, 258, 259, 260, XXV, XXXVI
Hein, Ingrid	XI, XXXII
Herrington, Nancy	XXI
Holden, Melinda	XXIV, XXXIII
Holland, Tom	IV, XVIII, XXVII
Hopper, Sheri Maxson	189, 190, 203, 204, 207, XXIV, XXX
Hulet, Patty	XXXV
Janelle, Al	FC, 105, XVI, XX
Johnson, Kathy	XV
Jurgens, Dave & Rebecca	XXXIII
Kan, Lisa	XI
Kennedy, Mary	114
Kimrey, Don	XIII
Klotz, Mary	152
Kulin, Eric	XXXII
Lang, Sharon	X
Lieberman, Marcia	XXIII
Liska, Laura	VIII
Liu, Robert K.	II, IV, VI, XVI, XXVII, XXVIII
Madera, Keri	VIII
Maher, Bruce St. John	XXVIII
Marchetti, Christopher	234, XXXI
Mellichamp, Budd	III
Nelson, Nanette	XXI
Norman, Wilbur	XXXVI
O'Dell, Jeffrey	II, XVIII, XXXV
Olson, John	XXII
Orr, David	X, XI, XVII, XXXIV
Overton, Robert	III
Pankey, Jeri	XI
Peacock, Janice	FC, I, III, VI, XV, XVII, XX, XXVIII, XXXII, XXXIII
Peterson, Bobby	XXXII, XXXIV
Picker, Alon	289, XXXVI
Pitts, Chad	VIII, XVII, XIX, XXII
Post, George	FC, 150, II, X, XXI, XXV, XXIX, XXXIII
Potek, Malcom	222, XXVIII, XXXVI
Powell, Dean	II
Radke, Paula	XVIII, XXVIII, XXXVI
Rich Images	FC, VII, IX, XI, XIV, XVII, XIX, XX, XXXII
Robbins, Wayne	XIX
René Roberts	XXI
Sage, Patricia	XVIII
Sakwa, Hap	XXI, XXIII, XXXV, XXXVI
Sanders, Larry	FC
Sawamoto, Emilo	V, XIV
Saylor, Lib	IX
Schmeers, Jake	XXVII
Schreiber, Roger	III, XXVII
Scovil, Jeff	X, XXXVI
Shapiro, Alex	V, VII
Smircich, Jim	163, V
Smith, Amy	V, XXI
Smith, Mavis	XXXII, XXXIV
Stegmann, Rob	XVI, XIX, XXXVI
Sundance Art Glass	08, 149, 194
Swigart, Lynn	VIII, XXXII, XXXV
Symons, Jill	V, IX
Tamura, Carl	BC, VI, XXIX
Telfner, David	VII, XIV, XX

Index

If you enjoyed this book, you maybe interested in Jim Kervin's other book that was co-authored with Dan Fenton on kiln casting of glass. That book is

Pâte de Verre and Kiln Casting of Glass 2nd ed.

With this book, you will learn the secrets of Pâte de Verre and kiln casting, which will permit you to break out of the flat world of glass fusing and expand your glass artistry into the world of three dimensions

You will discover how easy it is to make:

Sculptural work—Using the techniques presented in this book, you will learn how to model in a number of different media and how to transform that model into a finished glass sculpture.

Hollow vessels—With slight modifications, these same techniques will also allow you to form beautiful glass vessels with intricate details.

Beads—You will also learn further details on how to apply these techniques to make gorgeous glass beads and pendants that will really stand out in any necklace.

This is the most complete manual on Pâte de Verre and kiln casting available anywhere. It is a must for any glass artist seriously wanting to enter that field.

It contains pictures of work by the following kiln casting artists:

Mark Abildgaard
Anna Boothe
Linda Ethier
Newy Fagan
Mary Fox
Robin Grebe
Rachel Josepher Gaspers
Lucartha Kohler
Donna Milliron
Charles Miner
Seth Randal
Alice Rogan-Nelson
David Ruth
Kathleen Stevens
Janusz Walentynowicz
Mary Frances Wawrytko

And of course, the authors.

Here are some of the topics discussed in that book:

Modeling: You will learn the techniques for modeling with wax, clay, and other organic materials. You will learn how to make wax replicas of your models allowing you to make a casting series based upon a single original model.

Mold construction: You will learn about the composition of investments and what the different components do. You will learn how to orient your models in the molding process for best casting results. You will learn how to mix and cast you refractory investment molds. You will learn how to strengthen your molds. Lastly, you will learn how to prepare your molds for glass casting.

Casting techniques: You will learn about preparing the glass frit used in glass casting. You will learn to make and use glass pastes to their best advantage. You will learn how different glasses behave and which may be better for your work.

Kiln procedures: You will learn about the different steps in a firing schedule and how to determine which steps you should be using in your work. You will learn about the theory of annealing and how to apply it to all of your work. You will learn about how to control your kiln to get good results.

Safety: You will learn the safe use of your equipment. You will learn which materials are toxic and how to handle them. You will learn what to do about eye protection.

At 198 pages, 91 figures, and 12 tables this is not just a picture book—it contains a wealth of information on this subject. Whether you are a veteran glass caster seeking a specific piece of information or a newcomer looking for the basics, this book will answer your questions.

It also makes a wonderful instructional text for teaching glass casting and is currently being used by a number of schools around the world for just that purpose. It is the only book on the market that really goes into the safety aspects of glass casting.

Order your copy of ***Pâte de Verre and Kiln Casting of Glass*** today.

Look for it at your glass supplies distributor or contact me at:

GlassWear Studios
1197 Sherry Way
Livermore, CA 94550-5745
or call (925) 443-9139
or email glasswearstudios@comcast.net

Want to learn more about glass beadmaking?

Then you also want to find out about my Beadmaker Series, which was designed to serve as companion instructional material to this book.

Each of these 32-page, full-color booklets is jam packed with more information about making and decorating glass beads. Each booklet concentrates on one nationally-recognized glass beadmaker and gives an introduction to them and their work. The booklets include:

- biography of the artist and a gallery of their work
- discussion of some of their special beadmaking tools and techniques, and
- step-by-step descriptions on how to make some of their signature beads.

Each booklet is richly illustrated with both pictures and discussion to explain to you the secrets that this artist uses in making their works of art.

Current titles in the Beadmaker Series are:

The Wild and Wonderful World of Sharon Peters and Her Silly Sculptural Shapes

In the first booklet we are introduced to the witty work of Sharon Peters and her cartoony beads. Here you will learn how to plan out and execute beginning sculpture beads using her delightful creations as examples. We will start with how to develop a design and the steps by which you will put together your creations. Sharon will show you her favorite sculpting tools and how they are used to manipulate the glass. As you work your way through this booklet, you will find yourself becoming more comfortable stretching and shaping glass as you leave the surface of the bead with your sculptural components. The examples that you will see in this booklet are a fish, an ivory mouse, a twisty lizard, animal heads (cat, cow, and pig), and a sitting cat body.

The Fanciful Floral Beads of Leah Fairbanks and Her Gardens of Glass

In the second booklet we are treated to the beautiful floral beads of Leah Fairbanks. She will teach you how to make external floral decorations on the surface of you beads using stringers and canes. To increase the color and variation of these pieces she will familiarize you with making cased, ribbed, branch, and rainbow cane. You will learn secrets on how to apply these canes in such a way to form the petals of flowers and the foliage of plants. In addition she will share with us some of the background techniques that she uses in making her beads using foils, frits, and dichroic glass. The bead examples that you will see made in this book are a rose bead, a daisy bead, a sweet pea bead, a Monet bead, and a grape urn bead.

The Classic Bead Shapes of Jim Smircich and His Amazing Control of Heat

In the third booklet you will learn Jim Smircich's easy techniques to shape large classic biconic beads. He will reintroduce you to the fundamentals of surface tension, gravity, and heat base in forming beads. You will learn how to read the heat base of a bead to decide when to work it with your tools. You will observe his ergodynamic-approved work style, and tools to assist in sizing and shaping beads. He will introduce you to some chemistry tricks that you can use to make interesting and colorful creations. He will also teach you how to fume gold onto the surface of a beads. The examples that you will see demonstrated in this book are wavy beads, black web beads, black lace beads, melon beads, apple core beads, Van Gogh flower beads, shield buttons, and goddess pendants.

The Enamel and Electroform Decorated Beads of Kate Fowle Meleney

In the fourth booklet, Kate Fowle Meleney will teach you how to use enamels, color mixing, and electroforming in your work. She shows how optic molds can be used to construct ribbed canes, which she uses as barnacles on her colorful shell beads. Some of the alternate work style elements that you will learn from her are working in the center of a mandrel, paddling from above, and use of hot plates to preheat glass and components. You will learn all about enamels and techniques for applying them to your beads. You will discover the tools and secrets for electroforming thick copper coatings onto your beads. The examples that are shown in this booklet include a snail shell, a conch shell, an Anthromorph bead, a beach pebble, a petroglyph vessel, and a prehistoric goddess bead.

And this is just the beginning. More booklets are in the making. I am currently working with Heather Trimlett on a booklet discussing how to use the same skills from beadmaking to make amphorals, core-formed vessel, and stoppered vessels. I am also starting work on a booklet with Pati Walton on making aquarium and garden beads. Here you will learn to add depth to your masterpieces for more interest.

So if these booklets interest you, ask for them at your glass supplier or contact me for further information.

GlassWear Studios
1197 Sherry Way
Livermore, CA 94550-5745
or call (925) 443-9139
or email glasswearstudios@comcast.net